RELENTLESS STRIKE

ALSO BY SEAN NAYLOR

Not a Good Day to Die

Clash of Chariots
(with Tom Donnelly)

RELENTLESS STRIKE

THE **SECRET HISTORY** OF
JOINT SPECIAL OPERATIONS COMMAND

SEAN NAYLOR

ST. MARTIN'S PRESS

NEW YORK

For Duncan and Hannah Naylor

www.stmartins.com

Designed by Jonathan Bennett

Maps by Jeffrey L. Ward

Library of Congress Cataloging-in-Publication Data

Naylor, Sean.
   Relentless strike : the secret history of Joint Special Operations Command / Sean Naylor.
— First edition.
      p. cm.
   ISBN 978-1-250-01454-2 (hardback)
   ISBN 978-1-4668-7622-4 (e-book)
   1. United States. Joint Special Operations Command—History.   2. Special operations
(Military science)—United States—History.   3. Terrorism—Prevention—United States—
History.   4. United States—History, Military—21st century.   I. Title.   II. Title: Relentless
strike, the secret history of JSOC.   III. Title: Secret history of Joint Special Operations
Command.

   UA34.J65N39 2015
   355.4'60973—dc23

                                                                                    2015017796

Our books may be purchased in bulk for promotional, educational, or business use. Please
contact your local bookseller or the Macmillan Corporate and Premium Sales Department at
(800) 221-7945, extension 5442, or by e-mail at MacmillanSpecialMarkets@macmillan.com.

First Edition: September 2015

10 9 8 7 6 5 4 3 2 1

CONTENTS

AUTHOR'S NOTE

I began this project sure in the knowledge that researching and writing a book about a secret organization that controlled other secret organizations was going to be a challenge, and so it proved.

U.S. Special Operations Command—Joint Special Operations Command's administrative higher headquarters—declined to assist in the project, other than to answer the occasional question. Several people who figure prominently in the events described in this book declined requests to be interviewed. *Relentless Strike,* the first full-length history of JSOC, is therefore built on two foundations.

The first of these consists of interviews I did arrange with scores of sources, most of whom spoke "on background," meaning I could only identify them in a generic way, as in "a senior SEAL Team 6 source," rather than by name. The fact that many of my sources held several different positions during the period covered by the book complicated matters further when it came to attribution. In most cases, I used an attribution (for instance, "Delta operator") that applied to the position the source held during the events being discussed. This meant that sometimes the same individual might be referred to by different attributions in different chapters. However, a small number of individuals insisted that I refer to them by the same phrase (for instance, "retired special operations officer") throughout the book.

The second foundation upon which the book rests consists of published works by other writers. No book about JSOC could or should be written in a literary vacuum. As the endnotes indicate, this book stands on the shoulders of scores of others that have touched on the command in whole or in part. Several deserve specific mention. The first of these is Steven Emerson's *Secret Warriors,* which I found to be the most useful single volume about the covert operations of the 1980s. (At the outset

I intended for my book to concentrate on JSOC's post–September 11 history, but I soon realized that an extensive discussion of the first two decades of the command's existence would be necessary in order to provide readers with the context necessary to frame the events that occurred later.) For the chapters dealing with the creation of JSOC's fearsome industrial-scale killing machine in Iraq, I relied heavily on three books: *Task Force Black,* by Mark Urban, which, while focusing on British special operations forces, contained a wealth of information about the overall JSOC campaign; *The Endgame,* by Michael R. Gordon and General Bernard E. Trainor, a masterful narrative of America's war in Iraq, laced with telling details about the role played by JSOC; and *My Share of the Task,* by retired General Stanley McChrystal, who commanded JSOC during those critical years. The latter was one of several first-person accounts upon which I leaned for particular chapters. Others include *Kill bin Laden,* by Dalton Fury (the nom de plume of Delta officer Tom Greer), about the failure to get Osama bin Laden at Tora Bora, and *No Easy Day,* by Mark Owen (the pen name of SEAL Team 6 operator Matt Bissonnette) with Kevin Maurer, about the May 2011 mission that killed Osama bin Laden.

To the individuals at the heart of each of these foundations—the sources who agreed to be interviewed by me, and the authors whose work preceded mine—I am profoundly grateful.

PROLOGUE

As Marwan al-Shehhi turned United Airlines Flight 175 northeast above Trenton, New Jersey,[1] and pointed the hijacked Boeing 767 toward Manhattan and the already burning World Trade Center, the commander of the United States' premier counterterrorist force was concluding a visit to the U.S. embassy in Budapest.[2]

It was mid-afternoon in the Hungarian capital on September 11, 2001, and Army Major General Dell Dailey, head of Joint Special Operations Command, had just briefed senior embassy officials on a major—but highly classified—training exercise code-named Jackal Cave his organization was running across Europe.[3]

Jackal Cave was a "joint readiness exercise," or JRX, one of several that JSOC ("jay-sock") conducted each year. Like most JRXs, it was nested in an even larger "Ellipse" exercise run by one of the U.S. military's four-star regional commands, in this case European Command.[4] Some JSOC personnel viewed the JRXs as essential opportunities to rehearse critical capabilities. Others thought they were counterproductive wastes of time designed mainly to support JSOC's budget, which had been steadily growing for two decades.

Born from the wreckage of 1980's Operation Eagle Claw, the United States' failed attempt to rescue its hostages in Iran, JSOC was created that same year to give the United States a standing headquarters that could run similar operations in the future. But although its power, size, and influence had increased significantly since then, on September 11, 2001, the command remained a fringe presence on the U.S. military scene, with a narrowly circumscribed set of responsibilities that included short-term counterterrorist missions, operations to secure weapons of mass destruction, and very little else.

The exercise JSOC was running that damp, overcast afternoon in Hungary[5] typified the command's niche role at the turn of the century. The notional enemy was a hybrid force that combined elements of international organized crime and terrorism and was trafficking in weapons of mass destruction, or "loose nukes."[6] JSOC's forward headquarters for the exercise was split between Taszár,[7] a military airfield 150 kilometers southwest of Budapest, and Tuzla, Bosnia,[8] the latter a holdover from the command's recent history hunting Balkan war criminals. Bolstering the JSOC force were Hungarian military elements, as well as personnel from the U.S. Army's 10th Special Forces Group, with which JSOC had become close after years of operating together in the Balkans.[9]

One exercise aim was to validate a concept called advance force operations (AFO), which was also the name of a newly established staff cell in JSOC headquarters.[10] AFO's origins lay in the Operational Support Troop of the Army's Delta Force,[11] one of several secret "special mission units" JSOC controlled. (Another such unit, the Navy's SEAL Team 6, was reconnoitering the Croatian port of Dubrovnik, from where the "enemy" was trying to ship the nuclear material out on a boat.)[12] The AFO cell ran the sort of missions highlighted by this JRX: deep reconnaissance, often undercover, to prepare the way for possible "direct action"—kill or capture—missions by larger forces. To conduct these missions, the cell could pull operators from any unit that fell under JSOC.[13]

In Jackal Cave, the AFO undercover work was largely the responsibility of the Operational Support Troop, or OST, which had pioneered this concept in JSOC. The OST operators' role was to find the targeted individuals, allowing a larger—but still "low-vis[ibility]"—force to arrive in civilian vans wielding suppressed weapons and capture or kill them.[14] The aim in such a raid was to "get in and get out without drawing too much attention [so as to] be able to provide plausible deniability to the local government," said a Delta source.

"We were tracking 'terrorists,'" said a JSOC staff officer. "It was really a big tracking exercise, and then [we'd] bring an assault element in to take the target down."

That assault element was Delta's A Squadron, one of the unit's three ground squadrons. The squadron and a small Delta headquarters element had flown in the previous day from Pope Air Force Base, North Carolina, on two massive Air Force C-17 Globemaster III transport aircraft. The planes were still on the tarmac at Taszár, where JSOC had placed its joint operations center, or JOC (pronounced "jock").[15] (JSOC's permanent headquarters was at Pope, adjacent to Delta's home post of Fort Bragg.)[16] Other exercise participants took different routes to Hungary. The JOC personnel flew over in their own aircraft—two C-141 Starlifters referred to as J1 and J2 or, collectively, as the "J-alert birds"—while the OST operators at the heart of this low-vis exercise had taken commercial flights and used cover identities and false passports to infiltrate Europe. Some had also moved into position using the Air Force's "covered air" unit. That unit, known within JSOC as Task Force Silver, operated a variety of civilian airframes, from small propeller-driven planes to Boeing 727s, always hiding the military nature of its missions.[17]

By the afternoon of September 11, the exercise had barely begun. Like most JRXs, it was designed to meet the training needs of as many JSOC elements as possible. This necessarily required an elaborate scenario with many moving parts. When the first plane hit the World Trade Center, another C-17 had just touched down at Taszár, bearing four Little Bird helicopters belonging to the 160th Special Operations Aviation Regiment, an Army unit established, like JSOC, in the wake of Eagle Claw. Two of the regiment's MH-47E Chinooks had already arrived on a hulking Air Force C-5 Galaxy transport, which at 75 meters was almost 50 percent longer than even the C-17. The plane with the Little Birds taxied to a remote part of the airfield so those on board could follow Dailey's order to not offload the tiny attack and assault helicopters—there to support the Delta mission—anywhere they could be seen by non-JSOC personnel. The rest of the 160th's contribution to the exercise—principally a force of MH-60K Black Hawks and MH-60L Direct Action Penetrators (Black Hawks configured as attack helicopters, rather than as lift, or "assault," aircraft) led by Lieutenant Colonel Kevin Mangum, commander of the regiment's 1st Battalion—was staging out of Naval Station Rota in southern Spain. From Rota, the 160th crews were to fly Team 6 to assault a ship in the Mediterranean.[18]

The JSOC and Delta personnel at Taszár were meanwhile just settling into their temporary quarters at the end of a taxiway at the Cold War–era airfield in the Hungarian countryside. While the Delta squadron was as usual housed in a pair of large tents—a yellow and white "circus tent" apparatus that housed the squadron's operations center and a more conventional "fest tent" in which the operators stored their gear and slept[19]—the headquarters elements took over an old

Russian building that was an improvement over the tents JSOC usually used. Each unit and each JSOC staff section was assigned an office to use as an operations center or liaison cell. The JOC itself was in a larger room at the end of the corridor.[20] While the JSOC staffers wore their combat uniforms, the Delta operators at the airfield worked in T-shirts and athletic shorts or other civilian gear.

Some OST operators and one or two Delta staffers were already out and about, working in civilian clothes as they tracked "terrorists" through downtown Budapest.[21] Using small satellite radios, these urban reconnaissance experts sent back digital photographs of roofs, doors, windows, and other potential breach points in target buildings, allowing assault troop operators back in Taszár to figure out the exact amount and type of explosive charge required in each case.[22]

Operatives from the Defense Humint Service, the Defense Department's clandestine spy network, had traveled from other European countries and the United States to portray the terrorists. This was not unusual. OST and other JSOC elements that did clandestine work often used Defense Humint (short for human intelligence) operatives as both participants and mentors in exercises that involved low-vis tradecraft.[23]

The briefing over, Dailey and his senior enlisted adviser, Army Command Sergeant Major Mike Hall, were walking out of the conference room chatting with Major Jim Reese, a Delta officer who'd been pulled up to be AFO's operations officer. Eager to fetch something for Dailey, Reese jogged down the corridor to the room that served as AFO's operations center. "Hey boss, look at this," Air Force Staff Sergeant Sam Stanley told Reese as the Army officer walked in, indicating the pictures of the fires raging in the World Trade Center's twin towers on the television the tiny AFO staff always kept tuned to CNN or Fox News. His original errand forgotten, Reese took a moment to absorb the significance of what he was watching, then turned and ran back after his boss just as the red desk phone reserved for classified conversations began ringing.

Dailey and Hall were on their way to collect their IDs at the embassy's security desk when Reese caught up with them. "Hey sir, you need to see this," he told the general.[24] Alerted to the urgency in Reese's eyes, Dailey walked quickly back to AFO's operations center and fixed his gaze on the television screen for a few seconds before taking the red phone. On the line was his boss, Air Force General Charlie Holland, head of U.S. Special Operations Command at MacDill Air Force Base in Tampa, Florida.

Holland told Dailey to forget about the exercise and get back to Fort Bragg as fast as possible. Dailey got the message. After hanging up, he turned to Reese and Lieutenant Colonel Scotty Miller, the Delta officer running AFO, and told them he was canceling the exercise immediately and returning to Bragg, and that they were to do the same. "Get home any way you can," he said.[25]

JSOC was going to war.

UZBEKISTAN · Dushanbe · TAJIKISTAN

TURKMENISTAN

Mazar-i-Sharif · · Kunduz

AFGHANISTAN

Asadabad

Herat · Kabul ★ Jalalabad

Tangi Valley · Peshawar

Ghazni · Gardez · Parachinar · Islamabad ★

Highway I · Khost · Miram Shah

Tarin Kowt ·

Farah · Wana · PAKISTAN

Gereshk · Kandahar

Lashkar Gah ·

IRAN

× OBJECTIVE
RHINO

· Quetta

Indus River

AFGHANISTAN

0 Miles · 100 · 200

0 Kilometers · 200

· Dalbandin

INDIA

Jacobabad ·

© 2015 Jeffrey L. Ward

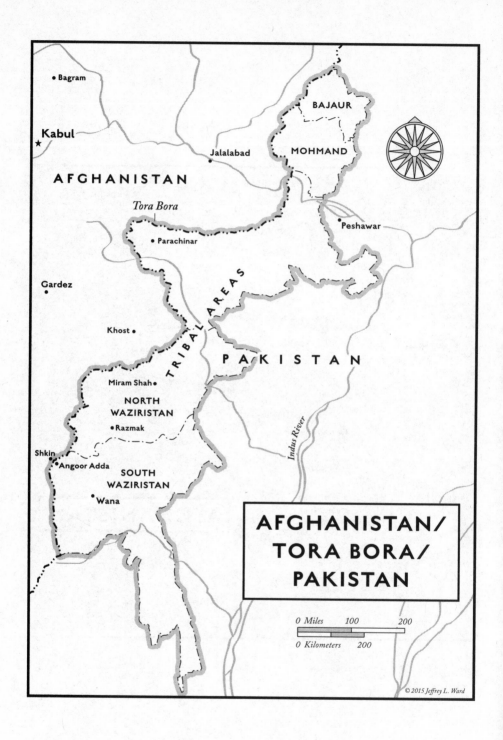

AFGHANISTAN/ TORA BORA/ PAKISTAN

- Bagram

Kabul
★

Jalalabad •

AFGHANISTAN

BAJAUR

MOHMAND

Tora Bora

- Parachinar

• Peshawar

Gardez •

TRIBAL AREAS

Khost •

PAKISTAN

Miram Shah •

NORTH WAZIRISTAN

• Razmak

Indus River

Shkin •
• Angoor Adda

SOUTH WAZIRISTAN

• Wana

0 Miles 100 200
0 Kilometers 200

© 2015 Jeffrey L. Ward

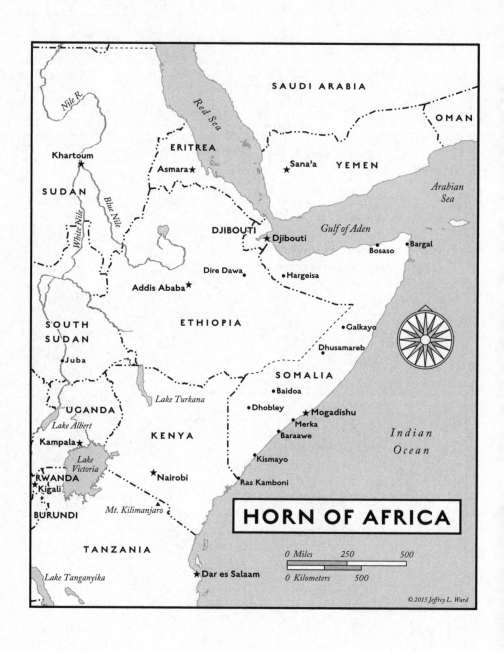

HORN OF AFRICA

0 Miles 250 500
0 Kilometers 500

© 2015 Jeffrey L. Ward

PART I

THE FERRARI IN THE GARAGE

1

A Phoenix Rises

It was a late summer afternoon in 1980, and America's most powerful men in uniform filed into "the Tank," the Joint Chiefs of Staff's sound-proofed conference room in the Pentagon, for a briefing that would mark a turning point in U.S. military history.

Already in the room, waiting patiently beside his flip chart stand, was Army Lieutenant Colonel Keith Nightingale, whose briefing the generals and admirals were there to attend. Nightingale was a staff officer for a top secret task force, and his charts and viewgraphs consisted largely of schematics, budget minutiae, and the other dry details involved in the establishment of a new organization.[1] But together they represented an attempt to conjure a phoenix from the ashes of bitter defeat.

America's mood that summer was grim. On April 24 the United States had launched Operation Eagle Claw, a bold attempt to rescue the fifty-two U.S. hostages held by Iranian revolutionaries in Tehran. The effort had been an ignominious disaster. With the assault force already deep inside Iran at a remote staging area called Desert One, President Jimmy Carter had aborted the mission at the commander's request because only five of the original eight helicopters critical to the mission were still in flying condition. Then, as the force was preparing to return to its base on the Omani island of Masirah, and perhaps try again twenty-four hours later, catastrophe struck. A helicopter crashed into a plane full of fuel and Delta Force soldiers. Eight servicemen and all hopes of merely postponing the rescue attempt until the next night died in the resulting fireball. By the time the force had made it home, pictures of the charred bodies and burned-out airframes at Desert One were all over the world's newscasts. The United States was humiliated.[2]

Most Americans, including many in the Carter administration, had despaired of rescuing the hostages in the wake of the Desert One fiasco.

But the men at the heart of Eagle Claw had not given up; nor had their president. Within seventy-two hours of the catastrophe, Carter told Army Major General Jim Vaught, the task force commander, to be prepared to launch again within ten days, in the *in extremis* case that the hostages' lives appeared in immediate danger. Such a swift turnaround had not been necessary, and the men spent the summer preparing for a second attempt, armed with the knowledge of what had gone wrong previously. In the process, they were hoping to help the United States regain not only its self-respect, but also its faith in the U.S. military and, in particular, its long-neglected special operations forces.

The new effort was code-named Snowbird. Separated from their families, who knew next to nothing about where their husbands and fathers were, the men gave serious thought to what had to be different this time around. Some of these things were tactical details, but others were larger concepts. Eagle Claw had been a pickup game, with each armed service claiming a role: the Army provided Delta Force and the Rangers as the ground rescue force; the Air Force contributed MC-130 Combat Talon transports, AC-130 Spectre gunships, and a small ground element called BRAND X; the Navy proffered an aircraft carrier from which the eight Navy RH-53D Sea Stallion helicopters launched; the Marine Corps, keen not to be excluded, provided the helicopter pilots. These forces were not used to working together. The headquarters that ran the operation was a similarly ad hoc organization commanded by Vaught.

The Eagle Claw veterans knew all that had to change, none more so than Colonel "Chargin'" Charlie Beckwith, the hard-bitten Delta commander. In the run-up to Eagle Claw, Beckwith had opposed the creation of any headquarters that might interfere with the direct line to the White House he desired for Delta. But after the trauma of Desert One, his resistance softened. Like others in Delta, he realized that having no specialized headquarters above the unit left it at the mercy of ad hoc arrangements in which it would have no say, for instance, in who provided its air support. Within a few weeks of returning, a group of senior Delta figures had sketched a design for what Beckwith called "a tier-type organization"—a command that encompassed all the units required for special operations missions of strategic importance, in which failure was not an option. In mid-May, Beckwith's main bureaucratic supporter, Army Chief of Staff General Edward "Shy" Meyer, ordered him to bring his proposed design for such a headquarters to Washington.[3]

A more formal and high-powered review of the Eagle Claw fiasco would soon reach much the same conclusion. On August 23 the Special Operations Review Group—six active and retired senior officers commissioned by the Joint Chiefs of Staff to examine Eagle Claw—released an unclassified version of its findings and recommendations. Led by retired Admiral James L. Holloway III, the group recommended "that a Counterterrorist Joint Task Force (CTJTF) be established as a field agency of the Joint Chiefs of Staff with permanently assigned staff personnel and certain assigned forces."[4]

The military brass put up fierce resistance. With the exception of Meyer, the service chiefs were very concerned that the creation of such a force would give the chairman of the Joint Chiefs of Staff his own private intervention force. The commanders of the military's regional commands around the world, called commanders-in-chief, or "CinCs" (pronounced "sinks"), feared that such a permanent task force would deploy to and conduct missions in their own areas of operations without them even knowing about, let alone approving, such actions. It was that venomous atmosphere in the Tank into which Nightingale, who served on Vaught's staff, walked a matter of days after the Holloway report's release.

But Nightingale was armed with knowledge that his high-ranking audience lacked. That morning, he, Vaught, and Colonel Rod Paschall, Vaught's chief of staff, had briefed Defense Secretary Harold Brown and Chairman of the Joint Chiefs of Staff Air Force General David Jones in Brown's office. Sitting side by side on a sofa, Vaught and his two staffers gave the two senior officials a preview of the briefing Nightingale was scheduled to deliver to the Joint Chiefs that afternoon. The briefing for the chiefs was a so-called decision brief, meaning it was intended as a starting point for discussion, with the individual service chiefs allowed to have input—which amounted to veto authority—over the details of the proposal.

Brown was well aware that the service chiefs, with the exception of the Army's Meyer, were unlikely to approve the creation of a counterterrorist joint task force. (Although the briefing focused on proposed bureaucratic arrangements for Snowbird, everyone concerned knew that the Holloway Commission's recommendation of a standing joint task force meant any structure created for Snowbird was almost certain to survive beyond another mission into Iran.) Brown interrupted the briefing. This could be difficult to get past the chiefs, he said. Would it be easier if it were made a directive from my office to the chiefs, rather than simply a presentation? Certainly, said those on the couch. Brown had a knowing smirk on his face. "I had anticipated that, so maybe I've solved some problems for you," he said, reaching for a typed document that codified the contents of the brief as a direct order to the services to take the actions laid out in the briefing. "Well, this is certainly going to make things a lot easier," said Vaught. Paschall just chuckled.

In the couple of hours between briefings, Nightingale converted his decision brief into a mere "information brief," then strode into the Tank to await his audience. The officers who entered and took their seats at the long table were Jones, the four service chiefs, and their operations deputies (the three-star officers in charge of operations and plans for each service). Using a flip chart stand to his right and a viewgraph screen to his left, Nightingale launched into his briefing without mentioning the morning's discussion with Brown. It slowly dawned on the chiefs and their operations deputies that Nightingale was speaking as if the new command was a fait accompli. The tension in the room rose sharply. "Wait a minute," said Deputy Chief of Naval Operations Vice Admiral Arthur Moreau. "This is an information brief, not a decision brief." Dead silence followed. Nightingale glanced at Vaught, who turned to Jones. "Yes, the secretary has made a decision," Jones confirmed.

"The Navy and the Air Force were just apoplectic," Nightingale recalled. Moreau and his boss, Chief of Naval Operations Admiral Thomas Hayward, "just went basically purple. They were really pissed. You could just see their blood pressure go up about 100 points." But Brown's preemptive action meant they had little recourse. "They just had to eat it," Nightingale said. For the fledgling command, it was an inauspicious beginning.[5]

Early one September morning Brigadier General Dick Scholtes, the 82nd Airborne Division's assistant division commander for operations, was already in his office at Fort Bragg, North Carolina, when he received a surprise visit from his boss, division commander Major General Guy Meloy. "You're going to be getting a call from the chief of staff in a couple of minutes," Meloy told him. Usually when the two generals discussed the "chief of staff," they were referring to the colonel who held that position in the division. But when the phone rang Scholtes found himself talking to Meyer, the Army chief of staff. "Dick, I want you to know you're leaving the division," Meyer said. "You're going to be leaving it very shortly.

I need you to come to Washington Thursday. I can't talk to you anymore about what's going to happen but I'll tell you all about it when you get up here Thursday."

Scholtes flew to Washington as directed. Already scheduled to meet Brown and Jones the next morning, Scholtes was told to head straight to the Pentagon for a meeting set for the oddly late hour of 9 P.M. After he had trouble getting past Pentagon security, someone finally came to collect the bemused general and lead him to a conference room beside Jones's office.

About thirty people were in the room. Most were strangers to Scholtes, though he would come to know some quite well. Beckwith, the Delta commander, was there, as was Commander Richard Marcinko, who was in the process of creating a Navy SEAL equivalent to Delta Force.

The officers told Scholtes they had a briefing prepared for him. Curious, he sat down. The briefing covered several options for a second attempt to rescue the hostages in Iran. Perplexed as to why he was being told all this, Scholtes sat through the first four or five, which all struck him as "absolutely asinine and outlandish," according to an officer who was there. (One involved rescuing the hostages and flying them on helicopters to a ship in the Black Sea, then tipping the empty helicopters into the water. Scholtes knew the Black Sea was dominated by the Soviets and therefore not a particularly welcoming environment for the U.S. Navy.)

No longer able to contain his curiosity, Scholtes asked why on earth they were briefing these schemes to him. Now it was his briefers' turn to be confused. "Didn't the secretary tell you about all this?" one asked. Scholtes replied that he wasn't due to see Brown until the following morning, but told them to continue the briefing and he'd wait for Brown and Jones to explain what this was all about.

On Friday the two senior officials made it all clear. His new job was to form the command that would include the nation's most elite special operations units, and to be ready to conduct another hostage rescue mission by October 31. As for other counterterrorist missions his new command should be ready to perform, Brown and Jones told him to be ready to discuss those once the Iranian mission had been completed. Scholtes's chain of command ran straight to Jones, the Joint Chiefs' four-star chairman—unique access for a one-star operational commander.

Scholtes was doubly shocked. First because, other than attending and graduating from the Special Forces Qualification Course as a young captain, he had no special operations experience, having opted to stay in the infantry mainstream rather than continue as a Special Forces officer. He never found out why Meyer selected him for the command. When he asked the four-star, Meyer simply answered: "Because I wanted you."

The imminence of the Halloween deadline also shocked Scholtes. It gave him "less than sixty days in which to pull this thing off," recalled a senior member of the command. "And we [had] no forces, no staff, and truly no capability."

Scholtes's new headquarters was located first at Bragg, the massive Army post in Fayetteville, North Carolina. Also home to XVIII Airborne Corps, 82nd Airborne Division, and Delta, which was housed in a nine-acre fenced-off facility that had been the post's stockade, the installation's huge size was an advantage in trying to hide a couple of small, secret organizations.

The new command started small: just Scholtes and an aide, working out of an office in Delta's compound furnished with a phone and very little else. Soon staff began to arrive, but only at a rate of one or two people a day. Scholtes was concerned.[6]

The new headquarters was acquiring a staff, and it already had a mission. But it lacked a name. In classified circles, the new command was referred to as the Counterterrorist Joint Task Force. But it needed a proper, official moniker. To that end, Scholtes and a couple of assistants detailed to him from Delta, Major Logan Fitch and Sergeant Major Walt Shumate, were tossing ideas around one day. "Why don't we call it 'Joint Special Operations Command,' because it's joint and it's special operations?" said Fitch. The others were fine with the suggestion, but when they ran it up the flagpole there was a problem. The Army bureaucracy opposed the name because the service's main field manual grouped a wide range of generic military tasks, including urban warfare, desert operations, and river crossings, under the heading of "special operations." The debate went back and forth between Bragg and the Pentagon, but eventually Fitch's proposal won the day. On the rare occasions it was discussed in public, Scholtes's new headquarters would be known as Joint Special Operations Command, or JSOC.[7]

The units that fell under the command were largely those deemed best suited to JSOC's counterterrorism mission, which officials at the time envisioned as small, high-intensity operations of short duration. As such, they did not include units like the Army's Special Forces groups that specialized in unconventional warfare (the use of proxy forces to foment rebellion in an enemy country), or other special operations forces designed primarily to operate against other militaries, rather than against terrorists.

At the core of the new command was Delta (full name: 1st Special Forces Operational Detachment-Delta), which the Army had formed under Beckwith's leadership in 1977 in response to the rising number of international terrorist incidents. Unlike Israel, West Germany, and the United Kingdom, the United States had no specialized force to handle such episodes until Delta's creation.

Beckwith modeled Delta on the British Army's Special Air Service, with whom he'd spent a year as an exchange officer in the early 1960s. Thus, instead of being divided into companies and battalions, like most U.S. Army units, Delta was broken into troops and squadrons. The troops were divided into teams of anywhere from three to six soldiers. Four teams made a troop, and three troops made a "sabre" squadron (the same term the SAS used). Only soldiers already in the Army were allowed to apply to Delta, guaranteeing the unit a more seasoned outlook than combat outfits filled with soldiers in their late teens and early twenties. But the key to Delta was its rigorous selection process. The unit looked for men who possessed not only extraordinary physical endurance, but also mental agility and the psychological ability to cope with ambiguity and the unknown. So its selection course combined increasingly difficult physical tests, culminating in "the Long Walk"—a grueling forty-mile hike across the Appalachian Mountains in West Virginia—with a battery of psychological examinations. If a prospective unit member made it over those hurdles, he still had to pass the "commander's board," in which the Delta commander and other senior unit figures peppered the candidate with off-the-wall questions in an attempt to unhinge him.

The small percentage of applicants who made it all the way through selection into Delta then went through a six-month operator training course in which they learned skills ranging from expert marksmanship and room clearing to how to take down a hijacked airliner, breach walls, and pick locks. They also learned espionage tradecraft, including elicitation, clandestine communications, surveillance, and how to live under a cover identity. Only after completing the course (which not all did) were the greenhorns considered full members of the unit who could call themselves "operators." They called Delta "the Unit."[8]

Eagle Claw was to have been Delta's first taste of actual combat.

Although the operators bore no blame for Eagle Claw's failure, they were acutely aware that they were 0 for 1 on "real-world" missions. They were hungry to even the score.

Backing up Delta were the Army's two (1st and 2nd) Ranger Battalions, based at Hunter Army Airfield, Georgia, and Fort Lewis, Washington, respectively. The battalions traced their lineage back to World War II, but had existed in their present incarnation only since 1974, when Army Chief of Staff General Creighton Abrams reactivated them with the intention that they would be the world's most elite airborne light infantry.[9]

Beckwith envisioned the Rangers compensating for Delta's lack of manpower on any mission requiring more than a handful of operators. He wanted the Rangers to help Delta get to and from an objective and to secure the perimeter while the operators took down the target. Beckwith called this his "donut theory," with the Rangers forming the donut's ring.[10]

Almost simultaneous with JSOC's creation, the Navy established a SEAL special mission unit that was the sea service's answer to Delta, and which would also report to Scholtes. The SEALs were the Navy's special operations forces, with roots in the service's World War II underwater demolition teams. In 1980 there were only two SEAL (Sea-Air-Land) teams, Team 1 on the West Coast and Team 2 on the East. Neither team was a dedicated counterterrorism force. In fact, less than a third of their platoons had received counterterrorism training. But Richard Marcinko had a vision. A colorful SEAL officer who, from a desk in the Pentagon, had been one of two Navy representatives on the Eagle Claw task force and was now working on Snowbird, Marcinko saw an opening for a SEAL team that would fill roughly the same counterterrorism niche for the Navy that Delta filled for the Army. He masterfully worked the Navy bureaucracy to establish such a unit and to get himself assigned as its first commander. He even got to name the unit. Because there were only six SEAL platoons that had received counterterrorism training and because he wanted to fool the Soviets into thinking there were more SEAL teams than there really were, Marcinko named his new command SEAL Team 6.

Marcinko and the Navy intended Team 6 to be the maritime equivalent of Delta, but there was a big difference between how the two units assessed and selected their members. Team 6 members didn't have to pass any formal tests or graduate from any courses to get into the unit. Marcinko chose SEALs for his new command based solely on his personal opinion of them, an opinion often formed during barroom interviews with prospective members. "The man liked to drink," said an officer who worked under Marcinko in Team 6. "To be with him, you had to drink—to be in the 'in' crowd." Marcinko acknowledged to an author his capacity to down large quantities of Bombay gin on the job, but added, "I use booze as a *tool*." Fairly or not, such behavior colored the opinions of Team 6 held by many others in the special ops community for years after Marcinko left the unit in July 1983.

Although the SEALs were maritime special operations forces, and Team 6's position as a coequal with Delta in JSOC was predicated on its "worldwide maritime responsibilities," from its inception, Marcinko was determined that his new unit not be pigeonholed or limited in any way. "As long as we carried water in our canteens, we'd be in a maritime environment—or close enough for me," he later wrote. This approach garnered the unit a role in Snowbird, in which they were earmarked for covert infiltration into Iran to destroy a series of military targets, but it also set the stage for three decades of friction with Delta over appropriate roles and missions for Team 6.[11]

The Air Force's initial contributions to JSOC were the 1st Special Operations Wing, based at Hurlburt Field in the Florida panhandle, and a secret unit of combat controllers—men whose job it was to act as battlefield air traffic controllers. The unit would go through many name changes. Until Eagle Claw it had been named BRAND X, but as JSOC stood up the Air Force renamed it "Det 1 MACOS," which stood for Detachment One, Military Airlift Command Operations Staff.[12]

Where capability gaps existed, units were created to fill them. Such was the case with the command's communications infrastructure, which the Pentagon told Scholtes the Joint Communications Support Element, a special ops communications outfit at MacDill Air Force Base in Tampa, Florida, would provide. Scholtes protested that JCSE was too "cumbersome" a unit for JSOC. After several months of arguing, he won permission to stand up the Joint Communications Unit at Bragg, with part of the unit assigned full time to JSOC.[13]

The lack of a special operations rotary wing aviation unit was an even more glaring weakness, given that the inability to keep enough helicopters mission-ready played a key role in the events that resulted in the fiery debacle at Desert One. But efforts were under way to fill that yawning void. A new organization, based around helicopters and aircrew from the 101st Airborne Division's 158th and 159th Aviation Battalions and dubbed Task Force 158, was training in great secrecy at the 101st's home post of Fort Campbell, Kentucky, as well as at the military's vast training areas in the Southwest.

Task Force 158 used the brand-new UH-60A Black Hawk utility helicopters that were replacing the UH-1 Iroquois, better known as the "Huey," in the 101st. To fulfill heavier lift requirements, the task force availed itself of some of the 159th's CH-47C Chinooks. Together these two airframes should have been able to perform any medium or long-haul lift or air assault requirements. But Vaught, who remained in command of the task force until Scholtes got JSOC off the ground, saw a need for a third type of airframe, one that could maneuver in Tehran's tight urban terrain, carrying small groups of operators or even functioning as a light attack helicopter. The active Army's inventory held no such aircraft. But Vietnam veterans were familiar with the OH-6 Cayuse, nicknamed the "Loach" (for light observation and command helicopter), a small, nimble airframe that still resided in a couple of National Guard units. Designed to carry just two pilots, the OH-6 was not armed. However, imaginative TF 158 aviators soon figured ways to fix small benchlike platforms called pods to allow assaulters to ride on either side of the helicopter and to equip the aircraft to fire miniguns and rockets. No longer "Loaches," both versions of the reconfigured aircraft were called Little Birds. The assault version (the one with the pods) was designated the MH-6 and the attack variant the AH-6.[14] There would be many twists and turns in the development of JSOC's world-class special operations rotary wing capability, but the Chinook, the Black Hawk, and the Little Bird would remain the basic Army special ops airframes for more than thirty years.

In July 1980, in a move that would have significant consequences, the Army established another secrecy-cloaked special operations unit but did not initially assign it to JSOC. Led by Colonel Jerry King, Vaught's chief of staff for Eagle Claw, the Field Operations Group (sometimes called the Foreign Operating Group) comprised about fifty Special Forces and military intelligence soldiers. The new unit's mission was to operate undercover abroad to gain the sort of intelligence for the military that the CIA had been unable to deliver for Eagle Claw, and to sabotage key

Iranian military infrastructure such as radar and communications facili-ties. In the summer and fall it successfully infiltrated several operatives into Iran to conduct surveillance and recruit agents.[15]

Halloween came and went with no orders to launch. Uncomfortable with the CIA's intelligence on the hostages' locations, Scholtes had told his bosses he was unwilling to do the mission on the basis of the Agency's "we can't tell you exactly [but] we think they're here, here, and here" intelligence. "We may end up killing a lot of people and getting a lot of our people killed and not getting anybody out," he said. Meanwhile, the lines of command between Scholtes's new organization and Vaught's headquarters, which was still in existence, were blurred. Each general seemed to think he would run the second rescue mission. The Pentagon officially transferred authority to JSOC on December 18, but Vaught continued to play a vague oversight role. "It was very ambiguous because both elements felt that they were in fact in command," Nightingale said. A personality conflict between the two generals didn't help, but their staffs nevertheless expected to be integrated for the mission, which they anticipated tough-talking Republican president-elect Ronald Reagan would green-light as one of his first acts in office.[16]

Although Scholtes had been assembling his staff since September, the Pentagon did not formally establish JSOC until December 15.[17] No cer-emony marked the creation of what would become one of the U.S. gov-ernment's most effective instruments of power. The command was completely focused on training for what everyone expected would be a second rescue attempt in Iran. On January 20, the day of Reagan's inau-guration, the task force was at Hurlburt Field running what a senior JSOC staffer called "the final dress rehearsal" for the mission. "We were hoping to launch the next week," he said. But within minutes of Reagan taking the oath of office, the Iranian regime released the hostages, who were immediately flown to Algeria and on to Rhein-Main Air Base in Germany. The Pentagon canceled the final rehearsal, frustrating JSOC officers, who saw it as a lost opportunity to put the task force through its paces.[18] But in the long run, that mattered little. The new command was up and running.

2

JSOC Gets Its Feet Wet

The peaceful resolution of the hostage drama gave Scholtes and JSOC time to draw breath and consider their role in the Reagan-era national security structure. A February 1981 memo from Caspar Weinberger, the new administration's defense secretary, directing each service to "maintain and continue to develop its own [counterterrorist] capabilities,"[1] not only helped solidify the position of JSOC and its constituent units, but more generally set the tone for the increased role the military's covert and clandestine actions would play in the 1980s.

In that context, it is important to note that JSOC still didn't have a monopoly over these actions. At the direction of "Shy" Meyer, the Army chief of staff, the Field Operations Group was renamed the Intelligence Support Activity, or ISA, and on March 3, 1981, became a permanent entity located in Arlington, Virginia, just outside Washington, D.C. But because JSOC was considered a purely tactical counterterrorist organization and ISA was to have wide-ranging national-level clandestine intelligence-gathering missions, the Pentagon did not place "the Activity," as it became known, under Scholtes's command. Instead King, who remained in charge, reported straight to the Army's assistant chief of staff for intelligence.[2]

A day before ISA's official establishment, and in conjunction with the CIA, the Army stood up a covert aviation unit code-named Seaspray, with a mission to move men and matériel in civilian, or at least, civilian-looking, rotary and fixed wing aircraft. Such missions and units are referred to as "covered air." Seaspray was the covered counterpart to Task Force 158, which had survived the hostage crisis denouement to earn a new name—Task Force 160—and a permanent home at Fort Campbell, Kentucky. But although TF 160 was also a secret unit, its function was purely military, while Seaspray could be used to clandestinely infiltrate

CIA or military intelligence operatives. The covered air unit soon amassed a small fleet of nine Cessna and Beechcraft King Air planes, as well as several Hughes MD500 helicopters (the civilian version of the Little Birds), which could be rigged with weapons and/or pods for operators if need be. The unit also acquired an innocuous cover name—1st Rotary Wing Test Activity—and a home at Fort Eustis, Virginia, conveniently close to Camp Peary, the CIA's training center better known as "the Farm." Like ISA, initially Seaspray did not report to JSOC.[3]

As new covert units proliferated, the two special mission units dedicated to direct action—Delta and SEAL Team 6—continued to evolve. For Delta, that meant learning to cope without Beckwith, who left the unit in October 1980. Meyer, the Army chief of staff, called Scholtes and suggested that he make Beckwith his director of operations. Although not a career special operations officer, Scholtes had great respect for the out-of-left-field mind-set with which Beckwith was trying to imbue Delta, but he still regarded the colonel as something of a loose cannon. He told Meyer that he would keep Beckwith on his staff as a special assistant, but had no intention of making him his operations officer. Beckwith retired shortly thereafter.

Scholtes also quickly became disenchanted with the hard-drinking, free-spending ways of "Demo Dick" Marcinko, Beckwith's Team 6 counterpart.[4] Marcinko had built his unit into a tightly bonded 175-man organization that pioneered new tactics to take down a variety of maritime targets, from oil rigs to cruise ships. Initially based at Naval Amphibious Base Little Creek, Virginia Beach, Virginia, before moving to nearby Fleet Training Center, Dam Neck, where it would remain, Team 6 trained hard—and expensively. The unit's annual small arms ammunition allotment was larger than that of the entire Marine Corps. But the resources lavished on the team and the sheer pleasure Marcinko took in flouting authority combined to antagonize just about every other officer in the Naval Special Warfare community and many beyond.[5]

So long as the largesse seemed focused on mission-essential training and equipment, Marcinko was on reasonably solid ground with Scholtes. But it wasn't long before the straight-arrow infantry general began to think things had gotten seriously off-kilter at Dam Neck. Events came to a head when Marcinko invited Scholtes to an evening function at the team headquarters at which several men were to be promoted. When Scholtes arrived, Marcinko told him Maine lobsters were on the menu.

Scholtes inquired as to how the team came by the lobsters. "I flew them down," Marcinko replied.

"The evening progressed and they got so shitfaced they couldn't stand up," said a senior JSOC official. Scholtes waited until the SEALs had had a chance to sober up the next day and then told Marcinko he was writing a letter of reprimand and sending it to the chief of naval operations, "because last night was an absolute disgrace." The CNO invited the JSOC commander to his office in Washington to talk. The admiral told Scholtes that Marcinko was the "best man" to lead Team 6. "He was outstanding to get this unit started, because he had to fight your system, he had to fight the Navy system," Scholtes replied. However, the general added, Marcinko was not the best choice to lead Team 6 into the future.[6]

By early 1981, JSOC's staff had grown to about eighty personnel. The command had already moved out of Delta's compound and into three World War II–era barracks that had a twelve-foot fence and round-the-clock civilian guard force, but just one secure phone line to Washington between them. Defense Secretary Caspar Weinberger agreed with Scholtes that JSOC needed new facilities and arranged a meeting between the general and some Pentagon bureaucrats he'd ordered to make it happen. In the meeting, Scholtes listed everything that he needed in his new headquarters. A Pentagon officially dutifully wrote it all down. But Scholtes overlooked one item: windows. As a result, his new headquarters was built on Pope Air Force Base (adjacent to Bragg) in record time, but with no windows.[7]

Within six months of Reagan's inauguration, Scholtes's Pentagon bosses gave JSOC a new mission that would come to dominate much of the command's training for the next two decades: countering the spread of weapons of mass destruction. They told the general to talk with Energy Department experts to determine the threat that terrorists might pose by gaining access to nuclear material, and to figure out ways to counter that threat.

JSOC's interest in weapons of mass destruction would grow, but during the early 1980s its focus was on the threat of nuclear-armed terrorists, rather than attacking enemy countries' facilities. "We never got into those [nation-state] types of scenarios," said a senior JSOC official. "Ours were small nuclear weapons held by terrorists in a hostage situation against one of our cities or against a U.S. facility." The command worked closely with the Energy Department and its national laboratories, running exercises everywhere from downtown Los Angeles to the Nevada desert to ensure they could all work together if terrorists ever gained access to a nuclear device. The exercises were invaluable for uncovering small flaws that could derail an operation. The L.A. exercise, for instance, which featured Delta operators working with a team from the national labs trying to secure and disarm a "nuclear" device held by "terrorists" played by FBI agents, revealed that "scientists with big beards have a hell of a time wearing a protective mask," the senior JSOC official said. This was a problem because Delta was using "a lot of tear gas in there." (The exercise was part of JSOC's three-year mission to help with security preparations for the 1984 Los Angeles Olympics. During the games themselves, JSOC positioned its joint operations center at Los Alamitos Army Airfield in Orange County, with a Team 6 element down the coast at Coronado. Team 6 also placed undercover operators with satellite communications on a cruise ship that was going to be at harbor in L.A. during the day but sail offshore to become a casino at night. JSOC wanted the SEALs, who had signed on as crew, on the ship so that they could communicate back to the JSOC in case terrorists took it over.)

At the Department of Energy's request, the Pentagon also tapped Delta and Team 6 to provide "red teams" to test the security of nuclear power plants in the United States. The operators had to base their plans on whatever "open source" information they could find in libraries. They found numerous weaknesses in the plants' security programs. "We had no trouble getting in them," said a JSOC staff officer. "But the more we did, the more they wanted." Often the units would break into a power plant's safe, only to find a consultant's report gathering dust inside that identified the same weaknesses the operators had just exposed. "They were wasting our time," the staffer said.

Modestly sized joint exercises soon became a regular occurrence for the headquarters and its subordinate units. "We tried to do an exercise every quarter and it was either a hostage rescue or a hit on a terrorist facility," a senior JSOC official said. Away from the larger exercises, the units were training constantly. Scholtes put JSOC on a readiness cycle, so each unit kept a small element ready to deploy on four hours' notice. The troops had to know the basics of the mission before they took off so that they could pack whatever mission-specific gear they might need, but any other details were to be briefed in flight. For larger operations, JSOC aimed to get more forces in the air within eight hours of being alerted, but rarely made that target due to the complexity of organizing the various air elements required for such missions.[8]

For all the training, what the operators really yearned for was a chance to test their skills in combat.[9] An opportunity seemed to present itself at the very start of JSOC's existence when, in late 1980, intelligence suggested Americans captured during the Vietnam War were being held in a prison camp in the jungle near the central Laotian town of Nhommarath. The "intelligence" took the form of RD-77 satellite and SR-71 Blackbird spy plane photos of a wooden stockade with what some analysts interpreted as the number "52" marked out on the ground, as if prisoners there were trying to signal U.S. overhead reconnaissance.[10] Not everyone was convinced. "I didn't see it," said a JSOC staffer who viewed the photographs. Nonetheless, at the direction of the Joint Chiefs of Staff, JSOC began tightly compartmented preparations for a rescue operation code-named Pocket Change and set for May 1981.

But the effort was complicated by the bizarre intrusion of retired Special Forces Lieutenant Colonel James "Bo" Gritz (pronounced "grites"). In March 1981 Gritz informed the White House he was planning his own rescue mission. The government told him to stand down, but he continued his efforts, this time (unbeknownst to JSOC) in collusion with the Intelligence Support Activity. Gritz's appearance on the scene, which had the potential to jeopardize the operation, pushed JSOC's timeline to the right, but the command continued planning. Scholtes considered on-the-ground confirmation of the presence of American prisoners essential before launching the mission. He wanted to assign the task of gathering that intelligence to a few Delta operators, but, to his displeasure, the CIA insisted on employing Laotian mercenaries for the purpose instead. The mercenaries returned to say they'd found no evidence of American prisoners, prompting a fierce debate over the reliability of their reporting.[11]

JSOC rehearsed extensively in Hawaii for the mission, which would involve a task force launching from the tiny Pacific island of Tinian in the Northern Marianas and using an abandoned and overgrown U.S. military airfield in Thailand as a forward staging base. With the airfield under control, C-5 transport planes would have landed, bearing JSOC's own version of a Trojan horse: white, civilian-style eighteen-wheel trucks, each hiding two TF 160 AH-6 Little Birds with folded rotor blades. As Delta operators made their way overland to the prison camp

TF 160 personnel would have driven the trucks close to the Laotian border, before stopping and launching the helicopters.[12]

TF 160 kept this rarely used technique—known in JSOC as "Smokey and the Bandit" after the 1977 trucker comedy starring Burt Reynolds—up its sleeve for decades, because it offered a clandestine way to move a lethal capability close to a target. "Our guys were trained and even had the truck licenses," said a TF 160 veteran. The unit had its own trucks, but locally obtained vehicles would suffice "with maybe a couple of days' work and some welding," he said. When the time came to launch the aircraft, the crew would roll them off the back of the truck and have them flying within three minutes. "You have to be really well trained," the TF 160 veteran said. "It's absolutely an incredible capability."

The Little Birds' role was to provide fire support to the Delta assaulters, and, in particular, to destroy the prison camp's three wooden guard towers. The delays caused by Gritz's interference meant it was now 1982. Army General John Vessey had replaced Jones as Joint Chiefs chairman. When briefed on the plan, Vessey refused to believe that the Little Birds could take out the guard towers. JSOC had replicas built at Fort A. P. Hill in Virginia and held a nighttime demonstration there for the chairman that ended with the AH-6s turning the towers into splinters, much to his amazement.[13]

Not for the last time, the preparations were for naught. The discovery that Gritz was still involved in planning a rescue effort—with help from ISA, no less—was bad enough, but then the story showed up in the press. "We were flying missions over [the camp] taking pictures of it every chance we got and after the newspaper article came out about Bo Gritz putting his team together, a week later, the next picture we got, there was nobody in the camp," said a JSOC staffer. "They deserted the camp. . . . That's what stopped the mission." However, a Delta officer involved in the planning said the mission was canceled because of a CIA report, which the Agency said was based on the word of a Marine detailed to the Agency who'd gone into Laos and gotten "eyes on" the camp, that no Americans were there. "I don't think there were ever Americans in there," the Delta officer said. A Pentagon special operations official said the mission was scrubbed because the Thai government withdrew its approval. Whatever the reason, the mission faded away, leaving in its wake rancor and bitterness,[14] but also a certain amount of relief. Army Colonel Don Gordon, the JSOC intelligence director, had strongly advised against an operation. "This is not worth it," he told Scholtes. "We lose half the force if we screw this thing up, [and] if you lose half your force in the middle of Laos you've got a problem." Nevertheless, JSOC was prepared to launch the raid, said a senior official at the command. "But thank God we didn't," he added.[15]

As preparations for the Laos mission continued through summer 1981, JSOC ran its first real-world mission at the end of July in the tiny West African nation of the Gambia. There, Marxist rebels had taken advantage of President Dawda Jawara's attendance at the royal wedding in Britain to launch a coup and seize more than a hundred hostages, including American, French, Canadian, British, Swiss, and German citizens. The Gambia had no military to speak of, so efforts to reverse the coup fell to neighboring Senegal and the Gambia's Western allies. JSOC flew a five-man team into Dakar, the Senegalese capital. Working from the U.S. embassy, the team coordinated with three SAS personnel Britain had sent into the Gambia. Once Senegalese paratroops had secured the airport in the capital city of Banjul, and the SAS had effected the release of the hostages, Delta's Major William G. "Jerry" Boykin and Sergeant First Class Tommy Corbett plus a radio operator flew in to organize their evacuation to Dakar on an Air Force C-141. The coup was over within a few days. JSOC hadn't seen combat, but had at least gotten its feet wet without embarrassing itself.[16]

✳

No proof ever emerged that American POWs were being held in Laos or anywhere else in Indochina, but one American soldier who did become a prisoner during this period was Brigadier General James Dozier. The Italian Red Brigades terrorist group kidnapped the general from his apartment in Verona, Italy, on December 17, 1981, setting in motion a crisis that exposed the bureaucratic limits of JSOC's power.

Ordered by Defense Secretary Weinberger to send a team to Italy to help with the search for Dozier, Scholtes dispatched a Delta element led by deputy Delta commander Colonel Jesse Johnson. But an extraordinary dispute between U.S. European Command, the State Department, and JSOC over whom Johnson was to report to slowed the team's work. The chain of command for JSOC—at the time considered a purely counterterrorist organization—ran straight from Scholtes to the chairman of the Joint Chiefs of Staff and from there to the defense secretary and the president. The exception was when a JSOC element had been deployed to a foreign country, but not yet committed to action. Then, the U.S. ambassador to the country was considered in charge. But when Johnson's team arrived in Italy, European Command, which otherwise ran all U.S. military operations in Europe, tried to assert its authority. The result was a messy and time-consuming dispute that the Joint Chiefs failed to settle. Further complicating matters, the Pentagon also deployed an ISA signals intelligence team to Italy. The team took to the skies in helicopters equipped with electronic directional finding systems that located numerous Red Brigades safe houses by locking on to the terrorists' radio transmissions.

The full-court press from Delta, the ISA, the National Security Agency, and the Italian authorities eventually located Dozier and his kidnappers in a Padua apartment, where Italian agents rescued him on January 28. The episode showcased the burgeoning skills of the United States' secret operators, but also highlighted the challenges of inserting them into a national security bureaucracy not designed to accommodate them.[17]

Scholtes fought frequent battles with that bureaucracy to keep his forces away from missions for which they were not designed. At the time, that included invasions of sovereign countries. "Boss, we've got some hellacious capabilities, but I'd hate to wipe them out—some of these really good, talented Delta or SEAL Team 6 operatives—for something that's not critical to their mission," he told Vessey.

This was a constant struggle for Scholtes and his successors. A case in point was the 1981 order the Pentagon gave JSOC to prepare to invade Suriname. The huge bauxite reserves in the former Dutch colony on South America's northeastern Atlantic coast meant that Alcoa, the massive U.S. aluminum firm, had major holdings in the country. A 1980 military coup that deposed the elected government and installed the brutal Dési Bouterse as a leftist dictator placed those properties—and, more importantly, the Western expatriates who worked on them—at risk. JSOC began planning an operation to oust Bouterse and free any Western hostages in late 1981, infiltrating operators undercover to reconnoiter possible targets and to photograph the route from the airfield to the capital, Paramaribo. "[Det 1 MACOS] people . . . went down to Suriname and surveyed all the airfields under the guise that they were birdwatchers," said a JSOC staffer. "We had lots of guys go down there. It was easy to get people in and out." JSOC was confident it could pull the operation off. "It really would have been a piece of cake," the staffer said. "Think of a little town with the worst police force you can think of and that's what they had."

But the mission began to expand, particularly when it became clear that Bouterse might take and hold Western hostages in several different locations. "The Rangers and Delta were part of the recovery for these people," said a Pentagon special operations official. "We'd have to go to several different locations and bring the expats to the airfield. At the same time we've got to take over the radio and TV stations in Suriname and grab the president. It was getting kind of complex." As a result, by 1982 the operation had evolved from one that involved only JSOC to one in which XVIII Airborne Corps would have a major role.

The JSOC tactical command post and representatives from the units in the invasion plan moved to Hurlburt Field, Florida, for six weeks. The Pentagon wanted the Rangers to conduct an airfield seizure, which was becoming their specialty, with XVIII Airborne Corps' 82nd Airborne and 101st Airborne (Air Assault) Divisions flowing in behind them. The two divisions were "preparing to move out," said a senior JSOC official. "I thought we were going to war." But in a dynamic to which JSOC would grow accustomed during the next two decades, the Reagan administration called off the 1982 operation late in the planning process. The administration remained interested in overthrowing Bouterse: in late 1983, after the CIA had considered and then dropped a plan to engineer a countercoup to topple Bouterse earlier that year, JSOC was still planning and rehearsing a carrier-launched full-scale invasion. Delta operators visited Suriname undercover on reconnaissance missions before the administration again decided against the operation. However, the prospect of a JSOC-led invasion of Suriname continued to surface for the remainder of the 1980s.[18] "That was always on the books," a Delta operator said.

Events in fall 1983 ensured that JSOC's planning effort for Suriname was not completely wasted, however. When a military coup October 14 in Grenada resulted in hard-line Marxists being replaced by even more zealous Marxists, President Reagan decided to invade the tiny Caribbean island nation. The initial plan had JSOC in the lead, with important roles for Delta, Team 6, both Ranger battalions, TF 160, and Det 1 MACOS. JSOC's plan borrowed heavily from the command's Suriname work. "For every target we had in Suriname, there was a like target in Grenada, so that speeded up our operations," a JSOC staffer said. "Suriname was kind of a big joke to us, but it really turned out to be the Grenada model." The Grenada operation, named Urgent Fury, would be JSOC's first combat mission, but placed the command in a role for which it was not designed: spearheading an invasion, rather than reacting to a terrorist incident.[19] Although ultimately successful, Urgent Fury was a fiasco that, like Eagle Claw, exposed the limitations of even the most elite units and had long-term ramifications for U.S. special operations forces.

On Friday, October 21, Scholtes briefed the services' three-star operations deputies in the Pentagon on how JSOC envisioned conducting the assault. He was due back October 23 to brief the Joint Chiefs, but that morning the Iranian-backed Islamic Jihad militant group killed 241 U.S. servicemen, including 220 Marines, in Beirut, Lebanon, by destroying their barracks with a truck bomb. The Marine losses prompted the Corps' commandant, General Paul X. Kelley, to petition Vessey for a prominent Marine role in the Grenada invasion scheduled less than forty-eight hours from then. Vessey relented. Carefully drafted plans had to be hastily rewritten as Vessey gave the Marines all targets in the northern half of the island.

The late addition of the Marines resulted in U.S. Atlantic Command changing the operation's H-hour (the mission start time) from 2 A.M., which had been JSOC's preference, to first light, allowing Grenadian forces and their Cuban allies to take JSOC forces under heavy, effective fire when they conducted their air assault and airborne missions. TF 160's Black Hawks were riddled with bullets as they tried to infiltrate Delta and Team 6 operators. U.S. forces, who outnumbered trained enemy forces on the island about ten to one, eventually triumphed, but with the loss of nineteen men killed in action, of whom thirteen were JSOC task force personnel. These included four Team 6 SEALs who drowned after a night parachute jump into the sea forty miles from shore and three Rangers killed when three Black Hawks collided as they landed during an air assault.

The operation was hobbled by a confused chain of command, a failure to properly prepare (U.S. forces conducted no rehearsals and invaded without any good maps of Grenada), poor to nonexistent communications between different elements of the invading force, and woefully inadequate intelligence. (Scholtes had refused ISA commander Jerry King's offer to have his unit conduct advance reconnaissance for the task force, because he had no faith or trust in him, a personality conflict that limited cooperation between the two organizations throughout the 1980s.) As many as a third of U.S. killed and wounded in action may have resulted from friendly fire.[20] The invasion was the United States' first major combat operation since the fall of Saigon and it revealed that much had been forgotten about the importance of unity of command and thorough preparation. The Pentagon had established JSOC in part to avoid a repeat of the ad hoc nature of Eagle Claw. But Grenada showed that while JSOC and its component units worked reasonably well together, there was still much progress to be made when it came to coordination with conventional forces.

JSOC was also hamstrung in this regard by the obsessive secrecy that permeated and surrounded the command. It was a principal factor behind the shambolic performance in Grenada, because many senior conventional force commanders were not even aware of JSOC's existence, let alone knew how best to employ its units. "It was so, so top secret that it was extremely difficult to do our job," said a senior JSOC official. The extraordinary level of secrecy that shrouded JSOC's missions, units, and personnel became a touchstone for the command and its subordinate elements, to the extent that an operator's commitment to this code of silence was considered a demonstration of his special ops bona fides. But Scholtes, like other JSOC commanders after him, chafed against it because of the constraints it placed on his operations. Indeed, it had come as almost a relief when the *Fayetteville Times* first reported JSOC's creation in October 1980.[21]

Grenada left deep scars in JSOC's collective psyche. Scholtes remained deeply embittered by the eleventh-hour interference in his plan.[22] Nor was he the only senior JSOC officer angered by the events surrounding the commitment of the elite forces to the fight. The Det 1 MACOS commander, Colonel John Carney, retired in disgust shortly after the operation.[23] Scholtes would eventually have an opportunity to air his frustrations in a way that counted. But not all the mistakes resulted from issues beyond JSOC's control. There had been several major errors internal to Scholtes's task force. Urgent Fury put JSOC on notice that the command and its subordinate elements still had a way to go to become truly effective combat units.

3

Frustration in the Middle East

The Pentagon's wholesale commitment of JSOC to combat in Urgent Fury proved an exception to the rule during the early and mid-1980s. Not that there weren't numerous crises—terrorist-related and otherwise—for which the command prepared, and sometimes deployed. But when push came to shove, the Reagan administration displayed a marked reluctance to commit its most elite forces to battle. Nowhere was this more so than the Middle East in general, and Lebanon in particular.

In 1981 Delta began routinely deploying two operators—one each from A and B Squadrons—on three-month stints as bodyguards for the U.S. ambassador in Beirut. The Lebanese capital was the most violent city in the world, with numerous armed militias vying for power and influence. After the United States deployed a Marine task force to Beirut as part of a "peacekeeping" force in 1982, some local factions, rightly or wrongly, viewed the United States as party to the conflict. On April 18, 1983, militants detonated a truck bomb in front of the embassy, shearing the front off the structure and killing sixty-three people. The blast wiped out virtually the entire CIA station. It also took the life of Sergeant First Class Terry Gilden of Delta's A Squadron, who was waiting for the ambassador with the rest of the chief of mission's dozen-strong security detail at the front of the building when the explosion killed them all.[1] Gilden was the first Delta operator killed in action.[2] When yet another bomb attack damaged the new U.S. embassy in September 1984, it was another A Squadron operator, Eagle Claw veteran Sergeant First Class Edward Bugarin, who pulled injured ambassador Reginald Bartholomew to safety.[3] (The action earned Bugarin a Soldier's Medal—the highest U.S. Army award for bravery not involving conflict with an enemy.)[4]

Protective detail deployments to Beirut continued into the late 1980s. Delta usually did not use them as cover for any other low-visibility activities. "When we went over for our protection missions, that's all we did," an operator said. But according to Eric Haney, an operator who later wrote of his experiences in Beirut, there were occasional deployments to Beirut for other missions, such as the time he and a partner successfully targeted a pair of snipers who had wounded several Marines.[5]

In his autobiography, Richard Marcinko also describes a December 1982 deployment of a dozen Team 6 operators to the Lebanese capital with a mission to analyze threats to the embassy and the Marines and recommend security improvements. In Marcinko's version of the story, he told a senior embassy official that the embassy was vulnerable to a car bomb, but the diplomat dismissed the SEAL officer's concerns and refused to take his advice, which was to station a "black box" device on the embassy roof that could detonate radio-triggered car bombs at a safe distance. The SEALs left Beirut the next day, about three months before the car bomb attack that destroyed the embassy, but not before they had tested their device by driving around Beirut until a house in a residential neighborhood "erupted" as they approached it. Marcinko implies the device he was holding caused the explosion. He describes a scene of devastation in which "dozens of Lebanese, some of them in pieces, lay in the street" as he watched others try and fail to rescue two women who were trapped in a car and burned to death.[6]

Intelligence officials later surmised that the organization responsible for the truck bombs that shattered the embassy and destroyed the Marine barracks that October was Hezbollah, the Shi'ite militant group also behind the spate of kidnappings of Westerners in Lebanon that began in 1982. Hezbollah in turn was largely a tool of Iran, the country whose actions had prompted JSOC's formation, and which the command would repeatedly confront over the next thirty years.[7]

The kidnappings drove JSOC to employ innovative countermeasures. "We were concerned about security for some of our ambassadors, so we were looking at how could we identify where they were if they were kidnapped," a senior JSOC official said. "We developed a tagging system based on the polar bear systems that were used in Alaska." The initial tag design was cylindrical, white, a few inches long, and was actually called the "polar bear." It worked on a line-of-sight basis, so JSOC needed an aircraft somewhere in the area to locate the tag. The Joint Communications Unit was at the center of the effort, which placed the tags in the belts, waistbands, or—for women—brassieres of ambassadors and any other individuals JSOC considered most at risk of kidnapping.[8]

Another new technology, the satellite fax, proved its worth in July 1983 when JSOC had to respond to a hostage crisis in Sudan. Two dozen Southern Sudan Liberation Front "rebels"—in reality little more than poorly equipped bandits—had taken five Westerners, including two American missionaries, hostage in the jungle of the Boma plateau in the southeastern tip of the country. Delta's Jerry Boykin led a small team to Khartoum and then Juba in southern Sudan to advise the Sudanese hostage rescue force, which by good fortune he and other JSOC personnel had helped establish a few months previously.

Meanwhile, a small ISA element located the rebels and their hostages by getting a fix on the shortwave transmitter they were using to negotiate with the Sudanese authorities. With the target location in hand, a Keyhole reconnaissance satellite was positioned overhead. But the satellite transmitted its photos back to Washington, not Sudan. This is where the satellite fax came into its own.

Boykin's team had arrived in Sudan with recent satellite imagery of the target area, which they had given to the CIA station chief in Khartoum, who in turn had passed it to the Sudanese military. But the details the hostage rescue force required—the location of guards, for instance—changed frequently enough to quickly render the photos out of date. After some urgent transatlantic phone calls to North Carolina, an officer in JSOC's operations directorate called the command's Washington office staff. It was a Saturday morning, but the staffers returned to the Pentagon and got hold of the latest Keyhole pictures. The staffers compared the new pictures with the originals in Boykin's hands, noted the differences—"where they could see people on the roof of a building or where a guard post had been established"—and then traced those differences onto a new piece of paper sized to the exact dimensions of the original satellite photos and faxed that image to Boykin's team, who used it as an overlay for their imagery. "It was very rudimentary, but it was effective," said a Delta officer.

After two weeks the Sudanese military made their move and rescued the hostages unscathed in an air assault mission that killed most of the kidnappers. As Boykin relates in his memoir, he and Delta Sergeant First Class Don Feeney flew down to Boma for the mission, but took no part in the action. It was one of a series of behind-the-scenes advisory efforts on JSOC's part that led to successful hostage rescues during the early 1980s. Others included a March 1981 operation by Indonesian commandos to free the passengers and crew of a hijacked Indonesian airliner at Bangkok airport, and Venezuelan forces' July 1984 storming of a hijacked Aeropostal jet in Curaçao.[9]

A frustrated Scholtes left JSOC in August 1984 to command 2nd Armored Division. He was replaced by another infantry officer, Army Major General[10] "Country" Carl Stiner, whose only previous special operations experience had been two years with 3rd Special Forces Group in the mid-1960s. Stiner took over a headquarters that had grown to about 120 people,[11] but which was still figuring out where it fit in the crowded national security structure. There were plenty of envious stares cast JSOC's way by conventional military leaders, who by nature and tradition are usually suspicious of "elite" units and resentful of organizations that receive a disproportionate share of the Pentagon budget, as JSOC and its special mission units assuredly did.

Other military organizations were not the only partners with whom it was in JSOC's interest to stay on good terms. The command also relied on the intelligence agencies to provide it with mission-critical information. Although Scholtes didn't much care for CIA director Bill Casey, JSOC's overall relationship with the CIA was good. The Agency kept a representative at JSOC's headquarters, but Scholtes's determination to keep his staff at a manageable size meant JSOC did not place a liaison at Langley.[12] JSOC also enjoyed a "good relationship" with the Defense Intelligence Agency, but the command's "best relationship" was with the National Security Agency, which specialized in collecting signals intelligence around the globe, a senior JSOC official said. "They were very good to us," he said. Hidden from the American people, that relationship would only improve over the next three decades.

Stiner took command of what he would later describe as "the best trained and most competent joint headquarters and the finest special missions units in the world." But although JSOC had seen fierce combat in Grenada and had undertaken numerous advisory and training missions abroad, the command had yet to conduct a major hostage rescue or other major counterterrorist mission—the sort of operation that was supposed to be its raison d'être. The following year, however, events in the Mediterranean twice almost put JSOC to just such a test. Two hijackings would reveal how far the command had come in less than five years, and how far it still had to go.

The first of these crises began June 14, 1985, when two Lebanese Shi'ite terrorists hijacked Trans World Airlines Flight 847 carrying 153 passengers and crew en route from Athens to Rome and forced the pilots to fly to Beirut, where they refueled and began a two-day pattern of shuttling between the Lebanese capital and Algiers, releasing most of the hostages before stopping permanently in Beirut June 16 with forty American men as their remaining captives. On the second stop in Beirut, on the morning of June 14, the hijackers viciously beat Robert Stethem, one of six U.S. Navy divers on the flight, before killing him with a shot to the head and dumping his body on the tarmac. The terrorists also took nineteen American prisoners off the plane and held them in Beirut while about a dozen more well-armed hijackers came aboard, including Imad Mugniyah, Hezbollah's youthful "enforcer," who would remain a major player in Middle East terrorism for more than two decades.

Meanwhile, the JSOC and Delta compounds were a blur of activity. A report on the television that Delta kept tuned to CNN at all times alerted the unit's watch officer to the crisis, who in turn contacted individual unit members at home via beeper, using a numeric code to tell them to prepare for a rapid deployment. Similar processes were under way at Dam Neck and Fort Campbell with Team 6 and TF 160, respectively. At JSOC headquarters, where officers first learned of the hijacking from BBC and Reuters reports, not from Washington, staff pulled up profiles of the Algiers and Beirut airports from the command's database. The various headquarters also put into practice a new telephone routine intended to keep everyone with a need to know up to speed on events. "When all this hijacking shit started, they built this system where once a plane's hijacked, phones ring everywhere that there are people that are supposed to be involved, and you can never hang up—somebody's got to stay on that phone," said a JSOC staff officer from the period.

Early that morning, the Joint Chiefs told Stiner to put a task force together and draw up a rescue plan. At Bragg, Dam Neck, and Campbell, troops were ready to go, but, not for the first or last time, the Air Force's Military Assistance Command had no planes or crews immediately available to deploy them. The Pentagon also wanted to wait to see where TWA 847 ended up before deploying the task force. That meant JSOC missed the best opportunity to rescue the hostages: when the plane was on the ground for the first time at Algiers, with only two lightly armed hijackers. By the time the Air Force was able to provide airlift and the Reagan administration had made a decision to launch the task force, the hijackers had killed Stethem. The task force flew overnight and landed on the morning of June 15 at Naval Air Station Sigonella on the Italian island of Sicily. Stiner planned to use the joint Italian-U.S. facility as an intermediate staging base and quickly set up an operations center inside a hangar. A pair of MC-130 Combat Talons (Air Force special operations variants of the venerable Hercules turboprop transport plane) flew in from England. A TWA Boeing 727 identical to that used by Flight 847 also arrived. Delta regularly trained on airliners awaiting destruction at an aircraft boneyard at North Carolina's Laurinburg-Maxton Airport, but the opportunity to rehearse the planned takedown using an exact replica of the hijacked airliner was priceless. TWA's loan of the 727 meant the operators could also use it as a Trojan horse to bring them unnoticed into either Algiers or Beirut. (If it came to that, the plan was for the Delta operators to land in "their" 727, put it nose-to-nose with the hijacked plane, free the hostages, "turn the other one around and fly off," said a Delta operator.)

The night of the 15th offered another opportunity for a rescue mission, although it would be a tougher challenge now that the terrorists had been reinforced. A couple of operators had infiltrated Algiers to keep watch over the target and report back to Sigonella over satellite radio. "They were in the bushes, they could walk up, put their hands on the fence and look at everything that was going on at the airfield and then go back in the bushes and talk to us," said a JSOC staffer. A JSOC officer in Sigonella was on the hangar roof—the only place the task force's satellite communications worked—talking to a general in the White House Situation Room. The JSOC officer told the general the task force was ready to launch the mission, but the White House needed to give the okay within the next hour and forty-five minutes or they would run out of the darkness deemed essential to the plan. The opportunity for JSOC to conduct its first set-piece counterterrorism operation beckoned. "This was the closest we'd ever come to being told we could do it," said a JSOC staffer. "We were getting excited." The Algerian government was steadfastly opposed to a military rescue, however. To the utter frustration of the operators and staff gathered in the hangar on Sicily, the White House never gave the okay. The next morning the hijackers ordered the plane flown back to their home base of Beirut, where they took the hostages off the plane, eventually distributing them around Hezbollah safe houses in southern Beirut.

Stiner moved the entire task force to the British Royal Air Force base at Akrotiri in Cyprus. By now the task force was almost 400 strong, including two Delta squadrons, about fifty Team 6 operators, plus elements of TF 160 and ISA (deployed on the authority of the DIA) and other military and intelligence personnel. (Seaspray helicopters and crews also deployed to Europe during the crisis.) The entire force was in one enormous hangar. The near-constant presence overhead of two Soviet reconnaissance satellites meant the operators could only train outside at night or during two one-hour periods of daylight.

Aided by information from a four-man team that had infiltrated Beirut via Black Hawk, as well as the Delta operators attached to the embassy security detail, JSOC drew up a series of elaborate rescue plans involving air assaults and AC-130 gunships, but the intelligence on the hostages' location was never solid enough to act on. (This lack of what JSOC referred to as "actionable intelligence" would remain a constant challenge for the command, particularly in Lebanon.) While the JSOC task force cooled its collective heels in Cyprus, the diplomats went to work. Sixteen days after the crisis began, Hezbollah released the hostages. In exchange, but never publicly acknowledged as such by the Reagan administration, Israel released 700 Lebanese Shi'ite prisoners it had been holding.

The TWA 847 hijacking had been another wrenching humiliation for the United States and an exercise in bitter frustration for JSOC. The terrorists had stayed one step ahead of the Americans throughout. They had realized that the keys to preventing a rescue attempt were to never remain in one place too long while on the plane, and to separate the hostages into small groups once off the jet.

At JSOC, there was aggravation that the operators had not gotten to Sigonella quickly enough to launch the first time the plane landed at Algiers, and had not been approved to launch after the jet returned there for a twenty-four-hour period. That frustration was exacerbated by information they received from debriefing hostages after their release. "When we take an airplane down, 80 percent of the holes to get into that airplane are in the first-class section," said a JSOC staff officer. "What they [the terrorists] had done is they had taken all the passengers and put them back in coach. And all the bad guys were up [in first class] sitting around bullshitting. . . . So it would have been like shooting ducks if they had just let us go that fucking night."

Upon his return to the United States, Stiner visited the Pentagon and spoke directly to the Joint Chiefs in the Tank. The JSOC commander did not mince his words. "We ought to be able to understand that the terrorists understand better than we do the timing of the decision-making process here in Washington and the time required for launching and getting to where they have perpetrated their action—and that they are operating within that cycle," he told the assembled brass. "Consequently we are always chasing our tail—and we always will be unless we do something about this situation. We are the most powerful nation in the world and if we cannot give this mission the appropriate priority—with dedicated lift assets—then we ought to get out of this business and quit wasting the taxpayers' money."

It was a tense, critical moment in JSOC's history. Stiner was gambling that Vessey and at least a couple of other chiefs would support him. He was right. Within several months, the Air Force placed multiple double-crewed C-141 Starlifters at Charleston Air Force Base, South Carolina, on the same alert status as the special mission units. JSOC finally had its J-alert birds.[13]

✳

In September, Stiner and a JSOC task force were back in the eastern Mediterranean, this time preparing for a shot at the Holy Grail of 1980s counterterrorist missions, a rescue of the U.S. hostages that Hezbollah was holding in Lebanon. The United States had received intelligence that the Shi'ite group might be about to release its American prisoners. Stiner was ordered to prepare to pick them up and return them to the United States covertly, but to be ready for a rescue mission in case things went badly. As it turned out, Hezbollah freed only one hostage, the Reverend Benjamin Weir. At midnight September 14 a car traveling Beirut's deserted streets slowed near the American University. Weir emerged in a tracksuit and was met by a Delta operator who took him to a spot on the coast before sending a coded message. Soon a helicopter appeared speeding across the sea, picked the pair up, and flew them to a waiting aircraft carrier over the horizon.

To the operators' frustration, however, there was to be no rescue of the other hostages. Shortly before deploying to the Mediterranean, JSOC had run a major rehearsal for a hostage rescue mission into Lebanon at Nevada's Nellis Air Force Range, which was home to Groom Lake, often referred to as "Area 51." JSOC often used the secret facility to replicate foreign military radar arrays, which it would then use to test its ability to penetrate them. Intelligence indicated Hezbollah was holding the hostages in Lebanon's Bekaa Valley, so JSOC "got the whole laydown of all the radars in that area and we went out to Area 51," said a JSOC staff officer. The operational concept had TF 160 helicopters launching at night from a carrier or another location in the area and flying below Syrian air defense radar into the Bekaa. "We put some trailers out there with 'hostages' in them and the Rangers and Delta were going to go in and rescue those 'hostages,'" the staffer said. In the event, a radar sweep caught the briefest of glimpses of the assault force, when a single helicopter climbed slightly too high. By the time the radar came around again, the aircraft had dropped out of sight. But with the exception of a JSOC visitor, no one in the radar control room had noticed. "We got in and got the guys and got them out and those radars never picked us up," the JSOC staffer said.

The exercise results delighted Stiner. Skeptics had told JSOC there was no way for a hostage rescue force to infiltrate the Bekaa. He believed the exercise proved them wrong. "He went to Washington and told them, 'We have that capability if you need us to do it,'" said the JSOC staffer. But infiltrating the Bekaa was only half the challenge. The other half, as always, was determining the hostages' exact location in the first place. There was intense debate over the intelligence community's ability to do this, even with the help of Delta operators who went into Lebanon undercover in late 1985. According to Stiner, the best chance to rescue the hostages came a few months after Weir's release, when the intelligence community believed it had identified a building in West Beirut to which Hezbollah had moved the hostages. JSOC found a similar building "in the western United States" and modified its interior to match that of the Beirut structure. The command rehearsed the rescue, but two weeks prior to the planned D-day, Hezbollah discovered and rolled up the agent network that had located the hostages. The mission was canceled. "There was never again sufficient credible intelligence to support a rescue attempt," Stiner wrote.

In 1986, ISA, which moved into new headquarters at Fort Belvoir, Virginia, in August of that year, developed another network of agents that provided allegedly detailed and accurate intelligence on the hostages' location. In June of that year JSOC conducted a hostage rescue exercise code-named Quiz Icing. But the command remained leery of any intelligence that it did not generate itself. With no intelligence it deemed actionable, JSOC remained on the sidelines.[14]

✳

Four months after their TWA 847 frustration, JSOC's operators experienced déjà vu when Middle Eastern hijackers again struck a Mediterranean target packed with Americans. But this time the terrorists were from the Palestinian Liberation Organization's Palestinian Liberation Front, and their target was the *Achille Lauro*, an Italian cruise ship with ninety-seven passengers, including eighteen Americans, and 344 crew members on board. Stiner was returning from a run the morning of October 7 when his intelligence officer met him at the gate to the JSOC compound and told him of the hijacking.

JSOC was now on its way to becoming a colossus. The JOC had become a state-of-the-art affair, incorporating secure communications to JSOC's subordinate units and all U.S. major commands, computer workstations for the staff, terminals connected to major news organizations, and an intelligence center manned by watch officers around the clock. The task force Stiner quickly assembled was a custom-designed amalgam of elite forces that had few if any equals in the world. It was also rather large.

Unlike the TWA hijacking, the *Achille Lauro* presented JSOC with a maritime target. This time SEAL Team 6 would have the lead role. Stiner told Dam Neck to alert assault and sniper teams plus special boat detachments. As usual, TF 160's standard alert package was part of the task force. At the time, the package included ten Black Hawks, six AH-6s, and four MH-6s. The task force also contained an Air Force special tactics element from Det 4 NAFCOS (Detachment 4, Numbered Air Force Combat Operations Staff—the renamed Det 1 MACOS), roughly a squadron's worth of Delta operators and Stiner's command group, which included the usual cells devoted to operations and plans, intelligence, communications, and medicine.

JSOC was on a four-hour "string," meaning it had to be able to get a task force appropriate for whatever no-notice mission it was handed in the air within four hours of being alerted. Specific mission requirements would dictate the exact makeup of that task force, but the perceived need to always take a significant slice of the JSOC headquarters, as well as TF 160's entire alert package and a series of other "enablers," guaranteed a large force would deploy. In the *Achille Lauro* case, JSOC was deploying a high-tech JOC, at least twenty helicopters and 500 personnel on a dozen transport planes, including four huge C-5s, in order to take down four lightly armed hijackers on a cruise ship. The command could argue that when the task force launched, its leaders couldn't be sure how the crisis would develop nor exactly what circumstances it would encounter on the objective, and so they needed the extra forces to hedge against risk.[15] But it was also clear, despite Stiner's claim that "this was a much larger force than was normally required," that by late 1985 the massive, unwieldy task force the command put together for the *Achille Lauro* mission was becoming the norm, rather than the exception. It was this formulaic approach, in which a big task force was deemed the solution to almost every problem, that critics would later say robbed JSOC of its ability to react nimbly, let alone to deploy clandestinely.

Already observers were critical of the time it took JSOC to deploy. Stung by the TWA hijacking fiasco, Reagan put his vice president, George H. W. Bush, in charge of a task force on combating terrorism. The staff director was James Holloway, the retired admiral who had recommended JSOC's creation after the Eagle Claw failure. Now tasked with evaluating the progress JSOC had made in the past five years, he was disturbed to discover that JSOC took as long as seventy-two hours to get going once it had been alerted. Holloway told Stiner that if the military couldn't accelerate JSOC's deployment timeline, it might as well shut the command down.[16]

Part of the problem was that until Stiner's bravura performance in the Tank a few months previously, JSOC had no control over the aircraft on which it deployed. This was still the case at the time of the *Achille Lauro* hijacking, because although Stiner had persuaded the Joint Chiefs to give the command its own dedicated airlift, the wheels of military bureaucracy had not yet turned far enough to make that happen.[17] As before, JSOC was left playing catch-up from the moment Stiner walked into his operations center the morning of October 7.

It took about eighteen hours, or until 1 A.M. October 8, to get the task force airborne. Even then, Team 6 was delayed for several hours because its C-141 suffered maintenance problems. Again, Stiner had the task force fly first to Sigonella, where he dropped off a small SEAL element and a couple of Little Birds, and then on to Akrotiri, which was barely big enough to handle the air armada headed its way.

The task force used the time in the air to plan.[18] In the best case scenario, the mission would be a classic "under way," so called because it involved the SEALs assaulting the ship while it was steaming ahead. This was a core Team 6 mission, and the unit trained for it repeatedly. Typically it involved blacked-out aircraft dropping SEALs into the sea at night alongside small Zodiac rubber boats several miles behind the cruise ship. The operators would clamber aboard the Zodiacs, ride up to the stern undetected (cruise ships are so loud it would be impossible for anyone on the ship to hear the Zodiacs approaching), then climb aboard using a scaling ladder hoisted up and hooked onto the ship's railing by a SEAL using a thirty-five-foot pole, as helicopters arrived bearing more SEALs. The concept was simple, but the execution could be terrifying in heavy seas for operators trying to first grab the swaying ladder in the darkness and then climb up while getting smashed against the vessel by large waves. Once on the ship, the SEALs were to kill or capture the hijackers and search the vessel for any hidden terrorists or explosives. Variations of this method involved the SEALs assaulting from MH-6s that would approach the stern just above sea level before flaring to hover above the fantail as the SEALs fast-roped down, and other SEALs or Delta operators reinforcing the initial assault force from helicopters landing on or hovering above the deck. The *Achille Lauro* offered an excellent chance of success. The ship's tapered stern could not be seen from the bridge, and the four hijackers would be tired and separated from each other trying to keep track of the hostages in three locations on the liner.[19]

But circumstances conspired yet again to rob JSOC of the chance to conduct a set-piece hostage rescue operation. The U.S. Navy lost track of the *Achille Lauro* as it headed east. When it finally stopped off Tartus, Syria, and broke radio silence, the hijackers murdered a disabled American passenger named Leon Klinghoffer, shooting him in the head and chest before having crewmen dump his body in the sea. Syria refused entry to the hijackers, who turned back toward Egypt. The Navy again lost track of the ship but Israel spotted it and relayed its location to the United States. JSOC's plan was to stage off a Navy ship just over the horizon from the *Achille Lauro* and to launch the attack after dark on October 9. The rotors of the helicopters taking the SEALs to their drop-off point at sea were already turning when Stiner learned the mission was off. The hijackers had surrendered to the Egyptian authorities "without preconditions." Furious U.S. officials suspected that either the Italians or the Egyptians had warned the PLO, whose leaders had become involved in the negotiations, that the Americans were planning a rescue mission.

Stiner ordered his force to head back to the United States. That movement was soon under way. But the drama wasn't over. With the Egyptian government's help, the hijackers tried to flee to Tunisia October 10 on an Egypt Air Boeing 737. Reagan ordered F-14s from the aircraft carrier *Saratoga* to intercept the flight and divert it to Sigonella, where the skeleton Team 6 force Stiner had left there surrounded it as soon as it landed shortly after midnight on October 11.

The aircraft carrying Stiner, his command group, and a couple of Team 6 platoons landed shortly thereafter. They soon discovered that in addition to the crew and four hijackers, the 737 was carrying eight to ten Egyptian commandos, an Egyptian intelligence officer in plainclothes, and two PLO officials, including PLO executive council member Abu Abbas, who U.S. officials suspected of masterminding the entire operation. As phone calls flew back and forth between Washington, Rome, and Cairo, a bizarre and potentially disastrous turn of events occurred when Italian troops and police surrounded the SEALs who were in turn surrounding the Egypt Air jet. The Italian authorities had decided to assert their authority over the hijackers, as it was an Italian ship they had hijacked. After much delicate negotiation between Stiner and the senior Italian general on the scene, and between Washington and Rome, a compromise was reached whereby the Italians would prosecute the four hijackers, but, to the Americans' frustration, the two senior PLO officials were allowed to leave Italy.[20]

For JSOC there was satisfaction that the command helped apprehend the four hijackers—all but the youngest of whom received lengthy prison sentences—mitigated by bitterness that Abu Abbas escaped justice. For the operators, there was again the frustration that came with being "spun up" for a mission that then evaporated before their eyes. JSOC and Team 6 would wait more than seventeen years for a reckoning with Abu Abbas.

✳

The following year, 1986, as part of a wholesale overhaul of the military's special operations structure, Congress held a series of hearings that allowed Dick Scholtes to finally have his say about the myriad problems that had bedeviled the JSOC task force in Grenada. Having waited almost three years for an opportunity to vent his frustrations, the two-star general retired from the Army in order to speak his mind. His August 5 testimony before a closed session of the Senate Armed Services Committee's Sea Power and Force Projection Subcommittee was widely considered "the most compelling" case Congress heard on the issue, according to Jerry Boykin's Army War College thesis on the subject. Scholtes's argument that conventional commanders ignorant of JSOC's unique capabilities had misused his forces in Urgent Fury, resulting in significant casualties, was critical in persuading Senators Bill Cohen of Maine and Sam Nunn of Georgia to introduce an amendment to the Goldwater-Nichols Department of Defense Reorganization Act that would change the course of U.S. special operations history. Among other steps, the Nunn-Cohen Amendment, passed as a rider to the 1987 Defense Authorization Act, created a four-star unified command—U.S. Special Operations Command, or SOCOM—that would be the equal of the military's geographic unified commands like European Command and Pacific Command, and would oversee JSOC. It also created an Assistant Secretary of Defense for Special Operations and Low-Intensity Conflict office in the Pentagon to oversee all special operations matters.[21] These steps were taken despite bitter resistance from the Joint Chiefs of Staff, who feared they would lead to the creation of a fifth service, but they laid the groundwork for JSOC's journey over the next two decades from the margins of the U.S. military to the centerpiece of its campaigns.[22]

4

Payoff in Panama

The TWA 847 and *Achille Lauro* crises were just two of at least eight "real-world" JSOC deployments in the three years following Grenada.[1] The possibility of invading Suriname arose again in late 1986, when the U.S. and Dutch governments planned a joint operation aimed at arresting Bouterse. The plan came to light in 2010 when Ruud Lubbers, prime minister of the Netherlands at the time of the planned invasion, disclosed it to a Dutch newspaper. The report said the United States was prepared to support the operation with ships, planes, and helicopters, but made no mention of U.S. troops on the ground. In fact, JSOC had a major role. The command had earmarked the Rangers for the airfield seizure mission, which had become their specialty. Delta was going to launch its attack from a Navy helicopter carrier and had conducted a couple of rehearsals for the operation, including at least one at Fort Jackson, South Carolina. However, Lubbers called off the invasion after becoming uncomfortable with the prominent Dutch role.[2]

The furious pace of training and operations continued into 1987, when Stiner changed command with Army Major General Gary Luck, who spent two years in Special Forces from 1963 to 1965, including time in Vietnam, but who had had no special operations assignments since then.[3] JSOC and its units trained all over the United States and the rest of the world, from the vast desert tracts of the American Southwest to the claustrophobic confines of metropolitan skyscrapers and Central American jungles.

With the command so busy, the Pentagon gradually expanded the size of its formations. Delta added a third "sabre" squadron of operators—C Squadron—and moved into a lavishly equipped new headquarters at Bragg's Range 19 complex in 1987.[4] The unit now had about 200 operators and 300 support personnel,[5] but a ruthless assessment and selection process meant it always had trouble keeping its squadrons filled.

In 1989 Delta expanded further when Seaspray became the unit's aviation squadron and was renamed E, or Echo, Squadron. Earlier in the decade, then JSOC commander Dick Scholtes had considered making a play to get the brand-new unit assigned directly under JSOC but decided against doing so "before they were fully qualified," a senior JSOC official from the period said. (By coincidence, Scholtes's son later served in the unit.)[6]

But Delta's absorption of the covert aviation element didn't mean Delta stopped working with TF 160. The two aviation units had very different capabilities and mission sets. "Echo Squadron's a much smaller capability [than the 160th]," said an officer familiar with both organizations. While the 160th was a purely military organization and made no effort to be clandestine, Echo Squadron provided a capability to support JSOC and the intelligence community with undercover pilots and civilian-looking aircraft that came with a full cover themselves, but which could be armed. Although now officially part of Delta, to avoid any public links to its higher headquarters the squadron remained at Fort Eustis. It continued to support all JSOC's special mission units and, on occasion, the CIA.[7] "This is a niche unit for very highly specialized missions," said an officer familiar with E Squadron.

SEAL Team 6 was also growing quickly. In 1987 the unit boasted about 225 personnel, of whom no more than half were SEALs. The unit's three assault teams—Blue, Gold, and Red—provided its cutting edge. Team 6 had also formalized its selection process, replacing the alcohol-soaked interviews of the Marcinko era with a six-month selection and training course. A fourth team, Green, ran the course, which roughly half the candidates failed to complete. A fifth team, Gray, operated the unit's boats. (Gray Team was originally manned by Navy construction battalion men—Seabees—but by the end of the decade SEALs were replacing them.) Within three years the unit's strength had grown to about 550 personnel. In 1989 Team 6 also adopted a new cover name, replacing "Marine Environmental Services Facility," or MARESFAC, with "Naval Special Warfare Development Group," often shortened to DevGroup or DevGru. In doing so the unit followed the usual rule of thumb in such matters: the blander the name, the more interesting the unit. (Delta would later go by "Combat Applications Group.") Events many years hence would make both SEAL Team 6 and DevGru almost household words in some quarters, but at the time the unit was only interested in burrowing deeper into obscurity.[8] "MARESFAC was getting kind of worn and it didn't seem like it really fit our mission very much anymore and it was too hard to maintain, so we changed it to something we thought nobody would ever have heard of and would give us a lower profile," said a senior Team 6 officer, chuckling. "It's funny in retrospect, but it made absolute perfect sense at the time."

The Navy unit's reputation had improved significantly after Marcinko handed off command to Captain Bob Gormly in July 1983. Within a year of Gormly taking over, the SEALs defeated Delta in a competitive shoot-off with rifles and handguns at Camp Mackall, North Carolina. "SEAL Team 6 took the handgun [and] the long gun—in every phase, they won it," said a senior JSOC official. "It set Delta back on their heels. . . . It was a wonderful thing . . . because SEAL Team 6 showed a new standard. As a result Delta had to start honing their skills to try to match that competition."

While Delta and Team 6 changed their cover names frequently in an effort to stay out of the limelight, perhaps no JSOC unit changed its real name as frequently as the Air Force unit that began as BRAND X in 1977. In 1987 it changed names for the third and fourth times, switching from Det 4 NAFCOS to 1724th Combat Control Squadron and then to 124th Special Tactics Squadron. By now the squadron combined combat controllers—airmen who coordinated air support for special operations forces—and pararescue jumpers (PJs), medical experts who specialized in personnel recovery (such as rescuing pilots shot down behind enemy lines). Like Delta, it had a hard time finding enough qualified personnel to fill its authorized spaces. A 1989 study validated a requirement for 220 personnel, but the unit only had fifty on hand.[9]

Together with Team 6 and Delta, the 124th was one of JSOC's three core special mission units. Also known as SMUs (pronounced "smoos") or "Tier 1" units, these were the formations that were assigned to JSOC and reported directly to the JSOC commander. A few years after JSOC's establishment, the Air Force also created a fixed wing covered air special mission unit that owned large civilian-style jets that flew around the world on covert missions for the command. Units that had a "habitual" relationship with JSOC, such as TF 160, the Rangers, and certain Special Forces companies that specialized in counterterrorism, were "Tier

2" units whose support the command had to formally request on a case-by-case basis, even though that support was virtually guaranteed. "Tier 3" units were any other military elements (special operations and non–special operations) that JSOC used from time to time. The 0300 ("oh-three-hundred") contingency plan, the basic plan for JSOC's original counter-terrorism mission, directed the tiering of the units. But financial politics also played a role. JSOC preferred for the Army to pay for Tier 2 units like the Rangers and TF 160, while equipping the Tier 1 units almost entirely via U.S. Special Operations Command Major Force Program-11, a congressionally mandated fund that allowed SOCOM, under which JSOC now fell, to pay for special operations–specific gear, as if it were its own service.[10]

The Army also expanded the Rangers significantly. In 1984 the service activated the 3rd Ranger Battalion at Fort Benning, Georgia, and established the 75th Ranger Regiment headquarters, also at Benning, to command the battalions.[11] Once Delta had three squadrons, each Ranger battalion paired up with a squadron and developed a routine training and deployment relationship.[12] (Team 6 elements eventually developed similar relationships with the Rangers, but not until many years later.)[13]

However, none of these organizations experienced the growing pains that TF 160 did. As was the case with Delta and Team 6, TF 160 was a new and unique organization, developing tactics and techniques literally on the fly. In particular, TF 160 was the first helicopter unit to routinely train in darkness using night vision goggles. But the night sky is an unforgiving environment for pilots flying ground-hugging "nap of the earth" flight profiles at more than 100 miles per hour. TF 160 (which officially became the 160th Aviation Battalion in October 1981, but which most JSOC personnel continued to call TF 160) was proud of its night-flying and night-fighting prowess. The unit's nickname was "The Night Stalkers." An early unit motto proclaimed "Death waits in the dark." But during the first years of the unit's existence the 160th crashed helicopter after helicopter striving to overcome the challenges of operating in darkness. In one grisly seven-month period in 1983, the battalion lost sixteen men and four helicopters.[14]

The unit also spent several years trying to hide in plain sight. Its cover was that it was part of the 101st Airborne Division, but its personnel all kept the same "relaxed grooming standards" enjoyed by Team 6, Delta, Seaspray, and other covert units: long hair, mustaches, and civilian clothes as often as not. But the training mishaps, combined with misbehavior by some 160th personnel on a 1984 mission in Colombia, brought all this to an end. Stiner delivered the news to the 160th personally. "Stiner came up and said, 'This is not working well with you guys being a covert unit and we're going to declare you as a special operations task force,'" recalled a 160th officer who was there. Thus, in 1986 the unit became the 160th Special Operations Aviation Group (Airborne), a name it kept until 1990, when the word "Regiment" replaced "Group."

The 160th refined its training methods, the crash rate declined, and the unit's reputation soared as it repeatedly demonstrated it could meet its standard of hitting an objective anywhere in the world "plus or minus thirty seconds" of the assigned time. Meanwhile, the 160th added a second and then a third battalion. But the battalions were not identical. The 1st Battalion had all the Little Birds. It also retained the TF 160 responsibility to provide JSOC with an immediate response force, called the "Silver Bullet" or the "Bullet package." As if to further muddy the nomenclature waters, that portion of a JSOC task force provided by the 160th, which often included nothing more than the Bullet package, was sometimes called TF 1/160 because it was based around the 160th's 1st Battalion. (However, the Chinooks in the package always came from 2nd Battalion.) The 1st Battalion commander even had a different reporting chain. The other battalions reported to the 160th commander (a colonel) and then to U.S. Army Special Operations Command (after its establishment in December 1989), but 1st Battalion's chain of command ran from the 160th commander to the JSOC commander.[15]

The Night Stalkers had the key role in two of the more interesting missions of the late 1980s—actions that showcased their lethality and versatility. In August 1987 the 160th deployed a small task force of two MH-6 and four AH-6 Little Birds to the Persian Gulf in Operation Prime Chance, which aimed to protect shipping—especially Kuwaiti oil tankers reflagged as American vessels—from Iranian mining efforts. Flying off converted oil servicing barges, the Little Birds' major actions occurred on the nights of September 21 and October 8, when they successfully attacked an Iranian mine-laying vessel and three small Iranian patrol boats respectively. Perhaps cowed by the losses they'd taken in these battles, the Iranians chose not to tempt the pilots of the 160th into combat again, but the Little Birds remained in the Gulf until June 1988.[16]

That same month, the 160th conducted Operation Mount Hope III, a mission to retrieve a Soviet-made Hind attack helicopter abandoned by Libyan armed forces at the Ouadi Doum desert air base in northern Chad. The aircraft was a very recent model and the United States was keen to get its hands on it, so much so that it kept watch over the stranded machine via satellite. Chad's government was willing to let the United States take it, but due to a maintenance problem the helicopter was not flyable. After what an official history described as "other U.S. government organizations" (usually a euphemism for the CIA) failed to recover the helicopter, JSOC was tasked with the mission. The command turned to the 160th, which rehearsed the mission by flying between White Sands Missile Range, New Mexico, and Fort Bliss, Texas, before deploying seventy-three personnel and two Chinooks to the Chadian capital, N'Djamena. On the night of June 11 the Chinooks flew 500 miles to Ouadi Doum, sling-loaded the Hind under one of them, and returned through a towering sandstorm to N'Djamena. All three helicopters were immediately loaded on a C-5, which took off soon afterward. The operation was a complete success and conducted under such tight secrecy that many in the 160th remained unaware of it years later.[17]

Eighteen months after the Chad mission, JSOC executed by far its largest and most ambitious operation up to that point when it took the lead role in Operation Just Cause, the U.S. invasion of Panama. This was to be the operation that finally gave JSOC a chance to show what it could do. It was when all the resources expended on the secretive command paid off.

Tensions between the United States and Panamanian dictator Manuel Noriega, which had been building since summer 1987, heightened after Noriega ignored the results of May 7, 1989, elections and had his forces beat up the winners. U.S. intelligence also knew Noriega was heavily involved in shipping cocaine into the United States. When Panamanian Defense Forces personnel killed a U.S. Marine officer and physically abused a Navy lieutenant and his wife in mid-December, President George Bush gave the order to depose Noriega, setting in motion an operation that had been long in the planning.[18]

As with Grenada more than six years previously, JSOC again found itself fronting the invasion of a small tropical country. But that's where the similarities ended. Just Cause was everything that Urgent Fury was not. In the intervening years, JSOC had become a larger, more experienced, and more robust organization, more at ease with the notion that the Pentagon might tap its unique, highly resourced units to do more than respond to hijackings and other terrorist incidents. The National Command Authority (the president and the defense secretary) was again directing JSOC to spearhead the invasion of a nation-state, but this time JSOC was comfortable with that mission.

Army Major General Wayne Downing, an infantry officer who'd headed the Ranger Regiment, assumed command of JSOC from Gary Luck shortly before the invasion. Together with Carl Stiner, who now led XVIII Airborne Corps and commanded the invasion task force, Luck had overseen the planning for the operation, which would put Downing, as JSOC commander, in charge of a 4,400-strong joint special operations task force[19] that included "white" (i.e., unclassified) special ops units not usually attached to the command, such as a 7th Special Forces Group battalion and SEAL Team 4. But at the heart of Downing's task force were the Rangers, TF 160, and JSOC's "black" special mission units, including about half of Delta's operators.[20]

At 12:45 A.M. December 20, H-hour for the invasion, four Little Birds landed one by one on the roof of Modelo Prison in downtown Panama City. It was the start of Acid Gambit, the code name for Delta's most dramatic mission of the invasion, the daring rescue of Kurt Muse, a forty-year-old CIA operative. It was also the mission that kicked off Just Cause. Operators jumped off, blew open a door on the rooftop, and flew down the stairs toward Muse's cell. Another operator, Pete Jacobs, rappelled down the outside wall until he was looking into Muse's cell windows, ready to shoot the guard Noriega had ordered to kill his American captive if the United States attempted a rescue. Inside, the operators encountered three guards. The first surrendered and lived. The other two made the mistake of resisting, and paid for it with their lives.

The operators grabbed Muse and stuffed him in the back of a Little Bird, but the overloaded MH-6 lost power taking off from the prison roof, clipped a low-hanging wire, and crash-landed in the street. The pilots took off again, but the helicopter was immediately shot down. All on board survived the crash, but were now trapped by the battle. After a nervous fifteen minutes with the fight for the capital raging around Muse and his rescuers, a U.S. Army M113 armored personnel carrier made its way to them and they escaped. Several operators were wounded in the rescue, but Muse was unharmed and eternally grateful. It was

Delta's first successful hostage rescue since the 1983 Sudan mission, and the first ever in which it was the main ground force.[21]

The rest of the JSOC task force, which was based in a hangar at Howard Air Force Base, about ten miles southwest of Panama City, was engaged in equally tough fighting. TF 160 lost two pilots and three helicopters. The plethora of aircraft aloft meant the combat controllers were called on to prove their worth, at one point coordinating the fires and movement of 171 different special operations aircraft in the sky. The Rangers saw heavy combat in airborne operations to seize Río Hato Airfield and Torrijos-Tocumen Airport, about sixty miles southwest and fifteen miles east of Panama City respectively. The Río Hato operation was particularly hazardous. The fifteen C-130s carrying the Rangers came in at a height of 500 feet. Panamanian forces raked the aircraft with automatic weapons fire, hitting some Rangers before they had a chance to jump and others during the twelve-second parachute descent. Meanwhile there was fierce hand-to-hand fighting in the terminal building at Torrijos-Tocumen. The Rangers eventually prevailed at each location, but at the cost of five of their brethren killed in action.[22]

A third airfield mission, to put Noriega's personal plane at Paitilla Airport in downtown Panama City out of action, was the one JSOC mission during Just Cause that would later be second-guessed. Although basically an airfield seizure with a twist, and therefore a classic Ranger mission, Downing assigned it to SEAL Team 4. For reasons that remain unclear even many years later, the SEALs chose to assault across flat ground, which left them silhouetted and relatively easy targets for the Panamanian forces guarding the plane. Communications problems meant they couldn't call in covering fire from the AC-130 gunship overhead. The SEALs ultimately succeeded in destroying the plane, but at a cost of four SEALs killed and eight wounded.[23] The "tactical blunder" at Paitilla was Team 4's responsibility, but it left a lasting stain on the reputation of the entire Naval Special Warfare community, including a Team 6 still trying to escape the taint of the Marcinko era, according one of the Team's officers. "I came in a decade after Marcinko and I completely felt that we had the Marcinko stink on us," he said. In the eyes of some at JSOC, the unit was guilty by association when it came to what happened at Paitilla. "That labeled us as inept at land warfare," the officer said.

Most of the fighting was over within twenty-four hours, but mopping up continued for several days. For JSOC, the key mission that remained was a harbinger of the operations that would define the command in the years ahead. That mission was to find Noriega, who had gone to ground during the invasion's first hours, evading Delta and Team 6 elements tasked with his capture. This led to what Stiner later described as "one of the most intensive manhunts in history," with Delta searching in Panama City and SEAL Team 6, led by Captain Rick Woolard, operating in western Panama and Colón on the Atlantic coast. To give his forces agile, responsive mobility, Downing used a small armor force made up of 82nd Airborne Division Sheridan light tanks, Marine light armored vehicles, and Army M113 armored personnel carriers. This was a first for many operators, but it would by no means be the last time in JSOC's history that conventional armor units were "sliced" to the special mission units. Delta conducted forty-two raids in seventy-two hours, going after Noriega's associates and dismantling his "Dignity Battalions," the gangs of armed thugs the dictator had established to strengthen his grip on the population. Operators kicked in the doors of safe house after safe house, immediately interrogated any Noriega cronies they found, and then launched new missions based on that intelligence.

These nonstop operations set a precedent for future missions in Afghanistan and especially Iraq. Although nobody in 1989 was talking about Noriega's "network," that's exactly what JSOC was attacking. But the Noriega manhunt also taught the command how difficult it can be to find someone who is on his own turf and doesn't want to be found. Despite the raids, Noriega stayed one step ahead of the task force until December 24, when he took refuge in the papal nunciature—the Vatican's embassy in Panama. Delta quickly surrounded the location, establishing a sniper nest in a luxury high-rise apartment that turned out to belong to boxer Roberto Durán.

After high-level negotiations between Washington and the Vatican,[24] Noriega surrendered on January 3, 1990, and was put on a Combat Talon for his flight to trial (on drug smuggling charges) and captivity in the United States. His signature red underwear, which he believed protected him from harm, ended up in a display case in Delta's compound at Bragg.[25]

For JSOC, Operation Just Cause was a major success and represented a remarkable turnaround from Grenada. "Panama was really where they stepped up to the plate," said a Special Forces general who did not serve in JSOC. There were several reasons why Just Cause was such an improvement over Urgent Fury. JSOC (and the rest of the U.S. forces) enjoyed some obvious advantages this time around. The tension with Noriega had been building for more than a year, so they had a long time to refine their plans. For instance, Delta built a three-quarter-scale replica of the Modelo prison at Hurlburt Field, Florida, and rehearsed Muse's rescue many times.[26] The 12,000 U.S. troops permanently stationed in installations across Panama gave the invading forces a greater understanding of the country and much better intelligence than was available to those who invaded Grenada. In addition, many JSOC troops actually infiltrated Panama quietly in the weeks preceding the operation.[27]

But JSOC and the Pentagon had also applied the lessons of Urgent Fury. There was no last-minute dickering by service chiefs to gain a bigger share of the operation. The chain of command was tight and the head of the operation, Stiner, understood JSOC's requirements intimately, as he had recently commanded the organization. The initial assault happened at night, maximizing the advantage conveyed by JSOC's ability to fight in the darkness. In almost all cases, units were assigned missions appropriate for them. For all those reasons, and with the exception of the Paitilla fiasco, Panama was the finest hour of JSOC's first decade.

There was one other way in which Just Cause set a precedent for future JSOC operations. It marked the major operational debut of the command's use of color-themed task forces as code names for its units. Thus Delta became "Task Force Green," Team 6 "Task Force Blue," TF 160 "Task Force Brown," and the Rangers "Task Force Red."[28] Some of the other color codes changed hands—the non–SEAL Team 6 Naval Special Warfare elements were "Task Force White" in Panama, but that moniker was soon given to the 24th Special Tactics Squadron (the new name for the 124th STS), for instance, and others were added. But the system endured formally or informally for another two decades, with special ops insiders often referring to Delta as "Green" or Team 6 as "Blue" in casual conversation. With the special mission units frequently changing their "official" cover names, the color codes just made things easier. JSOC headquarters soon acquired its own name in this system, taking the color the military uses to refer to anything multiservice or "joint"—"Task Force Purple."

5

Manhunts, Motorboats, and Mogadishu

If JSOC was at the very center of the action for Just Cause, it was anything but during Operations Desert Shield and Storm, the United States' response to Iraq's August 1990 invasion of Kuwait.

U.S. Central Command boss General Norman Schwarzkopf, responsible for American military operations in the Middle East, harbored a profound suspicion of special operations forces. JSOC had recently finished an exercise that stretched across Texas and New Mexico in which Delta, the Rangers, and TF 160 conducted a deep strike against a hidden strategic target deep inside a made-up country in southwest Asia. But despite entreaties from Stiner and Downing, he seemed determined to exclude JSOC from any role in the military effort to oust Iraqi forces from Kuwait. (Schwarzkopf made one exception, insisting a Delta bodyguard team augment the military police personal security detail the Defense Department had given him.) The four-star general dismissed Downing's suggestions to have JSOC launch a rescue mission for Americans trapped at the U.S. embassy in Kuwait City and to conduct direct action strikes deep into Iraq.

JSOC also did "a lot of planning" for the most sensitive mission possible: sending operators into Baghdad undercover to kill Iraqi dictator Saddam Hussein. "There was an effort to just solve the problem by taking out Saddam Hussein," said a Pentagon special operations source. The project was "sanctioned by the White House, [but] that was one of those things where you provide enough cutouts you can't track it back to the president," he said. JSOC considered a range of methods for killing Hussein, from shooting the dictator with small arms to having operators call in an air or missile strike. In the end, the officer said, the planning foundered on an all too common failing: "The intel just could not provide the proper foundations for being able to launch a mission like that."

JSOC finally elbowed its way into the war after Iraqi dictator Saddam Hussein's forces began firing Scud missiles into Israel on January 17, 1991. Fearful that Israel would retaliate militarily, thus breaking apart the fragile coalition of Arab and European states lined up against Saddam, Defense Secretary Dick Cheney and Chairman of the Joint Chiefs of Staff General Colin Powell pulled rank on Schwarzkopf and dispatched Downing and his forces to Saudi Arabia January 28, with orders to neutralize the Scud threat. Within about a week, Downing had deployed a 400-strong task force that included two Delta squadrons, a reinforced Ranger company, some Team 6 boat crews, a TF 160 package, and a JSOC command and control element. The task force based itself in northern Saudi Arabia at Arar, a small town with an airfield about fifty miles southwest of the Iraqi border.

The operators began cross-border operations February 6. Their mission was to shut down the Scuds, which were being fired from western Iraq, in any way they could. After coordinating with the British SAS, who were also part of the "Scud Hunt," Delta focused on the northwestern section of Iraq close to the Syrian border and conducted roughly fifteen missions into the desert looking for mobile Scud launchers. Each mission followed the same template. Helicopters would insert a team and one or two four-wheel-drive vehicles, sometimes hundreds of miles into Iraq. The operators would stay behind Iraqi lines for up to three weeks, holing up in hide sites during the day and hunting for Scuds at night, calling in air strikes on likely targets. While there were several firefights in which operators needed close air support to save them, the only casualties JSOC suffered were four MH-60 crewmen and three Delta operators killed when their helicopter crashed in bad weather near Arar. (In an indication of how long operators tended to stay in Delta, one of the dead, Sergeant Major Pat Hurley, was a Desert One veteran.)

After the war there was disagreement over whether Delta had been responsible for the destruction of any real Scuds, with suggestions that many targets were decoys. However, there was no disputing that once JSOC's campaign in western Iraq began, the number of Scuds fired declined by 80 percent, to an average of just one launch per day. The war ended with a comprehensive coalition victory February 28. The following week Schwarzkopf secretly visited Arar and spoke to the assembled task force. "What you've done is never going to be made public and we can't make it public," he intoned. "You kept Israel out of the war."[1]

It was a remarkable and ironic turnaround for a general who had worked assiduously to keep JSOC out of his combat theater. In future years, JSOC would make converts of many other senior conventional force officers. The operators, and those who came after them, would also have cause to revisit the tactics and locations of their brief foray to southwest Asia. In the meantime, they had business elsewhere.

⁂

On a warm, almost moonless night in the first week of October 1991, a small group of Team 6 operators climbed down a caving ladder thrown over the side of a Navy nuclear guided-missile cruiser, boarded four Zodiac F470 small rubber boats, and motored across calm Caribbean waters toward the coastline about 1,500 meters to the northeast. Wearing dark camouflage face paint and night vision goggles, the SEALs scanned the shoreline. They had only a three-hour window in which to execute their mission, and the beach they were approaching, in the shadow of Haiti's capital, Port-au-Prince, appeared deserted. But when the SEALs flashed red lens flashlights, the agreed-upon recognition code, they saw similar red lights winking up ahead. A short radio call confirmed the flashlights on the beach were being wielded by undercover operatives from the unit previously known as the Intelligence Support Activity, which many now referred to by its nickname: the Army of Northern Virginia. A few hundred meters from the shore the SEALs cut the outboard motors and paddled quietly the rest of the way. One of the boats headed left and another right, each carrying SEALs who were there to provide flank security. The two "pickup" boats, carrying operators from Team 6's Red Team, went straight ahead and landed on the beach. Waiting in the brush on the other side of fifteen feet of sand, right where they and their Army of Northern Virginia protectors were supposed to be, were what a source familiar with the mission estimated at about nine Haitians that the U.S. government felt it was imperative to rescue, and had turned to JSOC to make it happen.

(More than twenty years after the mission, sources who took part are divided about the identities of the "precious cargo"—as those rescued in such operations are called—and why the U.S. government was so keen to get them out of Haiti. The CIA had been in charge of that side of the operation. "The details of that were very compartmented," said an Army of Northern Virginia source, adding that not even the operatives from the Fort Belvoir unit knew who they were taking to the beach. "Our job was to be the driver and facilitate, get them to the right spot and hand them off," he said.

Some in Team 6 thought they were rescuing relatives of Jean-Bertrand Aristide, the populist Haitian president elected the previous year but deposed September 29 in a military coup. The coup leaders had already forced Aristide into exile, but his relatives had been forced to remain behind and were considered at risk. "My understanding at the time was it was members of Aristide's immediate family," said a Team 6 source. But the JSOC staff was under the impression that the people being rescued were a U.S. intelligence asset and his family. "It was a source that had been providing information to U.S. intelligence and it got too hot for them and they had to come out," said a senior JSOC officer. Another special operations officer familiar with the preparations for the mission said U.S. officials feared that Haitians suspected of helping the United States would suffer death by "necklacing," the practice of burning victims to death by forcing gasoline-filled tires around their bodies and setting the tires alight. Of course, these two accounts are not mutually exclusive. A third version of events, which appears in the autobiography of Dennis Chalker, a Team 6 senior chief petty officer on the mission, holds that the key individual being rescued was an eighteen-month-old baby girl who was a U.S. citizen. However, other, more senior, sources say that while the baby was part of the group rescued, she was not the reason for the mission.

Briefed ahead of time that he'd be taking a baby back to the ship, Chalker had come prepared. He had brought along his own daughter's baby carrier, repainted in black, along with a pacifier.

Team 6's commander, Captain Ron Yeaw, was heading a tiny command and control cell on the ship, but he could not have imagined that his unit's future was riding on the mission's outcome. Code-named Victor Squared, the mission was considered so important in Washington that Colin Powell was following it in real time from a Pentagon operations center. Powell was talking on a secure line with Major General Bill Garrison, the brand-new JSOC commander who was running the mission from the U.S. naval base at Guantánamo Bay, Cuba. (The Team 6 operators had also flown to Guantánamo and boarded the cruiser there.) But Powell was no friend of the SEALs, having held a grudge against them since at least the costly Paitilla Airport raid in Panama. His dislike only deepened in the aftermath of Iraq's invasion of Kuwait, when he suspected SEALs of telling the press about a mission they had wanted to conduct that Schwarzkopf had rejected. When Yeaw temporarily lost UHF satellite communications with his operators heading to the beach, Powell let the JSOC commander know he was on the verge of shutting down Team 6 for good. "Our command was on the chopping block," a Team 6 officer said.

Garrison believed in Team 6 and said as much to Powell. But the radio silence wasn't helping his case. Yeaw knew he could rely on the SEALs he had sent ashore, who included at least six chief petty officers and two senior chief petty officers, all experienced operators, but he too was keen to hear from them. After some very tense moments, the radio crackled to life. The SEALs reported they had picked up the family and were in the boats en route back to the blacked-out ship, which was sitting in the Port-au-Prince harbor. Soon everyone was on board the cruiser. The Army of Northern Virginia operatives cleaned up the beach and went back to their cars. The entire mission had taken a couple of hours. "Blue pulled it off, Bill Garrison was very satisfied and proud of the results, and defended Blue at the [Joint Chiefs of Staff] level the next time he had to brief them," said another Team 6 officer. "That was a seminal event, no doubt about it."

"If it weren't for the success of that mission," Garrison later told another officer, "SEAL Team 6 probably would have been dissolved."[2]

✳

Nine months later, JSOC found itself in the middle of another manhunt, when in July 1992 Delta deployed eight men to Colombia for Operation Heavy Shadow, the hunt for Colombian drug kingpin Pablo Escobar. As leader of the Medellín cocaine cartel and one of the richest men in the world, Escobar had terrorized Colombia for fifteen years, murdering anyone who got in his way, including Colombian presidential candidate Luis Galán. In 1991 he cut a deal with the Colombian government: he promised to turn himself in and be incarcerated with some of his closest allies in a luxurious, custom-built "prison." The government promised not to extradite him to the United States, which had indicted him on drug trafficking charges. But Escobar did not hold up his end of the deal and fled his gilded cage. President Bush had quickly signed off on the U.S. ambassador to Colombia's request that Delta help the Colombian authorities track him down.

The importance Delta—and by extension, JSOC—attached to the

mission can be gauged by the makeup of its team, which was led by Jerry Boykin, now a colonel and the new Delta commander, having succeeded Pete Schoomaker earlier that summer. The barrel-chested C Squadron commander, Lieutenant Colonel Gary Harrell, also deployed, along with Eagle Claw veteran Sergeant Major Deciderio "Jack" Alvarez and Sergeant First Class Joe Vega, both fluent Spanish speakers. They all inflated their ranks so as to earn respect from Colombian officers, who looked down on enlisted soldiers: Alvarez became a colonel, Harrell a general. Those in Colombia for extended periods also assumed different names.[3]

But the Delta operators were arriving a little late to the Escobar hunt. First on the scene was the Army of Northern Virginia. (The nomenclature associated with the unit was particularly confusing, even for the labyrinthine world of special operations naming conventions. In 1989 the Army officially changed its name from the Intelligence Support Activity to the Tactical Coordination Detachment. It was later known as the U.S. Army Office of Military Support. Despite its official cover names, the unit was often referred to by the names of the special access programs associated with it, including Capacity Gear, Centra Spike, Torn Victor, and Gray Fox. Perhaps because of the multiplicity of names, many of the relatively few people in the military community familiar with the unit called it the Army of Northern Virginia.) The unit, which in 1986 had moved into new facilities at Fort Belvoir, Virginia, was still not assigned to JSOC, but its relations with the command and the other special mission units had grown much closer since the fractious days of Dick Scholtes and Jerry King. Indeed, the JSOC commander who'd sent Boykin's team down, newly promoted Major General Bill Garrison, had previously commanded Delta Force shortly after serving as deputy ISA commander. Since 1989, the Army of Northern Virginia had maintained an intermittent undercover presence in Colombia using equipment covertly mounted on two small civilian airplanes—a Beechcraft 300 and a Beechcraft 350—to track Escobar by zeroing in on his radio and cell phone calls.[4]

For more than a year, JSOC rotated Delta and Team 6 operators through Colombia, keeping a force of about a dozen between Bogotá (the capital) and Medellín, Escobar's hometown. Their mission was supposed to be limited to training the "Search Bloc," the Colombian force going after Escobar and his henchmen. But the aggressive, action-oriented operators soon found ways to accompany their trainees on missions. All the while, the Army of Northern Virginia's aircraft and the Search Bloc were narrowing the focus of their hunt to a fifteen-block middle-class Medellín neighborhood. Escobar knew he was being tracked and that his calls were being listened to, so he kept his conversations short and always operated in a way that aimed to mislead the searchers about his real location.

But on December 2, 1993, he finally made a mistake, staying on the phone with his son for several minutes instead of the customary twenty seconds. The phone tracking devices the Americans had taught the Colombians to use led the Search Bloc straight to a two-story house. Escobar and his bodyguard were gunned down as they tried to flee across the rooftops. The shot that killed the drug lord entered his brain via his right ear. Persistent rumors suggested it was made by a U.S. operator, perhaps a sniper stationed on a nearby rooftop. No one has ever produced any evidence or witness that validates this claim and Boykin has gone on record to say Delta didn't pull any triggers that day.[5]

Whoever took the final shot, JSOC chalked Escobar's death up as mission success. It would also have long-lasting impact on the command, as it provided "the template" for how to use a quarry's cell phone to track him down, said a special mission unit member. Heavy Shadow also underlined the lesson learned four years earlier by the operators who had hunted Noriega through Panama City: finding a man of resources who is hiding in his hometown is a difficult task. As the search for Escobar was reaching its climax in fall 1993, another, much larger JSOC task force on the other side of the world was learning a similar lesson. That manhunt did not end quite as well.

⁜

In December 1992, U.S. forces deployed to Somalia as part of an international peacekeeping force charged with delivering humanitarian assistance to the famine-gripped East African nation. Operation Restore Hope, as the U.S. government dubbed it, was well intentioned but naive. The main problem gripping Somalia was not famine, but the clan-based civil war that had raged for more than a year. This violence, combined with endemic corruption, prevented the troops from delivering the humanitarian assistance to many who needed it. The United States withdrew most of its troops in mid-1993, but Mohammed Farah Aideed, a Somali warlord who controlled much of Mogadishu, the capital, viewed the United Nations–backed international force that remained as a threat. In August, with the capital deteriorating into a state of open war between Aideed's militia and the U.N. force, President Bill Clinton approved the deployment of a JSOC task force to Mogadishu to capture Aideed.

The roughly 450 personnel JSOC deployed included headquarters personnel to man the operations center, a reinforced company from 3rd Ranger Battalion, about sixty Delta operators, plus elements of Echo Squadron, TF 160, 24th STS, and a four-man sniper element from Team 6's Red Team. Other than a handful of SEALs on the JOC staff, the four snipers were the task force's only Naval Special Warfare representatives. Team 6's Blue Team had been under the impression that it would be the force to support Delta by establishing blocking positions and hitting ancillary targets. In what they thought was a preparation for that mission, Blue Team's operation had spent several weeks working with Delta at Bragg's urban warfare training site and on their own at a similar facility at the Marines' Camp Lejeune, in North Carolina. But during a JSOC capabilities exercise—a demonstration designed to impress visiting dignitaries—at Bragg in late August, the SEALs noticed C-141s taking off from Pope. It was the J-alert birds taking the task force to Somalia, leaving the SEALs at home. Wayne Downing, by then a four-star general and the commander of U.S. Special Operations Command, which was JSOC's higher headquarters, had decided to send the Rangers instead. The decision crushed the SEALs and added to their perception that the Army generals who dominated JSOC and SOCOM undervalued them. As if to rub salt in Team 6's emotional wounds, the Pentagon named the JSOC force Task Force Ranger to obscure the fact that Delta's C Squadron, commanded by Gary Harrell, was its centerpiece. TF Ranger's commander was Garrison, an officer steeped in covert operations since Vietnam, where he'd been part of the Phoenix Program that aimed to destroy the Vietcong infrastructure in South Vietnam. Straight out of central casting, the tall, laconic general was highly respected by his men and rarely without an unlit cigar clenched between his teeth. In Mogadishu the two-star general wore a lieutenant colonel's rank insignia in an effort to hide his role.

But although he projected confidence to his men, the seasoned covert ops veteran had confessed to serious misgivings about the mission when he visited an old friend in the Pentagon prior to the deployment.

"I hate it," he said, with his boots on his pal's desk. "This is not a good mission."

"It was unclear and unsatisfactory to him who was in charge of what," recalled Garrison's friend. "He had a premonition that he was going to get this thing hung around his neck if it went south."

As was the norm, the task force set up its JOC in a bullet-riddled hangar by the main airfield. At its heart, TF Ranger's mission was another manhunt. JSOC put the lessons learned in Panama and Colombia to use and launched half a dozen operations in August and September designed to strip away the layers of protection that surrounded Aideed. On the afternoon of October 3, based on an informant's tip, the task force launched a seventh mission, an air assault raid on a meeting of Aideed's inner circle at the Olympic Hotel in the Bakara Market neighborhood, the very heart of Aideed territory. The timing of the raid was not ideal—JSOC preferred to operate at night, rather than in broad daylight—but the transitory nature of the opportunity left the task force little choice.

The raid was going well, with the targets all captured and loaded into a ground convoy for the trip back to the airfield, when a militiaman shot down a TF 160 Black Hawk with a rocket-propelled grenade. About twenty minutes later another RPG shot down a second Black Hawk. What had been a routine, if dangerous, mission that should have lasted no longer than an hour descended into chaos. Task force elements were able to secure the first crash site, but not the second. Delta snipers Master Sergeant Gary Gordon and Sergeant First Class Randy Shughart, on another Black Hawk, volunteered to insert to try to hold off a mob of militiamen and enraged civilians at the second site. But after heroically defending the position against impossible odds, they died when the mob finally overran them. (The pair received posthumous Medals of Honor for their actions.) It was early the next morning before a rescue convoy finally reached the pinned-down troops.

The battle left eighteen U.S. soldiers dead and scores wounded (as well as many hundred Somali casualties). In addition, Aideed's forces captured a TF 160 pilot, Chief Warrant Officer 3 Michael Durant, the only survivor of the second crash, who they released October 14. (In a cruel coda to the battle, two days after it ended, a mortar round killed Sergeant First Class Matt Rierson, the Delta NCO who'd led the assault force into the Olympic, and badly wounded Harrell, Boykin, and Delta surgeon Major Rob Marsh as they stood talking outside the JOC.)[6]

Operation Gothic Serpent, as JSOC's Somalia deployment was named, had significant repercussions for the command. Although Garrison, Boykin, and many others in TF Ranger viewed the Mogadishu battle as a success, albeit one they had paid an extraordinarily high price to achieve, that perspective was not shared in Washington. Having taken its eye off the ball in Somalia, the Clinton administration had been shocked by the battle's carnage. Clinton doubled Task Force Ranger's size immediately after the battle, but, to the operators' immense frustration, he withdrew the force altogether shortly thereafter, with Aideed still at liberty. The fear of having a JSOC operation turn into a nasty political surprise would color the government's use of the command for years to come, leading to greater micromanagement and risk aversion.

The battle was, naturally, a searing experience for all involved. It dominated tactical training for Delta and the Rangers for the rest of the decade. "The Mogadishu scenario was 'it' in the unit until '01," said a Delta operator. "That's what you trained for because that was the last fight." Mogadishu veterans disproportionately rose to positions of authority in JSOC and the wider special ops world.[7]

There were also recriminations. As he had predicted, Garrison ended up paying for the bloody debacle with his career, while friction between Delta and the Rangers over the latter's conduct in the battle led to JSOC having to change the units' readiness cycles so that C Squadron was no longer tied to 3rd Battalion.[8]

The massive publicity accorded the battle, both in its immediate aftermath and several years later with Mark Bowden's bestselling book *Black Hawk Down*, which Ridley Scott turned into a successful film, made it even harder for JSOC to hide itself from the public, especially as the Internet began to dominate the information age.

A particularly keen observer from afar of events in Mogadishu was a young Saudi Islamist leader named Osama bin Laden, then living in Sudan. His organization, Al Qaeda, was five years old and had yet to make a name for itself, but its leader had great ambitions. The conclusion he drew from Mogadishu was simple: once they had taken a few casualties, "the Americans ran away."[9]

6

Forging Bonds in the Balkans

As the decade lengthened, JSOC's mission set grew. The combination of the command's sizable budget, demonstrated capability, and carefully cultivated aura of secrecy meant "JSOC was asked to solve problems nobody else could solve," said a retired special ops officer. The attitude of those in the very few rungs in the chain of command above JSOC seemed to be, "if it's really hard and it's really important let's ask JSOC to do it," said Mike Hall, who was the command's senior enlisted adviser from May 2000 to December 2001, having previously spent four years as the Ranger Regiment's command sergeant major. This applied even to missions for which the Marines or Special Forces or an infantry division might have been better suited. "Some of the things we were asked to do, maybe we weren't best for . . . but it sort of fell to JSOC because it was the no-fail, risk-averse environment from DoD," said Hall, who added that by sending the military's "very, very best" on a mission, Pentagon leaders were attempting to insulate themselves from criticism if the mission failed.

JSOC also retained its traditional 0300 mission to conduct counterterrorism operations abroad. Each JSOC unit was on a readiness cycle that kept one element prepared to be "wheels up" four hours after being alerted. In Delta, the unit on standby was called the "Aztec squadron," in Team 6 it was "the Trident" assault team, and in TF 160 it was the "Bullet package." Together they were called "the alert force."[1]

But in addition to being prepared to conduct what a retired special ops officer called the "standard reactive" 0300 mission set, which included hostage rescue and responding to a plane hijacking or the takeover of a U.S. embassy, JSOC continued to play a part in plans for much larger combat operations. Since its inception, "JSOC had always been the nation's strategic raiding force," said the retired special ops officer, citing

Grenada and Panama as examples. In September 1994, it appeared that the National Command Authority would order JSOC to repeat those exploits as the U.S. military prepared to invade Haiti to oust the junta that had deposed Aristide in 1991. A JSOC task force that included virtually all of Team 6 plus a Ranger contingent was ensconced on the aircraft carrier *America* ready to launch. Operators from Delta's Operational Support Troop had already infiltrated Haiti undercover and reconnoitered locations critical to the invasion. They took videos of the sites, which were then briefed back in extraordinary detail to the small elements preparing for their missions.[2] But at the last moment, under heavy pressure from a U.S. delegation that included former president Jimmy Carter, retired General Colin Powell, and Senator Sam Nunn, the junta's leaders decided to step down.

Although Team 6 was JSOC's main assault force, Delta operators had done the advance undercover work on land because their SEAL counterparts lacked such a capability. Within a decade JSOC units would be competing to conduct low-vis missions, but in the mid-1990s what the SEALs called "clan [short for clandestine] stuff" was not a Team 6 priority. That hadn't always been the case, however. In advance of the Panama invasion, Rick Woolard, the Team 6 commander, realized he had no good intelligence on one of his unit's likely targets—a favorite beach house of Noriega's at Río Hato. So Woolard cobbled together a few Spanish-speaking Latino operators who might be able to snoop around Panama without drawing attention. In what a senior Team 6 officer later described as a "totally unauthorized" mission, Woolard sent two of the operators to Panama undercover, along with a female supply petty officer, who posed as the romantic partner of one of the SEALs. The mission was a bust—the team couldn't find out anything useful about the beach house and Woolard recalled them—but the Team 6 commander saw the value of such a unit and kept the group of about half a dozen operators together. "They had brown skin so we called them the 'Brown Boys' and that eventually became Brown Cell," said a Team 6 officer.

The cell trained for deep reconnaissance and undercover operations, and endured through the rest of Woolard's tenure and that of his successor, Ron Yeaw. But by the time Captain Tom Moser took command of Team 6 in 1992, the attention paid to Brown Cell had become a source of discontent within the assault troops. Moser shut it down. The petty officer who was Team 6's first undercover female operative left the unit and the Navy in 1993 and joined Delta, which had heavily recruited her for its own small band of women operators. She spent several years there before returning to the Navy and retiring.[3]

Although JSOC was created to conduct the counterterrorism—or 0300—mission set that revolved largely around hostage rescue scenarios, from the mid-1990s until 2001, two very different missions dominated the command's world.[4] One of these was the hunt for Balkan war criminals, known in the command as PIFWCs (pronounced "pifwicks"): persons indicted for war crimes. Most were Bosnian Serbs accused of committing atrocities against Bosnia's Muslims.

The December 1995 Dayton Peace Accords that marked the end of the Bosnian war stipulated that war criminals would stand trial at a tribunal in The Hague. The challenge was finding and then nabbing them. With Bosnia divided into American, British, and French sectors, this entailed a complicated command and control setup in which an American-led intelligence-gathering task force was supposed to locate the hostages, before special operations forces—the nationality of whom depended on which country's sector of Bosnia the hostages were located in—were deployed to find them. If the mission was in the U.S. sector, then a JSOC task force would get the job.

The task force's first venture, Operation Tango, aimed to capture Simo Drljaca and Milan Kovacevic, two Serbian warlords accused of horrible war crimes in the town of Prijedor. Team 6 elements flew into the NATO base in Tuzla, Bosnia, on a C-17 transport. To hide from Serbian spies, they deplaned inside shipping containers that were taken inside a hangar, where the operators jumped out. After conducting surveillance of the pair's daily routines, the task force sprang into action on July 10, 1997. A combined force of Team 6 and British SAS operators killed Drljaca at a fishing retreat at a remote lake after he reportedly resisted arrest by shooting and wounding an SAS man. Simultaneously, 100 miles away, a Team 6 element posing as Red Cross personnel arrived at the hospital clinic where Kovacevic worked, talked their way past the receptionist, entered his office, and subdued him. The operators placed Kovacevic in a wheelchair, took him out a back entrance, and loaded him into a waiting truck.

Shortly after Operation Tango, the United States placed Jerry Boykin, now a brigadier general and fresh from a stint as deputy chief of the CIA's Special Activities Division (which included Ground Branch), in charge of the intelligence-gathering task force, whose overall mission to seize the PIFWCs was called Operation Amber Star. In theory, Boykin reported directly to Army General Wes Clark, the head of U.S. European Command and NATO's supreme military commander, but in practice he cleared everything through Army General Eric Shinseki, the NATO commander in Bosnia, before briefing Clark. From the moment they landed in Bosnia, the JSOC elements fell under Shinseki, who demanded reams of supporting intelligence before approving a mission. "It was a delicate and confusing situation," said a senior task force officer. Technically headquartered at European Command in Stuttgart, Germany, the task force (also called Amber Star) had two "command and control centers" in the Bosnian cities of Tuzla and Sarajevo as well as "a series of satellite centers scattered across the Balkans from which we could run our intel collection activities," according to Boykin. The task force focused on a list of a "dirty dozen" individuals. By March 1998, it had rolled up seven.[5]

The task force did not let up and was still grabbing war criminals in April 2001, when a group of at least six reconnaissance personnel (two from Team 6 and at least four from Delta's Operational Support Troop, including one woman) in two vehicles captured Dragan Obrenovic, a former officer in the Yugoslav army wanted for his involvement in the 1995 massacre of prisoners at Srebrenica.[6] "Some of the PIFWC snatches were kind of legendary," said a Delta source who served multiple tours in Bosnia, noting that the missions helped the unit develop new tactics, techniques, and procedures. Many operations involved intercepting and seizing someone traveling in a moving vehicle, often with bodyguards. The task force would surreptitiously attach a tracking beacon to the target's car. Delta was already experimenting with technologies that used an electromagnetic pulse to shut a car's battery down remotely. The unit also used a catapult net system that would ensnare car and driver alike. Once the car had been immobilized, operators would smash the window with a sledgehammer, pull their target through the window, and make off with him, shooting any bodyguards who posed a threat, while an outer security perimeter kept anyone who might interfere at bay. The operators had a name for these snatches: *habeas grab-ass*.[7]

Amber Star was the logical follow-on from the hunt for Pablo Escobar. The operators refined their man-hunting techniques, with an emphasis on low-vis operations. "It was a pretty steep learning curve," a Team 6 operator said. But the operators soon learned that to blend in they had to dress and act exactly like the locals. That might mean washing their hair less often, wearing locally bought clothes, smoking local cigarettes (even the special mission units' health-conscious athlete-warriors learned to smoke constantly when out on a mission), and doing close-target reconnaissance in locally purchased vehicles complete with the right license plates for whichever town they were in. Doing that sort of drive-by reconnaissance of a target's home might require the operators to drive from one safe house to another, where they'd swap vehicles before driving to a third location to pick up the "covered" vehicle they would use on the mission. "It takes a lot of discipline to do it right," the Team 6 operator said. "We were just starting to get it correct. It's a lot of stuff the Agency had figured out for years."

As in Colombia, the command worked closely with the CIA, whose job it was to find the PIFWCs, with JSOC brought in to capture the individuals once they'd been located. That division of labor led to frustration at JSOC headquarters. "We thought the Agency was fucked up and we were on a wild-goose chase 90 percent of the time in the Balkans," a retired special ops officer said. Nonetheless, the two organizations forged close relationships in the Balkans that would stand each in good stead after September 11. It was not unusual for Delta officers and CIA case officers to work side by side in an "R and S" (reconnaissance and surveillance) base with Army of Northern Virginia personnel and signals intelligence experts from the National Security Agency.[8] (The Army of Northern Virginia operatives were responsible for "infrastructure"—renting safe houses, buying cars, handling money, running sources.)

The personal connections that were forged in the Balkans between the special mission units and the CIA's Special Activities Division would prove crucial in the next decade. "The real bond between the CIA and Delta started in Bosnia, where [we were] face-to-face, working a real-world mission, getting to know each other, realizing once again that neither organization can do what they want to do without the other," said a Delta source. "That's the genesis of the whole relationship."

But no such bonds yet existed between the JSOC and CIA headquarters, however, according to Hank Crumpton, who was in charge of global operations for the CIA's Counterterrorist Center in the two years prior to September 11.[9] "Shockingly, in that period I basically had no interaction with JSOC," Crumpton said. "I had requested it, I had wanted it, I had needed their support, their resources, their air capability to get my teams into Afghanistan [in September 1999]. . . . And there was just really zero interest from DoD or the special ops command."

Although the U.S. news media barely registered JSOC's PIFWC missions,[10] the Clinton administration closely monitored them. The president himself authorized the January 22, 1998, mission in which Team 6 operators snatched Goran Jelisic, the so-called "Serb Adolf," outside his house in Bosnia's Serbian enclave, for instance, and was woken at 5:30 A.M. and told of its success.[11] But this level of political attention was accompanied by a requirement to keep friendly casualties low to nonexistent in the operations, which were usually "urban raids in dense population centers," said a senior special ops officer familiar with the task force. That in turn meant "your planning has to go into infinite amounts of detail."

It also led to an extraordinarily risk-averse environment in which JSOC commander Army Major General Bryan "Doug" Brown, who led the command from 1998 to 2000, and his successor, Major General Dell Dailey, a former 160th commander, felt compelled to deploy hundreds of personnel plus the JOC for each snatch mission. "So for picking up an old man who's walking between the bread store and his house, JSOC has to fly over, set up, and run the operation," commented a Delta source bitterly. By 2001, "everyone kind of acknowledged that you don't need to bring a squadron over to do a job that four people can do," said another Delta operator. However, Mike Hall, Dailey's senior enlisted adviser, said the general flew over to oversee operations not because he didn't trust the operators, but to act as a buffer between the operators and senior leaders in Washington uncomfortable with the thought of a lieutenant colonel running a national-level mission. "If he wasn't there as a two-star to deal with the bureaucracy, then those guys would have zero chance of executing that operation," Hall said.

Bosnia also gave JSOC's lesser known elements a chance to come into their own. Delta's Operational Support Troop, which did a lot of the unit's deep reconnaissance and undercover work, was heavily involved. The urban settings allowed the troop to take advantage of one of its secret weapons: its small number of female operators, who combined with male counterparts to form "guy-girl teams" that masqueraded as romantic couples while reconnoitering targets.[12]

The women occupied an almost unique role in the U.S. military. In early 1982, at the request of Delta commander Colonel Rod Paschall,

Army Secretary John Marsh authorized Delta to use female operators in direct combat roles. (They were banned from such jobs in the rest of the Army.) But that early experiment failed. Although four women graduated from a "modified" assessment and selection course, Delta's men were not yet ready for coed operations. "It didn't work out and they all kind of drifted away and the unit soon reverted to being an all-male preserve," said a Delta officer. However, mindful of the advantages mixed-sex couples enjoy on reconnaissance missions, where they are presumed to evoke less suspicion than "singleton" men or male duos, under Schoomaker's command, Delta tried again in 1990 and this time stuck with the program, despite continuing disapproval on the part of some male operators.[13] The difference this time was that the unit put more thought into the women's assessment and selection process, a Delta officer said. "It wasn't just about whether they could run a hundred miles," he said. "It was very physical, don't misunderstand me, but it was also a lot more emphasis on the psychological testing, so it worked out a lot better."

By the early 2000s OST had about half a dozen female operators, according to an experienced unit operator. The women "were every bit as capable" as its men, he added. "They were there for the same reasons the guys were—they wanted to serve their country and do missions." But he acknowledged his view was far from unanimous in Delta. "I didn't have the issues [with the women] that a lot of guys had," he said.

Delta's Echo Squadron also played a major role in Bosnia, albeit one hidden in plain sight. The covered air squadron was still a small organization in the 1990s with only about fifteen pilots, but its capabilities had grown since its Seaspray days. One technological development in particular had major tactical and operational consequences: the Wescam ball, which had already made an appearance in Mogadishu in 1993. A gyro-stabilized camera in a spherical mounting fixed to the underside of an aircraft, the ball could track a target and, using "basic line-of-sight digital radio secure technology," transmit live video of whatever it tracked back to the JOC, according to a Delta source. It quickly became JSOC's eye in the sky. The camera included a forward-looking infrared lens, a regular infrared lens, and a telescopic lens.

Echo fixed the Wescam balls to turboprop planes made by Schweizer, a firm that specialized in gliders and quiet reconnaissance aircraft. The Echo pilots would climb to altitude, then cut the engine and use the plane's long wingspan to descend in circles, before drifting away, flying out of the area, returning to altitude and repeating the process. "You couldn't hear a thing," said a Team 6 operator. The Wescam ball would be transmitting live down to operators riding in the back of a nondescript van. "We had little video screens watching the Wescam ball track cars and stuff right into our ambushes," said the Delta source. "They were at the forefront of all that technology that today is in Predators and everything else."

But Echo's value went far beyond the Wescam ball. The squadron had three basic missions: "sensor"—visual reconnaissance and surveillance missions involving high-tech gear like the Wescam ball; "shooter"—using civilian-style helicopters as attack aircraft; and "transport"—moving special mission unit operators and other sensitive personnel covertly. (The "sensor" mission originally included signals intelligence, but in 1987 the unit lost that part of the mission to the ISA, which also had a covered aviation element.)

The unit's pilots trained on a wide variety of rotary and small fixed wing aircraft, with a particular emphasis on the Soviet-designed Mi-8s and Mi-17s that allowed them to operate covertly in the many parts of the world where those airframes are ubiquitous. Sometimes Echo would rent helicopters abroad and convert them. At other times they'd steal them. Either way, the shooter or sensor packages would be secretly shipped to the U.S. embassy via diplomatic "pouches" (in reality, large boxes or crates), then Echo would marry up the airframes and the military gear out of sight in a remote airfield hangar. While Echo always operated undercover, that cover was often official: flying routine missions for a U.S. embassy, or, in regions where there were large U.S. military deployments, conventional military aircraft reconfigured to accommodate special mission equipment invisible to the casual observer. The squadron flew regular "signature missions" to different parts of the world where it might have to fly real-world missions someday, in order to condition those countries' security forces to the sight of the aircraft. Then if an actual mission required the unit's presence (and it wasn't already there), its arrival wouldn't raise too many eyebrows.

Of its three mission types, "shooter" was the one Echo executed least often. "We don't prefer arming" the helicopters, said a retired special operations officer, adding that ambassadors were unlikely to approve such missions.

Echo rarely if ever participated in JSOC's big quarterly exercises, now called joint readiness exercises, for fear of burning its cover, but it trained with Delta and Team 6 in more secluded settings on everything from jungle operations in Guyana with the former to cruise ship takedowns with the latter. The squadron also trained with the CIA's Special Activities Division. Indeed, that division's Air Branch was largely made up of former E Squadron pilots. The unit became so proficient that, according to a Delta source, by the late 1990s JSOC leaders became jealous of Delta's ownership of Echo and wanted the squadron to report directly to the joint command. Several cover and code names (Latent Arrow, for example) were associated with Echo and its special access programs, but by the end of the 1990s it was known in the wider military—when it was known at all—as Flight Concepts Division. On September 11, 2001, most Flight Concepts "assets" were still in the Balkans.[14]

✳

Most JSOC operations in the Balkans were designed to be low-vis (at least before the JOC staffers flew in all wearing special ops patches on their uniforms), but in 2000 the command came close to executing an operation there that more closely resembled the Grenada and Panama invasions than it did the clandestine and covert work in the Middle East or Colombia. That operation was Aurora Lightning, the code name for the invasion of the tiny country of Montenegro.

With a population of 620,000, Montenegro was very much the junior partner with the much larger Serbia in the Federal Republic of Yugoslavia, the rump state that remained after the violent breakup of Yugoslavia in the early 1990s. Montenegro was led by Western-leaning Milo Dukanovic, whose government Serbian leader Slobodan Milosevic repeatedly tried to undermine.

With critical elections pending in Montenegro in September 2000, the Clinton administration—apparently concerned that Serbian forces would take over Montenegro or at least depose and detain Dukanovic—ordered JSOC to plan for a major operation to safeguard Montenegro and its leader. Planning began in 1999. Late that year, under the code name Knocking Door, the command held a large rehearsal at Fort Campbell that included a "big, big airfield seizure that replicated the airfield" in Montenegro, said a mission planner. "It was a big package to go in there," so big that the operators took to calling the exercise "Knockers Galore," he said. "It wasn't going to be a permissive [uncontested] environment. It was semi-permissive at best, which is why we were going with so many guns." Under the guise of preparing for the "Y2K" computer bug, JSOC used an EC-130J Commando Solo aircraft to take over the frequencies of radio stations near Fort Campbell and broadcast a test message. The actual operation was to involve the Commando Solo seizing control of Montenegro's airwaves and broadcasting U.S.-controlled information over them. The plan was to "put the [Montenegrin] president in a van and have him broadcast up to Commando Solo, which would then broadcast out to the nation 'I am safe, blah blah blah,'" said a JSOC staff officer.

TF Brown's contribution included eight Little Birds and four Direct Action Penetrators, or DAPs (pronounced "dapps"), which were Black Hawks that functioned as attack helicopters, rather than troop carriers. The "Smokey and the Bandit" truck-mounted capability would be used to get some of the Little Birds into the fight. There were also plans to fly at least one Abrams tank into Montenegro. Fort Campbell was home to the massive 101st Airborne Division (Air Assault) and numerous smaller formations, but they had no say in what happened. "We came in and took over," said the JSOC staff officer. "All training on the ranges was canceled, everything; units were thrown off [training areas] so that JSOC units had free run of the entire base."

The plan evolved through summer 2000. At one stage it involved Team 6 assaulting at least five coastal defense cruise missile sites, before it was scaled back to an operation designed mainly to spirit Dukanovic and his family to safety. JSOC prepared multiple options. The preferred course of action was for Echo Squadron to fly the family out. Under that scenario, responsibility for safeguarding them would fall to Delta, which already had OST operators on the ground in Montenegro. Should that option fall through, Team 6 was prepared to pick up Dukanovic on the beach. On September 21, 2000, the *Saipan*, a helicopter-carrying U.S. Navy flattop, arrived in the Adriatic Sea off Montenegro to support Aurora Lightning. Shortly after the ship arrived on station, out of sight of land, Team 6's Red Team parachuted from three C-141s in mid-afternoon into the ocean close to the *Saipan* with six 40-foot, high-speed assault craft. Those "military cigarette boats," as a Team 6 officer called them, could race through choppy seas at up to 60 knots per hour. "We sunk our parachutes," said a SEAL. "No one ever knew about it." Meanwhile several Air Force Special Operations MH-53 Pave Low helicopters flew to the *Saipan* to provide assault aircraft, should they be needed.

But the internal frictions that so often plagued JSOC reared their head again. Dailey, the new JSOC commander, was in Tuzla with a Delta squadron and TF Brown. After talking with Schoomaker, by now the SOCOM commander, Dailey announced that the Delta squadron and TF Brown would fly to the *Saipan* and become the lead force for Aurora Lightning, with the SEALs relegated to a backup role. The JSOC commander then flew out to the *Saipan* with Delta commander Colonel Jim Schwitters, to be greeted by Team 6 operators quietly seething at being passed over yet again. But complications arose when TF Brown's munitions turned out not to meet the Navy's strict safety requirements, meaning the 160th helicopters couldn't land on the *Saipan*. In the end, it was all for naught. The elections went off without incident and what might have been JSOC's largest combat operation of the Clinton era faded away, leaving nary a shred of public evidence it had ever been considered.[15]

There was at least one long-term consequence of the late decision to favor Delta over Team 6. Dailey had told the SEALs that Delta was getting the mission in part because the Army unit's OST operators were already on the ground working undercover. Lesson learned, shortly thereafter Team 6 resurrected its Brown Cell concept for a subunit that specialized in clandestine activity. The new organization began as "a baby team," one operator recalled, but would grow to play an increasingly important role in the years ahead.[16]

7

Loose Nukes and Missed Opportunities

While JSOC honed its man-hunting skills during "real-world" operations in the Balkans, its training exercises increasingly focused on countering the spread of weapons of mass destruction (WMD). Known within JSOC as the 0400 mission, counter-proliferation had come to dominate the command, to the extent that by the late 1990s every joint readiness exercise scenario revolved around it.

Two main factors were behind the Pentagon's decision to throw money at JSOC to spend on counter-proliferation. One was the fear that the Soviet Union's breakup would result in "loose nukes" ending up in the hands of terrorists or "rogue" states like Iran, Iraq, or North Korea. The other was that after the 1991 Gulf War demonstrated that the U.S. Air Force could destroy anything on the earth's surface with "smart" bombs, the Pentagon assumed that enemies would seek to hide what they held most dear—especially their nuclear weapons programs—underground.

It fell to Delta to figure out how to penetrate these lairs, which were termed DUGs, for deep underground facilities, or HDBTs, for hard and deeply buried targets. A senior JSOC official summed up the challenge Delta faced: "If it was designed to defeat the biggest bomb that the United States Air Force had, how were you going to get in there with a few men and be able to defeat that system without killing yourself?"

Delta concluded that the best way to do it was using high-tech drilling and breaching equipment wielded by well-trained, experienced soldiers. "Drill and blast, that's the name of the game," said a Delta source. After initially training operators to do it, the unit changed course and recruited Special Forces engineer sergeants and a handful of other soldiers to form a heavy breaching section, which at its height numbered no more than about twenty soldiers assigned to the unit's Combat Support Troop. The heavy breachers were specially selected but did not go through Delta assessment and selection nor the operator training course through which all those who make it through assessment and selection must pass. The section worked with private firms to have some of the world's best drilling equipment designed to its specifications.

The breachers spent long hours experimenting with explosives, and a lot of time away from home getting "special schooling," a Delta source said. "These are the guys in the unit who had gone through all the basic atomic energy training." However, he said, even that training has its limitations. "You can go through all the training you want, but the last thing we're going to be recovering is a U.S.-made atomic bomb. It's going to be jury-rigged [and] foreign-made."

Delta operators also delighted in confounding JSOC exercise planners by figuring out ways to penetrate the facilities that didn't involve drilling and blasting. "We'd have the rest of the troop or squadron scour this place for access points and most of the time it was a simple fix," said an operator. "One time we used a high-lift jack, lifted the door off its hinges, it fell in. It took like six minutes. The JSOC folks are like, 'That's a six-hour door!'" On another occasion, during a joint readiness exercise at an old Russian nuclear weapons storage depot in Poland, the heavy breachers had barely gotten their drills and explosives unpacked when operators found an air shaft and fast-roped down it into the facility to open the door from the inside.

In a rare on-the-record interview in 1997, JSOC commander Army Major General Michael Canavan told *Armed Forces Journal International* that the command was at "about a 60 percent solution" with regard to its counter-proliferation mission. "Right now we're as good as our equipment," he said. "Our biggest challenge is getting into these deep underground shelters. Once you get in that environment, you run into real problems in terms of seeing, in terms of communication, in terms of breathing." By the late 1990s the concept had expanded beyond "drill and blast," according to a commander of one of JSOC's colored task forces. "There are all these fast-burning lasers and all kinds of fancy things that they are trying to do besides explosives to get into hardened buildings that are underground," he said. "It's a huge effort."

The challenges of the 0400 mission were extensive and went beyond the physics of how to penetrate concrete that was x meters underground and y meters thick. "You start to look at [operating in] tunnels," a retired special ops officer said. This required "battery-powered vehicles" so there would be no emissions, as well as being able to operate without line-of-sight radio signals. In addition, all the 0400 mission kit had to fit on a variety of military aircraft, and the crew for those aircraft, whether they were Air Force planes or the 160th's helicopters, had to be able to fly in while wearing fully sealed nuclear-biological-chemical protective gear.

The JSOC task force would be augmented on these missions by civilian nuclear experts from the national laboratories—known as the Lincoln Gold team—who were on alert, just as JSOC units were. Sometimes the mission would require a direct real-time video link back to Department of Energy experts in the United States. The final and most dangerous piece of the mission fell to explosive ordnance detachment personnel recruited by Delta and Team 6 especially for this purpose, but the retired senior special ops officer said it would be a mistake to assume their job was little more than deciding which wires to snip. "It isn't cutting wires like you see on TV," he said. "It's much more hard science."

In the early 1990s Iraq's presumed nuclear weapons program was JSOC's priority target. Saddam Hussein "became the living, breathing model" of the madman bent on destruction that Delta and (especially) JSOC hypothesized in their increasingly elaborate Joint Readiness Exercise (JRX) scenarios, which typically climaxed in James Bond style with Delta's heavy breachers racing to burrow into a nuclear facility hidden beneath the desert after Rangers had seized an airfield always conveniently located nearby, a special operations source said. (An enemy T-72-tank-equipped heavy division would also be within a few hours' drive of the facility, so the Delta breachers and their civilian expert colleagues would be toiling under pressure, knowing the tanks were closing in.)[1]

Delta had a secret advantage in planning operations against Saddam's nuclear facilities: it had undercover operators visiting them regularly as part of the United Nations inspection teams. Their presence, if not their identities, was not a real secret to the Iraqis or the United Nations, which requested military personnel for its teams. (Other countries, among them Russia, also included special ops forces in their contribution to the inspection teams.) There wasn't a Delta presence on every inspection mission, but the norm was for two operators to go on the missions, which, including train-up and debrief, could last as long as three months. "If the Iraqis pushed back hard, or if it was going to be a long mission, we'd go," a Delta source said. The operators were there in part to acquire a basic familiarity with Iraq, and also to be available should the U.N. team run into trouble. But of course, the trips were very useful in enabling JSOC to plan how it would take down any Iraqi weapons of mass destruction establishments if ordered to do so. Intelligence personnel would brief the operators before they went on what to expect and what to look for at the Iraqi facilities. The operators therefore took careful note of everything they saw, on the assumption that even if they weren't tasked to assault that particular facility, they might get ordered to assault similar ones.[2]

Toward the end of the decade, the focus of the WMD exercises shifted somewhat. The primary target against which the scenarios were modeled became the Libyan facility at Tarhuna, a vast complex built into a rocky hillside. Muammar Gaddafi's regime claimed it was a waterworks project, but the U.S. government, in the person of Director of Central Intelligence John Deutch in February 1996, accused Libya of "building the world's largest underground chemical weapons plant."[3]

"We looked at it for a long time and the IC [intelligence community] was convinced that it was some sort of WMD production facility," said a Delta staff officer. "It was clearly pushed to the world as a great waterworks project but the geospatial information just didn't support it." (A decade later, however, some observers would cast doubt on the conclusion that Tarhuna ever was a chemical weapons plant.)[4]

As the new century loomed, suspected Iranian and North Korean nuclear facilities also featured in JSOC's planning and exercise scenarios, as did the spread of biological weapons such as anthrax. But some missions the regional U.S. military commanders-in-chief dreamed up for JSOC were little more than wishful thinking.[5] "People have unfeasible notions about what you can accomplish with small teams," said a retired special operations officer. A raid against a WMD facility in North Korea or Iran would have needed the support of at least two divisions' worth of conventional troops, he said.

While Delta's heavy breachers were the core of that unit's counterproliferation capability, Team 6 leveraged the Navy's traditional strength in explosive ordnance disposal, or EOD, to earn itself a key role in JSOC's mission to "render safe" any WMD device. Not only did Team 6 have the lead for any shipborne nuclear, biological, or chemical threat, it also had a particularly important part to play on the domestic side of JSOC's mission. The unit was on a one-hour string to deploy a team to Andrews

Air Force Base, just across the Maryland border from Washington, D.C., to advise civilian officials on how to handle a WMD threat in the national capital region. Originally Delta's, by 1998 JSOC had given the mission to Team 6 in part because Dam Neck was closer than Bragg to Washington, but also because of Team 6's strong EOD capability. "The SEALs were cleared all the way up to frickin' nuclear to disarm manually," but could also "reach back" to experts at the national laboratories, a JSOC staff officer said. In most cases it wouldn't be SEALs doing the technical work, but Team 6's EOD personnel, typically an officer and four enlisted men.

The "render safe" mission did not require the special mission units to completely neutralize a device, just to "render it safe for movement" by ship or aircraft to the tiny Johnston Atoll in the Pacific, where it would be made "final safe," a Team 6 officer said. (Biological or chemical threats might be taken to Utah's Dugway Proving Ground.) In a worst-case situation in which even Team 6's experts were unable to stop a ticking bomb, the task force commander would face "an emergency destruct decision," the officer said. "It's going to fuck things up and people up. We've been through that one [in a joint readiness exercise] as well."

As part of its domestic counter-proliferation mission, JSOC participated in congressionally mandated Top Officials Exercises, or TOPOFFs, designed to test the U.S. government's ability to handle WMD crises in the United States. The first TOPOFF, held in spring 2000, involved multiple simultaneous WMD scenarios across the country,[6] including a bomb hidden in Anacostia, a poor Washington, D.C., neighborhood. "A device was going to be planted, the SEALs were going to have to find it," said the JSOC staff officer. To eliminate the chance of terrorists detonating either the bomb or an anti-handling device attached to it via a cell phone signal, Doug Brown, the JSOC commander, wanted to shut down a large part of the capital's cell phone coverage. The command's information operations office drafted a cover story blaming the cell phone blackout on a power failure. At "the eleventh hour" the Department of Justice blocked the move, the staff officer said. The workaround was to place the device on a boat and direct the anti-cell-phone technology away from the city.

By the late 1990s, in an effort to avoid having to conduct the sort of dramatic, last-ditch missions envisioned in the JRX scenarios, Team 6 had begun to think differently about counter-proliferation. The new approach, called "pathway defeat," involved preempting threats by intercepting or otherwise interfering with an enemy's ability to obtain precursor materials like centrifuges needed to create weapons of mass destruction. By then, even the counterterrorism mission was morphing into counter-proliferation, or CP. "We started seeing less desire to take hostages and more desire to commit atrocities and it was believed that it was going to go towards CP," said a senior Team 6 officer. "We didn't think we'd see an aircraft with hostages anymore. The *Achille Lauro* wasn't happening again. Instead it was something [terrorists] were transporting [on] a ship."

Team 6's counter-proliferation mission meant an influx of money, enabling the unit to buy a couple more Beechcraft King Air civilian-style planes, doubling the unit's fleet of the small turboprop aircraft. The original aircraft transported leaders and staff to meetings at JSOC headquarters. The new planes were intended to fly the SEALs to Andrews quickly. Team 6 also purchased the *Del Monte*, a disused cargo ship the unit used for static training. Training on the *Del Monte* was mostly unrelated to WMD, "but [the ship] was paid for with WMD money," a Team 6 officer said. The money for the ship and the planes was but a small fraction of the "hundreds of millions of dollars a year" a Delta source said the Pentagon was shoveling into JSOC's coffers for the counter-proliferation mission, which had become the command's highest priority. "All the way up to 9/11 it was the premier mission," he said. "It was the can't-fail mission." That money was helping to make JSOC a very rich, powerful organization. As the Delta source put it, the command had "tons of fucking cash."

The resources the American taxpayer was—largely unwittingly— lavishing on JSOC were spent in part on exercises across the globe. By the mid-1990s, quarterly joint readiness exercises were planned two years in advance. At the end of the decade, "every JRX we did for three years for both Green and Blue was WMD," a Team 6 officer said. Roughly a third of the exercises were abroad, in locations as diverse as Panama, the Bahamas, Poland, Israel, and Jordan.[7] In the latter case, Delta "infiltrated hundreds of kilometers in the desert [using] a combination of off-road vehicles and our . . . Nissan pickup trucks," an operator recalled. The Jordan JRX lasted three weeks and, like numerous others, was aimed at penetrating "hardened targets" in the desert, another participant said.

JSOC also held many exercises in the military's immense facilities in the American Southwest, which had the advantage of roughly replicating the flat desert that was home to many WMD targets while offering protection from prying eyes. Among the installations used were White Sands Missile Range and Kirtland Air Force Base in New Mexico, Dugway Proving Ground in Utah, and the Nevada Test Site for nuclear weapons, where the tunnels were 3,000 meters long.[8] These exercises were not risk-free. In 1992 twelve Ranger and Air Force special operations personnel died when their Air Force MH-60G Pave Hawk helicopter crashed in bad weather into the Great Salt Lake en route between Hill Air Force Base and Dugway during an exercise. The casualties included the commanders of 1st and 3rd Ranger Battalions and the Air Force's 55th Special Operations Squadron.[9]

The command also continued to train regularly in cities such as New York, Los Angeles, and Philadelphia. "My first time in New York, I rode a Little Bird that buzzed the Statue of Liberty," a Delta operator said. Although always coordinated with local authorities, the secrecy that surrounded these exercises often provoked thousands of panicked phone calls from residents about "black helicopters" and explosions in their neighborhoods.[10]

But the epic scale of the counter-proliferation scenarios and the command's decision that, according to a retired special operations officer, "every component of JSOC was part of the WMD mission," meant JSOC was in danger of becoming a prisoner of its own exercise process, unable to conceive of an operation that didn't involve almost every facet of the command and a cast of thousands. The quarterly exercises began to inspire a mixture of scorn and apprehension among participants. "Everybody just dreaded these things," said a Delta source.

The JRX concept's value "depended on where you sat" in the JSOC world, said a Delta staff officer. "To the individual, younger operator the value of the training was not as good because you could get better training day to day on the range," he said. But at higher levels of command, "it was absolutely necessary to exercise that whole thing and get all the pieces moving." However, he acknowledged that some of his peers feared JSOC was losing the very nimbleness the special mission units were supposed to embody. "It became the massive staff drills," he said. "It became the cookie-cutter process; you had to do it, you couldn't vary from it." He blamed the "inflexibility" on the Rangers who dominated the JSOC staff. They were more likely to think like conventional infantrymen and plan a real-world operation a certain way "because this is how you did it in exercises—it's that muscle memory, task, conditions, standards type stuff," he said. But others saw value in having Rangers—who were renowned planners—in the JOC. The reactive nature of the 0300 and 0400 missions placed a premium on quick planning, noted a retired special operations officer. "JSOC was a fucking planning machine," he said. "It could plan anything fast."

Some operators blamed the reluctance of the National Command Authority (the president and the defense secretary) to send JSOC into action on the unwieldy, "all or nothing" mentality that seemed to have gripped the command's planners. They had a point, but the behemoth that JSOC's standard deployed task force had become was far from the only factor. In the wake of the September 11 attacks, Bob Andrews, the acting assistant secretary of defense for special operations and low-intensity conflict, hired respected historian Richard Shultz as a consultant to research why Washington had never used JSOC to conduct the sort of counterterrorist missions for which it had been formed. Shultz came up with nine "showstoppers," as he called them, which he outlined in a classified study for Andrews and an unclassified article published in *The Weekly Standard*. The article quoted Pete Schoomaker, who had commanded Delta, JSOC, and, between 1998 and 2000, U.S. Special Operations Command, lamenting the failure to commit his forces to battle. "It was very, very frustrating," he said. "It was like having a brand-new Ferrari in the garage, and nobody wants to race it because you might dent the fender." One of Shultz's "showstoppers" was indeed what he called "big footprints," his phrase for the huge task forces JSOC would put together for operations, which in some cases scared off civilian policymakers. But others included the military hierarchy's disdain for special operations forces and, crucially, "risk aversion."[11]

There are no better examples of this risk aversion than what befell Delta's plans to capture or kill Osama bin Laden in 1998 and 1999. (And no better example of irony: had Delta been successful then, JSOC might never have garnered the resources, the authorities, and the roles that put it at the forefront of the U.S. military effort over the next decade.)

In 1998, Delta spent two weeks drawing up a plan to snatch bin Laden by inserting operators and vehicles onto a dry lake bed near the Al Qaeda leader's compound outside Kandahar and then either seizing bin Laden at home or ambushing his convoy on the road between Kandahar and Khowst.[12] If the task force opted to ambush the convoy, Delta would have provided the ground force while six or eight snipers from Team 6's Red Team riding on MH-6 Little Birds would have the mission to stop bin Laden's vehicle using Heckler & Koch 21 light machine guns firing 7.62mm "slap rounds," which had tungsten penetrators cased in plastic. The SEALs had already boarded an Air Force plane containing several Little Birds and their crews at Oceana Naval Air Station, close to Dam Neck, and were preparing for takeoff to conduct the mission when they got word it had been scratched.[13] The Clinton administration had decided to pursue what it considered less risky options in its pursuit of bin Laden.[14] On August 7, 1998, after the Delta plan had been shelved, Al Qaeda attacked the U.S. embassies in Kenya and Tanzania, killing more than 200 people, including twelve Americans, and wounding several thousand. Two years earlier bin Laden had declared war on the United States.[15] Now he was delivering on that grim promise.

In 1999, Delta planned again to target bin Laden. This time, the mission was to kill him. Four undercover OST operators would infiltrate (or "infil," in JSOC-speak) Afghanistan, identify bin Laden using binoculars, then call in either a smart bomb from a jet or Hellfire missiles from a pair of AH-6 Little Birds on his position. (A Combat Talon would have flown the helicopters onto the same dry lake bed.) The operators and the Little Birds rehearsed the mission at White Sands Missile Range. A TF Brown source familiar with the plan doubted that a Hellfire, a shaped charge weapon designed to penetrate tanks, would have created enough shrapnel to kill bin Laden if he was in a cave. But a Delta source thought chances were good that they would catch him in the open. "That plan would have worked," he said. Neither got a chance to find out. After the operators were kept on standby for several months, the mission was called off, with consequences that would not become clear until two years later when Delta and the Little Birds assembled again, this time on a damp afternoon in Hungary.[16]

PART II

A NEW ERA DAWNS

8

"Fairly Ponderous and Enormously Heavy"

With U.S. airspace closed to international commercial flights for several days after 9/11, it had taken the better part of a week for the hundreds of JSOC personnel spread across Europe to find their way home from Jackal Cave. The travel difficulties served to remind them that their world had just changed, permanently. As if to reinforce that message and motivate them for the challenges ahead, the pilots of a C-5 taking 160th personnel back to Fort Campbell flew directly over Manhattan, so the aviators could gaze down at what one described as the "smoking hole" that had been the World Trade Center. Along with the absence of any other aircraft in the sky, the sight "really drove home the reality" of the attacks, he said.[1]

The Delta and JSOC compounds to which many of the JRX participants returned were abuzz with anticipation. "Everybody was running around," said a JSOC staffer. "Everyone was amped." However, he added, "there was a lot of uncertainty of what we were going to do, where we were going, who was in charge."

For Delta, there was a near-term requirement to be ready to respond if terrorists hijacked more commercial airliners. "That kind of occupied a lot of the initial thought process," said an operator. "But . . . for us, that was, 'Okay, all you've got to do is give us the scenario. We're trained, we've got all our equipment, the Aztec squadron is prepped and waiting.'"

For a few hours, it seemed as if Delta would get that chance. Shortly after the government allowed normal commercial flights to resume on September 14, rumors flew that another jet had been hijacked and was sitting on the tarmac at Dulles Airport outside Washington, D.C.[2] Hijackings in the United States were usually the purview of the FBI's Hostage Rescue Team, but after September 11 there was a sense at Bragg that the old rules might no longer apply.[3] "We flexed on that and got ready to deploy the aircraft takedown team up there," before the truth that there was no hijacking reached Bragg, said the Delta source.

Meanwhile, Delta's operators brainstormed. To deter future hijackings, they suggested that the government, in conjunction with the FBI and the airlines, "leak out that there are Delta operators on board almost every flight and then do a fake takedown" using role players "in a first-class compartment that's all stooges" on an otherwise regular commercial flight, said the Delta source. A "terrorist" would attempt a hijacking before operators in plainclothes took him down "with hand-to-hand or something," the source said. "Get that out [via the media]. Get inside their heads." The aim was to "at least make [Al Qaeda] think twice and begin to think, 'Hey, they're on to us, there's special mission unit guys on every airplane.'"

But with Delta commander Colonel Jim Schwitters offering only luke-warm support for the proposal, Dailey vetoed the idea.[4] This typified the relationship between the JSOC commander and Delta, which was marked by a mutual distrust. "Dailey already had ideas on things and was unwilling to accept ideas that were starting to percolate up," the Delta source said.

Responsibility for fleshing out Dailey's ideas fell to a planning cell the general established within a few days of returning to Pope. Dailey staffed the cell with about twenty to thirty personnel from JSOC and its component units, but rather than keep it at Pope, he put it in some drab offices in the Ranger Regiment's gray cinder block headquarters at Fort Benning. By now it was clear Al Qaeda was responsible for the September 11 attacks. Defense Secretary Donald Rumsfeld was pressuring the military for retaliation options. The cell's job was to identify targets that JSOC could strike as soon as possible, and then plan missions against those targets.[5] But that was easier said than done.

Based in landlocked Afghanistan, Al Qaeda was sheltered by that country's Taliban regime. A harshly Islamist group that had seized power in 1996, the Taliban had been nurtured by Pakistan's powerful Inter-Services Intelligence agency as a hedge against Indian influence in Afghanistan. Drawn almost exclusively from the Pashtun ethnic group that dominated the country's southern and eastern provinces, by September 2001 the Taliban controlled all Afghanistan, save for the northeastern corner. There, the Northern Alliance, which drew its support from Tajiks, Uzbeks, and Hazaras, fought a bitter defensive struggle. But on

September 9 Al Qaeda had dealt the Alliance a crushing blow, assassinating its legendary military leader Ahmad Shah Massoud.

As it became increasingly clear that the Taliban would not turn over bin Laden and other Al Qaeda leaders to the United States, as demanded by President George W. Bush in a September 20 address to Congress,[6] it became equally apparent the United States was going to go to war in Afghanistan. The only questions were when and how.

The Taliban's ragtag armed forces—officially Afghanistan's military, but in reality little more than a collection of Pashtun militias—offered few major targets for the vast, high-tech military machine now focusing its attention on the impoverished Central Asian country. There was a small antique air force that the United States and her allies would soon put out of action, but no major early warning radar systems, armored divisions, or naval shipyards against which to deliver devastating attacks. The same was true, on a smaller scale, of Al Qaeda, a terrorist organization whose strength lay in its members' dedication, not in any particular piece of hardware. Other than its key leaders, whose location the U.S. intelligence community was frantically trying to divine, Al Qaeda possessed little worth bombing or raiding.

At the Pentagon, Rumsfeld was quickly becoming frustrated by the shortage of options that the military was presenting him.[7] "We were being pressured enormously by Rumsfeld to do things and come up with ideas," said a senior member of the Joint Staff (a headquarters staff in the Pentagon that supports the Chairman and Vice Chairman of the Joint Chiefs of Staff).

That pressure soon cascaded down to Tommy Franks, the bluff Army general who ran Central Command, or CENTCOM, which encompassed the Middle East, Pakistan, and Afghanistan, and to JSOC, its component units and the planning cell. "All the organizations were told: *Try and find targets*," said Mike Hall, Dailey's senior enlisted adviser. The warrant and senior noncommissioned officers who labored in the intelligence "shops" at JSOC and its special mission units scoured maps, imagery, and intelligence reports for anything that might be of value to the Taliban or Al Qaeda that JSOC could strike.[8] They passed what they found to the planning cell, but the fact was there weren't many good targets to be had in Afghanistan, for JSOC or anyone else. This would soon lead to a clash between Dailey's preference for the sort of elaborate, set-piece operations to which the joint readiness schedule of the

1990s had accustomed the command, and the desire of others in JSOC, particularly in Delta, for less visible, more patient work to hunt down Al Qaeda's leadership.

For the planning cell, eighteen- to twenty-hour workdays in over-crowded offices cluttered with papers, maps, laptops, and printers were the norm. "Dailey would come in, give a little bit of guidance, a little bit of focus, and then he'd leave," said a planner. The mood was "100 percent mission focus and figuring out how we could best meet Dailey's intent, right or wrong," the planner said. "You woke up and that's all you did and you just quit when you were too tired."

The limited menu of targets from which to choose was not the only constraint under which the planners worked. They also were hostage to the twin tyrannies of time and distance. In keeping with JSOC's modus operandi at the time, the missions had to begin and end during the course of a single night, or, in JSOC-speak, one "period of darkness."[9] JSOC's operational approach, honed over dozens of JRXs, was to establish an intermediate staging base, or ISB, close enough to the target that the mission could be launched directly from the ISB, but secure enough to host the joint operations center. The most obvious location would have been one of the numerous military airfields along Pakistan's border with Afghanistan. But Pakistan would only allow support flights—such as combat search and rescue missions or quick reaction forces—to be staged out of its territory. Direct action missions were out of the question.

That left the three Central Asian republics that bordered Afghanistan to the north: Turkmenistan, Uzbekistan, and Tajikistan. The planners con-sidered using Termez, an Uzbek town near the border, but eventually deci-ded to assume JSOC would stage out of Kharsi-Khanabad, another Uzbek air base. Any targets would therefore have to be in northern Afghanistan.

By Monday, September 17, relying on work done in the years prior to 9/11, JSOC's intelligence analysts had produced a list of six potential tar-gets.[10] All but one were petroleum facilities or airfields within forty-five miles of the border. The exception was a fertilizer plant in Mazar-i-Sharif, Afghanistan's fourth largest city, about forty miles south of the Uzbek border.[11] It was that target to which Dailey took a particular shine and on which he told his planners to focus.[12]

※

While his planners wrestled with the challenges of mounting a series of assaults on a landlocked country on the other side of the world, Dailey was summoned to Washington to brief the president on the missions JSOC was proposing. Bush had originally been scheduled to visit JSOC, but that trip was canceled out of concern it would give away the nature of the planning under way. Instead, Dailey would brief Bush, Vice President Dick Cheney, Rumsfeld, and the Joint Chiefs in the Pentagon on September 17.[13] (The White House and the Defense Department kept the reason for the president's visit under wraps, instead telling the public that Bush and Cheney were at the Pentagon to get briefed on the call-up of 35,000 military reservists. The visit would be remembered mainly for Bush's comment to reporters that bin Laden was "wanted—dead or alive.")[14]

Rumsfeld's office faxed a copy of Dailey's PowerPoint slides to the White House less than an hour before the briefing was set to start. The National Security Council staff had only a few minutes to review the presentation before the presidential motorcade pulled out of the driveway. Frank Miller, a special assistant to Bush and NSC senior director for defense policy, grabbed the slides and glanced through them. He was immediately troubled by a line on a slide that listed options for action in Afghanistan: "Thinking Outside the Box—Poisoning Food Supply."[15]

"That struck me as wrong," Miller said. "Poisoning food supplies would harm innocent civilians and we just weren't going down that road." It also could be interpreted as implying the possible use of biological weapons, which the 1972 Biological Weapons Convention banned the United States from possessing. Miller quickly checked with a colleague who knew more than he did about the convention. "We agreed that this was not a good thing," Miller said. When the motorcade reached the Pentagon he grabbed his boss, National Security Adviser Condoleezza Rice, who'd been in another vehicle but was also due to attend Dailey's briefing. "I showed her the slide," Miller said. "I said, 'This is completely wrong—I don't know what they're talking about, it could potentially get into the areas of the BWC. We don't do this.'" Rice agreed strongly, but the start of the briefing was only minutes away.

"We walked upstairs to the secretary's office and she put the slide in front of Rumsfeld and said, 'You're not going to show this slide to the president of the United States,'" Miller said. "And he looked at her and took it and walked away without saying a word. And in fact the slide did not get shown in the briefing."

Off-the-wall ideas such as poisoning the Afghan food supply flourished because JSOC was having tremendous difficulty finding viable targets. A senior member of the Joint Staff attributed this, in part, to a tension between the "culture of JSOC at the time, which was fairly ponderous and enormously heavy in its orientation," and "the melodramatic reaction of people like Rumsfeld after 9/11 to just 'do something.'"

"The conflict between the two and the pressure . . . probably produced some fairly bizarre notions," he said. Indeed, Dailey repeatedly complained to subordinates that "we've got no targets," said a Delta source. "So he goes up [to Washington], yanks that out of his ass—*poison the fucking food supply.*"

Among the possible missions Dailey did brief in the Pentagon was a Ranger raid on an airstrip attached to a hunting camp southwest of Kandahar owned by a United Arab Emirates military official, but the JSOC commander's priority was an attack on the fertilizer factory, which the planners had named Objective Goat. "This fertilizer factory had gained some legs, and it was obviously gaining legs because Dailey wanted it to," said a planning cell member. After Dailey delivered the last slide, the room fell quiet. "It was sort of dead because the president's there and all the generals, they're waiting for him to say something," said Mike Hall, Dailey's top NCO, who was the only enlisted service member there. Bush locked eyes with Hall. "Sergeant Major, some people are going to get hurt," the president said. "Is it worth it?" Although he had reservations about the initial targets, Hall thought the president was asking about the wider military operation in Afghanistan, so he answered that he thought it was.

The focus on the fertilizer factory was hugely controversial within JSOC. Dailey's rationale was that Al Qaeda might be using it to produce chemical weapons. CIA human intelligence suggested the production of urea and ammonia, both used in the manufacture of such weapons. Imagery indicated the site was surrounded by seven guard towers and other fighting positions. Intelligence analysts said the towers were manned by a security force of fifty personnel working in shifts. That was enough for Dailey.[16] Tommy Franks was likewise persuaded.[17]

But the planning cell dismissed this notion. "None of us had a lot of confidence in that target," said a cell member. The notion that Al Qaeda was producing chemical weapons was a "giant leap" from the available intelligence, he said. "I just remember us going through the motions, going, 'It's got to get better than this.'"

Several senior figures on the JSOC staff and in Delta, the unit slated to lead the assault, shared the planners' disdain for the target and couldn't believe Dailey was allowing it to consume JSOC's time and energy while strategic targets like bin Laden and other Al Qaeda leaders were still at large in Afghanistan. "We were like, 'We've got to think outside the box here, guys,'" said a Delta source. "'Let's get away from this . . . JSOC mentality of setting up another massive JRX, and let's do things that matter.'" Instead, he said, "We spent all our time planning this massive raid on that empty target." The critics thought JSOC should focus on hunting bin Laden and working with the CIA to insert teams with the Northern Alliance. Coherent change detection, a technique that measures the differences in images of the same location captured by satellite-mounted synthetic aperture radar, supported their skepticism of the fertilizer plant.[18] "The coherent change detection sensors were all focused on this thing," the Delta source said. "So after four days, this thing that was being briefed to the president as, 'Yes, there are guards there, we believe the guard force is small but highly trained, they patrol the perimeter and that part is going to require some combat power'—well, coherent change detection detected no movement . . . no vehicles, nothing."

One of the loudest voices arguing against the Mazar target was that of Lieutenant Colonel Pete Blaber, a tall, lean former Ranger who'd joined Delta a decade earlier and had a reputation for speaking his mind. The personality conflict between Dailey, who, not unusually for a career special operations aviator, favored a process-oriented approach,[19] and Blaber, a supremely self-confident climbing and hiking enthusiast who viewed the military decision-making process as something close to a waste of time,[20] would reverberate through the next two years of JSOC's history. But for now Dailey held the whip hand as JSOC's two-star commander while the naysayers wore the oak leaves and eagles of majors, lieutenant colonels, and colonels, so the plan to attack the fertilizer factory moved inexorably forward.

*

It was late evening in the cramped, windowless space that served as the planning cell's main briefing room. The utilitarian furniture was strewn with empty coffee cups, full spit cups, and open laptops bearing red stickers warning that classified information was contained therein. Maps covered the walls. About fifteen sleep-deprived men sat in the harsh electric light listening to a tall, dark-haired colleague in his mid-thirties.

Seated were the operations officers from most of JSOC's units, a few staffers from the command, as well as Colonel Joe Votel, commander of the Ranger Regiment, and Dell Dailey. Briefing was Major Tom DiTomasso, Delta's B Squadron operations officer and the planning cell's senior Delta representative. As a lieutenant, DiTomasso had led a Ranger platoon in Mogadishu, the last high-profile JSOC battle. Now he was proposing how to fight the next one.

The target was the fertilizer plant. Under pressure to find a target JSOC could hit soon, Dailey had selected the target but told the planners he was open to ideas about how to strike it. DiTomasso's plan was classic Delta: stealthy, elegant, and lethal: a small number of operators would freefall parachute into the area, hit the factory hard and fast in specific locations, and then have TF Brown pick them up with the mission complete. "It was very low-vis," said an officer who was there. "They'd never have known what hit them and from where."

The plan impressed several of those listening, but not Dailey, who wanted a much bigger extravaganza as JSOC's first mission of the war. "What in the hell kind of bullshit is that?" yelled the JSOC commander. "We ain't doing that."

"Dailey absolutely like a laser blew Tom out of the water," said the officer. "Essentially stripped him in front of God and everybody about what a dumb idea that was." Those present got the message. Despite his professed openness to out-of-the-box thinking, Dailey wasn't interested in tactical solutions that weren't big, JRX-style operations. "He eviscerated Tom right then and there for a plan that most people thought could have worked," said the officer. The planners went back to work, under the strong impression that for JSOC's first combat operation of the twenty-first century, stealth and secrecy were not only not required, they were to be avoided.[21]

✳

On September 19, Dailey visited Benning, where the planning cell and other key individuals were holding a series of scaled-down rehearsals (called "rock drills") of the raid on Objective Goat and other proposed missions. The plan had morphed to one in which thirty-six hours of air strikes would precede a nighttime air assault on Kunduz Airfield in northeast Afghanistan (deemed a psychological operations target) and near-simultaneous strikes by fixed wing and helicopter gunships against a petroleum plant. On the third night, Delta and the Rangers would stage out of Kharsi-Khanabad, raid the fertilizer factory, take chemical samples, and then depart via one or more MC-130s that would land close by, before the Air Force dropped a BLU-82 "daisy cutter" bomb to destroy the complex. The mission was due to take place as soon as September 26.[22]

The strike against the factory was a key element of the plans Franks and Dailey briefed to Rumsfeld and the Joint Chiefs in the Pentagon September 20. But serious doubts persisted.[23] The two generals were due to brief Bush the next day.[24] Deeply dissatisfied with what he'd heard, Rumsfeld had Undersecretary of Defense for Policy Doug Feith draft a memo to set the stage for the president. The memo made clear not only the priority now attached to the fertilizer plant target, but the shaky foundations upon which the plan rested. "We may come up empty-handed," it said. "Can't count on finding proof of chemical weapons production in the fertilizer factory that is our prime target."[25]

Early the next afternoon, Franks and Dailey traveled to the White House to brief the president. Also present were Vice President Cheney, Rumsfeld, Chairman of the Joint Chiefs of Staff Army General Henry "Hugh" Shelton, and Air Force General Richard Myers, the Joint Chiefs vice chairman who would succeed Shelton when the latter retired in October. "The secret JSOC part of the operation" was "a big part of the plan," according to Shelton. But the briefing was also notable for a shift in emphasis since Shelton presented options to Bush and the National Security Council at Camp David September 15. That brief had focused on possible conventional military attacks—mostly cruise missile and air strikes—and left the president and his advisers underwhelmed. But now Franks proposed inserting Special Forces teams into Afghanistan to advise and assist the Northern Alliance in their war against the Taliban and Al Qaeda.[26] Such a mission would be a classic example of "unconventional warfare," which means using guerrilla forces to overthrow a hostile government and is a doctrinal Special Forces mission. While Dailey and his staff had been focused on the fertilizer factory, plans were under way to make their "white" special ops counterparts the centerpiece of the war in Afghanistan.

But no matter how thin the evidence that anything nefarious was occurring at the fertilizer factory, JSOC not only kept planning to assault it, but that plan became increasingly elaborate. Under Dailey's direction, JSOC was reverting to what it knew best: a massive JRX-style operation involving as many of its component units as possible.

Some argued for missions that went beyond this restrictive template. Lieutenant Colonel Steve Schiller, TF Brown's operations officer, proposed using a small force to seize Bagram air base, about forty miles north of Kabul. A former commander of the 160th's Little Bird gunship company, Schiller wanted to stage Little Bird raids and other missions from Bagram into northeastern Afghanistan, where bin Laden was presumed (correctly) to be hiding. But Dailey had no interest in taking the air base early on, let alone launching Little Bird missions from it. A former Black Hawk pilot, the general was skeptical that Little Birds, with their limited range and power, had much to offer in a vast country consisting largely of deserts and mountains.[27]

Although the planning cell's Delta and Team 6 representatives had thus far taken the lead in proposing operational concepts, Dailey's putdown of DiTomasso had a predictable effect. "Tom essentially after that, I don't want to say shut down, but [his attitude was], 'Okay, why don't you just tell me what you want and that's what we'll do,'" said a planning cell member. "And kind of from that point forward, Dailey did end up driving that train on the target sets."

Several factors drove Dailey's preference for big, highly synchronized operations. One was that the command had been moving in that direction for many years. With Dailey, "that's what you're going to get, because that's the way JSOC had been through the '90s," said the planning cell member. "And to be fair to JSOC, if you train to these big, complex ones, it makes the smaller ones easier to do."

Another was Dailey's aviation background. Military aviation culture is "to mitigate risk on every level, because any aircraft accident is a significant emotional event," said a TF Brown officer. "Most of us that are aviators are pretty process-oriented, because that's the way you get to success: through some very significant level of detailed planning, not double-checked but triple-checked," said another TF Brown officer who knew Dailey well. "That's kind of beat into you from the time you start in the 160th."

Dailey's perceived risk aversion would only have been exacerbated by a third factor: the JSOC intelligence analysts' wildly exaggerated estimates of the enemy threat in Afghanistan. Again and again in the weeks after 9/11, intelligence briefings focused on implausible worst-case scenarios, rather than what some of the best troops in the world might reasonably expect to face from a poorly equipped rabble.[28]

But the fourth factor behind Dailey's insistence on making JSOC's first missions such elaborate affairs was perhaps the most important: pressure from Franks, Rumsfeld, and Bush for a mission that would send a message not only to the Taliban and Al Qaeda but also to the American public that the United States could reach out and put troops anywhere it wanted in Afghanistan. This appealed to Dailey, who was particularly fond of influence, deception, and psychological operations. Together such missions fell under the rubric of information operations, or IO.[29]

Planning continued even after a September 22 brief by the Ranger Regiment's intelligence officer that Goat might be empty and the plant might close. But as the plan became ever more complex and other targets presented themselves, the date for the raid kept slipping to the right. It was now slated for October 12. (Another factor behind the frequent postponements was a desire to conduct the air assault on as dark a night as possible. By shifting the date closer to mid-October, the planners were ensuring JSOC's first mission in Afghanistan would take place under a cloak of darkness.)

The Ranger intelligence briefing was part of another rock drill Dailey attended that gave an indication of the difference in scale between DiTomasso's original proposal and the sort of plan the JSOC commander preferred. The latest version of the plan to assault a target most observers thought was empty would require a minimum of about 160 ground troops and twenty-four aircraft.[30]

But the clock was ticking for the fertilizer factory mission. During a video-teleconference the previous evening, Dailey told the planners to think about possible targets in southern Afghanistan. Three days later, the planners learned Central Command was considering five targets for JSOC. While the factory remained first on the list, three of the others were in southern Afghanistan. JSOC's focus was shifting south. Another September 24 announcement explained why: the command no longer planned to locate its intermediate staging base in Central Asia. The requirement for missions to be completed during the course of a single night remained, but two new staging options meant the assault forces would be coming from the south, not the north.[31]

✳

With the United States still negotiating with Afghanistan's Central Asian neighbors for use of their air bases, Pakistan unlikely to allow large numbers of U.S. troops into its restive tribal areas adjacent to Afghanistan, and Rumsfeld impatient to put boots on the ground in Afghanistan, Tommy Franks had been working on other options. "We needed to stage SOF [special operations forces], particularly the elite SMU troopers of the Joint Special Operations Command, close enough to strike al Qaeda in their mountain redoubt in southeast Afghanistan," he wrote in his autobiography. "And we needed to stage them soon."[32]

The solution came to Franks as he studied a map of the region projected onto a screen in his headquarters' "war room." He returned to his office and called Chief of Naval Operations Admiral Vern Clark on a secure line. "Vern, we're going to need an aircraft carrier for some unusual duty," he told the Navy officer.[33] On September 27 the *Kitty Hawk*, a Yokosuka, Japan–based carrier, was conducting sea trials and exercises in the Philippine Sea when it was alerted for Operation River City—its role in JSOC's war in Afghanistan. After dispensing with most of its aircraft in order to clear space for JSOC forces, the carrier sailed for the northern Arabian Sea.[34] Positioning the *Kitty Hawk* there would allow JSOC to get to and from targets in southern Afghanistan within one night by crossing over the deserts of southwestern Pakistan and southern Afghanistan, thereby avoiding the risky flights over 10,000-foot mountains that an attack on the Taliban heartland from Central Asia would have necessitated.[35]

Operating from a carrier was nothing new for JSOC, which had used the *America* during 1994's operation to remove Haiti's military junta. More recently, about six months before September 11 during a JRX centered in Qatar, JSOC had put forces on a flattop that then sailed up the Persian Gulf before launching a helicopter attack on a target in Kuwait. Flying off carriers was standard operational procedure for TF Brown, which trained for such missions about once a year. JSOC called a carrier used thus an afloat forward staging base.[36]

But not even a carrier could accommodate the massive operations center JSOC hauled around the world, nor could a flight deck handle all the fixed and rotary wing aircraft the command was preparing to deploy. For those, Franks had another location in mind, one that was 700 miles from Afghanistan, but which had a special resonance for JSOC: Masirah Island off the coast of Oman in the Arabian Sea.

It was from Masirah that on April 24, 1980, a Delta assault force launched on three Combat Talons en route to the landing site in Iran named Desert One. That mission had ended in fiery disaster. But anguished memories aside, Masirah retained the advantages that had made it an attractive base for Operation Eagle Claw: a runway capable of handling large Air Force transport aircraft, relative proximity to the combat zone, and total seclusion.

Following September 11, Central Command, which, like U.S. Special Operations Command, was located at MacDill, had worked to gain access to Masirah for the war in Afghanistan.[37] By September 20, Oman's ruler, Sultan Qaboos bin Sa'id, had given permission to stage special operations troops and aircraft there, including AC-130 gunships.[38]

Word that JSOC might have both Masirah and a carrier available from which to launch attacks had reached the planners September 18, but with no confirmation they had continued to assume any missions would originate in Central Asia.[39] News that the attacks would be launched from the south spelled the beginning of the end for the plan to assault Objective Goat. Years later, nobody could remember exactly when JSOC stopped planning to hit the factory; they were just glad that it did. "As people asked questions, it just didn't pass scrutiny," said Hall. "Of course, it turned out to be a fertilizer factory."

⚔

During this period a potential mission arose that in retrospect seems bizarre but which JSOC took very seriously. U.S. intelligence sources reported that bin Laden had left Afghanistan and made his way to Southern Africa. The intelligence was specific enough that Delta's A Squadron spent several days planning an operation based upon it, before being told to stand down when the intelligence didn't pan out.[40] "That sidetracked us briefly," said a Delta source.

⚔

A couple of days after returning from Budapest, Jim Reese, the AFO operations officer, left JSOC headquarters for a run. He returned to find Dailey and Holland, who was visiting from MacDill, waiting for him. Dailey told him to go home, pack some civilian suits, and fly up to Washington. There he was to visit the Pentagon to receive guidance before driving to Langley, Virginia, and reporting to Director of Central Intelligence George Tenet. Reese was to be JSOC's point man at the CIA.[41]

Reese was perfect for the job. "He brings people together," said a Delta operator who'd worked with him for years. Delta officers nicknamed him "Serpico" due to his resemblance to the Al Pacino character in the movie of the same name, while NCOs called him "Hollywood," often shortened to "The 'Wood," on account of his good looks and gregariousness. But he was also operationally savvy and possessed infectious self-confidence.[42]

Reese flew up early the week of Monday, September 17, and went straight to the Pentagon, where he met with Rumsfeld's deputy, Paul Wolfowitz. "Are you the Delta guy?" Wolfowitz asked. "Yes sir," Reese replied. "Go report to George Tenet," Wolfowitz said. "Bridge the gap between DoD and the CIA."

A Defense Department driver took Reese to CIA headquarters, where he arrived late in the afternoon still carrying his suitcases. Security guards then took him straight to a crowded conference room on the seventh floor, where Tenet's daily 5 P.M. meeting with his senior staff was just starting. A man in his mid-sixties with steel-colored hair and an engaging smile sitting near the head of the table noticed Reese standing in the doorway looking lost. "Are you the Delta guy?" he said. "Yes sir, I am," Reese replied. "Come up here, sit next to George," said the man, pointing to a chair next to Tenet. The person welcoming Reese to the CIA was A. B. "Buzzy" Krongard, the Agency's number three, whose son was a SEAL officer.

Reese sat quietly as analysts briefed Tenet. His job was to facilitate the CIA's coordination and cooperation with special operations forces, as well as to help the Agency plan its campaign in Afghanistan. To help him, Reese immediately asked for and received Sam Stanley, his radio operator from the AFO cell, while the Army assigned him a military intelligence officer named Captain Kara Soules. The CIA put his tiny team in the Counterterrorist Center, or CTC, where they worked closely with the center's director, Cofer Black; Hank Crumpton, who Black had picked to run the war in Afghanistan; and Jose Rodriguez, the CTC chief of staff. All welcomed the military trio warmly, making sure they had full access to everything the Agency was doing.[43]

The easy cooperation between Reese's team and the CTC personnel at Langley was at variance with the frustration Rumsfeld was expressing in the Pentagon over the military's need to wait for the CIA to blaze a trail with the Northern Alliance before sending in Special Forces teams. The defense secretary "later declared it inexcusable that the Defense Department couldn't use its numerous and costly forces until the CIA shook some hands," according to Feith.[44] In his autobiography, Rumsfeld is careful to say his relations with Tenet were good,[45] but others said that warmth did not extend to the secretary's views of the CIA at large.

Rumsfeld displayed "incredible impatience and disgust with the CIA," said a senior member of the Joint Staff.

It irked Rumsfeld when Franks told him as late as October 15 that Special Forces teams were waiting for the CIA's okay to enter Afghanistan.[46] But the delays were actually down to the military chain of command. The CIA was more than ready to welcome the participation of JSOC and other special ops forces in the Afghanistan operation. As late as October 4, Gary Schroen, who led the first CIA team into Afghanistan, complained to Crumpton that he had "begged and pleaded with each of the commands—Delta, Special Forces, SEALs, Gray Fox—to send a team to join us," to no avail.[47] (Gray Fox was the latest code name for the Army of Northern Virginia.)

JSOC's operators were likewise champing at the bit. While still in Budapest, Blaber had called "Phil," who headed the CIA's Special Activities Division. Would Delta be able to send a couple of operators in with the Agency teams preparing to infil into Afghanistan, Phil asked. "Of course," replied Blaber. "Count us in."[48] (Blaber was no stranger to the challenges of planning for missions in Afghanistan. In 1998, as OST commander, he helped plan Delta's bin Laden capture mission.)[49]

But at all levels of command above the operators, from Delta through JSOC, SOCOM, and CENTCOM, there was hesitation about whether and how to commit the military's most elite forces. "They were totally against us sending guys in with Schroen and crew [on the grounds it was] too risky," said a Delta source involved in the discussions. To the operators' intense frustration, neither Central Command nor JSOC were keen to deploy forces into Afghanistan until combat search and rescue, or CSAR ("see-sar"), helicopters could be positioned close enough to come to their aid. "CENTCOM and JSOC were against anything without CSAR," the Delta source said. "Meanwhile the CIA is sending into Afghanistan guys with an average age in their forties, most of whom with little to no military experience."

Loath to put his people under another organization's command, Dailey was therefore opposed to attaching JSOC personnel to the Agency teams going into Afghanistan. Schwitters, the Delta commander, was of like mind. "And if 'the Unit' commander's against it, how is a guy like Dailey ever going to be for something?" the Delta source said. (Not all Delta operators shared this view of Schwitters, an Eagle Claw veteran. One experienced unit member noted that Schwitters was nicknamed

"Flatliner" due to his even-keeled temperament, which some could mistake for a lack of enthusiasm. Schwitters "was all about getting us involved," but wanted to ensure Delta's unique skill sets would be used for legitimate missions, rather than hollow shows of force, he said.)

Some in Delta argued for deploying an entire squadron into the Panjshir Valley, the fastness in northeastern Afghanistan still held by the Northern Alliance. The CIA's Schroen, already in the Panjshir, supported the plan, saying Delta could "use the valley as a staging area for raids on Al Qaeda leaders behind enemy lines."[50] But this initiative also foundered on the rocks of Dailey's skepticism.

In the minds of some operators, Dailey was anxious to avoid Delta taking the lead, particularly without a JSOC headquarters in close proximity. Prior to becoming an aviator Dailey had been an infantry officer in the Rangers, and some JSOC personnel perceived a favoritism toward the Rangers and the 160th on the part of their commander. Hall acknowledged a widespread belief in the special mission units, Delta in particular, and that Dailey was biased against them, but said this was a misperception on the operators' part. "He had a very deep respect [for the operators]," Hall said. "Sometimes he wasn't very good at expressing it, unfortunately. Because he didn't speak the language, he wasn't one of them."

One of the strongest advocates for putting a squadron into the Panjshir, Blaber continued to mount an insurgency against what he considered Dailey's intransigence and lack of imagination. He was not alone. A couple of other operators as well as Phil and one or two others at the CIA kept lines of communication open, working every angle to try to get Delta into the fight. At first, Blaber called Phil on Delta's red classified phones, but after JSOC banned its people from talking to their CIA contacts without going through the Agency's liaison officer at JSOC headquarters, he was forced to call Phil from outside the Delta compound on an untraceable calling card.[51] Eventually the CIA operatives got tired of waiting. "They just got sick of it," said a Delta source. "They were like, 'Forget it, man, I'll see you over there.'"

Meanwhile, at JSOC headquarters there was similar frustration with Central Command. Relations between Dailey and Franks were cordial, but the same could not be said for their staffs. The need to go to war in Afghanistan had caught CENTCOM cold and the four-star command was struggling to respond. "They didn't seem to be a heck of a lot of help to us, and [were] almost a hindrance," Hall said. Only part of that could be put down to "the JSOC arrogance" rubbing CENTCOM staffers the wrong way, he said. "I'm not sure anybody at CENTCOM thought this was really, really serious other than General Franks. . . . We thought he was pretty much switched on [about] what had to happen, but you certainly didn't have that level of confidence from his staff."

Indeed, some at JSOC still doubted that they'd be called into action, despite the scale of the September 11 attacks and all the feverish activity since. Memories of being "spun up many, many times before," only to be dialed back down, were too fresh and too strong, said Hall. Opinion "was probably evenly split" over whether they would be sent into battle, he said. "A lot of us old guys . . . really wondered if there would be the national will to do that, quite frankly. . . .

"It was Schoomaker that always talked about the Ferrari that was kept in the garage," Hall said, referring to the former JSOC commander's comments in Richard Schulz's "Showstoppers" article. "Most of us had grown up in that environment. We figured the Ferrari's still going to be in the garage." But this time the skeptics were wrong. The garage doors were opening and the Ferrari was about to be taken for a drive. A very long drive.

9

Risky Missions and Empty Targets

The vastness of the moonless night sky swallowed the turboprop drone of the four blacked-out Combat Talons high above Pakistan's Baluchistan province. Headed north, the planes crossed into Afghan airspace at about 11 P.M., October 19, skimming low across the Registan Desert. On board were 199 Rangers with a mission to seize a desert airstrip and thus send a message to the world that the United States was able to put troops on the ground in Afghanistan at will. Within days, the Pentagon would release a video of the operation—produced by a psychological operations unit—to the media, but without the essential context that the airfield seizure was supporting a simultaneous mission taking place about 100 miles to the northeast. There, Chinooks and Black Hawks were slicing through the darkness carrying more than a squadron of Delta operators plus a Ranger company on the night's main effort: a surprise attack on Taliban leader Mullah Mohammed Omar's residential compound in the Taliban's hometown of Kandahar, a mission that would be the farthest air assault in history. After five frustrating weeks, this was the night that the U.S. military's ground war in Afghanistan would begin, and JSOC was taking the lead.[1]

At MacDill Air Force Base, Tommy Franks watched as icons representing the MC-130s inched across a map on a giant plasma screen in the Central Command joint operations center. Dell Dailey called with an update from Masirah: "Missions on target in nine minutes." Despite early indications that both targets were empty, "the freshest reconnaissance imagery revealed the Taliban had installed a security force at Objective Rhino," Franks would later say. (One planner said the pictures showed "people," but not necessarily a "security force." Other sources did not recall this imagery at all.) Now Franks checked with Dailey. "Any activity on the ground, Dell?" Franks asked. "Negative, sir. No issues, no drama," Dailey said calmly.[2]

But JSOC was taking no chances. A Predator unmanned aerial vehicle had already destroyed two armored vehicles on the target.[3] Now, as the Rangers on the Talons made last-minute adjustments to their gear, ahead of them fiery orange blossoms punctuated the darkness of the arid plateau. Global Positioning System–guided 2,000-pound bombs dropped by B-2 stealth bombers were finding their marks. Circling AC-130 gunships also softened up the target, pounding it with 105mm cannon fire. "Initial reports were that eleven enemy had been killed and nine were seen running away," according to an official history.[4]

The Rangers' morale was high. The elite infantrymen saw themselves as the tip of the United States' spear, ready to exact revenge for September 11. They had spent the last ten days sitting on a desert island becoming increasingly frustrated as their leaders worked to keep them focused. Now the time for action was finally at hand. They were just minutes from making the first Ranger combat parachute assault since December 1989's Panama invasion. On each plane, the nervous soldiers together recited the Ranger Creed, the twelve-sentence articulation of the regiment's ethos, ending with the defiant chant: "Rangers lead the way!"[5] Then, after almost four hours in flight, with the aircraft nearing the target and jumpmasters barking orders, they stood up and lumbered forward in ungainly fashion, under the awkward weight of their rucksacks strapped to their thighs, their reserve parachutes on their chests and main chutes on their backs. The Talons were a mere 800 feet above the ground, so low that an influx of dust coated the Rangers as the doors opened for the jump.[6] Outside, the only illumination came from flares the aircraft dropped to ward off the threat of heat-seeking missiles and from fires already burning on the objective.[7] For this jump the Rangers would use a door on each side of the aircraft. After finishing their verbal and hand signal commands, the jumpmasters told the Rangers to "stand by" and turned and readied themselves in the doors. As the muted lights above and beside the doors on the first aircraft turned from red to green, the jumpmasters stepped out into the night.[8]

❋

The Masirah airstrip from which the Rangers had taken off had been transformed over the previous fortnight from a deserted stretch of tarmac to a high-tech hub of military activity. A few days into October, massive C-5 transport aircraft carrying everything required to build JSOC's space-age joint operations center began touching down every ten minutes on the runway at the northern end of the forty-mile-long island. In the searing desert heat and stifling humidity, a tent city began to rise.[9] The JSOC advance party deployed from Bragg October 6. Most of the JOC staff followed a day later. The first of eight C-5s transporting TF Brown landed October 8. To deceive any interested parties about JSOC's plans, Dailey directed troops to deploy wearing woodland green camouflage and then change into desert uniforms once they were at Masirah. The Rangers landed in chartered airliners. Combat Talons from the 1st Special Operations Wing arrived. Dailey himself flew over October 10.[10] Twenty-one and a half years after the debacle that resulted in JSOC's creation, America's most elite special operators were back on Masirah. It was from here, hidden from the prying eyes of the news media, that Dell Dailey planned to run JSOC's war in Afghanistan.

Within a few days, engineers had completed construction of the operations center from which Dailey would oversee combat operations 700 miles away. Consisting of scores of air-conditioned tents arrayed in a spoked-wheel design, the JOC was a testament to the wealth and computing might of the world's one remaining superpower. Inside, the tents were festooned with the communications gear the staff required to stay connected to operators and headquarters around the globe. As with everything else to do with JSOC, little expense was spared. "Within twenty-four hours of our plane touching down, we were watching the BBC on seventy-two-inch plasma flat-screen TVs," wrote Blaber, who, along with about fifty other Delta operators was among the first to arrive. However, all those laptops, squawking satellite radios, and video screens offered only the illusion of understanding, according to the Delta ops officer. "There was just one thing missing," he wrote. "We had no situational awareness of Afghanistan, Al Qaeda or UBL."[11]

Despite the size of the tented Taj Mahal JSOC was building at Masirah, the command deployed only a fraction of its ground forces: one Ranger battalion (the 3rd); a squadron-plus from Delta (B Squadron, commanded by Lieutenant Colonel Chris Sorenson, plus A Squadron's second troop, or A2—an assault troop); less than a third of the 160th's 1st Battalion, plus a few 2nd Battalion Chinooks; and Team 6's Blue Team. All came with headquarters elements that reported to the JSOC joint operations center. On September 17 JSOC had sent out an "alert force update" with orders to maintain forces ready to conduct 0300 global counterterrorism missions, so the Aztec, Trident, and Bullet packages remained on alert at their home stations, along with roughly half the JSOC staff, ready for any other crisis that might rear its head.[12] Those elements that deployed forward acquired a new name: Task Force Sword.

Time on the island was to be fleeting for some of the new arrivals, however, because after steaming more than 6,000 miles in twelve days, the *Kitty Hawk* neared Oman October 10, ready to receive its complement of about 600 JSOC personnel.[13] These included the Delta and Team 6 tactical elements; 3rd Ranger Battalion's B Company; all twenty Task Force Brown Black Hawks and Chinooks and their crews; and a small Task Force Sword command and control element. While the helicopters and crews self-deployed to the carrier, most others flew out to the ship on a C-2A Greyhound turboprop aircraft.[14] By October 15 the JSOC forces were in place aboard the carrier.[15]

Task Force Sword's operational security demands, which to outsiders sometimes appeared to border on paranoia, required the *Kitty Hawk* crew to maintain a five-mile exclusion zone that no other ship was allowed to enter. The sailors began to refer to the ship as the "stealth carrier." Nor was life for the task force elements aboard the *Kitty Hawk* without its challenges. Unlike 1994's Haiti operation, when the Navy took all the jets off the *America* and turned the carrier into a floating platform just for JSOC, this time a small number of jets, including eight F/A-18C Hornets remained on the *Kitty Hawk,* flying missions over Afghanistan night and day and playing havoc with the "battle rhythm" of the Task Force Sword personnel, who were on a reverse cycle—working through the night and trying to sleep through the roar of fighter-bombers launching off the deck during the day. Although the *Kitty Hawk* had sailed to the northern Arabian Sea with only fifteen of the ninety or so planes and helicopters it could hold, those aircraft still jostled for space with Task Force Brown's Black Hawks and Chinooks. "It was very hard for us and them to juggle twenty-four-hour operations of two totally different types of mission," said a Brown aviator. "We made it work, but it was a lot of work."[16]

⚜

On both Masirah and the *Kitty Hawk,* planning was under way in earnest for JSOC's first missions of the post-9/11 era.

On September 20, President Bush had delivered a televised address to a joint session of Congress in which, without naming the command, he hinted at the role JSOC would assume in the months and years ahead. "Americans should not expect one battle, but a lengthy campaign unlike any other we have ever seen," he said. "It may include dramatic strikes, visible on TV, and covert operations, secret even in success."[17] For JSOC, the ultimate covert special ops organization, the irony was that the command's first missions would fall into the former category, rather than the latter. After the demise of the plan to assault the fertilizer factory, Central Command proposed two targets[18] that quickly became JSOC's priorities. One came directly from Franks: a desert airstrip about 100 miles southwest of Kandahar built for Sheikh Mohammed bin Zayed, the United Arab Emirates' military chief of staff. A keen falconer, the sheikh had had a 6,400-foot paved runway installed in a dry lake bed to give him access to a nearby hunting camp. After the September 11 attacks he alerted Franks to its existence and suggested U.S. forces use it to reduce the number of troops they might need to deploy to Pakistan. Franks wanted the Rangers to seize the airfield so the United States could use it to deploy a Marine task force into southern Afghanistan.[19] The airstrip, which planners quickly dubbed Objective Rhino, also appealed to JSOC planners because it offered the possibility of putting a helicopter forward arming and refueling point there.[20] The other target, named Gecko, was Mullah Omar's compound on the north side of Kandahar city, the Taliban's base of power.

The Rangers had been examining the possibility of seizing Rhino about a week after September 11,[21] when there were still hopes Pakistan might allow the United States to launch raids from its territory. They planned to use a company-plus of Rangers to take the airstrip, which JSOC could then use as a forward support base. Once the fertilizer factory faded into oblivion and Masirah and the *Kitty Hawk* entered the equation, the planning cell at Benning turned its attention to first Rhino, then Gecko, as the most likely candidates to fulfill the chain of command's desire for a highly visible "boots on the ground" mission. Rhino was to be a Ranger mission while Delta would be the lead force assaulting Gecko.

The plans for the two missions evolved over the course of four weeks. Although Rhino was the first of the two targets to emerge, it soon became a supporting element to the assault on Gecko: a place where the helicopters involved in the latter mission could consolidate, refuel, and rearm. In late September the planners' intent was for the Rangers to take the airstrip forty-eight hours before a combined Delta and Ranger air assault on Omar's compound. D-day for the Rhino mission was set for October 14. But as with the canceled assault on the fertilizer factory, that date continued to slide to the right. As it did so, the plan changed. Now the raids were to take place simultaneously. That caused another late alteration to the plan. Less than a week before the missions launched, both were planned as air assault (i.e., heliborne) missions.[22] The Gecko raid would involve the Delta and Ranger elements aboard the *Kitty Hawk* flying 575 miles straight to the target on Chinooks and Black Hawks.[23] The Rhino assault force, made up of 3rd Battalion Rangers, was to land in three Chinooks launched off the *Kitty Hawk,* supported by three other MH-47Es—one for combat search and rescue, one carrying a quick reaction force, and one configured as a "fat cow" refueling aircraft. Two DAPs—the Black Hawks configured as attack helicopters—would provide fire support. But as the size of the Ranger force assigned to Rhino steadily grew, planners realized there weren't enough helicopters to run each operation as an air assault.[24] The Rangers would have to jump in. So it was that Rhino, originally planned as a "somewhat minimal" helicopter assault to support Gecko, morphed into a substantial and telegenic airborne operation launched from Masirah.

The desire on the part of Dailey, Franks, and Bush for a televised spectacle undoubtedly factored into the decision to make the Rhino raid a parachute assault. "I absolutely remember Dailey talking about the president wanting footage," a planner said. But some observers suspected that a hankering for glory, rather than any tactical necessity, was also behind the increase in the Rhino assault force, which eventually included both Lieutenant Colonel Stefan Banach, the 3rd Battalion commander, and Votel, the regimental commander, as well as other headquarters personnel (even the 3rd Battalion chaplain) jumping in to command and control a force consisting of little more than two infantry companies. It had been almost twelve years since the Rangers had jumped into Panama and, the cynics said, the chance to gain their "mustard stains"—the coveted gold stars on their jump wings that denoted a combat jump—was apparently irresistible to some. "Numerous [personnel] that normally would not be involved in an operation like that that did it purely to get a combat jump," said a Masirah source. But Command Sergeant Major Walter Rakow, the regiment's top enlisted man, who did not make the jump, denied this was Votel's motive. "That was not Votel's reason for going," he said. Rather, with Rangers in several different locations that night, "the commander felt that his best position to work from would have been from Rhino." Votel saw his role as communicating with the operation's other moving pieces and Masirah while Banach focused on "the ground fight," Rakow added.

To many experienced operators on the *Kitty Hawk,* on Masirah, and back at Bragg, the growing size and complexity of the missions, with their many moving parts and refuelings, bore an unsettling resemblance to the operation whose failure had given birth to JSOC. Indeed, attacking Omar's compound would require the Chinooks and Black Hawks to fly farther than the Sea Stallions had in Eagle Claw, with each helicopter needing two aerial refuelings en route to the target, another while the assaulters were on the objective, a fourth refueling on the ground at Rhino, and a further two aerial refuelings en route back to the carrier.[25]

The risks inherent in such long-haul, complex missions over denied territory were one factor behind a growing opposition in Delta and JSOC to conducting the Gecko and Rhino raids at all. "We really didn't want to go to Desert One again as the primary option," a retired special operations officer said. Franks himself described each assault as "a moderate-to-high-risk operation." However, he added, "I had confidence that the Rangers and the SMU operators could handle themselves deep in enemy territory."[26]

But there was another reason voices in Masirah were raised against the proposed raids: intelligence suggested each target was empty. "When an intelligence officer first presented 'the targets' to us in a briefing, he nonchalantly added that there wasn't any enemy on either target," Blaber wrote.[27] "A lot of people were of the opinion that it was probably a dry hole," said Hall. "I think we would have been surprised if Mullah Omar was on Gecko. I think we would have been surprised to find anything significant on Rhino."

In his autobiography, Franks said Central Command had "chosen" not to bomb Omar's compound, "hoping it would serve as a magnet for Omar and his deputies." But he cited no intelligence indicating the target was occupied. Rather, the CENTCOM boss gives two other reasons for assaulting Gecko and Rhino: an expectation that JSOC forces would find a wealth of exploitable intelligence on Omar's compound, and the desire to conduct a surprise attack in the Taliban "heartland," thus demonstrating that the United States "could strike anywhere, at any time of our choosing" while fixing the Taliban's reserves in the south, preventing them from reinforcing the northern positions that the Northern Alliance would soon be attacking with help from their American friends.[28]

Although Franks claimed credit for the decision to have the task force assault Gecko and Rhino, the idea of attacking empty targets in order to send a message to the Taliban was pure Dailey, the self-styled information operations expert. "He believed that if we raided empty targets in Afghanistan and filmed the raids for the world to see (he always said CNN), we would have some kind of morale-breaking effect on the enemy," Blaber wrote.[29] But using the JSOC task force to raid Gecko and Rhino just to show the Taliban that U.S. forces could do it rubbed many in the command the wrong way. "This was a demonstration mission, which is not exactly what JSOC ought to be used for," said a retired special operations officer.

Several senior JSOC officials advised Dailey against conducting the raids.[30] "I gave that counsel to the general, I absolutely did," based on the level of risk and the likelihood that the targets would turn out to be "dry holes," said Mike Hall, Dailey's senior enlisted adviser. "You were hanging some people out there in the middle of nowhere with not tremendously good plans to back them up," he said. "I just did not think it was a good idea. . . . I'm not sure anybody really thought Omar was there and I just thought it was a lot of risk with so many enemy forces so close by."

To a Delta operator familiar with the planning, the decision to raid the airstrip and Omar's compound originated from the same misguided thought process that came up with the fertilizer factory target: "That got killed off and so what do we do? *Let's go raid Mullah Omar's empty house and this empty airfield out in the middle of the desert.*" Although others, including Franks, suggested the targets originated with Central Command, the operator blamed Dailey for the decision to proceed, which he described as "monumental recklessness that can't be emphasized enough."

But Dailey overrode these objections, to the dismay of senior Delta personnel. "It's like a nightmare unfolding in front of us," said the operator. "There were no fucking off-roads at this point. The plan was the plan." This view was not unanimous, however. A planner who had opposed the fertilizer plant mission was less worried about this one. "Of course we were concerned, because the time/distance issues and the amount of aircraft made it extremely complex and extremely difficult," he said. But he added that the detailed planning "prepared us extremely well for having the ability to pull this off."

The JSOC commander's determination to drive on with the missions reflected his faith in the units involved, according to his senior NCO. "General Dailey had a tremendous amount of confidence in those organizations, especially the special mission units, but also the Rangers," Hall said.

JSOC also tried to find a mission for Team 6. Some planning went into a possible assault on what a TF Brown source described as "a set of power line stanchions that they wanted to take down"—named Objective Badger—about twenty-five miles southeast of Gereshk on Highway 1 between Kandahar and Herat. However, Rumsfeld withheld approval. Instead the Blue operators on the *Kitty Hawk* busied themselves preparing for a much higher profile mission: a hostage rescue from under the Taliban's noses in Kabul itself.[31]

※

Planning for Rhino and Gecko entered the final phase. Another rock drill was held on Masirah October 14.[32] The operation was growing more complex by the day. As was often the case with JSOC, the complexity revolved around the helicopters. The distance a helicopter can fly depends on a variety of factors, including the altitude at which it's flying, the air temperature, the weight of any passengers or cargo, and the amount of fuel in its tanks. Keeping these in balance so the aircraft had enough fuel to get where they needed to go, but not so much that the fuel's weight overly restricted what could be carried, challenged TF Brown's planners and meant the helicopters did not top up their tanks when being refueled, but instead "managed" their fuel levels to ensure they could still carry their passengers. For the Gecko raid, in order for the Black Hawks to carry the gas they needed, they could only take five operators each. "Those five operators were probably planning to be 300 pounds apiece, with all their kit," said a TF Brown source. The distances the aircraft would have to fly to and from Gecko and the number of operators they'd be carrying required an exquisitely choreographed refueling ballet, with the helicopters being refueled in midair by turboprop MC-130P Combat Shadows, which in turn would cycle back and forth to a KC-135 Stratotanker jet at a higher altitude for their own aerial refueling. (It was this need for the MC-130Ps to hit the KC-135, and the timing of it, that required the helicopters to land at Rhino for one of their refuelings.)[33]

A couple of days before the raids two AC-130s flew from Masirah on a path that took them over Rhino and Gecko before returning to the island. Although the gunships hit what a TF Sword source described as "targets of opportunity" en route to and from the objectives, they made the flight to confirm the mission timeline and to desensitize anyone on the ground to the sound of the planes overhead.

The flights detected no enemy on either objective, yet in a bizarre twist the closer the missions loomed, the more paranoid the intelligence briefings became about what the task force might encounter on the targets.[34] Having initially suggested the targets were empty, intel folks now warned the operators to "assume" there might be enemy forces on Rhino equipped with advanced night vision goggles. Much talk centered on the Taliban's air defenses, which—in the absence of hard evidence to the contrary— some alarmists in the intelligence community were hyping out of all proportion to the actual threat. A September 28 briefing warned that Rhino was mined, and that a ZSU 23-4—a tracked, radar-guided, four-barreled antiaircraft weapon—was on the objective. The planners were particularly focused on the threat from Stinger and Redeye antiaircraft missiles that the United States had given the Afghan mujahideen during their 1980s struggle against Soviet occupation forces. An October 1 briefing said Kandahar was defended by "a picket line" of man-portable air defense missiles. "There is a ring of fire around Kandahar," an intelligence officer warned. "It consists of concentric circles of rockets, hand-held missile launchers, and antiaircraft guns."[35]

If true, these weapons represented a serious threat to the fixed and rotary wing aircraft that would carry the assault forces to Rhino and Gecko. The mission was going to require every Combat Talon at Sword's disposal. Even the quick reaction force (QRF), which consisted of a Ranger element and a pair of AH-6 Little Birds, would have to remain three hours away on Masirah because no aircraft were available to stage them closer to the objectives.[36] "The plan was, if something happens and the QRF needs to be launched . . . the [M]C-130s that were supporting the mission at Rhino would have to fly all the way back to Masirah and pick us up and take us back out there," said a Little Bird pilot. "So there was nothing 'quick' about the QRF."

In preparation for the missions, Sword moved its primary medevac and combat search and rescue assets to a Pakistani military airfield in Jacobabad, about 300 miles southwest of Kandahar. Staff on Masirah also drew up plans to establish a forward arming and refueling point (FARP) and emplace a Ranger platoon on the night of the missions at a small Pakistani airfield about forty-five miles south of the Afghan border at Dalbandin. (The FARP was for emergencies. If Gecko went according to plan, there would be no need for any aircraft to refuel there.)[37]

Unlike the Delta operators, who all had prior military experience before being selected into "the Unit," many Rangers were first-term enlistees and therefore much younger than their special mission unit counterparts. This was their first combat operation and they were wondering when the "combat" part of that phrase was going to apply. "Are we going to do something, Sergeant Major, or what?" they asked Rakow after a week cooling their heels on Masirah. Rakow and other senior NCOs told the younger soldiers to get used to it. "We had to talk to Rangers about the reality of combat, that sometimes there's huge periods of boredom interspersed with high levels of activity," he recalled.

Now, with action just hours away, the Rangers paused to listen to Rakow and Votel deliver speeches. The two were a study in contrasts. Rakow's was brimming with testosterone, reminding his audience that what they were about to do—leap into the darkness from a perfectly good airplane to possibly confront their nation's enemies—was what the country paid them to do, and what they lived for. "If your dick ain't hard getting ready to do this then you ain't alive and breathing," he told them.

Later Votel would gently chide Rakow for using such language with a few women in the audience, but for now the regimental commander turned to the troops. His speech was also an expression of pride in his soldiers, but was less bombastic than his sergeant major's. The regimental commander told his men he was looking forward to making a combat jump with them that night, and cautioned them to stay focused on their part of the mission, which he reminded them was connected to a wider set of operations. After the speeches, the Rangers—not for the last time that evening—recited the Ranger Creed, which the proximity of combat had imbued with extra significance. Eager to get on with things, the Rangers got rigged up, loosely attaching their gear, which they would tighten during the flight.[38] The regimental chaplain invoked a blessing on the task force and the soldiers walked onto the planes.

The need to produce a televised spectacle meant a four-man psychological operations team[39] joined the Rangers on the aircraft, one of numerous additions that meant there was no space for the two Little Birds that had originally been part of the plan. "We really don't need you because there's not much of a threat there," the Sword staff told the crews. This caused some griping among the AH-6 pilots, who suspected standard operational procedure was being ignored to ensure more paratroopers got a combat jump. (The AH-6s were integral to most airfield seizures, taking to the air to provide security as soon as Rangers cleared the objective and the Talons landed.)

※

The Combat Talons above Rhino were in trail formation, separated one from the other by several thousand feet, so the sticks of paratroopers floated down roughly on a line that began beyond the end of the runway and ended at the compound itself.[40] After landing, the Rangers quickly gathered and stowed their parachutes to ensure the airstrip was clear for the planes and helicopters due there soon. Although braced to encounter resistance, only one "enemy fighter" (in the official history's words) appeared. Fire from several of 3rd Battalion's C Company soldiers quickly cut him down. C Company went on to clear the compound, which had sustained surprisingly light damage from the AC-130 fire. Meanwhile, A Company, together with an attached sniper team secured nearby locations and set up preplanned blocking positions to fight off any counterattacks. The Rangers swept through the compound. It was empty, rendering superfluous the repeated loudspeaker broadcasts in three languages from the psy ops team telling any Taliban to surrender.[41]

Airfield seizure was, of course, the quintessential Ranger mission.[42] But the presence of combat cameramen on the ground and of a Navy P-3C Orion command and control plane overhead underlined the priority given to the operation's propaganda role. (The Orion was transmitting video of the assault in real time back to a psychological operations detachment at Masirah.)[43]

The Rangers cleared Rhino so quickly that fourteen minutes after C Company entered the compound, an MC-130 landed with a team from JSOC's elite Joint Medical Augmentation Unit (JMAU). The team was there primarily to treat any combat casualties from the two missions, but its only patients at Rhino were two Rangers injured on the jump. Six minutes later came the sound of rotor blades churning the night air.[44]

꙰

As the Rangers floated down to Rhino, Franks's attention was on Gecko, from where a Predator was beaming live video of the assault back to his Tampa headquarters as well as to Masirah. "The sheer speed of the insertion was unbelievable," the CENTCOM boss would later write. "The big tandem-rotor helicopters swept in from two directions, so low that the pilots flying in night vision goggles had to pop up to clear the compound walls. As the dust billowed, the operators pounded off the tailgates and moved toward their objectives, firing on the run."[45]

But the infiltration was not quite as smooth as Franks implied. The AC-130 that was supposed to quickly take out the guard tower missed with its first several shots before finally hitting the target. Someone shot at the inbound helicopters without effect about a kilometer short of Gecko, while smoke from the AC-130's "pre-assault fires" obscured much of the compound as the helicopters arrived, preventing the DAP flight lead, Chief Warrant Officer 3 Casey Ragsdale, from firing Hellfire missiles at his preassigned targets.[46] (Ragsdale was piloting one of four DAPs committed to the Gecko assault.)[47] And in an accident that foreshadowed events on an even higher profile mission nine and a half years later, "the second Chinook in clipped a wall," said a Delta source who watched it happen.[48] The MH-47E, call sign CRESCENT 93, was carrying A2 operators, including Pat Savidge, the troop sergeant major and acting commander, whose presence earned him the dubious distinction of having crashed in all three of the 160th's basic airframes (the other two being the Little Bird, during the Kurt Muse rescue in Panama, and the MH-60 Black Hawk, during jungle training, also in Panama).[49] The Chinook got banged up several times as it tried to land, said another Delta operator. The accident ripped away most of the landing gear and caused a hydraulic fluid leak, but the helicopter was able to take off again. While the other helicopters went into a holding pattern until the operators were ready for exfil, Dailey ordered CRESCENT 93 to fly to Jacobabad. The A2 operators would get picked up by "the flying spare" that TF Brown always included in its plans for just such circumstances.[50]

As for Franks's comment about operators "firing on the run" as they came off the helicopters, an experienced Delta man who watched the whole mission said it didn't ring true. "Nobody was shooting inside that place," he said.

Central Command had chosen not to bomb Gecko, partly in an

attempt to lure Omar and other senior Taliban leaders there and partly out of a desire not to destroy "the trove of intelligence" Franks hoped to find.[51] But the ploy hadn't worked. Led by ground force commander Chris Sorenson, the Delta operators found themselves scouring an empty target, just like their Ranger counterparts at Rhino. "There certainly wasn't a heck of a lot of great intelligence that came off of there," Hall said.

Later accounts, including Franks's autobiography, gave the impression that the Delta operators encountered resistance. "The Taliban had attempted to defend the sites, as we had expected," Franks wrote, referring to Gecko and Rhino. "Several of our men had been wounded, some of the enemy killed."[52] In a *New Yorker* article published a couple of weeks after the missions, Seymour Hersh wrote that during a running firefight with the Taliban, "Twelve Delta members were wounded, three of them seriously."[53] But several sources with firsthand experience of the mission denied all of this. "None of our men were wounded in the raid," wrote Blaber,[54] Delta's operations officer at the time. "We didn't medevac anyone out of that target," said a retired special operations officer. Even Franks, in the days after the mission, said, "We had no one wounded by enemy fire," appearing to contradict his own yet-to-be written book.[55]

According to a Delta source, the stories of operators getting hurt stemmed from two separate episodes that had nothing to do with the Taliban: the crash landing, and an incident in which operators got too close to one of their own grenades when it exploded as they were clearing the compound. "Somebody decided to throw frags instead of bangers,[56] and when they chucked a frag into a room, it was like a thin tin wall, and the frags peppered them, so they ate their own frags," he said.[57]

None of this prevented one of two AC-130s overhead opening up on what had been called in as "an enemy bus fleeing from the target." The gunship, which boasted a stabilized 105mm howitzer plus 40mm and 25mm cannon, locked on to the bus with its targeting system and followed it away from the compound before firing. "The 105s were exploding left and right," said a source who watched it happen. "The bus skidded to a stop." The AC-130 crew watched their sensor screens, on which warm objects, such as humans, show up darker. "Out came this single file of black blobs out the front right door. They were running down the middle of the road, again, 105s exploding on both sides of the road."

A Delta officer on the plane as a ground force liaison watched events unfold with growing unease. Something didn't feel right. "They did not starburst out of the bus [as trained guerrillas would], they ran down the middle of the road," the source said.

"Who called the target in? Was this target called in by the ground force?" the Delta officer said, before calling the operators on the ground himself to find out. "Negative, we've not seen a bus," they replied. Then a voice from the other AC-130 came on the net and said that crew had called in the target. The AC-130 crew that had already fired—and was about to fire for effect—reexamined the target. "You could see that there were double blobs, one slightly smaller than the big one, they were kind of attached," the source said. "I think they're holding hands," the Delta officer said. "I think that's a parent with a child—Cease fire! Cease fire!"

The cease-fire call was controversial. "It was a big deal because . . . that was the one target to shoot at out of Gecko that night," a Delta source said. "By the time they got back they were still kind of pissed and then they reviewed the tapes and saw that it was women and children."

Whether or not any actual Taliban were on the objective—and the evidence suggests there were not at the time of the mission, although as many as eight armored vehicles had been seen nearby earlier that day[58]—some were on the move nearby. Staff in Masirah monitoring the Predator feed could see tanks approaching. At 11:55 P.M., the operators called for the helicopters to pick them up twenty minutes later.[59] Protected by the circling AC-130s, the raiders were able to fly away before the tanks got close enough to cause any trouble, the retired special ops officer said. The Delta operators left a few NYPD and FDNY baseball caps as calling cards on the objective. "It was basically a 'Fuck you—we've been here,'" said a Task Force Sword officer.

The Gecko assault force flew straight to Rhino, refueling there before returning to the *Kitty Hawk* at sunrise.[60] Although questions remain as to whether the assault force took any fire on Gecko, there is no doubt the helicopters were fired at on their flights across Pakistan to and from the objective. "When they went across Pakistan is when they got shot at the most," said a 160th pilot, adding that the fire likely came from civilians in the tribal areas near the border, rather than from the Pakistani military. Once the helicopters had departed Rhino, the Rangers gradually collapsed their perimeter, boarding two Combat Talons that had landed on the airstrip. Once the last Talon landed, task force members picked up the infrared airstrip markers that had helped guide the planes in, got on the aircraft, and left. The Rangers had spent five hours and twenty-four minutes on the ground.[61]

Back in Tampa, Franks was about to call Myers, the new chairman of the Joint Chiefs, when Dailey called with bad news.[62] Task Force Sword's luck that evening had run out at Dalbandin, where 26 B Company, 3rd Battalion Rangers, and two 24th STS operators had flown in from the *Kitty Hawk* on Black Hawks to establish a forward arming and refueling point and a quick reaction force to support that night's missions. TF Sword had received word that somehow the locals had learned Americans were coming to Dalbandin, so the Rangers conducted their arrival there as an air assault, rather than as a more routine landing, even though they were still in Pakistan, a notional ally. As the second Black Hawk in—call sign RATCHET 23—was repositioning, it kicked up a dust cloud that obscured the landing zone, creating what aviators call a "brownout" and disorienting the pilots. The helicopter hit the ground hard and rolled onto its right side, pinning several Rangers who'd been aboard the helicopter underneath the fuselage. Despite their colleagues' best efforts, two Rangers—Specialist John Edmunds and Private First Class Kristofer Stonesifer—were killed.[63]

News of the accident hit the task force like a punch in the gut, but Dailey stayed calm. "To Dell Dailey's credit . . . he responded relatively well to serious incidents like that," said a Task Force Sword officer. "He was able to compartmentalize that specific thing and not allow it to drive the rest of the mission." But others instantly flashed back to the Eagle Claw disaster, which had also occurred as a helicopter repositioned in a brownout at a FARP.[64] "The first thing that people said was, 'Jesus, we're going to have another freakin' Desert One,'" recalled Rakow.

In addition to sadness over the sheer tragedy of the losses, the accident was a source of intense frustration in the 160th. A senior Night Stalker noted that the regiment traced its origins to the aftermath of Desert One. With pre-mission comparisons between the Rhino/Gecko operation and Eagle Claw fresh in aviators' minds, there had been a focus on operating safely at the Dalbandin forward arming and refueling point. "It amazed a lot of people that that's where that accident happened," he said.

✴

As the Rangers and Delta operators flew back to Masirah and the *Kitty Hawk*, in the JOC a fifteen-soldier team from the 9th Psychological Operations Battalion was editing six hours of raw footage from the Rhino mission into a three-minute clip to be forwarded to the Pentagon. Propaganda, after all, was the mission's raison d'être: to demonstrate the United States' ability to put troops wherever it pleased in Afghanistan. Rumsfeld, who had not watched the missions in real time, but had stayed up to date over the phone, wanted the film available to the U.S. television networks for their evening news broadcasts later on October 20. He got his wish. At a lunchtime news conference that day in the Pentagon, Myers aired the clip, which would be shown on every major news program in the United States and around the world.[65]

The Joint Chiefs' chairman stayed on message throughout his press conference. He offered little detail about the missions, saying nothing about Masirah or the *Kitty Hawk*, but continually reinforcing his point. "U.S. forces were able to deploy, maneuver and operate inside Afghanistan without significant interference from Taliban forces," he said. In case the reporters didn't get it the first time, he repeated the point some minutes later: "One of the messages should be that we are capable of, at a time of our choosing, conducting the kind of operations we want to conduct."[66]

Assessments of the value of the Gecko and Rhino missions were as divided after the fact as they had been before.

"It was disappointing when they conducted that operation that they didn't catch more, but I have to say that the operation had strategic value," said a senior member of the Joint Staff. "That changed the way Omar thought about the conflict and the word I heard was that he was terrified that he was not safe and his sanctuary was violated. The operational and tactical effects of a strategic operation are that he becomes isolated, insular, communications are constrained, so that when other things take place . . . they have more limited ability to react to those things."

But to the skeptics, the raids had been worse than a waste of time: they had placed troops' lives at risk for nothing more than a propaganda effort that resembled a joint readiness exercise. "So many guys almost died so many times on both targets, for no fucking reason," said a Delta source who monitored the operation in real time. "That was just a complete JRX done for the sake of the cameras."

Understandably, the Rangers' mood was somber, the twist of fate that took the lives of two of their buddies serving as a wake-up call for the young soldiers. The task force held a memorial service for Edmunds and Stonesifer at Masirah October 23.[67] Then the Rangers turned their minds to the future. They would soon be back in action.

10

"Carte Blanche"

At 10:30 P.M. on November 13, the silence of another moonless Afghan night was disturbed by the thrumming of a single Combat Talon's four turboprops 800 feet above the desert about fifty miles southwest of Kandahar. From the plane tumbled forty dark shapes that floated to earth in a matter of seconds after parachute canopies blossomed above them, barely visible against the night sky.

The parachutes belonged to thirty-two Rangers from 3rd Battalion's B Company and an eight-man 24th STS element. Their mission was to seize a desert landing strip named Bastogne and prepare it to receive two Combat Talons, each loaded with a pair of AH-6 Little Bird gunships, a mobile forward arming and refueling point, and the pilots and other personnel to man them. The Little Birds were then to fly off to attack preplanned targets. Bastogne was the Rangers' second combat parachute assault of the war,[1] but unlike the seizure of Objective Rhino, this mission was most certainly not a propaganda exercise. There would be no Pentagon press briefing about it, ever. Rather, the Bastogne mission was the latest step in a campaign of deception and destruction Task Force Sword had decided to wage across southern Afghanistan.

The details of that campaign would remain secret for years, but even the broad brushstrokes had not been imagined when, with the Gecko and Rhino raids finally out of the way, the staff on Masirah pondered Sword's next move. There was no long-term plan. Everything was a seat-of-the-pants decision. "After we did this first mission, we went, 'All right, what are we going to do now?'" said the retired special ops officer.

The first days after the October 19 missions saw a flurry of administrative activity as the task force conducted after-action reviews and prepared for the arrival of Franks, who secretly visited Masirah and the *Kitty Hawk* October 22. The Delta elements on the *Kitty Hawk* quickly returned to Masirah, but Brown, Team 6, and Ranger elements remained on the ship. Possibly as a result of meeting with Franks, Dailey issued new guidance October 22 instructing Sword planners to draft "a campaign plan" with missions centered on Kandahar.[2] Operators and planners on Masirah brainstormed. Delta personnel resurrected their 1998 plan to ambush bin Laden as a basis for planning new missions. Key to the original scheme had been landing Combat Talons on one or more dry lake beds around Kandahar. "We determined that we could land large fixed-wing aircraft (C-130s) on these dry lakebeds in the middle of the night without anyone seeing or hearing us," Blaber wrote of the 1998 effort.

Before Sword could launch any such missions, Dailey apparently had a change of heart. In the first week of November, he ordered the task force to start planning immediately for redeployment to the United States. By then it was clear that, enabled by 5th Special Forces Group, the CIA, and U.S. airpower, the Northern Alliance's campaign against the Taliban was gaining traction, leaving JSOC, supposedly the United States' premier special operations organization, on the sidelines. Aghast that JSOC might leave the theater with the Al Qaeda and Taliban leaders—and thousands of their forces—still at large, Blaber and others of like mind put together a few concepts on the fly and forwarded them up the chain. Somehow they persuaded those at the top, Dailey included, to allow them to proceed. "Only because they were so beaten down and in such dire straits with . . . CENTCOM did JSOC headquarters go, 'Okay, we're willing to try anything' and turned the whole thing over to us for those next few days," said a Delta source. "At this point, the staff of our higher headquarters was ready to approve just about anything we brought to them—and they did," according to Blaber.[3] "Anything we wanted to try for years, we finally got carte blanche to do it," said another Delta source.

For once, JSOC unleashed the power of its operators' imaginations. In short order, they produced concepts with two aims: to "develop the situation"—in other words, to gain a deeper understanding of the situation on the ground—in southern Afghanistan, and to convince the Taliban that there was a greater U.S. presence along the southern stretch of Highway 1 (the ring road that connects most major Afghan cities, including Kabul and Kandahar) than there actually was. The latter aim meshed perfectly with Dailey's penchant for deception operations. Unlike the unconventional warfare campaign being waged by Special Forces and the CIA in northern Afghanistan, which involved tight coordination with the Northern Alliance, Sword's operations in the south were unilateral missions. Rather than taking and holding territory, the intent was to distract the Taliban and prevent them from concentrating their forces in Kabul and Herat.[4]

Although the ultimate goal was to clandestinely infiltrate teams of operators, the first fruits of the brainstorming sessions required no boots on the ground. A couple of nights after Dailey announced that Sword would be going home, a series of parachutes dropped from a Combat Talon flying over the hills outside Kandahar. Attached to the parachutes were large blocks of ice. The idea was that once the parachutes landed the ice would melt and the chutes would blow across the landscape until someone found and reported them, sowing seeds of paranoia in the Taliban's minds as they wondered where the paratroopers might be. "We later learned that the phantom parachute drops not only confused the enemy, they also terrorized the enemy," Blaber wrote.[5]

Within a few days of the ice block deception, the dark shadows drifting to earth were real operators, conducting some of the most daring missions JSOC had executed in years: high-altitude, low-opening (HALO) freefall jumps.

Although glamorized in video games and movies, actual combat HALO missions—in which operators jump from as high as 34,900 feet and freefall for as long as roughly two and a half minutes before opening their parachutes just a few thousand feet aboveground in order to minimize the chance of being observed—are rare. When a reinforced team from Delta's B3 troop (B Squadron's reconnaissance troop) led by Major Brad Taylor HALO'd in northeast of Kandahar to call in air strikes against Taliban and/or Al Qaeda targets fleeing southwest from Kabul, Tom Greer, at the time a major in Delta and commander of A1 Troop, called it "the first nighttime combat HALO . . . parachute jump since the Vietnam War." The "death-defying" jump was "one of the riskiest missions" of the war, said a Delta source. "It had everything: cold, night, the unknown, high winds, all that stuff," he said.

The team's mission was to establish an observation post in some high ground near the road. But it immediately went awry when Christopher Kurinec, nicknamed "CK," was badly hurt as he landed. Kurinec had "jumped the bundle,"[6] meaning that in addition to his own gear he had the team's "bundle" of supplies (usually water, ammunition, and medical kit) strapped to him when he jumped. Because the extra weight increases the speed at which the operator hits the ground, the bundle makes an already difficult task that much more awkward. For that reason, the operator with the bundle is usually one of the team's most experienced freefall jumpers.[7] Despite Kurinec's injury, the team drove on with the mission, climbing to the place they had picked out for their observation post and in the process discovering an operator from a previous generation had apparently shared their assessment of the spot's usefulness. "They got up into the side of the mountain there, set up their OP in a little cave overhang, and they found a can from a Soviet K-ration, which at the time we imagined very likely was a Spetsnaz [Soviet special operations] guy who had been in that same cave, same [observation post]," said a Delta source.

Team 6's Blue Team and the Rangers' Regimental Reconnaissance Detachment also got in on the freefall act (with a SEAL badly injuring his knee in a jump to secure a landing strip),[8] but the unit that did the most HALO jumping during this period was 24th STS, whose mission was to validate each desert landing strip using a tool called a penetrometer to ensure the soil could support the weight of the Combat Talons. "The STS was clearing every one of those and they loved that mission. That was their heyday right there," said a Delta operator closely involved with the operations. "I would estimate they probably did at least ten separate jumps in."

All these jumps were done to enable the arrival of Combat Talons bearing a mobile ground force or Little Bird gunships. These missions followed Delta's rough operational concept for 1998's canceled bin Laden raid: Talons would land on dry lake beds, then offload wheeled vehicles, operators, and AH-6 and MH-6 Little Birds. Such was the case with the Bastogne mission. Special mission unit operators (almost certainly from 24th STS) had scouted the landing strip ahead of the Rangers' jump, while the Regimental Reconnaissance Detachment HALO'd in ahead of the main Ranger body and stayed until the B Company paratroops landed, according to Rakow. "That was the first HALO operation in a combat environment that they had done," he said.

Some HALO missions were a precursor to mounted Delta operations. "They'd set up the landing zones, make sure they were straight, make sure they were good," said a JSOC staff officer. "Then you brought the

Talons in to bring the mobility guys in." The "mobility guys" were operators manning Delta's Pinzgauer six-wheel-drive combat vehicles. These rugged machines could carry a payload of almost 3,300 pounds cross-country, had a range of about 435 miles, and featured a variety of weapons on forward, center, and rear mounts. Delta had been using Pinzgauers for years and was constantly working with the manufacturer to upgrade them.[9]

The Pinzgauer missions "weren't raids, they were insertions," the JSOC staffer said. "They spent a week on the ground then we pulled them out" using Combat Talons or Chinooks. The operators' primary mission was not blowing things up, but reconnaissance—getting the lay of the land and locating Taliban or Al Qaeda forces.

But despite the emphasis on understanding the environment, there was still plenty of direct action, much of the intelligence for which came from the CIA. "In the beginning, I remember particularly in southern Afghanistan, we didn't have the reach," said the Agency's Hank Crumpton. Only "tiny numbers of CIA officers" were operating in that part of the country, he said. So the Agency turned to JSOC. "I remember us identifying targets with Predators, with human sources, with satellites, and just funneling this to JSOC and saying, 'Go get 'em.' So they weren't under our control, we were just identifying targets and they were putting the packages together. And it was their authorities, their command and control." But Sword also coordinated with the CIA to use the Agency's armed Predators (the military had none of its own) to strike an average of one or two moving vehicles a night in late October and early November. "The [Predator] missions were unbelievable," said a source who monitored the strikes from the JOC. "Every night there were Taliban guys or [or other enemy] guys trying to get out being hunted down and destroyed."

✳

The mid-November missions came as a blessed relief for one Sword element in particular: the Little Bird crews, for whom the post–September 11 period had been a two-month exercise in frustration. Like their Delta counterparts, they had been surprised at how long they had to wait before finally departing for Masirah on October 6. "I thought something as big as 9/11, within a day or two we would have been wheels up going somewhere to go whack some bad guys, but that's not how it ended up working out," said a Little Bird pilot. By the time TF Brown deployed,

Dailey had cut the Little Bird element down to two pairs of AH-6 gunships and crews, plus a spare airframe, and the same number of MH-6 assault Little Birds. The 160th had seen no combat since Somalia in 1993, so for those picked to deploy, "there was the excitement and anticipation of actually going out and doing something . . . and getting revenge for what had just happened," the Little Bird pilot said. "You could see how disappointed the others were that they were staying behind."

Once at Masirah, the Little Bird crews watched their Black Hawk and Chinook colleagues depart for the *Kitty Hawk*. When planners cut the AH-6s from the airfield seizure mission, the Little Bird pilots began to wonder if their chance for action was evaporating.

After the October 19 missions, the Little Bird contingent became more proactive in their effort to find themselves a mission. Schiller, the Brown operations officer, again tried to persuade Dailey to seize Bagram as a base from which to stage Little Bird missions. The proposal met with no more success than it had before the deployment.

Every day Chief Warrant Officer 3 Rob Rainier and CW4 John Meehan, the AH-6 flight leads, would discuss possible targets with the Task Force Brown intelligence director, plan an operation to attack those targets, then brief that plan to Mangum and Dailey. Each time, Dailey vetoed the plan because it involved not only landing MC-130s at a desert landing strip, but parachuting a fuel blivet, ammunition, and a detachment of soldiers to establish an even more distant forward arming and refueling point. "Basically, after about the third or fourth one, he said, 'We are not putting any FARPs in—FARPs are dangerous,'" said a Little Bird pilot.

Dailey's refusal to countenance any mission that involved jumping a FARP into the desert disappointed the pilots, for whom the tactic was second nature. The regiment had a jump-qualified airborne support detachment for just such occasions. "We've trained hundreds and hundreds of times for it," an AH-6 pilot said. The ability to perform such missions was why the Night Stalkers' full name is the 160th Special Operations Aviation Regiment (Airborne). But Dailey was having none of it, citing the risk of having a force of fewer than twenty soldiers stuck out in the desert, reliant on TF Brown's MH-60s and 47s to pick them up.

In the second week of November Meehan and Rainier finally arrived at a winning formula. They found a couple of viable targets: military installations that still appeared active but which had yet to be bombed and were on nobody else's target list. Instead of jumping the FARP in, they would have MC-130s land in a dry lake bed and refuel them. Ironically, while the Night Stalkers frequently trained to parachute a FARP into a combat zone, the Little Bird pilots had never practiced operating from a dry lake bed. But the MC-130 pilots assured them the planes could handle the surface, so the TF Brown men presented the plan to Dailey.

The JSOC commander approved it, but with an attitude that he was "throwing the guys a bone," a TF Brown source said. The mission, Dailey told the Little Bird crews in a meeting, was "just one step above Range 29," a reference to the range the AH-6s used for gunnery practice at Campbell. When the experienced AH-6 flight leads pushed to get the quick reaction force for the mission staged closer to the target than Masirah, Dailey pushed back, saying, "Hey, look, do you guys want to go on a mission or not?"

As with all helicopter missions, the aviators were required to brief a combat search and rescue (CSAR) plan and an evasion and recovery (E and R) plan to Mangum. It was a very short brief. "We had no CSAR," recalled one of the pilots. "When we briefed the E and R plan, that was E and E [escape and evade] back to the dry lake bed—that's your [only] choice, and if you get there after sunrise, there's nothing going to be there."

The AH-6 crews knew their targets were of no great strategic importance and could have been struck with much less risk by jets or AC-130 gunships, but desperate to get into the fight, they willingly accepted the hazards. Not only had they yet to see action in Afghanistan, only one of the eight Little Bird gun pilots in Masirah had any combat experience at all, "so this is busting everybody's cherry," one pilot said. Because JSOC had never disclosed the AH-6s' presence to the Omani government, TF Brown had kept the tiny attack helicopters hidden behind cheesecloth sheets in their hangar. Now they were finally being unleashed. The 160th had a famous motto: *Night Stalkers Don't Quit*, often shortened to *NSDQ*. But the AH-6 crews had their own saying—*Six Guns Don't Miss*—and they were itching to prove it.[10]

❉

As the first Rangers hit the ground at Bastogne, a little more than an hour behind them another two MC-130s were following the same route. Each carried a pair of AH-6s and crews, a Ranger security element plus the fuel, munitions, and troops for a mobile FARP. A TF Brown medic and a maintenance test pilot were also on the aircraft.

On the lead Talon, the AH-6 company commander Major Al Pepin walked around shaking everyone's hand and wishing them good luck. Otherwise, each man was alone with his thoughts. Meehan's copilot, CW3 Gary Linfoot, was surprised at how routine the flight felt, just like a training mission. *This is the first combat mission, I should be a little more nervous,* he thought. That sense of normalcy vanished at 11:45 P.M. as the plane descended out of the night sky on its final approach to the lake bed. The special tactics team had ensured the landing strip could handle the Talons and marked it with infrared landing lights, but when the pilot of the Talon carrying Linfoot landed, "he hit so hard it seemed like that AH bounced off the deck even though it was strapped down," the AH-6 driver recalled. Within moments the air in the plane was thick with the lake bed's talcum-powder-like dust. *This is definitely going to be a little bit more exciting than I thought it was going to be,* Linfoot realized. The Talon slowed to a halt and the troops swiftly unloaded the helicopters and FARP, before guiding the plane off the runway to clear space for the second MC-130E, which landed at midnight, disgorging its cargo just as quickly.

Within fifteen minutes of the second Talon landing, the four Little Birds were ready to take off. But as each helicopter's five rotor blades began to turn, the challenges of using the lake bed as an airstrip became immediately apparent. The whirling rotors whipped the powdery dust into clouds that enveloped the helicopters. Such brownouts are extraordinarily dangerous during takeoffs and landings. If the pilot becomes just slightly disoriented and tilts his helicopter, the rotor blades may strike the ground, shearing off and flying through the air, destroying the helicopter and anything—or anyone—else they encounter. The pilots had trained for brownouts, but never for the sort of towering dust clouds with which they had to deal that night.

Most Little Bird pilots prefer sitting in the right-hand seat, but despite being the pilot in command Meehan had allowed Linfoot, his copilot, to sit there for this mission. As Linfoot "pulled pitch"—pulling up on the collective lever, which increased the rotor blades' pitch, creating lift and allowing the helicopter to take off—he immediately browned out. Unable to see the ground or the sky, he "went inside," focusing on his instruments and relying on them to keep the Little Bird level as it lifted off the ground. "John's calling out the altitude and I'm just pulling the guts out of it without over-torquing it, and when we cleared the cloud

I was not facing the direction I started off," Linfoot said. "I was 90 degrees to the left or something."

Emerging from the cloud at an altitude of 200 to 300 feet, the pilots headed north to their first objective, briefly relieved to be out of the dust and flying toward the targets. But their struggles with the unforgiving Afghan environment were only just beginning.

Flying over the flat, featureless lake bed on any night would have challenged an experienced helicopter pilot. But TF Brown's planners had chosen that particular night because Dailey, still fearful of the Taliban's vaunted air defenses, insisted the Little Bird missions occur only on moonless nights; in aviator-speak, nights of "zero illum." The total darkness compounded the pilots' problems.

"I bet they invented darkness in Afghanistan," Linfoot said. "Flying over that dry lake bed, I tell you, it was something. . . . It was flat as paper and so dark you can't really tell where earth ends and the sky begins. The horizon kind of becomes blurred, almost like you're flying inside of a golf ball." Like all 160th pilots, the AH-6 crews were experts at flying in night vision goggles, which worked by magnifying ambient light. But by choosing the last night of a waning crescent moon, TF Brown had given the goggles almost none to work with, leading Linfoot to question whether they had really gained an edge by flying in such pitch blackness. "There comes a point where maybe you haven't stacked the deck in your favor any longer," he said.

Once beyond the lake bed, Linfoot decided to cheat a little by turning his infrared "pink light" on for a second to illuminate the ground and reorient himself now that the previously featureless terrain was dotted with rocks and scrubby vegetation that showed up more clearly in the goggles. He did so just in time to see a rocky finger of land flash by only a couple of feet below his skids. A moment later, CW3 Jim Hosey flying the "Dash-2" (the trail aircraft or "wingman" in any two-aircraft formation) actually skimmed off the rocks, almost losing his skids to the unseen outcrop. The first combat AH-6 mission in eight years was only minutes old, not a round had been fired, and yet four pilots had just cheated death by a few feet.

Any Taliban or Al Qaeda fighters out there with access to their own night vision goggles would have been able to see the "pink light," but Linfoot continued to flash it occasionally to help keep his bearings. He judged this a risk well worth taking. Unlike most future missions in

Afghanistan and Iraq, the Little Birds were on their own. There was no stack of intelligence, surveillance, and reconnaissance (ISR) aircraft above them to warn them of trouble ahead, nor any jets or AC-130 gunships to protect them if enemy fire or maintenance issues forced a helicopter down. The "Six Guns" were hanging it out there a long, long way from home.

About twenty-five minutes after taking off, the helicopters approached the small town west of Kandahar where their first target—Objective Wolverine—was located.

With Linfoot still at the controls of the lead aircraft, flying at an altitude of 300 feet, Meehan navigated, using a small green map light mounted beside him to check the paper map on his lap while calling out what he was seeing around him. Meehan soon spotted Wolverine—a walled Taliban compound containing vehicles, radar equipment, and other gear. At that point he took the controls and went into the classic AH-6 attack profile, "bumping up" about 100 feet to dissipate the helicopter's forward airspeed and give the pilots a better view of the target before nosing over into a 45-degree angle, which is better for handling the aircraft and reducing the "beaten area" where the aircraft's munitions would hit. The 4,000-foot elevation, warmer than expected temperatures, and the amount of fuel the helicopters required to reach the target meant each Little Bird was limited to one rocket pod containing seven 70mm Hydra 70 rockets and one GAU-19 three-barreled .50 caliber Gatling gun with about 500 rounds of ammunition, set to fire at a rate of 1,000 rounds per minute. (When unconstrained, an AH-6 would typically fly with two rocket pods and two 7.62mm miniguns.)

Meehan let loose with a burst of .50 cal, then added a rocket for good measure, before breaking off and coming back around. Hosey and Pepin in the Dash-2 followed up with a similar attack. The target was large enough that during the planning, the teams had divided it between themselves by drawing a "line of death" (officially, a "restricted fire line") through the middle using overhead imagery, so each team now attacked its own half of the target independent of the other team. All four helicopters made several strafing runs, or turns, over the target, their stubby wings spitting rockets and streams of heavy machine gun fire that destroyed the compound and the gear therein. The Little Birds took no return fire and saw nobody on the target, but they later learned that a signals intelligence platform (probably a Navy EP-3 Aries aircraft flying over Pakistan) overheard a Talib on the objective saying: "I don't know where they're coming from, [but] I can hear them and they're killing us."

With the target in smoking ruins and little ordnance left on their wings, the Little Birds returned to Bastogne, where the toughest part of the mission awaited. After locating their individual landing points marked by infrared chemical lights, the pilots again had to delicately negotiate another nerve-racking brownout, this time in reverse as they tried to land. Much to the relief of all concerned, the pilots nailed the landings.

With each team of two Little Birds having its own FARP manned by an armament specialist, a fuel handler plus a crew chief for any maintenance issues, all moving with the smooth, well-rehearsed choreography of a Formula One pit crew, it took less than ten minutes to refuel and rearm the helicopters and get them on their way to the next target: a Taliban compound they had named Objective Raptor.

After another white-knuckle flight across the high desert, the four AH-6s found the target, which was also filled with vehicles and other gear. Again the pilots strafed the target several times, this time striking a fuel dump that exploded. The glow of the burning fuel "washed out" the pilots' night vision goggles, forcing them to call the mission quits a little early and head back to the landing strip with Raptor in flames behind them. They landed, again with great difficulty, at 3:15 A.M. With help from the crew chiefs and armament soldiers, the pilots quickly folded the rotor blades up and pushed the small helicopters up the ramps onto the Combat Talons, which had conducted a midair refueling while the Little Birds were away. Within about forty-five minutes, the Talons were headed back to Masirah, leaving the desert to its cold, dry silence.[11]

Less than three days later, Task Force Sword launched another series of missions in southern Afghanistan. These differed from the raids on Wolverine and Raptor in that while those were direct action missions against assigned targets, the next set of missions were considered "armed reconnaissance," or, to the gun pilots, "search and destroy." In a touch of irony, the collective name Task Force Sword assigned to the missions did not quite reflect the episodic nature of JSOC's efforts at this stage of the conflict, but within a few years would define the command's approach to warfare. The missions were called Operation Relentless Strike.

After Sword reconnaissance elements found a patch of desert that could support the weight of heavily laden Combat Talons, the operation began on the nights of November 16 and 17 when MC-130s touched down on that desert landing strip—now named Anzio—and dropped off forty-eight Rangers and 24th STS personnel plus six Desert Mobility Vehicles (modified Humvees armed with an M240 machine gun and an M2 .50 cal machine gun).[12]

Another two MC-130s dropped off the AH-6 package. The Six Guns' mission that night was to patrol along Highway 1 looking for targets of opportunity. The two teams split up, but flew roughly the same flight paths, with the second team never more than about twenty miles from the other, so that either team could quickly come to the aid of the other if necessary. This time Meehan was in the lead bird's right seat and Linfoot in the left. They soon came across a Taliban motor pool full of armored personnel carriers and T-55 tanks. "We just start making run after run, and John, he's smacking the hell out of these tanks, hitting them with the .50, hitting them with the rockets, he's having a great time," recalled Linfoot. "As he's coming in, I look over and say, 'Hey, are you going to let me have any of this action?' He just kind of chuckled and went and made a few more passes, hit some more stuff." After firing all seven of his rockets, Meehan decided to leave the target and press on with just the small amount of .50 cal ammunition they had left.

Ahead on Highway 1, they spotted two vehicles: a flatbed truck with something on the back and a pickup carrying about ten men. "Let's see what those jackasses are up to," Meehan said, pulling the helicopter parallel to the mini-convoy with the vehicles off to the left. Linfoot had a clear view of the trucks, and told his copilot the object in the bed of the lead vehicle was a double-barreled 23mm antiaircraft gun. Meehan came back around, went into the bump, and then attacked, getting a direct hit on the antiaircraft gun with his last .50 cal rounds. Sparks flew from the flatbed, followed by secondary explosions as the 23mm rounds cooked off. As for the pickup, "they came to a screeching halt, all the dudes bailed out of that thing and they started hightailing it to the high ground out there to the left side," Linfoot recounted.

But Meehan and Linfoot were now "Winchester"—the universal aircraft code meaning out of ammunition—on both rockets and .50 cal, as were Hosey and Pepin in the Dash-2. The only weapons the pilots had at their disposal were their personal M4 assault rifles and a few hand grenades. But keen to finally engage Taliban they could actually see, Linfoot grabbed his M4 and began shooting at the running figures. The scene was not quite as bizarre as it might appear. Little Bird pilots often trained to engage foes from the helicopter with their personal weapons. Since Mogadishu, the regiment had replaced the 9mm Heckler & Koch MP5 submachine gun with the 5.56mm M4 as the pilots' personal weapon, but had yet to equip the rifles with the laser sights used by other special ops units. Linfoot was thus reduced to firing short bursts and trying to track his rounds by the sparks they'd make as they hit the ground.

The dozen or so Taliban began to scatter, so to keep them corraled in a killing zone, the two helicopters set up a "wagon wheel," flying in a counterclockwise circle with the left-seaters firing at the enemy fighters. Soon the left-seaters were running low on M4 ammunition. There was only one option left if they wanted to keep up the attack. "We pull out the hand grenades and start dropping these hand grenades," Linfoot recalled. "It was kind of funny because the guys, they tried to split up, we'd drop the hand grenades and that would kind of force them back into the kill zone and we'd shoot some more, pull out some more hand grenades and do the same thing."

At that point, Rainier, who was about twenty miles to the east, came up on the teams' internal radio network to report that his team hadn't seen anything left to shoot and were done. "We're about 50 percent [on ammo] and returning back to the FARP," he said. "How's it going where you're at?" Flying in the Dash-2, Pepin, the company commander, got on the radio, but accidentally transmitted his reply over satellite, so it came in loud and clear in the JOC on Masirah. "We're currently Winchester on [.50 cal] and rockets, engaging with M4 and hand grenades," he said. Eyebrows went up in the JOC. Irritated, Dailey turned to Mangum. (The two officers, both graduates of the U.S. Military Academy at West Point and both Black Hawk pilots, were very close.) "Kevin, why are your AHs dropping hand grenades on these guys?" Instead of answering, Mangum, known as "the Bulldog," turned to Schiller, who had recently given up command of B Company, and asked him the same question. "I guess that's because they're out of .50 cal and rocket," Schiller replied. The answer did little to mollify Dailey and Mangum, who displayed "huge angst" over the AH-6 pilots' decision to press home their attack with the only weapons remaining at their disposal, said a source in the JOC.

Back on the "wagon wheel," the pilots were having fun. The Taliban on the ground were focused only on survival, not firing back at their unseen tormentors. "They were just trying to get the hell out of there," said

Linfoot. "They couldn't see us. They heard the AHs and shooting but they had no idea what was going on. . . . We were giggling our asses off."

After Linfoot had seen several Taliban drop, and with secondary explosions from the flatbed truck still illuminating the desert, the crews decided to return to the FARP. They were still due to make one more sortie. As the FARP team gassed up and rearmed the helicopters, Linfoot grabbed an armament soldier. "Bring me more M4 magazines and grenades because we're all out," he said. The soldier gave him a *What the hell are you guys getting into out there?* look, then ran off, returning with every magazine he could scrounge.

On their second turn, the teams flew along a road that ran south from Highway 1 to Lashkar Gah, the capital of Helmand province. In the lead aircraft Linfoot was at the controls and Meehan was pointing out the airspeed, saying, "Make sure you keep it above 60 knots," which Little Bird pilots regarded as their magic number because not only did the helicopter behave more efficiently above that speed, but it made it harder for someone on the ground to identify and fire at the aircraft's location from the sound alone. "This is bullshit, there's nothing out here," Linfoot had just told Meehan when the cockpit lit up as tracers from another 23mm antiaircraft gun flashed underneath the aircraft. "I could hear and feel the gun going off right next to us, just loud," Linfoot recalled. "Couldn't tell what was going on, I just knew somebody was shooting at us. I couldn't tell where from but they were right on us." Linfoot continued straight for a split second, but Hosey in the Dash-2 had seen the weapon. "Break right, break right," came his voice over the radio.

The Little Birds broke right, wheeled around, went into the bump and came hard at the gun, which was next to a mud building and represented a deadly threat. As they attacked with rockets and .50 cal, the pilots could see several Taliban around the gun, all firing back at them. More than one rocket-propelled grenade streaked past the AH-6s. The Little Birds made three or four turns flying and firing into the hail of bullets and RPGs before deciding discretion was the better part of valor in this instance. The team withdrew and contacted an AC-130 gunship in the area. They gave the gunship crew the grid and talked them onto the target, which the AC-130 obliterated with its 105mm howitzer. The Little Birds returned to the forward arming and refueling point, where the brownout conditions were almost as bad as at Bastogne, and the crews loaded the helicopters onto the Talons for the flight to Masirah.[13]

While the AH-6s had been out hunting, the Rangers, from A Company, 3rd Battalion, patrolled for several hours to make sure no Taliban forces were reacting to their presence. They then drove across the desert to check another proposed landing strip, named Bulge. The Rangers established 360-degree security around Bulge as the 24th STS airmen assessed the suitability of the site. The airmen decided Bulge could also handle MC-130s, and was not nearly as dusty as Bastogne and Anzio. The Rangers moved the vehicles to a hide site from which they could observe the landing strip, covered them with camouflage netting, brushed away their tracks, established a watch, and awaited the morning.

The next day, November 18, TF Sword directed the Rangers to prepare for helicopter operations from Bulge that night. Once darkness fell, the Rangers secured the landing strip while the special tactics airmen laid infrared landing lights along the runway. At 8:30 P.M., two Combat Talons landed with the same cargo of Little Birds, FARP, and personnel as at Bastogne and Anzio, along with a resupply package for the task force holding Bulge. Again, the Little Birds were airborne within minutes, this time without any brownout drama.

Rainier's team was the busier that night, hitting several fuel trucks and military vehicles along Highway 1, while Meehan's team took some small arms fire from a compound they then attacked. After two sorties, the AH-6s were loaded back onto the Combat Talons, which had returned from an aerial refueling, and flew off into the night. The Rangers and airmen collected the landing lights, removed any evidence of U.S. forces' presence, and settled in for the night at the hide site, sending out dismounted patrols.

The next night saw a repeat performance, the only difference being the routes flown by the Little Birds and the fact that the Rangers put their observation posts "farther out on higher ground to provide better early warning," according to the official history. There was also a new target category. On previous missions, the AH-6 pilots had understood their rules of engagement to allow them to engage any military equipment or anyone shooting at them. For this mission, the TF Brown intelligence director told them that any tank or vehicle that could hold liquid was fair game. With that in mind, they destroyed fuel tanks at an airfield near Lashkar Gah as well as a fuel truck in the area. Once the Little Birds returned from their second turn, the Combat Talons started landing at 1:15 A.M. The helicopters and FARP were taken out first, with the last Talon lifting off with the final load of Rangers and vehicles at 2:51 A.M.[14]

Not to be outdone, the MH-6 assault variants of the Little Bird also saw action that week, conducting a series of what a pilot called "hide site operations" with Delta's B Squadron. As with the Pinzgauers, the Little Birds would arrive with aircrews and Delta operators aboard Combat Talons that landed at desert landing strips—often the same strips used for the AH-6 missions. Between the Pinzgauers and the Little Birds, a JSOC staff officer estimated that Delta conducted four to six "search and destroy" missions.

The task force took no fatal casualties, but at least one B Squadron operation took a nasty turn when an MH-6 bringing a team of operators back to the desert landing strip browned out and rolled over. "A guy got his leg caught underneath the skid, it was kind of ugly," said the staff officer. "Nobody died but there were some pretty serious injuries." It could have been even worse, but for a stroke of luck. The pilot in command of the MH-6 was a maintenance test pilot and for no good reason at all had his maintenance test pilot checklist—"which is pretty thick," as another Little Bird pilot put it—on the helicopter. "In the crash sequence, somehow that checklist became dislodged from the cockpit and actually ended up on the ground, between the ground and the skid, which prevented the skid from taking the guy's leg off," the Little Bird pilot said.[15]

Those mid-November missions represented the only action the Little Birds would see in Afghanistan for many years. The men who flew them would participate in hundreds of other perilous missions in Iraq during the coming decade of war, and some would pay a high price for the privilege of doing so, but they considered those first missions unique because of the autonomy the crews enjoyed, and the knowledge that they were very much alone above the Afghan desert.[16] Comparing the Little Bird actions in November to later operations, Rainier described them simply as "the most dangerous mission that we did."

11

Precious Cargo

Operation Relentless Strike was over, and so was Sword's campaign in southern Afghanistan. Supported by Special Forces and the CIA, the Northern Alliance had taken Kabul without a fight November 14. But the war was far from finished. The Taliban retreated southwest to Kandahar as Al Qaeda's leaders and thousands of troops headed south and east toward mountain redoubts. "The south was still wide open," said a JSOC staffer.

That was the situation when, on November 17, with Sword's desert landing strip operations in full swing, Dailey gathered his senior commanders and staff in Masirah in his Spartan living quarters to make a major announcement. "We are not leaving Afghanistan," he said. Instead, he told them, TF Sword had a new mission: hunting bin Laden and Mullah Omar. More than two months since September 11, JSOC finally had the strategic mission for which the operators had been hankering. Thus began the man-hunting campaigns that would define JSOC for the decade to come. At a minimum, this would require an expansion of the advance force operations presence in Afghanistan, he said. But it would also spell the end for Sword's campaign around Kandahar. The JSOC commander then outlined three potential courses of action for tailoring the force that would deploy to Afghanistan.

The light option would be two AFO elements—designated North and South—plus a small direct action force made up of nothing larger than troop-size elements. The medium option would involve squadron-size assault task forces as well as a special operations command and control element to liaise with conventional U.S. military headquarters in Afghanistan. (The light and medium options would also need a TF Brown contribution.) The heavy option would add a Ranger company, the Sword headquarters, and a larger TF Brown contingent. Dailey made it clear he opposed the heavy option, as he was concerned that it would lead to "mission creep." To nobody's great surprise, he opted for the middle course. Although Sword would now establish a presence at Bagram, as others had been urging for weeks, Dailey told his audience he had no intention of moving the JOC to Afghanistan anytime soon, and planned to run JSOC's war in Afghanistan from Masirah for months to come. He also stressed the need to maintain the command's readiness system, called the Joint Operations Readiness and Training System (JORTS), in which units were on a cycle of individual training, unit training, alert, deployment, and reconstitution. "They didn't want to mess up the JORTS cycle," said a source who attended the meeting.[1] This led some in the task force to conclude that Dailey was prioritizing a peacetime training cycle over wartime requirements.

War in southern and eastern Afghanistan, where Pashtuns were the dominant ethnic group, presented the United States with different challenges than those it confronted in the north, where the Northern Alliance represented a ready-made military partner. Northern Alliance leaders had little stomach for a war in the Pashtun heartland, whence the Taliban drew their strength. The Alliance warlords were more concerned with establishing themselves in Kabul. To defeat the Taliban on their home ground, the United States would need Pashtun allies.

As in the north, the CIA took the lead in deciding which figures to work with and promote in the Pashtun regions. In the case of one Pashtun leader in particular, the Agency's decisions were to have far-reaching ramifications for Afghanistan, the U.S. war effort, and JSOC.

In early November, Agency officials came to Jim Reese, JSOC's representative at Langley, with an urgent request. An important Agency source was in trouble in Afghanistan and needed to be pulled out fast. "Can you support us with helicopters?" they asked. After JSOC's air planners on Masirah told Reese no aircraft were available, he went over their heads to Dailey. "This is an opportunity for us, right here, to establish who we are, how fast we can move, how agile we are, and support the CIA in what they see as a critical task," Reese told the JSOC commander. "We have to bring our elements of critical national power at JSOC to bear to help them. Right now that's Task Force 160." Dailey needed no more convincing. "Jim, roger that, execute, and I'll put the execute order out," he said.[2]

When Reese told Cofer Black, the Counterterrorist Center director beamed.[3] An hour later, Black informed George Tenet at the CIA director's daily 5 P.M. staff meeting. "It was almost like the first string quarterback had run [back onto the field] out of the locker room after being hurt, because they were struggling how to figure this out," said a source in the meeting. "I remember Cofer telling Tenet, 'JSOC is going to bring our guys [out] and they're going to support us.' You could see everyone just going, 'Yes!'"

JSOC's willingness to fly to the rescue of the CIA source "was a big deal," Crumpton said, adding that the Agency's Mi-17 helicopters ("all two of them") were not available for the mission. "It was absolutely a big deal."

On November 3[4] two Black Hawks[5] carrying heavily armed Team 6 operators and a bearded case officer[6] nicknamed "Spider" from the Ground Branch of the CIA's Special Activities Division[7] slipped into Afghan airspace, flying fast from the *Kitty Hawk* straight for the central province of Uruzgan. There, anxiously awaiting them, were Spider's Afghan source and a small group of supporters. Since October 8, when the source and three companions had crossed from Pakistan into Afghanistan on two motorbikes, they had been trying to rally Pashtun tribesmen against the Taliban. It was a dangerous mission.[8] The Taliban had captured and executed renowned Pashtun mujahideen commander Abdul Haq that month for doing the same thing.[9] In fact CIA officials deemed the quartet's project so risky they decided not to send their own people in with the Afghans. Instead they gave their source what Crumpton described as "a sack of money" and a satellite phone so he could at least keep in touch with Spider. Four weeks later the source used that phone to call for help as the Taliban who'd been hounding his tiny band through southern Afghanistan finally cornered them in the mountains of Uruzgan.[10]

Overwatched by two direct action penetrators and an ISR aircraft beaming pictures back to Masirah, the helicopters neared the valley where the source was holed up. Spotting the prearranged signal of four fires marking the corners of their landing zone, the Chinooks landed and the Afghans climbed aboard, led by a distinguished-looking forty-three-year-old man with a neatly trimmed salt-and-pepper beard and a prematurely bald scalp under his turban.[11] The Night Stalker pilots took off again heading for Pakistan, where they landed at Jacobabad, now partially occupied by U.S. forces.[12] There would be other close calls for the source, but for now he was safe. The CIA breathed a collective sigh of relief, for the Afghan with the regal features in the back of the helicopter was no run-of-the-mill source, nor was he another power-hungry warlord. No, Spider's source was the CIA's best hope for the future of Afghanistan. His name was Hamid Karzai.

When asked how long the CIA had had Karzai on its payroll, Crumpton demurred. "I can't address that," he said. "I can confirm that we gave him money when he infiltrated back into Afghanistan on the motorbike."

But Karzai had been a known quantity to the Agency and other Afghanistan watchers going back to the 1980s, when he was an idealistic aide to Sibghatullah Mojaddedi, leader of a moderate Afghan resistance group in the Pakistani frontier city of Peshawar.[13] In the intervening years, his stature had grown. Crumpton recalled meeting with "some of our Afghan allies . . . including Massoud" in 2000. "Say the Taliban was gone," Crumpton asked the battle-hardened Northern Alliance leaders, "who could be a leader of Afghanistan?" Their answer was unanimous. "They all said 'Karzai,'" Crumpton said. "There really was not much discussion of anybody else. So we knew early on that he was really the only—imperfect though he may have been—really the only choice for attempting to unify the Afghan tribes and the Afghan ethnic [groups]."

In this context it's easy to see why the CIA considered Karzai's rescue so crucial, and why the United States was determined to take Karzai back into Afghanistan, this time with more support. Again, the Agency turned to JSOC to make it happen.

On November 14, the same day the Northern Alliance entered Kabul in force, TF Brown Black Hawks flew Karzai and Spider back into Afghanistan.[14] The two men were a study in contrasts. In his mid-forties with fair hair and a Fu Manchu mustache, the skinny, fit Spider was an affable former Marine officer and one of Ground Branch's most seasoned operatives. He was well known to JSOC operators from time spent together in Somalia and the Balkans.[15] At forty-three, the mild-mannered Karzai was of a similar age, but despite his association with the more royalist mujahideen elements during the Soviet war of the 1980s, he had no background as a warrior. The two had been working together for less than six months,[16] but Spider had already succeeded in forging a bond with the Afghan. It was Spider, according to CIA director George Tenet, whom Karzai had called when things looked grim in Uruzgan and who immediately contacted CIA headquarters to argue that "Karzai represented the only credible opposition leader identified in the south" and his "survival . . . was critical to maintaining the momentum for the southern uprising."[17] "Even then, he was the guy Karzai totally trusted," said a Delta source. "The whole Karzai thing was about a personal relationship between those two that then went on for many, many years afterwards. But he wouldn't have done any of that if it weren't for Spider."

(A Special Forces source on the Karzai mission disputed this version of events. To this source, it appeared Spider was not keen on going into Afghanistan with Karzai, and the sole reason the Agency staked its claim with Karzai was he was their only Pashtun option after Abdul Haq's death.)

Also on the flight of five Black Hawks escorted by two DAPs were nine members of a Special Forces A-team, about seven CIA operatives and three TF Sword personnel—two Delta operators and an Air Force combat controller. The Sword trio had a vague mission and were a controversial last-minute addition to the passenger list. Spider told Captain Jason Amerine, the A-team leader, that they were there at Task Force Sword's insistence to spot "emerging" Al Qaeda targets. "Sword isn't going to let us fly without them," Spider said. But one of the operators told Amerine that their inclusion had been Spider's idea. Either way, the helicopters were already maxed out for weight, so the Delta operators' sudden arrival meant Amerine had to tell two of his men they were being left behind for now, with Spider leaving one of his team. The rejiggered group climbed aboard two Air Force special operations MH-53 Pave Low helicopters at Jacobabad for a late afternoon flight to a small desert airstrip that Sword had taken over close to the Afghan border. There, with Rangers guarding the perimeter, they waited until sundown, when the telltale beat of rotor blades told them the Night Stalkers were approaching. After loading their gear onto the Black Hawks, the motley group flew off, protected by jets high in the sky as well as by the 160th's constant ally—the all-enveloping darkness.[18]

⁂

As the combined CIA and special ops contingent escorted Karzai into southern Afghanistan, another drama that had demanded much of Sword's attention was finally drawing to a conclusion.

On August 3, the Taliban had arrested two American women—Dayna Curry, thirty, and Heather Mercer, twenty-four—working in Kabul for

Shelter Now International, a Christian aid organization. Within a couple of days, the Taliban had taken six other Westerners on the organization's Kabul staff into custody. The Taliban put all eight in a Kabul prison and threatened to try them for proselytizing. They faced possible death sentences if convicted. International efforts to negotiate their release came to naught.

After September 11, as it became clear the United States was going to war in Afghanistan, concern for the prisoners mounted.[19] The first CIA team into Afghanistan worked closely with the Northern Alliance intelligence arm to ascertain the details of their imprisonment. The Agency hoped to bribe Taliban officials into releasing them. One plan involved paying a senior Taliban official $4 million to spirit the eight Westerners out of Kabul and up to the Northern Alliance. Another would have the Agency pay eight prison guards $1 million each and move their families to the Panjshir Valley prior to the operation, in which the guards would move the prisoners to a prearranged helicopter pickup zone near Kabul. To Gary Schroen, the senior CIA man on the ground in Afghanistan, neither plan seemed realistic.[20] It was starting to look like U.S. forces would have to mount a unilateral rescue operation.

As the military's go-to force for hostage rescue, JSOC—and Delta in particular—was monitoring events closely. Just after midnight on October 26, three Delta operators arrived by helicopter in northern Afghanistan to work with the CIA on putting a rescue plan together.[21] Schroen was underwhelmed by his first encounter with the operators: "They were all younger than the other teams' Special Forces soldiers we had met so far, and none of them had any real idea of the situation on the ground in Afghanistan."[22] (Schroen's assessment of their ages seems a little off. One of the operators was Major Jim Reese, the experienced officer on a week's break from duty at Langley. Another was Sergeant Major Manny Pardal, described by a JSOC staff officer as "a very, very sharp guy," who had enlisted in the Army in 1984, so must have been at least in his midthirties. He was assigned to Delta's Operational Support Troop.)[23] After being thoroughly briefed by the CIA, the trio visited the front lines to gauge the challenges they would face smuggling the prisoners—now viewed as hostages by the Americans—to safety.[24]

As the three operators considered their options, they were in frequent communication with A Squadron, which, having assumed the Aztec role from B Squadron, was still at Bragg, ready to be brought forward if needed for a rescue mission. The operators in Afghanistan sent back Predator imagery of the routes to and from the prison. The Taliban controlled all roads with mobile checkpoints. Noting that the only forces to enjoy freedom of movement after dark in Kabul were small Taliban and Al Qaeda elements in Toyota pickup trucks, Delta planners decided to emulate their foes and bought a dozen Toyota pickups. The unit's mechanics set to work modifying the vehicles to fit a dozen specific mission parameters while others in Delta acquired turbans and other Afghan and Arab clothing items with which operators might disguise themselves.

To convince the powers-that-be in Delta and JSOC that the mission was viable, A Squadron operators found a photo of Taliban fighters in a pickup, then juxtaposed it on a PowerPoint slide with a photo of a Delta assault team in one of the new Toyotas wearing similar clothes and carrying AK-series assault rifles and RPGs. They added a caption that read, "At less than 10 percent illumination, what does the enemy actually see?" and sent the slide to Blaber, the Delta operations officer, in Masirah. He liked the concept and took it to JSOC headquarters. "A few hours later we had approval," wrote Greer, whose troop, A1, was at the heart of the planning.

The rest of the rescue mission task force comprised Delta's A3 troop and Team 6's Gold Team, which had the Trident role at the time. Together these elements included about fifty to sixty operators. They planned to infiltrate Kabul at night by pretending to be an Al Qaeda convoy. "We had no illusions of being able to pass any close inspection or talk ourselves past a sentry, but all we needed was just to avoid being recognized at a distance," wrote Greer. "If our ploy worked, we would continue to roll toward the hostage location. If not, we would eliminate the guards with our suppressed weapons to keep things quiet from neighborhood ears. We did not want a Mogadishu-like confrontation."[25]

Schroen's CIA team had meanwhile interviewed the father and uncle of a young male Afghan Shelter Now employee whom the Taliban had incarcerated at the same prison as the Westerners. The Taliban allowed the two men weekly visits to meet their relatives. The men were able to provide the Agency with detailed descriptions of the jail's interior and exterior layouts.[26] Armed with this information, Delta's engineers built a mock-up of the prison at Bragg, where the rescue force conducted dozens of assault rehearsals using both nonlethal training ammunition and live rounds.

Greer was guardedly optimistic about Delta's chances of success.[27] But Schroen was distinctly unimpressed when briefed by the operators at his headquarters. According to Schroen's account, the plan involved a Delta convoy driving from Northern Alliance lines to Kabul, "fighting their way through Taliban defensive positions and checkpoints" to the prison, freeing the hostages, and then driving back out of the city to be picked up by "military helicopters." But a Delta source familiar with the plan said Schroen did not describe it accurately. Rather than risk the complicated passage of lines necessary if they drove down from the north, the operators would fly with their civilian pickup trucks on about six Combat Talons into a remote landing strip to the south of the capital at night. Then, under the cover of darkness, they'd drive to Kabul that same night and free the hostages, putting them on MH-6 Little Birds that would fly them north to safety. Delta often rehearsed hostage rescues with Little Birds. Standard practice was to jam the hostage in the tight space behind the pilots' seats with at least one operator sitting on each pod for protection.

Also unmentioned by Schroen, the plan called for most of the assault force to remain behind in Kabul, incognito. The Delta operators who had designed and rehearsed the mission thought the plan was more elegant than Schroen did. They were confident it would work. The only reason they never got the green light to execute the plan was because the Taliban moved the hostages, one said. But Schroen insisted that the operators attached to his team were not proud of the plan. "I think even they realized the plan was both impossible and lame," he wrote. "We never heard any more from the three Delta operators on rescue plans."[28]

Nonetheless, the trio stuck around while the CIA team, now working under Gary Berntsen, who had replaced Schroen as the senior Agency representative in-country November 4, continued refining its own plan to free the Shelter Now prisoners. "We were trying to basically suborn the prison commander to get them out," Crumpton said. "That didn't work." Sword personnel in Masirah and on the *Kitty Hawk* took over the military side of planning a rescue, with the Team 6 element on the carrier as the main ground force. They named it Angry Talon. But a hesitant chain of command held them back. The task force had figured out the hostages' new location, "but nobody wanted to fly into Kabul with three Chinooks, in the middle of a city that's an unknown threat," said a Sword planner. "We knew they were there and we had a plan to go in there, but no one [said] 'Let's go to the prison,' because we didn't think we had quite the right assets to go after it with helicopters." After drawing up the plan in late October, the staff on the *Kitty Hawk* put it aside, waiting for even better actionable intelligence. Working through various Northern Alliance and Taliban intermediaries, the Americans were still able to keep close tabs on the location of the hostages, who were being moved between two different prisons in Kabul. But the Taliban's sudden evacuation of Kabul beginning November 12 rendered any plan centered on the city moot.[29]

That evening, the Taliban bundled the eight prisoners into a truck and drove them west out of Kabul as Northern Alliance advance elements entered the city. Their captors forced the hostages to spend the night in a frigid shipping container before driving them on to a small jail in Ghazni, seventy-five miles southwest of the capital.[30] All the way, the CIA had a source on their tail, using a mobile phone to update his Agency handlers.[31] That source was in Ghazni on November 13 when the hostages' nightmare finally came to an end with a furious pounding on the door of the room where they were being held. It burst open and there stood "a scruffy, beardless man in ragtag clothing" with a rifle in his hand and ammunition belts across his chest. "Aaazaad! Aaazaad!" he shouted. "You're free! You're free!" The Taliban had fled.

Anti-Taliban locals cared for the hostages over the next twenty-four hours, while their leader, Georg Taubman, found a satellite phone and contacted the U.S. embassy in Islamabad,[32] setting the wheels in motion in Masirah and on the *Kitty Hawk*. Task Force Sword prepared to execute Operation Angry Talon. The actionable intelligence for which they had been waiting was now coming in. On the morning of November 14 on Masirah and the *Kitty Hawk,* staffs and operators who, in keeping with Sword's reverse cycle, had gone to sleep just a couple of hours earlier, were awoken and sprang into action. But the mission would stretch the task force. With the Karzai infil also slated for that evening, Sword would be conducting two national-level missions into Afghanistan using Team 6 and Brown assets during the same period of darkness.

In mid-afternoon, three Chinooks took off from the *Kitty Hawk,* headed for Pakistan. They were starting on one of the farthest helicopter missions ever flown. The lengthy high-altitude flight ahead limited each helicopter to 5,000 pounds of cargo, or fifteen combat-loaded SEALs. Because one aircraft was "the flying spare," included in case one of the others was shot down or suffered a mechanical emergency, that meant a total of thirty Team 6 operators for the mission. Although the immediate threat to the hostages had lessened, the SEALs were flying into an anarchic situation with very little understanding of what was happening on the ground. They needed to be ready for anything.

After a three-hour flight the Chinooks landed at Jacobabad, where a smoky haze covered the airfield. Shortly thereafter, two MC-130s from Masirah landed and married up with the Chinooks. They were the refueling aircraft for the mission and had also brought along Schiller. As Angry Talon's air mission commander (Mangum was performing the same role for the Karzai infiltration) he jumped aboard the Chinook piloted by blond, barrel-chested CW3 Dean "Beef" Brown, flight lead for the mission.

After coordinating with the Air Force combat search and rescue crews at Jacobabad, the Chinooks and the MC-130s took off as darkness fell, a five-hour flight ahead of them. Ghazni lay about 360 miles due north of Jacobabad, but in order to minimize time in Afghan airspace, Beef Brown plotted a route that had the helicopters fly northeast, parallel to the Indus River, before doing an aerial refuel and turning north-northwest through the Sulaiman Mountains, steadily climbing to an altitude above 11,000 feet. It would be one of the longest helicopter missions ever flown. An icy draft blew through the helicopters, the doors of which were fitted with miniguns and therefore always open. As the temperature plummeted to near freezing, air crewmen shivered, wishing they'd brought warmer clothes than their flight suits, jackets, and gloves—gear that had seemed excessive when boarding the aircraft in the 90-degree-plus heat of the Masirah midday sun. The radios were silent but for the trailing Chinook's calls every five minutes letting Brown know the flight was still intact.

Flying west-northwest, the Chinooks traversed the Pakistani tribal areas and crossed into Afghanistan. Soon they began losing altitude as they identified the wide valley in which Ghazni sat. The JOC in Masirah called to let the crews know the plan for the linkup with the hostages and their benefactors was still on track. Locating the hostages promised to be the biggest challenge. The aircrews had no way of communicating directly with the hostages or the CIA source with them. Everything had to be passed through Masirah. Prior to departure, Schiller had arranged with the CIA representative in the JOC to have the hostages wait on a main road close to a soccer field on the town's southern edge. They were to light a fire as a means of signaling their location to the helicopters. Now the JOC was telling him the fire would be lit fifteen minutes before the helicopters were due to touch down. A few minutes later the JOC called back to say the CIA source with the hostages had been in touch: he was driving south with them in his vehicle and would be ready for pickup in twenty minutes.[33]

But this gave the rescue force a misleading impression that the plan was going smoothly, when in fact the situation on the ground was chaotic. The hostages were under extraordinary stress as Taubman coordinated the rescue with the Islamabad embassy while negotiating with obstinate local commanders to take the Shelter Now personnel to the pickup zone. For a while it seemed the locals would not allow the hostages to leave the compound in which they'd been held. But at the eleventh hour, with the embassy insisting the helicopters were already en route and it was imperative the mission take place that night, the local leaders relented and escorted the eight foreigners to the pickup zone (PZ).[34]

A Predator was buzzing over Ghazni, relaying images back to Masirah. The helicopters had no access to its transmissions, so staffers passed directions to them based on what they were seeing on the screen in the JOC. But the Predator feed to Masirah suffered from a lengthy delay. Added to the satellite radio delay of the staffer in the JOC describing what he was seeing to the aircrews, the information being passed to the pilots—"Turn left now!" "You're right above the PZ!"—was about thirty seconds late and therefore useless. After several passes 200 feet over the pickup zone with no sign of a fire surrounded by nine or more people, the frustrated flight lead crew turned the satellite radio off. There was still no sight of the hostages. Tension was building on the helicopters. Their fuel levels allowed only thirty minutes to locate the hostages, pick them up, and take off. Then they faced an hour-long flight in order to make an urgent midair appointment with an MC-130 just east of the Pakistan border. With Taliban still marauding through Ghazni, the risk to the helicopters grew with every passing minute. Brown ordered his trail aircraft to fly an orbit a couple of miles to the west, which reduced the Chinooks' signature over the town and put a helicopter in an overwatch position with a wider field of view.

The tactic appeared to have worked when Chalk 2's pilot, CW3 Frank Mancuso, spoke up. "I have a vehicle moving south on the main road, twelve o'clock, one mile," he announced. "It appears to have about ten people in the back of the truck—that must be our group." Ordering Mancuso to stay overhead, Brown landed ahead of the moving vehicle. The SEALs stormed off and set up a roadblock. When the truck came to a stop, there was disappointment and knife-edge tension: it contained only armed Afghan men. They claimed to be anti-Taliban fighters when questioned by Commander Mitch Bradley, Team 6's Blue Team commander, adding "We love America!" repeatedly for good measure. The SEALs assumed they were lying and were actually Taliban fighters, but let them go and quickly reboarded the helicopter.

The Chinook took off. The helicopters now had less than ten minutes before they would have to leave in order to make their refueling rendezvous. Wracking their brains trying to figure out how to locate their "precious cargo," the Night Stalkers scanned the ground for the fire that was supposed to serve as a beacon. But the planners had not accounted for the fact that on a cold night in Afghanistan many fires would be visible, lit by locals for light and warmth. Telling one from the others seemed an impossible task.[35]

The hostages had lit none of those fires, however. Somehow the word to build one never reached them. "We knew the helicopters were not looking for a fire," Curry and Mercer said somewhat incongruously in their written account of the episode. Instead, they were sitting on the PZ straining their ears for the sound of helicopters and getting increasingly desperate. After what seemed an eternity but was actually about fifteen minutes, the hulking shapes of two twin-rotor aircraft appeared overhead, circling the PZ and twice making a low-level sweep directly over them before flying off a little. Frantic, the women serendipitously took it upon themselves to light a fire using their headscarves as fuel, hoping to draw the aircrews' attention to themselves, apparently ignorant that this was the plan all along. The Afghans with them threw planks onto the blaze. The detainees were on the verge of giving up when the helicopters returned, hovering directly overhead, before maddeningly flying away again.[36]

As Brown flew over the town's mud houses, investigating as many of the fires as possible in the hope of some form of recognition, Mancuso came up on the net. "I have a fire on the main road down the street from the soccer field," he said. "They appear to have about ten people huddled around it. Two appear to have burkas as well." Brown landed in the soccer "field," which was nothing but dirt, causing a massive brownout that briefly disoriented the SEALs as they left the helicopter. An aviator who had noted the hostages' location jumped off the bird and grabbed the SEAL commander by the shoulder. "Follow me!" he yelled, and led the SEALs to the corner of a wall and pointed down the street to the group gathered around the fire. The lead SEAL gave him a thumbs-up, then quickly briefed his men before they advanced toward the anxious figures.[37]

Twenty agonizing minutes after the helicopters had initially flown away, several dark shapes appeared out of the darkness and approached the hostages. "Covered in gear, they looked like Martians," recalled Heather Mercer. "Are you the detainees?" yelled a SEAL. "Listen and do exactly what we say!"[38]

The aircrew sat and waited. Even hostage rescues in which no bullets are fired can be time-consuming affairs. It wasn't just a case of grabbing the people to be rescued and throwing them on the aircraft. "That only happens in the movies," said a JSOC source. The SEALs needed to positively identify the detainees by comparing them to photographs and to search them (in case their captors had hidden explosives on them). Already at "bingo" fuel—the point at which it was essential to depart in order to make the refueling rendezvous in Pakistan—Beef Brown called the MC-130 pilot and persuaded him to move the refueling point into Afghan airspace, reducing the time the Chinooks would need to fly there. That move was technically against orders, so nobody coordinated it with the JOC, in case someone on the Sword staff tried to overrule it.

In less than fifteen minutes, the SEALs returned with all eight hostages. They lifted off, and the three helicopters made a beeline south, "running on fumes," as a TF Sword source put it, as the MC-130 flew as fast as it could toward them. The rendezvous came off perfectly and the Chinooks made the three-hour flight to Jacobabad, where they landed at dawn, pulling up to the back of another MC-130 with a medical team on board in case any hostage needed immediate medical care.[39] For the Shelter Now personnel there followed reunions with their families and, in the case of Curry and Mercer, a phone call from President Bush.[40] For Task Force Sword, it was mission complete.

It could be argued that as far as hostage rescues go, Angry Talon was almost a nonevent. There was no shooting and by the time the rescue occurred, the Shelter Now personnel weren't even prisoners. That didn't stop Dailey transmitting a "Congrats to the Blue shooters" message across the command, which provoked scorn among some Delta operators.[41] "There was no rescue," said one. "It was more like picking up a downed pilot in the middle of nowhere." Of course, it could also be argued that a rescue mission in which no bullets were fired represented the most elegant solution to the crisis. The onset of war had done little to diminish the rivalry between Team 6 and Delta, which would reassert itself—at times with venom—over the years ahead.

✳

At this early stage of what President Bush was already calling the "war on terror," JSOC had not fully come to terms with the fact that its world had changed permanently. The command was "designed to do in-and-out operations, not sustained combat," and the Sword JOC was therefore structured and manned for sprints, rather than marathons, said a retired special operations officer. On reverse cycle since early October, the staff on Masirah was under tremendous strain. "We worked for eighteen hours, nineteen hours a day and then crashed when daylight hit," he said.

Dailey wanted to rest his troops. The arrival off Pakistan of the Marines' Task Force 58 offered him a chance to do so. "By the end of the month, the level of lunar illumination would exceed the special operations forces' comfort zone, presenting an opportunity for an operational pause between 20 November and 8 December," according to an official Marine history. On November 25, five weeks after the Rangers seized Objective Rhino, Task Force 58 flew in to the airstrip intending to continue the fight in southern Afghanistan as, in the Marine history's words, "Task Force Sword prepared to withdraw from the battlefield."[42] But a source in Masirah said the pause had more to do with Sword's new orders to hunt for bin Laden and Mullah Omar than it did with the lunar cycle. Nonetheless, the decision to curtail Sword's campaign in the south deeply frustrated the operators creating havoc in the deserts and hills surrounding Kandahar. "Just as we were learning everything and getting more and more confident/brazen in our ability to go right up into Kandahar, we pulled the plug on it," said a Delta source. "We were like, 'operational pause'? Why would we pause right now? It's not like this is so complex we need a break so we can wrap our heads around it."

Three Sword operators who weren't withdrawing from the battlefield were the trio who had accompanied Karzai, Spider, Amerine, and their men into Uruzgan the night of November 14. They included two seasoned

OST operators: Sergeants Major Morgan Darwin and Mike "Flash" Johnston. While many of their Delta colleagues had yet to hear a shot fired in anger since September 11, these three had seen more than their fair share of action during their first few days in-country. Barely forty-eight hours after arriving, the tiny band of U.S. fighters—supported by a withering aerial barrage—had destroyed a Taliban convoy racing to re-take Tarin Kowt, Uruzgan's small capital.[43] (Having come down with a nasty case of dysentery, Darwin rode in the convoy to Tarin Kowt "kit-ted out for combat while hooked to an IV," according to one account.)[44] From there the Americans and Karzai's band of fewer than 200 lightly armed and even more lightly trained Pashtun irregulars drove south to Shawali Kowt, ten miles from the center of Kandahar city on the north bank of the Arghandab River. There, the combined force of U.S. special operators, CIA operatives, and Karzai's Pashtuns fought a back-and-forth battle with the Taliban for control of the only bridge across the river for miles in either direction.[45] To the surprise of Amerine's team, who had now been joined by a battalion headquarters element, in the middle of the fight, on the night of December 4–5, TF Sword delivered Delta's A2 Troop and three Pinzgauers via MH-47 to give the Karzai force more firepower and mobility.[46]

Later that day, the Delta operators were lucky to survive a tragedy that almost changed Afghanistan's history. An airman attached to the Spe-cial Forces battalion headquarters mistakenly called in a bomb on his own position. Three SF soldiers and at least twenty Afghans died in the acci-dent, with many others seriously injured. In the aftermath of the attack, the Delta operators—all of whom had extensive medical training—were invaluable in tending to the wounded and securing the site's perimeter. Karzai was in a building 100 meters from the blast and emerged with only a small cut on his face from flying glass. (Spider had dived on him to shield him when the bomb hit.) About fifteen minutes after the ex-plosion, Karzai received a call on his satellite phone from a BBC reporter telling him a conference of Afghan factions in Bonn arranged by the United States had named him head of the interim Afghan government.

Despite the setback, the Taliban resistance at Shawali Kowt evapo-rated. Two days later, Karzai, whose reputation among Pashtuns had been growing rapidly since the Tarin Kowt battle, entered Kandahar in tri-umph.[47] The last major city in Afghanistan—and the one that was the Taliban's power base—had fallen. Unnoticed by the news media, Delta's

A2 troop had remained with their Pinzgauers in southern Afghanistan. When Mattis's Marines arrived at Kandahar airfield on December 14,[48] the Delta operators "met them, turned the key over, and took off," said a JSOC staff officer.

✻

Up in Kabul, things had also been moving fast. After the successful Shelter Now hostage rescue removed their original raison d'être in Afghanistan, two of the original three Delta operators who arrived October 26 to work with the CIA had been attached to an Agency team that Berntsen sent to Jalalabad in pursuit of Al Qaeda forces fleeing east. In their place, Berntsen wrote, Central Command deployed another small "JSOC advance team" to work with Berntsen and "to prepare the ground for a large JSOC contingent to follow"[49]—a classic AFO mission.

The new team's leader was Lieutenant Colonel Mark Erwin, the wiry, brown-haired commander of Delta's Operational Support Troop.[50] Erwin had been a star NCAA Division I soccer player for his alma mater, Wake Forest University in Winston-Salem, North Carolina, leading the nation in scoring in 1983. After entering the Army in 1984 as an infantry officer,[51] Erwin had been selected for Delta. But after commanding a B Squadron troop his career had stalled, at least temporarily. He had been passed over for squadron command by the special mission unit board, while the regular Army had not selected him to command a maneuver battalion. Instead the Army had selected Erwin for a less prestigious basic training battalion command at Fort Jackson, South Carolina, said two Delta sources. Rather than lose Erwin from Delta, unit commander Jim Schwitters and his deputy, Colonel Ron Russell, gave him command of the Operational Support Troop in order to evaluate him and then, based on his performance, put him back in front of the special mission unit board, the source said. That job found him seated beside Berntsen on the evening of November 20, driving the forty miles north from Kabul to Bagram air base in a new blue Ford pickup flown in for Erwin and his three-man team. (The ruined base, fought over for years by the Taliban and the Northern Alliance, had been in American hands since October 21.) As they motored carefully past the rusted hulks of Soviet tanks, Erwin told his Agency counterpart about his soccer background. Berntsen was suitably impressed by Erwin, past and present: "He was now in his late thirties and hard as nails."[52]

There had been a few bumps in the road, but JSOC and the CIA were demonstrating an ability to work well together downrange. Sources in both organizations said the Karzai missions exemplified the benefits to be gained from a close—some would say symbiotic—relationship between the Agency and the military's most elite special operations units. At the core were personal links forged in the Balkans. "The real bond between the CIA and Delta started in Bosnia . . . face-to-face, working a real-world mission, getting to know each other, realizing once again that neither organization can do what they want to do without the other," said a Delta source. "That's the genesis of the whole relationship. That thing with Karzai was an extension of it."

Crumpton found JSOC's cooperative attitude a refreshing change from the Agency's recent experience butting heads with Rumsfeld in the Pentagon. "It was all driven by mission, and the further you got away from Washington, the easier it was," he said. "I can't say enough good things about Dell Dailey. . . . I can't say that about DoD, but I can say that about JSOC." There would be further tensions between the two organizations as they shouldered the bulk of the responsibility for the secret wars across the globe, wars the U.S. government was only now beginning to contemplate. But things were off to a reasonable start.

✳

Erwin and Berntsen were driving to Bagram to meet Franks, whose C-17 landed shortly after the pair had arrived at the base, and the two moved up to the runway to await the general. Berntsen's account hints at the importance Franks attached to JSOC's AFO effort: "With the engines still running, the back hatch opened and a dozen U.S. soldiers with helmets, weapons, and night vision goggles spilled out. One of them crossed the fifty meters of apron to shake the Lt. Colonel's hand, then escort him back to the C-17." Only after conferring with Erwin for a couple of minutes did Franks, with the JSOC officer by his side, stroll over to greet Berntsen, the senior CIA officer in-country.[53]

As Franks was meeting with JSOC's advance force leader in Bagram, Dailey was planning the next phase of JSOC's war in Afghanistan. Kabul had fallen and the Taliban were retreating in disarray to Kandahar, but the United States' top three high-value targets—bin Laden, his deputy Ayman al-Zawahiri, and Taliban leader Mullah Omar—were still at large. In addition, thousands of Al Qaeda and other foreign fighters remained in the field, massing in the mountains of eastern Afghanistan. The opportunity presented itself to destroy Al Qaeda's leadership and crush its fielded forces. But rather than consolidate his own forces in an effort to finish the campaign in short order, the JSOC commander opted for a more conservative approach.

Dailey thought that by withdrawing some of his force, he could deceive Al Qaeda into believing all U.S. special ops forces had departed the battlefield. He pulled the Rangers' 3rd Battalion, Delta's B Squadron, and most of TF Brown back to the States, replacing them with 1st Battalion, the rest of A Squadron, and a small AFO element, who deployed to Afghanistan.[54] After flying its JSOC contingent to Masirah December 6 and 7, the *Kitty Hawk* returned to Japan.[55] The move confused the Sword staff and was poorly received in Delta, where operators were openly skeptical that "the bad guys would let down their guard," as Greer put it. "The naivete of that idea still boggles my mind today," he wrote more than six years later. "'Aren't we at war?' we asked. Why were we not pouring all available assets into Afghanistan, rather than withdrawing our strength?"[56]

But as he prepared to deploy to Afghanistan from Bragg in late November 2001, Greer had little time to dwell on the vagaries of his higher command. The mission of a lifetime awaited him in the mountains of eastern Afghanistan.

12

Rumsfeld Falls for JSOC

On September 24, as Pete Blaber and his colleagues were stewing in the Delta compound, 300 miles up Interstate 95 Don Rumsfeld was in a packed Pentagon conference room also getting impatient with the military brass.

Less than two weeks previously, in the hours after the September 11 attacks, with smoke still billowing through Pentagon corridors, the defense secretary had moved to the Executive Support Center, a suite of rooms protected against electronic eavesdropping and designed to host the most senior Defense Department officials during a crisis. From there, surrounded by other senior Pentagon officials, he had spoken via videoteleconference with Charlie Holland, head of U.S. Special Operations Command. As SOCOM commander, Holland's job was to prepare U.S. special operations forces for operations overseas. JSOC fell under SOCOM for administrative purposes, but SOCOM did not command overseas missions conducted by JSOC or any other U.S. special operations forces. JSOC's operations were run under the auspices of the National Command Authority (the president and defense secretary), with responsibility sometimes delegated to the regional commander-in-chief, who also ran any non-JSOC special operations missions. But Rumsfeld seemed unaware of this distinction, and tasked Holland to come up with a plan to strike back at Al Qaeda. "I don't want you to wait around for a 100 percent plan," he told the Air Force general. "This is going to be an iterative plan. Come up here with a 50 percent solution so I can look at it."

Now Holland was in the Pentagon to answer Rumsfeld. Dozens of senior defense officials and their aides had gathered to hear the SOCOM commander. Thirteen days had passed since Al Qaeda had struck America. The U.S. military, which Rumsfeld commanded, had yet to hit back.

The defense secretary was expecting his top special operations officer to specify how that might happen. He was to be bitterly disappointed.

"Holland started out saying, 'You tasked us to get some possible targets for us to go after Al Qaeda,' then he talked about Al Qaeda or extremist elements in the tri-border area in South America, in the Philippines, Mauritania, and then some transshipment points off the Somali coast, loading weapons and stuff," said an official in the Office of the Secretary of Defense (OSD). As Holland spoke, "Rumsfeld was getting sort of excited about the idea of being able to go to Bush and say 'We're going to hit these sons of bitches tomorrow night all around the world.' So then Rumsfeld said, 'When can we get these guys? . . . Let's hit them,' because what Rumsfeld wanted to do originally was to [get] back at Al Qaeda with a series of blows around the world to show our reach."

But Rumsfeld's question didn't elicit the answer he wanted. "Well, you know, we don't have the actionable intelligence to go after individual leaders in those areas," Holland said. "We don't know who they are or where they are." His comments "took Rumsfeld by surprise," the OSD official said.

Another nasty shock was waiting for the secretary. When would the first Special Forces A-teams fly into Afghanistan from Uzbekistan and link up with the Northern Alliance, he asked. "Well, when the CIA gives us clearance," Holland replied. "That got Rumsfeld's goat, too," the OSD official recalled. "Rumsfeld said, 'You mean we have to get clearance from the CIA to go in there?' And Holland said, 'Yeah,' sort of lamely. And everything sort of fell apart there."

The meeting began to break up, but there was still time for one more awkward, telling exchange between Holland and Rumsfeld that simultaneously revealed the SOCOM commander's reluctance to seize the initiative and the defense secretary's ignorance of special operations. Although he was on his second tour as defense secretary, neither SOCOM, JSOC, nor any of the special mission units had existed during his previous tenure in the mid-1970s. During the course of the meeting it had become clear that Rumsfeld thought Holland had direct command of special operations forces around the world, according to the OSD official. Rumsfeld was wrong, but on the basis of this assumption, he announced a far-reaching decision.

Holland was chatting with another special operations official when

Rumsfeld approached the pair. "This is a global fight, and I want you to be the global commander," he told the general. Holland, a mild-mannered, nonconfrontational officer, wasn't keen on that idea, which would have required him often to go toe-to-toe with the regional commanders-in-chief. He preferred to work through the theater special operations commands—offices inside the regional commands that reported to the CinCs. Holland also knew he had no real command authority over forces overseas. But the SOCOM commander wasn't about to correct his boss. Instead, Holland's response was along the lines of "Yes, I hear you," not "Yes, I will," said an OSD official who observed the exchange.

"So Rumsfeld that day learned that we didn't have actionable intelligence, we needed a global command capable of fighting a global war, and that we relied on the CIA to tell us when to go in," the official said. Those three lessons would shape much of the defense secretary's approach in the coming months, the OSD official said. "Rumsfeld had just gotten a sobering look at how tough it was going to be."[1]

✳

Even in those early weeks, it was apparent that the Bush national security team—and Rumsfeld in particular—was envisioning a greatly expanded role for JSOC and its higher headquarters, SOCOM. In his September 20, 2001, address to Congress, the president had declared a global war on terrorists. "Our war on terror begins with Al Qaeda, but it does not end there," he said. "It will not end until every terrorist group of global reach has been found, stopped and defeated."[2]

Those words were easily spoken and would reverberate for many years, but the U.S. military machine, the most expensive and powerful ever built, was not designed for such a conflict. Caught tragically off guard by the September 11 attacks, Bush and his advisers were searching for an answer to the problem of how to wage a global conflict against non–nation-state actors. JSOC, a specialized counterterrorist force with boundless self-confidence, a can-do attitude, and peerless operational capability, all suffused with the aura of secrecy, seemed to offer the perfect solution. The Bush team grasped at it desperately.

The day after Bush's address, Dailey issued updated guidance via video-teleconference. He told his staff to work on "global targeting." The JSOC commander added that "the president knows more about our organization in the first eight months [of his tenure] than the previous administration knew in the last eight years."[3] The prevailing view was "we're in business," said a Delta source. "This is a war and we got the right president. . . . This is what we came in for. It was very exciting."

Rumsfeld wanted SOCOM to run the "war on terror" in part because he didn't trust his regional commanders-in-chief "to adopt a global view of the war," according to Doug Feith, the undersecretary of defense for policy.[4] The secretary was frustrated with what he perceived as outdated thinking on the part of many of the conventional military leaders. The irony was that in his search for a dynamic and innovative alternative he turned to Holland, whose reputation was that of an officer reluctant to buck the system or threaten the consensus.

Holland had already shot down at least one innovative concept since September 11. JSOC's forces in the Balkans had learned quickly that "unity of effort" with other government agencies, especially the CIA, was a key to success. The best way to formalize that would have been to create a joint interagency task force, or JIATF (pronounced jie-att-iff), that reported to the defense secretary but included a CIA representative as deputy commander. "That was in almost every AAR [after-action review] that we wrote," said a Delta operator with much Balkan experience. The JIATF concept would soon become almost synonymous with JSOC, but in September 2001 it was an idea whose time was yet to come. Holland quickly vetoed it. "We came back from [Europe] and our first concept was to make JSOC a JIATF and bring in the interagency," said a retired special ops officer. "But Holland didn't want to do that."

This was in keeping with what sources uniformly described as Holland's go-along-to-get-along leadership style. At well over six feet tall, the gray-haired pilot with more than 5,000 flight hours—including more than 100 combat missions[5]—under his belt cut a towering figure as he strolled the corridors of power in the Pentagon, Capitol Hill, and his own headquarters at MacDill Air Force Base. But those who worked closely with him in the months after September 11 said he appeared more worried about upsetting the other four-stars than eager to assume the mantle of leadership Rumsfeld wanted to bestow upon him. This was particularly true of his relations with the regional commanders-in-chief. Congress had established SOCOM as a headquarters with responsibility only to train and equip special operations forces that the president, the CinCs, and U.S. ambassadors could use for operations. Now Rumsfeld was asking Holland to run a global war. That made the general, who had been appointed to his position by Defense Secretary Bill Cohen at the tail end of the Clinton administration, very uncomfortable.[6]

Holland was "likable" but not well suited for his present boss, said a senior member of the Joint Staff. "He might have been good for Secretary Cohen, but he was anything but for Secretary Rumsfeld." A brief exchange during a Pentagon meeting several months after the September 24 briefing exemplified this personality conflict. "I don't have the authority, Mr. Secretary," Holland told his boss. "I didn't hear you ask me for the authority, General," replied Rumsfeld acidly. "Everybody sort of looked at their feet and said, 'oh shit,'" said Bob Andrews, the acting assistant secretary of defense for special operations and low-intensity conflict, who was in the room.

JSOC chafed under Holland's conservatism. "We were very aggressive with what we wanted to do, and he was less aggressive," the retired special operations officer said. JSOC sent director of operations Army Colonel Frank Kearney and Lieutenant Colonel Scotty Miller to the Pentagon to brief Rumsfeld on how SOCOM could take the lead in the "war on terror," but Holland got ahold of their slides ahead of time and changed the brief's content. "Holland didn't like the fact [that the brief] told people how it could be done," said the retired special operations officer. "Basically he didn't want to take the lead."

But the result of Holland's resistance to turning SOCOM headquarters into a war-fighting command was that that role in effect devolved to JSOC. "General Holland immediately turned to JSOC for everything," the retired special operations officer said. "The opportunity was there for SOCOM to take over the 'war on terror' and they chose not to and chose to turn the combatant command [i.e., SOCOM] into a support function for JSOC," an OSD source said. Dailey soon became a frequent visitor to Rumsfeld's office—a rare privilege for a two-star whose headquarters was more than five hours' drive from the Pentagon.[7]

As indicated by the briefing Kearney and Miller were set to give Rumsfeld, key personalities at JSOC headquarters took an entirely more expansive and ambitious view than did Holland of the possibilities afforded by the newly declared "global war on terror." In a classified "vision statement" called *JSOC XXI*,[8] a team led by Delta veteran Lieutenant Colonel Bennet Sacolick and Lieutenant Colonel William C. "Bill" Mayville, respectively chief of current operations and chief of plans and training in the command's operations directorate, outlined a future for

JSOC that entailed "getting out of Fort Bragg, having global resources, global reach, prepositioned forces," said a special ops officer who was briefed on the document. "It was Sacolick's vision," said a JSOC staffer. That vision was of a "holistic approach, instead of all direct action," the staffer said. "It's more boundary spanning, problem solving, bringing the interagency together." But to reach this goal, JSOC required even more resources. "They understood sooner than anyone else that this [war] was not going to go away, and the country needed more than they had to give . . . and Rumsfeld understood that," said a special operations officer on the Joint Staff.

⁂

The more Rumsfeld learned about JSOC, the more he was drawn to the command. His first exposure to JSOC was the morning of March 27, 2001, when Dailey, Hall, and a couple of special mission unit senior enlisted personnel had given him and Wolfowitz an introductory briefing on the command in a Pentagon conference room. Rumsfeld's handlers had told the JSOC team they would have only twenty minutes with the secretary, but the meeting stretched to a couple of hours. "He had a bunch of questions and Wolfowitz had a bunch of questions," said Hall, who added that much of the conversation revolved around the type of people who served in JSOC units. "It turned into a great capabilities brief."

A few months later, Rumsfeld got a chance to witness some of those capabilities firsthand during a visit to Fort Bragg. On a warm, sunny November 21—the day after Franks had met with Mark Erwin and Gary Berntsen in Bagram—the defense secretary visited the Delta compound to take in a stage-managed JSOC "capabilities exercise"—a demonstration designed to impress visiting dignitaries. Delta operators typically viewed these exercises as "a pain in the ass," because they robbed the unit of precious training time, according to then Major Tom Greer, whose A1 troop was responsible for the show that day. But this time was different. The nation was at war and the man who signed off on every combat deployment had appeared on Delta's doorstep. "We wanted to impress the hell out of Rumsfeld," Greer wrote in his memoir, *Kill Bin Laden*, which he published under the pen name Dalton Fury. In this respect, the exercise was an unqualified success.

The visit began with Delta operators portraying terrorists "ambushing" the bus carrying Rumsfeld and his party, before more operators—playing themselves—stormed the bus and "rescued" the VIPs. (To Rumsfeld and most of his party, the "ambush" was a complete surprise. In on the secret were the secretary's bodyguards—to ensure they didn't pull their weapons and fire real bullets to defend him—and an individual with a heart condition.)

Shadowed by Holland, Doug Brown—now a lieutenant general and head of Army Special Operations Command—and Air Force Brigadier General Greg Trebon, JSOC's deputy commander and the host for the JSOC portion of the trip, Rumsfeld toured displays and watched a demonstration of "super marksmanship with .50 caliber sniper rifles," said Andrews, who accompanied Rumsfeld on the trip. "Essentially it was a Delta show," as Andrews put it, but the other JSOC units got to showcase their abilities. In Team 6's case, this included a demonstration of the unit's HALO freefall technique, which the Navy operators regarded as one of their specialties. "These guys put on a parachute infiltration of a single agent into an area, where he skydives out at high altitude, lands, jumps out of his jumpsuit, and has a business suit on and a briefcase and walks down the street," Andrews said. This impressed Rumsfeld, as did a live-fire hostage rescue scenario in a shoot-house.

The JSOC visit ran long, just like the Pentagon briefing in March, cutting into time set aside for a visit to Army Special Operations Command. The JSOC hosts "liked to cheat . . . [and] were deliberately taking more time than they were" allotted, another Rumsfeld aide said. But the tactic paid off. About an hour into the trip, Rumsfeld spoke to Greer, the main briefer. "What we really need is small groups of folks, say two to four people, that can go anywhere in the world and execute discreet missions against these people [i.e., Al Qaeda]," he told the Delta officer. In his book, Greer relates how "shocked" he was that Rumsfeld seemed ignorant of the fact that his desired capability had existed in Delta "for many years." The special operations brass at the exercise quickly reassured Rumsfeld that he already had a force that could do what he had just described.

The visit was a critical inflection point in how Rumsfeld perceived JSOC and its potential role in the forthcoming campaign. "He probably would have stayed there forever if I had let him," said the second Rumsfeld aide. "I had to finally pry him out of there. But he was very intrigued by the capabilities [and] by the quality of the people that they had doing this stuff. . . . They got their money's worth out of the dog-and-pony show." As Andrews said, "It was enough for him to say, 'This is where I want to put my money, this is where I want to invest some effort.'"[9]

But despite—or perhaps because of—his repeated exposure to brief-ings on the high-end counterterrorism that was JSOC's forte, Rumsfeld's understanding of special operations remained superficial and unbalanced. He did not recognize the value of unconventional warfare and foreign internal defense (helping an ally defeat an insurgency), which were the specialties of Special Forces as well as SOCOM's psychological opera-tions and civil affairs units. To Rumsfeld, the value of special operations lay only in the spooky and lethal activities JSOC exemplified, not in training foreign militaries or standing up local militias.[10] "There were some things that Rumsfeld said and did that indicated that we, his staff, had not fully and well explained to him the nature of special operations forces," said Andrews, a former Special Forces officer. "He didn't under-stand and we didn't try to beat into him an appreciation of counterin-surgency as foreign internal defense, UW [unconventional warfare], the 'white' stuff."

"Rumsfeld . . . didn't care about setting up networks, he didn't care about establishing forward operating bases, he didn't want to hear all that shit," said a Special Forces officer who briefed the secretary frequently. "He just wanted a way for bodies to show up." The result was Rumsfeld's almost blind faith in JSOC. "He didn't truly understand us, but he trusted us," Hall said.

JSOC's administrative chain of command ran through Holland to Rumsfeld. But the SOCOM commander's reluctance to take control meant JSOC became "almost an independent military force for Rums-feld," said a senior Joint Staff officer. Above Rumsfeld, there was only one more link on the chain of command: the president. For JSOC, there-fore, a whole set of circumstances had fallen into place serendipitously: the emergence of a global terrorist threat; a defense secretary frustrated with the conventional military's business-as-usual mind-set and drawn to what he perceived as the more decisive and innovative approach of spe-cial operations forces; and an action-oriented president heavily influ-enced by a vice president infatuated with covert operations. After years spent honing its skills with the help of steadily climbing budgets, JSOC's rocket was on the launch pad. The stage was set for liftoff.

✳

In the late afternoon of October 30, 2001, the Defense Department's most senior military and civilian officials gathered in Rumsfeld's con-ference room for a Joint Staff briefing on how to expand the war against

Al Qaeda beyond Afghanistan. The briefers were Rear Admiral John Stufflebeem, the Joint Staff's deputy director for global operations, and Colonel Jeff Schloesser, a former commander of the 160th's 1st Battalion who had just taken charge of a new Joint Staff planning cell for the "war on terror."

The briefing quickly bogged down in a debate over the definitions of terms like "defeat" and "destroy." Rumsfeld, who seemed to exist in a perpetual state of impatient frustration, made clear his dissatisfaction with what he saw as the glacial pace of the military's efforts to widen the war. "There is no need to wait until after Afghanistan is complete," he said. "As I've said a hundred times already, I would dearly love to attack in another AOR [area of responsibility] now." The rest of the briefing fell flat and Rumsfeld rose to take a call from the president. "I could have written this briefing myself," he said as he exited.[11]

Rumsfeld had gotten his point across. From that point on, "we became much more expansive," said a Joint Staff source. "At that point I fully understood—and I think so did all the other senior military leaders—what he was trying to get at." But as the secretary had learned from Holland's September 24 briefing, there were legal and practical hurdles to overcome before he could dispatch special operators around the globe to attack terrorist targets on a moment's notice.

Nested in the Joint Staff's strategic plans and policy directorate, Schloesser and his small staff held a series of video-teleconferences with the regional commanders-in-chief. The upshot of those discussions was the discovery that the military lacked the legal authorities to deploy forces into the countries about which it was most concerned: Yemen, Somalia, Kenya, Sudan, Pakistan, Iran, Georgia, the Philippines, and South America's tri-border area (where Paraguay, Argentina, and Brazil meet). In some cases, particularly Yemen and the Horn of Africa countries, these were places to which the military feared Al Qaeda leaders and their forces might flee as they lost their Afghan sanctuary. "We don't really understand that Pakistan's going to become quite the safe haven that it actually proves to be," said a Joint Staff officer. "Everybody's thinking that bin Laden, Zawahiri, and everybody else is going to move out and that they're going to move fairly freely."

While Pentagon staffers worked feverishly to get special operations forces—which usually meant JSOC elements—the authorities they needed to operate in these countries, the Defense Department issued a series of what the military called "execute orders" allowing the regional commanders-in-chief to take certain steps within their areas of responsibility.

On December 1, Schloesser gave a briefing to Rumsfeld titled "Next Steps in the War on Terrorism" that laid out a series of options for where to take the war next. These included "maritime interdiction operations" (boarding, searching and seizing, or destroying ships) in the Mediterranean and off the Horn of Africa; operations to deny terrorists safe haven in Somalia; missions to disrupt Islamist terrorist logistics in Bosnia and Kosovo; helping the Philippine armed forces defeat the Abu Sayyaf Group; and actions in Yemen and Sudan.

Much of the discussion concerned the Army of Northern Virginia, the intelligence and advance force operations unit. "In all these areas there are some preparatory operations that would have to be done," said a source who attended the briefing. Much of that work—advance force operations on steroids—was the Army of Northern Virginia's responsibility.

✳

Over the course of the next year, the Joint Staff worked on three major interconnected initiatives that combined would go a long way toward empowering JSOC for the campaign ahead: gaining JSOC the (U.S.) legal authority to operate in specific countries; giving the command the authority and the resources to target the Al Qaeda senior leadership; and creating an intra-governmental system to enable "time-sensitive planning" so that if the intelligence community or JSOC located a high-value target, the government could get a decision brief to the president fast enough for him to approve a mission to capture or kill that person before the target moved beyond reach.

All these came together in a document known as the Al Qaeda Senior Leadership Execute Order, or AQSL ExOrd. The ExOrd originated with an order from the Joint Staff's director of strategic plans and policy, Army Lieutenant General George Casey, to Schloesser to spend the weekend of June 29–30, 2002, developing a plan to capture or kill Al Qaeda's two top leaders—bin Laden and Zawahiri—and seven other senior figures in the group.

A Joint Staff officer deeply involved in the staff work described the strategy as "cutting off the head of the snake." During that first year after the September 11 attacks, Schloesser's planning cell, in concert with the Joint Staff's operations and intelligence directorates, was "trying to understand how do you defeat an organism or a network," the officer said. "First of all we said, 'Hey, we can do it by [eliminating] leadership.'" That approach, so enticing to policymakers because it seemed to offer a neat and relatively cheap solution to the intractable global problem of violent anti-Western Islamism, also perfectly matched JSOC's skill set, something not lost on Rumsfeld.

On July 1, 2002, the defense secretary sent a memo to Feith, titled "Manhunts." "How do we organize the Department of Defense for manhunts?" the memo asked. "We are obviously not well organized at the present time." The memo reflected a critical moment for Rumsfeld and JSOC, according to Andrews. "Once he fastened on the manhunt thing, he looked at that as the silver bullet against terrorism and he built a unit [JSOC] that can do manhunts," he said. With Dailey already aware of the secretary's interest in this approach, Joint Special Operations Command was also rewiring itself for manhunts. When Jim Reese returned from Afghanistan that spring Dailey sent him to Israel to speak to officials there about their experiences with man-hunting, and in particular the years-long effort to track down and kill the Palestinian Black September terrorists who murdered eleven Israeli athletes at the 1972 Munich Olympics. What JSOC came to realize, according to an officer at the command, was that effective man-hunting required both military capability and legal authorities. "If you have the authorities to do things, and then the capability, look out," he said. "It's all about authorities and capability."

The next several years would prove that a so-called decapitation approach to counterterrorism was no silver bullet, but in the spring and summer of 2002 its limitations were far from clear. "Eventually you'll find that we got that partly wrong," the Joint Staff officer said. "We understand that fairly fast, but AQSL has a life of its own."

The formula was known as "two-plus-seven" but in reality it quickly expanded to "two-plus-seven-plus-thirty," best envisioned as a series of concentric circles with bin Laden and Zawahiri in the bull's-eye. The ring around them consisted of seven key Al Qaeda facilitators, surrounded by an outer ring of thirty slightly less senior but still important Al Qaeda operatives. Schloesser's strategic planning cell and the Joint Staff intelligence directorate maintained the list. As one of the seven was captured or killed, the next in line from the outer thirty would take his place in the diagram. "Eventually, I think essentially almost all of them are captured or killed," said the Joint Staff officer. "And so they change out."

The AQSL ExOrd's birth was labored, involving multiple briefings to Rumsfeld and Bush over the course of the next year. Throughout the process, it was clear that JSOC would have the authority to execute the order, with Holland exercising oversight as the "supported CinC." Just as Holland had feared, this phrase created friction with his fellow four-stars. "'Supported CinC' means he is going to get the support of all the [regional] combatant commanders," said the Joint Staff officer. For the first time, the SOCOM commander had the power to deploy JSOC forces into a regional commander-in-chief's area of responsibility without asking for permission. "He can basically say [to the regional combatant commander], 'We're coming [and] we need this kind of level of support,'" the Joint Staff officer said. "Most of them did not like that. Franks did not like it at all, was very much against it."

The CENTCOM boss aired his grievances in summer 2002 when Rumsfeld brought the CinCs back to the States for a conference at the Defense Intelligence Agency headquarters at Bolling Air Force Base in Washington, D.C. The subject of Holland's role as the "supported CinC" arose. Pointing at Holland, Rumsfeld told the four-stars that he knew they were all opposed to the change. "I don't care," the secretary said, according to a staff officer who observed the conversation. "That's not my concept of doing business." "Franks then speaks up, kind of like he's speaking for everybody else," the staff officer recalled. The Army general objected strongly to the notion of JSOC operating without his say-so in his area of responsibility. But Rumsfeld brooked no dissent on the issue. "Franks takes a beating," the staff officer said. "Rumsfeld, if he wasn't clear enough when he pointed at Holland the first time, he makes it absolutely clear."

Franks's opposition was finally quashed on November 13, 2002, during an "off-site" meeting of the senior military leadership in a modern auditorium at Washington, D.C.'s, Fort McNair. Myers, Marine Lieutenant General Pete Pace (the new vice chairman of the Joint Chiefs), the four service chiefs, the regional "combatant commanders" (Rumsfeld had banned the phrase "commander-in-chief" as of October 24), Army Lieutenant General John Abizaid, who was the director of the Joint Staff, and Casey. During a briefing on how Holland's newfound authorities would increase JSOC's role, "Franks pushed back pretty hard," complaining about "the centralization" of special operations forces under SOCOM, said an officer who was present. "He argued forcefully that he needed most of JSOC to fight in the CENTCOM AOR [area of responsibility] fighting CENTCOM targets." By then, U.S. forces were deployed not only in Afghanistan, but also in small numbers working with Jordanian special operations forces training Yemeni security forces, as well as in Kuwait, preparing for a possible invasion of Iraq. In response, and in what the source said was "a somewhat uncharacteristic move for General Myers," the chairman "shut him down and basically just said, 'The president's decided that we're doing this,' and that was that." (Franks's objections were ironic, because in the end he got just what he wanted, which was the preponderance of JSOC's effort committed to his region.)

But Franks and the other regional combatant commanders were by no means the only flag officers digging in their heels when it came to expanding JSOC's role via the AQSL ExOrd. The Joint Staff, and in particular the intelligence directorate, headed by Rear Admiral Lowell Jacoby, "non-concurred" with its implementation. (Although it might seem odd to outsiders, it is not unusual to have the Joint Staff as a corporate body take issue with products that originated within one of its own directorates.) Wolfowitz also had some legal questions about the ExOrd, and the Joint Staff's new vice director of operations was dispatched to brief the deputy defense secretary one weekend to persuade him of the ExOrd's utility. "He sat down that evening with Wolfowitz and went through it, probably page by page, and convinced the depsecdef that it was worthwhile," said another Joint Staffer. The officer who worked so hard to sway Wolfowitz was a lean, hatchet-faced brigadier general who had spent the early 1990s on the JSOC staff and the later years of the decade commanding the Ranger Regiment. He may not have realized it at the time, but in the new century no officer would benefit from the AQSL ExOrd more than he would. His name was Stan McChrystal.

✳

Embedded in the AQSL ExOrd was the time-sensitive planning concept, which was the brainchild of the Counterterrorism Campaign Support Group (CTCSG), an organization Myers had established in October 2001 to support JSOC. "Its main purpose was to interface, coordinate, and collaborate with the Joint Staff and the National Command Authority to expedite decision-making," said a Joint Staff officer who worked closely with it. Working out of trailers at Pope and led by

Special Forces Colonel David Schroer, who doubled as JSOC's director of global long-range plans, the group was "basically an interagency task force built to support JSOC," said the Joint Staff officer. The group's chain of command was fuzzy. Holland and Dailey thought Schroer worked for SOCOM, but Rumsfeld was adamant that the CTCSG was an "extension of him and the Joint Staff," said another officer familiar with the group. Rumsfeld gave Holland no veto over the group's creation or its recommendations. In other words, in all but name the CTCSG was the joint interagency task force that Holland had tried to block. It became "how JSOC actually pulls itself into Washington, and then how Washington tries to influence JSOC," said the Joint Staff officer.

By the spring of 2002, despite his admiration for JSOC's operators, Rumsfeld had become frustrated with the command itself, "because JSOC had a standard way of doing business, and Rumsfeld could not break them of that," said an officer who attended meetings with the secretary. In particular, Rumsfeld thought it took too long for JSOC elements to deploy in response to fleeting intelligence. But the fault did not lie entirely with JSOC. The military's planning system, as well as the need to clear such deployments through numerous other government agencies, also served to slow the process to a walking pace. This issue came to a head in a Pentagon meeting attended by senior Defense Department figures and the deputies of other government agencies that had a counterterrorism role. Rumsfeld chided CIA deputy director John McLaughlin for what the secretary perceived as the Agency's failure to deliver timely intelligence on the location of Al Qaeda targets. But McLaughlin argued that the blame lay with the Pentagon. "It's because you're too . . . slow," the CIA man told Rumsfeld. "The world is not like that. This isn't the buildup to D-Day, where you get a little intelligence and more and more and more [before acting]. This is, 'You get something and you're either there or you're not.'" McLaughlin was right. The fastest that the Pentagon could get JSOC combat forces to a regional combatant commander using the military's expedited planning process was seventy-two hours, and "that was like if everybody was running down the hallway with a big lighter in each hand setting their hair on fire," said the officer who attended meetings with Rumsfeld. "McLaughlin would just laugh and say, 'If you think that I'm going to get the nugget [of intelligence] and be able to pass it to you guys and let you have seventy-two hours' planning to do something, you're nuts.'" Rumsfeld turned to Schroer then and there and told him to fix the problem.

Within a couple of days Schroer and a handful of subordinates had drafted a process that, by relying on secure video-teleconferences, liaison officers at all the key agencies, having non-JSOC personnel "read in" on the command's programs, and an alert roster of about 100 personnel across the government, could have a recommendation for the president twelve hours after getting the initial intelligence. The CTCSG's role in this process extended beyond JSOC, however. Its charter was to come up with a recommended course of action from the entire Defense Department. Sometimes that course of action might be an air strike rather than the deployment of Dailey's JOC and a Delta squadron. As such, Schroer's staff included F-18 and B-52 pilots as well as one of the Navy's most knowledgeable officers on the Tomahawk cruise missile.

JSOC now had the authority to go after Al Qaeda and its allies in about a dozen countries, although the exact rules under which it could do so varied from place to place. The command was soon conducting advance force operations in many of the countries. "It's a massive increase in JSOC's authority to do things," said a Joint Staff officer. "It elevates JSOC to being a critical component of this whole war on terrorism, or, one could argue, the critical component to the war on terrorism," he said. "From it . . . in the space of two and a half to three years, JSOC's resources and staffing and their connections to all the intelligence organizations and all the supporting organizations for intel are magnified several times over."[12]

The AQSL ExOrd was the key to giving JSOC the authority to wage a global campaign. "When we got an execute order to go after Al Qaeda senior leaders, that became the document" that codified JSOC's transformation, a retired special ops officer said.

※

For all the effort Schroer's Counterterrorism Campaign Support Group put into expediting the joint and interagency planning process, there was little point having the president approve a mission within twelve hours of receiving actionable intelligence if JSOC wasn't able to respond in a timely manner. Events in spring 2002 suggested that the command had yet to internalize the need for greater agility in the post–September 11 world.

Solid intelligence reports out of Iraq's Kurdish region indicated hundreds of Al Qaeda–linked militants displaced by the U.S. military action in Afghanistan had joined a terrorist group called Ansar al-Islam (Supporters of Islam) in the village of Khurmal. The intelligence further suggested that the hardened fighters in the camp were experimenting with biological and chemical weapons, including ricin. The Pentagon considered a range of air strikes to destroy the camp, but each had drawbacks: cruise missiles might destroy the camp's buildings and kill terrorists, but they would also kill families believed to be living there and might spread any toxins; a bombing raid would likely destroy the toxins, because of the bombs' more powerful warheads that burn at hotter temperatures, but would otherwise share the disadvantages of the cruise missile strike. Neither option would give the Bush administration any proof that the terrorists were working on weapons of mass destruction.[13] "If you want to be discriminating and you want to bring back evidence, then you have to have boots on the ground," said a senior Joint Staffer.

So the Joint Chiefs tasked JSOC—through SOCOM—to present options for attacking the camp. JSOC's response left them sorely disappointed. "What they came back with was a massive large slow option that would have taken a month and a half and [was] completely impractical to the objective," said the Joint Staffer. JSOC's proposal involved staging out of Turkey and "involved C-5As, C-141s, the covered aircraft," he said. "It was huge and took a long time to build up and would have deceived no one."

For reasons that would remain unclear, in the last week of June, the president decided against an attack, despite the Joint Chiefs' unanimous support for action. The week after Bush made his decision, Rumsfeld expressed his displeasure with JSOC's proposed courses of action, which were all "mini-JRXs," according to a special operator briefed on them. "I'm really disappointed," Rumsfeld told a special operations officer. "You've got to do better than this. . . . If I wanted a D-Day invasion I could call the 82nd. Why can't you come up with things that don't involve six C-17s?"[14]

While any JSOC mission into Khurmal would have involved risks, the decision to take no action also incurred risk. Among the terrorists who had arrived in Khurmal from Afghanistan—after, in his case, sojourns in Lebanon, Syria, and Iran—was a thuggish Jordanian who had been running a training camp in Herat. Unknown to all in the West but a few analysts who closely tracked militant Islamism, his name—Abu Musab al-Zarqawi—would soon echo around the Middle East while his hands dripped with the blood of JSOC operators.[15]

⚌

Dailey's preference for large, infrastructure-laden deployments was a contributing factor—but not the only one—behind a widely held view at Bragg, MacDill, and the Pentagon that by summer 2002 the demands of the "war on terror" were straining JSOC to its limits. Although Afghanistan was the only high-profile campaign in which the command was fighting, the AQSL ExOrd and other Pentagon initiatives meant new theaters beckoned in the Horn of Africa, Yemen, and elsewhere. JSOC's staff numbered about 800, and in November 2001 the Army had given the command another general officer—Brigadier General John Scales, a Vietnam veteran and reservist with no previous JSOC experience—to enable the command and control of multiple deployed task forces. But JSOC still had to keep an alert force at home in the United States for the 0300 counterterrorism and 0400 counter-proliferation missions. And in the background, the possibility of a major war in Iraq loomed closer.[16]

The command was also the victim of its own success. As Franks's protests later that year demonstrated, the regional CinCs' appetites for JSOC's forces—by reputation the military's most elite units—were unbounded. Indeed, on July 19, 2002, a Rumsfeld order to CENTCOM stated that Franks could use the JSOC task force in his area of responsibility only for hunting the "two-plus-seven" Al Qaeda targets and neutralizing weapons of mass destruction.[17]

On August 15, Myers flew down to JSOC for a series of meetings. Brigadier General Eldon Bargewell, a former Delta commander now on the SOCOM staff, came up from MacDill to brief the chairman. Bargewell told Myers there was deep concern at SOCOM that the "war on terror" was pulling resources and attention from two missions in particular: the 0400 counter-proliferation mission and Power Geyser, the code name for JSOC's—really Team 6's—domestic mission to protect top government officials when so ordered.[18]

Team 6 was also providing Hamid Karzai's security detail in Afghanistan, a topic that came up during an October 10, 2002, Pentagon briefing by Bargewell to Rumsfeld that Holland, Franks, Myers, Pace, and Dailey all attended. A partial solution to the strain JSOC was under could be achieved simply by pulling some JSOC elements out of Task Force 11 (the renamed TF Sword) if higher-priority missions presented themselves, Rumsfeld said. The discussion then turned to JSOC's 0300 counterterrorism response mission. Despite his previous briefings on JSOC's mission set, Rumsfeld seemed confused about 0300's purpose. "Bargewell spent a fair amount of time giving him an explanation," as well as articulating SOCOM's view of why a highly classified strategic reconnaissance mission in Indonesia for which Pacific Command had requested JSOC forces was not an appropriate mission for the elite operators, said an officer who was in the room.

Not for the first time, Rumsfeld also inquired after the Army of Northern Virginia, referring to the unit by its latest code name. "Has anyone really got Gray Fox involved in the GWOT?" he asked, using the acronym for the "global war on terror." "Yes," Holland replied. "They'll start next week."[19] The secret unit had, of course, already been heavily involved in Afghanistan, but Rumsfeld was concerned that the unique unit had not been committed to the wider war the United States was now waging around the world. The fact that Holland was replying at all to this question was an indication that things were changing for the unit. Although manned by a mix of special operations and intelligence personnel, the Army of Northern Virginia fell under the Army's Intelligence and Security Command for administrative purposes and was considered a strategic asset of the U.S. military. But if Rumsfeld and his aides had learned anything during the previous year, it was that the "war on terror" would place a premium on intelligence, particularly signals and human intelligence, the specialties of the Fort Belvoir unit, which had a squadron dedicated to each discipline. Rumsfeld wanted the unit where he felt it could be most effective in the new fight, and that was under SOCOM, where they could work more closely with JSOC. (Up to that point, although the Army of Northern Virginia sometimes supported JSOC missions, it also performed other non-JSOC tasks for the regional commanders-in-chief.)[20] The defense secretary had secured an agreement by early fall 2002 from the CIA's McLaughlin under which small special operations teams could enter countries where the United States was not at war "and work essentially for the chief of station," said a source in the room when the deal was made. The Army of Northern Virginia's operatives would be perfect for such missions.

A debate ensued over whether to assign the unit directly to JSOC.

Those against such a move argued that the unit needed to be kept focused on strategic targets, rather than the tactical ones that often occupied JSOC. Four courses of action were considered: to keep the unit under Intelligence and Security Command; to move it under the Joint Staff's direct control; to assign it to SOCOM with SOCOM retaining operational control; and to assign it administratively to SOCOM but with operational control given to JSOC. On December 9, 2002, over the Army's wishes, Rumsfeld chose the fourth option.[21] However, it took the military bureaucracy until 2004 to make the shift.[22] As the unit came under JSOC's control, it gained its own color name: Task Force Orange. Most JSOC personnel soon referred to the unit as "TFO" or "Orange."

✳

It was mid-January 2003 and Dave Schroer was standing before Rumsfeld and the senior brass in the Pentagon. A couple of days earlier, Schloesser had told Schroer to prepare a briefing requested by the secretary on the implications for JSOC's contribution to the "global war on terror" if the United States invaded Iraq, and to recommend how to prosecute the global war if such an invasion occurred. Based on what Schloesser told him, Schroer designed his briefing to answer the question, "Can we do Iraq and continue the GWOT?"

Schroer looked out at a sea of faces that belonged to the most powerful men in the Defense Department: Rumsfeld; Wolfowitz, who had been aggressively advocating a war to topple Saddam Hussein; the Joint Chiefs; the heads of the Joint Staff's directorates; Doug Brown, now the deputy SOCOM commander; Bargewell; and Air Force Lieutenant General Victor "Gene" Renuart, CENTCOM director of operations, among others. Schroer described how the campaign would look if it proceeded on its current trajectory. He noted that there were about half a dozen "forward operating locations" that special operations forces were already establishing or should be creating soon, in places like the Philippines and the Horn of Africa. In addition, forces were still in Afghanistan, and JSOC needed to keep an alert force ready for the 0300 and 0400 missions, he said.

Then Schroer turned to what would happen if the forces needed to invade and occupy Iraq were removed from that plan. Were that to occur, it would be impossible to sustain the global war, even as "an economy of force," Schroer told his audience. ("Economy of force" is the U.S. military's term to refer to the allocation of the minimal force necessary to sustain a secondary effort.) In particular, an invasion of Iraq would result in a critical shortage of special operations helicopters available for the global war, he said. "When you looked at what folks said they needed for Iraq, you were nowhere close," said a source in the room. "So either you stopped most of the five or six [forward operating locations], or you short-sheeted Iraq."

As Schroer continued his briefing, he could tell that he wasn't getting through to the secretary. "I don't understand, what are you telling me?" Rumsfeld said. Schroer gave him the bottom line: "You can't do it—you can't get there from here." The Counterterrorism Campaign Support Group's recommendation was "Do not do Iraq now."

The reaction in the room was "almost comical," said the source who was there. "There were flag officers looking for places under the table to dive." Schroer suddenly realized the decision to invade Iraq had already been made, and he was the only person in the room who didn't know it.[23]

13

Bin Laden Slips Away

Not long after dawn on December 9, 2001, a convoy of ten white Toyota pickup trucks was bouncing over a rutted dirt road heading south from the city of Jalalabad in eastern Afghanistan's Nangarhar province. A casual observer might have remarked on the relative newness of the vehicles, but otherwise would have seen nothing unusual about a convoy of trucks carrying several dozen scruffy, bearded fighters, long hair flopping from under their traditional Afghan *pakool* caps.[1] In this part of the world, most men had guns, and those of substance traveled with a well-armed entourage. For the last several years Taliban convoys had become commonplace in Nangarhar, as had those of Al Qaeda fighters, whose leader had something akin to a country estate in the mountains up ahead.

But if a passerby had the opportunity to take a closer look, he'd have noticed that the trucks' interiors were a little unusual. They had been stripped for action, with the backseats and anything else superfluous ripped out to lighten the vehicles and create more room. The pickups were now small enough to squeeze onto a Chinook and light enough to fly on small fixed wing aircraft. Delta's engineers had even made them sturdy enough to be airdropped from a Combat Talon.[2]

As for the passengers, some were indeed local Afghan militiamen, but many others were assaulters and snipers from Delta's A1 and A3 troops, respectively. The weapons the operators gripped under their blankets were not the AK-series assault rifles ubiquitous in these parts, but SR-25 sniper rifles and M4s spray-painted in camouflage patterns and tricked out with laser designators and holographic sights. Other cutting-edge technology was stowed in their rucksacks or the many pockets of their customized gear.

The convoy was nearing the end of what an operator described as a "hellacious" thirteen-hour drive from Bagram, broken only by a couple of hours' break at a Jalalabad safe house. Now, with the mountains looming ahead, the trucks suddenly pulled over and stopped. The operators dismounted and turned their gaze south, focusing on a small dot in the azure sky far ahead of and above them, a Combat Talon flying through a patch of the heavens that until then had been the domain of B-52s and fighter-bombers. As they watched, an even smaller speck tumbled from the plane, floating toward the mountains under a parachute barely visible from the road. Most of the operators watching realized that up close, that speck was the size of a car and contained 12,600 pounds of explosive. One of the largest conventional bombs in the world, the BLU-82 daisy cutter had been designed to clear landing zones in the Vietnamese jungle. Now the United States was employing it to seal caves in the Afghan mountains. For several seconds the watchers held their breath. When the bomb detonated, the effect was underwhelming. The ground did not shake as expected, nor did the sound of a massive explosion reach the operators' ears. What one described as a "nice mushroom cloud" rising over the snowcapped peaks was the only indication that a major blast had just shaken the mountains several miles ahead.

The troops got back on the trucks and continued south. The sleep-deprived operators were exhausted but impatient to get to their destination. They represented the most elite troops the United States had to offer, but the most important battle of the war had started without them, at a place called Tora Bora.[3]

✳

More than twelve weeks after September 11, JSOC was finally on the hunt for Osama bin Laden. The command had developed a certain man-hunting expertise through its pursuits of Noriega, Escobar, Aideed, and the Balkan war criminals. But until Dailey's November 17 change-of-mission video-teleconference, finding the Al Qaeda leader was considered strictly the CIA's job. "No one tasked JSOC" to go after bin Laden in the weeks after September 11, a retired special operations officer said. "The CIA thought that was their mission and they didn't need any goddamn help doing it." To an extent, this was a repeat of the Balkans, where the CIA did much of the work locating the targets, with JSOC elements deploying to execute the culminating raids.

In time, JSOC would gain a reputation as the nation's premier man-hunting organization, but in late 2001 it lacked the intelligence infrastructure required for such missions. "JSOC was a reactive, 'you've got the intelligence for me, I will execute this hard target' organization,'" the retired special ops officer said. "Intelligence wasn't JSOC's strong point."

As it turned out, the CIA was doing its job reasonably well, and by late November had received multiple reports that bin Laden had retreated to his mountain base in Nangarhar.[4] That base's name was destined to become a catchphrase, in the United States, at least, for missed opportunity: Tora Bora.

Bin Laden's presence there should have come as no surprise to the U.S. forces on his trail. The Al Qaeda leader's historic association with Tora Bora was no secret. He knew the area intimately and felt secure there. It is a truism regarding hunted individuals that they tend to go to ground where they feel most at home. Bin Laden was no exception.

In the first weeks after September 11, Al Qaeda's leader had mostly divided his time between Kabul and his headquarters outside Kandahar, opting for Kabul once the bombs started falling. But when the Taliban fled the capital in mid-November, he withdrew to the region he knew best: the Jalalabad area. Nestled in a broad valley that terminated at the fabled Khyber Pass into Pakistan, the city had been bin Laden's home after he moved his headquarters to Afghanistan from Sudan in 1996. About thirty miles to the south, on the northern slopes of the Spin Ghar Mountains, lay Tora Bora, which functioned as both a beloved vacation home and a military redoubt for the Al Qaeda leader. The mountains' southern slopes were in Pakistan, the border of which jutted into Afghanistan in a twenty-mile-wide protuberance known as the Parachinar salient. Bin Laden had first gotten to know the area—and the Pashtun warlords, tribal chiefs, and village elders who ran society there—during the 1980s war with the Soviets and their Afghan communist allies. He had gained combat experience near there in 1987's battle of Jaji. He had also financed and built a rudimentary road from Jalalabad to Tora Bora and on to the Pakistan border. After constructing what amounted to a settlement above the snow line at Tora Bora, he would take his sons on regular seven-to-fourteen-hour hikes into Pakistan, telling them: "We never know when war will strike. We must know our way out of the mountains."

Now bin Laden's multinational force, composed mostly of Arab and Central Asian fighters, was retreating to Tora Bora from battlefields the newly enabled Northern Alliance had forced them to abandon. Soon they were at work digging trenches and stockpiling food at the base, which was organized around modest bunkers and smallish caves, rather than the Bond-villain subterranean lair imagined by some in the West. Sometime in the week prior to November 25, bin Laden and Zawahiri left Jalalabad in a convoy of four-wheel-drive vehicles that took three hours to ascend the Spin Ghar foothills and reach Tora Bora. It was there that bin Laden planned to make his final stand in Afghanistan.[5]

⚹

As November gave way to December, Delta's A Squadron (minus A2 Troop, which was already in Afghanistan) boarded two C-17s at Pope Air Force Base and flew to Masirah. The newly arrived operators stayed on the desert island just a few days, getting brought up to speed by their outgoing B Squadron counterparts and receiving Dailey's guidance before flying on to Bagram on December 5. The dilapidated and heavily mined air base had spent much of the past decade on the front lines of the various Afghan civil wars, changing hands several times, and its cratered runway, pockmarked buildings, and junked aircraft symbolized the backward steps Afghanistan had taken in that time. Few structures had complete roofs and none had running water or electricity, but Delta's engineers went to work to create conditions that could support operations.[6] The Afghan winter had just begun to bite.

A lead element under A1 troop commander Major Tom Greer drove down to Tora Bora December 6. The newly arrived Delta operators were keen to get started, but the reality was they were already two weeks late to the fight. Two weeks previously, as soon as Berntsen had received what he viewed as actionable intelligence placing bin Laden in Nangarhar, the CIA team chief and Erwin had gone to Bagram to discuss their options with Colonel John Mulholland, the 5th Special Forces Group commander, and another Special Forces officer assigned to the CIA. Scrutinizing a map of eastern Afghanistan spread over the hood of a Humvee, they wrestled with the operational dilemma before them.[7] Their nation's number one enemy was likely ensconced in the Spin Ghar Mountains, defended by an estimated 1,500 to 3,000[8] fanatically loyal fighters. Rooting him out would ordinarily require a large infantry force. But the special operations officers had no large U.S. infantry force at their disposal. (There were 10th Mountain Division troops in Uzbekistan and Marine forces in Kandahar, however.) The United States had two major paratroop infantry units: the Ranger Regiment and the 82nd Airborne Division. Each maintained a battalion ready to deploy at short notice, either of which could have been dropped into or near Tora Bora within a couple of days. (Indeed, there had been a plan to drop an entire 82nd brigade to seize Kabul's airport, had the Northern Alliance advance ground to a halt outside the capital.)[9] But CENTCOM never seriously considered using large U.S. infantry formations to seal Tora Bora. Up and down the military chain of command, generals and their civilian bosses had become prisoners of their recently formulated conventional wisdom, which was that the introduction of large military formations into Afghanistan would automatically engender fierce hostility and outright resistance from the local population, and that the Afghan mountains posed impossible logistical and tactical challenges for U.S. troops. The speed with which the Northern Alliance had been able to roll back the Taliban once the United States had applied the vital formula of CIA money, Special Forces know-how, and airpower had also seduced the decision makers into believing they could destroy Al Qaeda and the Taliban without the deployment of thousands of infantrymen.

But the Northern Alliance leaders were busy helping themselves to the fruits of power in Kabul and had no interest in helping the Americans fight the Taliban on their own turf: the Pashtun provinces of eastern and southern Afghanistan. Most Pashtun warlords were loyal to the Taliban, so in an effort to rent an army with which the United States could assault bin Laden's mountain fastness, the CIA was forced to ally with three less well known and barely vetted militia chiefs in the Nangarhar region, spending several million dollars of U.S. taxpayer money in the process.[10]

Berntsen was about to move a small element to Nangarhar to work with the militias and develop the situation. He asked Mulholland, whose Special Forces teams had done so much to help the Northern Alliance, to support the plan, such as it was, with a single A-team. (A fully manned A-team, officially known as an operational detachment-alpha, has twelve soldiers.) But the 5th Group commander, who had yet to lose a soldier in Afghanistan, was extremely reluctant to commit his forces into the relative unknown of Nangarhar. He agreed to send the team in a week, if Berntsen's men had survived that long. The next day, November 18, Berntsen sent eight men, including three JSOC personnel, to Jalalabad.[11]

After linking up with Hazrat Ali, a militia boss the CIA was paying, the Agency team spent a week north of Jalalabad before moving south on November 25 as intelligence increasingly indicated that bin Laden was at Tora Bora. They established a base in an abandoned schoolhouse at the foot of the Spin Ghar Mountains. Once they'd familiarized themselves somewhat with the environment and their new allies, and with no other U.S. forces in the area, on December 4 Berntsen and Erwin sent four Americans into Tora Bora: a Delta operator, a 24th STS combat controller, a former Delta operator now working as a CIA contractor, and a former Special Forces soldier with the CIA's Special Activities Division. After hiking for the better part of two days with their local guides, they found an ideal observation post and called in air strikes on Al Qaeda positions for fifty-six hours straight.[12]

Once A Squadron's main body arrived at the schoolhouse, the U.S. forces at Tora Bora included the CIA team, a Special Forces A-team Mulholland had finally provided, a few combat controllers from 24th Special Tactics Squadron, and a small Army of Northern Virginia signals intelligence element. But the Delta operators from A1 and A3 Troops comprised the main U.S. combat force. There were also about a dozen operators from the British Special Boat Service, the rough equivalent of SEAL Team 6. A3 lacked a commissioned officer, and was led instead by the troop sergeant major, Bryan "Butt Monkey" Morgan, so Greer became the overall ground force commander. The senior enlisted man and most experienced operator present was A Squadron's command sergeant major, Greg "Ironhead" Birch. Squadron commander Lieutenant Colonel John Alexander remained in Bagram.[13]

※

From the outset, the CIA men on the ground in Nangarhar did not think that the formula that had worked thus far would succeed at Tora Bora. They had no faith in their putative Afghan "allies." To stand a good chance of killing or capturing bin Laden, they knew they would need a more tactically proficient and reliable force, an assessment they relayed repeatedly—with growing alarm each time—to Washington.[14] As a result of these warnings, at the end of November Hank Crumpton found himself in the Oval Office briefing Bush and Cheney, a map of Tora Bora and the surrounding area spread out on the floor. Realizing the military chain of command had not conveyed the CIA's concerns to Bush, Crumpton got to the point. "We're going to lose our prey if we're not careful," he told the president, before urging the immediate deployment of U.S. forces to Tora Bora. Bush appeared surprised. The Pakistanis had promised him they would seal the border. The president asked if the Afghan militias at Tora Bora were "up to the job." "Definitely not, Mr. President," Crumpton replied. "Definitely not."[15]

On December 3, "Dusty," a member of Berntsen's team who was a retired Ranger and Delta operator, recommended inserting a Ranger battalion—about 800 men—to seal the south side of the mountains. Legendary CIA operative and former Special Forces soldier Billy Waugh, also on Berntsen's team, echoed Dusty's counsel. Berntsen endorsed the request and relayed it to Crumpton at Langley.[16] Another team member called Crumpton directly from the base of Tora Bora to repeat the request. The next morning Crumpton called Franks and passed on the message. Franks was noncommittal, concerned that no planning had been done for deploying any substantial infantry force.[17] (Given that, according to Franks himself, Pakistani president Pervez Musharraf had told him a month previously that bin Laden might already be at Tora Bora,[18] it's hard to know who Franks had to blame but himself for the failure to plan for that eventuality.)

Franks was obsessed with not repeating the Soviets' mistake of deploying large conventional formations into Afghanistan. Like President Bush, Franks also had a misplaced faith in the willingness and ability of Pakistani military—the Taliban's patrons—to seal the border. "Our friends in Islamabad wanted the terrorists dead or captured just as much as we did," he later wrote.[19] For his part, Rumsfeld never received a request for more forces from either Franks or Tenet, according to the defense secretary's autobiography.[20]

The attitudes of Dailey, Mulholland, and, to a lesser extent, John Alexander, reflected Franks's caution. The Delta officer ruled out any Delta teams infiltrating Tora Bora by helicopter, at least on the Afghan side of the border. A Mogadishu veteran, Alexander was leery of using helicopters in a role that put them at risk of being shot down. The Al Qaeda forces in Tora Bora were equipped with 14.5mm antiaircraft guns, 12.7mm heavy machine guns, and RPG-7 rocket-propelled grenades, any of which could turn a multimillion-dollar TF Brown Chinook into a smoldering heap of wire and metal. Instead, Alexander proposed a helicopter insertion of several Delta sniper teams onto the Spin Ghar range's southern slopes via Pakistan. This view found support with Greer and his men. "Having Delta guarding the far side of the mountain passes, closing the ring, would have made a huge difference," Greer wrote. A higher echelon of command "way, way above us" denied the plan, he added. (Alexander also wanted to drop CBU-89 cluster bombs to mine the passes, but this option too was denied, likely at the four-star level or higher, in part because some international partners threatened to withdraw their forces if the United States used such munitions.) However, like his bosses, Alexander was an advocate of letting the Afghans take the lead, something with which his troops on the ground strongly disagreed.[21]

Mulholland's orders to the members of the one A-team he allowed to venture onto the Tora Bora battlefield were that they were authorized only to engage in "terminal guidance operations"—i.e., calling in air strikes. On no account were they to maneuver against the Al Qaeda forces in front of them.[22] Dailey was equally cautious, repeatedly ordering the Delta operators to let the Afghans take the lead. In the December 2 meeting with A Squadron on Masirah, the JSOC commander conveyed "an impression of hesitancy" to Greer. "Somehow I got the impression the general was not too keen on Delta venturing up into the mountains," the Delta officer wrote. To Greer's disappointment, Dailey ruled out the use of Rangers as a quick reaction force, preferring to leave even that role to the local hires. Greer thought the idea that an untrained Afghan militia could compensate for the Rangers' absence "was a complete pipe dream."[23]

There were no easy options available to the generals. Air-dropping or air-assaulting troops to encircle the Al Qaeda forces would have stretched U.S. air-to-air refueling resources and would have required repeated and dangerous resupply missions. The landscape of snowy gorges and steep-sided 14,000-foot mountains was extraordinarily tough—"the most formidable terrain that we fought in," according to Lieutenant Colonel Mark Rosengard,[24] Mulholland's operations officer—and well defended by hard-core fighters who were using every additional day granted them by the U.S. generals' inaction to improve their fortifications. But the United States military, especially JSOC's superbly trained and equipped forces, had a variety of means of infiltration at its disposal and access to the best cold-weather gear in the world, not to mention the ability to call on an almost limitless supply of smart bombs from the jets overhead. It's hard to believe that had those forces been committed to the fight in the mountains, they would not have prevailed against militants drawn in large part from the desert nations of Arabia.

Left to fend for themselves, the JSOC operators and CIA operatives performed heroically. They first took over two observation posts the Special Forces team had been manning, then braved heavy machine gun and mortar fire to push farther into the heart of the Al Qaeda positions. As the CIA men had warned, the Afghans displayed little appetite for the fight, retreating every night from ground taken during the day.[25] (It didn't help that the entire operation was occurring during Ramadan, during which pious Muslims do not eat or drink between sunup and sundown. This left the Afghans weak and dehydrated during the day and even less eager than usual to stay on the battlefield overnight.)[26] Greer and his men found it hard to contain their frustration. "It was just over two months since 9/11, and for the most important mission to date in the global war on terror, our nation was relying on a fractious bunch of AK-47-toting lawless bandits and tribal thugs," he wrote.[27] This was where Mulholland's refusal to commit any forces to work with the Afghans cost the United States. Unlike Special Forces soldiers, each of whom was specially trained to work with indigenous allies, Delta operators received little or no such training. Greer had received none.[28]

Day after day, night after night in early December, the operators ground their way forward, always relying on the aircraft overhead and fickle Afghan allies for their protection. No Delta operator used his rifle to kill any Al Qaeda fighters during the battle.[29] Having had several weeks to array themselves, bin Laden's troops held the high ground and were dug into well-defended positions of tactical advantage. They even had a small armor force.[30]

But Greer's men also had what he described as a "secret weapon"— the Army of Northern Virginia signals collectors, who included at least one Pashto speaker and who were "regularly" picking up and, where possible, triangulating, bin Laden's radio calls.[31] Getting the Delta operators into a position to profit from that information was proving difficult, however, given the orders to do no more than support the Afghans. In the unlikely event that this approach gave them an opportunity to confront bin Laden, Dailey's guidance to the operators was direct. "It was made crystal clear to us that capturing the terrorist was not the preferred outcome," Greer wrote.[32] Meanwhile, Berntsen continued to urge the deployment of more JSOC forces, telling Langley at the end of the first week of December, "We need Rangers now! The opportunity to get bin Laden and his men is slipping away!!"[33] As usual, his pleas fell on deaf ears at CENTCOM.

On December 10, Army of Northern Virginia personnel intercepted a radio transmission that stated "Father [i.e., bin Laden] is trying to break through the siege line." Promising as that was, later that day another intercept gave the U.S. force an eight-digit grid reference point for bin Laden's position, the most detailed information the United States had had on his location since the late 1990s, according to Greer. The Delta officer led a thirty-three-man, nine-vehicle team into the mountains to try to capitalize on it. But any hopes the operators had that Hazrat Ali's forces had surrounded bin Laden's position were dashed when the "allies" abandoned the battlefield to break their fast.[34] At the same time, a three-man JSOC team called Jackal was in extreme danger, having ventured far behind Al Qaeda lines to call in a series of devastating air strikes before being spotted and taken under machine gun fire. All but five of their Afghan militiamen fled. Jackal's combat controller, nicknamed "the Admiral," passed the code word for a team escaping and evading: "Warpath. Warpath. Warpath."[35]

With night closing in, bin Laden "fading like a ghost," and Jackal's whereabouts unknown (the team was out of radio contact), Greer faced a dilemma: pursue bin Laden or search for his missing team. He chose the latter, figuring "we'll have another shot at bin Laden." Jackal finally made it to safety under their own steam that night, but the opportunity to kill bin Laden, if it had ever existed, was gone.[36] The battle stalled. To the Americans' disgust, on December 12 one of the Afghan militia leaders took it upon himself to arrange a twenty-four-hour cease-fire to allow Al Qaeda to surrender. Of course, as the Americans soon surmised, the surrender was a hoax, but it gave whatever Al Qaeda remnants had yet to flee across the border to Pakistan vital breathing space before the bombing resumed.[37]

By December 14, Delta had pushed several thousand meters into Tora Bora over the course of seventy hours.[38] Berntsen made another impassioned request to Dailey for more U.S. ground troops during a December 14 meeting in Kabul. The JSOC commander again refused, for fear of alienating the Afghan forces whose dubious allegiance the CIA was renting. Dailey's caution did not sit well with the CIA officer. "I don't give a damn about offending our allies!" he yelled at the general. "I only care about eliminating Al Qaeda and delivering bin Laden's head in a box!"[39] With bad weather interfering with air support, Greer asked Dailey to send the Ranger mortar teams at Bagram to Tora Bora, so the

U.S. forces would at least have some fire support available, but Dailey turned even that request down. (Meanwhile, Mulholland refused to let the A-team he'd sent down reenter the battlefield after they'd come out to refit, and then relieved the team leader into the bargain.)[40]

Sporadic fighting continued for another couple of days, but the battle for Tora Bora was essentially over. The international coalition opposing the Taliban had dropped more than 1,100 precision-guided munitions (otherwise known as "smart bombs") and more than 500 "dumb" gravity bombs, managing to kill at least 220 Al Qaeda fighters and capture a further fifty-two in the process. (U.S. and British forces suffered no casualties.) Greer claimed the real numbers of enemy dead were "much higher," but admitted "several hundred others probably managed to run from the field." The bottom line, as he acknowledged, was that bin Laden, Zawahiri, and hundreds of their best fighters had gotten away.[41]

The U.S. military chain of command's extraordinary reluctance to commit the forces necessary for victory was a major factor in bin Laden's escape. The Al Qaeda chief's resourcefulness and knowledge of the mountains was doubtless another. But a couple of eyewitness reports offer the intriguing suggestion that bin Laden may have had outside help. At least one Delta operator observed Mi-17 helicopters—a model flown by Pakistan's armed forces—flying very close to the border at the Agam Valley pass, the single egress point from Tora Bora to Pakistan that didn't involve climbing to 14,000 feet. The helicopters appeared to be making a quick trip into Afghanistan. "They were in, they were out," the operator said, adding that he suspected they were flying bin Laden to safety in Pakistan, but he had no way of proving that. However, Greer wrote that an Afghan fighter told a different Delta operator that he'd seen a helicopter he took to be Pakistani flying in fast and low to land in the Wazir Valley several days earlier. Both operators were sure the helicopters in question were not American.[42]

When A Squadron came out of Tora Bora, some operators were crowing about how many enemy fighters the air strikes they'd called in had killed up in the mountains, until Greg "Ironhead" Birch reminded them they hadn't killed the one man they'd been sent in to kill. Their mission, therefore, was a failure, he told them. The senior Delta officer on the battlefield agreed. Tora Bora "must be viewed as a military failure," according to Greer. Nonetheless, he wrote, Dailey "relayed the necessity that we paint a picture of victory."[43]

The failure prompted bitter recriminations from the operators. One said that relying on the Afghans as the main force at Tora Bora and on the Pakistanis to seal the border were "100 percent" mistakes. The "gutless" U.S. commanders' failure to seal the border was inexplicable to the operators, for whom preventing enemy "leakers" from an objective was standard operating procedure. "Not one American life could be risked to gain anything," said an operator. "Not one guy could be hurt. They didn't want us going forward on the front line with the Afghan army. They wouldn't give us reinforcements. . . . Every day we were calling for people. . . . We should have dropped the entire 82nd to seal the border. Think about what that would have done to change the war."

Another operator, who did not take part in the battle but was familiar with the area, said Greer's decision making was not above reproach and that the on-scene Delta commander should have established positions above the Agam Valley pass. "Anyone who looked at the map was like, 'Get to this pass right here and we could be armed with Hostess Ho Hos and just fucking drop 'em from the rocks above and they can't get through that pass," he said.

"The truth is [that] a little bit of risk will get you success," said the first Delta operator. "No risk, no reward, and those guys chose the 'no reward' route."

The squandering of the opportunity to destroy Al Qaeda at Tora Bora was a strategic catastrophe for the U.S. military, one it would compound three months later.

14

"Patton's Three Principles of War"

After Tora Bora, A Squadron moved to Kandahar and thence, briefly, to Tarin Kowt, the capital of Uruzgan province in the south, in search of Mullah Omar.[1] But in January, barely a month after the squadron had deployed, Dailey replaced it, not with Delta's C Squadron (whose operators were "borderline suicidal they weren't in the fight yet," as an Army special ops source put it), but with Team 6's Red Team. Dailey's decision to use SEALs rather than Delta in a landlocked country raised eyebrows in JSOC and hackles in the Delta compound, but stemmed from the commander's view that the United States was now engaged in a global war that might last decades. Committing Delta to Afghanistan full-time would exhaust the unit within nine months, Dailey thought. He knew the Army special mission unit had the edge over Team 6 on land, but was sure the SEALs could handle the Afghanistan mission.

A name change accompanied the end-of-year unit rotation. Task Force Sword became Task Force 11, the first of many such changes intended to obscure JSOC's role in the wars of the new millennium.

There were also leadership changes at all levels. By early 2002, Dailey had returned to Pope Air Force Base and handed the Task Force 11 reins to his deputy commander, Air Force Brigadier General Gregory Trebon, a special ops pilot with vast experience in the air but none running manhunts or other tactically complex ground operations. Another key personnel switch saw Pete Blaber replace Scotty Miller as head of advance force operations in Afghanistan. A former commander of Delta's B Squadron, Blaber had extensive man-hunting experience in Colombia and the Balkans. Highly respected by both peers and subordinates, he was an independent thinker who often found himself in conflict with Dailey's cautious approach. Nonetheless, whether Dailey realized it or not, in making Blaber the AFO commander, he was giving the Delta officer a chance to put his unconventional approach to work in the real world.

Amid all the changes, Dailey kept one thing constant. Despite the fact that the United States now had access to any base in Afghanistan, the JSOC commander insisted his joint operations center remain on Masirah, 700 miles from the action.

※

By the time Blaber arrived at Bagram in the first week of January, the trails of bin Laden, Zawahiri, and Mullah Omar had gone cold. U.S. leaders suspected Al Qaeda still had significant forces in the field. They just didn't know where. Blaber quickly reorganized his forty-five-man AFO element, dividing them into six teams—three in the south and three in the northeast—that he pushed out to safe houses in the hinterlands to combine with CIA and Special Forces personnel in "pilot teams." Task Force 11 had divided its in-country forces between Bagram and Kandahar, but Blaber wasn't interested in staying at Bagram and instead established himself in the Ariana hotel, the new home of the CIA's Kabul station. It was there, at the end of January, that the deputy station chief told him that intelligence suggested Al Qaeda forces were massing about ten miles south of Gardez in eastern Afghanistan's Paktia province, in a place called the Shahikot Valley.

The conventional U.S. forces trickling into Afghanistan were also tracking the reports emanating from Paktia of an Al Qaeda buildup there. Together with the special operators, they began to plan an operation to destroy those forces. Central Command again insisted that Pashtun militia take the lead in the operation, but chastened by the failure at Tora Bora, Franks's headquarters this time permitted the inclusion of U.S. infantry in order to prevent Al Qaeda fighters from escaping. Those infantry forces consisted of a battalion each from 10th Mountain and 101st Airborne Divisions, which for the purposes of the operation to come were brought together under the 101st's 3rd Brigade. (The divisions' names were misleading: 10th Mountain was a regular light infantry unit and the 101st was a helicopter "air assault" division, rather than a paratroop formation.) Two A-teams from John Mulholland's Special Forces task force would train the Afghan militia. Major General Franklin "Buster" Hagenbeck, the 10th Mountain commander, would be in charge of the operation. However, Hagenbeck had no official command and control authority over AFO or any other Task Force 11 elements.

Central Command allowed such an ad hoc approach to what would be the United States' biggest battle of the war up to that point for several reasons. First, after more than two months with no real combat to speak of in Afghanistan, some planners were skeptical of the intelligence that a large Al Qaeda force remained in the Shahikot. Second, CENTCOM continued to insist that local forces take the lead, even if that put the operation's overall success at risk. Third, Franks and Rumsfeld were already husbanding forces for the expected invasion of Iraq, which meant starving the Afghan war effort.

Through January and February staffers from all the task forces worked on the plan, the essence of which was that the Afghan militia would sweep into the valley from the southwest as the main effort, while U.S. infantry companies air-assaulted into the valley's northern and eastern edges to prevent Al Qaeda forces, presumed to be occupying villages on the valley floor, from escaping. They named the operation Anaconda.

In February, Blaber moved his base of operations to the Gardez safe house. From there, he would command one of the most daring special operations missions in JSOC's history.

At Gardez, he was reunited with Spider, whom the CIA had sent to manage the Agency's side of the operation, and with whom Blaber had worked in the Balkans. It was clear to Blaber, Spider, and the SF officers at Gardez that it would be necessary to put U.S. eyes on the target in the Shahikot in order to discover what secrets the valley held. Confident he could infiltrate reconnaissance teams into the Shahikot, Blaber brought over two such teams from Delta's B Squadron for just that purpose. But before Blaber sent anyone anywhere near the Shahikot, he insisted that they steep themselves in the area's military history and familiarize themselves as much as possible with the region by closely studying maps, reading recent intelligence reports, and talking to the local militia. Like Tora Bora, the Shahikot ("Place of Kings" in Pashto) had been a mujahideen stronghold in the 1980s. Blaber knew many lessons from that war would still hold true in 2002. A staunch opponent of the "stovepiping" of intelligence by which U.S. government agencies kept information from others by arguing that they didn't have a "need to know," Blaber spoke instead of a "need to share," and practiced what he preached. Putting his command post in Gardez ensured that he, Spider, and the Special Forces officers were all on the same page.

Before Blaber sent his teams into the Shahikot itself, he wanted to conduct a "proof of concept" reconnaissance mission to further define the art of the possible when it came to moving on foot through the mountains in the middle of the Afghan winter. (He was strongly opposed to helicopter infiltrations of reconnaissance teams, on the grounds they were too predictable and ran too high a risk of compromise.) Between February 20 and 26 Blaber sent the two Delta teams on what he called "environmental recons." India Team, which included two B3 operators, a Team 6 SEAL, and an Army of Northern Virginia operative, approached the Shahikot from the south, trudging through driving wind and heavy snow to within 3,000 meters of the valley before turning back. Juliet Team, consisting of three B3 operators, a Team 6 SEAL, and a 24th Special Tactics Squadron combat controller, explored the valley's northern approaches in equally arduous conditions that would have stymied lesser operators. The environmental recons proved that the high altitude and bad weather actually gave the well-equipped AFO operators an advantage: the Al Qaeda forces did not expect Americans to brave the elements and penetrate their lines in such conditions, and had focused their surveillance on vehicular routes to the Shahikot.

Events were now moving fast. D-day for Anaconda was set for February 28. Blaber knew he needed to have his teams in place overlooking the valley before the attack began. He also knew that, superb as they were, the two reconnaissance teams he had would not give him the coverage he wanted. He persuaded Captain Joe Kernan, the Team 6 commander, to loan him a five-man reconnaissance team called Mako 31 for the operation. With bad weather delaying D-day until March 2, Blaber launched his three teams the evening of February 27.

This time, Juliet's five operators would not be on foot. They were riding super-quiet all-terrain vehicles equipped with infrared headlights and a variety of navigational aids as they approached from the north, heading toward their desired observation post on the Shahikot's eastern ridgeline. Because passes that had seemed navigable from overhead imagery turned out to be impenetrable, they were forced to ride at midnight through a small village supposedly garrisoned by at least 100 Al Qaeda fighters. They made it through, only to find themselves in a minefield, which they escaped by steering their ATVs along a 45-degree exposed rock slope for several hundred meters. They continued on, ascending through increasingly thick snow, invisible under the moonless night sky to the fighters they spotted manning two heavy machine gun positions about 4,000 feet above them. Finally, after covering twelve kilometers in nine hours, they were in position.

India Team, which for this mission consisted of just the two Delta operators and the Army of Northern Virginia signals intelligence collector, was moving on foot, but found the going much less arduous than the environmental recon. After walking seven kilometers, India Team reported at 5:22 A.M. that it too had reached its observation post, located at the valley's southwestern corner. Mako 31, which included three SEALs, a Navy explosive ordnance disposal expert, and a combat controller, faced an exceptionally tough hike over 8,000-foot ridgelines and through knee-deep snow to get into position on a finger-shaped ridgeline jutting into the southern end of the valley. Movement was so tough the team had to stop a little short of the observation post as dawn beckoned, resting up until they could cover the final thousand meters the next night. Nonetheless, by dawn, Blaber had passed three teams through Al Qaeda's lines of defense and positioned them in or near the Shahikot Valley. It was an enormous success, the value of which would become even clearer during the next three days. It also validated his approach, which combined tactical boldness with painstaking preparation.

The next day, the teams' reports proved beyond doubt the presence of a large Al Qaeda force in the Shahikot: enemy positions and movement on the western ridgeline, radio communications monitored by the two Army of Northern Virginia personnel, and, just after noon, the sound of marksmanship training from a village on the valley floor. Blaber reported all this and more to Bagram and Masirah, but despite the news that the enemy were in the high ground as much as they were on the valley floor, the commanders made no changes to the plan.

Just after first light on March 1, two Mako 31 snipers crept 500 meters to check out the exact spot the team and Blaber had selected for their observation post. Peering around rocks to get their first glimpse, they made a startling discovery: Al Qaeda had already occupied the position. There was a gray-green tent that could sleep several people and, fifteen meters away, a heavy machine gun positioned to overwatch the narrow southeastern entrance to the valley through which every infantry-laden Chinook and Black Hawk was due to fly in twenty-four hours. The ranges would have been such that the Caucasian heavy machine gunner the SEALs observed and photographed could hardly have missed. Mako 31's infiltration, and, in a larger sense, Blaber's belief in the value of human reconnaissance and the abilities of his men, had saved Anaconda from disaster.

Early the next morning, Mako 31's three SEALs moved stealthily to within twenty meters of the tent, intending to wait until 5:30 A.M.—one hour before the air assault was to begin—before eliminating the Al Qaeda position. But when a fighter emerged at 4 A.M. and spotted them, it was game on. As five militants poured from the tent, the SEALs opened fire, only for two of their rifles to jam as soon as they'd fired a single round. The third SEAL held the enemy off as his colleagues quickly cleared the jams and resumed firing. They dropped three of the tent's occupants before calling for fire from an AC-130 overhead, which took care of the others with a few well-placed 105mm rounds.

The rest of Operation Anaconda's first day did not go as well for the Coalition. The combined Afghan militia/Special Forces column named Task Force Hammer descended into chaos after a Special Forces warrant officer and two Afghans died in a friendly fire attack from the same AC-130 crew that had destroyed the Al Qaeda observation post. When a planned series of bombing runs on the valley's humpbacked western ridgeline did not materialize, and Al Qaeda mortars opened up on them, Task Force Hammer's attack stalled before reaching the valley. Although the infantry was supposed to be the supporting effort, the air assault continued as planned. But when the infantry companies landed on the valley floor they found themselves under much heavier fire than they anticipated, pouring down from Al Qaeda positions in the mountainsides. One 10th Mountain platoon, plus its company and battalion command posts, were pinned down for most of the day in the southern end of the valley.

During those difficult hours, the AFO presence in the high ground, hidden from the enemy, was a major factor in preventing the infantry from being overrun. Together the teams gave Blaber a better picture of the battlefield than any other commander enjoyed, and from their perches they were able to call down punishing air strikes on Al Qaeda positions. Indeed, Hagenbeck was on the verge of pulling his troops out of the battle before Blaber jumped on the radio and changed his mind, telling him via the AFO liaison officer in Bagram (none other than Jim Reese) that this was "the battlefield opportunity of a lifetime" and he intended to keep his teams in the Shahikot decimating the enemy through air strikes until there was no more killing to be done. Instead of withdrawing completely from the valley, Hagenbeck pulled out two elements that had been pinned down in the south and west and repositioned the other platoons. Incredibly, other than the Special Forces' friendly fire casualty, the U.S. had suffered no troops killed in action up to that point.

But the battle began to turn for AFO the next morning when a bunch of SEALs arrived at Gardez. They were not AFO personnel, but Team 6 operators desperate for action, having seen almost none since arriving in-country. Over Blaber's objections, Trebon ordered him to insert the SEALs that night and to turn his whole AFO operation in the Shahikot over to Team 6 as soon as possible. These orders ran contrary to Blaber's whole approach, which stressed the importance of operators familiarizing themselves with the environment before infiltrating. The careful preparations that lay behind the AFO teams' success were lost on those following the operation from Bagram and Masirah, from which inserting teams into the mountains and calling in accurate air strikes must have appeared easy. When the SEAL commander immediately established separate communications with Team 6 in Bagram and Task Force 11 in Masirah, cutting Blaber out of the loop, command and control of the most successful part of Anaconda began to fray.

The SEALs wanted to put a team on the highest point overlooking the Shahikot, the top of a mountain named Takur Ghar. Breaking one of Blaber's foundational rules, they were going to insert the team that night via Chinook. "Slab," the team leader, planned to land at an offset location and climb Takur Ghar, but a series of delays meant the infiltration occurred much later than planned. He had been ordered to get in position by dawn, and there wasn't time to ascend the mountain on foot and still make that deadline. Slab reluctantly told the pilots to fly his team straight to the top of the mountain. When they did so, they discovered, just as Mako 31 had, that the enemy was already there. Two RPGs tore into the aircraft, shredding its electrical and hydraulics systems. In an extraordinary display of skill, the pilot managed to get the stricken helicopter airborne and fly it 7,000 feet before having to put it down at the Shahikot's northern end. But in the confusion as the helicopter lifted off the peak, one SEAL, Petty Officer First Class Neil Roberts, jumped or fell out the back.

A fog of confusion and miscommunication then descended upon all headquarters trying to control events in the Shahikot. This was the inevitable result of the bifurcated command and control system, under which the senior U.S. officer, Hagenbeck, had no control over Task Force 11. Trebon, who was visiting the Team 6 operations center in Bagram, compounded the problem by taking command and control authority from Blaber and Reese, who had better situational awareness of events in the Shahikot than any other officers. Trebon retained "command" for himself but handed "control" to his desert island headquarters 1,100 miles from the Shahikot. The six-foot-five brigadier general, nicknamed "Chewbacca" on account of his height and bushy, rigorously combed gray hair, placed his faith in Task Force 11's high-tech communications systems and Predator imagery, rather than on the officers best prepared for this crisis.

As a result, although Al Qaeda forces killed Roberts about ninety minutes after he landed in their midst, almost half an hour later another Task Force Brown Chinook returned Slab's team to the top of Takur Ghar in a valiant but vain attempt to rescue their comrade. A blizzard of fire met the helicopter. It was able to drop off the SEALs and get away, but the operators found themselves in a hellacious nighttime firefight, outnumbered and outgunned on the top of a frigid mountaintop. Two were badly wounded and 24th STS Technical Sergeant John Chapman appeared to be killed. What happened next caused a rift between units in JSOC that took years to repair. Under heavy fire and with no time to exhaustively check for vital signs, the fact that Chapman was not moving nor showing any signs of life convinced the SEALs he was dead. Realizing they had bitten off more than they could chew, they withdrew over the lip of the mountaintop and slid down the steep side of Takur Ghar.

Meanwhile, a confused Task Force 11 headquarters in Masirah ordered the quick reaction force—1st Platoon, A Company, 1st Ranger Battalion—led by Captain Nate Self to launch. But nobody told Self or the aircrew that they were flying to a heavily defended enemy position where the two previous helicopters had taken heavy fire, a mountaintop the SEALs had already vacated.

On that mountaintop, a fierce firefight was under way between an individual in a bunker and two other combatants maneuvering against him. The individual in the bunker killed one with an expert shot, but was killed by the other. A Predator unmanned aerial vehicle overhead captured the entire episode. Colonel Andy Milani, a 160th officer later tasked by Dailey to investigate the Takur Ghar fight, concluded that

there were only two possible explanations: confused Al Qaeda personnel were fighting each other, or Chapman was still alive and, wounded
and alone on the mountain, was taking it to the enemy. (However, another source who watched the video noted that the fighter in the bunker
was firing his weapon on full auto, which would be very unusual for a
special mission unit operator, and that Chapman's rifle had a suppressor,
which the man in the bunker's did not.) Whatever the truth, forty-five
seconds after the bunker combatant's resistance was finally ended, the
Chinook carrying Nate Self and half his men loomed over the mountaintop. The quick reaction force had arrived.

On the mountainside below, Slab saw the Chinook approaching. He
tried desperately to raise the helicopter on his radio (the only one of his
team's that still had battery power), but the quick reaction force was using a different frequency than the one to which his radio was set. He
frantically switched over to a new frequency, but it was too late. At that
moment, as the Chinook flared to land, Al Qaeda greeted it with a brutal fusillade, killing a crew chief and a Ranger, while wounding a pilot
and another crew chief. The helicopter landed with a bump, the ramp
dropped, and the Rangers charged off, straight into a hail of bullets. Two
more fell, killed instantly, as the other Rangers sought cover where they
could and returned fire. For the next several hours the battle raged on
the snowy mountaintop, as the Task Force 11 staff on Masirah struggled to figure out what was happening. For the first time, an armed CIA
Predator was used as close air support for ground troops when the unmanned aerial vehicle destroyed a troublesome Al Qaeda bunker with a
Hellfire missile. The little band of Rangers, aviators, and airmen fought
bravely, steadily gaining the upper hand over the Al Qaeda fighters.
When the second half of the quick reaction force arrived on foot, having landed farther down the mountain, the Rangers assaulted and cleared
the top of Takur Ghar, taking no further U.S. casualties.

But before Self could arrange a medevac for his casualties, Al Qaeda
counterattacked from a neighboring ridge separated from the peak by a
saddle. This attack seriously wounded two more Americans: a 160th
medic and an Air Force pararescueman. Bombing runs from an endless
stack of jets subdued the counterattack, but Trebon, with support from
Dailey, who was monitoring the operation from JSOC headquarters at
Pope, refused to send medevac aircraft to pull the wounded out until after
dark. Senior Airman Jason Cunningham, the pararescueman wounded

in the counterattack, died in the intervening period. He was the last U.S. casualty on Takur Ghar.

Anaconda would continue officially for two more weeks, but the Takur Ghar battle was the last heavy fighting. The coalition forces—especially the three AFO reconnaissance teams—had inflicted scores, possibly hundreds, of casualties on the Al Qaeda forces. But as at Tora Bora, hundreds of others escaped to Pakistan, including the militants' presumed leader in the Shahikot, Tohir Yuldeshev, who headed Al Qaeda's Central Asian franchise, the Islamic Movement of Uzbekistan. The operation served as a warning of the dangers of relying too heavily on technology. Overhead imagery systems had not detected many Al Qaeda positions, including those on Takur Ghar, and communications systems failed repeatedly at key junctures. But Anaconda also validated Blaber's approach to strategic reconnaissance, which he summed up by referencing what he called "Patton's three principles of war": "Audacity, audacity, and audacity." This served to expose the deep rift between Delta's way of doing business—as exemplified by Blaber—and the micromanagement favored by Dailey and Trebon.[2] That rift would widen during another daring operation in a different theater the following year.

PART III

BUILDING THE MACHINE

15

Invasion

On an April night a small white propeller aircraft descended out of the darkness about 115 miles northwest of Baghdad. The plane had been in the inventory for years but had never before been used for a clandestine infiltration. Now its two Echo Squadron pilots were a hundred miles behind enemy lines searching through their night vision goggles for a place to land. There was no airfield—not even a dirt strip—nearby. But they weren't worried. Up ahead, on the only paved road for miles around, they spotted the glow of an infrared chemical light a 24th Special Tactics Squadron operator had placed where he wanted them to touch down. Aligning the aircraft with the thin black ribbon across the desert, the lead pilot lowered the plane until the wheels screeched on the tarmac and the aircraft came to a rest. Out stepped a lean, athletic man in his early forties. In Delta they called him "Panther" and he was arriving to take charge of a small task force with a big mission. That was nothing new for him. What was unusual was the makeup of his force. For the first time since the Panama invasion a U.S. special operations force was taking tanks into battle, and Pete Blaber was going to lead it.[1]

※

Although the U.S. military's failures at Tora Bora and Anaconda meant Al Qaeda's leadership and thousands of its fighters had escaped to Pakistan, it was clear to most in JSOC that the next phase of the Bush administration's "war on terror" would not be a covert campaign against its enemies strategizing in Pakistan's tribal areas, but an invasion of Iraq. The JSOC staff was discussing a potential role for the command in such an operation by the end of 2001. Real planning for it began shortly after Anaconda, when the staffers returned to Pope Air Force Base from Masirah, and, together with their Delta counterparts, were busy dusting off Desert Storm plans and after-action reports for reminders of lessons learned twelve years previously.[2] Task Force Brown's aircrews had little doubt where their next battles lay. "All of our training exercises, all of our scenarios were built off an Iraqi scenario" once the unit returned to Fort Campbell in December 2001, a Little Bird pilot said.

December 2002 found the JSOC staff in Qatar taking part in Internal Look, CENTCOM's war game of an Iraq invasion.[3] Within three months, Dailey had established his joint operations center at Arar, the same airfield JSOC used during Desert Storm. There, out of sight of the news media and never officially acknowledged, a substantial force was gathering. Not only did it include the usual color-coded elements that formed a JSOC task force, but also a significant contribution from the conventional Army: an infantry battalion from the 82nd Airborne Division, a Patriot air defense missile unit, and a High-Mobility Artillery Rocket System, or HIMARS, battery. (A truck-mounted version of the Army's tracked Multiple Launch Rocket System, HIMARS could also fit on a Combat Talon. Its mobility made it an ideal fire support platform for a raiding force.) Together, the elements assembling fifty miles from the Iraqi border were called Task Force 20.[4]

Most of the 160th's 1st Battalion was involved, other than those crews required to stay home and maintain the Bullet package of helicopters ready for a no-notice JSOC mission. "Those guys, they were hating life," said a Little Bird pilot. "They thought they were going to miss all the action, that this was going to be a fight that was going to be over in a couple of months and they'd miss the war."

Delta was to be the main special mission unit, having handed Afghanistan off to Team 6 by late 2002.[5] The unit's C Squadron, led by Lieutenant Colonel Bill Coultrup, was at Arar waiting for the action to start. But Delta commander Colonel Ron Russell had suffered a brain aneurysm while running around the airfield. With deputy commander Colonel Chuck Sellers back at Bragg, Dailey made Blaber, the unit's operations officer, Delta's acting commander in theater. Team 6's Gold Team was also there.[6]

If Delta provided Task Force 20's rapier, the Ranger Regiment provided its muscle. The Rangers were there in force because Dailey was planning the command's pièce de résistance, an airborne seizure of Baghdad airport—a classic joint readiness-exercise-style mission for which the task force had conducted large-scale rehearsals at Forts Benning and

Bragg prior to deployment. For JSOC's other assigned mission—hunting for Iraq's fabled weapons of mass destruction—Dailey's preferred option was to keep his force at Arar and launch heliborne raids from there.

Blaber, unsurprisingly, disagreed. Just as he had with regard to Afghanistan, the Delta officer advocated putting forces on the ground in Iraq to "develop the situation." Dailey and his more cautious staffers recoiled from this suggestion. Anxious about the risks that sending a raiding force into Iraq would entail, they had no interest in sending a small, lightly armed and armored task force into Iraq's vast western desert. They would remind Delta operators eager to launch into Iraq of the case of Bravo Two Zero, the eight-man British SAS patrol in Desert Storm that was compromised, leading to the deaths of three operators and the capture of four others. To Delta, Dailey's attitude was simple: *You can't operate behind enemy lines.*

Blaber thought Dailey and his nervous staffers were overestimating the risks. "Guys, you're fighting a past war again," the Delta officer told them in a briefing at Arar, before listing five assets available to Delta in 2003 that were not available in 1991: precision-guided munitions in the form of the shoulder-launched Javelin antitank missile, which would allow operators to engage tanks from stand-off range, and Joint Direct Attack Munitions, or JDAMs, which were "smart" bombs dropped by jets; small unmanned aerial vehicles a raiding party could launch to check for dangers over the next terrain feature; new, highly mobile trucks that carried generators and large quantities of fuel; trained dogs (with air-conditioned kennels) to help secure a perimeter; and battlefield interrogation teams to produce instantly actionable intelligence. Together these assets were "game-changers," he told the staffers. Blaber's men knew it. The operators were itching to roam across western Iraq. "We begged, borrowed, and begged some more just to get in," a Delta source said.

Dailey threw Blaber a bone and agreed to let him send a small task force organized around Coultrup's C Squadron across the border as part of the Scud-hunting mission that Central Command had given 5th Special Forces Group, which had set up shop at Jordan's Prince Hassan Air Base, also known as H-5. In mid-March, Blaber, Coultrup, and Colonel Frank Kearney, who was still the operations director for JSOC and Task Force 20, flew there on covered aircraft from Arar to meet with 5th Group commander John Mulholland and his 1st Battalion commander Lieutenant Colonel Chris Haas, with whom Blaber had worked closely before and during Anaconda. British SAS and SBS elements also attended the meeting.

Dailey's guidance to Blaber was clear: "You have one mission: find Scuds." (Because Scuds could be used to fire chemical warheads, U.S. military personnel often used the word to refer not just to the missiles but Saddam's WMD program.) But Blaber and his colleagues had other ideas. The acting Delta commander's order to Coultrup was classic Blaber: "Develop the situation." Despite Dailey's expectation that Delta would limit itself to poking around missile sites in the western desert, Blaber had designed Coultrup's force to go all the way to Baghdad.

"So this was like a secret mission, but secret from our own people, because we knew we weren't going to find any WMDs and we weren't going to find any Scuds," a Delta source said. New communications technology could reduce their vulnerability, he told the other commanders. Noting that they all carried Iridium satellite phones, Blaber suggested they type each other's numbers into the speed dial. If one task force came under attack, its commander should immediately text the word "baseball" to the others, who would converge on the location, thus reducing the risk of having small elements operating independently in the desert. "We will become a swarm," Blaber said.[7]

✳

On the moonless night of March 19, TF Brown pilots fired the first rounds of the war against Iraq. Their targets were the scores of small buildings known as visual observation posts from which Iraqi forces monitored the western and southern borders with Jordan, Saudi Arabia, and Kuwait. Flying from Arar, a pair of DAPs headed northwest to destroy the posts facing Jordan, while ten Little Birds—eight AH-6s and two MH-6s—flew north and northeast to take out the posts along the Saudi border. The Little Birds were divided into "Black Swarm" teams. In tactics developed the previous year during exercises across the American Southwest and at Fort Knox, Kentucky, each MH-6 was teamed with four AH-6s, divided into two pairs. As they approached the border, the pairs would separate, one pair going into a holding pattern while the other attacked the border posts with the MH-6, which would spot targets with its forward-looking infrared (FLIR) sensor and use a laser designator to identify them for the AH-6s. (All Little Birds had been fitted with FLIR systems since returning from Afghanistan, but the

AH-6 crews had removed theirs to allow the aircraft to carry more munitions.) Once the first pair of AH-6s had fired all their ammunition, the second pair would take over. The tactic was a variation on that used in Prime Chance, the 1987 operation against the Iranians in the Persian Gulf, with an important twist: each Little Bird team could call on a pair of Air Force A-10 Thunderbolt II ground attack aircraft (better known as "Warthogs") to take care of larger targets with Maverick missiles and 30mm cannon fire.

The rules of engagement allowed the pilots to target any Iraqi with a weapon. Firing sometimes from two or three miles away, the DAPs and Little Birds cut down dozens of people. Resistance was minimal and ineffective.[8] An AH-6 pilot said his team took no return fire. "It was pretty much like shooting ducks in the water," he said.

Friendly fire was perhaps a greater threat to the helicopter crews. Before the missions, TF Brown planners and crews were given maps overlaid with the paths of each cruise missile strike scheduled for that night, "so we didn't fly into one," said a pilot. The squiggly lines "looked like a jellyfish," he said. But the maps were to ensure that the crews weren't the ones getting stung. "We had to plan our flight routes around it because basically they're flying at our altitude," the pilot said. "You didn't want to be in formation with one of those."

As the DAPs and Little Birds were systematically destroying the visual observation posts and the first bombs were falling on Baghdad, a seventeen-vehicle column from Arar blasted a hole in the forty-foot berm marking the border and crossed into Iraq, the first U.S. ground force to do so. Inside the fifteen Pinzgauers and two SUVs (included for their low-vis characteristics) were about seventy-five personnel, including Delta's entire C Squadron, led by Coultrup. Pete Blaber's dream was alive. Task Force Green was in the fight.[9]

⁜

The flights targeting the visual observation posts marked the start of the U.S. invasion, but the aircrews were not the first JSOC personnel to cross the border. Prior to the invasion, a single U.S. intelligence operative—a former Delta operator still working for the unit—climbed into a black SUV in Amman, Jordan, and began the fifteen-hour drive to Baghdad, where he would become JSOC's only nonofficial cover agent in the enemy capital.

Born and raised in Eastern Europe, the agent had high Slavic cheekbones and eyes that became slits when he smiled. He had moved to the United States as a teenager, joining the Army in the 1970s before being selected into Delta early enough to take part in Eagle Claw. An operator who served with him in the early 1980s recalled "a funny, out-going guy" with a heavy accent. "He was so East European," the opera-tor said. "He slouched a little bit, he wasn't real buff. But he ran—he was fast." The East European remained in the Unit through the 1980s, joined Operational Support Troop in the early 1990s, then disappeared into the training, evaluation, and operational research (TEOR) de-partment, where older NCOs went when they no longer wanted to put up with the rigors of being in an operational squadron. For that reason, other operators sometimes referred to TEOR as "travel everywhere or retire." But the department, manned largely by personnel with technical and technological expertise, was responsible for supplying operators with one-of-a-kind gear, particularly for covert missions. "If you need a cam-era that can hide in a 'rock' or you need to have an attaché case rigged with a microphone on it," you visit the department, said a Delta source. "They developed all kinds of cool breakthrough products, the founda-tion of which were always off-the-shelf technology."

At some point the East European left the uniformed Army to become a nonofficial cover operative, or NOC (pronounced "knock"): an intel-ligence officer working under a cover identity as something other than a U.S. government employee (in the East European's case, as a business-man). This is one of the most hazardous types of intelligence work, be-cause the operative does not enjoy diplomatic immunity. The East European continued to report to Delta in his new role, but few of his old comrades knew about it. "This is totally compartmented at the Unit," said a Delta source. The agent rarely, if ever, visited the compound. An operator who had served with him in the 1980s had no idea that he'd become a nonofficial cover operative. "I just made an assumption that he'd moved on," the operator said.

For years he "lived his cover," spending time in his native country, even returning there for medical treatment as well as to meet sources. He trav-eled globally, including weeks-long trips to Latin America, Iran, and Turkey to build his cover, in addition to Iraq, which he visited repeat-edly in the 1990s to support Delta's counter-proliferation mission, in par-ticular the Unit's role in the U.S. component of the United Nations inspections. "Everybody else who did the inspections had nothing even close to being that deep or protected," said a Delta source.

The East European had his own case officer at Delta, an Army major, but the former Delta operator also had the authority to recruit and task agents himself. "Businessmen and people in the military were the people he was talking to," a senior JSOC officer said. "He was trained sufficiently enough to make contact with folks, give them covert communications," and teach them basic tradecraft such as how to perform dead drops and use the simple cameras he gave them. The East European never revealed his American background, even when recruiting his sources, the officer said. His agents never realized they had been recruited by an American.

After the September 11 attacks, intelligence and special operations officials wondered whether they were maximizing the opportunity the East European represented. "In late '01 . . . there was a lot of discussion about . . . leveraging him more and better," said an intelligence officer. "He was an asset that everybody realized may not have been leveraged in the most opportune ways."

Already in his fifties when the United States invaded Iraq, the East European had a cover his native country helped maintain, even giving him access to its Baghdad embassy. "This was a rare program in 2001–2002," the senior JSOC officer said. Nonetheless, the East European was one of about seven or eight nonofficial cover operatives JSOC and its special mission units were running in the first years after the September 11 attacks. These included at least two agents who went to Iran, the officer said: the East European, whose missions "were mostly designed to . . . look for opportunities to recruit [sources] in the Iranian military," and an Iranian-born U.S. citizen working for the Army of Northern Virginia.

Now the East European was on one of his most dangerous missions. He was not alone on the long drive from Amman to Baghdad, but his companions "were unwitting," the senior JSOC officer said. In other words, they were unaware that the vehicle in which they were riding was no ordinary SUV. The National Security Agency had outfitted it with a variety of hidden receivers that the agency's technicians could remotely tune to survey cell phone and push-to-talk FM radio network traffic. This, in turn, enabled the NSA to focus on specific emitters. When they reached Baghdad, as directed, the East European parked it close to an

Iraqi intelligence headquarters and left it there. Because the vehicle's hidden receivers could collect with a lot more sensitivity than satellites or airborne collection systems, the NSA used them to tip and cue those other sensors. In addition, the receivers could capture a large chunk of the radio frequency spectrum in Baghdad and transmit it back to be unraveled at the NSA's Fort Meade, Maryland, headquarters. "We were desperate back in 2003" for information on the Iraqi leadership's thinking and intentions, the senior JSOC officer said. The hope was that, for instance, the receivers would enable the NSA to figure out which frequencies senior Iraqi government officials' personal security details were using. "If you were trying to establish every time that Saddam Hussein's PSD [personal security detail] drove around Baghdad, this was a way of doing that," he said. "The Iraqis were notoriously poor at opsec [operational security]," often not changing their frequencies for years, he said. But although the East European successfully positioned the vehicle and the technical side of the mission worked, the JSOC officer didn't recall the effort producing "a lot of intel."

"That was not really our op," he said. "We were the delivery guys."

After dropping the vehicle off, the East European's task in Baghdad was to figure out and transmit Saddam's location for targeting by U.S. air strikes. In several cases, he conducted what a former Pentagon special operations official called "a GPS walk-by," strolling through Baghdad while wearing a Global Positioning System tracking device and pressing a button that transmitted his exact coordinates via satellite as he passed a potential target location. Such missions entailed enormous risk, not only from the Iraqi security services if the agent was compromised, but from the bombing campaign itself. Protecting him required careful, up-to-the-minute planning of the air strikes. One such strike was launched based on intelligence he provided, but Saddam was not at the targeted location.

The East European's efforts were largely in vain. "He had not recruited any sources that were giving him the whereabouts of Saddam," the senior JSOC officer said. A Delta source said the agent's European background was not much help. "It would have been better if he had been an Arab American, because no matter what embassy you're with, if you're not an Iraqi, walking around in those days would be a death sentence," he said, adding that the agent was able to provide JSOC task force leaders with little more than "environmentals"—general information about what they could expect in Baghdad. Once U.S. troops had occupied Baghdad, the East European drove back to Amman. "It's perhaps another opportunity that wasn't fully taken advantage of, but nothing really of substance came of it," the Delta source said.

When the East European's case officer moved to a job at the Defense Humint Service in the summer of 2004, and was not replaced, the East European followed him, according to an intelligence source. This represented a loss to Delta—"the guy was irreplaceable," said a Delta source—and played into the larger issue over whether special mission units should run nonofficial cover agents. By the end of the decade, the CIA was spending between $1.5 billion and $1.8 billion a year to maintain its officers' cover, and senior Pentagon leaders were hugely frustrated at the Agency's inability to deliver actionable intelligence in places like Iran, Iraq, and Syria.

Even in the 1990s, putting operators undercover was "difficult . . . unless you're lucky enough to have been born and raised in another country and have a credible missing part of your life," a Delta source said. Because soldiers go on the Department of the Army Special Roster when they join Delta, essentially hiding them from the public, the East European fulfilled both requirements. "Then you need an ally who's going to cover for you" and create a history for that missing part of the operator's life, "which they did." In the twenty-first century, creating that sort of deep "cover for status"—i.e., a plausible reason for an intelligence operative to repeatedly visit or live in certain countries—for JSOC personnel had become almost impossible "because it requires immersion and time," the source said. "It's just impossible to make that happen without all that other stuff in place."

As for the vehicle packed with top secret antennae? "I want to say the vehicle was destroyed," the senior JSOC officer said, but added that he could not be sure. "That vehicle was not exfil'd and we didn't target it" for an air strike, he said.[10]

✳

As per Dailey's orders, Task Force Green's first task was to check out a number of possible weapons of mass destruction and Scud sites in the west, before moving on to the Haditha Dam, a vast Soviet-designed structure on the Euphrates River 130 miles northwest of Baghdad that U.S. generals viewed as another potential WMD hiding place. Unlike his bosses, Blaber, who remained at Arar, was skeptical Saddam had stashed any WMD in remote sites in the western desert. The Delta officer thought it more likely the Iraqi strongman would keep such weapons, if he had them, closer to the seat of power in Baghdad. Another mission beckoned. In the weeks prior to the invasion, U.S. signals intelligence had intercepted an Iraqi general's phone calls as he drove along Highway 12 to and from the Syrian border, raising the possibility that the general was reconnoitering an escape route for the regime's leaders. Blaber ordered Coultrup to block the routes to Jordan and Syria in an effort to prevent Saddam, his sons, and other senior leaders from escaping the noose that the Coalition would soon tighten around Baghdad.[11]

For several days Task Force Green raised havoc in western Iraq, ambushing Iraqi military convoys and clearing suspected weapons of mass destruction sites, none of which held anything remotely suspicious.[12] In the meantime, as the 3rd Infantry and 1st Marine Divisions raced toward Baghdad in the fastest military advance in history, it was becoming increasingly clear in Arar that the armored columns could take the airport without JSOC's help. Despite Dailey's desperate attempts to hold on to it, Task Force 20's set-piece mission to seize the Iraqi capital's airport was evaporating before his eyes. "He was jamming a marshmallow in a piggy bank there trying to get an airfield seizure mission," said a Delta source. On March 23 the Rangers learned that the mission, which had been scheduled for the next day, was canceled. Attention now focused on Task Force Green, whose foray into Iraq Dailey had only grudgingly approved. "Suddenly it's like this is *the* JSOC mission," the Delta source said. Colonel Joe Votel, still in charge of the Ranger Regiment, which would have been the main force seizing the airport, found himself looking for a new mission. "Pete, I don't have a mission. Is there anything my guys could do for you?" he asked Blaber. "How many guys are you talking about?" the Delta officer replied. "A whole regiment," Votel said. "Yeah, we can use it!" was Blaber's reply. Dailey quickly attached Votel's 1st Battalion to Task Force Green.[13]

The Rangers were soon in the thick of the action, much of which involved seizing desert landing strips and military airfields. On the evening of March 24, 3rd Ranger Battalion's C Company seized Objective Roadrunner, a desert landing strip near Al Qaim close to the Syrian border, in a parachute assault.[14] The Rangers secured the strip while a small Delta element, supported by a pair each of MH-6s and AH-6s, operated from there, interdicting lines of communication. (Task Force Brown's

DAPs had finished their portion of the mission to destroy the visual observation posts on March 20, while the Black Swarm teams continued through March 23, pushing a little deeper into Iraq every night. From then on, Brown focused on supporting the Task Force 20 ground forces.)[15]

Task Force Green conducted raids on two airfields, H-2 and H-3, in western Iraq's Anbar province, and 1st Ranger Battalion seized another pair of airfields, Sidewinder South and Sidewinder North. The latter missions began the night of March 23 when the battalion's A Company plus a small battalion command element crossed into Iraq in newly fielded ground mobility vehicles (GMVs), driving twelve hours to a desert landing strip called Objective Coyote. The Rangers were fortunate to arrive in daylight, because the objective was strewn with unexploded ordnance. The company and battalion commanders were deep in the planning for the assault on Sidewinder South, which included the village of Nukhayb and a small military garrison as well as the airfield, when the dust storm that slowed the entire invasion hit on March 24. The Rangers at Coyote could do little other than seek shelter for two days. When the storm abated on the evening of March 26, the Rangers mounted up and drove thirty-five miles to the objective, which they cleared over the course of twelve hours, encountering little resistance.

Leaving a small element at Nukhayb, A Company returned to Coyote, where a C-17 landed on the night of March 27, disgorging 1st Battalion's C Company and a Humvee-mounted 82nd Airborne Division antitank company. With one platoon remaining at Coyote, C Company moved to Nukhayb to relieve the remaining A Company elements, who then assaulted Sidewinder North, at the village of Mudaysis on the night of March 29, supported by a 120mm mortar section, AH-6 gunships, and A-10 ground attack jets. They again encountered little resistance and after destroying weapons and munitions caches returned to Arar via Coyote.[16]

Task Force Brown, 2nd Ranger Battalion, and Team 6's Gold Team got a much hotter reception when they raided the Al Qadisiyah Research Center, otherwise known as Objective Beaver, on the night of March 26. Located on the southern shore of the man-made lake north of the Haditha Dam, the research center was a suspected biological and chemical weapons facility. The raid was a classic JSOC set-piece operation: Rangers from 2nd Battalion's B Company landed in four MH-60K Black Hawks and established four blocking positions, isolating the facility. Two MH-47E Chinooks delivered the Gold Team assaulters next to the target building, while a pair each of DAPs and AH-6s provided fire support, as did two MH-6s used as Gold Team sniper platforms. Another two Chinooks would be close by, prepared to infil an immediate reaction force.

After refueling and picking up four Gold Team snipers, the Little Birds launched from Roadrunner, which was only thirty-five miles from Al Qadisiyah. The larger Task Force Brown aircraft flew straight from Arar, refueling in midair, before dividing into two groups. The Chinooks and Black Hawks flew through a hail of bullets as they converged on the target, while the DAPs attacked the town's power station two and a half miles away, in the process setting the oil in the transformers aflame. "It looked like a nuclear bomb went off," said an MH-6 pilot.

Fierce resistance, including armor-piercing rounds, met the assault force at the research center. The Chinook and Black Hawk door gunners responded with devastating minigun fire, and AH-6 pilot CW4 John Meehan expertly put a rocket through the front door of the government building from which much of the firing was emanating, suppressing the threat instantly. The Rangers' luck held until the fourth Black Hawk landed at its assigned blocking position. A bullet flew into the cabin and hit a Ranger in the back, passing through his chest before getting stuck in his body armor. With a crew chief and a Gold Team SEAL fighting to keep the Ranger alive, the pilots took off and made a beeline back to Roadrunner, where a C-130 equipped as a flying operating theater was waiting with a surgical team.

As the second of the two Chinooks carrying the main assault force landed, gunfire peppered the aircraft, striking a crew chief above his jaw. The Chinook crew dropped the ramp and the assaulters stormed off. The pilots took off immediately with two soldiers working furiously on their critically wounded colleague stretched out on the floor. In the middle of the flight the crew chief stopped breathing, necessitating five minutes of CPR before he recovered. The helicopter landed beside the flying operating theater at Roadrunner and the crew chief joined the wounded Ranger in surgery. Both soldiers survived, thanks to the calmness and lifesaving skills of their colleagues.

Back at Al Qadisiyah, the assaulters combed the research facility for forty-five minutes, looking in vain for WMD. The Little Birds and DAPs circled overhead, the MH-6s' snipers picking off individual targets while the other aircraft used chain gun and rocket fire to destroy threatening vehicles. After less than an hour on the objective, the assault force and the Rangers departed on the Chinooks and Black Hawks, returning to Arar after stopping to refuel at Roadrunner.[17]

The next night, March 27, it was 1st Ranger Battalion's A Company's turn to conduct a parachute assault. This time, the objective was the military airfield known as H-1, or, to the Rangers, Objective Serpent. Three C-17s' worth of Rangers dropped onto the target, but, other than antiaircraft fire that forced the transport pilots to take evasive action en route the Rangers met no opposition. They did, however, suffer almost a dozen injured landing on the rocky ground.[18] The airfield was now available to stage other missions across western Iraq. Blaber just happened to have one in mind.

The acting Delta commander's analysis told him the Iraqi defense of Baghdad hinged on four critical locations where, according to U.S. intelligence maps, Saddam had concentrated his forces: Haditha; the area around his hometown of Tikrit, ninety-five miles northwest of Baghdad, and the neighboring town of Baiji thirty miles farther up Highway 1; Ramadi, about sixty miles west of Baghdad; and Baghdad's southern approaches. He likened these to four fence posts, and said that pulling down one post would cause the fence to collapse. Blaber thought the northwestern fence post—Haditha Dam—was the most vulnerable to attack by his forces. It was isolated and surrounded by flat, empty terrain. If Task Force Green could rip that post out, he thought, the Iraqis would believe they were surrounded and the other posts would collapse. "Let me take the fence posts down," he told Kearney, Task Force 20's operations director. "If I can pull down this corner post I can pull the whole thing apart." Kearney agreed.[19]

But before Task Force 20 could focus on Haditha, it had a high-profile rescue to conduct. Iraqi forces had captured six U.S. soldiers when they ambushed the 507th Maintenance Company's small, disoriented convoy in Nasiriyah March 23. (Eleven U.S. soldiers died in the firefight.) One of the six soldiers captured was Private First Class Jessica Lynch, a nineteen-year-old from West Virginia. The Iraqis held her separately from the others. In late March, an Iraqi lawyer informed Marine elements and a Special Forces A-team in Nasiriyah that Lynch was being held in the city's main hospital, where his wife was a nurse. Once the lawyer presented photographs proving this, Task Force 20 went into high gear planning a rescue. A joint operations center was established at Tallil air base, about twelve miles southwest of Nasiriyah. The task force expected a heavy fight as the headquarters of the local Saddam Fedayeen, a militia fiercely loyal to Hussein, was in the hospital basement. For two days staff worked around the clock to put together a plan that involved Rangers, Marines, Task Force Brown, Team 6, Delta, and the Army of Northern Virginia. The rescue force would total 488 personnel. Two Ranger colonels were running the show: Frank Kearney, JSOC's operations officer, who was in charge of planning the rescue, and Joe Votel, the regiment commander, who led the mission. Team 6's Gold Team had the lead role. The task force persuaded the Iraqi lawyer to return to the hospital and covertly film the route from the facility's main front door up the stairs to Lynch's room. He dropped that film off with Marines, who passed it back to Task Force 20. The SEALs assigned to go straight to her room studied the video intently so they knew every step they'd have to take once inside the hospital.

At 1 A.M. April 1, the first phase of the rescue began with Marines launching a diversionary attack south of the Euphrates, which dissects Nasiriyah. (The hospital was on the north side of the river.) The Marines also cut the city's power. The hospital's generators quickly switched on, making the building easily visible in the surrounding darkness. Then the assault force flew in. First came four Little Bird gunships, which encountered no Iraqi opposition but plenty of friendly fire from the Marine diversion. Then a pair of MH-6s with three Gold Team assaulters on each pod landed inside the hospital compound, right in front of the main door. The assaulters stormed into the hospital, with one thought: get to Lynch's room before any harm could befall her. An MH-60K Black Hawk inserted Gold Team snipers on the roof. Another landed with a medical team. There weren't enough TF Brown helicopters for all the missions, so Marine CH-46 Sea Knight helicopters flew in the Rangers—2nd Battalion, augmented by A Company, 1st Battalion—whose mission was to isolate and secure the objective. The Marines deposited the Rangers some distance from the hospital, forcing them to move on foot to their positions, a movement they referred to as the "Mogadishu Mile" in reference to the grueling run Rangers and Delta operators made at the end of the October 1993 battle in Somalia. A combined ground assault force that included Gold Team operators in six-wheel-drive Pandur armored vehicles, Ranger GMVs, and Marine tanks approached from the north. Overhead, an AC-130 circled.

The expected resistance failed to materialize because the Fedayeen had vacated their positions shortly before the raid. But not knowing this, the Team 6 operators were taking no chances. When they burst into Lynch's room she screamed from fright because SEALs were blasting locks off other doors in the corridor with shotguns to make sure no Fedayeen were hiding behind them. "She's freaking out because she thinks we're there to kill her," said a Team 6 operator. To calm her, the SEAL element leader removed his U.S. flag Velcro patch and gave it to her. "We're Americans," he said. "We're here to take you home."

When the assaulters made the radio call with the code word that meant they had found Lynch safe and sound, a cheer went up in the JOC. The operators quickly got Lynch on the waiting Black Hawk, which flew her straight to Tallil, from where a plane took her to Kuwait.

Back at the hospital, workers led the operators to the morgue, where they found the bodies of two of Lynch's less fortunate colleagues. Locals said more Americans were buried in shallow graves in the soccer field next to the hospital. The Rangers investigated and found this to be true. "It was basically just dirt thrown over them, limbs still sticking up out of the ground," said a Task Force 20 planner. With no shovels, the Rangers had to dig the corpses out with their hands, a process that lengthened the mission far beyond what planners had anticipated. By daylight they had uncovered a total of nine bodies, all victims of the ambush of the 507th. (Marines rescued the remaining prisoners April 13 in Samarra.) The Rangers put the bodies on their vehicles and returned to Tallil. "The Rangers came back from that just beat down hard," said the planner. "That was a tough one for them."[20]

※

While the Task Force 20 staff wrestled with the Lynch rescue, Task Force Green was at H-1, preparing to assault the Haditha Dam about fifty-five miles to the northeast. The tactical approach would be a reprise of that used by Juliet Team in Anaconda: a night movement on all-terrain vehicles. The force was extraordinarily small considering the size of the enemy force guarding the target—just nine ATVs, each carrying no more than two operators.[21] Defending the dam were four Iraqi armor companies with roughly forty-four T-55 tanks and BMP-1 armored personnel carriers, an infantry company of about 120 troops, an estimated fourteen South African GHN-45 155mm howitzers, numerous mortars, several truck-mounted Roland air defense missile launchers, and scores of antiaircraft guns. Another 6,000 Iraqi troops were less than twenty miles away.[22] It was a target straight out of a JRX scenario, except in the JRX it would be half of JSOC assaulting the objective. Coultrup was sending fewer than twenty operators.

But the assault force's small size proved an asset, as did the ATVs' super-quiet mufflers and their drivers' night vision goggles, which enabled the Delta operators to penetrate the Iraqi lines unheard and unseen. As Blaber monitored their progress using Blue Force Tracker, a system that used GPS signals sent from the ATVs to create an icon for each vehicle on his computer screen, the operators used laser designators to mark targets for the attack jets overhead. As had been the case in Afghanistan, the use of special operators to "lase" targets for U.S. airpower proved a powerful combination. A mix of laser-guided bombs and satellite-guided Joint Direct Attack Munition (JDAM) bombs destroyed twenty-three armored vehicles, seventeen ZSU 23mm air defense guns, plus a collection of trucks and some buildings. The operators withdrew as quietly as they had arrived, and then returned for a similar performance the following night.

As successful as Green's forays had been, however, Blaber was now thinking bigger. The Delta officer realized the little task force lacked the manpower to seize and hold the dam, so he asked for a Ranger battalion to take over at Haditha. But Blaber wanted more than that, much more. He envisioned a force that in addition to sealing the escape routes to Syria and Jordan could rampage up and down Highway 1 north of Baghdad in an effort to convince the Iraqis that a large armored force was approaching the capital from the northwest. Blaber suggested the force could also start to build a human intelligence network in Iraq, a recognition that the Coalition's intelligence picture was sorely lacking. He knew his small band of marauders would need to grow in order to fulfill his vision, so in addition to the Ranger battalion he requested another Delta squadron to deploy with Pinzgauers to join Task Force Green. Then he added the kicker: he wanted a tank company as well.[23]

The request was extremely unorthodox. With the exception of the Panama invasion in 1989, since World War II special operators had rarely worked closely with armored forces.[24] Kearney, Dailey's director of operations, was in favor, and even Dailey was "partially amenable," according to one party to the discussions, because he was under pressure to demonstrate some value from his highly resourced task force. Blaber played two of his aces: the persuasive talents of his trusted sidekick from

Anaconda, Jim Reese, who was a liaison in the Kuwait headquarters of Army Lieutenant General David McKiernan, the conventional ground force commander; and the high regard in which Tommy Franks had held Blaber since Anaconda. "Dailey was against it, everyone was against it, but Jimmy got McKiernan and McKiernan only had to say one thing to Franks and he was all over it," said a Delta source. Frustrated with his conventional commanders, whose attack had temporarily stalled, the CENTCOM commander was eager to reward initiative and had enthused over TF Green's Haditha raids. Sure enough, Blaber got everything he asked for. Delta's B squadron scrambled at Fort Bragg and, within hours, was on two C-17s winging its way direct to a desert landing strip in Iraq.

Meanwhile, on March 31 in Samawah in south-central Iraq, Captain Shane Celeen, commander of C Company, 2nd Battalion, 70th Armor Regiment, from Fort Riley, Kansas, received an order he was not expecting. He was to leave a platoon with the infantry battalion task force to which he was attached, load his remaining tanks on transporters, and move with all due haste south to Tallil Air Base, from where C-17s would fly his tanks north to H-1. There he was to link up with Task Force Green. When the promised transporters failed to show, Celeen ordered his company to move out under its own power. Five hours later, they reached Tallil. Celeen flew up to H-1 first to brief the special operators on his company's capabilities and requirements. Because a C-17 can only carry one M1A1 Abrams tank, it took fifteen sorties over three days to deliver Celeen's ten tanks, three M113 armored personnel carriers, five trucks, one Humvee, and one fire support vehicle. Once at H-1, they acquired a new name: Team Tank. Within two hours, they were on the road again, en route to Mission Support Site Grizzly, the temporary home between Haditha and Tikrit where Blaber's expanded task force was assembling.[25]

As Celeen began the fruitless wait for the tank transporters, a 140-man, seventeen-vehicle column organized around 3rd Ranger Battalion's B Company was approaching the fifty-seven-meter-high, almost six-mile-long Haditha Dam complex. It was before dawn on April 1.

The Rangers' mission was to secure the dam to ensure the Iraqi regime didn't destroy it or otherwise use it to create a flood downriver. After shooting a handful of armed guards who failed to immediately surrender—the only initial resistance—they began clearing the administrative building at the dam's western end. Other than the discovery of twenty-five civilian workers, this was uneventful. But the Iraqi soldiers' courage seemed to rise with the sun. Iraqis on the western side of the river began firing RPGs. A Ranger sniper on the dam put his rifle sight to his eye and saw three men who had unwisely chosen a propane tank as cover. When the man clearly holding an RPG stood in front of the tank, at a range of 900 meters, the Ranger staff sergeant pulled the trigger. His first round sliced through the targeted gunner and continued into the propane tank, igniting it and instantly killing the other two men.

Next a truck full of armed men came hurtling toward the Rangers on a road that ran along the top of the dam. A GMV .50 cal machine gunner fired several hundred rounds into the vehicle, stopping it and killing five of its occupants. The others dismounted and engaged the Rangers in an hour-long firefight, at the end of which three Iraqis were dead, five had surrendered, and three who were seriously wounded had jumped over the side of the dam and come to rest 100 meters down a steep embankment. On the scene was 3rd Battalion Command Sergeant Major Greg "Ironhead" Birch, who had been Delta's A Squadron command sergeant major at Tora Bora. He and Sergeant First Class Jeffery Duncan, B Company's 2nd Platoon sergeant, knew the wounded Iraqis were certain to die unless the Rangers rescued them. Birch was wearing a brace on each leg after breaking his left ankle and fracturing his right tibia six weeks previously in a jump at Fort Bragg, but that didn't prevent him from joining Duncan in a 100-meter sprint down the slope to the stricken Iraqis, while under heavy fire from a ZSU antiaircraft gun to the south. By the time the pair reached the Iraqis, two had died. After providing the surviving Iraqi first aid, the two Rangers carried him back up the slope, still under fire. But despite the Rangers' best efforts, he died from his wounds shortly thereafter. Nonetheless, the actions of Birch and Duncan earned each a Silver Star.

The other two platoons also saw action during those first hours of April 1. The twenty-seven men of C Company's 3rd Platoon took their objective, the hydroelectric power station on the dam's southwest side, after a brief fight in which the only Ranger casualty was a vehicle mechanic with a gunshot wound to his toe. B Company's 1st Platoon was the last in the order of movement. Its mission was to establish a blocking position on a hilltop on the southwestern approach to the dam. The platoon's soldiers were surprised to find an entire military facility that hadn't appeared on their maps. Consisting of a dozen buildings, it appeared to be an antiaircraft training headquarters. Judging by the half-cooked eggs on a stove, its soldiers had abandoned it at the first sound of gunfire. But 1st Platoon had little time to investigate. Enemy mortar fire was soon falling on the hilltop as scores of fighters poured out of Haditha village to the south, occupying prepared positions from which they began firing at the Rangers. In response 1st Platoon used its ground mobility vehicles' heavy machine guns and Mark 19 40mm grenade launchers to keep the Iraqi fighters' heads down while calling in close air support from two AH-6s. The Little Bird gunships rained .50 cal, minigun, and rocket fire on the Iraqis, destroying the mortar sites, killing an unknown number of Iraqi fighters, and igniting a natural gas pipeline that burned for several days. As they had during the first missions in Afghanistan, the Little Bird pilots also engaged the enemy from the cockpit with their M4 rifles. After a lethal half hour, the vicious combination of AH-6 and Ranger fire broke the Iraqi counterattack as the sun was rising.

Believing the Little Birds had taken care of the mortars that had been firing at them, 1st Platoon's Rangers were surprised to be taken under mortar fire again shortly thereafter. Then they noticed telltale puffs of white smoke coming from a small island about 2,000 meters away in the massive lake to the dam's north. A single Javelin antitank missile ended that threat.

That night, the Rangers cleared the wing of offices on the dam's east side, but at dawn April 2 they had to repulse a determined attack by several groups of roughly a dozen men each. Iraqi mortars resumed their harassment of the Ranger positions, along with the first of more than 350 heavy artillery rounds the Rangers would endure over the next several days. Later that evening an Iraqi force used dead space and RPGs to pin 2nd Platoon down, before A-10 attack aircraft again came to the Rangers' aid with a couple of well-placed 1,000-pound bombs. The artillery fire peaked April 3 with a barrage that seriously wounded a Ranger specialist, who was soon evacuated to H-1 on a Task Force Brown Chinook that landed on the dam to pick him up in the midst of the bombardment. He was one of four Rangers wounded during the battle. But the worst fighting at Haditha Dam was over. Team Tank's April 6 arrival sealed the victory, allowing the Rangers to turn their attention to making sure the dam continued to function.[26]

No Rangers were killed at the dam, but their A Company colleagues manning a checkpoint eleven miles to the southwest were not so lucky. On April 3, a man drove a car up to the checkpoint and stopped. A pregnant woman got out and yelled that she needed help. It was a trick. As several Rangers stepped forward, the car exploded, killing Captain Russ Rippetoe, the company's fire support officer; Staff Sergeant Nino Livaudais, a squad leader; and Specialist Ryan Long, a rifleman. Two other Rangers were badly wounded. The woman and the driver also died, making the attack one of the first suicide bombings of the Iraq War.[27]

※

Meanwhile, in the week since the cancellation of the Baghdad airport mission, Dailey had been scrambling, looking for new set-piece missions for his task force. He had retained his interest in tactical missions that he believed would have a disproportionate effect on the enemy's will to fight. But as in the opening stages of the Afghan war, this led him to order assaults on targets suspected to be empty, so the raids could be filmed for propaganda purposes. Such a mission was planned for the night of April 2, when Dailey intended to launch a Gold Team air assault against an unoccupied palace that had belonged to Saddam Hussein. But this time his prioritization of such missions would be shown up in the worst possible light.

As Task Force Green maneuvered north from Haditha, it had attracted the attention of about 100 Fedayeen acting as a quick reaction element for the regime's forces in Tikrit and Baiji. On April 2, as TF Green hunkered down in a sand-dune-encircled hide site, the Fedayeen attacked, driving toward Coultrup's small force in SUVs and pickup trucks supported by mortar fire. The Delta operators destroyed the first two SUVs with Javelin missiles, then took cover behind a ridge as the Fedayeen called up reinforcements. A vicious firefight ensued in which two Delta operators were wounded: one was hit by a bullet that broke his jaw; the other—Master Sergeant George "Andy" Fernandez, who had only joined Delta in November—was struck just under his body armor. Fernandez was critically wounded and bleeding heavily. Coultrup called Arar, urgently requesting a medevac flight.

Back in the joint operations center full of squawking radios and wall-mounted plasma screens, Blaber and Delta Command Sergeant Major Iggy Balderas were in constant contact with the C Squadron commander. Task Force Brown had Chinooks on alert and ready to fly the mission. Balderas immediately asked them to conduct the medevac. He didn't really have to request their assistance. "The pilots were begging to fly it," said a Delta source. "They knew someone was dying." But the 160th's strict crew rest regulations meant that if the Chinooks flew the medevac, they would be unavailable for that night's raid, so Dailey would not allow them to fly to the aid of Fernandez. Instead, to the intense frustration of the Delta men, other crews were woken after only three hours' sleep, and other helicopters prepped for the mission. The U.S. military often described the first sixty minutes after a soldier was seriously wounded as "the golden hour," meaning that if the military could get that soldier to trauma care during that period, his chances of survival exponentially improved. It took the backup crews forty-five minutes to launch.

The flight that finally took off from Arar included two MH-60K Black Hawks for the medevac mission and two direct action penetrators to protect them and provide fire support to the beleaguered ground force. Pushing their aircraft to the limit, the pilots flew most of the ninety-minute flight at fifty feet above the desert. When they arrived over Task Force Green's position, the pilot of the trail DAP was surprised to see Delta operators on the defensive, taking cover behind the ridge. The DAPs spent the next fifty-five minutes hammering the Fedayeen with their chain guns and rockets. Shortly after the helicopters showed up, two A-10s appeared on the scene. One dropped a 500-pound air-burst bomb on a group of Fedayeen in a ravine. By the time the DAPs' fuel levels compelled them to leave, virtually all the militants were dead.

The Kilos had landed as close to the Delta operators as possible, but Coultrup told the pilots to reposition the aircraft at a safer landing zone. As soon as they did, the operators drove their casualties over. The Task Force Green member shot in the face came aboard one helicopter, but the crews were dismayed to see operators also carrying a stretcher on which lay a body covered with an American flag. Fernandez had bled to death. He was the first Delta operator killed in action since Mogadishu.

That night the Black Hawks that Dailey had kept at Arar flew the SEALs on the raid against the empty palace. A combat camera crew filmed the mission and the tape was flown to a psychological operations unit in Kuwait. It was never used.[28]

⌗

Over the course of several days in the first week of April, Blaber's expanded task force coalesced at Grizzly, an ideal home for a band of marauders operating behind enemy lines. A collection of one-story modern buildings at the base of a deep wadi but just a few hundred meters from the highway connecting Haditha and Baiji, it had been a secret weapons testing facility prior to the U.S. invasion. The special operators had done their homework and knew from Iraqi contacts that the site was a restricted area. "That was part of what would make it so perfect for us," a Delta source said. "Iraqis were used to not going out there." The force gathering at Grizzly included Delta's B and C squadrons; 1st Ranger Battalion; Team Tank; and a pair each of AH-6 and MH-6 Little Birds. As soon as Blaber alighted from the Echo Squadron plane that landed on the road in the middle of the night, he took personal charge of the cohort and gave it a new name, borrowed from the teenage gang that fought the invading Soviet military in the movie *Red Dawn*: Task Force Wolverine.[29]

Resting up during the day, the Wolverines would sally forth at night to reconnoiter, harass, and destroy. But not long after Blaber arrived, they endured two harrowing events during an otherwise successful attack on the huge K-2 airfield near Baiji the night of April 8/9.

In the middle of the assault, a Ranger Reconnaissance Detachment Humvee darted in front of the tanks without warning. Under fire, a tank crew mistook the Humvee for an enemy vehicle and destroyed it with a 120mm main gun round, killing the detachment's 24th STS combat controller, Staff Sergeant Scott Sather. He was the first airman to die in the Iraq War.[30]

Shortly thereafter, Celeen, the Team Tank commander, was maneuvering through a wheat field in support of the attack when his tank dropped into a forty-foot hole, flipping as it fell to land on its turret. Relatively unscathed except for the loader, who almost lost a hand, the four-man crew was nonetheless in a nightmarishly claustrophobic plight: every way out of the tank was blocked by the sandy earth. While Celeen and his gunner provided first aid to the loader, driver Private First Class Christopher Bake struggled out of his hatch and used his hands to dig his way through the sand. He eventually emerged, to the relief of other Team Tank soldiers who had arrived to guard the site. Celeen and the gunner passed the injured loader through Bake's tunnel and then used it to escape. The tank was declared a total loss.[31]

※

A week of successful marauding north of Baghdad gave Blaber and Coultrup confidence that they could conduct a show of force mission on the outskirts of Tikrit, Saddam Hussein's fiercely loyal hometown. On the evening of April 11, Blaber gathered the 100 or so men at Grizzly who would be going out that night. He reminded them that their mission was not to seize terrain or destroy a specific objective, but rather it was to fool the Iraqi forces in Tikrit into believing that a large U.S. armored formation surrounded them. Blaber had no intention of getting sucked into a fight in the town itself. "We want to get close enough to the enemy that they can see us, but we don't want to get decisively engaged," he told them, according to his book, *The Mission, the Men, and Me.* "Keep your back to the desert at all times."

The Wolverines emerged from their lair into a cold, moonless night. Leading the way across the desert were a dozen Pinzgauers and SUVs. The vehicles approached Highway 1, the eight-lane freeway that separated Tikrit from the desert, and crept under a massive cloverleaf intersection. At a given code word, the five Team Tank M1A1s still in working order after ten grueling days of desert warfare moved forward and took up positions on the cloverleaf ramps overlooking the town. At the sight of the tanks, Tikrit burst into angry life, muzzle flashes of all calibers lighting up the night. The Wolverines replied in kind. The tanks' main guns were far more powerful and accurate than anything the Iraqis might throw at them, but there were many more Saddam loyalists in Tikrit than there were Wolverines in Iraq, let alone on the cloverleaf. The volume of Iraqi fire grew steadily.

Wire had become wrapped around the treads of one of Celeen's tanks, preventing it from moving. Five Delta operators ran out from their cover, each heading for a different tank to help select targets, steady the crews' nerves, and, in the case of the immobilized tank, try to untangle the wire. Monitoring the battle from Grizzly, Blaber directed Task Force Brown gunships about 100 miles away to move to Coultrup's location. The C Squadron commander reported an estimated 500 enemy gunmen armed with heavy weapons and RPGs. He could see rooftop bunkers and dug-in fighting positions in the barricaded streets. It was as if the Tikritis were just daring the Wolverines to come and fight them on their home turf. Coultrup, the Mogadishu veteran who knew firsthand what can happen to a JSOC task force outnumbered and cut off in an urban fight, recommended pulling back as soon as he could get his entangled tank moving. Blaber agreed and told him to withdraw to Grizzly as soon as possible.

Suddenly, Dailey came on the radio. He was still at Arar, but had been monitoring the Wolverine radio traffic. "Negative, negative, negative," he said, in a transmission monitored by every member of Task Force Wolverine, including those fighting for their lives at that moment. "You are not to pull out of that city. I want you to keep moving forward into the city and destroy the enemy." Blaber would later speculate that Dailey wanted his troops to engage in a "thunder run" through Tikrit similar to those that 3rd Infantry Division's 2nd Brigade had made through Baghdad in the previous several days. After reminding the JSOC commander that the Wolverines were on a "show of force" mission and repeating the gravity of the situation they were already in, Blaber told Dailey he'd already ordered Coultrup to pull back into the desert.

The JSOC commander was silent, but moments later Blaber's secure satellite phone rang. It was Votel, the Ranger Regiment commander and Dailey's second in command at Arar, trying to persuade Blaber to change his mind. Blaber just repeated the arguments he'd made to Dailey and hung up. Votel called back, this time with a warning, clearly based on his knowledge of how Dailey was thinking. "If you don't . . . move through that city, your . . . future as a commander might be affected," he told Blaber. The acting Delta commander was unmoved. "Pull back to the desert as ordered," he told Coultrup. In a second Dailey was on the radio again. "What did you say?" he yelled, furious. "You listen to me, I told you to—" At that point, Dailey's radio shorted out. The general ripped off his headset, flung it down, and stomped out of the JOC.

After freeing the entangled tank, the relieved Wolverines followed Blaber's order and withdrew to Grizzly with no casualties.[32]

⁂

The Wolverines spent the next ten days conducting a variety of missions: searching in vain for Scott Speicher, the Navy pilot shot down during the first Gulf War; checking out a suspected WMD facility that turned out to be a barbecue pit; and conducting a series of raids around Baiji. The task force also captured five of Saddam's bodyguards, several Iraqi government ministers, and the Iraqi air force chief of staff, while never missing an opportunity to spread the false story that they were the advance guard of a multi-divisional attack from the west.[33]

Dailey's preoccupation with weapons of mass destruction became a factor whenever the Wolverines or another Task Force 20 element passed through the massive arms storage areas often located close to Iraq's military airfields. At H-2 airfield, for instance, there were eighty-eight aircraft-hangar-size magazines, each stuffed with crates of munitions from floor to ceiling. "I need a thorough check of each of those to make sure there's no WMDs in them," Dailey told TF Wolverine. "What do you mean by 'thorough'?" came the reply. "Go through every box," Dailey said. "Okay, roger, we're just finishing up right now actually," said a Delta operator, no doubt shaking his head wryly.

"These generals were consumed [with the thought] that there were WMDs laying around," a Delta source commented. "Logic said, 'You're out of your fucking mind.' Nobody stores the object of their desire, the family jewels, in a place that they can't control."

One mission in which Dailey showed no interest was assigning anyone to guard those arms depots. When the operators had moved on, they would sometimes arrange for Predator drones to stay behind and watch in case enemy fighters were using them as hide sites. What the Predators showed instead was that Iraqis were looting the depots. "It was like watching ants raid a picnic basket," said a Delta source. When Blaber reported this to Dailey, with a proposal that Task Force 20 use its troops on loan from the 82nd Airborne Division to guard the storage sites, the general rebuffed the suggestion. That was a job for the conventional Army, not his task force, he said. "But they're not here, we're the only ones up here," Blaber reminded him, to no avail. Task Force 20 left those arms depots wide open, a decision that placed thousands of U.S. soldiers at risk. "It was all those artillery rounds that ended up being IEDs," said a Delta source, in reference to improvised explosive devices—the homemade bombs insurgents later used to kill and maim American soldiers. "That's where they came from."[34]

It was a threat with which JSOC's operators would soon become familiar.

16

The Deck of Cards

It was nighttime on June 18, 2003, and three helicopters were flying fast and low across Iraq's western desert. Out of sight far ahead was their quarry, a small convoy of SUVs driving at breakneck speed toward the Syrian border near Al Qaim. In the Task Force 20 operations center on the outskirts of Baghdad, all eyes were on the screen showing footage of the convoy being beamed in real time from a drone. The task force knew the mobile phone numbers being used by the vehicles' occupants. Those phones' call patterns led about half Task Force 20's intelligence analysts to believe Saddam Hussein was in one of the vehicles. That information very quickly made its way to Donald Rumsfeld, who got on a secure phone line straight to the JOC. His guidance was clear: "You're not going to let Saddam drive across the Syrian border."

Although the task force had been tracking the convoy across Iraq, it was late launching the helicopters from the northern city of Mosul. Now, two DAPs and a Chinook full of Delta operators and Rangers were in hot pursuit. Somewhere ahead of them, the most wanted man in Iraq might be trying to make his escape. In the Chinook were Major Clayton Hutmacher, the air mission commander, and a Delta officer nicknamed "Bricktop," the ground force commander. The Task Force Brown pilots were pushing the helicopters as fast as they could, but their target had too much of a head start and crossed the Syrian border before the task force birds could catch it.

Rumsfeld ordered the task force to intercept the vehicles in Syria. In the JOC, Delta Lieutenant Colonel John Christian, the new task force commander, relayed the convoy's latest grid location to Hutmacher and Bricktop. They called back concerned. Although many Saddam loyalists had fled to Syria, from where U.S. officials presumed they were pulling the strings of the nascent Sunni insurgency in Iraq, until now Rumsfeld had sanctioned no missions into Syria, where a U.S. raid could spark a major international incident. "Do you know this grid's in Syria?" Hutmacher and Bricktop asked. "Yes it is, and you're authorized," Christian replied. As the JOC fed the officers on the Chinook new location data for the convoy, their concern only mounted. Bricktop called back again: "Hey, these grids are in Syria." Christian tried to set his mind at rest. "Bricktop, you're authorized to pursue."

With Rumsfeld still on the line, the three helicopters crossed the border.[1]

⁂

After the fall of Saddam Hussein's regime, albeit with Saddam himself still at large, Dailey's instinct was to get his force back to the States as quickly as possible. A senior JSOC officer later characterized the mindset at the top of the command thus. *"We don't need to be here anymore. The main effort is go back and practice. . . . The war's over. There are no weapons of mass destruction."*

But first, JSOC had some unfinished business to which to attend. Abu Abbas, the Palestinian mastermind of the *Achille Lauro* hijacking in 1985, had escaped justice when the Italian government let him go. He had eventually settled in Baghdad. From there, sheltered by Saddam, he had been running the Palestine Liberation Front while still functioning as a member of the Palestine Liberation Organization's executive committee. With U.S. forces encircling Baghdad, Abu Abbas had made several unsuccessful attempts to flee to Syria. Once Task Force 20 reached Baghdad, finding him became a priority.

On the morning of April 14, U.S. intelligence tracked Abu Abbas to a farm on the western bank of the Tigris on Baghdad's southern outskirts. From a hangar at Baghdad airport, Task Force 20 quickly planned and launched a classic direct action mission. Rangers from 2nd Battalion's A Company moved out in a ground convoy and isolated the farm, blocking all possible routes of escape or reinforcement. As two AH-6 gunships covered the ground force, four MH-6 Little Birds deposited Team 6 Gold Team operators who stormed the compound.

They were too late. Abu Abbas had driven off in his black Range Rover minutes previously. The assaulters questioned the people on the objective, seized one of the terrorist leader's passports and several weapons, and waited in vain for his return, before heading back to the airport after a few hours.

Task Force 20 would not have to wait long for another chance to grab Abu Abbas. By day's end, intelligence indicated the Palestinian was in east Baghdad's Fateh Square neighborhood. Again the task force moved out, this time borrowing twenty-four Bradley Fighting Vehicles and four M113 armored personnel carriers from 3rd Infantry Division to transport the Rangers to their blocking positions. Two AH-6 gunships and five MH-6s carrying the assault force dodged wires and other obstacles to arrive simultaneously with the ground convoy. Rangers from 2nd Battalion's B Company cordoned off the objective. Team 6 operators swept through the target building but found nothing of interest while 1st Battalion's B Company cleared structures on the opposite side of the street, detaining every man they found. One detainee immediately stood out: a six-foot-tall, 220-pound man with a notably casual demeanor. When the assaulters returned to his comfortable apartment, they found several passports and $35,000 in cash. The task force had its man.[2]

Despite Dailey's wish to take the task force home, the National Command Authority had other plans. Oblivious to the fertile ground the invasion had created for an Islamist insurgency to take root, the Bush administration was focused on destroying all remnants of Saddam's Ba'ath Party and capturing or killing the leading figures of his regime still at large. Thus, on May 16, Paul Bremer, the head of the U.S.-dominated Coalition Provisional Authority, which served as Iraq's transitional government, issued CPA Order No. 2, disbanding the Iraqi army. As Iraq teetered on the brink of chaos, JSOC's mission was to go after "the deck of cards"—the top fifty-five members of the Saddam regime, memorialized on an actual deck of playing cards distributed to U.S. forces ahead of the invasion. Within that deck, the task force's primary focus was the ace of spades: Saddam Hussein himself.[3]

Task Force 20 set up its JOC at what had been an Iraqi Special Republican Guard base at the capital's main airport, now renamed Baghdad International Airport (BIAP, pronounced "Bye-App"). The compound badly needed cleaning up before Task Force 20 moved in, which is how it acquired its nickname. Dailey, standing in the airport terminal with some JSOC staff, referred repeatedly to it as "that nasty-ass military area." A logistician mentioned the phrase in notes that got wide distribution in the task force, and "Camp Nama" was born.[4]

The deck of cards mission notwithstanding, Dailey still pulled

80 percent of the task force out of Iraq. Delta's B and C Squadrons went home. A Squadron took their place. The task force's other principal elements were most of 2nd Ranger Battalion, a small Task Force Brown detachment, and the JOC staff. Delta remained Task Force 20's central assault force, but there was a shift in command. Blaber returned to the States, to be replaced by John Christian, who commanded the unit's Combat Support Troop, which contained the heavy breachers and the rest of the unit's counter-proliferation specialists. Tall and endowed with a deep, booming voice, Christian's strikingly large head topped with silver hair earned him his Delta nickname: "Buckethead." His role would be to run the JSOC task force on a day-to-day basis from Nama.[5]

But A Squadron was not based at the airport, which was too far from central Baghdad, the site of many of its missions. Instead, Delta put its squadron headquarters at a large Ba'ath Party villa in the Green Zone, the chunk of central Baghdad adjacent to the Tigris that the international Coalition walled off to serve as a safe haven for Coalition and Iraqi leaders. The squadron also had a troop in Mosul and smaller elements at BIAP and Tikrit, but for the early stage of the occupation, Delta's base was at the villa. Named after the unit's only casualty since September 11, the building was known as Mission Support Site Fernandez and boasted a pool, a gym, and enough space that each team was spread between two bedrooms. Task Force Brown kept aircraft and crews on a stretch of blacktop behind the villa, while the British SAS, known early in the Iraq War as Task Force 14 and later as Task Force Black, moved into the villa next door.[6]

✳

Task force operators quickly realized they were missing something vital to any manhunt: actionable intelligence—the sort that could be used to launch a mission immediately. The CIA was unprepared for the nascent insurgency, which senior Bush administration officials were still attributing to Saddam regime "dead-enders." "There was no intel" when A Squadron arrived, a Delta operator recalled. It became the job of the Delta cell at BIAP to sort through the Agency's cables and turn them into targets to be divided between Task Force 20, the "white" Special Forces, and the conventional Army. "All the staff officers in JSOC say intel drives operations, right?" said the operator. "It was just the fucking opposite. We had no intel, so operations were driving intel [because of] what we found on these targets. We'd pick on a sweater and we'd pull that string. And sometimes you pull a string on a sweater and it's nothing and sometimes it unravels, and over time that intel picture starts to develop."

As Delta began to develop its own source networks, friction grew between the operators and Agency case officers. According to Delta operators, they were far more comfortable than their CIA counterparts with the risk that accompanied low-vis missions in a high-threat environment. Delta acquired a fleet of beat-up local cars to carry them unobtrusively to meetings with sources. The CIA "would go pick up sources we'd been working for a while in three black [Chevy] Suburbans," an operator said. "The source would turn up dead the next day . . . [But] if it wasn't three black Suburbans, they couldn't do it."

✳

On June 11, the Rangers took advantage of what for JSOC was a rare opportunity: a set-piece battle against a large, unsuspecting enemy force. U.S. intelligence had alerted the task force to the presence of a large terrorist training camp near Rawa in Anbar, about thirty miles from the Syrian border. The 101st Airborne Division had been preparing an assault on the position, but intelligence indicated the terrorists were readying a major attack on Coalition forces and the 101st needed more time to plan, so the mission was given to Task Force 20. In less than twenty-four hours, 2nd Ranger Battalion's B Company and Task Force Brown's Little Bird guns launched under the cover of darkness.

Two platoons air-assaulted onto the terrorist training camp—Objective Reindeer—located in a deep wadi, while another drove 175 miles from BIAP in ground mobility vehicles along with the battalion mortars to arrive simultaneously with the air assault. Jets dropped six air-burst Joint Direct Attack Munition bombs on the position, but the militants had plenty of fight left in them. Fierce point-blank combat with grenades and automatic weapons ensued. Withering AC-130 and AH-6 gunship fire supported the Rangers. When the dust cleared, eighty-four enemy fighters lay dead. No U.S. soldiers were killed, but one lost his leg to a grenade. The militants also shot down an AH-64 Apache gunship helicopter that arrived with a relief force from the 101st. Rangers rescued its crew. Along with 2,000 RPGs and fifty RPK machine guns, the Rangers found eighty-seven SA-7 surface-to-air missiles at the site. The task force's victory and the lopsided casualty figures were a testament to the "bilateral" training the Rangers and Task Force Brown conducted routinely.[7]

A week later, the task force found itself in a race to the Syrian border against the convoy thought to contain Saddam Hussein. The convoy won that race, but with Rumsfeld's okay, the helicopters crossed the border and chased it down a couple of miles into Syria. In a confusing situation, the heliborne JSOC troops, supported by an AC-130 gunship, interdicted the vehicles but also got into a firefight with Syrian border guards, in which several guards were wounded. Saddam Hussein was not in the convoy, but relatives of his were. "I think they were cousins of his," said a source who tracked the battle in Task Force 20's JOC. The task force also conducted an air strike against a group of farmhouses on the Iraqi side of the border, killing at least one person—a pregnant woman—and shot up a Bedouin truck, killing at least two people, according to Patrick Andrade, a photographer embedded with 3rd Armored Cavalry Regiment, which was called to deal with the aftermath of the Task Force 20 mission. A Delta source estimated Syrian casualties at between ten and twenty. "As we approached the Syrian border, everyone just figured, 'We're on a movement to contact, start firing at everything that moves,'" the Delta source said. Other unconfirmed reports said as many as eighty Syrians died. The task force troops flew the wounded Syrians to a U.S. medical facility in Iraq, where they were treated before being repatriated.

Franks visited Baghdad the next day and reacted with typical bravado after Task Force 20 officials briefed him on the incident. "The Syrians can either make a big deal out of it or a small deal out of it," he said. "And if they make a big deal out of it, we'll show them what a big deal is." Syrian protests were restrained. From the task force's perspective, "everyone moved on," said the Delta source. "It was almost a nonevent."[8]

✳

Delta's A Squadron spent the rest of its tour hunting Saddam. They didn't find him, but on July 22 they got a chance to take down his sons, Uday and Qusay Hussein, who were also still on the run. After being turned away from Syria, they found temporary refuge in Mosul in the home of a sometime supporter of their father. But spooked by the presence in his house of the second- and third-most-wanted men in Iraq (and, perhaps, tempted by the $30 million reward on offer for the pair), their host let Coalition forces know that the brothers were at his home, along with Qusay's fourteen-year-old son and a bodyguard. Delta delayed the mission until the next day as operators gathered a blocking force from the

101st and tried to visually confirm the targets. On July 23, with the building surrounded in broad daylight, an A Squadron sniper nicknamed "Noodle" killed Qusay with a shot through a window. Then a six-man team from A2 Troop with Ivan, a military working dog, entered via the carport and tried to assault up the stairs. But the brothers' well-trained bodyguard, in all likelihood a member of the Special Republican Guard, which Qusay led, drove the operators back with AK fire and a grenade, wounding at least two of them. The bodyguard also killed the dog, which had paused to attack Qusay's corpse. After the operators withdrew, the bodyguard shot and wounded a soldier attached to the 101st company who was standing casually by a Humvee.

Reluctant to attempt another assault, the operators instead asked the 101st to take the building under fire with heavy weapons. OH-58D Kiowa Warrior helicopters from the division's 2nd Squadron, 17th Cavalry Regiment fired rockets at the building, while the ground force peppered it with about ten TOW missiles. The barrage worked. When A2 reentered the building, they found Uday and the bodyguard dead. Qusay's son was still alive—holding a rifle—until an operator shot him. In the operation's aftermath, task force troops reportedly showed more respect to Ivan's corpse than they did to the bodies of the two brothers.

Proud of their role in the brothers' demise, A2's operators had a group photo taken with the source holding a fake check signed by George W. Bush. The squadron command sergeant major, "Grinch," had ball caps made for his men embroidered with the aces of hearts and clubs, Uday and Qusay's respective ranks in the deck of cards.[9]

Less than a month later, on August 17, the task force captured Ali Hassan al-Majid al-Tikriti, better known as "Chemical Ali," a cousin of Saddam responsible for gassing Kurds who rose up against the regime in the 1991 Gulf War's aftermath. The deck of cards' king of spades, Ali was the fifth-most-wanted man in Iraq.[10] "We had been tracking Chemical Ali's girlfriend," said a Delta source. "We had her on sigint, had her on humint, and we found her gathering passports for Chemical Ali and all the rest of his family to go to Syria—fake passports. So we finally picked her up one night and pretty much told her, 'Hey, you either tell us where he is or you're going to go away for a long time.'" The woman quickly gave up Tikriti's location: a tall apartment building "a couple of blocks" from Delta's squadron in downtown Baghdad. The operators waited until very early morning, then picked or forced the lock on his door and silently entered the apartment. They found Tikriti sound asleep in bed. Using the barrel of his M4 assault rifle, an operator nudged him. Tikriti opened his eyes to see the green glow of several operators' night vision goggles staring down at him. "He pissed his pants right there in bed," the Delta source said.

But as the task force worked its way down the list of fifty-five "former regime elements," a different enemy was setting flame to the kindling provided by an Iraqi population humiliated by a foreign occupation. Two days after Chemical Ali's capture, a suicide car bomber attacked Baghdad's Canal Hotel, headquarters of the United Nations effort in Iraq, killing Sérgio Vieira de Mello, the U.N. special representative in Iraq, and at least twenty-one others. A similar attack on the hotel on September 22 caused the United Nations to pull out of Iraq altogether. The bombers were sent by a new entrant into the Iraq armed conflict, the Jordanian Islamist Abu Musab al-Zarqawi.

Into the growing anarchy stepped a new JSOC commander. On October 6, Dell Dailey handed off command to Major General Stanley McChrystal in a bland ceremony in a parachute packing facility on JSOC's compound at Pope Air Force Base.

In light of the events of the next several years, it's interesting that command of JSOC wasn't McChrystal's first wish at that stage of his career. He had hoped to be given the 82nd Airborne Division and wondered aloud about whether he was the right choice to lead JSOC.[11] But at forty-nine, McChrystal had already built an impressive résumé that in retrospect made him a perfect candidate to head the organization. His multiple tours in the Rangers, culminating with two years commanding the regiment between 1997 and 1999, combined with almost three years as a staffer in JSOC's operations directorate (including the 1991 Gulf War), had taught him how JSOC worked; his most recent assignment as the Joint Staff's vice director of operations had given him an insight into the inner workings at the highest levels of the Pentagon. But as McChrystal was only too aware, one item missing from that résumé was any time spent in the special mission units, many of whose members were, as he admitted, still of the opinion that the JSOC headquarters was as much a hindrance as a help.[12]

A few days after taking command of JSOC, McChrystal flew to Tampa to meet with General John Abizaid, who had replaced Franks as CENT-COM commander, and General Doug Brown, who'd taken Holland's place at Special Operations Command. The meeting with Abizaid produced two agreements. McChrystal requested, and Abizaid agreed, that he would deal with McChrystal personally on any issue to do with JSOC forces in the Central Command region, even if a deputy, rather than McChrystal himself, was running the show in Iraq or Afghanistan at the time. Second, McChrystal agreed to Abizaid's request to conduct a major operation in eastern Afghanistan, where Central Command had reports of the presence of senior Al Qaeda leaders.[13]

Within three weeks of taking command, McChrystal departed for an orientation tour of JSOC elements in Iraq and Afghanistan.[14] The forces he visited were by now stretched thin by the nonstop commitments of the "global war on terror." When Zarqawi's terrorist bombing campaign in Iraq took hold in late summer, the Pentagon directed Delta to prepare to assume a security role at the U.S. embassy in Baghdad. This threatened to burden the unit, just as the requirement to provide bodyguards for Karzai had hampered Team 6 in Afghanistan, so Delta pushed back hard, telling Rumsfeld he had to choose between having his premier counterterrorist force protecting the embassy or actually fighting terrorists in Iraq.[15] The tasking soon went away, but the ongoing commitment to Iraq was straining JSOC, which now had to man task forces in Afghanistan and Iraq as well as a headquarters and an on-call force in the United States ready to respond to an 0300 counterterrorism or 0400 counter-proliferation mission. "We were tapped out," a retired special operations officer said, adding that JSOC had to request help from the services' special operations components—Air Force Special Operations Command, Army Special Operations Command, and Navy Special Warfare Command—to help fill its manpower needs.[16]

Stunned by the indecisiveness at the highest levels of American command in Iraq, McChrystal focused on problems within his powers to fix. After visiting JSOC's sixteen-person team in Mosul and a similar cell in Tikrit, he realized his 250-person task force in Iraq was divided into isolated elements with little connectivity to each other and no efficient process for turning potentially valuable documents and digital devices seized on missions into intelligence to be cycled back to the strike elements—the Delta troops and Ranger platoons—to drive more raids. As if to underline the growing threat to U.S. forces, on October 25 an insurgent RPG downed the trail aircraft in the flight of two TF Brown Black Hawks returning McChrystal from Mosul to Baghdad. Because the general had left most of his party in Baghdad, the aircraft was empty except for the crew, all of whom survived.[17]

During those first months after the fall of Baghdad, JSOC had access to only one Predator, and even that was flown by pilots back in the States. But the senior Delta officers in-country, first Blaber and then Christian, realized they had at least a partial solution to the lack of aerial intelligence, surveillance, and reconnaissance (ISR) at their fingertips: the helicopters of the unit's E Squadron, equipped with the Wescam ball. "We said 'Let's get the fucking Wescam ball over here,' and that was a major breakthrough in Iraq," recalled a Delta source. E Squadron shifted its main effort to Iraq, deploying its small air force of fixed wing planes, standard Army Black Hawks, and at least one Mi-17, all affixed with the Wescam ball and other top secret sensors. (A standard Black Hawk, without an air-to-air refueling probe that is a 160th Black Hawk's unique signature, provided a sort of cover in Iraq, as regular Army aviation units were flying so many of them.)

It soon became the norm for an E Squadron Black Hawk with the call sign "Birdseye" to go up for eight hours every night to provide ISR support to the task force's missions. The helicopters didn't support daytime missions, as the risk of being seen and compromising missions was too great, but flying at about 8,000 to 10,000 feet, they were invisible at night. "They'd be blacked out," said a special operations aviator. "You couldn't even hear them." The Birdseye pilots would narrate what they were seeing on their video, which they also transmitted in real time to task force vehicles on the ground and back to the JOC. This mission fell to E Squadron for a simple reason: its crews were the only personnel that the operators on the missions trusted to be able to know what tactical information they needed. "It always boiled down to who did Green trust to give them what they wanted," said the special ops aviator.[18]

Through fall 2003, the task force stuck assiduously to their assigned mission, hunting "former regime elements," as around them Iraq descended into bloody tumult. For Delta, the primary focus was Saddam Hussein. By December, A Squadron, now led by Mark Erwin, sensed they were closing in on their quarry. "We were getting a lot of intel," said an operator. "We had rolled up on our rotation anybody who was even remotely close to Saddam: chicks he liked to bang, their husbands, his butler, his tailor, his inner circle, his cooks. We had gone through all those guys and we knew we were getting close."

⁂

In November McChrystal moved to Bagram to oversee what became Winter Strike, the operation he'd promised Abizaid. Winter Strike was in some ways the last hurrah of the JRX-style mind-set that held sway under Dailey. "We went there and set up the Taj Mahal," a JSOC staff officer said. The Afghanistan task force, which had shrunk to about 200 personnel, increased tenfold. But the massive operation was a bust. McChrystal's forces—Rangers and Team 6 SEALs, mostly—swept through Nuristan and Kunar provinces without snaring any senior enemy leaders. The new JSOC commander quickly realized that this sort of large, laboriously planned operation was not the route to victory.[19]

Then, with McChrystal back at Pope and nine days after Coultrup's C Squadron had replaced A Squadron in Iraq, the task force there got its big break when it captured Mohammed Ibrahim Omar al-Musslit, a trusted Saddam confidant, in Baghdad on December 12. Under intense interrogation, Musslit coughed up the information that the deposed dictator was in the town of Dawr, across the Tigris from his hometown of Tikrit. The next day, C Squadron moved north to Tikrit, bringing Musslit with them.

By this point in the war, JSOC had expanded its command structure to accommodate two full-time, one-star deputy commanders. With three flag officers, JSOC could keep one each in Afghanistan, Iraq, and Pope. Rear Admiral Bill McRaven was the deputy commander running JSOC operations in Iraq. He called McChrystal from the BIAP operations center and told him that the task force had actionable intelligence on Saddam's whereabouts.

That night, based on further information that Musslit had reluctantly divulged, the task force raided an objective consisting of two farms on the river's east bank. McChrystal and the JSOC headquarters staff watched the operation in real time on a Predator feed displayed on a large screen in the JOC. After seizing two brothers, one of whom was Saddam's cook, the operators knew they were on to something. Under rigorous questioning at the site, Musslit finally indicated a floor mat outside one of the farmhouses. Moving it aside, the troops discovered Saddam's hiding place, a tiny six-foot "spider hole." The bearded, disheveled ex-dictator appeared, looking up at the operators. Through an interpreter, the operators asked his identity. "I am Saddam Hussein, the duly elected president of Iraq, and I am willing to negotiate," he answered. "President Bush sends his regards," a Delta operator shot back.

There was no negotiation to be done. The task force soldiers pulled him out, checked his body for telltale tattoos—dealing roughly with the slightest resistance on his part—and bundled him aboard a Little Bird for a short flight to a Coalition compound in Tikrit.[20] The ace of spades was in the bag.

✳

For the Delta operators, a brief period of relative calm followed Saddam's capture.[21] "We were literally down in Baghdad going to dinner and drinking tea out in the cafés, for about six weeks," recalled a unit member. But at higher levels in the task force and at JSOC headquarters, there were already suspicions that capturing Saddam, while an important target for political reasons, was not the key to ending the violence in Iraq. As early as October 2003, Scotty Miller, now Delta's deputy commander, had concluded that the ongoing violence did not represent the death throes of the former regime, but a new, tenacious insurgency.[22] It was also soon clear that that insurgency, while rooted in the grievances of Iraq's Sunni population, was being nourished from abroad. Task force personnel noticed that an increasing number of detainees they pulled off objectives were not Iraqis, but foreign Islamist fighters flowing into Iraq across the Syrian border. By the end of 2003, a JSOC advance force operations task force had established a base in western Iraq in an effort to keep track of this influx.[23] As task force intel analysts pored over the available data, one name kept cropping up: Abu Musab al-Zarqawi. A comer in the world of Islamist terrorism, the thirty-seven-year-old Zarqawi had run a militant training camp in Afghanistan and was now seeking to make a name for himself in Iraq, running a group called Jama'at al-Tawhid al-Jihad (the Organization of Monotheism and Jihad). By fall 2003, Major Wayne Barefoot, Delta's assistant intelligence officer, had identified Zarqawi as a key enemy figure.[24] Before the year was out, he would inform McChrystal of his assessment that not only was Zarqawi in Iraq, but that the Jordanian was constructing an insurgent network in the country.[25] McChrystal brought Barefoot with him from Baghdad to Riyadh in Saudi Arabia to brief his findings to CIA director George Tenet.[26]

In retrospect, the realization that an Islamist insurgency had taken root in Iraq seems like a foregone conclusion, but at the time it did not permeate all levels of JSOC simultaneously. As with the rest of the U.S. military in Iraq, many task force members at first mistook the war being waged by Zarqawi's group, soon to be known as Al Qaeda in Iraq, for a Ba'athist "Saddam insurgency," a Delta source acknowledged. "It really turned out to be [Al Qaeda in Iraq]," he said. "It took us a little bit to figure that out, but once we did, then it was on."

Iran hostage-rescue task force commander Major General Jim Vaught and Delta Force commander Colonel "Chargin'" Charlie Beckwith in discussion at the airbase in Wadi Kena, Egypt, prior to the launch of the ill-fated Operation Eagle Claw. [U.S. Army]

Brigadier General Dick Scholtes, JSOC's first commander, greets Vice President George H. W. Bush during the latter's visit to JSOC on January 5, 1982. [White House]

A 160th Special Operations Aviation Regiment Chinook carrying a Soviet-made Hind helicopter away from the Oadi Doum airbase in northern Chad during Operation Mount Hope III in 1988. [U.S. Army]

Defense Secretary Donald Rumsfeld visits JSOC in November 2001. The tall four-star general in the background is Charlie Holland, commander of U.S. Special Operations Command. [Defense Department]

SEAL Team 6 operators prepare their Pandur armored vehicles prior to the April 1, 2003, rescue of Army Private Jessica Lynch in Iraq. [U.S. Navy]

A task force member grabs a just-captured Saddam Hussein after JSOC had tracked him to his spider hole on a farm outside his hometown of Tikrit. [U.S. Army]

Stan McChrystal, the general whose vision and intensity transformed JSOC into a global manhunting machine. [U.S. Army]

A Task Force Brown MH-6 Little Bird flying over Iraq with SEAL Team 6 operators on the pods ready for action. [U.S. Navy]

SEAL Team 6 operators conducting a freefall jump from a C-17 Globemaster. Team 6 considered freefall missions their forte, and proved it during the rescue of Jessica Buchanan. [U.S. Navy]

SEAL Team 6 operators silhouetted as their high-speed assault craft rises out of the water. Many operators suffered long-term health problems from the pounding they took during such training. [U.S. Navy]

SEAL Team 6 operators during a night mission in Afghanistan. [U.S. Navy]

SEAL Team 6 commander Captain Brian Losey briefs Navy Secretary Donald Winter on the capabilities of the Sentry unmanned aerial vehicle during a 2007 visit by Winter to Team 6's Dam Neck headquarters. [U.S. Navy]

A Task Force Brown MH-60 Black Hawk landing on a rooftop in an Afghan valley to drop off SEAL Team 6 operators. Afghanistan's mountainous terrain frequently required the Night Stalker pilots to prove their reputation as the military's best. [U.S. Navy]

President Barack Obama congratulates JSOC commander Vice Admiral Bill McRaven after the success of Operation Neptune's Spear, the mission to kill Osama bin Laden. [AP Photo/Charles Dharapak]

JSOC commander Lieutenant General Joe Votel greets Defense Secretary Chuck Hagel, April 23, 2014, during a visit by Hagel to JSOC headquarters at Fort Bragg, North Carolina. [Defense Department/Erin A. Kirk-Cuomo]

Lieutenant General Tony Thomas, who became JSOC commander in July 2014. [U.S. Army]

17

Building a Network

It was still dark when Master Sergeant Don Hollenbaugh heard the call to prayer echoing from a minaret 300 meters to the north. The haunting sound unsettled the Delta operator. "This is not going to be a good day," he told Staff Sergeant Dan Briggs, a twenty-eight-year-old Delta medic kneeling beside him on a street corner in northwest Fallujah. "This could get ugly quick."

At 4 A.M. that morning, six Delta soldiers and roughly forty Marines from E Company, 2nd Battalion, 1st Marine Regiment had quietly advanced on foot about 300 meters in front of Coalition lines. The Delta contingent included Hollenbaugh and Sergeant Major Larry Boivin, Combat Support Troop's operations sergeant and senior heavy breacher respectively; three A Squadron snipers; and Briggs. A fourth sniper occupied a building to the rear, from which he could overwatch the patrol's route and warn of any movement ahead. Hollenbaugh and Boivin were there at the Marines' request to provide added firepower of a specific type: thermobaric AT4 rockets. The AT4 was ubiquitous in U.S. Army and Marine Corps infantry formations, but Delta's thermobaric rounds were not and were thus the envy of the Marines. Shoulder-fired from disposable launchers like all AT4s, they worked by rapidly driving up heat and pressure in any confined space into which they were fired. Used properly, they were enormously destructive. The Delta soldiers had already trained the Marines on the weapon and supplied them with rounds, but the Marines still didn't feel comfortable employing the thermobarics, so had asked Hollenbaugh and Boivin to accompany the patrol into Fallujah to fire the rounds themselves. "They didn't feel like the training was sufficient," Hollenbaugh said. "And given the lethality of those weapons, I think that was a good call."

After holding static positions on the city's edge for several days, the U.S.

troops were worried that the insurgents had figured out their "blind spots"—locations from which the militants could launch attacks unseen from Coalition lines. The early morning patrol was an effort to "mix up the battlefield . . . so that the snipers could change their lanes and if need be, we could put these thermobaric weapons to use," Hollenbaugh recalled. As he knelt and whispered to Briggs, the Marines were clearing and occupying a pair of houses north and south of an intersection. The Delta soldiers entered the southern one and took positions on the flat rooftop, which measured about ten meters by fifteen meters. The Marines did the same on the northern rooftop and on the houses' other floors. Low walls surrounded both rooftops. Using sledgehammers, the Americans spent the hour before dawn knocking holes in them to create fighting positions. The Marines were expecting a fight. They would not be disappointed.

At first light, a rocket-propelled grenade exploded against the southern house, followed a few minutes later by a burst of machine gun fire. As Hollenbaugh peered out of his fighting position another RPG hit a few feet below, close enough that he felt the heat and the spray of grit on his face. "Luckily, I had one earplug in and eye protection on," he recalled. He quickly put the second earplug in. "Hey, keep watch over my sector, I'm going downstairs to see where this thing came from," Hollenbaugh told Boivin.

Emerging outside, he crawled up on a wall to examine the "splash" mark the RPG had made on the house. The experienced operator could tell the rocket had been dipping by the time it impacted, meaning it had been fired from some distance away. Hollenbaugh mentally traced the angle of fire as far as he could see, then raced back upstairs to get a longer view. Spotting a small dark hole in some rubble about 300 meters away, he figured that was the RPG gunner's position. He fired several M4 rounds into the hole and told the Marine forward observer to mark it as a potential mortar target.

For the next hour or so, insurgents probed the U.S. positions and traded occasional shots with the Americans. The Delta sniper team leader, J.N., decided to pull his men back to the other sniper's position, from where they could better utilize their rifles' range. After speaking with Hollenbaugh, E Company commander Captain Doug Zembiec sent two Marines to the roof to replace the snipers. Between himself, Boivin, Briggs, and the two Marines, Hollenbaugh calculated there were enough men on the roof to cover all sectors of fire, especially considering the presence of the Marines in the northern house and the Delta snipers to the rear.

Within a couple of minutes of the two Marines arriving on the roof, the volume of insurgent fire suddenly increased as word of the Americans' location spread. More than 300 militants arrived by the truckload to join the fight. Thousands of bullets and scores of RPGs tore into the walls of both houses. The insurgents "really believed this was the full-on invasion of Fallujah," recalled Hollenbaugh. "They were just throwing everything they had at us." Using alleyways and positions in neighboring houses, insurgents got close enough to hurl grenades onto the northern rooftop, wounding several Marines. Hearing their screams, Briggs left his position and, together with the forward observer, sprinted across the no-man's-land between the two buildings to help treat and evacuate the wounded, exposing himself to enemy fire at least six times.

The situation was now perilous for the Americans, outnumbered ten to one by insurgents who were moving along the walls of the two buildings in an effort to surround them. Shouting to be heard above the din, the U.S. troops rained fire and threw grenades down on their attackers. On the southern roof Hollenbaugh, Boivin, and the two Marines were fighting hard to hold off the insurgents—a tough job for only four men. Then a grenade landed on the roof and exploded, grievously wounding both Marines, one of whom stood up. "He's got his hands on his face and blood's coming through his fingers, it's just ugly," Hollenbaugh recalled. Concerned that the Marine was exposing himself to insurgent fire, the Delta master sergeant hustled him into the crowded stairwell, before returning to the other wounded Marine, an NCO whose name he never learned. Lying facedown, the Marine pointed with his right hand in the direction of where he thought the more junior Marine was still lying. "Take him first, take him first," he told Hollenbaugh, who was impressed with the Marine's selfless bravery. "This guy's crawling backwards and he's just leaving a streak of blood, so you know he's hurt really bad," he said later. "I already got him," the operator told the Marine, as he grabbed his belt, yanked him to his feet, and moved him to the stairwell.

With Boivin still covering his sector, Hollenbaugh moved between his own fighting position and those left vacant by the Marines' departure, firing his M4 and tossing grenades. Another incoming grenade exploded on the roof, with shrapnel catching Boivin behind the ear and in the back of his arm. "Don, I'm hit," he yelled. Sitting by the stairwell opening, which was surrounded on three sides by walls, Hollenbaugh worked to patch Boivin up quickly. Reaching into a "go bag" that the Delta guys had brought, which contained grenades, spare magazines, a signal kit, and medical supplies, he grabbed Kerlix gauze bandages and green do-rags. He packed the Kerlix into the head wound, tied it off with do-rags, and told Boivin to turn and face him. "You look really cool," he teased the heavy breacher. Despite the nasty wound, Boivin—later described by Hollenbaugh as "a tough, tough individual"—was about to return to the fight when both men noticed what looked like a mouse moving under a clumped-up blanket the Marines had been using to shield themselves from the sun. Realization came to each soldier simultaneously. Staring at each other in wide-eyed alarm, they yelled the same word: "Grenade!"[1]

✳

With Saddam captured and Winter Strike concluded, in January John Abizaid held a conference at his Tampa headquarters to which he invited representatives of the key organizations fighting the war against Al Qaeda, which was largely playing out across Central Command's patch of the globe. Attendees included McChrystal; SOCOM commander Doug Brown and his deputy, Vice Admiral Eric Olson; CIA director George Tenet; as well as NSA and Joint Staff representatives. Abizaid expressed his belief that the United States had taken its eye off the ball in the campaign against Al Qaeda, and, in particular, the hunt for the terror organization's leaders. The officials seated around the table committed themselves to work together more closely and with greater imagination.

McChrystal had already decided that for JSOC to reach its full potential, it would need to leverage the strengths of other government organizations, particularly those in the intelligence business. Before the conference ended, McChrystal announced his intention to create a joint interagency task force (JIATF) that would incorporate representatives of as many intelligence agencies as he could persuade to send personnel downrange to fill it. The JIATF had been McRaven's idea, but McChrystal instantly saw its potential. He correctly perceived that taking analysts out of their cubicles in suburban Washington, D.C., and putting them in the same tent in a combat zone on the other side of the world would enable them to turn raw data into actionable intelligence that much faster, and loosen the bonds of parochialism that often hindered true collaboration between government entities in the United States. Within weeks, McChrystal established JIATF-East on the JSOC compound at Bagram, under the leadership of former Delta A Squadron commander Lieutenant Colonel John Alexander.[2]

The JIATF's purpose was to look beyond Afghanistan's borders in an effort to draw an accurate picture of the enemy networks and the movement of targeted individuals within those networks, with particular attention paid to bin Laden and Zawahiri. It wasn't all plain sailing at first, particularly when it came to persuading the CIA personnel to open up. In the early days at Bagram, police tape separated Agency analysts from their military counterparts. Military folks were not allowed past the tape.[3]

✳

As JIATF-East began to map the jihadist networks that spread across Central Asia and the Middle East, Team 6 was involved in a mission on the other side of the world to peacefully remove the leader of a nation with which the unit had some history: Haitian president Jean-Bertrand Aristide. It was shortly after a military junta had deposed Aristide in 1991 that Team 6 had rescued some mysterious individuals from a Haitian beach—the mission that saved the unit from being dissolved. The U.S. military had ousted the coup leaders and reinstalled Aristide as president in 1994. But ten years later, in February 2004, the SEALs were back, this time enforcing U.S. policy by helping to persuade Aristide to leave again after a heavily armed rebellion that appeared to have U.S. support had taken over much of the country.

"TF Blue went down," said a senior JSOC officer. "We were in communications with the team leader constantly. They were coached to try and go in and almost negotiate his removal. They weren't directed to forcibly pull him out. He [the team leader] was more or less going there with the Department of State—I think the ambassador was involved, there may have been others too—and it was designed basically to provide security and protect [Aristide] and escort him out and ensure that he got out."

But a Team 6 officer said that although the small SEAL element, which included a master chief named Pete Kent, did not use physical force, their discussions with Aristide left little doubt as to what his options were. Kent told the Haitian politician, "Get on the plane now!" the Team 6 officer said. "I was told that to avoid bloodshed I'd better leave," Aristide told CNN. White House press secretary Scott McClellan strongly denied this at the time. But several officers familiar with the mission said the Team 6 personnel were influential in getting Aristide on the plane, which ultimately took him to exile in the Central African Republic. "That's when McChrystal told me, 'We need more guys like that master chief, because he could sell a fucking bad bucket of stones to somebody,'" said an officer.[4]

(Two years earlier Kent had achieved a certain level of notoriety as one of then interim president of Afghanistan Hamid Karzai's bodyguards during a September 5, 2002, assassination attempt on the president. Karzai's SEAL Team 6 bodyguards shot the would-be assassin, as well as two Afghans who were wrestling with him. In the course of the fight, a round ricocheted and hit Kent in the head, lightly wounding him, but forced him to take his shirt off and wrap it round his head as a bandage. The photo of him naked from the waist up, brandishing an assault rifle, with a shirt around his head was picked up by many news outlets.)[5]

❋

Meanwhile in Iraq it was becoming clear that the campaign against the "former regime elements" had run its course. A new enemy more capable and far more dangerous than any of Saddam Hussein's henchmen had emerged: Abu Musab al-Zarqawi. In January, "Zarqawi became our primary focus," McChrystal wrote.

Zarqawi's group had embedded itself in Fallujah, a religiously conservative city of 285,000 in the Sunni heartland of Anbar province about thirty miles west of Baghdad. The city was part of the 82nd Airborne Division's area of operations until March 2004, when the 1st Marine Division relieved the 82nd as the "landowning" conventional force responsible for the city. But neither unit had the manpower to keep the lid on insurgent activity in Fallujah, which had become a no-go area for U.S. forces.[6] Residents threw rocks at low-flying Little Birds on daylight missions in mid-January. By February, they were aiming more dangerous projectiles. A shoulder-launched surface-to-air missile narrowly missed a Little Bird flight just south of Fallujah on February 26. A few days later in the same area, a similar missile—later determined to be an SA-14—brought down an AH-6, destroying the helicopter and injuring the pilots.[7] It was on this cauldron of anti-Coalition sentiment that the task force focused its attention in spring 2004.

The task force almost got lucky with one of its earliest missions into Fallujah. In February, McChrystal accompanied a Delta strike force on a night raid on a suspected Zarqawi safe house in the middle-class Askari neighborhood in the city's northeast. (The JSOC commander made a habit of going along on such raids, believing they gave him a better feel for the war and allowed him "to build relationships and mutual trust" with his troops.) But Zarqawi eluded them, probably jumping into a dark alleyway from a second-floor window as the operators closed in. Just as with the decision not to proceed with Delta's 1999 bin Laden mission, JSOC's history and that of the unit might look very different had the task force captured Zarqawi that night in Fallujah, before the Jordanian's goal of inspiring a Sunni-Shi'a civil war in Iraq had gained traction.[8] As it was, the operators continued to make frequent forays into Fallujah and Ramadi throughout March, hunting Zarqawi and his lieutenants. They ran into trouble on the night of March 24 when insurgents ambushed a mounted Delta patrol outside the city. With operators forced to shelter behind their vehicles, a firefight ensued, the ferocity of which can be judged by the fact that somehow a detainee managed to escape. Two troops were wounded before the operators could withdraw.[9]

Less than a week later came the event that would sear the word "Fallujah" into the American consciousness, when insurgents ambushed four employees of the security firm Blackwater as they were driving through the city, killing all four and stringing two of their corpses up over the bridge across the Euphrates. The incident recalled 1993's battle of Mogadishu, when Somalis had dragged fallen task force soldiers' bodies through the streets. The episode's fallout prevented Delta commander Colonel Bennet Sacolick from attending a commanders' conference that McChrystal hosted the first week of April at Bagram. The commanders, deputy commanders, and senior enlisted advisers of JSOC's units, as well as McChrystal's senior staff officers, attended the conference. With his force dispersed across the globe, McChrystal held such gatherings regularly to ensure his immediate subordinates understood his intent. The JSOC commander left no doubt that he was dissatisfied with the task force's level of knowledge of their enemies. "We fundamentally do not understand what is going on outside the wire," he told his men.

McChrystal, who was bouncing between Pope, Bagram, and Baghdad during this period, flew to the Iraqi capital with his staff on April 5, arriving as the Marines launched an attack to rid Fallujah of insurgents.[10] (Major General Jim Mattis, commander of 1st Marine Division, had counseled a patient approach after the Blackwater incident, but with anger and a desire for revenge coursing through the American body politic, Army Lieutenant General Ric Sanchez, the senior U.S. military leader in Iraq, ordered him to attack.)[11] At the urging of Delta's Fallujah team leader, one or two of the unit's operators linked up with Marine platoons entering the city. The aim was to add a little more lethality and combat savvy to the Marine elements, but because the operators enjoyed superior communications links with each other and the task force JOC, they were able to give their higher headquarters superb situational awareness of events on the battlefield. By his own admission, McChrystal "became addicted to this ground-level reporting for the rest of the war."[12]

Four Marine battalions began to sweep through Fallujah. But the same political forces that had forced Mattis to attack before he was ready abruptly changed tack after Arab media outlets reported that the initial stages of the assault had killed hundreds of civilians. On the advice of Paul Bremer, the head of the Coalition Provisional Authority, President Bush decided the attack had to stop, an order Abizaid delivered to Mattis April 9.[13] Surprised by the halt, McChrystal realized he had not established close enough links to Mattis's headquarters. He sought to rectify that oversight by placing liaison officers not just with Mattis's Marines, but in as many conventional unit headquarters as possible. Many regular units were reluctant to accept the JSOC representatives, however, so the process took almost a year. McChrystal's approach mirrored his strategy with other government agencies. He placed more than seventy-five liaison officers in Washington and 100 elsewhere, including on the staffs of Joint Chiefs chairman Myers, CIA director Tenet, CENTCOM boss Abizaid, and the U.S. ambassadors to Afghanistan and Pakistan. The liaisons were limited to four-month tours, to prevent them losing touch with the battlefield. McChrystal had come to two conclusions. The first was that not just in Iraq but across the globe, JSOC was confronting a networked enemy—one that went by many names, but shared values, goals, personal connections, and, in many cases, people. McChrystal's second realization was that to have any chance against Al Qaeda's global brand of Sunni Islamist militancy, JSOC would have to create its own network by availing itself of the knowledge, the man-power, and, sometimes, the legal authorities that resided in other parts of the military and the U.S. government. "It takes a network to defeat a network" became McChrystal's mantra.[14]

‎ ❊

The Marines' pause in Fallujah became a withdrawal to the city's out-skirts at the end of April. Although a hastily cobbled together local security force called the Fallujah Brigade replaced them, the reality was that Zarqawi's men controlled the city. It was on April 26, a few days before the withdrawal, that Hollenbaugh, Briggs, Boivin, and the Ma-rines of Echo Company found themselves in a desperate fight to avoid being overrun.

Spying the grenade as it rolled under the blanket, the already wounded Boivin dived down the stairwell, crashing into Zembiec and his radio operator. Hollenbaugh had just enough time to duck behind the stair-well wall before the grenade exploded harmlessly. But he noticed it had been thrown from roughly the same area as the previous two. Grabbing a grenade of his own from a pouch on his body armor, he pulled the pin while walking toward that side of the roof. "About three quarters of the way there I let the spoon fly, counted *one, two, three* and threw it down hoping to get the guy," he recalled. "Never saw any grenades come up over that [wall] again, but you just don't know." He then did a quick tour of the roof, moving from hole to hole, firing multiple single shots from his M4 when he saw a target or a suspected insurgent position. He turned to check on Boivin, who was sitting in the stairwell with his head in his hands. "Larry, are you okay?" Hollenbaugh yelled. "Yeah, Don, I'm okay," Boivin replied shakily. But he was very pale. The original dressing had come loose and he was bleeding heavily. Hollenbaugh redressed the wound with new Kerlix, taking even more care this time and tying it off so tightly that Boivin worried it might crush his skull.

Boivin descended to an open-air patio on the second floor and con-tinued to fight from there with the Marines. Hollenbaugh remained on the roof and fought on alone, shifting from position to position, staying in one place only long enough to squeeze off a few rounds or toss one of the sixteen grenades he'd brought. Twelve were regular M67 fragmen-tation grenades, but four were thermobarics. Essentially a smaller, hand-thrown version of the "thermo" AT4 round, a thermobaric grenade needed to land in an enclosed space for optimal effect. With insurgents in neighboring houses, Hollenbaugh hurled his thermobaric grenades at their windows. "A couple" hit the target, he said. Dodging grenades, RPGs, and bullets, the experienced operator needed all his tricks to keep the insurgents at bay. When a Humvee arrived to evacuate the wounded, insurgents fired a well-hidden machine gun at the medics from an upper-floor window of a building to the south. Unable to see the machine gun itself from his position on the south wall, Hollenbaugh identified its location from the visible gases emanating from its barrel. He fired against the alley wall at an angle that he calculated would send the ricochets into the window. The gun went quiet. Hollenbaugh turned his attention to an insurgent-occupied house to the northeast. "I started putting rounds into the building," he said. "Skipping bullets in off the floors and the walls."

After an hour, Hollenbaugh was down to his last magazine and his final thermobaric AT4. His ears were ringing from the multiple explosions around him; his throat and nostrils were filled with the smell of gunpowder smoke, RPG accelerant, and the sweet tartness of C4 explosive; and his boots were tracking his colleagues' blood across the dusty rooftop. The machine gun opened up again. He had just grabbed his last AT4 when Zembiec appeared on the roof. "Hey Don, it's time to go," the Marine captain said. "Let me shoot this," the Delta operator replied, shouldering the AT4. Zembiec knelt down behind him, too close to the launcher's back blast area for Hollenbaugh, who motioned for him to move forward, then fired. The rocket flew just inside the edge of the machine gun nest window and exploded. "It shut the gun up," Hollenbaugh said later. Satisfied, he followed Zembiec down the stairs. It was then he realized that everyone else had long since pulled out (eleven Marines having departed on stretchers). Only his one-man impersonation of an infantry squad had prevented the insurgents from storming the southern building. "It never came into my mind that I was alone," he said later, telling *The Fayetteville Observer*. "I am glad someone did a head count."

A single Marine, nineteen-year-old Lance Corporal Aaron Austin, died in the firefight. For their roles, Hollenbaugh and Briggs received the Distinguished Service Cross and Boivin the Silver Star.[15]

The Marines' withdrawal and the predictable collapse of the Fallujah Brigade shortly thereafter gave Zarqawi the run of the city. In a late May meeting at the Coalition's Camp Fallujah on the edge of the city, a frustrated Abizaid let McChrystal know he expected his task force to take the lead in striking back. "We need to hit some targets," he told the JSOC commander, slamming his fist on the table. But with no Coalition troops in Fallujah, the task force relied on Predators to track insurgent movements. By now, JSOC was rotating forces through Iraq about every ninety days. From April through June 2004 Mark Erwin's A Squadron was on point as Task Force Green. Wanting more from the Predator coverage, the squadron's team leaders put their heads together and came up with a new system. They placed an experienced operator alongside the intel analysts monitoring the Predators' real-time video feed around the clock. Once a drone caught sight of a suspect, the operator would have the pilots back in the United States follow the target relentlessly, keeping careful notes of his movements. "We would follow these guys all over—*went in this house with two guys, got in this car, changed cars here*—and plot all this on a map," said a Delta source. At shift's end, the operator passed the logbook to his relief, so the task force was able to build a detailed picture of the suspect's "pattern of life." According to McChrystal, this new way of operating meant both analysts and operators felt as if they "owned" the mission, "which in turn increased activity on the ground by moving targeting decisions down the ranks." The system wasn't perfect yet—there weren't enough Predators to track every target, for one thing—but it was the beginning of what JSOC came to call the "Unblinking Eye."[16]

The new technique paid off almost immediately. In mid-June, a Delta intelligence analyst studying recorded Predator footage noticed a truck blocking a Fallujah street. Directing the drone back to that spot, he saw men moving weapons from a house to a pair of trucks. One drove off heading east. The Predator tracked it. When Green operators intercepted the truck near Baghdad without a fight, they found in it enough AKs, belted ammunition, fragmentation grenades, rockets, ammo vests, and medical supplies to equip a hundred fighters. The operators detained two men and a thirteen-year-old boy who were in the truck, brought them back to Mission Support Site Fernandez, and interrogated them.[17] The boy said they had drunk tea with Zarqawi very recently and told the operators where.[18] Meanwhile, the Predator returned to the original blocked-off street, from where it followed cars and trucks to a southwest Fallujah house exactly where the truck drivers had told Task Force Green the rest of the arms cache was being moved. Some operators were sure Zarqawi was there or in one of two other buildings they were watching. The task force dubbed the house Objective Big Ben and planned to bomb it the night of June 18, then raid it to exploit any intelligence in the rubble.

Delta's operators were on the verge of launching when Lieutenant General Jim Conway, commander of the 1st Marine Expeditionary Force, told McChrystal the potential for civilian casualties meant that he didn't want JSOC to bomb the house, nor did he want Delta driving Pandurs into the city. After talking with McChrystal, Erwin canceled the mission, unwilling to risk insurgents swarming the convoy without the armored vehicles' protection and firepower. McChrystal then gained permission— presumably from Sanchez or Abizaid—to hit Big Ben with a precision air strike after all. At 9:30 the next morning, the strike destroyed the building. To the relief of McChrystal, whose task force's credibility was on the line, after a few tense seconds the arms cache began exploding, validating the target. The bombing killed an estimated twenty people, mostly Tunisian jihadists. Zarqawi, however, was not among them.[19]

Another upshot of Big Ben did not reflect well on the task force. A couple of days after the operation, one of the truck drivers that Task Force Green had captured arrived at the Camp Nama detention center. A routine medical screening found suspicious burns on him. A quick investigation determined that in their zeal to get the drivers to talk, four operators had been involved in shocking at least one driver with a Taser.[20] The task force chain of command quickly punished the four: two were expelled from Delta for a year (which later became a permanent expulsion for one of them); the others received letters of reprimand from Sacolick, but were still in the unit as of 2013.[21]

In his autobiography, McChrystal described the episode as an isolated incident and said neither he nor his subordinate commanders ever ordered troops to mistreat detainees, or tolerated those who did.[22] But others in and around the task force at the time said that explanation strained credulity, that the problem was far more prevalent than McChrystal suggested, and that the operators punished were "scapegoats."[23]

Several news stories and documents released under the Freedom of Information Act lend credence to this view. A March 2006 *New York Times* article reported that the task force's treatment of detainees was bad enough that in August 2003 the CIA barred its personnel from Nama.[24] In December 2003, retired Army Colonel Stu Herrington had highlighted the excesses of the JSOC task force (then called Task Force 121) in a report for Major General Barbara Fast, the senior U.S. military intelligence officer in Iraq. To research the report, Herrington and two other intelligence officials toured U.S. detention facilities in Iraq for a week in early December. "Detainees captured by TF 121 have shown injuries that caused examining medical personnel to note that 'detainee shows signs of having been beaten,'" Herrington wrote, before concluding that "It seems clear that TF 121 needs to be reined in with respect to its treatment of detainees." (When Herrington asked an officer in charge of interrogations at a high-value target detention facility whether he had alerted his bosses to his concerns that Task Force 121's prisoners appeared to have been beaten, the officer replied, "Everyone knows about it.")[25]

Part of the problem was that prior to September 11, 2001, JSOC typically trained for operations of such short duration that its personnel were not used to having their own prisoners, let alone being responsible for squeezing actionable intelligence from them.[26] This was compounded by the fact that, like the rest of the U.S. government, JSOC had very few trained interrogators, and almost none fluent in Arabic.[27]

JSOC used its cocoon of secrecy to shield itself from a series of investigations into overall U.S. military conduct with regard to detainees, repeatedly rebuffing investigators seeking access to Nama and other task force facilities.[28] But at McChrystal's behest, JSOC deputy commander Air Force Brigadier General David Scott conducted a classified review of procedures at Nama, resulting in administrative punishment for more than forty task force personnel and ending the career of the colonel in charge of Nama at the time.[29]

Media attention focused on Nama, but detainee abuse also occurred at smaller facilities where task force elements would hold detainees for as long as a few days before sending them to Nama. As the Taser incident indicated, this was particularly the case with Mission Support Site Fernandez in the Green Zone.

Fernandez functioned as the operations center and main living quarters for whichever Delta squadron was deployed to Iraq. It had two floors. The upper floor held the operations center and sleeping quarters, with each assault team of six to eight operators taking one bedroom.[30] The lower floor—which operators sometimes called the basement—was divided into interrogation rooms and a room converted into a holding facility. These were built during one of A Squadron's first Baghdad tours, said a Delta source who estimated the holding room measured twelve feet by twelve feet. Along its walls, engineers built what he described as about twenty "stand-up closets" that prevented a prisoner from physical relaxation—"so a guy can't squat, he can't sleep, all you can do is stand." Another Delta source seconded this description.

Under pressure from their chain of command to get information immediately from the detainees in the basement, Delta operators routinely resorted to abusing them, the first Delta source said. Trained interrogators or intelligence personnel were rarely if ever present. "We might go talk to the intel guy and he gives us the twenty questions he has and then we go down there and fucking get [the answers] from [the detainee]," he said. The second Delta source said the failure to push trained interrogators down to the lowest echelons was a major factor behind the abuse. "A lesson learned from this is we should have . . . had the right guys doing it and not the operators," he said. "Instead we let the operators do it, and you've got a commando sergeant major saying, 'Get this fucking shit now.' There was a lot of consternation in A Squadron about that. . . . [They] could have said, 'It's an illegal order, I'm not going to do it.' However, that's easier said than done."

The first Delta source defended Delta's harsh methods, which he said were "a necessary evil" that were not only an inevitable by-product of the emotions produced in close quarters combat, but also effective. "You can't go out and catch these guys who shot your buddies and expect we're going to fucking hand them tea and crumpets," he said. "Saddam wasn't caught on tea and crumpets. Saddam was caught on ass whuppings." Trained interrogators such as Herrington were critical of the notion that detainee abuse produces better intelligence than a more patient approach of building a relationship with a prisoner. But the pressure to produce immediate results meant there was no time for such niceties, the operator said. "When you got a year to crack someone's brain, your technique is best," he said. "When you've got minutes to save American lives, that shit don't fucking work."

The operator was particularly aghast at what he viewed as his chain of command's efforts to blame the detainee abuse on a few "rogue" personnel. "You know how much scrutiny you're under as a Delta Force operator? You think you can just go rogue? You think you can do something without orders?" he said. "The detainee abuse happened in the fucking basement of the house we all lived in, at the bottom of the stairs, under the commander's bedroom. . . . Everybody who lived in the house knew what was going on." Indeed, sometimes residents on the upper floors heard screams coming from the basement, he said. "There's times I'd go down there and tell people, 'Hey, keep it the fuck down, I'm trying to relax up here,'" the operator said.

Other Delta operators took strong issue with the suggestion that this behavior was par for the course in the unit. "You never thought of beating somebody up or applying physical torture to anybody," said an experienced operator who was in Delta during the Iraq War's opening stages. "The culture of the unit wasn't anything like that." He cited the case of an operator forced out of Delta for kicking a Balkan war crimes suspect struggling in a net that operators threw over him after pulling him from his car. Another operator who made multiple deployments to Iraq in 2003 and 2004 said only a very few individuals in the unit abused detainees and that they did so without any authorization, tacit or otherwise, from above. "None of the leaders that I know there, not a one, do I think would allow that," he said. "It's a small few who did that and those who got punished deserved it."

But documents, press reports, and interviews with special operations troops leave little doubt that JSOC personnel engaged in widespread detainee abuse during the first thirteen months of the American occupation of Iraq.[31] Already under scrutiny because of the warnings from Herrington, the CIA, the FBI, and others, this practice may have been in its final days by spring 2004, anyway. But in late April news of conventional soldiers' abuse of detainees at Abu Ghraib prison hit the headlines, resulting in a much closer examination of all U.S. forces' treatment of prisoners. As described by Delta operators, their chain of command's attitude changed immediately. One special operations officer likened what happened to "a game of musical chairs." The operators punished for the Taser incident happened to be those left standing when the music stopped.

In midsummer 2004, McChrystal made a change that went some way toward solving his Camp Nama problem. He simply moved his entire headquarters to the sprawling Balad air base, almost fifty miles north of Baghdad. There, he built a new "clean and sterile" detainee facility that he described as "clearly the most important building constructed during" the move. This facility remained off-limits to the International Committee of the Red Cross, but McChrystal made it "internally transparent" within his growing "network" by allowing carefully controlled visits by partner agencies and, on occasion, allied representatives.[32] Whether it was the move to Balad that made the difference, or a heightened sensitivity to the potential political fallout from incidents of detainee abuse, reports of such transgressions declined sharply once the task force moved north.[33]

There were practical reasons for moving the JOC to Balad—the Iraqi government was taking control of Baghdad airport—but also psychological ones. After ten months in command, McChrystal's concept for how JSOC should operate had crystallized, and he wanted to start from a clean slate as he turned that vision into reality.[34]

18

"JSOC on Steroids"

With the move to Balad under way, McChrystal held a commanders' conference at Bragg in late July. Attended by JSOC's senior staff officers and component unit commanders, the conference was McChrystal's chance to outline the direction in which he intended to take the command. That direction was away from the large set-piece operations that for so long had dominated JSOC's thinking. Instead, McChrystal wanted to expand the capability to operate on the left side of a spectrum that had large-scale joint readiness exercise-style operations at the right end, and small, completely clandestine missions on the other. "He wanted to go blacker, faster, smaller," said a source familiar with the meeting. McChrystal expressed preferences for smaller tailored packages for such missions and for a Joint Readiness Training paradigm, in which JSOC elements trained together on specific tasks, but without the massive joint readiness exercise umbrella. In this context, he announced his intention to review the "internal role" of all JSOC's tiered units. The JSOC commander also left subordinates in no doubt about where they stood in the long war now under way. JSOC, he told them, was now the nation's "main effort" in the "war on terror."[1]

The JOC McChrystal built in a corner of Balad air base was the physical embodiment of his insistence on a networked, flattened command structure in which organizations shared information with each other instead of hoarding it in their own "stovepipes." Housed in a massive concrete clamshell-shaped hangar dating from Saddam's time, the operations center had an entry control point at one end and offices for McChrystal and other senior figures at the other. Between these, separated by a plywood wall, were two big rooms that functioned as the nerve centers for the Iraq task force and for JSOC globally. Each had a right-angled horseshoe of desks at the center facing a wall of flat video screens, with rows of workstations behind and to the sides of the leaders and senior staff officers who occupied the horseshoe.

In the Iraq task force operations center, the task force commander—usually the Delta commander—and his staff sat at the horseshoe. In the rows behind them sat about sixty more operations officers, intelligence analysts, and liaison officers from other commands. The JOC's space-age, high-tech appearance invited comparisons to science fiction. "We used to call it the Battlestar Galactica," said an officer who spent several tours in the Iraq task force JOC. Others called it the Death Star. The officer estimated there were thirty to fifty individual workstations in the JOC, all facing nine "monster TV screens . . . probably sixty-inch TVs arranged in a grid square." A separate feed ran on each screen. One might have a list of the day's missions, another the feed from Echo's Birdseye aircraft above an ongoing assault, a third the video from another intel asset, and so on. "All of a sudden something would start happening on a target, people would focus on that one screen," the officer said. The staff called it "Kill TV." Next door in McChrystal's global ops center, called the Situation Awareness Room, the JSOC commander—or, in his absence, one of his two one-star deputies—sat at the head table with his command sergeant major and intelligence and operations directors on one side and representatives from other agencies and the Iraq task force on the other.[2]

John Abizaid, who had been McChrystal's brigade commander a decade before when McChrystal commanded an 82nd Airborne battalion, was a strong supporter of the JSOC boss's desire to turn his command into a "network." But, as McChrystal acknowledged, others he needed to buy into the concept—particularly in the intelligence community—took longer to come around. He pressed ahead regardless, hoping that as the task force produced results, leaders in other agencies would want to leverage its success. To help accelerate the process, he made the entire JOC facility a sensitive compartmented information facility, or SCIF (pronounced "skiff"), so folks from different agencies and task forces could share top secret data quickly and openly—a complete reversal from the mind-set that traditionally dominated special ops and intelligence organizations.[3]

McChrystal or one of his two one-star deputies were always in Iraq, but from fall 2003 Delta had day-to-day responsibility for running the Iraq task force. (When he focused Delta on Iraq, McChrystal also put

JSOC's Afghanistan task force under the alternating command of Team 6 and the Rangers.)[4] By late summer 2004, the Iraq task force was divided between the headquarters at Balad, usually led by the Delta commander or his deputy, a Delta squadron task force headquartered at Mission Support Site Fernandez in Baghdad, and smaller Ranger, Delta, and Team 6 elements in Mosul, Tikrit, and other towns, with Task Force Brown's helicopters in support. The British SAS's Task Force Black, based in the Green Zone next door to the Delta squadron, wanted to work closely with JSOC, but the British government's concerns over JSOC's treatment of detainees meant the SAS continued to concentrate on hunting former Saddam regime elements long after McChrystal had refocused on Zarqawi.[5]

The size of the force would grow over the next several years, commanders would shift locations, and the organizational chart would change repeatedly. But this was all in keeping with McChrystal's precept that it was important for his force not to become wedded to a particular organizational construct or geographic setup. Rather, he wanted his command to be able to adapt on the fly, moving troops and command and control nodes from base to base as the enemy situation morphed.[6]

McChrystal was running a global enterprise, but after first favoring Afghanistan with time and resources for Winter Strike, he had decided to prioritize the campaign against Al Qaeda in Iraq. "Things were really heating up in Iraq," said a senior JSOC staff officer. "We shifted the main effort." Having established his state-of-the-art command center at Balad, taken stock of the challenges confronting him, and taken the measure of the men and women under him, by fall 2004 McChrystal had the pieces in place to realize his ambitious agenda for JSOC and to pit his nascent network against Al Qaeda in Iraq. As the staff officer put it, "That's when JSOC became the JSOC on steroids."

※

Perhaps no individual other than McChrystal himself was more responsible for turning JSOC into an information age war-fighting machine over the next couple of years than Colonel Mike Flynn, who replaced another Army colonel, Brian Keller, as JSOC's intelligence director in July 2004. A wiry, black-haired Rhode Islander equipped with a razor-sharp mind and a willingness to challenge conventional wisdom, Flynn had already enjoyed an impressive career, serving as intelligence director for the 82nd Airborne Division and XVIII Airborne Corps, including a tour in Afghanistan in the latter position when McChrystal was the Corps' chief of staff. But this would be his first special operations assignment.[7] McChrystal understood the central importance of intelligence in counterinsurgency and had put in what the military calls a "by name request" for Mike Flynn to become his intelligence chief.[8]

When Flynn took charge of JSOC's intelligence shop, the command's intelligence capabilities were on the cusp of a quantum leap forward. This revolution was a necessary step in achieving McChrystal's vision. For the task force to get inside Al Qaeda in Iraq's decision cycle, it needed to drastically increase both its intake of all sources of data and the speed with which it molded that information into actionable intelligence. This in turn required improvements in how JSOC obtained and processed all the different types of intelligence, such as imagery intelligence and signals intelligence. But lacking access to significant volumes of either in early 2004, when McChrystal refocused the task force on Zarqawi, Delta made human intelligence a priority.

"We said, 'Okay, we're on it,'" said a Delta source. "We got AFO going, our [reconnaissance] going, every guy that had been trained as a case officer. We knew we've got to find sources, start hunting." Delta had advantages over the CIA in building source networks in war-torn Iraq: not only were its operators more used to working in a combat zone, but they could more easily plant themselves on small bases from which the conventional military was operating all over Iraq.[9] By early 2004, the CIA was also positioning small numbers of officers on military bases,[10] but tension had continued to grow between the Agency and JSOC over the latter's exploding intelligence requirements and capabilities. Later that year, in an effort to build bridges with the Agency, McChrystal made Flynn his liaison at the CIA's Baghdad station,[11] which was now the largest in the world.[12]

Delta's ability to conduct low-vis operations using its fleet of locally acquired cars was impressive, but the unit was determined to go one better. In the absence of an effective Iraqi intelligence service, Delta created its own. The unit recruited and trained carefully selected Iraqis to conduct intelligence operations on the task force's behalf. Perhaps borrowing the CIA's name for the Afghans the Agency hired for one of its counterterrorism pursuit teams in Afghanistan, Delta called its Iraqi agents the Mohawks. Delta used these brave Iraqis, who numbered in the dozens and for the most part lived on Coalition bases, to conduct close-target reconnaissance—in essence, getting as close to a person or building of interest to JSOC as possible—where sending in non-Iraqis would entail too high a risk. For such missions, the Mohawks sometimes used Delta's "camera cars"—local vehicles in which the unit's "techs" had installed hidden cameras in much the same way that major auto manufacturers disguised backup cameras in their vehicles. "It's the same color as the car but it's still a camera," an operator said. In addition to close-target reconnaissance, the Mohawks' other primary mission was source recruitment. They also elicited information simply by talking with family members and other acquaintances on the telephone. Sometimes they would accompany conventional forces on patrol, which allowed the Mohawks to enter houses, talk with locals, and even recruit sources without attracting attention.

Non-Delta personnel familiar with the Mohawk program gave it high marks. A task force intelligence source called the program "very important" and "probably the best relationship [we had] as far as enabling Iraqis." It was actually safer to have a Mohawk live on military bases in Iraq, where he could hide in plain sight among the large number of local hires working there, than it was to meet him in a safe house or other location outside the wire. "He knows the area, he's vetted," the intelligence source said. "He can work his own cover story . . . better than if he's seen coming out of a house in the neighborhood that's directly tied to the U.S." Mohawks lived at Mission Support Site Fernandez in the Green Zone, at the task force's base in Mosul, and at other installations across Iraq. But living on the bases only slightly mitigated the obvious and substantial risk involved in being a Mohawk during a time of open warfare between the Coalition and the Zarqawi-led Sunni insurgency. Despite the care Delta took to teach the Mohawks proper tradecraft, the Iraqi agents sometimes paid a heavy price for siding with the task force.[13] "Occasionally we'd get the reports of one of the Mohawks being kidnapped and I know a couple of them got killed," said a task force officer.

The Mohawks also targeted insurgents using Internet cafés in operations run by Delta and two even more shadowy units. All followed roughly the same template: Mohawks would enter the Internet café without arousing suspicion and upload software onto the computers. Sometimes the software was of the keystroke recognition type, at other times it would covertly activate a webcam if the computer had one, allowing the task force to positively identify a target.

The insurgents often thought they were exercising good communications security by sharing one account with a single password and writing messages to each other that they saved as drafts rather than sending them as email. But the keystroke tracking software meant JSOC personnel in the United States were reading every word. The task force would wait until the target established a pattern, then act. "When you're ready to deal with him, when that password is [typed] it would trigger a 'Shitbag 1 is at café 6 at computer 4, go get him' [order]," said a source familiar with the missions.

Locally recruited Iraqi agents—or sometimes low-vis U.S. operators—would track the insurgent far enough away from the Internet café to minimize the chances of other enemies figuring out how the Americans had located their target. (Often, operators would identify the target's most likely route away from the café and lay in wait to ambush him.) As with most task force missions, the operators usually snatched the wanted individual without a fight. "Generally when the shootout happened it was either, A, foreign fighters that wanted to fight, or, B, you fucked something up," said a Delta operator. "We snatched tons of dudes that had guns on them. Why didn't they shoot? Because we didn't give them time." Delta ran "hundreds" of missions like this, he said. But Delta wasn't the only unit using these tactics. They were pioneered by a Delta offshoot called the Computer Network Operations Squadron, which was the brainchild of two technologically gifted Delta soldiers in the unit's Technical Surveillance Element called Scott and Keith who by the late 1990s were experimenting with what would later be called cyber operations. "They started as just two dudes in the [Delta headquarters] building that were computer savvy, and then it grew from there," said a Delta operator. "Before I even had email, they were hacking email. And they were incredibly effective."

Scott, a Special Forces weapons sergeant turned Delta communications expert from California, was a technological savant with a particular interest in—and aptitude for—supervisory control and data acquisition (SCADA) computer systems, which run processes in multiple industrial facilities simultaneously. Higher-ups recognized the potential in what a JSOC staff officer described as his "unbelievable talent." "This was just a dude who said he could hack some email and then the next thing you know he's running his own program, getting funded," the Delta operator said. In the first years after the September 11 attacks, the "program" became a stand-alone unit. It started as a small yet effective troop, but by 2007 had grown into the Computer Network Operations Squadron—headquartered in Arlington, Virginia, with a troop at Fort Meade and another at the CIA's Langley headquarters—and reporting straight to the JSOC commander. The military kept CNOS in JSOC "because we want it to operate in areas that are not necessarily . . . where we're currently at war," said a military intelligence officer. "We want it to operate around the globe [pursuing] national objectives." By 2006 the unit was "cruising" but heavily committed to the wars in Iraq and Afghanistan, according to two other sources familiar with the unit.

For some of the most dangerous—and kinetic—cyber operations in Iraq, the squadron provided information to the Interagency Support Activity, a short-lived unit created in early 2006 after an Afghanistan proof-of-concept the previous year. It consisted of: Mohawks; CIA Ground Branch paramilitary personnel and contractors; Delta, Team 6, and Orange operators; plus a few Canadian and British operators. Although notionally a combined JSOC-CIA force, the unit reported to the Agency's Baghdad station chief. "This was how the pesky networks were broken in Iraq," said a source familiar with the Activity's missions. "The ones we couldn't get with sigint and we couldn't get with humint, basically the really disciplined ones." One Activity team targeted the leaders of Sunni insurgent rings managing the flow of foreign fighters into Iraq from Syria. The other went after the heads of Shi'ite networks run by Iranian intelligence.

The Activity teams lived in a collection of safe houses separated from each other and from other Coalition forces. When on a mission, the six or so Americans on each team dressed as Iraqis. Fair-toned personnel wore skin-darkening makeup. Their Internet café missions followed the same pattern as Delta's, with one crucial difference: the Activity teams, which did not have the layers of backup and enablers that habitually supported JSOC's strike elements, always planned to kill their targets. "I do not know of one who was captured," said the source familiar with the missions, which were even more secret than Delta's. "Under forty-five people in the country knew this was going on," the source said.

The Activity lived a short, violent life. The CIA disbanded the teams in September 2006, partly because the general level of violence in Iraq was increasing and the Activity was taking casualties, partly because JSOC was eviscerating the Sunni networks to such an extent that targeting Internet cafés was no longer yielding results, but also because the United States decided it had better uses for the teams' talented Iraqi sources.[14]

Task Force Orange also got into the act, using two Hispanic operatives who spoke excellent Arabic. "They could walk into any Internet café and pass themselves off as a college student or a low-level businessman," said an officer familiar with Orange missions. "If it was a more cosmopolitan section of Baghdad, we would target those [cafés]. If it was one of the more suburban areas where everybody knew everybody going in and out of that Internet café then we wouldn't try to do it. But the NSA and the CIA would come to us and say, 'Okay, here's a map. We need this place, this place, this place, and this place all covered.' And we would send guys out and they would do that in a heartbeat."

Despite the intrepid Internet café operations, however, the breakthroughs that made the biggest difference for JSOC were in the areas of imagery and signals intelligence. In both fields, the task force needed far more aircraft, particularly of the fixed wing variety, than it had in late 2003. McChrystal and his staff worked hard to lay their hands on aircraft that were ready for intelligence, surveillance, and reconnaissance (ISR) missions or could be reconfigured for them. Under McChrystal, the staff became more involved than it had been under Dailey in supporting the strike forces, especially in regard to making ISR aircraft available. "He realized his job as the big boss was to give assets to the smaller bosses," a Delta source said. The task force's ISR fleet went from Echo's single helicopter in mid-2003 to forty aircraft of fifteen different types within the next two years.[15] The aircraft belonged mostly to Echo, Task Force Orange, and Task Force Silver (the Air Force covered air unit), and together were known as "the Confederate Air Force" (perhaps in a nod to Orange's nickname as "The Army of Northern Virginia").[16]

McChrystal's unquenchable thirst for ISR coverage, together with the control JSOC had gained over the unit it now called Task Force Orange, had major ramifications for the Fort Belvoir special mission unit. By 2004 more than half of Orange, and a lot more than half of its aircraft, were committed to Iraq. "Our capability was just that more advanced, we provided that resource that you really couldn't get with anything else," said a field grade officer familiar with Orange's operations. But in order to commit Orange to the war in Iraq, McChrystal had to overcome powerful bureaucratic opposition, particularly from the National Security

Agency, which had paid for many of Orange's capabilities in the expectation that they would be used for the NSA's national-level missions, rather than in down-and-dirty urban fights in Iraq. "The NSA did not want to have the aircraft in Iraq," said the officer. "They wanted to do other things [with them]."[17] Opposition to the reorientation of Orange also came from high inside the special operations world. "That organization wasn't designed to do tactical intelligence for JSOC—they pirated it," said a retired special operations officer. "This was supposed to be a strategic asset that was doing serious stuff."

Orange bought six single-engine turboprop aircraft, stripped the insides, and refilled them with signals intelligence gear.[18] The unit experimented with putting the packages on Black Hawks, but found that for the sensors to work properly, the helicopters could get no further than 3,000 feet aboveground and a mile or two away from the target—close enough to be spotted by alert insurgents. The planes, however, could perform the mission at up to 15,000 feet above ground level and five miles away.[19] "You had no idea I was around," the field grade officer said.

While much of the Confederate Air Force provided real-time imagery of targets, Orange's aircraft were there to provide signals intelligence, primarily targeting the insurgents' use of Iraq's burgeoning cell phone networks. Before the U.S. invasion, there were almost no privately owned cell phones in Iraq, as they were illegal under Saddam Hussein.[20] But the toppling of the dictator resulted in exponential growth of the cell phone market. By May 2005, about 1.75 million Iraqis had cell phones, a number that continued to grow.[21] Mid- and lower-level Iraqi insurgents, particularly those fighting for Zarqawi, seemingly could not resist the immediacy of communicating by cell phone. As a result, McChrystal's network expended much energy on developing and using technological means to exploit a potentially rich source of signals intelligence.

The cell phone networks made such a fat collective target that several different organizations inside and outside the task force attacked it, including Delta (and particularly Echo Squadron), Orange, and the NSA. During the first three years the task force achieved several cell phone-related technological breakthroughs that together represented what a Task Force Brown officer described as "a game-changer."

The Confederate Air Force planes carried gear that when flown close to a cell phone tower allowed those on board to log in passively and see a real-time record of every phone making a call. Task force personnel could then search for numbers in which they were interested, and the database would tell them if those phones were in use, and if so, where. "We'd pinpoint the location, we'd go hit the target," said an operator. The cell phone tower info might guide the task force to a particular city block. At that point, the operators would use an "electronic divining rod," a handheld paddlelike sensor that could be programmed to detect a specific phone and would beep increasingly loudly as it got closer to the device.[22] The divining rod could even detect a phone that had been turned off, although not one with the battery and SIM card removed. Indeed, not only could the task force's electronics specialists find a phone that had been turned off, they also figured out how to turn it on remotely so it became a microphone, broadcasting everything it was picking up back to the task force. They could also "clone" a cell phone without having the original phone in their possession, allowing the task force to send and receive texts, for instance, as if they were the phone's owner. In addition, Delta made extensive use of handheld SIM card readers that allowed operators who found a cell phone while searching a suspect's home to quickly remove the card, copy it in the machine, and put it back in the phone, often without the suspect realizing it had been taken out and copied. Sometimes operators would pretend they hadn't even found the phone, to hide the fact that they now had a record of all its owner's contacts.[23] Operators invented software that allowed it to conduct "nodal analysis" that quickly mapped out insurgent networks based on an analysis of insurgents' cell phone traffic.[24]

The NSA placed all the signals intelligence information on the Real Time Regional Gateway (RTRG), an interactive signals intelligence clearinghouse that task force personnel could query using phone numbers they'd just derived from raids, and be rewarded with a set of new leads that the system would spit back. According to authors Dana Priest and William M. Arkin, the RTRG also allowed task force members to monitor signals intercepts as they were happening and led to "a tenfold increase" in the speed with which operators gained access to the intelligence.[25]

Despite the NSA's objections to JSOC's co-opting of Orange, the agency became a critical partner in the effort to break Iraq's cell phone networks open as a source of intelligence. By late 2003, an NSA cryptologic support group was collecting the metadata—dialing information, but not the content—of all calls made in Iraq. After McChrystal moved his headquarters to Balad, the NSA put a liaison team in the command center.[26] Realizing that their cell phones made them vulnerable, the insurgents recruited what a task force officer described as "pretty sophisticated communications engineers" to protect them from surveillance. In 2003, they had already figured out how to reconfigure high-powered cordless phones into a sort of walkie-talkie network. "They thought they had this private little communications hotline . . . that no one could read because it wasn't operating at a cell phone level, but we figured that one out pretty fast," said the officer. "That was a major coup, finding it . . . and then using that information." It was a short-lived success. By the next year, the insurgents had all but given up using the technique.

Through 2004, McChrystal's force of personality gradually melded all these disparate parts—the motley fleet of ISR aircraft; the growing ability to use insurgents' digital communications against them; the "Death Star" JOC at Balad, increasingly peopled by staffers and liaisons from other parts of McChrystal's network; the unsurpassed skill and tenacity of special mission unit operators, the Rangers, and the Night Stalkers—into a dynamic process that became known as F3EAD: Find, Fix, Finish, Exploit, Analyze, Disseminate. Finding and fixing involved the ISR assets identifying and then locating a target—usually a person—in time and space. Finishing—capturing or killing—the target was the job of the direct action forces: the special mission unit operators, Rangers, and Task Force Brown aircrews. Exploiting and analyzing the mission's intelligence haul, which could mean anything from deciphering papers, phones, and computer gear to interrogating prisoners, was the work of operators and, especially, intelligence personnel at all levels. Immediately after that analysis was concluded—which might take weeks in 2003 and a couple of hours by 2006—the results were disseminated around the network to drive more operations. At its core, the process required a much tighter and smoother coordination between intelligence and operations than had been the norm, even in JSOC.

It's worth noting that veterans of the hunts for Pablo Escobar and Balkan war criminals argued that McChrystal and Flynn were essentially reinventing a wheel that those much smaller task forces had already designed. Published accounts that "attribute to McChrystal and Flynn this great transformation where now we integrate things" ignore history, a Delta source said. "It's like, dude, that's Colombia." Similarly, "the multi-agency sharing of intelligence and technology, [the] breaking down of the walls between the different interagency partners that was done later [by McChrystal in Iraq] was demonstrated under [Jerry] Boykin's leadership" during JSOC's hunt for Balkan war criminals in the 1990s, said a senior special operations officer familiar with those missions.

The F3EAD acronym did not roll off the tongue, but it was still easier to say than to do. Lives were lost and much blood spilled as the task force ramped up its operational tempo, fighting to get inside the Zarqawi network's decision cycle. Getting JSOC to adopt the McChrystal/Flynn mind-set was not without its challenges. As the task force amassed intelligence on a target, there was often tension between those who wanted to keep watching it to see what more they could learn about the enemy network and those who wanted to strike the target immediately, even if it meant exposing assets that had led to the target in the first place.[27] These arguments were usually settled on the side of those wanting to act quickly, on the grounds that there was as much or more intelligence to be gained from striking a target than there was from simply watching it. "Strike to develop" became a task force catchphrase.[28] "Our fight against Zarqawi was, at its heart, a battle for intelligence," McChrystal later wrote.[29]

But once JSOC had perfected the F3EAD "machine," it became self-sustaining, said a Special Forces officer who observed the process first-hand. Occasionally, the task force would tinker around the margins of the model, "but while they were doing that the machine kept running," he said. "Unless you could prove you could do something better, you didn't fuck with the machine."

19

Snake Eyes

The Euphrates lapped against the sides of the small boats as, cloaked in darkness, they pulled up to the riverbank beside the farm in Anbar province. The men in the boats wore kaffiyehs and looked from a distance like local farmhands. But they weren't. They were Delta operators on a mission to capture a top Zarqawi lieutenant—a mission of the type others said would never succeed.

The man they were after, Ghassan Amin, was close enough to Zarqawi to have recently arranged for a relative to host the Al Qaeda in Iraq supremo for five days. Amin was Zarqawi's enforcer in Rawa, a strategically important town on the north bank of the Euphrates that he ran as his personal fiefdom. With its bridge across the river, Rawa was key terrain for Zarqawi. Whoever controlled the town could influence the flow of foreign fighters from Syria into the dense urban battlefields of Fallujah, Ramadi, and Baghdad. His forces having destroyed the Rawa police station, Amin's effective counterintelligence network allowed him to terrorize the town's population of about 20,000. "He . . . used to publicly execute one person—snitch—per week in the market," said a senior special mission unit officer. "We saw him on a Predator shoot a source [of ours] right in the head in his vehicle. He was a bad, bad guy."

He was also very difficult to catch. "We couldn't figure out how to get the guy," the officer said. But intelligence that Amin owned a farm west of Rawa on the banks of the Euphrates gave Delta operators an idea. "Some of our sources said, 'Hey, they're coming up to harvest season and he goes down and he visits the farm certain days literally to watch the workers bring the harvest in,'" the officer said. An assault troop in C Squadron led by Captain Doug Taylor, a former enlisted Delta operator who had received a commission from Officer Candidate School and returned to the unit, proposed snaring Amin by driving up to the Euphrates from

Al Asad air base, floating down and across the river in small boats, then posing as workers on his farm. It was a classic out-of-the-box Delta plan: simple, yet elegant. It was also the type of plan that rarely got approved. But the United States was not winning in Iraq. Unconventional ideas that senior commanders would previously have dismissed were now getting a fair hearing. "By that time we had carte blanche to do anything we liked," said a Delta source. Taylor's plan was given the green light. So it was that he and his men—including several Arabic speakers—found themselves sneaking onto Amin's farm before the day heated up. It was the morning of April 26, 2005.

The operators quickly sequestered the real farmworkers in the farmhouse. Taking the farmhands' places, they worked the fields—even driving a tractor—and waited. After some time, their prey approached. "Ghassan Amin and his two henchmen drove right up to the guys," said the special mission unit officer. Amin walked to within a couple of feet of an operator and greeted him in Arabic, before belatedly realizing his mistake as the operators whipped out their weapons and took him and his cohorts prisoner. The Delta ruse worked so well that the operators were able to capture several of Amin's Al Qaeda associates in Iraq that day on the farm. "It's like something out of the movies," said the special mission unit officer. "Many higher officers would [say], 'Well, you can't be putting Arab garb on and driving tractors out in the field and have anyone fall for that.' Person after person came down to the farm, into the bag."

The Delta source was more specific in his movie reference, alluding to Kevin Costner's famous quote in *Field of Dreams*. "If you build it, they will come," he said. "They came and they came and they came."

The operators eventually sped away with their captives, having successfully completed one of the more colorful Delta missions of the war on terror. Amin, for his part, was cool to the last. "I should have known it was Americans," he said when he realized he'd fallen for a trick. "Iraqis never work that hard."[1]

※

As the Ghassan Amin mission indicated, by late spring 2005, JSOC's war in Iraq was moving west, in response to the flow of foreign jihadists entering Iraq from Syria. Although the task force estimated that no more than 150 foreign fighters were arriving in Iraq per month, McChrystal had concluded they were playing an outsized role in the Sunni insurgency, which JSOC assessed as having between 12,000 and 20,000 fighters. The foreign jihadists, young men with no familial concerns or patriotic interest in seeing a prosperous Iraq, provided a disproportionate share of the insurgent leadership (with Zarqawi himself—a Jordanian—as the prime example) and almost all the suicide bombers cutting bloody swaths through Iraqi market squares. Once in Iraq, insurgent groups moved them through "ratlines" of safe houses in the towns along the western Euphrates Valley, from Al Qaim, the dusty industrial town on the Syrian border, to Rawa, Haditha, Hit, Ramadi, Fallujah, and Baghdad.[2]

Realizing that the task force's knowledge of foreign fighter networks beyond Iraq's borders was too shallow, in December 2004 McChrystal established a counterpart at Balad to Bagram's Joint Interagency Task Force-East, specifically to map those networks and to identify high-value targets abroad. The catalyst for the creation of what he dubbed JIATF-West was the December 21 suicide bombing by a young Saudi jihadist of the dining facility at Forward Operating Base Marez in Mosul. The attack killed twenty-two people, including Sergeant Major Robert O'Dell, an Orange operative on a team deployed to Mosul to help the task force element there get a better handle on the foreign fighter problem. Already aware that he needed to gain a greater understanding of the web of imams, financiers, ideologues, facilitators, and fighters that stretched across and beyond the Arab countries and was feeding jihadists into the meat grinder the Iraq War had become, after the Marez bombing McChrystal moved quickly. Within twenty-four hours he had flown from Bagram to Balad and established JIATF-West under Tom DiTomasso's leadership.[3]

While JIATF-East focused on Pakistan, Central Asia, and Afghanistan, JIATF-West's area of coverage included the Levant, the Arabian Peninsula, East Africa, North Africa, Europe, Iraq, and Iran (which it shared with JIATF-East). The two JIATFs stayed small, with staffs of fifteen to twenty-five. Using a "newsroom" open-plan office design, the JIATFs worked to develop what they called a "common operating picture" that was shared with all the government agencies with a stake in counterterrorism. The JIATFs mapped the jihadist networks, but also combined intelligence from many sources to create target folders on wanted individuals. These five-page folders included a biography of the person, a diagram of his social network, a detailed description of his pattern of life, and solid intelligence on his location. Packaged together, that information allowed U.S. decision makers to choose between four courses of action: to continue to do nothing other than keep tabs on the individual; to work with partner nations and their security forces to kill or capture the target; to turn the data over to another country and let it handle the problem; or to act against the target unilaterally.[4]

But as JIATF-West steadily built its picture of the foreign fighter network outside Iraq, a sharp difference was appearing between JSOC's view of the enemy inside the country and the perspective of Multi-National Force-Iraq (MNF-I), the international coalition's conventional military command headed by U.S. Army General George Casey. McChrystal's staff was convinced that Al Qaeda in Iraq, and particularly Zarqawi's access to the foreign fighter networks, presented the biggest threat. Unconvinced, during the first half of 2005 Casey's headquarters continued to focus its attention on "former regime elements."

There were other sources of tension between McChrystal's task force and the conventional U.S. military forces in Iraq. Conventional commanders tired of having their patient efforts to build relationships with Sunni communities in their areas of operation disrupted by destructive task force raids over which they had no control. The regular military was also jealous of JSOC's disproportionate share of scarce, in-demand ISR assets, particularly Predators. It didn't help that although Casey outranked McChrystal, the task force's chain of command ran directly to Central Command in Tampa, rather than to Multi-National Force-Iraq.[5] In other words, the U.S. military's two principal war-fighting commands in Iraq were fighting different wars.

A rapprochement of sorts was achieved in May. A devastating series of well-coordinated attacks by Zarqawi's men across Anbar and Baghdad in April caused Casey to belatedly recognize the extent of the threat posed by Al Qaeda in Iraq and designate the organization as the Coalition's number-one enemy. At about the same time, in a conversation with Casey, McChrystal offered to shift his task force's focus to the west to support a major conventional effort to combat Zarqawi's forces closer to the Syrian border.[6] The move guaranteed an even bloodier confrontation between JSOC and Al Qaeda in Iraq. McChrystal was dramatically raising the stakes, but felt he had no choice.

By fall 2004, the JSOC commander had determined that what he termed "a strict decapitation" strategy—i.e., one aimed only at capturing or killing Zarqawi and other very senior insurgents—was unlikely to succeed. Instead, he focused the task force on eviscerating Al Qaeda in Iraq's middle level of leaders. By stripping Al Qaeda in Iraq of its experienced day-to-day management structure faster than it could be replaced, McChrystal aimed to knock the Zarqawi network off its stride. Flynn's radical redesign of the task force's intelligence structure enabled this, but it was nonetheless a very labor-intensive approach requiring a massive increase in operational tempo. At the time, JSOC's Iraq task force's ground elements consisted of a Delta squadron headquartered with an assault troop in Fernandez (Task Force Central) but with teams distributed around Sunni cities like Tikrit and Mosul, with Ranger elements in support. (The Delta/Ranger element in Mosul became Task Force North.) To enable him to expand westward while keeping the pressure on the rest of Zarqawi's network, in summer 2005 McChrystal brought in a second Delta squadron from Bragg, and installed a SEAL Team 6 troop and squadron command cell plus a Ranger platoon at Al Asad as Task Force West. He also deployed an almost complete Team 6 troop from another squadron to Iraq, broke it up, and spread its operators around different Green teams. All this involved moving some Team 6 and Task Force Brown forces from Afghanistan to Iraq.[7]

McChrystal's announcement of his plan to "surge" forces into Iraq in order to facilitate a campaign in the western Euphrates Valley did not go over well with the task force's combat elements. "Not a lot of people were on board with McChrystal's expansion," said a Task Force Brown source. "They felt we were already too involved in Iraq." McChrystal acknowledged that Delta operators met his "highly controversial decision" with "initial intransigence." The general's relations with Delta had been characterized by mutual wariness since he had taken command of JSOC. Visiting the unit compound at Bragg soon after assuming command, he felt like an outsider, which he was, having never served there. Many in Delta had traditionally viewed JSOC headquarters as one that added much bureaucracy and little operational value. But McChrystal had at least two things working in his favor: as a Ranger, he was an alumnus of the regiment from which Delta drew an increasing percentage of its operators; and he wasn't Dell Dailey. Many in Delta found McChrystal's aggressiveness a welcome change from what they perceived as Dailey's overly cautious approach. Nevertheless, when McChrystal gathered his commanders in May 2005 to explain his rationale for the surge, he encountered little enthusiasm. Delta officials' immediate concern was that operations in western Anbar would put them much farther from immediate medevac and other support than their missions in Baghdad had. But they were also worried that deploying two of Delta's three ground squadrons simultaneously would disrupt—perhaps permanently—the carefully controlled schedule that kept one squadron deployed, one on alert at home, and one resting, refitting, and training.[8] "Green thought they were already getting tapped out," said the Task Force Brown source. The surge west also required a considerable effort from Task Force Brown, which had most of its aircraft at Balad with a small detachment at Fernandez. Built as it was around just the 1st Battalion of the 160th, Brown did not have the flexibility that Blue, Green, and Red enjoyed by virtue of each having three separate ground maneuver elements.[9]

Nor was everyone gung ho about the increased tempo at which McChrystal expected teams to operate. While individual squadrons, battalions, and lower echelons all had their own personalities and approaches, some in Delta were reluctant, first, to expand their target set to include lower-ranking Al Qaeda in Iraq fighters, and, second, to hit objectives immediately, rather than observe them to gain intelligence. Of the three primary assault forces—Delta, Team 6, and the Rangers—Delta, manned largely by operators in their thirties and forties, was the unit most associated with "tactical patience." This created particular problems in Iraq and then Afghanistan when McChrystal placed Ranger battalion commanders in charge of task forces that included Delta teams.[10] But McChrystal would not be denied. Through a combination of his forceful personality and the support of key subordinates like Chris Faris, the Delta command sergeant major, and Scott Miller, who replaced Sacolick as Delta commander early that summer, McChrystal made the surge work.[11] "You've got to give McChrystal credit because he fought through all of that, all the resistance . . . and essentially won," said the TF Brown source.

The stakes were high. McChrystal warned Abizaid the task force's casualty rate would likely rise. But McChrystal also knew "failure in Iraq was tangibly close." Responsibility for naming the move west belonged to John Christian, back in Iraq for another tour as task force commander. The moniker he chose captured the nature of the gamble: Operation Snake Eyes.[12]

Delta began mounting raids from Al Asad in late May. The surge forces began arriving in July 2005, but by then McChrystal's grim prediction regarding casualties had come true. In a May 31 raid on what McChrystal described as "a fortified enemy position" in Al Qaim, Sergeant First Class Steven Langmack became the first Delta operator killed in action in more than two years when small arms fire struck him down. The thirty-three-year-old Special Forces communications sergeant had only joined Delta the previous year. McChrystal's reference to the "fortified enemy position" is instructive. The insurgents were getting wise to Delta's tactics and were strong-pointing their safe houses in expectation of task force raids. Two and a half weeks later, B Squadron operators assaulted another house in Al Qaim, unaware the insurgents had built a bunker inside it. A volley of automatic weapons fire met the operators as they stormed in, killing Master Sergeants Bob Horrigan and Michael McNulty. The assault team withdrew and called in an air strike on the building, but the damage to the unit's sense of invincibility had been done.[13]

The June 17 assault marked the first time that Delta had lost more than one operator on a mission since Mogadishu. The three "deaths hit the unit like a shudder," McChrystal wrote. The loss of Horrigan was a particularly tough blow. "That rocked a lot of guys," said a Delta source. Hugely respected and well liked in Delta, among Horrigan's many exploits was his infiltration of Afghanistan's Shahikot Valley as a member of AFO's India Team during Operation Anaconda. A former Ranger and Special Forces soldier, the forty-year-old Horrigan was on his last combat deployment, due to retire in a matter of months to focus on his booming custom knife-making business. A military plane flew about forty of Horrigan's Delta colleagues plus McChrystal—in whose Ranger company he'd served as a private in the 1980s—to his funeral in Austin, Texas.[14]

✳

In mid-2005, four major changes to task force operations were taking place simultaneously: the expansion to the west, the surge of JSOC forces into Iraq, the shift from a "decapitation" strategy to one focused on mid-level insurgents, and an increasing willingness to conduct daytime operations. The reason for the last change was simple: "The bad guys were getting smart to our night tactics," said a Task Force Brown source. "We'd been hitting targets all over Baghdad for probably a year." Most of those raids keyed off signals intelligence from monitoring insurgents' cell phones. Al Qaeda in Iraq had gotten wise to this. "They quit turning cell phones on at night," the Task Force Brown source said. "They just stopped operating at night. They started operating during the day. So McChrystal said, basically—obviously with TF Green influence—'Hey, we need to start hitting these targets during the day.'"

Combined with the westward expansion, this had major implications for Task Force Brown. Whereas in Baghdad Delta typically sent a ground assault force (GAF) mounted in Pandurs to an objective, distances in the west were so vast that often only a helicopter assault force (HAF) would suffice. (These phrases soon became acronyms and then verbs in JSOC-speak: operators would talk of "GAFing" or "HAFing" to a target.) But the potential move to daylight ops represented "a significant emotional event" for the TF Brown crews, "who didn't want to fly during the day, being known as Night Stalkers," the Brown source said. Used to flying missions at night, when their helicopters were more easily hidden from insurgent small arms and RPGs, the Night Stalker pilots pressured Task Force Brown's commander, Lieutenant Colonel Steve Schiller, to push back against McChrystal and Task Force Green. Schiller took their arguments straight to the top. "If you're going to do this, we're going to have helicopters shot down," he told McChrystal. The general replied that he was willing to assume that risk.[15]

As Task Force Brown split its force between day-alert and night-alert crews and the pilots came to terms with their increasingly dangerous mission profile, losses were mounting for Delta, a unit singularly unaccustomed to taking casualties. On August 25, a task force convoy traveling through the town of Husaybah next to the Syrian border struck an IED (improvised explosive device—an insurgent-manufactured booby trap) made of three antitank mines stacked on top of each other. The explosion devastated a B Squadron team, killing three soldiers immediately: Delta operators Master Sergeant Ivica "Pizza" Jerak, forty-two, and Sergeant First Class Trevor Diesing, thirty, as well as Corporal Timothy Shea, twenty-two, of 3rd Ranger Battalion. A third Delta operator, Sergeant First Class Obediah Kolath, was mortally wounded and died August 28 after being flown to the military hospital in Landstuhl, Germany. The blast badly wounded several other operators. The team leader was blown out of the vehicle but survived.[16]

The fight in Anbar became the bloodiest test of wills that Delta had faced in its history. During one squadron's three-month tour, "almost 50 percent of the entire force had been wounded on that one rotation—an astronomical number," said a Little Bird pilot. The fact that many of these casualties were taken chasing lower-level targets only heightened the frustration of some Delta operators. But McChrystal's sheer willpower, combined with the strength of character for which Delta screens all applicants, meant that the task force drove on regardless of the cost. "McChrystal was relentless in not letting it affect anybody," said a task force officer. "He stayed on his task and pressed on."

By now, McChrystal's zeal had become an obsession. In October, he began his third year as JSOC commander, having spent most of the first two forward. He gave those around him the impression that the only thing that mattered in his life was the fight against Al Qaeda in Iraq, and that it was the only thing that should matter in theirs. It was a message that he drove home in meetings, video-teleconferences, and one-on-one conversations with subordinates, once telling a commander who was trying to ensure some home time for his troops, "I need them to realize that they don't have a life—this is their life." This unwavering determination was a double-edged sword, inspiring many but rubbing others the wrong way. "That dude's hard as fucking nails and probably the best war-fighting general we've had . . . since Patton," said one of McChrystal's color task force commanders. "But his shortcoming there was he expected that out of everybody, and he didn't realize that not everyone . . . [had] the drive to perform at that level." The general summed up his view during a visit to B Squadron at Al Qaim on August 28, 2005. "I told the men that day what I believed and what had come to be my life," he wrote. *"It's the fight. It's the fight. It's the fight."*[17]

※

Throughout 2005, JSOC's task force in Iraq continued to refine its tactics, techniques, and procedures as it ramped up its operational tempo. As the number of raids rose dramatically, so did the amount of material seized on those raids. Under Mike Flynn's direction, the task force changed what it did with this material, which had originally been nobody's priority—assault teams had tossed it into trash bags to which they affixed sticky notes. That changed by summer 2005. Flynn established and filled a series of workspaces at Balad where specialists mined every piece of pocket litter (the items lifted from detainees' pockets) and digital device taken off a target. The JSOC intelligence director ensured that the leader of an assault team that captured a suspect took part in the detainee's interrogation, so he could explain the exact circumstances under which the suspect was taken and any material seized.

A major breakthrough came when McChrystal and Flynn met a man called Roy Apseloff while visiting CIA headquarters. Apseloff ran the Defense Intelligence Agency's National Media Exploitation Center (NMEC) in Fairfax, Virginia, and offered to help JSOC derive useful intelligence from material taken in raids. The task force gained control of a massive amount of bandwidth, thus enabling it to immediately email NMEC the contents of everything seized on a mission. In Fairfax, Apseloff's thirty-strong staff used innovative software not only to access the data even from broken hard drives, but to link it together to create a better picture of the insurgent networks. Apseloff's team was responsible for what McChrystal called an "exponential improvement" in the task force's ability to process the raw material it was capturing into actionable intelligence.[18] The task force "created a social network database, and every raid made the database better," said a Special Forces colonel.

Meanwhile, as McChrystal and Flynn had reformed the task force's detainee operations, the CIA, DIA, and FBI had all reconnected with JSOC after keeping the task force at arm's length over concerns regarding detainee abuse.[19] From its difficult beginnings, McChrystal's effort to build "a network to defeat a network" was surpassing perhaps even his own expectations. At the height of the campaign against Al Qaeda in Iraq, there were nearly 100 CIA representatives and eighty FBI personnel ("Fox Bravos," in JSOC-speak) in Balad.[20] "McChrystal had a remarkable ability to bring everybody inside the tent and make them feel like a team player," said a retired Special Forces colonel who saw him at work. "He'd co-opt them so in some respects when they went back to [their] agency they became his ambassadors and advocates." The sheer adrenaline rush that came with participation—even from the relatively safe confines of Balad—in the task force's operations was a major factor in gaining support from these representatives from other government agencies. "For the average civil servant," said the retired colonel, tours with the task force were "a pretty strong narcotic."

McChrystal's decision to design a JOC conducive to collaboration was paying off handsomely. "Everybody wore different hats, but they all seemed to be working together," said an officer who visited the task force in Balad. "It just didn't seem like it was very compartmented, which is how I had always envisioned that world." The officer was also struck by how the task force, and therefore the JOC, stayed on reverse cycle for years on end. "It's odd when you go during the daytime and there's like no one there," he said. "And then you're there [at night] when things start happening and the place is buzzing, it's just hopping."

⁎

Although the task force's main effort was Anbar, its components elsewhere were not letting up. Delta's Task Force North element in Mosul was also hanging it out there in a big way. "In Mosul they were gunning a lot of dudes down on the streets," said a Delta operator. "They'd ID a guy, catch him driving, and just fucking shoot him in traffic and keep driving." This account appears to contradict McChrystal's memoir. "No raid force under my command ever went on a mission with orders not to capture a target if he tried to surrender," the general wrote. "We were not death squads."[21] But another task force source's description of a Delta team's daytime mission in Mosul seems to confirm the operator's contention. The team used a small civilian van to get close to their target, the second source said. The van was decorated in typical fashion for that part of the Middle East, but a special covering in the rear windows made the vehicle appear full of blankets, when in fact it was driven by operators disguised as locals with more operators concealed in the back. Hiding in plain sight, the Delta operators drove through the Mosul traffic with their quarry in view. "They were able to, using that vehicle, pull right next to his vehicle and then slide the door back and make the hit on this terrorist," the task force source said. After shooting the target and someone with him, the operators grabbed the bodies and brought them back to the base.

As the year lengthened there were signs that McChrystal's gamble in the west was paying off. The number of suicide car bomb attacks declined about 80 percent between July and December 2005, something McChrystal attributed to Operation Snake Eyes.[22] But at the end of each busy period of darkness, when McChrystal, Flynn, and Miller retired to their stiff green Army cots to catch a few hours' sleep as dawn broke, each knew that somewhere out beyond the wire, Zarqawi still loomed.

20

Killing Zarqawi

In late June 2005, McChrystal was back in the United States hosting a JSOC commanders' conference at Gettysburg, Pennsylvania, when he received a summons to the White House to brief a National Security Council session on Zarqawi. On June 29, the general found himself in the White House Situation Room briefing the president and what amounted to his war cabinet. When McChrystal concluded, Bush fixed him with his eyes. "Are you going to get him?" The JSOC commander's response was firm. "We will, Mr. President," he said. "There is no doubt in my mind."[1]

As the National Security Council meeting indicated, Washington increasingly saw the complex struggle in Iraq, which combined traditional insurgency, Islamist terrorism, sectarian civil war, tribal conflict, and a proxy war between the United States and Iran, as a war with one man's organization: Abu Musab al-Zarqawi's Al Qaeda in Iraq. To a degree, Washington merely reflected the thinking in Casey's Baghdad headquarters, which over the course of a few months had shifted from doubting that Zarqawi was playing an important role to believing that removing him from the battlefield would collapse the insurgency.[2]

The task force had already missed a golden opportunity to test that theory. On February 20, 2005, after learning that Zarqawi was due to travel down a stretch of highway along the Euphrates between Ramadi and Rawa during a certain time window, the task force set up an elaborate ambush. But Zarqawi was late, and the U.S. troops had relaxed their guard by the time his vehicle came into view. Zarqawi's driver blew through a Delta roadblock and approached a Ranger checkpoint at high speed. A Ranger machine gunner had the AQI leader in his sights and requested permission to fire, but his lieutenant denied the request because he did not have "positive ID" of the vehicle's occupants. To the intense frustration of other Rangers at the checkpoint, Zarqawi's vehicle flew past, with the Jordanian staring wildly at them. He was close enough for them to note he was gripping a U.S. assault rifle and wearing a Blackhawk! brand tactical vest. "He was shitting his pants," a special operations source said. "He knew he was caught."

A Predator kept Zarqawi in sight as Delta operators on the ground roared after him. Realizing they were being chased, Zarqawi and his driver turned onto a secondary road. With the Delta team about thirty seconds behind, Zarqawi jumped out and ran for it, leaving his driver, laptop, and $100,000 in euros to be captured. Staffers in the operations center tried to follow Zarqawi with the drone, but at that moment its camera suffered a glitch, switching from a tight focus on Zarqawi to a wide-angle view of the entire neighborhood. By the time the frantic staffers had refocused the camera, their target had vanished.[3]

There would be other close calls for Zarqawi, but for the next fifteen months he and the task force were locked in a deadly contest, as JSOC's operators and intelligence analysts raced to devour the middle ranks of his network before he could replenish them, in the hope that this would stall his campaign and lead the task force to him. Zarqawi, meanwhile, was trying to ignite a full-scale sectarian civil war before the task force destroyed his organization, which he had presciently designed to function as semi-autonomous regional and local cells.[4] Zarqawi and McChrystal each encouraged their respective organizations to take an entrepreneurial approach to warfare. McChrystal was renowned for promoting a sense of competition among the various strike forces at his disposal in Iraq, allotting the precious ISR assets to whichever commander came up with the most compelling target.[5]

In early January 2006, the task force's luck began to turn. Iraqi forces captured Mohammad Rabih, aka Abu Zar, an Iraqi native and a senior Al Qaeda in Iraq leader. The task force had briefly been on his trail the previous summer, only to fall victim to a ruse: in late August, Abu Zar had faked his own funeral, complete with his apparently grief-stricken mother. Task force sources in the crowd believed the funeral was genuine, so the task force stopped looking for Abu Zar. Now he had turned up in Iraqi government hands. The task force used Defense Department channels to persuade the Iraqis to transfer Abu Zar to JSOC's detainee facility at Balad, where he soon told interrogators that Zarqawi's number two, Abu Ayyub al-Masri, would sometimes stay in a particular cluster of buildings in Yusufiyah, twenty miles southwest of Baghdad. The task force saw nothing untoward about the buildings. However, one intelligence analyst was convinced Abu Zar wasn't lying and continued to observe the area whenever aircraft were available.[6]

While that analyst kept watch over Yusufiyah, a significant event in JSOC's history went almost unnoticed by the public. On February 16,[7] McChrystal was promoted to lieutenant general but remained in command of JSOC. By elevating the JSOC commander's position to three-star rank, Rumsfeld had at a stroke raised the prestige and leverage of the command, and created space underneath the commander for more subordinate flag officers. JSOC's command structure soon expanded to accommodate a two-star deputy commander in addition to a pair of one-star assistant commanders.

But while McChrystal was pinning on his third star, Zarqawi was finalizing his plan to ratchet up Iraq's sectarian tensions several more notches. On February 22, explosives planted by his fighters destroyed the golden dome of the Shi'ite Al-Askari mosque in Samarra, one of Shi'a Islam's most sacred places. Inevitably, the bombing initiated an intense cycle of Sunni versus Shi'a violence. Entire neighborhoods switched hands as populations coalesced along sectarian lines. Zarqawi had again stolen a march on the Coalition. By spring 2006, the task force's hunt for Zarqawi had become a higher JSOC priority than its search for Osama bin Laden and Ayman al-Zawahiri. "Who's the biggest threat right now?" said a special operations source at the time. "In military terms, bin Laden has been neutralized. He's not going anywhere. He can't really move. His communications are shallow. . . . Zarqawi is a bigger threat."[8]

As the bodies piled up in Baghdad trash dumps and floated down canals, McChrystal rallied his troops. On March 18, he told subordinates that the task force was "supported and well resourced," but the lack of apparent progress in Iraq had people back home worried. He derided those people as "quitters." Less than two weeks later, on April 1, he reminded his commanders that their mission was to "win here in Iraq."[9] The route to that victory included pressuring Al Qaeda in Iraq's lines of communication from Syria and Saudi Arabia. The task force would occasionally undertake raids into Syria and more frequently conduct clandestine intelligence operations in the country. There were no raids into Saudi Arabia, but JSOC had people there working on a secret intelligence operation in which Saudi militants captured in Iraq would be taken back to their homeland, and then persuaded "to somehow go back to Iraq as a double agent," said a task force officer.

＊

As insurgents figured out that the task force preferred to work at night, they began conducting more business during daytime. "You'd watch them on ISR during the day run around freely, make all their runs and drop their messages, take the dudes out, put them in the trunk, take them out to the desert, and execute them," said a Little Bird pilot. The task force responded by increasing use of a favorite tactic of both Delta operators and Little Bird pilots: air vehicle interdiction, or AVI.

By March 2006, Task Force Brown had divided its Little Bird crews into day and night teams, so as to always have a team ready for a no-notice AVI mission. There were several ways to conduct such missions, but a typical vehicle interdiction involved two AH-6s, two MH-6s with snipers on the pods, and a pair of MH-60K Black Hawks full of operators. The mission began with an ISR aircraft tracking an insurgent vehicle. The pagers the pilots carried buzzed. Checking the numeric code, the pilots saw a row of 1s: "launch now." The flight leads raced to the operations center for a quick briefing on the type of vehicle they'd be chasing, its location, and who was in it, and then went straight to the aircraft, where the operators were waiting. The helicopters launched and the race was on. The insurgents' only hope was to drive into a heavily populated neighborhood where the task force would be loath to shoot for fear of harming noncombatants. "If the vehicle went into a populated area, we'd just pull off and hold out in the desert and wait for him to start moving again," said a Little Bird pilot. "If he was out in the open desert, it was game on."

After chasing down the vehicle, either the Black Hawk door gunners or the AH-6 pilots fired red tracer warning shots in front of it, to give the people in the vehicle a chance to surrender. If the insurgents took that opportunity, the Black Hawks landed behind and beside the vehicle, and the operators quickly zip-tied the insurgents and searched the vehicle while the MH-6s landed the snipers to set up blocking positions on the road. But if the vehicle occupants attempted to fire at the helicopters, the snipers on the MH-6 pods, the Black Hawk door gunners, and the AH-6 gunships were ready to render any show of resistance futile and fatal. By spring of 2006, the Little Birds were launching as many as five AVI missions a day. "If you were an adrenaline junkie it was pretty exciting," said an AH-6 pilot. Or, as a Delta operator put it: "All the [A]VI shit was always awesome."[10]

Al Qaeda in Iraq leaders knew that their hunters were the United States' most elite forces. They were also easily identifiable—they wore beards and used aircraft and vehicles like Little Birds and Pandurs to which no other military units had access. The insurgents came up with nicknames for their nemeses: they called the operators "Mossad," after the vaunted Israeli intelligence service, and referred to the Little Birds as "Killer Bees" and "The Little Black Ones."[11]

＊

That spring, the task force continued to hunt insurgents moving along Anbar's ratlines while also focusing on the "belts" around Baghdad—the suburbs and rural areas surrounding the city. Coalition presence was lower in the belts than in the cities, and Al Qaeda in Iraq used them as rear support areas from which to terrorize the capital. This was particularly the case with the southern belt, which encompassed the towns of Yusufiyah, Latifiyah, Iskandariyah, and Mahmudiyah. Sometimes known as the "Triangle of Death," JSOC paid particular attention to this area in early 2006.[12]

Smack in the heart of this triangle was the group of buildings in Yusufiyah that Abu Zar had pinpointed and that a savvy, determined intelligence analyst had been monitoring for three months. On the afternoon of April 8, his patience paid off when the screen in front of him showed a line of cars pulling up to one of the buildings. That was enough to launch the daytime vehicle interdiction team on a raid. When the C Squadron operators landed at the objective shortly before 2 P.M., the men in the building opened fire. Five militants died in the fierce firefight that followed. No task force personnel were killed, but an MH-6 pilot was shot in the foot, and another got plexiglass in his face when his cockpit took a round. Both aircraft were damaged. One returned to base immediately. The operators gathered a large amount of intelligence material. (The house also held a van that had been turned into a mobile bomb.) Meanwhile, as the helicopters were en route to the objective, task force analysts had seen more vehicles arriving at a nearby building. A second raiding party launched, arriving at the target compound at 4:11 P.M. The dozen men they found there put up no meaningful resistance and were soon bundled aboard helicopters and flown back to Mission Support Site Fernandez.[13]

While interrogators went to work on the new detainees, who were soon flown to Balad, more raids followed. In the early hours of April 16, elements of B Squadron of the SAS, which had only begun hunting Al Qaeda in Iraq targets as an equal component of JSOC's task force in late March, assaulted Objective Larchwood IV, a farmhouse on the outskirts of Yusufiyah. The "blades," as SAS operators are known, were met with a burst of gunfire. After initially withdrawing, they quickly resumed the assault with renewed vigor, killing five militants, three of whom wore explosive suicide belts. The blades shot two before they could blow themselves up. The third detonated his bomb, killing only himself and injuring nobody else. The SAS detained five other men, one of whom was wounded, and suffered five wounded themselves. But there were other casualties in the house. A woman was killed. Three others and a child were medically evacuated to a U.S. military hospital in Baghdad. One of the detainees turned out to be AQI's administrator for the Abu Ghraib region, who was the individual the SAS had targeted in the raid.[14]

Among the materials the British seized in the farmhouse was a video shot by Al Qaeda in Iraq's propaganda wing that showed a black-pajama-clad Zarqawi firing an M249 squad automatic weapon, a light machine gun used by U.S. forces. Nine days later, AQI released an edited version of the video, prompting the U.S. military to publicize the raw footage, which showed Zarqawi's inexperience with the weapon and his willingness to ignore a muezzin's call to prayer, which can be heard in the background. The video also included a scene of Zarqawi seated beside an M4 assault rifle with an M203 grenade launcher attachment. The SAS blades had seized just such a weapon—presumably the same one—on Larchwood IV. It had apparently been lost by their maritime counterparts, the Royal Marines' Special Boat Service, in a bungled mission during the 2003 invasion, but its presence in the farmhouse told the task force it was getting closer.[15] Indeed, intelligence suggested that Zarqawi himself had been about a thousand meters away.[16]

✳

The task force continued grinding away at Zarqawi's network. Although almost every raid was conducted in the hope that the targets would surrender peacefully, the results were often extraordinarily violent. On April 25, the same day Zarqawi released his video, the task force raided Objective Johnson Village, another Yusufiyah safe house. As they approached, a man ran out brandishing "a shoulder-fired rocket," according to a Central Command press release. Operators shot him dead. A fierce gunfight ensued between other militants who emerged and the operators, who, supported by the helicopters, killed four more. Still taking fire from the building, the operators called in an air strike that leveled it. In the rubble, they found the bodies of seven men and a woman. Each man wore webbing holding two loaded magazines and two grenades. But the fight had not been without cost for the task force. The insurgents killed Sergeant First Class Richard J. Herrema, twenty-seven, a Delta operator, in the opening exchanges.[17]

JSOC's task force was essentially the U.S. military's offensive arm in Iraq, at least as far as operations against Zarqawi's network were concerned. While the task force's operations tempo was now approaching what McChrystal and Flynn had first envisioned, the JSOC commander wanted to gird his troops for a fight he did not expect to end soon.

"This has been, and will be, a long and serious war," he wrote in a memo to his entire force (one of about five he issued during his command), which was published on JSOC's intranet. "Although initial structures and TTPs [tactics, techniques, and procedures] have evolved tremendously from where they were even two years ago, we are still operating with manning and operating processes that need to be improved to be more effective and professional. We must increasingly be a force of totally focused counter-terrorists—that is what we do. This is as complex as developing a Long Term Strategic Debriefing Facility that feeds our in-depth understanding of the enemy, and as simple as losing the casual, 'I'm off at my war adventure,' manner of dress and grooming. In every case it will not be about what's easy, or even what we normally associate with conventional military standards. It will not even be about what is effective. It will be about what is the MOST effective way to operate—and we will do everything to increase the effectiveness even in small ways. If anyone finds this inconvenient or onerous, there's no place in the force for you. This is about winning—and making as few trips to Arlington Cemetery en route to that objective."[18]

On May 11, he reiterated the message to his subordinate commanders, reinforcing the "fanatical importance" with which he expected them to treat the fight. This was the essence of McChrystal. "He expected everybody to be as fanatical about the task at hand as he was," said one of McChrystal's commanders. "Life is hard right now," McChrystal continued. "Take this [war] and make it the cause."[19]

Life got even harder for Task Force Brown three days later, when Lieutenant Colonel Joe Coale, Delta's B Squadron commander, ordered a mid-afternoon assault on Objective Leadville, another building near Yusufiyah. Again the assaulters faced withering fire the moment the Black Hawks landed beside the objective. Pinned down by heavy machine gun and mortar fire, the operators fought back, with the crew chiefs on the circling Black Hawks pouring minigun fire onto the insurgent positions.

Back at Mission Support Site Fernandez, they woke Task Force Brown's night team early to fly down to relieve the helicopters in the fight, but as the fresh Little Bird crews neared Yusufiyah, they ran into an ambush and the AH-6 piloted by Major Matt Worrell and CW5 Jamie Weeks was shot down, killing both men on Mother's Day. Several other helicopters were so damaged that they had to land. The ground force managed to finally secure the objective and detain four men. They also treated and evacuated four injured civilian women, but the fighting was so fierce they didn't leave the area until darkness had fallen and they had called in a series of air strikes on surrounding buildings.

There was plenty of fallout from the Leadville fight. Joe Coale was replaced as B Squadron commander with Tom DiTomasso, meaning the latter was also the new Task Force Central boss. The battle also marked a turning point in how the task force dealt with heavily defended targets. From then on Delta and Task Force Brown placed less priority on capturing targets and were more willing to use overwhelming firepower early in the fight.[20] "I started telling our guys, hey, if you're going in on a target and someone's shooting at you, fucking kill him," said a task force commander. Another factor behind this mental shift was the frustration the operators experienced at repeatedly encountering and detaining the same people on objectives, because the Iraqi authorities kept releasing them.[21]

But McChrystal's strategy of eating away at the rings of defense surrounding Zarqawi was paying off. So was his determination to professionalize the task force's interrogation capabilities. By the third week of May, after being subjected to several weeks of skilled, manipulative interrogation, the administrator that the SAS had captured on April 16 and an Al Qaeda in Iraq operative detained at the second April 8 target in Yusufiyah had detailed the group's command structure around Baghdad and identified Abd al-Rahman as Zarqawi's spiritual adviser. For three weeks, the task force monitored Rahman in the hope that he'd lead them to Zarqawi.

He did.

On June 7 a drone tracked Rahman as he was driven north in a silver sedan out of Baghdad. At Mission Support Site Fernandez, DiTomasso and his lead analyst watched as Rahman deftly switched vehicles in heavy traffic, jumping into a small blue truck in a skillful but futile attempt to throw off any surveillance. In Balad, Mark Erwin—by now a full colonel, deputy Delta commander, and Iraq task force commander—directed ISR aircraft from all over Iraq to converge on the area north of Baghdad. It was Erwin's A Squadron that had missed getting Zarqawi because of a drone camera glitch in February 2005. He was determined not to miss out again. The aircraft followed the truck to Baqubah, where Rahman transferred to another truck and continued on to a two-story house in Hibhib, a village only a dozen miles from McChrystal's Balad headquarters. Analysts, operators, and staffers in Fernandez and Balad watched in rapt attention as a stout man in black walked out and took a late afternoon stroll down the driveway before returning to the house. It had to be Zarqawi. An assault team prepared to launch from Fernandez, but Erwin wasn't comfortable with a heliborne raid. Worried that the only good landing zone was so far from the house that Zarqawi might escape into a large grove of date palms, Erwin discussed the situation with McChrystal, then decided to bomb the target and have the Delta team land immediately thereafter.

A series of mishaps nearly derailed the plan. A Task Force Brown helicopter engine failed to start at Fernandez. Then, one of two F-16s that the task force planned to use to bomb the house had to break off for an air-to-air refueling; the other swooped toward the house but didn't release a bomb, because Task Force Central hadn't worded the bombing command properly. Finally, at 6:12 P.M., the second F-16 dropped a laser-guided 500-pound bomb on the house and followed it less than two minutes later with another bomb. The house disintegrated. A cheer erupted in the Balad operations center. Eighteen minutes later, Delta operators arrived on Little Birds to find Iraqi police loading Zarqawi on a gurney. Holding the police at gunpoint, the operators realized Zarqawi was still alive, but suffering from severe internal blast injuries. He died in front of them.[22]

The next several days were a blur of energy for McChrystal and the Iraq task force. The bombing, which also killed Rahman, another man, two women, and a girl, was the trigger for the task force to launch synchronized raids that night on the three vehicles in which Rahman had ridden en route to the house and the fourteen buildings he'd visited while under surveillance. The aim of the raids was to crush what one JSOC staffer called Zarqawi's "internal network" in one night.[23] The task force also plundered the rubble in Hibhib for intelligence, which added to the spike in missions. A particularly satisfying find was a handwritten document saying that the American strategy in the Triangle of Death was succeeding and senior Al Qaeda leaders could no longer count on it as a refuge.[24]

Zarqawi's death caused an inevitable sense of satisfaction at all levels of command, from Task Force Central to the very top. President Bush rang McChrystal on the night Zarqawi died to congratulate him.[25] But any hopes that his death would signal an immediate downturn in the violence went unfulfilled. Al Qaeda in Iraq quickly promoted Abu Ayyub al-Masri, the Egyptian who had been Zarqawi's deputy, to replace his late boss, and the monthly civilian death tolls for the second half of 2006 all rose above the highest monthly tally (June) for the first six months of 2006, a trend that continued well into 2007.[26] McChrystal's assessment was blunt: "We had killed Zarqawi too late."[27]

As the violence spiraled ever higher, the task force strove to keep pace. By 2006, the "Unblinking Eye" concept that began with Delta's A Squadron and a single Predator in early 2004 had reached full fruition. At Flynn's direction, the task force aimed to have up to three ISR aircraft watching a target simultaneously. Indeed, it often had enough of such aircraft over Baghdad and the major cities in Anbar that when a car bomb went off, analysts could pull the video feeds from aircraft overhead and watch them in reverse, to trace the car's route back to its start point.[28] The dynamo that McChrystal and Flynn had built was now operating almost on automatic. In August 2004, the task force had conducted eighteen missions. In August 2006 it conducted more than 300.[29] Strike forces now aimed to conduct the "analyze" and "disseminate" parts of the F3EAD process within an hour of coming off target. "McChrystal would say, 'We have to operate at the speed of war,'" said a Ranger officer. "'Faster, faster, faster.'"

The task force was growing. It routinely included a "white" Special

Forces company that specialized in direct action missions. Each Special Forces group had such a company, called a combatant commander's in-extremis force, or CIF (pronounced "siff"), because it was designed to give a regional combatant commander an on-call counterterrorist force in case the JSOC task force was unavailable. The CIFs, which had a training relationship with Delta, all rotated through Iraq in support of McChrystal's task force. In 2006, McChrystal also gained an 82nd Airborne Division paratroop battalion, known as Task Force Falcon. With its reinforcements thrown into the fray, his task force continued its furious pace through the fall.[30] But one of its most notable fights was a defensive one. On November 27, a daytime air-vehicle interdiction mission targeting an Al Qaeda in Iraq foreign fighter facilitator went awry when an RPG downed an AH-6 between Taji and Lake Tharthar about fifty kilometers northwest of Baghdad. (The assault force was en route to a larger site in the desert to wait for the target's vehicle when this happened.) Outnumbered and outgunned by insurgents who arrived in truck after truck, the assault force found itself with no shelter in the flat desert. The force's remaining AH-6, piloted by CW5 Dave Cooper, did much to hold them off, repeatedly strafing the insurgents. Cooper was credited with turning the tide of the battle, and later received a Distinguished Service Cross for his efforts. The ground force remained at the site until darkness, but tragedy struck when an F-16 supporting the embattled force flew too low and crashed, killing its pilot.[31]

Other raids that month focused on Ansar al-Sunnah, a Kurdish-led Islamist group that was allied with, but not formally part of, Al Qaeda in Iraq. The Coalition's efforts to reconcile some Sunni insurgent groups, thus isolating Al Qaeda in Iraq, included an effort to divide Ansar al-Sunnah from AQI.[32] But although JSOC (and much of the rest of the U.S. national security community) had focused almost exclusively on Iraq's Sunni insurgency, in particular on Al Qaeda in Iraq, since 2004, a different threat was emerging. Arguably a greater threat to U.S. forces and interests in the region than Iraq's Sunni insurgency, it was an enemy that would hark back to JSOC's birth, but for which its Iraq task force was singularly unprepared: Iran.

21

A New Campaign Against an Old Enemy

It was July 25, 2004. Violence was escalating in Iraq, the Taliban were reasserting themselves in Afghanistan, and JSOC was already deploying operators to the Horn of Africa and Yemen. But for the first day of the three-day JSOC commanders' conference that Stan McChrystal was holding at Fort Bragg, the country under discussion was Iran, and the conversation was right out of the late 1990s: how to defeat hard and deeply buried targets, in this case the underground shelters that U.S. intelligence believed housed Iran's nascent nuclear program. Intelligence also indicated that no air-delivered weapon could penetrate deep enough to reach those bunkers, thought to be a hundred feet or more beneath the surface. The National Command Authority had turned to JSOC for solutions.

By now, Team 6 was JSOC's lead unit for counter-proliferation. But any raid on Iranian facilities would also involve Delta, in part because JSOC was considering simultaneous raids on two separate sites, and also because the assault force would need Delta's heavy breachers to gain access to the bunkers. However, even a cursory examination of the challenges associated with such an operation gave the commanders pause. Unlike a lot of counter-proliferation operations for which they planned, this was not a mission to "render safe" a device held by a few terrorists, but a large-scale operation that would require JSOC to secure two major facilities. It would take a lot of troops, probably more than the special mission units and the Rangers could muster.

The commanders and their planners also considered from where such a mission might launch: Iraq, Kuwait, Qatar, or a carrier in the Persian Gulf. All had disadvantages. The upshot was that when it came to a direct action mission against Iran's nuclear sites, "no one really wanted to do it," said a source familiar with the discussion. As the unit with primary responsibility for counter-proliferation missions, Team 6 had done its homework. This wasn't the first time the unit had been directed to develop options for a raid into Iran. Shortly before the Iraq War Team 6's Red Team conducted several rehearsals for a possible mission to seize a suspected weapons of mass destruction facility on the outskirts of Tehran and then hold it for up to twenty-four hours, while being resupplied by "speedball" low-altitude parachute drops. The mission's purpose would be to locate indisputable proof that Iran was developing nuclear weapons. "We trained for weeks for it," said a Team 6 source. But the proposed mission, which would have been an extraordinarily perilous undertaking, was not popular with the Team 6 operators. "I remember us all thinking, 'This is stupid. Why are we going to go do this?'" the source said. "And then it all just kind of fizzled away."

This time, Team 6 instead advocated a clandestine approach aimed at intercepting or disrupting material the Iranians needed for their nuclear program before it reached Iran from North Korea or elsewhere—a strategy based on the "pathway defeat" concept the SEALs had been refining since the late 1990s. The campaign to prevent Iran from producing nuclear weapons would continue in the shadows.[1]

✳

As the July 2004 conference indicated, even as JSOC's number one target remained Al Qaeda and its associated groups, in the background loomed Iran, the would-be regional superpower distinctly uncomfortable with U.S. forces occupying the countries on its eastern and western borders. In the immediate post–September 11 period, JSOC was running at least two undercover agents into Iran, but that was far from enough to gain any sort of holistic understanding of the massive target set that country represented.

This became clear when it emerged that about ten leading Al Qaeda figures, including bin Laden's son Saad, had fled Afghanistan for Iran in fall 2001, as U.S.-backed Northern Alliance forces swept the Taliban from power. The Iranian government—no friend of the Taliban or Al Qaeda—placed them under house arrest in the city of Chalus, about 108 miles north of Tehran on the southern shore of the Caspian Sea. The Pentagon tasked JSOC to plan a mission to seize the Al Qaeda personnel. Planners considered infiltrating Team 6 operators via submersible or helicopter. "The SEALs really definitely wanted to do it . . . because it would have proven a few of their new technologies," said a Joint Staff source. But, as had been the case so often before, all attempts to plan a raid foundered on a lack of intelligence. JSOC simply did not know the Al Qaeda personnel's exact locations. The command conducted several rehearsals in Texas before Chairman of the Joint Chiefs General Richard Myers canceled the mission on the grounds that the risks—both tactical and political-military—exceeded the potential gains.[2]

The U.S. invasion and subsequent occupation of Iraq gave JSOC more opportunities to penetrate Iran. After the invasion, Delta and Orange did quiet work along the Iranian border, particularly in Kurdistan, where Delta quickly made connections with the Asayish—the Kurdish intelligence organization that had one or more spies reporting on the Iranian nuclear program. Delta enlisted the help of other Iraqis as well in its twin campaigns against AQI and Iran's covert operatives, but "the guys with the greatest access and placement were the Kurds," said a task force officer. "They delivered some fucking huge targets to us." Delta wasn't the only unit working with the Asayish. "There's a long history between Orange and the Kurds going back to at least the early 1990s," said a special mission unit officer. JSOC personnel also worked with the Mujahideen-e-Khalq (MEK), a militant Iranian exile group that had based itself in Iraq after falling afoul of the ayatollahs' regime in Tehran. The State Department had placed the MEK on its list of designated terrorist organizations, but that didn't stop JSOC from taking an attitude of "the enemy of my enemy is my friend" toward the group. "They were a group of folks that could transit the border, and they were willing to help us out on what we wanted to do with Iran," said a special operations officer.

But JSOC was keen to get more of its own people into Iran.

In 2003, tantalizing information reached the command that caused Dailey and then McChrystal to direct the advance force operations cell to examine ways to infiltrate Iran. JSOC heard that Iran had moved Saad bin Laden and the other Al Qaeda exiles from Afghanistan to a comfortable "country club"-like facility in downtown Tehran, according to a JSOC staff officer. The two JSOC commanders wanted the AFO cell to determine the feasibility of entering Iran, going to the prison in Tehran, and confirming that Saad was being held there. Inside JSOC, it was considered a very high-risk mission. But the AFO personnel were surprised to discover that someone could drive to the Iranian border, show an American passport, get a ten-day tourist visa, and enter the country immediately, whereas if the same person applied for a visa through an Iranian embassy or consulate, "then they're going to pull your Social Security number, then they're going to do the background diligence on you," said a source familiar with the operation. Nonetheless, the AFO cell's assessment was that it would take at least a year to be able to work up a "legend" (a spy's claimed biography—his cover story) and a cover that would allow a special mission unit operator to enter Iran, get to the prison, gather information, and then leave without attracting suspicion.

McChrystal wasn't happy. "I need it sooner than that," he said that fall. When the AFO cell came back to him a month later with the same assessment, this time backed up by the new Orange commander, Colonel Konrad "KT" Trautman, McChrystal told Trautman he wanted Orange to take a closer look at how the mission might be conducted sooner.

But while Orange planned, the growing concern over Iran's suspected nuclear program changed the mission from reconnoitering the prison to determining whether fissile material was being produced at certain sites. By spring 2004, Orange had selected a two-person male-female team for a proof-of-concept mission and figured out an effective cover for them. McChrystal approved the plan and sent it up the chain of command. But because it involved undercover operatives on a clandestine mission into a country with which the United States was not at war, Orange also needed the CIA's approval, which proved harder to obtain. "We had a really difficult time getting it approved by the Agency," said an officer. "They had their own equities to protect." After the CIA agreed, President Bush gave his okay. The mission finally launched in fall 2004, a delay that appeared to prove the AFO cell correct in its assessment of how long it would take to prepare for such an operation. The operatives' cover was strong enough to get visas through an Iranian consulate, so they dispensed with the idea of driving up to the border and instead flew commercial into a major Iranian city and checked into a hotel. They spent several days taking taxis around and outside the city, and determined that it would not be difficult to get close enough to the suspected nuclear sites to take a soil sample. But on this occasion, they chose not to. "That wasn't the mission," said the source familiar with the operation. "[The mission] at the time was just to get in and get out." Upon their return to the United States, the operatives briefed President Bush on their mission, who was duly impressed.[3]

The United States' occupation of Afghanistan gave U.S. forces access to that country's border with Iran from late 2001 onward. But for several years, risk aversion restricted almost any effort to take advantage of that for human intelligence purposes. It wasn't until 2007 that JSOC started a program to penetrate Iran using trained Afghan surrogates. "It was kind of one of those things . . . that the rest of the world assumes that we're [already] doing," said a special operations officer. Nonetheless, the Defense Department considered the program so hush-hush that the officer recalled being ushered into "the room within the room within the room" in the Pentagon to receive a briefing on the topic. The officer's reaction to the briefing was, "You mean we're not doing this already?"

✳

Striding out of the Baghdad International Airport arrivals terminal, dressed in a suit and fresh off the flight from Tehran, the fifty-something Iranian was looking for a taxi on a warm April night in 2009. As he scanned the street, a small plane high above the airport filmed him, transmitting video in real time to a strike force of Rangers and SEALs, who had parked four Stryker wheeled armored vehicles and two nondescript Toyota HiLux trucks in a covered area used by taxis waiting to pick up fares at the airport. The Iranian dialed a number on his cell phone. Using data from that call, the Rangers confirmed his identity within moments. Loading into the HiLuxes, about half a dozen Rangers moved a short distance forward before dismounting quickly and encircling the Iranian. Surrounded by heavily armed soldiers from one of the world's premier light infantry regiments, the Iranian did not appear in the least flustered. He just laughed, before coming up with perhaps the worst insult he could think of. "Are you guys Jews?" he asked (probably equating "Jews" with "Israelis"). "What?" the Ranger platoon leader asked. The Iranian said he asked "because surely the Americans aren't stupid enough to detain me."

His self-confidence was no false bravado. The situation typified a Gordian knot of a problem the United States faced in Iraq. The Rangers' target was a senior figure in Iran's powerful covert operations organization: the Islamic Revolutionary Guard Corps' Quds Force. Carrying a diplomatic passport, he had come to Iraq as part of Iran's campaign to destabilize its neighbor by distributing training, bombs, and money among not only Shi'ite militias—the natural allies of the Shi'ite theocracy that governed Iran—but even Sunni insurgent groups. However, the Quds Force's vast web of alliances throughout Iraq's Shi'ite political structure meant any American moves against its operatives were matters of extraordinary sensitivity. The Quds Force operative had laughed at his would-be captors, said a U.S. officer, "because he knew he was protected."[4]

Established during the Iran-Iraq War of the 1980s, the Quds Force combined the roles of intelligence collection and covert action for Iran, taking the lead in the Islamic Republic's special operations and proxy wars in the Middle East and beyond. It was the power behind Lebanon's Hezbollah organization and now sought to weaken Iraq and kill U.S. troops in the country. The Quds Force was divided into departments or corps, with each corps having a geographic area of responsibility. Department 1000, or the Ramazan Corps, was in charge of operations in Iraq. It was the Quds Force commander, Qassem Suleimani, rather than the foreign minister, who set Iran's Iraq policy.

Suleimani wielded power in Iraq via a complex and shifting web of proxy forces. These included: the Badr Organization, which began as the Iranian-funded and -led armed wing of the Supreme Council of the Islamic Revolution in Iraq, or SCIRI; firebrand cleric Moqtada al-Sadr's militia, Jaish al-Mahdi (JAM, or the Mahdi Army), and in particular, its even more extremist and violent offshoots referred to by the Coalition as "special groups"; Asaib Ahl al-Haq (the League of the Righteous); the al-Gharawai Network in southeastern Iraq's Maysan province; and Khatab Hezbollah. Suleimani found the Badr Organization (previously called the Badr Brigades or the Badr Corps) particularly useful. Badr and its parent organization, SCIRI, had a historic relationship with the Quds Force dating back to their years spent exiled in Iran during Saddam Hussein's rule. They also had close ties to many Iraqi members of parliament. The Quds Force used the Badr Organization for intelligence collection as well as militia activities, with its proxies in the organization passing information directly to Quds Force handlers.

Iran's strategic goal of destabilizing Iraq created some strange bedfellows, with the Quds Force—the covert arm of Iran's Shi'ite theocracy—even cozying up to Sunni insurgent networks. "It was 100 percent 'Are you willing to kill Americans and are you willing to coordinate attacks?'" said an officer who studied the Quds Force's approach closely. "'If the answer is "yes," here's arms, here's money.'" The officer compared this approach to that employed by the CIA in the 1980s, when the Agency armed and funded the Afghan mujahideen in their war against Soviet occupiers and their Afghan communist allies. The Quds Force also conducted information operations in Iraq, working via the Internet and the news media, with the goals of: influencing any status of forces agreement between the U.S. and Iraqi governments governing the future role of U.S. forces in Iraq; effecting a reconciliation between warring Shi'ite factions; and focusing those Shi'ite groups on attacking only Coalition forces.[5]

In early 2005, the Quds Force introduced a new weapon onto the Iraqi battlefield: the explosively formed projectile (EFP), a sort of roadside bomb that sent a jet of molten copper slicing through Coalition armored vehicles. EFP use increased 150 percent in 2006, inflicting 30 percent of U.S. casualties from October through December.[6] By early 2007 some U.S. intelligence estimates held that as many as 150 Iranian operatives were in Iraq.[7] For several years large sections of the U.S. government had seemed in denial[8] about the extent of the Quds Force's activities, but after years of reluctance to confront the Iranians, the U.S. chain of command could no longer ignore the toll in blood extracted by the Quds Force. In summer 2006 Rumsfeld directed McChrystal to use special operations forces to target Shi'ite death squads.[9] George Casey, the MNF-I commander, who had no authority to give orders to JSOC forces, followed up with his own request for McChrystal to go after the Shi'ite groups, especially those supported by Iran.[10] "It came down from the top once we . . . started recovering EFPs in Sadr City that were stamped from Iranian manufacturing facilities," said a Ranger officer, referring to the teeming Shi'ite neighborhood in east Baghdad.

JSOC began targeting Iranian proxies in Iraq in October 2006.[11] The new missions were collectively described within the command as "countering malign Iranian influence." Between November 2006 and January 2007, McChrystal's task force conducted two such missions.[12] In the first, on December 21, operators descended on Objective Clarke, the Baghdad compound of SCIRI leader Abdul Aziz Hakim. Inside the compound they found and detained Iranian Brigadier General Mohsen Chirazi, who directed all Quds Force operations in Iraq, and the colonel who served as the Quds Force's chief of operations. After strong protests from Iranian and Iraqi political leaders, JSOC released the pair nine days later.[13]

In the second mission, the task force launched a combined air and ground assault on Objective Twins, an Iranian diplomatic compound in the northern Iraqi city of Irbil, in the early hours of January 11. The Delta operators were hoping to snare Mohammed Jafari, the deputy head of Iran's Security Council who was playing a key role in the Iraq campaign, and General Minjahar Frouzanda, the Revolutionary Guard's intelligence chief. Neither target was present in the walled compound, however. Instead, the operators detained five lower-ranking Revolutionary Guard personnel who became known as "the Irbil five," and who provided valuable intelligence under interrogation.[14]

The Quds Force struck back January 20, with a carefully planned attack on the Karbala Provisional Joint Coordination Center, a compound manned by U.S. and Iraqi troops in central Iraq. The League of the Righteous, one of the Iranians' most dangerous proxy forces, carried out the attack, driving eight black SUVs and wearing U.S. uniforms to gain access to the compound. They killed one U.S. soldier on the spot and kidnapped four, only to execute them shortly thereafter while making their escape.[15]

By the time General David Petraeus replaced George Casey as commander of Multi-National Force-Iraq on February 10, 2007, what had been a one-sided campaign on the part of the Quds Force and its Iraqi agents had become a war. "It was clear [from] theater-level and above intelligence that these guys were active proxies for Iran—they were doing Iran's bidding in Iraq," said an Army civilian who spent time in Iraq. "When Dave Petraeus was commander in Iraq, he was determined to stop that." As usual, when the problem seemed beyond others' ability to solve, the force to which the Pentagon turned was JSOC.

But after Rumsfeld (in one of his last decisions before resigning effective December 18, 2006) ordered him to go after the Iranians, McChrystal struggled to figure out how to accommodate what was essentially a doubling of his mission. His Iraq task force, at the time called Task Force 16, was fine-tuned to go after Sunni insurgent networks, with a particular focus on Al Qaeda in Iraq. All its intelligence analysts, interrogators, and even operators had become experts on that target set, which was keeping them fully occupied. By early 2007, JSOC estimated its forces had killed about 2,000 Sunni insurgents. But that hard-earned expertise was of limited utility against the Iranians and their proxies, at least according to some in JSOC. A Task Force 16 interrogator "wouldn't know the first question to ask one of these guys," said a senior special mission unit officer. John Christian, the Task Force 16 commander at the time, asked not to be given the additional mission of targeting the Quds Force and its allies, for fear TF 16 would lose its laserlike focus on Al Qaeda in Iraq. McChrystal shared his concern. The general did not want to add the Shi'ite groups to Task Force 16's target set, nor to split off some of that task force to focus solely on those militias.[16] "We were getting bled out in Baghdad by the EFPs that were being brought over by Iran . . . but McChrystal wasn't willing to pull assault forces from what he perceived to be the real fight strategically," said a Ranger officer. "So he asked for additional assets."

Those "assets" came largely from the "white" or "theater" special operations task force working in Iraq, which was known as Combined Joint Special Operations Task Force (CJSOTF, pronounced "see-juh-so-tiff")-Arabian Peninsula and included Special Forces A-teams and SEAL units. Colonel Kevin McDonnell, commander of 5th Special Forces Group, led the task force, which also included SEAL Team 4, led by Commander John Burnham. McDonnell reported to Major General Frank Kearney, the former JSOC operations director who now commanded all non-JSOC special operations forces in Central Command's area of responsibility.

Realizing that he needed far more resources to handle both target sets, McChrystal's solution was to request personnel assigned to the CJSOTF, which had already been targeting Sadr's Mahdi Army. But when McChrystal made his move, "the threat was it would subsume the entire CJSOTF," said a retired special forces officer. Concerned that the JSOC boss wanted to bring the entire CJSOTF under his command, Kearney and McDonnell resisted McChrystal's efforts to strip away theater special operations units from the task force for his own purposes. "Kevin [McDonnell] saw that [JSOC's] appetite was such that once it got its teeth into you, it could quickly eat you up," the retired officer said. In a tense arrangement, the mission to counter the Iranians was handed to McDonnell from January to March 2007, reporting to McChrystal. But intense friction between the two officers meant that didn't work, so in April command of the counter-Iranian task force was moved to Balad and given to a former Delta squadron commander on the JSOC staff.[17] McDonnell gave up some headquarters personnel, "a SEAL platoon or two," and "some technical things" to the new task force, the retired officer said.

The new task force was named Task Force 17. Its mission statement was simple: "TF 17 defeats IRGC-QF [Islamic Revolutionary Guard Corps-Quds Force], their proxies and surrogate networks in Iraq IOT [in order to] disrupt malign Iranian influence." In layman's terms, Task Force 17's mandate was to go after "anything that Iran is doing to aid in the destabilization of Iraq," said a Task Force 17 officer. The task force was to work along three "lines of operation": disrupting the Quds Force's networks in Iraq "through kinetic targeting" (i.e., via kill-or-capture missions); using captured intelligence materials to enable nonkinetic pressure to be brought to bear on key Shi'ite leaders; and isolating the Quds Force from its Iraqi proxies. Task Force 17's assault forces at first were a couple of Burnham's SEAL platoons and a Special Forces CIF company. Its campaign against the Quds Force was called Operation Canine.[18]

In addition to the challenges inherent in trying to find, fix, and finish enemies who did not want to be found, fixed, and finished, Task Force 17 faced political obstacles that TF 16 did not. While Iraq's Shi'ite political leadership was only too happy to have McChrystal's ruthless machine grind away at the Sunni insurgency, there was enormous sensitivity over the targeting of Shi'ite groups, even those who were clearly murdering other Iraqis. The political connections of some of the most savage Shi'ite militia leaders meant there was "an unofficial list of Shiites whom we could not knowingly target," McChrystal wrote. This dynamic would act as a brake on Task Force 17 throughout its existence. But nonetheless the new task force quickly made an impact.

For months Task Force 17 had been hunting Laith and Qais Khazali, brothers who ran the League of the Righteous. Qais, at thirty-three the older of the two, had worked for Moqtada Sadr's father, Grand Ayatollah Mohammed Sadeq al-Sadr, before the latter's 1999 assassination by Saddam Hussein's regime. After throwing his support behind Moqtada following the U.S. invasion, Qais had split off in June 2006 to found the League of the Righteous. His political connections meant Task Force 17 was not supposed to launch a raid to grab him. The same did not apply to his brother, however, and in mid-March an intelligence tip fixed Laith Khazali in the southern Iraqi city of Basra. Task Force 17 named the location Objective Setanta and on March 20, 2007, a combination of the SAS's G Squadron and SEALs led by Burnham flew down to Basra and, supported by conventional British troops, detained Laith and seven other men without a fight. One of those seven, they almost immediately realized, was Qais. When Burnham called McChrystal with the news, the latter decided Qais was too big a fish to release.

The task force's analysts immediately went to work on the large amount of captured material, while interrogators puzzled over one of the detainees—a middle-aged Arab man who acted deaf and mute. The analysts quickly found a document that named Azhar al-Dulaimi as the leader of the Karbala attack, tied the brothers to the attack, and proved that the Quds Force had provided significant support for it. The document helped persuade Iraqi prime minister Nouri al-Maliki to keep the brothers behind bars. Within two months, the task force had killed Dulaimi in northern Baghdad and the supposedly deaf and mute man had begun to talk, revealing himself to be Ali Mussa Daqduq, a senior Lebanese Hezbollah operative brought in by the Quds Force to help the League of the Righteous.[19]

Daqduq's role was typical of the Quds Force's efforts to use cutouts to do its dirty work in Iraq. In order to preserve a fig leaf of plausible deniability for the Iranian regime, the Quds Force used a "train the trainer" concept, bringing members of its Iraqi proxy forces to Iran and Lebanon to receive training, often from Hezbollah instructors, before sending them back to Iraq to train others.[20] "We were confused there about the actual delineation between the Quds Force and the splinter networks, and that's intentional," a Task Force 17 officer said.

The task force followed that success up with an April 20 raid that netted Abu Yaser al-Sheibani, second in command of the Sheibani Network run by his elder brother Abu Mustafa al-Sheibani, who was a former member of the Badr Brigades. The network had been smuggling EFPs to militias like the League of the Righteous from Iran for the Quds Force for more than two years. But Task Force 17 had to wait five months for its next high-profile capture, when it detained Mahmud Farhadi, a Quds Force lieutenant colonel who commanded one of the three camps along the Iran-Iraq border from which the Ramazan Corps ran its Iraq campaign. The task force captured Farhadi, who was posing as an Iranian trade representative, in a September 20 raid on a hotel in the northern Iraqi province of Suleymaniyah. (The Iranian government protested Farhadi's seizure vehemently, closing the northern border for a period.)[21]

The captures—particularly those of the Iranian operatives—caused the Quds Force to reassess how it conducted its Iraq campaign. Rather than scale down or end its destabilization efforts, Suleimani increasingly sought to put an Iraqi face on the campaign. As a result, the Sheibani Network and other Iranian proxies grew in size.

In October 2007, Ranger Regiment commander Colonel Richard Clarke took command of Task Force 17. This was significant because it was the first time the Rangers had been given command of a JSOC task force at the O-6 level (the pay grade that equates to captain in the Navy and colonel in the other services). Underneath Clarke, a SEAL commander (an O-5) ran the operations, with two Ranger platoons (about ninety soldiers) and two SEAL platoons (about thirty-two personnel) under him (plus a Ranger company headquarters and a SEAL troop headquarters), all based at the massive Victory Base complex beside Baghdad airport. Task Force 17 also included a SEAL reconnaissance team in Baghdad, and a Ranger reconnaissance team in Al Kut, about 160 kilometers southeast of the capital. McChrystal blended the assault forces, so that each company-level assault force included a SEAL platoon and a Ranger platoon working for either the SEAL troop or the Ranger company commander. This was double the size of Task Force 16 assault forces, in which a single Ranger platoon would be a strike force. Some of those forced to work under this paradigm resented it on the grounds that it unnecessarily limited the number of assault forces.[22] There was no need to have seventy-five personnel on a single raid, according to a Ranger officer. "It was four assault forces that were forced into two," he said.

One reason Task Force 17's forces were organized this way was that the SEALs lacked vehicle crews, limiting their mobility. In other locations, they'd use helicopters to air-assault to an offset location a short distance from the target. But in Baghdad's dense—often hostile—environs, that wasn't always possible. "You can't offset in Sadr City," the Ranger officer said. The imperfect solution, he said, was "to get Rangers to drive them."

Almost immediately, the Rangers were embroiled in a controversy stemming from an October 20 mission that exposed the thin political ice on which Task Force 17 was skating. That night Rangers from B Company, 2nd Ranger Battalion, launched a ground raid into Sadr City to get a Shi'ite special groups leader. The Rangers missed their target, and then found themselves virtually surrounded by Shi'ite militants in the dense urban jungle. With the support of helicopter gunships, the task force fought its way out block by block, killing an estimated forty-nine militiamen without suffering a single fatality. "It was like the Mogadishu Mile [in] and then the Mogadishu Mile out," a Ranger officer said. "There was a substantial amount of collateral damage."

The political backlash from conducting a large, violent operation in the heart of Shi'ite Baghdad was immediate. U.S. forces could virtually level entire neighborhoods in a Sunni city like Fallujah without upsetting Iraq's

Shi'ite leaders, but kinetic action, even on a much smaller scale, in Sadr City crossed a line. Petraeus was worried. Maliki, a Shi'ite whose government had a distinctly anti-Sunni bent, was enraged. His government accused U.S. forces of killing fifteen civilians in the raid. From January 2008 on, Task Force 17 was no longer authorized to enter Sadr City. To the deep frustration of its personnel, it had to wait for targets to leave the rectangular Shi'ite neighborhood before striking.[23] "The concept that we would allow a safe haven blew my mind," said the Ranger officer.

To some observers, the Sadr City operation exemplified Task Force 17's overreliance on firepower at the expense of precision. "Whenever they did anything, they tended to shoot the shit out of everything," the retired Special Forces officer said. "Either they shot everything up, killed the wrong person, captured the wrong person who was related to someone, or didn't coordinate with the locals." But despite the Rangers' aggressive posture, which was on full display in Task Force 16 and in particular in Task Force North when it was under Ranger battalion command, Task Force 17 never came close to matching Task Force 16's operational tempo.

Politics was partly responsible. "My teams needed immense freedom to operate in order to achieve the desired operational tempo," McChrystal wrote. But Petraeus had to balance his desire to counter the Iranians with Maliki's need to keep the Shi'ite militias from turning on his government. As a result there were standing restrictions on Task Force 17 operations in the provinces that had been turned over to Iraqi control (there were nine by the end of 2007), as well as the province of Qadisiyah and the cities Hindiyah, Najaf, and Karbala, in addition to Sadr City—"all their safe havens," as the Ranger officer put it. Before striking a target Task Force 17 needed to get it approved on the day of the raid all the way up the chain of command to Petraeus.[24]

"TF 17 was very political," said a Ranger officer who served in it. "There were a lot of times when we detained a senior-level Quds operative who had a diplomatic passport. . . . We'd get called and Maliki would shut down JSOC for a day, and say 'Until he's in my compound, all JSOC operations are closed.' Not just [TF] 17. All. And so obviously, McChrystal would get pissed and then I would have to drive some dickhead to the Green Zone and he'd get released the next day." However, he said, complaints that political concerns kept the task force from hitting Shi'ite targets were misplaced. "Don't let anyone fool you that the weak optempo was politically driven," he said. "It was incompetence." In particular, he blamed the "white" (i.e., non–Team 6) SEAL officers' inexperience with real-time signals intelligence. "The targeting was a joke."

This inexperience only exacerbated another problem: the fact that when it came to signals intelligence, surveillance, and reconnaissance assets, Task Forces 16 and 17 were "in competition over the same resources," as McChrystal put it.[25] JSOC never gave Task Force 17 the priority it allotted to the task force going after Al Qaeda in Iraq. "At 17 you're at the bottom of the totem pole," said the Ranger officer.

By 2008, Task Forces North and West, in Mosul and Al Asad respectively, were Task Force 16's priority, but Task Force Central, in Baghdad, still conducted more missions than Task Force 17, much to the amusement of TF Central's Rangers, who missed no opportunity to mock their TF 17 colleagues. Clarke, the Task Force 17 commander, followed the JSOC model of allowing his subordinate commanders to run day-to-day operations. But he repeatedly expressed his frustration with his assault forces' inability "to get out the door." Despite these hurdles, Task Force 17 prosecuted about sixty raids in a ninety-day cycle in early 2008, probably the high point of its short history.

In spring 2009, interrogations of Quds Force and Shi'ite militia detainees revealed that the senior Quds Force operatives were not sneaking across the border into Iraq like their AQI counterparts in Syria, but instead were arriving on commercial flights from Tehran. It was a eureka moment for Task Force 17. U.S. intelligence persuaded the airlines to supply the passenger manifests for each flight from Tehran, which were quickly passed to the Task Force 17 operations center. TF 17 assumed Quds Force operatives would be flying undercover, but within three days the real name of one of its highest priority Quds Force targets showed up on the manifest. It was that man that the Rangers detained as he got into his taxi, flex-cuffing him, and putting him in the back of a Stryker for the short drive to Victory Base, adjacent to the airport.

What followed typified the challenges that Task Force 17 faced. For a few hours, the task force interrogated the operative, as they had other Quds Force personnel. "We don't torture them," said a TF 17 officer. "We don't beat them. We're going to take all their personal effects, strip them down, and then interrogate them and put them in jail." Quds Force detainees' pocket litter and electronic devices such as laptops sometimes held useful intelligence, the officer said. The Iranian that Task Force 17 detained that night in April 2009 did not have a laptop, but was carrying several phones and important documents. As usual, however, the detainee's status as a Quds Force operative meant his detention was brief.[26] Word of his capture was quickly reported up the chain of command and from there to Iraqi prime minister Nouri al-Maliki. "He was handed over to the Iraqis and then he was released the next day," the Task Force 17 officer said. Maliki then stood Task Force 17 down until it agreed to clear its target list through him daily.

✳

As JSOC sought to fill the gaps in its knowledge of the Quds Force's reach into Iraq and the Levant, it was able to draw heavily on intelligence from another country that paid close attention to the militant Shi'ite threat in the Middle East: Israel. JSOC had access to Israeli intelligence because in the middle of the decade, Delta established a cell in Tel Aviv specifically to exchange intelligence with Israel. Doug Taylor, the Delta officer who'd led the 2005 mission in which Delta operators dressed up as farmhands to capture Ghassan Amin, ran the cell for a long time. "He, in particular, was able to work the information exchange and make relationships with the Israelis that allowed us to trade intelligence with them for intelligence they would trade to us," said a senior special mission unit officer.

The cell swapped intelligence on Sunni Islamist networks active in southern Lebanon, Jordan, and Iraq that JSOC had gained in Iraq for Israeli intelligence on Hezbollah and other Shi'ite groups in the Levant and Iraq. JSOC had the right to make the trade because, in the U.S. intelligence community, organizations retained release authority over intelligence that they had produced. While the Israelis got useful intelligence out of the deal, they may have had another goal in mind, according to the senior special mission unit officer. "I think their intent all along was to keep pushing us against the Iranians . . . in terms of trying to get us to interdict Hezbollah in other areas around the globe for them," he said. Eventually Orange took over Taylor's cell, due to that unit's longstanding relationship with the Israelis.

But despite the Israelis' extensive penetration of the Shi'ite militant networks, the intelligence tip that led Task Force 17 to the Khazali brothers' safe house in Basra in March 2007 did not come from Tel Aviv, but from London, courtesy of Britain's MI6 intelligence agency. "It was an MI6 source in the Levant [who] knew exactly where it was in Basra," said the senior special mission unit officer, adding that the tip's value could be judged from the fact that other than those detained at the site, presumably, the number of "bad guys" who knew the safe house's location could likely be counted on the fingers of one hand.[27] There was a certain symmetry to the British role in Khazali's detention, in that the brothers were released—Laith in June 2009 and Qais in January 2010—in exchange for the release of Peter Moore, a British information technology consultant kidnapped (along with his four bodyguards, who were then murdered) on May 29, 2007, as he worked to install software to track the billions of dollars in foreign aid pouring into Iraq's treasury.[28] "It got very diplomatic, to the point where it was out of JSOC's control and the British government was negotiating," said a Task Force 17 officer. Equally frustrating for Task Force 17 veterans, in November 2012 the Iraqi government released the Hezbollah operative captured with the Khazali brothers, Ali Mussa Daqduq, whom the United States wanted charged with war crimes for his role in the execution-style killing of the four U.S. soldiers kidnapped in Karbala.[29]

The political restrictions that had hobbled Task Force 17 from its outset became even more onerous as the United States lowered its profile in Iraq and turned as much responsibility as possible over to the Maliki government. Between February and August 2009, by which time Army General Ray Odierno had replaced Petraeus as the Multi-National Force–Iraq commander, "they only did three missions because of restrictions placed on them by the four-star," said the retired Special Forces officer.

But for a small number of Shi'ite targets, JSOC found a way around the political restrictions by killing its enemies without leaving any U.S. fingerprints. The command did this using a device called the "Xbox." Developed jointly by Delta and Team 6, the Xbox was a bomb designed to look and behave exactly like one made by Iraqi insurgents, using materials typically found in locally made improvised explosive devices. Its genesis was the training that Delta and Team 6 explosive ordnance disposal (EOD) personnel went through to learn how to disarm the homemade bombs. After capturing some intact on the Afghan and Iraqi battlefields, the EOD troops set about taking them apart. It wasn't long before they realized they could build them as well. "So they're reverse-engineering the whole thing," said the senior special mission unit officer. A collective light went on in some corners of JSOC when leaders realized the possibilities inherent in this capability.

At first, the officer said, JSOC's bomb makers used components typically found in the Afghanistan-Pakistan theater: "Chinese circuits and Pakistani parts . . . and explosives from old Soviet munitions, et cetera." The intent was to create a device that if it were sent to the FBI's Terrorist Explosive Device Analytical Center in Quantico, Virginia, the Bureau's experts would mistakenly trace the bomb back to a particular terrorist bomb maker because of certain supposedly telltale signature elements of the design that JSOC's explosive ordnance disposal gurus had managed to re-create.

But the Xbox was different from regular IEDs in several ways, in order to reduce risks to operators and civilians. First, unlike many IEDs, such as those detonated by vehicles running over pressure plates, it had to be command detonated, meaning an operator somewhere was watching the target and then pressing a button. Another design requirement was that the Xbox device had to be extremely stable, to avoid the sort of premature explosions that often kill terrorists. JSOC wanted to use the device to kill individuals, rather than crowds. "You're just going to get the one guy in the car, you're not looking to blow up forty people in a marketplace," said the senior special mission unit officer. "You've got authority for military force against one by-name guy. You've got to get positive ID and positive detonation in a place where you're not going to get collateral damage. [For instance,] smoke the guy while driving his HiLux pickup in an area that there's no U.S. or Coalition presence."

Most insurgents JSOC killed this way were Task Force 17 targets in southern Iraq—"a variety of folks that were running [the] Quds Force EFP pipeline and stuff in through the south," the senior special mission unit operator said. But the missions were conducted by operators from the squadron Delta had created in 2005 to replace and take the mission of Operational Support Troop. (Confusingly, the new reconnaissance squadron was initially called D Squadron, until Delta created a fourth line squadron about a year later and named it D Squadron, with the reconnaissance squadron renamed G Squadron.)[30] JSOC used reconnaissance operators, who are typically some of Delta's most experienced, because getting the device into position, by placing it in the target's vehicle, for example, was "a lot of work," he said. It usually involved surveillance of the target for days on end, understanding his pattern of life—his daily routines—so that the operators could predict when they would be able to gain access to his vehicle unobserved. When that time window opened, "then, like out of the movies, you're picking the locks and going over walls and alleyways, very shortly placing that stuff in there," he said.

The special mission unit officer acknowledged the possibility that JSOC might choose to use the Xbox on other battlefields—and might already have done so. "We have successfully used this in places where you're not flying a Predator, you don't want to launch a missile, you don't necessarily want to do a raid," he said. "So if you get authorization for the use of military force then you want something very precise against a target." But although the Xbox began with EOD personnel re-creating devices from the Afghan theater, it was not used there, where Team 6 was the lead special mission unit. "We co-developed it with Delta, but it was only being used in Iraq," said a senior Team 6 source, who questioned the morality of using the device: "[It's] a great tool, but as many of us have said—hey, we're no different than the enemy if we're just blowing people up with booby traps."

⁂

Task Force 17 continued to operate for several years, but was closed down long before U.S. troops left Iraq at the end of 2011. Despite all the challenges the task force faced, it achieved some success, albeit fleeting. "Previously they [i.e., Quds Force] were running in EFPs and U.S. currency by the truckload," said a Ranger officer. "Post–TF 17 they were using ratlines and having to do what al Qaeda was having to do up north, so there was some level of success there. We saved a lot of Coalition lives by reducing the EFP footprint all around Sadr City, but it was never going to be [the equivalent of] TF 16."

Meanwhile, in 2007 Task Force 16's main effort shifted to Mosul, where McChrystal had placed a Ranger battalion in command of Task Force North, the first time the Rangers had been given command of a battalion or squadron-level task force.

In the wider war, there was a sense by late 2007 that the tide was turning in favor of the Coalition. Petraeus had asked for and received a "surge" of five additional combat brigades—more than 20,000 troops. As those forces flowed in and were committed mostly in the Baghdad area, the Coalition was also making headway splitting Anbar's Sunni tribes and associated insurgent groups away from AQI in what became known as the "Sunni Awakening."

In June 2007, Mike Flynn left JSOC to become Central Command's intelligence director. A year later McChrystal changed command after almost five years on the job, far longer than the tenure of any previous commander.[31] The JSOC he left behind bore little resemblance to the organization he had taken command of in October 2003. Its budget, authorities, and the size of its headquarters staff had all expanded exponentially. (In 2002 the size of the JSOC staff was about 800. By the end of 2008, that had ballooned to about 2,300.)[32] The command's battlefield role had similarly evolved. Accustomed to fighting on the periphery of major conflict, JSOC had taken a central role in Iraq, albeit one that the U.S. military did its best to obscure, never acknowledging the command or its special mission units by name when discussing their operations. Several factors had combined to enable JSOC's rise to prominence: the fact that Zarqawi allied his group with Al Qaeda at a time when the U.S. military considered the destruction of Al Qaeda its most pressing mission meant JSOC—often called "the national mission force"—was likely to have a starring role; the rapid growth of cell phone networks in Iraq, and the insurgents' concomitant use of the same, were invaluable in helping McChrystal's task force find and fix the enemy; the same was true of the Internet café phenomenon in Iraq, and the fielding of the Predator unmanned aerial vehicle in growing numbers.

McChrystal was, of course, also fortunate to have at his disposal units composed of men and women who brought an unparalleled combination of professionalism, skill, imagination, courage, and drive to their work. But this is something to which all previous JSOC commanders could lay claim. And there was no guarantee that the various technological advantages JSOC brought to the fight would ever amount to a winning combination. Like the German architects of blitzkrieg in the 1930s, who took tools—the tank, radio communications, fighters, and bombers—and combined them in ways that others had not imagined, what set McChrystal apart was, first, a vision for how to meld all the tools at his disposal together, while flattening his organization and breaking apart the "stovepipes" that kept information from being fully exploited, and, second, the force of personality required to make that vision a reality.

What that meant was that during the U.S. military's darkest days in Iraq, in 2005, 2006, and 2007, when the country seemed on the way to becoming a charnel-house, JSOC was virtually the only American force achieving success (leading President Bush to declare to author Bob

Woodward, "JSOC is awesome").[33] The crucial role that McChrystal and his JSOC task force played in rocking Al Qaeda in Iraq back on its heels when the terrorist group had seemed on the brink, if not of victory in the traditional sense, then certainly of pushing Iraq into an indefinite period of bloody sectarian conflict, would remain largely unrecognized for years. But its growing size and increasingly important role were robbing JSOC of its ability to hide in the shadows. In less than three years, the man to whom McChrystal passed command, Vice Admiral Bill McRaven, would preside over JSOC's highest profile success. But first, he had matters to address on Iraq's borders.

PART IV

A GLOBAL CAMPAIGN

22

Close Target Reconnaissance in Syria[1]

The four helicopters scythed through the air, two Black Hawks full of Delta operators covered by a pair of AH-6 Little Birds, all headed for the Syrian border near Al Qaim. The aircraft were flown by Night Stalkers, but it was broad daylight—4:45 P.M. on October 26, 2008. They were on their way to kill a man.

That man was Abu Ghadiya, the nom de guerre of Badran Turki Hishan al-Mazidih,[2] an Iraqi of about thirty years of age who ran the largest foreign fighter network in Syria. During the peak of the Iraq War in 2006 and 2007, JSOC estimated Abu Ghadiya was running 120 to 150 foreign fighters[3] (including twenty to thirty suicide bombers) a month into Iraq. Thanks to a spy in Abu Ghadiya's camp and to signals intelligence facilitated by an Orange operative's repeated undercover missions to the area, JSOC had been carefully tracking him for months. The task force knew that he occasionally visited Iraq to maintain his bona fides with the fighters, but his regular base in the area was a safe house in Sukkariyah, a village near the town of Abu Kamal, six miles across the border from Al Qaim.

It was to that village the helicopters were now flying. Thousands of feet above, a Predator cast its electronic eye on the objective, transmitting what it saw back to Al Asad, where task force staff crowded around the few computer screens that had the live video feed. (The Task Force West operations center lacked its Balad counterpart's lavishly high-tech accoutrements.) As the helicopters crossed the border, the mission fell under CIA command.[4]

꙰

The raid on Sukkariyah had been nine months in the planning, but it became the only public evidence of a highly successful clandestine campaign

313

waged inside Syria by Orange and other JSOC elements since the earliest days of the Iraq War.

JSOC's history in the Levant stretched back to the work done by Delta and the Army of Northern Virginia during the 1980s. Since then, Delta had maintained a close relationship with Israeli special operations forces, with operators sometimes wearing Israeli uniforms when working in the Jewish state,[5] while the unit later known as Orange had gradually deepened its network in the region. After the September 11 attacks raised U.S. awareness of Islamist terror threats, in 2002 Rumsfeld gave JSOC the green light to conduct missions in both Syria and Lebanon. The United States had deep concerns about the Quds Force's operations in the region as well as Hezbollah's huge influence in Lebanon. Special mission unit operators rated Hezbollah, not Al Qaeda, as the "A-team" when it came to Islamist terrorism. "You don't want to mess around with Hezbollah," said one. "They make Al Qaeda look like a joke."

Beirut was no longer the battleground it had been in the 1970s and 1980s, but danger still lurked in the shadows. An Army of Northern Virginia operative almost learned this lesson the hard way in October 2002 out walking near the Lebanese capital's famous corniche. Returning from a mission in a nearby country, he was passing through Lebanon in order to conduct activities to maintain his nonofficial cover when three men tried to force him into a car as he took a short cut back to his hotel. The operative, whose background was in Special Forces but who was unarmed, fought back. He managed to wrestle a .22 caliber pistol away from one of the attackers and escape, shot in the midriff. Unwilling to break his cover by going to the U.S. embassy, he called instead, and was put through to the regional medical officer (who worked out of the embassy). Following the doctor's advice, "he literally sewed himself up in the hotel room and then continued with his full counter-surveillance routes," said a special mission unit source. The operative then went through the laborious process required to cover his tracks before departing Lebanon without breaking cover (other than the call to the embassy), despite suffering from a gunshot wound. He crossed multiple international borders before receiving medical care, a feat of tradecraft and endurance that insiders discussed in whispered tones years later. "Putting people in and getting people out of those environments [requires] very elaborate steps to ensure that they are clean [i.e., with cover intact and not under surveillance] coming out," said the special mission unit source. "He went through all those elaborate steps and that's why it's legendary."

As to who had attacked the operative and why, a JSOC staffer familiar with the episode said they were most likely street criminals who saw him as a target of opportunity, rather than Hezbollah members who suspected he was more than he seemed. But an Army spokesman told the author that the operative received a Silver Star "for gallantry in action against an enemy of the United States during the period 19–21 October 2002."[6] The citation for the Silver Star, however, was classified.[7]

After returning to the United States, the operative briefed Rumsfeld on his exploits. His unit, meanwhile, ensured that in the future operatives under nonofficial cover would have better access to emergency health care.

The close call did little to inhibit JSOC or its newest subordinate unit, Orange, from undertaking equally dangerous missions next door to Lebanon in Syria. JSOC had plenty of reasons for wanting to get inside Syria after the September 11 attacks. One was the knowledge that Syria had chemical weapons and was trying to achieve nuclear capability, perhaps with help from Iran, whose Quds Force was gaining influence in Syria. The 2003 invasion and occupation of Iraq soon heralded a new concern: Sunni insurgent groups' use of Syria as a way station en route to Iraq for volunteer militants from the broader Muslim world.

As in Lebanon, there was a significant role for Orange, which in 2003 was just beginning the shift in mind-set and, ultimately, culture that its move to JSOC entailed. The unit's change of command that summer helped accelerate things. The outgoing commander, Colonel Tom Tutt, was an old-school military intelligence officer more comfortable with treating Orange as a national intelligence asset to be used against strategic targets. His replacement, Colonel "KT" Trautman, who had been Tutt's deputy and Orange's sigint squadron commander, thought differently. "He was very tactically focused," said one officer. "He very much wanted to get into the fight." In particular, Trautman wanted to modernize the unit's signals intelligence platforms to enable Orange to provide direct, real-time support to JSOC task forces conducting direct action missions. Another officer said Trautman's approach had the support of the unit's rank and file. "Everybody in that organization wanted to get into the fight" and knew remaining a "strategic" asset would have meant "you stay on the sidelines," he said.

Up to that point, the unit's case officers—personnel certified to recruit sources—were typically human intelligence specialists who had not graduated from its assessment and selection course. Not being traditional operatives, they were viewed rather skeptically in the unit. "The leadership always wanted to get rid of case officers," said one special mission unit veteran. But once the Army of Northern Virginia came under JSOC, the need for case officers grew. In an effort to meet the demand, Orange expanded the number of selection course graduates it sent to the CIA's field training course at the Farm. The unit also increased the number of personnel it accepted from the other (i.e., non-Army) services (a process that had begun in the late 1990s).

Something that didn't change was Orange's frequent role as the tactical arm of the NSA, which funded most of the unit's signals intelligence budget via the Consolidated Cryptologic Program. Another constant was the unit's obsession with secrecy. "Everybody in the unit was on the Department of the Army Special Roster, which means they didn't exist," said a retired special ops officer. Orange was still headquartered at Belvoir, but its three squadrons—"Operations" (sometimes referred to as "Humint" or "Ground"), "Sigint," and "Mission Support," as well as its supporting aviation elements—were spread around the Washington area, in some cases operating from clandestine locations including an office building near Fort Meade.

In 2003, Orange had teams in Saudi Arabia, the Horn of African and South America, among other locations. "Outside of Afghanistan and Iraq, Orange had everything else in the world," said a special mission unit officer. "Everything. That unit was maxed out." Partly because the other units were so tied up in Iraq and partly because Orange itself was adopting a more tactical pose, the unit's ground squadron, made up largely of Special Forces soldiers, tried to muscle its way into a direct action role, or at least that was how it appeared to other units. This led to friction with Delta and Team 6 operators, who had long regarded such missions as their sole preserve. "Everyone thinks they're a trained shooter," complained a Delta operator. "Orange doesn't want to do AFO anymore. They want to be the finishing force. . . . When they go somewhere to do the find and the fix, they're trying to fuck the Unit out of the finish. It'll never work."

That, however, was not the case in Syria. There, the personnel Orange sent in were unarmed and were largely commercial cover operatives, meaning they posed as businessmen and had what a special mission unit veteran called "established presence" in the region. (Until 2003, all the Army of Northern Virginia's commercial cover operatives were in Operations Squadron's B Troop. The squadron's other three troops, A, C, and D, used only official cover. Then D Troop, which had only been reestablished in the late 1990s after a long hiatus, saw its mission change from one that used official cover to one that availed of nonofficial cover. Its operatives went abroad using commercial cover in places like Jakarta, Sulu Province in the Philippines, and Morocco. But D Troop had a hard time getting official backing for missions into denied areas like Syria, which remained the preserve of B Troop.) During the middle of the decade, Orange had fewer than a dozen personnel operating under commercial cover, about half a dozen of whom were conducting the Syrian operations.

Those missions actually began in the months prior to the March 2003 invasion of Iraq. The intent was to ensure the United States had "eyes and ears all around Iraq" by the time the conventional forces drove north across the Kuwait-Iraq border, said a JSOC staffer. By late summer 2003, Orange operatives and other JSOC personnel were infiltrating Syria to focus on two target sets: any evidence that Saddam Hussein's regime had moved weapons of mass destruction to Syria ahead of the allies' invasion of Iraq; and the foreign fighter networks already establishing roots in Syria to support the Iraq insurgency. Rumsfeld had to personally approve the missions, which were carried out under the auspices of the CIA's chief of station in Damascus. Tasked to locate the foreign fighter safe houses and get proof that the networks were operating in Syria, the operatives were not starting from a blank slate. They were often led to a particular safe house by a suspect's IP router address that U.S. intelligence had already obtained. Because the United States wanted to keep this ability secret, while still proving to the Syrian regime that it knew what was going on at a particular location, the operatives' mission was to gather more tangible evidence, often by photographing safe houses, hotels, mosques, and bus stops used by foreign fighters. These missions combined high technology with classic espionage tradecraft: cover identities and counter-surveillance practices that included ducking into public bathrooms to change disguises—including wigs—to throw off any tail. "I go in a public restroom, do a quick [disguise swap] and I come out as a seventy-year-old man because I've got the bald head," said a special mission unit veteran. In theory, anyone tailing the hirsute man who entered the bathroom would ignore the bald guy coming out. Meanwhile, "you're off and onto public transportation, going to do an operational act." Sometimes that act was even more dangerous than secretly photographing jihadists in public. On occasion, operatives would pick the locks of Al Qaeda safe houses, filming and photographing what was inside, and presumably copying the contents of any digital devices they found. "They had guys on the ground basically breaking into the people's apartment and getting information," said a special ops source familiar with the missions. "Talk about close target recce. . . . That's pretty frickin' ballsy. . . . Two people with a lockpick kit and a camera. If they would have been caught, they were done."

The operatives also placed automatic cameras and other recording devices disguised as everyday items to monitor safe houses and other locations. One new piece of gear they used was the Cardinal device, developed by the Defense Intelligence Agency's science and technology department and operated in conjunction with the National Security Agency, which programmed the devices to work in groups that configured and reconfigured their own networks.[8] Designed to take photos only when triggered by movement sensors, the device stored the pictures before transmitting them via satellite uplink at preset times. "The original plan was to use them for establishing patterns of life," a senior JSOC official said. However, the device was neither popular with operatives nor productive in terms of actionable intelligence.

Another new piece of kit the operatives employed was a camera designed to evade detection by the security cameras the jihadists used at their safe houses. "Those [security] cameras can see infrared cameras," said a source familiar with the operations. (Many cameras use infrared for some functions.) "So if you plant a camera to spy on them, they can see the infrared source, the camera. So we developed a camera that did not use [infrared]." Although JSOC tested the new cameras in 2004 in very low light conditions in Afghanistan, they were designed for clandestine operations in an urban environment. On at least one occasion, the new cameras worked spectacularly. "We caught guys going into a Syrian office building, I believe it was in Damascus, and they were like head dudes of this fighter network," said the source. "The State Department walked into [Syrian president Bashar] Assad and friggin' put the photographs down . . . and said, 'You're supporting this. This is the evidence right here. Here are the friggin' pictures.'"

Indeed, the United States used intelligence that JSOC obtained in Syria as leverage with the Assad regime, presenting it to Damascus in demarches in an effort to pressure Assad to crack down on the foreign fighter networks. Sometimes this was done indirectly via Jordanian government intermediaries and at other times by the U.S. government itself, including on at least one occasion, by Secretary of State Condoleezza Rice (who had moved to the position in January 2005). But not wanting to reveal to the Syrians that American troops had been spying in their country, the U.S. government told Damascus that the material had been seized in raids on foreign fighter safe houses in Iraq. Disguising and altering the material to conform to that cover story represented a "delicate art," a special mission unit veteran said. JSOC and the CIA went to great lengths to figure out whether to actually change the documents and photos, or to keep them as they were and tell the Syrians, "This was pulled off this guy's Nokia 3200 cell phone in Baghdad—this is the guy's name, here's his bus ticket; he laid this all out on who was assisting him. Here's all the evidence. Do something about it. We know they're coming through here." Sometimes this required technological wizardry. For instance, if the cover story for a photograph taken by an operative in Aleppo was that it was pulled off a foreign fighter's iPhone in Baghdad, it might need to be digitized so that it looked like an iPhone photograph. The Assad regime remained completely ignorant that the intelligence being presented to them was obtained by undercover U.S. troops in Syria. The demarches met with mixed success. The Syrians would only take action if the United States could tie the presence of particular jihadists passing through Syria to a threat to the Assad regime.

This deception was one reason why the United States sometimes chose to use military personnel under a combination of official and nonofficial cover for these missions rather than the more traditional method of paying local sources to conduct them. A second was to protect the technical intelligence upon which the missions were based. "Do you want to let a recruited source or agent know how much data you've got, particularly when some of that stuff's come from NSA collection et cetera?" said the special mission unit veteran. "Because of the sensitivity of the information . . . it really needs to be an American doing this." A third reason was that the United States needed to have absolute trust in the intelligence coming out of Syria. So, although Orange had an increasing number of Farm-trained case officers who were certified to recruit and pay sources, the Syria missions did not involve that. They were "almost all CTR [close target reconnaissance], close-in signals intelligence or close-in collection of data," said the special mission unit veteran.

In the early days operators from the small unit that became Computer Network Operations Squadron sometimes augmented the Orange operatives.[9] In at least one case in Syria, a CNOS operator entered Syria as an employee of an international organization. At other times, capitalizing on the popularity of Internet cafés in the Middle East, CNOS operators often posed as businessmen who dealt with communications technologies like cell phones or computers. CNOS also targeted the Iraqi refugee camps in Jordan, most likely using local sources to access the camps.

The Orange operatives' ethnicities would not have immediately marked them as Westerners. The operatives included one or two women, who never went in solo, but accompanied male operatives as part of a pair. Having a man and woman work in tandem proved even more useful in parts of the Arab world than it had in the Balkans. The special mission unit veteran noted that jihadists used women in certain roles in the Middle East because male security personnel were less likely to search under their all-covering garb. "Two can play at that game," he said. But two-person missions were the exception, rather than the rule. Orange's Syria deployments were "mostly singleton and most without any backup," he added.

As the program matured, Orange deepened its operatives' cover, in some cases moving them and their families from the United States to countries closer to Syria, which required the Army secretary's approval and the agreement of multiple geographic combatant commanders and station chiefs. The governments of at least some of those countries had no idea that U.S. spies were living under commercial cover there. (The U.S. ambassador and CIA station chief in each nation had to sign off on such arrangements.) The commercial cover operatives never resided in Syria itself, however.

As with their East European counterpart in Delta, the Orange operatives under commercial cover were unknown to many even in their own chain of command and their missions were tightly compartmented even within JSOC. When intelligence generated by the missions was discussed in JSOC's video-teleconferences, "they'd never say where the intel came from," said an officer. Even in higher-level discussions, the most detailed description would be "Orange assets in Syria," he said.

The missions into Syria were also kept from almost everyone in the U.S. embassy in Damascus. "The chief of station, the ambassador will know they're in there and maybe the chief of ops in the station, and that's about it," the special mission unit veteran said. The operatives had an emergency action plan if they were compromised. "Your best course of action is not to break cover," he said. "Always stick to whatever and whomever you're portraying and the legend." Even if the Syrians caught the operatives and threw them in jail, they were forbidden from acknowledging that they were American spies. It would be up to the U.S. government whether or not to claim them.

The Orange operatives in the Levant were working in areas where spies for Israel were "constantly getting rolled up," the special mission unit veteran said, which partly explained why the missions into Syria and Lebanon were "episodic." If, for instance, the Syrian security services pulled in a network of Israeli sources for questioning, JSOC would want to know what tipped the Syrians off before sending its own operatives back in. Perhaps in part because of this caution, no Orange operative or mission in Syria was compromised, a remarkable record, "since Syrian intelligence is really good," the special mission unit veteran said. "They're looking for spies all the time." But there were some close calls. In one case an operative "had a recording device battery kind of melt and explode and just burn the shit out of [his] pocket" while he was on Syrian public transport, the SMU veteran said. "He just held his pants out and it was just like burning the tar out of them as he's riding this bus out of there."

The missions enabled JSOC to build a detailed picture of the network that moved jihadists from Aleppo and Damascus airports through the Syrian section of the Euphrates River Valley until they crossed into Iraq near Al Qaim. After several years, one name stood out as Zarqawi's master facilitator in Syria: Abu Ghadiya.

The United States tried to bring diplomatic pressure to bear on Syria, sending Dell Dailey (the State Department's coordinator for counterterrorism from June 2007 to April 2009) on a tour of Arab capitals asking governments to use their leverage with the Assad regime. The U.S. government also gave its Iraqi counterpart intelligence about Abu Ghadiya's activities, leading the Iraqis to lobby the Syrians to do something about him. The Syrian government initially refused to take action, perhaps because keeping Abu Ghadiya in position allowed the regime to closely track the foreign fighter network in its country. "He ran the network," said a senior JSOC official. "It was easier for Syrian intelligence to keep their eyes on him." Frustrated with the Syrians' inaction, Petraeus himself volunteered to fly to Damascus and confront Assad about Abu Ghadiya. President Bush rebuffed the offer in a video-teleconference with the general. In the end, the Assad regime tired of Abu Ghadiya's presence within their borders and let the U.S. government know it would essentially look the other way if U.S. forces targeted him. The Bush administration handed the mission to JSOC.

But to some, it appeared that JSOC needed a little prodding to strike Abu Ghadiya. By 2008 both Central Command and U.S. Special Operations Command had established interagency task forces at their respective Tampa headquarters to track foreign fighters. (Scott Miller headed SOCOM's.) They prioritized Abu Ghadiya on the grounds that multiple intelligence sources had identified him as the principal facilitator of foreign fighters headed to Iraq, and removing him would help create the pause in the foreign fighter flow that Petraeus wanted. Working together, the two task forces drew up a concept of operations for a mission against Abu Ghadiya. But the Tampa task forces had only "asking authority," not "tasking authority." They couldn't issue orders to other organizations. When they asked JSOC to act, JSOC demurred, arguing it didn't have enough assets to conduct a raid while maintaining its operational tempo in Iraq. But JSOC attempted to present CENTCOM and SOCOM with a catch-22, claiming that because Abu Ghadiya was already on its target list, nobody else could launch a mission against him. This didn't sit well with acting CENTCOM commander Lieutenant General Marty Dempsey. He told JSOC, essentially, "if you don't do something, we will," said a CENTCOM source. That threat caused JSOC to prioritize Abu Ghadiya.

For at least nine months, JSOC focused its intelligence collection on the foreign fighter kingpin. The planners knew that although he made his home in Zabadani,[10] about thirty kilometers northwest of Damascus, he repeatedly visited the safe house near Abu Kamal, sometimes traveling on into Iraq. They hoped he'd enter Iraq while under surveillance, but he never did. The alternative was to strike while he was at the safe house. An Orange operative made multiple solo trips to Sukkariyah undercover to keep tabs on Abu Ghadiya. Among his tasks was to position and move equipment that allowed the NSA to precisely locate Abu Ghadiya's cell phone in a particular building. JSOC also had access to a spy in Abu Ghadiya's inner circle who was originally recruited by Syrian intelligence.

In planning a strike into Syria, albeit one just a few miles over the border, the task force intelligence analysts had to determine the likely reaction times of the Syrian air force, border guards, and air defense networks. While the United States had given senior Syrian officials in Damascus a heads-up that a raid might be in the offing, the Syrian troops along the border were none the wiser. But Syrian air defenses were oriented on Israel and Turkey, not longtime ally Iraq, while U.S. intelligence reported that Syrian air force pilots were flying no more than a handful of times a month. "They weren't sitting on strip alert," said a military intelligence source. Task force planners estimated that the operators could spend at least ninety minutes on the objective before trouble arrived—"an enormous amount of time for the task force," he said.

But for JSOC to launch, the spy in Abu Ghadiya's camp had to report that the wanted man was at the safe house. Abu Ghadiya's cell phone also had to be on and emitting from that location. There were several false starts. "A lot of us spent a lot of sweat equity planning it and actually going out to Al Asad multiple times to get this guy," said the military intelligence source. It finally all came together on October 26, 2008.

The Task Force Brown crews had about thirty-six hours to prepare for the mission. After crossing the border, the flight to the objective lasted no longer than fifteen minutes. Located in a tiny hamlet, the target building was a single-story flat-roofed structure. The helicopters took no fire as they approached. The Black Hawks landed, disgorging operators who sprinted to the building, where they suppressed resistance from Ghadiya and a handful of his fighters within ninety seconds, killing between six and twelve militants[11] without suffering any wounded or killed themselves. The operators spent about an hour doing "sensitive site exploitation," which amounts to collecting as much material of intelligence value as possible, before calling for the Black Hawks to return, loading Abu Ghadiya's body aboard a helicopter,[12] and flying back to Al Asad. As the intelligence analysts had predicted, no Syrian security forces showed up while the operators were on the ground.

While Orange continued to operate in the Levant, its presence there declined within two years as Iran became a higher priority. Delta, however, increased its commitment to the region.

23

Back to Mogadishu

It was January 2002 in Afghanistan. Snow covered the mountains that surrounded Bagram air base, where, in a frigid electrical closet, FBI special agent Russ Fincher and New York Police detective Marty Mahon were interrogating Ali Abdul Aziz al-Fakhri, a Libyan known by his nom de guerre, Ibn al-Shaykh al-Libi. One of the highest-level Al Qaeda figures captured by that point in the war, Libi had run the group's Khalden training camp in eastern Afghanistan. Fincher and Mahon built a relationship of trust with Libi, who talked freely. In particular, he divulged what a military source who was in Bagram at the time described as Al Qaeda's "multi-phased" plans to regroup after being forced from its safe haven in Afghanistan. The first phase was to flee across the border to Pakistan's tribal areas, but to be prepared for further movement. Assuming they would not be safe for long in the tribal areas, Al Qaeda leaders' ultimate goal was to reconstitute their force in the next best potential sanctuaries: Yemen and Somalia.[1]

History and geography argued in favor of believing Libi. East Africa and Yemen had been the sites of Al Qaeda's most sensational attacks prior to September 11, 2001. On August 7, 1998, the group staged almost simultaneous truck bomb attacks on the U.S. embassies in Nairobi, Kenya, and Dar es Salaam, Tanzania, killing more than 200 people, the vast majority of them locals. On October 12, 2000, Al Qaeda conducted a suicide boat attack on the *Cole*, a U.S. Navy destroyer, killing seventeen sailors and blowing a hole in the ship while it was at harbor in the Yemeni port of Aden. The United States knew, therefore, that Al Qaeda already had roots in the region. It also knew that Yemen was Osama bin Laden's ancestral homeland.

Sure enough, in 2002 U.S. intelligence noticed small numbers of second-tier Al Qaeda figures moving back and forth between the

Afghanistan-Pakistan theater and the Horn of Africa and Yemen, traveling by boat from Oman, past Yemen, and across the Bab-el-Mandeb Strait, which separates the Red Sea from the Gulf of Aden, before following the coast of Djibouti down to Somalia. When Al Qaeda also began transferring money into the region—a key indicator that operational planning might be occurring—U.S. leaders became alarmed.

But with a war under way in Afghanistan and another planned for Iraq, the Bush administration decided to wage its campaign against Al Qaeda's East African and Yemeni branches largely in the shadows, using the two weapons upon which it would increasingly rely in the years ahead: the CIA and JSOC.[2] For the first four years of the campaign in the Horn, the CIA would take the lead. The Agency gave the campaign a name that recalled JSOC's past experience in Somalia: Operation Black Hawk.

⁂

Starting in early 2002, small teams of U.S. operatives began to conduct missions into Somalia. The first trip was by car, from Addis Ababa, the Ethiopian capital, to Hargeisa, Somalia's second largest city and the capital of the autonomous Somaliland region in the country's northeast. Shortly thereafter the U.S. operatives began flying to Baidoa, a city in southwest Somalia. On these first trips the operatives would start their missions unarmed, before renting AK-series assault rifles once they were on the ground in Somalia. In 2003 the operations center for the clandestine campaign in Somalia switched from Addis Ababa to the Kenyan capital of Nairobi. The teams would drive to Nairobi's Wilson Airport and climb aboard a chartered Bluebird Aviation turboprop that would fly them to the K50 Airport, about fifty kilometers southwest of Mogadishu. Although two Bluebird planes would crash into each other a couple of years later, it's still the case that for the Americans aboard, the flights were probably the least dangerous part of missions that demanded professionalism, courage, and coolness under pressure.

In those early days, the teams combined at least two CIA case officers, two Army of Northern Virginia operatives, and an interpreter. Once the planes landed, the teams would travel to and through Mogadishu in small convoys escorted by fighters loyal to one warlord or another. Different patches of the anarchic city were controlled by different warlords, requiring much coordination to ensure safe passage as the convoys crossed the boundaries between the warlords' territories.

Those warlords were the key to Operation Black Hawk. The CIA was paying them to kill or capture the twenty or so most senior members of Al Qaeda's East Africa cell. If the warlords captured one of these targets, they were to turn him over to the Agency, which would send—or "render"—him to a U.S. ally or one of the CIA's secret prisons. The man in charge was John Bennett, the Agency's highly regarded Nairobi station chief, a former Marine infantry officer who in 2010 would become the head of the National Clandestine Service—the CIA's top spy. Bennett did not travel to Mogadishu, but his leadership was critical to the effort. "The relationship with the warlords was built through . . . Bennett," said an intelligence source familiar with the missions. "It was through his sheer willpower and personality. He could do it and nobody else could."

Bennett also worked well with, and was respected by, JSOC. On those first missions, the military personnel were Army of Northern Virginia operatives, whose primary role was to provide security as the CIA gathered and validated human intelligence. But the operatives came into their own as they began to install gear around Mogadishu to monitor the city's cell phone traffic, which NSA satellites could not capture. "The problem was you cannot do intercept through a lot of national asset capability," said an officer familiar with the unit's operations in the Horn. "You have to be there on the ground, for a lot of this stuff is very tactical in nature, it's very temporal. You have to be Johnny on the spot." Just as in Syria, these devices, which were sometimes placed in warlords' homes, had to be serviced and moved regularly as new cell phone towers sprang up and old ones were repositioned. The CIA had its own signals intelligence capability, which it jealously guarded, but it was keen to augment its tiny fleet of signals intelligence aircraft in the region with a modular signals intelligence package that could be rolled on and off a rented plane. The Agency wanted the package to collect cell phone traffic from an airborne position up to four or five miles from the target area. However, significant technical difficulties were involved in making such a system work without integrating it into the plane's airframe. Developing the capability took several years, and the help of Orange (as the Army of Northern Virginia was now known), after which the modular capability was made available to both organizations.

The CIA used a carrot-and-stick approach to working with the warlords, handing them suitcases full of hundreds of thousands of dollars, but with the implicit threat of U.S. air strikes if they betrayed the United

States. "They were risky missions," said the intelligence source. "You could never actually trust the warlords—they're subject to the highest bidder." But the Americans were bluffing about the air strikes. No U.S. aircraft were nearby, not even drones to monitor the missions. The escape and evasion plan in case a team got into trouble was "Get to the coast and hope for the best," said a JSOC staffer. At the time, the staffer noted, the Navy had no ships in the Indian Ocean, and the closest "fast-mover" jets that might provide close air support were five hours away, in Qatar.[3]

After Bennett left in August 2003, the CIA station's focus began to shift and its appetite for risk waned, according to a JSOC source stationed in Nairobi. For two years, the CIA operatives who flew into Mogadishu never left the plane, holding their meetings with the warlords on the Bluebird. During one such meeting, the warlord pointed out of the window to four white female reporters going about their business. His point was clear: *Those unarmed Western women aren't scared to work in Somalia—why are you?* The three-man JSOC teams that accompanied such flights but were also confined (on the ambassador's orders) to the aircraft were now filled by a couple of Team 6 operators in addition to an Orange signals intelligence soldier. Ironically, the Agency treated the operators as "hired guns," but banned them from bringing rifles on the missions, said a SEAL. The Orange operative would either position his phone-monitoring device at the airport near Mogadishu or would have an Agency source emplace it.[4]

While the CIA was in overall charge of the Black Hawk missions, the JSOC personnel reported to a Team 6 or Delta officer in Nairobi who oversaw a small interagency team established in mid-2003 under JSOC auspices, staffed with intelligence and law enforcement personnel and working out of two small rooms in the embassy. He in turn worked for the Orange commander, who between 2003 and 2005 was Konrad Trautman. (Just as McChrystal had given Iraq to Delta, he had placed Orange in charge of the Horn and Yemen.) JSOC doubled its tiny resources in the Horn between 2003 and 2005, focusing more tightly on intelligence collection and target development. These efforts meant "we gained a lot of understanding of what was going on," a senior intelligence official said.[5] McChrystal began conducting Horn of Africa–specific video-teleconferences that connected operators, ambassadors, and CIA station chiefs with officials in Washington. He also placed a small team in Addis Ababa as part of this effort to thicken JSOC's network in the Horn.

JSOC was seeking to target Al Qaeda and its associates in the Islamic Courts Union, an Eritrean-financed Islamist force that had gained control of much of southern Somalia. Conversely, by the middle of the decade, the Nairobi CIA station seemed more interested in collecting intelligence for its own sake than on hunting Al Qaeda. "The Black Hawk team was not interested in CT [counterterrorism], they were interested really in foreign intelligence collection," said a Team 6 operator, adding that the warlords got the better part of the deal. "They were paying these warlords vast sums of money for nothing," he said. "From my perspective it was a complete failure. I'm sure from the Agency's perspective it was not."

(A JSOC staffer took issue with the operator's account, and said Team 6 deserved some blame itself. Orange "had safe houses all over Somalia by the time Blue came in," he said. "All that went [away]." A U.S. intelligence officer, meanwhile, disputed the notion that the CIA's Nairobi station became less interested in counterterrorism after Bennett's departure. "Every day [the new chief of station] was hammering, 'What have we done on CT?'" he said.)

The CIA had also decided that there weren't enough targets being developed in Somalia to keep its Predator fleet in nearby Djibouti, a tiny Muslim country that had agreed to host U.S. forces. The drones went away.[6] But the U.S. military was building up its forces in Djibouti, creating Combined Joint Task Force–Horn of Africa in November 2002. That task force ostensibly focused on civil affairs missions and on strengthening the capacity of allies in the region. It also gave the small but growing JSOC presence in Djibouti a larger organization in which to hide.[7]

In late summer 2005, the Black Hawk teams got permission to occasionally get off the planes and go into Mogadishu again. The CIA tried to extend the rule that banned rifles on the planes to the missions in which operators—from Team 6, Delta, and Orange—disembarked and went into Mogadishu, sometimes staying overnight at the residence of Bashir Raghe Shiiraar, a secular warlord. The Agency argued that the warlord militias would provide enough protection. An incident at a Somali airfield soon exposed the emptiness of that promise. A Black Hawk team that included a couple of Team 6 operators was sitting on the plane for a warlord meeting when a rocket-propelled grenade flew across the runway. The warlord's forces who were supposed to be protecting the Americans disappeared. The SEALs, who had been carrying their rifles broken down in their packs, quickly put the weapons together, got off the plane, and seized the highest ground they could, which was a berm around the airfield. Whoever had fired the RPG disappeared. The CIA officers said nothing about the weapons.[8]

The friction between the Agency and JSOC in the Horn extended to the highest levels. In 2005 McChrystal visited the embassy in Nairobi. The station chief let it be known ahead of the visit that McChrystal "had better be prepared to get down on bended knee." When the meeting took place, the station chief, a short man with a "huge ego," according to a source who worked close to him, condescended to the JSOC commander. McChrystal, who as Ranger Regiment commander had overhauled the regiment's hand-to-hand combat program, sat and listened. "When the guy stopped talking, McChrystal finally says, 'Hey look, if you ever talk to me that way again, I'm going to come around this desk and beat the shit out of you,'" said a source who was in the room. "And that changed the whole tone between the two of them. It became that old cartoon Spike and Chester, Spike's the bulldog and Chester's always jumping over him saying, 'Can I be your buddy, Spike, can I be your buddy?' All of a sudden [the station chief] now wants to be McChrystal's buddy. It was disgusting actually but I'm thinking to myself, 'That's all it would have taken—just threaten the guy physically.' Classic move."

By late 2005, the Orange operatives' courage and professionalism had earned the respect of their peers in the Horn. "Orange did a great job," said a Team 6 operator. At any one time, there were between two and six operatives—i.e., those personnel who went into Somalia with the signals intelligence gear—in Nairobi. They were there on typical JSOC three-to-four-month rotations, using fake last names with thin official cover while there. Orange had selected a few personnel for the mission whose ethnicity would not draw attention, meaning a greater range of covers was available to them. "A lot of them you wouldn't recognize as Westerners," said a special mission unit member. For instance, one operative was a black American who, in civilian clothes, could pass as an African and spoke fluent Swahili, he said.

Of course, these covers came with their own risks. During the 2005 to 2006 winter, an operative who resembled a member of Kenya's ethnic Indian merchant class was shot in the abdomen late at night at a gas station as he filled the tank of his SUV in an affluent part of Nairobi near the U.S. embassy. The operative was rushed to a nearby hospital and survived. "Of course, this sent everyone spinning to [figure out], have we been compromised? Are people following us?" said the special mission unit member. However, in part because the robbers stole the operative's wallet, the consensus was that he was the unfortunate victim of a crime of opportunity.[9]

With every trip into Mogadishu's urban jungle, the Orange operatives strengthened the United States' ability to keep tabs on its enemies in the Horn. But events beyond JSOC's control would soon undo much of that work, while ultimately offering the command new opportunities.

⌗

As with the Horn, JSOC's post-September 11 presence in Yemen started small. In summer 2002, three Delta operators under official cover, including a male-female team, arrived in the country on a classic advance force operation. Their job was to begin to gain an understanding of the political-military environment and how transnational factors were affecting it.[10] Two Army of Northern Virginia operatives had actually preceded them, arriving in February 2002. By the end of the year, the unit had been placed under JSOC and become Task Force Orange, but the plan to ramp up the military's clandestine force in Yemen had already suffered a couple of setbacks.

First, Yemeni officials seized some of the Army of Northern Virginia's critical signals intelligence technology when it arrived at Sana'a airport, hidden in a larger shipment of gear for U.S. theater (i.e., non-JSOC) special operations forces that were training Yemeni troops. The kit was essential for the unit's mission, but the U.S. embassy refused to pay the import duty that the Yemenis demanded, in the belief that it was a shakedown. Complicating matters was the fact that neither the Yemeni officials nor U.S. ambassador Edmund Hull understood what the gear was for. "He wasn't cleared for that," said a military source with Yemen experience. (In his memoir, Hull referred to the Yemenis refusing entry to pallets that the U.S. government considered to enjoy the same protection as diplomatic pouches, and listed "radios, weapons, and blood" as among the "equipment" items the pallets contained.) Following the loss of the gear, JSOC personnel were involved in a car crash in early summer 2002 that killed a Yemeni. They had to leave the country. It took several months, Hull's involvement, and the payment of what the military source termed "blood money" before JSOC was allowed back in.

Meanwhile, Hull was resisting what he described as "a great deal of pressure" from Washington for unilateral U.S. combat missions in Yemen. The ambassador opposed air strikes on the grounds that they would "inevitably" result in high numbers of civilian casualties. He acknowledged that special operations forces might "theoretically" provide "a more surgical option," but added that "planning always entailed options for massive support for the special [operations] forces should they become trapped." As with its proposal for attacking Ansar al-Islam's camp in Iraqi Kurdistan earlier that year, JSOC's insistence on a massive JRX-style operation became an insurmountable stumbling block. By the fall, JSOC's numbers began to climb again, but in September it only had six or seven personnel in Yemen. The U.S. counterterrorism mission in Sana'a at the time was clouded by a multitude of actors and differing chains of command.[11] There was a team from Central Command's special operations headquarters, which commanded the theater special operations forces; the small JSOC element; the CIA station; and a national intelligence support team that included a cryptologic support group from the National Security Agency.[12] The JSOC and intelligence personnel were trying to locate Al Qaeda targets, particularly those associated with the *Cole* attack. But there was competition between the CIA and the military over who could get permission to strike first, if one of those targets hove into view. "The Agency was a little faster," said the military source with Yemen experience. "Probably a lot faster."

This became clear on November 3, 2002, when the NSA detected a call made on a phone associated with Qaed Salim Sinan al-Harethi,[13] a Yemeni Al Qaeda member who was suspected of helping to plan the *Cole* attack. The United States had been trying to locate Harethi all year using cell phone tracking technology. They had located him at least once before that summer, but while the U.S. and Yemeni governments were planning a strike, the United States monitored a call to Harethi's phone from the Yemeni defense ministry, warning him. Not surprisingly, he disappeared and stopped using that phone. "He went chilly for about three months," said the military source. Now, for whatever reason, the experienced jihadist had chosen to use it again. This time the Agency was taking no chances. A Predator flew from Djibouti and destroyed the car, which was being driven through the desert in Marib province, about 120 kilometers east of Sana'a, killing Harethi and five fellow passengers. It was the first known lethal drone strike outside Afghanistan.

Orange kept a small team in Yemen, operating out of the embassy, but the next few years were relatively quiet from a counterterrorism point of view. That began to change on February 4, 2006, when twenty-three Al Qaeda members tunneled their way to freedom from the Political Security Headquarters jail in Sana'a.

＊

Meanwhile, back in the Horn, Orange's signals intelligence missions were paying off. "It definitely led to us being able to have much more precise information about what was going on," said the senior intelligence official. "Those operations gave us pretty good insight into what Al Qaeda was doing in East Africa. They saw it as another safe haven, they saw the opportunity to establish training camps, and they did. And it allowed us to start to plan [counterterrorism] operations against a couple of the key targets."[14]

The gear that the operatives used was not much to look at—"essentially it's a box and an antenna"—but emplacing it required significant expertise, said the special mission unit member. "You just can't put it anywhere to get the collection you want. So you really have to go in and survey both the physical geography and the electron environment." Figuring out the best places "to collect against your signals of interest" was laborious and time-consuming work. "Electronic communications engineers, they love that sort of problem," he said. "But if you're in a place like Mogadishu, it's a dangerous place to be out, figuring that stuff out." However, the need to safeguard the technology meant some otherwise optimal locations were ruled out. "You really want it in a controlled place," the special mission unit member said. "You don't want to lose that stuff." On some occasions, the operatives settled for "the least bad place to put them," he said. Of course, once the machines were up and running, someone had to translate the intercepted phone calls. Orange used a combination of its own personnel and contractors—"just phenomenal linguists" who not only understood Somali dialects but "had been doing it so long they could immediately recognize targeted or key individual voice characteristics," the special mission unit source said.

Despite JSOC's increasing ability to track targets in Somalia, the command mounted no successful air strikes or raids into the country during the first half of the decade. During that period, warlords paid by the CIA helped render "seven or eight" Al Qaeda figures out of Somalia, said an intelligence source with long experience in the Horn. Reluctant to put these detainees on trial in the United States, for fear of divulging the intelligence "sources and methods" that led the CIA to them, the Agency transferred at least some of them to its "Salt Pit" secret prison in Afghanistan.[15]

While Orange's technologies helped locate Islamists targeted for rendition, the CIA's warlord allies were letting it down on the wider battlefield. The Islamic Courts Union steadily gained ground during the first half of 2006, finally taking control of Mogadishu the first week of June, when it ran the secular warlords out of town.[16]

The warlords' defeat was a disaster for U.S. policy, for the CIA's strategy, for JSOC's operational ambitions, and for Orange's signals intelligence program. Not only did Orange—and therefore JSOC and the National Security Agency—lose access to the locations where it had been setting up its devices, it also lost a couple of the devices themselves when the Islamic Courts Union fighters overran the positions in which they'd been positioned. The devices, of which Orange had fewer than ten in its inventory, were not disguised. "This is clearly Western intelligence agency equipment, which was the biggest concern," said the special mission unit member. "So losing those was not good." The loss of the kit not only meant "a loss of collection," but also that the United States' enemies in Somalia, realizing that they were being listened to, might start engaging in deception when talking on their cell phones. "So you've got all sorts of problems created by that," he said. It took about a year for JSOC to regenerate its signals intelligence capability in Somalia.[17]

Part of JSOC's problem was that, just as Dave Schroer had predicted to the Defense Department leadership in early 2003, the demands of the Iraq War had forced JSOC to neglect the Horn of Africa. Now, three years after the invasion of Iraq, the growing Al Qaeda presence in the Horn and Yemen so alarmed senior military and intelligence leaders that they were prepared to take risks in Iraq and Afghanistan in order to deploy more ISR assets to the Horn.[18] In late 2006, however, the JSOC presence in Kenya consisted of no more than a dozen military personnel: two or three Team 6 operators; a technical surveillance equipment support service member, also from Team 6; one or two Orange signals intelligence squadron personnel; a Joint Communications Unit radio expert; and an officer to command the team, which operated out of the Nairobi embassy. Only the SEALs and the Orange personnel would go into Somalia.[19]

‼

The Team 6 operators were in trouble and they knew it. There were just a couple of them, plus a 24th Special Tactics Squadron combat controller, embedded in a larger unit of the security services of northeastern Somalia's autonomous Puntland region, and they had bitten off more than they could chew. It was June 1, 2007. They had been on the hunt for a multinational group of Al Qaeda fighters who had arrived a few days earlier in the Somali town of Bargal, on the very tip of the Horn of Africa, having traveled up the coast from southern Somalia. But the hunters had become the hunted. Outnumbered and outgunned, the operators turned to the combat controller as a last resort.[20]

The operations that led up to the Battle of Bargal began in late December 2006, when Ethiopia invaded Somalia in response to the growing strength of the Islamic Courts Union. (Ethiopia's traditional enemy, Eritrea, had been funding and supplying the Islamists.) In a December 6 cable, U.S. Ambassador to Ethiopia Donald Yamamoto accurately predicted that Ethiopia would invade later that month and that the incursion might "prove more difficult for Ethiopia than many now imagine." But oddly, although JSOC had been building up a small force at Dire Dawa in eastern Ethiopia throughout late 2006, presumably in preparation for combined operations with the Ethiopian forces in Somalia, the invasion took JSOC by surprise. "We should have been leaning forward to capitalize on this, and we did nothing," said a senior military official. JSOC was forced to scramble. It took until late March or April to deploy about a dozen operators to link up with the Ethiopians in Somalia. Most were from Team 6's Gold Squadron, along with a few Delta and 24th Special Tactics Squadron operators. Split into two- and three-man teams and inserted into Ethiopian infantry units, their mission was to advise and assist the Ethiopian forces, who were ousting the Islamists from Mogadishu and driving them south toward the Kenyan border. Even that tiny deployment, which required Rumsfeld's approval, created heartache among Washington policymakers who were fearful of a repeat of 1993's costly Mogadishu battle. "It was very uncomfortable," the intelligence official said, adding that if McChrystal had had his way, JSOC "would have gone with a much bigger capability and been much more aggressive."[21]

The command also stationed two AC-130 gunships at Dire Dawa, to which the Ethiopian government consented on the condition that their missions and presence on Ethiopian soil remain secret. At least one gunship was soon in action, striking a column of suspected Islamic Courts Union and East African Al Qaeda fighters on January 7 near the port of Ras Kamboni in southern Somalia. The main target of the attack, Aden Hashi Ayro, leader of the Islamic Courts Union's al-Shabaab militia, was wounded but survived and escaped. Another series of air strikes in the same area followed two days later. But a third mission near the Kenyan border a little more than two weeks later proved to be the gunship deployment's undoing. The early morning strike targeted Ahmed Madobe, a deputy of Islamic Courts Union head Hassan Turki, but only succeeded in wounding him and killing eight of his companions. A few hours after the strike, a helicopter landed carrying Ethiopians and Americans who seized him and took him to a facility near the Somali city of Kismayo, where they interrogated him and treated his wounds.

The Washington Post reported on the raid on January 24, infuriating the Ethiopian prime minister, Meles Zenawi, who had stressed the need for operational security and urged the United States to keep a "light footprint" in the area. Meles asked that gunships leave Ethiopia and for the United States not to engage in military strikes in Somalia, but to pass targeting information to his forces instead. In a January 25 cable, Yamamoto said he agreed with Zenawi that the gunships should depart. "Heavy press interest has made it difficult to secure and protect the AC-130 operations," he wrote. The gunships left shortly thereafter.[22]

Planned as a quick in-and-out operation to dislodge the Islamists, the Ethiopian invasion soon bogged down into an occupation. The JSOC operators spent only a few weeks with the Ethiopians before pulling out, their most serious casualty a SEAL who came down with malaria. By then, JSOC had opened an "outstation"—a small base or safe house from which a handful of operators and support personnel worked with local forces—in Bosaso, a port on Puntland's northern coast. "That was a relationship that started with the Black Hawk teams that we pretty much took over," said a Team 6 source. It was a team from Bosaso that found itself pinned down in Bargal on June 1. Out of other options, the 24th STS combat controller called the one source of U.S. firepower nearby: the *Chafee*, a Navy destroyer off the coast. The *Chafee* fired more than a dozen rounds from its five-inch gun. That naval gunfire—rare in the twenty-first century—enabled the U.S. and Ethiopian troops to break contact and get away.[23]

JSOC's missions in Somalia were taking on a lethal aspect. The aim increasingly became to kill targets, rather than to capture them. But that shift required a much bigger support presence in Nairobi to enable JSOC's small teams in Somalia. Accordingly, the task force presence in the embassy quickly grew to about seventy people as intelligence analysts and other support personnel arrived. But as 2007 wore on, the relationship between JSOC and the Ethiopian military began to fray. This was in part because the Ethiopians did not want to be seen as U.S. proxies, but also because the priorities of the United States and Ethiopia overlapped, but were not the same. Ethiopia's primary goals were to oppose the threat posed by the Islamic Courts Union and to prevent its bitter enemy Eritrea from using the group as a proxy to attack Ethiopia. The United States was focused on killing a handful of people at the top of the East Africa Al Qaeda cell, and had little interest in killing large numbers of Islamist foot soldiers. "If we wanted to kill a couple of thousand guys, we could have done that pretty much any time," said the senior intelligence official.[24]

The Ethiopian invasion essentially reinstalled Somalia's Transitional Federal Government, but the TFG controlled very little territory and was wholly reliant on its foreign backers. Meanwhile, from JSOC's perspective, the situation in Somalia was worsening. Put another way, the more force JSOC applied to the problem in Somalia, the more work the command found for itself. U.S. intelligence concluded that up to 300 Islamist fighters arrived in Somalia in summer 2007.[25] JSOC believed that a similar number of militants were training in just two camps near Ras Kamboni.[26] Operators also accompanied Kenyan forces to the border in order to help the Kenyans intercept senior Islamists trying to slip into their country.[27]

Although the decision to move assets from Iraq and Afghanistan to the Horn meant there were now Predators and manned ISR aircraft flying over Somalia from Djibouti, it was nowhere near the sort of coverage to which JSOC was accustomed. In contrast to JSOC's "Unblinking Eye" in Iraq, "in Somalia, it was a blink all the time," the senior intelligence official said. There would be days on end when task force commanders in the Horn had "no overhead collection capability," the official added.[28]

The lack of airborne signals and imagery intelligence collection might not have been so painful for JSOC had the Defense Intelligence Agency not turned its nose up at a golden opportunity several years earlier. In 2002, after a Defense Humint officer made an approach through an intermediary, a fiery Islamist leader named Sheikh Hassan Dahir Aweys let it be known that he was open to establishing a relationship with U.S. intelligence. Aweys would go on to become the spiritual adviser to the Islamic Courts Union and al-Shabaab, a man in regular contact with the United States' highest-priority targets in the Horn. "All Aweys wanted," said a special mission unit officer, was "respect." But in 2002 mid-level Defense Humint managers had "no interest" in pursuing a relationship with him, the officer said. "It wasn't sexy. . . . Aweys was a nobody. Few of us believed he was destined for greatness, loosely defined."

The fact that the U.S. government had already designated him a supporter of terrorism didn't help. "They didn't want us meeting with an actual terrorist," said the officer, many years later. "It was still early in the game. Nowadays nobody would think twice about it."

As the situation in Somalia worsened, a human intelligence source with the access and placement of Aweys would have been invaluable. "We could have been in his camp in 2002," said the special mission unit officer. "It would have been a lot of work for an unknown return, but looking back through a better lens, we probably should have [done it]. . . . That was a missed opportunity."

∗

With the AC-130s gone, JSOC turned to the Navy when it needed to strike high-value targets. On March 3, 2008, the task force tracked Saleh Ali Saleh Nabhan, a twenty-eight-year-old senior East Africa Al Qaeda figure, to a compound in Dhobley in southwestern Somalia. JSOC had been on Nabhan's tail for five years. Now they had him in their sights. There then followed what the senior intelligence official described as an "unbelievably painful" decision-making process as JSOC shoved its request to strike Nabhan through the upper layers of the U.S. government. Finally, President Bush signed off. A Navy vessel fired two Tomahawk cruise missiles at the compound, destroying much of it. JSOC's intelligence had been good. Nabhan was indeed at the compound, but he escaped the blasts. McChrystal later complained that the task force made a mistake in only firing two missiles ("to be conservative") when four would have done the job. "The miss was a bitter lesson for me," he wrote.

Eight weeks later, there was almost a case of déjà vu for the task force.

This time the compound was in Dhusamareb in west-central Somalia, and the target was Ayro, the al-Shabaab leader. Another torturous bureaucratic struggle ensued. "The confidence [the Bush administration] wanted was almost 100 percent, because they didn't want to have this compound destroyed with a whole bunch of women and children getting lined up," the senior intelligence official said. That meant the task force had to confirm Ayro's location as close as possible in time to the missile launch. Flying out of Djibouti, a Chain Shot aircraft—a secret variant of the Navy P-3 Orion sub-hunter—provided real-time video of the compound. President Bush gave his okay and at least four Tomahawks flew across Somalia. Sitting in his headquarters in Balad on May 1, McChrystal watched a screen nervously waiting for the explosions, "worried about the potential impact of a second failed strike on [JSOC]'s standing and its hard-won freedom of action." But this time, JSOC made no mistake. The missiles devastated the compound, hitting at about 3 A.M. and killing Ayro and several colleagues. JSOC's "freedom of action" was safe, but it would have to wait for its reckoning with Nabhan.[29]

24

Victory in Mosul?

It was another hot early summer night. Sweat trickled from under the helmets of the Rangers creeping north through the back streets and alleys of north Mosul.[1]

They had left their Stryker vehicles on the south side of a canal almost two kilometers behind them, so as to not alert their target as they approached his home, which, like those of many insurgent leaders, was not easily accessible by vehicle in any case. Parking so far away entailed significant risks. If the Rangers took fire en route to their objective, they wouldn't be able to reply with the Strykers' heavy machine guns, nor quickly evacuate any casualties on the vehicles. But the target that night was worth the risk. While the Coalition referred to Abu Khalaf as Al Qaeda in Iraq's emir of Mosul, he was really the organization's number two, second only to Abu Ayyub al-Masri, the Egyptian who had taken charge after the death of Zarqawi. For six years the task force had hunted Abu Khalaf without success. Today, for the first time, it had located him and was striking before he had a chance to slip away. During the previous few months, Task Force North had launched a series of raids that had steadily dismantled Al Qaeda in Iraq's infrastructure. The Rangers knew that now, June 24, 2008, they had a chance to strike a devastating blow against the network. This was the most important mission in which almost any of them had participated, and it exemplified not only the machine that Stan McChrystal had created and then passed on to Bill McRaven, but how far the Rangers had come since their assault on Objective Rhino less than seven years before.

Two files approached Abu Khalaf's house from the rear, a route selected in part to hide them from guards on the roof. As they moved quietly through the streets, one of two small civilian-style aircraft high overhead "sparkled" the objective, confirming its location for the Rangers by briefly illuminating it with an infrared light that looked like a spotlight in their night vision goggles, but was invisible to the naked eye. Various units flew such aircraft over Mosul, but it was usually Orange operating two-seater Cessnas or similar propeller aircraft packed with imagery and signals intelligence collection gear. If any insurgents ran from the building and somehow escaped the Rangers' cordon, one of the aircraft would track them with a pulsating infrared spotlight so that they could be dealt with after the initial assault.[2]

Tonight's was a platoon mission. One of the platoon's four squads had stayed to guard the vehicles. The other three squads of eight men each moved to the objective, hugging walls and staying in the shadows as they neared Abu Khalaf's house, which was in the middle of a block. One squad would take the lead in the assault, breaching and entering the house with the platoon sergeant, the unit's most experienced soldier. Another stayed in reserve to the front of the objective, in case it was needed to reinforce the assault. The remaining squad split into two teams of four, each taking position on a corner of the block to isolate the objective, not allowing anyone to leave or enter the area.

Less than ten minutes after leaving the vehicles, the Rangers reached the release point, which was a block from the objective. The four-man sniper-observer team and the isolation squad split off. The rest of the assault force paused at the corner, out of sight of the house. A block farther back were Colonel Michael "Erik" Kurilla, commander of 2nd Ranger Battalion and Task Force North, and the company commander, a major.[3] Kurilla was there to observe the mission. He knew the stakes were high. The major was officially the ground force commander, but his primary role was to keep Task Force North's operations center in the loop and request additional assets, if needed. It was the platoon leader's fight.

The entire assault force was itching to move. Every second they waited increased the chance of compromise. But the platoon leader, a captain who was the assault force commander, wanted to wait until the sniper-observer team was in position on a roof adjacent to the objective. The team's role was to ensure that the Rangers had "as many eyes and muzzles over all the apertures of the house as possible," said a Ranger on the mission. The four Rangers on the team were moving as fast as they could, shimmying from one flat rooftop to another across a thirty-foot-long lightweight graphite ladder. After examining pictures of the neighborhood, the team leader had picked a site his men could reach without being seen. The only problem was that they had to cross seven rooftops to get to it.

The assault force knelt and waited. The tension mounted. The Rangers were kitty-corner from the home of the most powerful insurgent leader in northern Iraq, out of direct line-of-sight of the objective but bathed in streetlights. "There's a sense of urgency to get to the breach," recalled a Ranger. But the platoon leader had done 200 missions with the sniper team leader, a sergeant first class, and knew that he could depend upon him. Finally, the team leader called to say that his team was in position. The trip across the rooftops had taken all of nine minutes, a pace that was "unbelievable, when you think about what's involved, moving four guys across one ladder," said the Ranger. "But . . . it feels like it's an eternity when you're sitting on a fairly well lit street corner at 11 P.M. in one of the most hostile cities in Iraq."

The lead assault squad and the platoon sergeant ran across the street and got ready to breach. Like many insurgent leaders' homes, Abu Khalaf's compound was defended by a high wall and heavy steel gate. His thick front door provided further protection. The Rangers would need to breach each simultaneously. The squad leader scampered up a ladder he'd placed against the exterior wall and dropped down into the compound, where he moved quickly to place an explosive charge on the door. The others readied the charge on the gate or climbed ladders to cover the squad leader as he set the door charge.

Whispering into a small microphone on his shoulder, the sniper team leader reported that two "military-age males" had been lying on the roof of the objective, but one had just stood up, having presumably heard the assault squad getting into position, despite the Rangers' efforts at silence. The captain checked a screen slung over his chest that enabled him to watch real-time video from the aircraft overhead. He too saw the man moving on the rooftop. At that moment, the platoon sergeant's voice came over the radio: "Three, two, one, breach."

A blur of movement and violence ensued.

Grabbing a pistol, the man standing on the roof took a couple of steps toward the building's front. That was as far as he got before the sniper team leader fired two rounds into his skull, killing him instantly, as the breaching charges exploded with a deafening bang. The other guard on the roof reached for an assault rifle. Below, the Rangers rushed through the door, which opened into the living room. "Good breach," said the platoon sergeant into his mike. "Eagles moving in. Foothold." In other words, the squad had blown through both gate and door and was inside the house. (In radio chatter, U.S. personnel were "Eagles.")

When "clearing" a building—i.e., moving through it and eliminating any threats—Rangers flowed through the structure like water, scanning each room in a synchronized choreography that was the result of hundreds of repetitions in training and combat. Only if they found any military-age men would the Rangers pause momentarily to leave a couple of soldiers to watch that room as the others continued through the building. It was not unusual for the Rangers to clear a compound in less than twenty seconds.

The living room opened to a hallway that led to a corridor with several bedrooms. In the first, the squad leader and a young Ranger found a man and woman sleeping on mats. Using memorized Arabic, the squad leader, who was a battle-hardened staff sergeant, and the other soldier—a twenty-one-year-old specialist armed with a light machine gun called a squad automatic weapon—told the couple to put their hands up. Neither did. The two Rangers repeated the order, as their colleagues checked the corridor's other rooms, finding two women and several children. But instead of putting his hands above his head as ordered, the man in the first room made as if to reach inside his robe. The squad leader's finger tightened on the trigger of his M4. He had less than a second to make a life-or-death decision.

⚒

By 2008, JSOC's successes elsewhere had caused the command's main effort in Iraq to shift to Task Force North. Having been squeezed out of Baghdad and Anbar, Al Qaeda in Iraq was increasingly focused on Mosul. Task Force North's strike forces were two Ranger platoons and a Delta troop. After weighing the units' strengths, Kurilla settled on a division of labor: the Delta troop would concentrate on helicopter assaults and vehicle interdictions in the Sinjar desert between Mosul and the Syrian border to the west, while the Rangers focused on urban ground assaults in their Strykers.

In the first half of the year, this combination subjected Al Qaeda in Iraq to an unrelenting campaign that targeted its foreign fighters, its financial and spiritual emirs, and its military leaders. The task force's operational tempo built to as many as eight missions a night. A strike force would hit a house based on signals intelligence that there was a cell phone linked to an insurgent leader inside. Once the strike force found the phone, analysts would load its contents into computers packed with advanced network mapping software, and combine what they found with what had been learned from questioning detainees. "The analysts would then push out a bunch of additional targets immediately, so we could then destroy that whole cell in one period of darkness," said a Task Force North source. "That wasn't happening in 2004 and 2005."

Abu Khalaf was Task Force North's highest priority target, but its analysts had never been able to link a cell phone to him. "That's why he'd been alive for six years," the source said. "He didn't even have couriers that were allowed to use phones."

The keys to finally running Abu Khalaf to ground were National Security Agency cyber sleuths and Task Force North's Mohawks, who in this case were Kurdish spies being run by the Delta troop. Suspecting that insurgent leaders were communicating by sharing an email account and writing draft emails that they never sent, but which their colleagues could read so long as they had the right username and password, the NSA had built a query that alerted it whenever the same username and password information were entered in different countries—like Pakistan, Syria, and Iraq—within the span of a few hours. From this, the NSA got username and password information for those accounts, allowing Task Force North's Mohawks to upload software onto computers in Mosul's Internet cafés that would alert them whenever someone typed in one of these username and password combinations. Analysts soon knew that they were tracking a senior Al Qaeda in Iraq leader from the contents of one of the accounts, but they didn't know his identity. Finally, someone with that username stayed logged on at a Mosul café long enough for the task force to get a Mohawk there and positively identify him as Abu Khalaf as he walked out of the café and strolled through an adjacent market.

Trailed by the Mohawk and a task force aircraft, the terrorist went back to his house, which became Objective Crescent Lake, simply because Crescent Lake was Khalaf's code name in the task force's targeting matrix. It was now mid-afternoon and Kurilla's instinct was to assault it immediately. But his operations officer persuaded him to keep the house under observation and map out Khalaf's network by having aircraft follow whoever left the house. There was a risk in this: one of those people could be Abu Khalaf, and Task Force North might lose him.

The task force quickly got two drones over the house. By 2008, this was routine for JSOC forces in Mosul, who were used to controlling as many as fourteen surveillance aircraft over the city at one time. In the task force headquarters at Forward Operating Base Marez, leaders and analysts watched as, sure enough, early that evening, Abu Khalaf left his home and returned to the market, where a black sedan picked him up. Kurilla was getting anxious. Even with the task force's exquisite surveillance assets, it was easy to lose a target as his car weaved in and out of traffic, or as he switched vehicles. But the highly trained imagery analysts kept their eyes on the car as it took Abu Khalaf back to his neighborhood, where he met with two men for thirty minutes in the courtyard of a house before getting back in the sedan and returning home.

It was getting dark. The task force put a plan together for two simultaneous assaults that night. One platoon would take down Abu Khalaf's home, the other would target the compound he had just left. After a quick series of briefings and planning sessions, the Rangers loaded onto the Strykers and rolled out of the gate.

※

The squad leader made his decision. He pulled the trigger, shooting the man in the head. Realizing what his squad leader was going to do, the specialist did the same, firing a burst with his squad automatic weapon. Their reaction "was aggressive," said another Ranger later, with studied understatement. If it turned out that the man was unarmed, there would be consequences.

The squad leader reported the room "clear and secure" and left the specialist to guard the woman. Above them, the sniper team leader shot and killed the second gunman on the roof. But as soon as the squad leader had left the room, the woman dove toward the body of her husband. Again the specialist had to make a split-second decision. Again his instinct told him to pull the trigger. He fired a short burst and the woman's head split apart. With the squad momentarily distracted by the firing, a figure darted from the last room left to be cleared and ran up the stairs clutching a pistol. He burst out of the cupola, only for the sniper team leader to put two bullets in his head. The gunman's lifeless body toppled back through the cupola and fell to the ground floor, crashing into a Ranger, the impact tearing the latter's night vision goggles from his face.

Abu Khalaf was dead.

The Rangers had been in the house for less than thirty seconds.

With the house finally cleared and all the adult males killed, the Rangers began the exploitation phase of the mission. An examination of the dead man in the first bedroom revealed a suicide vest. Had the two Rangers not fired when they did, they and perhaps several of their comrades would have died. Honed in nine combat deployments, the squad leader's instinct had saved numerous lives, as had the specialist's decision to open fire on the woman. She was the first woman that platoon had shot in about 200 missions. That there had been shooting at all was unusual. Only about 10 percent of the platoon's missions involved gunfights.

The Rangers also found about $120,000 in U.S. currency that Abu Khalaf had received from the man he met earlier that day—an Egyptian doctor who, the task force learned via signals intelligence, was in Iraq to work on some type of chemical attack. (Al Qaeda in Iraq had been trying to mount a chemical car bomb attack on a Coalition base for months.) The Rangers were elated. Kurilla, in particular, was "fired up," said a soldier who was there. They had achieved a huge victory with a perfectly executed mission. The assault's impact could be gauged from message traffic the task force intercepted over the next few weeks. "I'm tired of running," said one AQI fighter. "I have no place to sleep. They hunt me every day. I can't keep doing this."[4]

In conjunction with operations by conventional U.S. and Iraqi forces, Task Force North kept hammering at Al Qaeda in Iraq. The result was a two-thirds drop in car bomb attacks from March to June of 2008, from 234 to seventy-eight. For suicide car bombs, the drop was 59 percent, from twenty-seven to eleven.[5] Numbers such as these, combined with the successful assaults on Abu Khalaf and other senior figures, caused some outside JSOC to declare victory.[6] With its own cell that fused intelligence of different types from diverse sources, Task Force North's operational tempo was far beyond what had been imagined in the early days of the revolution started by McChrystal and Flynn. From a total of eighteen JSOC missions across all Iraq in August 2004, in the spring of 2008 a single Task Force North Ranger platoon averaged more than sixty raids a month. But as the capability peaked in Iraq, things were starting to change.

On June 13, Bill McRaven replaced Stan McChrystal as JSOC commander. McRaven was a SEAL officer with a reputation as a deep thinker, based in part on his time at the Naval Postgraduate School in Monterey, California, where he designed—and was the first graduate from—the special operations/low-intensity conflict curriculum. He turned his thesis into a book, *Spec Ops—Case Studies in Special Operations Warfare: Theory and Practice*, in which he presented his own definition of special operations, one that paid homage to the direct action missions that were the forte of JSOC and the SEALs, but which ignored the unconventional warfare approach that was the specialty of Special Forces: "A special operation is conducted by forces specially trained, equipped, and supported for a specific target whose destruction, elimination, or rescue (in the case of hostages), is a political or military imperative." With the exception of a brief spell at Team 6 as a junior officer, McRaven's career before he became an admiral had been entirely in non-JSOC jobs. But his stint after September 11 as director of strategic planning in the Office of Combating Terrorism on the National Security Council staff (working for retired general and former JSOC commander Wayne Downing) gave him invaluable insight into how national security decisions were made at the highest levels of government.[7]

McRaven was by no means an unknown quantity at JSOC, however, having served as the organization's deputy commander for operations during the middle of the decade. And while there were subtle differences between his command style and that of McChrystal—some observers thought McChrystal drove his subordinates slightly harder[8]—by and large McRaven continued where McChrystal had left off in terms of continuing to flatten and broaden the organization.[9]

After taking command, McRaven initially positioned himself in Balad. But JSOC's—and the U.S. military's—priority was shifting to Afghanistan.[10] In Iraq, JSOC kept up the pressure, but with fewer forces and more political constraints. The task force was now working closely with Iraqi commandos, a recognition that even the "black" special operations war was taking on more of a local flavor. But there were missteps. In a mission aimed at a Shi'ite "special group" in central Iraq's Babil province on June 27, JSOC forces killed an innocent security guard who was a cousin of Nouri al-Maliki, the Iraqi prime minister. In early July, in an apparent effort to mollify Maliki, Petraeus brought him to McRaven's Balad headquarters, where operators and leaders gave him an overview of the task force's capabilities—a highly unusual display for a foreign leader.[11]

For the final three years of the United States' war in Iraq, JSOC, like all U.S. military forces, was subject to the status of forces agreement (or SOFA)[12] between the U.S. and Iraqi governments. The agreement's requirement that JSOC obtain warrants for most targeted individuals before launching raids, and the Iraqi government's habit of releasing most terrorist suspects detained by JSOC, created intense frustration at all levels of the command's forces in Iraq. The situation regarding JSOC's targeting of Shi'ite militias and their Quds Force benefactors remained even more tenuous. Quds Force operatives were on an Iraqi government "restricted target list," meaning JSOC could not detain them without a warrant from Maliki's government, which rarely, if ever, provided one.[13]

By early 2010, most of the task force had shifted to Afghanistan. But the units that remained had one more major success to come, when on April 18 a combined JSOC-Iraqi special operations raid killed Masri and three other insurgents in a safe house on the border between Anbar and Salahuddin provinces.[14]

That raid aside, for JSOC no less than the rest of the U.S. forces, the 2011 withdrawal marked an anticlimactic end to its war in Iraq. McChrystal and other senior U.S. military leaders had always argued that JSOC's campaign was designed to hold the terrorists and insurgents at arm's length, to keep them on the back foot, to allow time for a political solution. There can be no doubt that the JSOC task force in Iraq achieved extraordinary successes against Al Qaeda in Iraq and its allies. But absent a holistic political solution in Iraq, and given the reality that the U.S. military presence was destined to end, those gains were always likely to be temporary. By the first week of January 2014, the organizational descendants of Al Qaeda in Iraq were back in control of Fallujah.[15]

For many in the task force, the frustrations that accompanied the status of forces agreement prompted jealous glances toward their colleagues in what had long been the secondary theater in the "war on terror." "The SOFA agreement," said a Ranger officer. "This is when everyone was like, 'Pack it up, boys. Let's go to Afghanistan.'"

25

Rangers Step Up in Afghanistan

After Operation Anaconda, in spring 2002, a debate took place at the highest levels of JSOC over whether—and how—it should proceed in Afghanistan. "The debate really was: what is our role here in Afghanistan?" said a senior JSOC officer. "Are we going to position troops forward here always, to be on the prowl and look for Al Qaeda senior leaders?" That approach didn't make much sense to some at JSOC. "The trail had run cold by 2002, after Tora Bora," said the officer. "There wasn't, in many ways . . . a very clearly defined mission. So do we want to now, with the cold trail, leave the nation's premier mission forces in these shit holes in Bagram or up in Kabul? And the answer in many cases, [was] no."

Concerned that its troops' highly perishable skills would atrophy if they were left with little to do in Afghanistan, JSOC drastically downsized its force there. A small task force headquarters remained in Bagram. As Delta became consumed by the Iraq War, the Afghanistan-Pakistan theater became Team 6's domain, with a small Ranger element in support. But although the September 11 attacks had been planned there, and the Al Qaeda leaders that had survived the operation to oust the Taliban from power were thought to be hiding just across the border in Pakistan, Afghanistan became a strategic backwater from the point of view of Washington and, therefore, of JSOC. Team 6 kept a squadron headquarters and a troop of operators there. The other operational parts of the JSOC task force consisted of little more than a Ranger platoon, three Task Force Brown Chinook helicopters and two Predator drones. Beyond hunting Al Qaeda, Team 6 operators had one other mission in Afghanistan: providing a personal security detail for Hamid Karzai, Afghanistan's new president.[1] "Karzai owes his life to their skills," said the senior JSOC officer.

By early 2004, the task force headquarters was housed in a large set of connecting tents at Bagram. JSOC's mission in Afghanistan was to hunt senior Al Qaeda figures, who had disappeared from view in the wake of Tora Bora. But task force leaders knew there was little chance of them gaining actionable intelligence at Bagram. "The mind-set was, you've got to be active when seeking out intel, and how are we going to be able to find these folks if we're not going out there and actually looking for them," said a special operations officer who spent time at Bagram during this period. The Rangers appeared to have little to do there, he said, so the task force "came up with this concept of the Ranger Action Plan, where the Rangers would go through a village and meet with the village elders and kind of go door-to-door and see what was going on." It was a mission more suited to Special Forces than young, aggressive Rangers, and it didn't turn up any valuable intelligence, he said.

One Ranger mission on April, 22, 2004, did, however, cost the regiment the life of its most famous member and threaten the careers of several officers in his chain of command. On that date 2nd Ranger Battalion sent a mounted patrol through Khost province that resulted in a confusing firefight in which Corporal Pat Tillman was killed by friendly fire.[2] Tillman had walked away from a successful career as a player with the NFL's Arizona Cardinals to enlist in the Army and join the Rangers, together with his brother Kevin. Although the Tillmans assiduously avoided the limelight after enlisting, their story had attracted a lot of favorable publicity for the Army, and in particular, to the Ranger Regiment. Even though some Rangers on the patrol knew immediately[3] that he had been killed by friendly fire, in a series of mistakes that spawned a controversy that continued for years after Tillman's death, the Rangers and JSOC reported that he had been killed by the enemy. That official line persisted long after the truth was known, with the Pentagon finally notifying Tillman's family on May 28 that he died at the hands of his fellow Rangers. It seemed as if the incident might derail the career of Stan McChrystal, but he was cleared of any wrongdoing.

✳

During the war's early years, special mission unit (SMU) operators emplaced disguised listening devices and cameras along the Pakistan border in an attempt to sniff out bin Laden and Zawahiri. "The SMUs didn't like doing that sort of work," said a senior JSOC officer. "They were difficult to put in, they were risky." They were also ineffective. "Nothing was ever actioned on those devices," he said, adding that their value declined even further as Predators and other ISR aircraft became more readily available.

Around 2005, JSOC also began contributing small numbers of Team 6 operators and, eventually, Ranger noncommissioned officers to form Omega teams with CIA Ground Branch officers. These were combined CIA-JSOC teams that trained and commanded the Agency's Counterterrorism Pursuit Teams—Afghan units that reported to the CIA, not to the Afghan government. In many cases they were the same Afghans that the CIA and Special Forces had recruited in late 2001 and early 2002 to chase the Taliban and hunt Al Qaeda. Originally known as the Afghan Combat Applications Group (a play on Delta's 1990s cover name, "Combat Applications Group"), the unit began life at a brick factory on the outskirts of Kabul, which was significantly expanded in 2003 and later housed a secret CIA prison.

The group soon numbered several hundred fighters. As it grew, and the Agency realized the importance of agents in the provinces who could blend in, the CIA divided the group into regionally and ethnically homogenous subunits. The Agency put these "pursuit teams" at its bases in Asadabad, Jalalabad, Khost, Shkin, and Kandahar, among others. At each location the CIA had a chief of base, Ground Branch operatives, and independent contractors (often former U.S. special operations personnel) training and leading the pursuit teams. The Agency gave each pursuit team a different name: the team at Jalalabad was known as the Mustangs, while the Asadabad team was the Mohawks. The Omega teams at each location were numbered: Omega 10, Omega 20, Omega 30, and so on. "We always sent at least two Blue shooters to each one of those, each deployment," said a senior Team 6 source. Team 6 operators were welcome on the Omega teams in part because they were all qualified to call in close air support.

Some pursuit teams grew very large (the team at Khost numbered 1,500), but for the most part they and their Agency handlers focused on minor insurgent and criminal kingpins in the areas around their bases. The CIA's ambition to have the teams conduct missions in Pakistan ran into problems because the Afghans lacked basic military skills.[4]

During the decade's middle years, one of JSOC's two one-star deputy commanders was usually in Bagram. The one-star had formal command of the JSOC forces in-country, but his day-to-day job was to deal with the other Coalition flag officers. Tactical command of the Afghanistan task force alternated between Team 6 and the Ranger Regiment, with either the commander or deputy commander of one of those units in Bagram at all times. But no matter which colonel or Navy captain was running the show, there wasn't much going on. Operators called those years "the dark times," said a senior Team 6 operator. "We'd do a [ninety-day] deployment and you might get one mission." By late 2005, it was clear something had to change. The Afghanistan task force was an all but forgotten offshoot of JSOC. During the daily operations and intelligence video-teleconferences that McChrystal held to bind his global network together, the Iraq task force leaders would get up and walk away when it came time for the Afghanistan task force leaders to brief, so limited were the latter's operations. "We were truly the B team," said a senior Team 6 officer.

What changed was a massive expansion of the target set that the task force was allowed to pursue.

Since arriving in Afghanistan in late 2001, JSOC forces had focused exclusively on Al Qaeda targets. That meant that even if solid intelligence linked an individual to the Taliban, the JSOC task force was forbidden from launching a mission against that person. "If there was no link [to Al Qaeda] there, we weren't doing it, period," said a senior Team 6 operator. "No matter how hard we fought for it: 'Hey this guy's a financier for the Taliban'; 'It doesn't matter, we're only here for Al Qaeda because this is the national mission force.'" This approach, along with the priority JSOC gave to Iraq, "basically took the pressure off the insurgency and let them build a strong base," the operator said.

McChrystal finally directed his task force in Bagram to go after Taliban targets as well. Having focused exclusively on Al Qaeda, it took the task force a little time to get smart on the Taliban, but once it had done so, its operational tempo increased dramatically, to an average of three missions a night. "It was a very ripe target set," said a senior Team 6 source.

By the time the task force turned its attention to the Taliban, the guerrillas "were very well established" and confident enough to move in large formations, said another senior Team 6 operator. But sometimes the Taliban were overconfident. Such was the case during Operation Niland II, a battle in late summer 2006 near Kandahar. A Predator had picked up a long line of fighters moving from one village to another. "It is a full serpentine column of dudes moving out, and they're moving at a good clip," recalled an operator. A troop from Team 6's Blue Squadron geared up and, together with a Ranger platoon, flew from Bagram to Camp Gecko in Kandahar (Mullah Omar's old compound now used by the CIA and Special Forces), where they continued to study the Predator feed, waiting for the order to launch. When the Taliban column halted at a compound, the SEALs and Rangers stood down, because they didn't want to take the collateral damage risks that an assault on a compound holding more than 100 people would incur. Back in Bagram, Captain Scott Moore, the deputy Team 6 commander who was running the Afghanistan task force, decided to use Air Force A-10 Warthog ground attack aircraft to strike the column as it moved through a valley. "As soon as they get back on the road and they clear the compound, they roll the A-10s in to strike," the operator said. But the jets missed their targets. The Taliban fighters scattered. Moore sent in the ground force, while continuing to pound the militants with air strikes. By now an AC-130 gunship was overhead, firing at the insurgents with its 105mm howitzer and 20mm cannon. The Rangers set up a blocking position at one end of the valley while about twenty or twenty-five SEALs swept through from the other end.

The result was a massacre. By battle's end, the task force estimated that 120 Taliban lay dead (most killed by air strikes), with the Rangers and SEALs having taken no casualties. But Moore was worried about the implications of reporting such a high number of enemy dead. "We can't say 120, the Pentagon will freak," he told his operations officer, a Ranger, who passed a lower number—eighty—up the chain of command.[5]

Even with authorization to target the Taliban, the task force never reached the operational tempo of its Iraq counterpart, for several reasons. One was the rural nature of the insurgency in Afghanistan, and the size of the area in which the Taliban operated, which prevented quick turnarounds of the sort possible when striking several targets in the same Baghdad or Fallujah neighborhood. At McChrystal's direction, the task force established more outstations to lengthen its reach. Despite this, virtually every mission required a helicopter assault, which in turn required helicopters, for which demand exceeded supply in Afghanistan. Another factor was the shortage of ISR (intelligence, surveillance, and reconnaissance) aircraft.[6] "The big one was ISR," a senior Team 6 source said. "We [didn't] have the support there to build those networks, to go after the little guy to work our way up the ladder." A third factor hampering the task force was what the Team 6 source described as "a certain degree of talent management" on JSOC's part when it came to which staffers it deployed to which theater. During the middle of the decade, "the cream of the crop's going to go to Iraq," he said.

Nonetheless, the task force mapped out the various Taliban groups that were sowing chaos in eastern and southern Afghanistan's Pashtun provinces. "We knew those networks very well, so it was very network-centric targeting," a senior Team 6 source said. At about the same time that Captain Brian Losey turned over command of Team 6 to Scott Moore in 2007, McChrystal decided to put Team 6 in charge of Afghanistan indefinitely, with the Ranger Regiment leadership running Task Force 17's operations against Quds Force and Shi'ite militia targets in Iraq. McChrystal also leaned on his task force in Bagram to ramp up their operational tempo. "The one thing I learned from McChrystal was if you can't get quality, get quantity of missions," said a senior Team 6 source. "'Even if you can't find the guy you're going after, continue to pressure the network,'" McChrystal would tell subordinates, he said. "Which meant, if you're not going out, you're wrong." The task force duly complied with McChrystal's directive. In 2008, it hit 550 targets, killing about 1,000 people.[7]

As was also the case in Iraq, such a high operational tempo, when combined with the pressure to launch raids based on incomplete intelligence, resulted in the task force assaulting a lot of targets where no insurgents were to be found. Even when successful, JSOC's raids created problems for the conventional units in whose areas of operations the missions were conducted. The task force would arrive in the night, assault or bomb a target, and leave. The next morning the townspeople would wake up to see a smoking pile of rubble where a house used to be, and turn their anger on the local "landowning" conventional Army or Marine commander. This in turn led to friction between the conventional military and the JSOC task force. "Sometimes our actions were counterproductive," McChrystal later acknowledged.[8]

Despite the vastly increased target set, Afghanistan's immense scale still hampered the task force, which was largely based at Bagram. Most operations required long helicopter flights to and from the objective, limiting the number of missions possible per night. In 2007, McChrystal told the task force to solve the problem by making more bases. So the task force built itself two new compounds: one at the Coalition's massive base at Kandahar airfield, and one at Forward Operating Base Sharana in Paktika province, between Kandahar and Bagram. McChrystal also deployed another Ranger platoon to Afghanistan.[9]

Team 6 used its years in Afghanistan to hone its tactics, which "had evolved over the years into being as sneaky as we could, so we could keep the element of surprise until the very last second," said Matt Bissonnette, the Team 6 operator writing under the pen name Mark Owen. He noted that Team 6 had given up "flying to the X"—i.e., landing right at the objective—in Afghanistan. "We were more comfortable being dropped off and patrolling to the compound." Contrary to the unit's reputation among some in the military as shoot-'em-up cowboys, Team 6 also learned early to creep into buildings and catch their targets off guard whenever possible.[10]

It helped that Team 6 had conducted nonstop rotations to Afghanistan—and particularly its eastern provinces—since late 2001. "They are the only tier that more or less has been in the same region for a decade," said a Ranger officer in 2012. "And so those [operators] . . . have a phenomenal understanding of that terrain, a phenomenal understanding of risk mitigation in terms of mission planning, maneuvering in those mountains, and so they have become very effective out east."

But Team 6's domination of the Afghanistan task force was ending. By late 2009, McRaven had tweaked the McChrystal-era arrangement that placed each special mission unit in charge of a combat theater or another portion of the globe. In doing so, he would write another chapter in the storied history of the 75th Ranger Regiment.

✳

No JSOC unit evolved more during the post–September 11 period than the Ranger Regiment, which went from being simply the muscle behind the special mission units' scalpel to an organization that assaulted the same set of targets as those units. As part of this evolution, the Regimental Reconnaissance Detachment was expanded to become the Regimental Reconnaissance Company, and took on many of the same characteristics and advance force operations–type missions as Delta's G Squadron and its Team 6 counterpart, Black Squadron. In fact, the regiment created reconnaissance platoons in the Ranger battalions because JSOC kept calling the regimental-level reconnaissance unit away for special missions, mostly in Afghanistan. The changes were reflected in the regiment's abandonment of its signature "high and tight" hairstyle in favor of the regular Army's grooming standards during Colonel Craig Nixon's tenure as regimental commander between 2003 and 2005. (The rules for the Reconnaissance Detachment were even looser. Its members were allowed civilian-style haircuts and to grow beards—what the Army calls "relaxed grooming standards.")[11]

The fact that McChrystal, a former Ranger Regiment commander, was running JSOC was no doubt a factor in the elevation of the Rangers. But so was the wealth of combat experience that the unit had built up during the first years after September 11. When McChrystal put a Ranger battalion commander in charge of Task Force North in Iraq, it was the first time Delta operators had worked under a Ranger officer at the battalion/squadron level. Then he put the regimental commander at the head of Task Force 17, the first time that the Rangers had been in charge of a task force at the colonel/Navy captain level. But stymied by politics, 17 was always the secondary task force in Iraq. In the summer of 2009, however, having taken command of JSOC from McChrystal the previous year, Bill McRaven went one better, putting the Rangers in charge of a theater: Afghanistan.

Several factors underpinned McRaven's decision, which he had been planning since the winter of 2008–2009, according to JSOC officers. The Taliban were clearly resurgent, leading to a perceived need for more strike forces in Afghanistan. McRaven could find those additional strike forces most easily in the Ranger Regiment, which had several times more shooters than either Delta or Team 6. The impending drawdown in Iraq also meant that more Ranger companies were available to deploy to Afghanistan. The admiral also told subordinates that with the conventional Army surging forces into Afghanistan, it made sense to put a Ranger officer in command of the JSOC task force. Rangers are, after all, infantrymen. McRaven figured that a Ranger officer would already know many of the Army battalion, brigade, and division commanders deploying to Afghanistan, enabling greater coordination between the two forces.

McRaven's idea was to shift the Ranger Regiment commander, Colonel Richard Clarke, from Iraq, where he had been running Task Force 17, to Bagram, and to replace Clarke with the SEAL captain who commanded Naval Special Warfare Group 2, the "white" SEAL organization that had been contributing platoons to Task Force 17. Meanwhile, McRaven planned to put the Team 6 commander in charge of JSOC's operations in the Horn of Africa and Yemen.[12]

By mid-2009, the Ranger Regiment was in command of JSOC forces in Afghanistan, which now included: a Team 6 squadron minus (i.e., a squadron command cell, but less than a full squadron's worth of operators) in the east; a Delta squadron minus in the north (which was just setting up at Mazar-i-Sharif); and a Ranger battalion in the south. More importantly, in the eyes of junior leaders, Ranger platoons were doing the same sort of missions as Delta or Team 6 troops. While no Ranger officer would make the case that a Ranger infantryman had the same level of individual training or skills as a special mission unit operator, "on the ground in we had the same job," said a Ranger officer. "That's where Regiment changed. We went from kind of the stepchild to [where], at least in Afghanistan, we were equal."

The United States' Iraq War was winding down, and that freed up units and other assets for JSOC's Afghanistan task force. No longer was Afghanistan the sideshow for the U.S. military in general and JSOC in particular. It was now the main effort. But there was a sense, particularly among Ranger officers, that compared with the conventional U.S. forces in Afghanistan, the task force now had so many resources that it had to show results. "Ranger platoons had more helicopters than friggin' infantry brigades had," noted a Ranger officer.

In August 2009, Erik Kurilla became the regimental commander and, therefore, the overall task force commander in Bagram. (When Kurilla was not physically present, the deputy regimental commander, Colonel Christopher Vanek, would run the task force.) Just as he did in Mosul as the Task Force North commander, Kurilla was keen to raise JSOC's operational tempo even higher. But doing that required the regional task forces to "lower the threshold" for targeting, said a Ranger officer. "You couldn't just go after very senior, high-level guys," he said. "You had to go after everybody that was a potential target. . . . So any type of IED cell . . . that we could target, we would target." However, this decision caused the FBI to pull its agents from strike forces in Afghanistan. "They were there for Al Qaeda," not the rank-and-file Taliban, the officer said.

The different regional task forces—and therefore the different units around which they were organized—had target sets that were almost unique to them. Team 6's strike forces in the east focused on foreign fighters; in the north, Delta concentrated on what were code-named the "Lexington" targets, which were primarily Al Qaeda and the Islamic Movement of Uzbekistan; the Ranger-run Task Forces South and Central targeted the Haqqani Network and other Taliban groups. (There was always one Ranger battalion deployed to Afghanistan. Its commander ran Task Force South, based at Kandahar airfield, while the executive officer oversaw Task Force Central at Forward Operating Base Salerno, in Khost, which is actually in eastern Afghanistan.) For a while, Delta also had a troop functioning as a vehicle interdiction strike force in Kandahar, reporting to the Ranger battalion commander. "They were absolutely laying it down, to the tune of ten to twenty-five EKIA [enemy killed in action] per op," said a Ranger officer.

The Marines were the "landowning" conventional force in Helmand province, which stretches almost 300 miles from the Pakistan border to central Afghanistan. The Corps targeted the senior Afghan insurgents who lived year-round in Afghanistan, while the Rangers would target the leaders who went back and forth across the Pakistan border. Although the Rangers in the south had Strykers and, later, more heavily armored Mine-Resistant, Ambush-Protected, or MRAP, vehicles in the south, they rarely used them because of the distances they had to cover and the threat of roadside bombs. Instead they relied on helicopter assaults almost exclusively. "We were completely dependent on helicopters," said a Ranger officer. "More helicopters equaled more missions."

But JSOC found targeting in the south more difficult than in the rest of Afghanistan, and much more challenging than it had been in Iraq. Southern Afghanistan lacked a robust cell phone infrastructure, and the Taliban soon got wise to how JSOC used the networks that did exist for targeting. Taliban leaders removed the batteries from their cell and satellite phones at the end of the day, and forced cell phone providers to shut down their entire networks at night, reducing to almost nothing the signals available for the task force to zero in on. "It was hard," said a Ranger officer. South of Kandahar there were no cell phone networks anyway. As a result, signals intelligence was "limited at best," a Ranger source said. However, senior insurgents in the south did use satellite phones, which the National Security Agency collected on, he added. (As in Iraq, the Rangers went to some lengths on raids to hide the importance of phones to the targeting process, for instance by using words like "handset" and "selector" instead of "phone" when talking to each other while searching a house. "If I have the ability to lead them to believe they were turned in by an informant, then I'm going to do that," the Ranger source said.)

The signals intelligence challenges served to raise the value of intelligence, surveillance, and reconnaissance (ISR) aircraft, particularly those with imagery capabilities. The strike forces would zero in on their targets' phone signals during the day. Once they had located the individuals, they would follow them using a combination of Predators and manned aircraft flown by military pilots and contractors. "You had to be very, very effective during the day, or you didn't go out at night," said a Ranger source. Squad leaders—staff sergeants whose traditional job was to control seven or eight infantrymen—were now spending their days in the operations center, on the phone with pilots flying the Predators (remotely) and other ISR aircraft.

The JSOC task force headquarters in Bagram distributed the ISR aircraft among the regional task force commanders, who in turn decided how to allocate those resources between their different strike forces. Colonel Mark Odom, the Ranger battalion commander in Kandahar during the 2009–2010 timeframe, used two criteria: what were his operational priorities, and which strike forces were getting out and doing missions. "If we could get another mission, another statistic, then he would give us [the assets]," said a Ranger. "It was all about generating the optempo."

How much of that operational tempo was driven by military necessity, and how much by a desire just to post numbers for the sake of the statistics, became "a very controversial question across Task Force, because Red [i.e., the Rangers] ran it," said a Ranger source, alluding to the view commonly held by Team 6 and, particularly, Delta, that the Rangers often failed to exercise tactical patience. For instance, while the Ranger chain of command would want to launch a mission as soon as ISR aircraft had located someone exhibiting a suspicious pattern of life, such as visiting a mosque and then a compound associated with the Taliban, "a Green officer would develop it, say 'Let's see where the guy goes the next three nights,'" the Ranger source said.

"There was a lot of pressure," the Ranger source said. The battalion commander would ask, "Why aren't you executing this target? Are you sure it's not good enough?" If the strike force commander replied, "Sir, we have no fidelity on this target," the battalion commander would be insistent. "I don't care, you're going," he'd say. As a result, the Ranger source said, in early 2010 "every strike force is going out almost every night." Pressure from above meant that the Rangers hit a lot more "empty holes"—objectives where there were no Taliban present. As the operational tempo increased, "the percentage of jackpot went down," meaning the percentage of raids that netted their targets declined to where as many as 30 percent of the Kandahar strike force's raids came up empty, a figure that rose to 40 or 50 percent for the strike forces in outlying areas, a Ranger officer said. Ranger commanders at the task force level "knew they were kicking in tons of doors that they shouldn't," but other than handing out cash to homeowners whose property they had damaged, they evinced little concern. "Red doesn't care," said a Ranger source. "Odom wants results, and if that means we're going to kick in the wrong guy's door, so be it."

Others in the JSOC community were convinced that this approach created more enemies than it removed from the battlefield. "We will lose because of it," said a senior Team 6 source. But a Ranger officer stationed in southern Afghanistan saw it differently. Odom felt "a moral obligation" to use the considerable assets at his disposal to help the conventional forces bogged down in a grinding counterinsurgency campaign, noting that Delta and the Rangers have closer links to the conventional Army than other JSOC units do. "Every frickin' Green and Red guy was in the regular Army, so we know how hard it is," the Ranger officer said. "We feel like we have to help them. We can't just sit by and be like, 'Oh, that target's not good enough for us.'"

"What the Rangers would do is target what the conventional Army landowning brigades wanted them to go after," agreed a senior Team 6 officer. Those targets were typically lower-level homemade bomb networks, rather than the senior leadership that the JSOC task force should have been targeting, he argued. The Rangers' efforts "to make friends across Afghanistan in the Army way" allowed the enemy to regroup, he said.

The Rangers had a harder time making friends with the Marines. There were "massive arguments" between Task Force South and the Marine headquarters in Helmand, according to a Ranger officer. "They wouldn't give us the airspace that we needed to bring in AC-130s or A-10s," he said, referring to the task force's fixed wing gunships and the conventional Air Force's close air support aircraft, respectively.

In 2007, the Ranger Regiment added a fourth company to each Ranger battalion, at least partly in response to McChrystal's desire to have three more Ranger strike forces in-country. Each Ranger company had three platoons, which became strike forces in Afghanistan. Prior to 2007, a

Ranger battalion had three companies, meaning it could field nine strike forces. By adding a fourth company, each battalion could bring twelve strike forces to Afghanistan. In contrast, Team 6 and Delta rarely had more than two troops each (with each troop functioning as a strike force) in Afghanistan at any one time.

A Ranger platoon was almost twice the size of a Delta or Team 6 troop, which gave it more firepower and more flexibility as a strike force. With attachments like dog handlers, snipers, mortars, a tactical psychological operations team, a combat camera unit, and an explosive ordnance detachment, a Ranger strike force would number about sixty or sixty-five personnel. Support and administrative personnel meant a Ranger outstation would have about 100 people in it.

In the spring of 2010, Kurilla decided to capitalize on the amount of firepower a Ranger strike force could bring to bear by keeping two 2nd Battalion platoons in-country for an extra two months. He combined the two platoons into Team Darby, named for Brigadier General William Darby, who was influential in the establishment of the first Ranger battalions during World War II. Kurilla had big plans for Team Darby, which was part of a larger JSOC surge that arrived in summer 2010, in concert with the conventional buildup in the country. Delta deployed an entire squadron, with a troop at Forward Operating Base Sharana in Paktika, a troop in Kunduz in the north, and a troop that roamed where the action was. Team 6 remained steady with a troop in Jalalabad and another in Logar. The Rangers added a company headquarters and two platoons. "This was Kurilla's big plan," said a Ranger officer. "Kurilla was going to have extra Rangers the whole time. The regular Army was surging, so Kurilla was going to surge."

Team Darby was renamed Team Merrill, a 120-soldier force named after Brigadier General Frank Merrill, who led a long-range jungle penetration force in Burma in World War II. Team Merrill's mission was very different from that of the single platoon-size strike forces into which the rest of the Rangers in Afghanistan were organized. "The idea is we're going to do movement to contact, we're going to do clearing operations," said a Ranger who fought in Team Merrill. "We're not going to do single human targets. We're going to go to the very, very worst places and we're going to clear those areas."

Team Merrill conducted operations in Kandahar province's Arghandab, Zhari, and Panjwai districts, and the Khost-Gardez pass in eastern

Afghanistan. Unlike other strike forces, the team would spend up to a week figuring out which areas to hit, and then launch a night raid. But the fights in which it found itself were so big that the team was usually still in combat at daybreak, which would lead to an even bigger fight during the day. Initially, the team did not come supplied for such lengthy battles and had to rely on airdrops. During one such daylight resupply in Zhari, the Taliban shot down a Task Force Brown Chinook, albeit with no fatalities. (The task force was able to repair the helicopter and fly it away.)

Kurilla quickly made Team Merrill his main effort in Afghanistan. "They [were] the biggest show in town," said a Ranger officer. In addition to two Ranger platoons, Team Merrill included a radio intercept unit from regiment headquarters. "They're not as special as the Orange guys, but same idea," said a Ranger, adding that the unit "had all the boxes for intercepting" the Taliban's handheld Icom VHF radios, "so this all becomes about VHF traffic."

The size of the firefights into which Team Merrill was getting during daylight hours got Kurilla thinking. "This is when the lightbulb goes off in Kurilla's head—if we stay out during the day, we get into an even bigger fight, meaning we went from killing five guys to killing fifty guys," a Ranger said. So instead of being dragged reluctantly into daylight fights, Team Merrill planned for them.

The missions evolved from both platoons clearing an area, to one platoon air-assaulting in to do the clearing while the other established a command post in a compound. It would spend all night turning it into a strongpoint, knocking holes for firing ports in the walls, digging a trench for the mortars, and setting out Claymore mines. The compounds were family houses. At first the Rangers let the families stay in them, but it soon became clear that was too dangerous for the civilians, as the house became a magnet for Taliban fire. Thereafter, the Rangers would "give them a bunch of money and boot them out, because their place is going to get destroyed," a Merrill veteran said. "It turns into World War II." The payoff to a subsistence farmer for getting kicked out of his home with his family and then having that home destroyed was usually "a couple of thousand" dollars, the Merrill veteran said.

Team Merrill began encountering Iraq-style house bombs—entire homes rigged to explode—in the Taliban strongholds in which they fought. When Rangers discovered such booby traps, they got very "kinetic" as the military would say, very fast. "You go up to one building and it's booby-trapped and we back away and we level everything," said a Ranger officer. "We're dropping bombs and firing HIMARS [High-Mobility Artillery Rocket System] at a rate that's ridiculous. In Arghandab on multiple nights we leveled villages. Empty villages, but we leveled villages."

The Rangers on Team Merrill did not feel bound by even JSOC's rules of engagement, which were looser than those that governed conventional units. "The rules go out of the window with Merrill," recounted a Ranger source. "When the sun comes up, when the fighting starts, if there's a male outside, we're going to kill him. . . . We would hear intercepts on the VHF radios and we couldn't triangulate it, but we'd be like, 'Well, it sounds like those guys over there,' and then we would just kill them. We were in massive fights, so it's not like we were murdering out of vengeance. It was more like we were in a fight and the enemy looked like the friendlies."

After tough fighting in Kandahar province during late summer 2010, Team Merrill conducted a series of operations in Helmand. "The Taliban in Helmand are organized and effective fighters," using mortars, RPGs, and recoilless rifles, said a Ranger who fought there. The Rangers listened to intercepted radio calls as Taliban observers adjusted mortar fire on U.S. positions. "These guys were not playing," he said.

Team Merrill had a variety of ways to kill Taliban, the most lethal of which flew. "We had everything," said a Ranger. "At night, Little Birds, AC-130, A-10s." During the day, the Rangers could call on Apache attack helicopters and A-10s, as well as larger bombers. But these fights took a toll on the Rangers too. In a "massive fight" called Operation Matthews in Helmand on October 1, 1st Battalion suffered more than a dozen wounded and lost Sergeant First Class Lance Vogeler, who was on his twelfth combat deployment, to Taliban fire. "On that day we dropped fifty bombs," said a Ranger. "We emptied two B-1 bombers."

As winter bore down, Team Merrill moved north to conduct operations in Kunduz province to support the Delta task force based in Mazar-i-Sharif. By now, JSOC's regional task forces were competing for the team to operate in their areas, because it brought so many ISR and close air support aircraft with it. "They did some pretty amazing missions—the tough, difficult fights," said a senior officer in the headquarters of the International Security Assistance Force (ISAF), the official name of the Coalition military effort in Afghanistan. "They went right into the most remote places where these guys were hanging out and really stirred things up."

But the team's mounting losses meant some Rangers became very conflicted about its operations. "For a Ranger, it's good and bad," said a Merrill veteran. "This is the highlight of what a Ranger wants to do. He wants to get in these massive fights, kill as many people as he can kill, destroy as much as he can destroy, but at the same time, we start to take serious casualties."

At least twenty Rangers were killed in Afghanistan in 2010 and 2011. Scores more were seriously wounded. By late 2011, the Afghanistan task force, now run by Colonel Mark Odom, had abandoned the Team Merrill concept. "They lost a bunch of guys, and that was it," said a Ranger officer. "It stopped."

In 2011 the operational tempo issue also reared its head again, creating what a Ranger officer called "a toxic relationship" between the Delta troop at Sharana and the Ranger-led Task Force Central headquarters at Forward Operating Base Salerno in Khost. Again the cause was the more aggressive approach taken by the Rangers, when compared with some special mission unit strike forces, who thought the Rangers were not exercising enough tactical patience. Of JSOC's fourteen strike forces in Afghanistan at the time, ten were Ranger platoons, while two were Delta troops and two were Team 6 troops. However, only at Sharana was a special mission unit troop working directly for a Ranger officer, in this case 2nd Battalion's executive officer. The Delta troop commander finally became so resistant to the Ranger chain of command's insistence that his operators mount raid after raid that he all but stopped his troop from doing any operations. As a result, a platoon from 2nd Battalion's A Company was moved to Sharana "to hit Green's targets for them," a Ranger source said. When it came time for the next rotation of units, Delta declined to send another troop to Sharana. The replacement troop went to Kunduz instead, giving Delta two troops in the north.

"The optempo thing becomes ridiculous," said a Ranger officer. The strike forces were conducting a raid a night, which was very low compared with the height of the Iraq War, but a lot for Afghanistan. "Red goes too far," said the officer. "Green gets really, really pissed off. They don't believe that going out every night is valuable, because you're kicking in people's doors that aren't bad. . . . One out of every two missions resulted in grabbing the wrong guy."

Organizational egos were also a factor. "Green was running it [in Iraq], Green was winning," said the Ranger officer. "In Afghanistan, Green was marginalized. Green came in at the end and got Task Force North. They got the least amount of ISR, they got the least amount of [close air support]. Out of all four [regional JSOC task forces], they were the least important. Green I don't think was used to being the least important."[13]

Delta's presence in Afghanistan increased as its Iraq commitments subsided, allowing it to put a squadron headquarters at the airfield in Mazar-i-Sharif. Its task was to prevent Al Qaeda establishing a sanctuary in northern Afghanistan. The German army provided the Coalition's main conventional force in northern Afghanistan, but the U.S. military held out little hope that the Germans could take care of business. "The Germans weren't going to do it, obviously, or didn't have the means," said the senior ISAF staff officer. "Our guys obviously did."

Delta's area of operations extended east to Kunar province, targeting the Islamic Movement of Uzbekistan, among other groups, said a Special Forces officer with multiple tours in Afghanistan.

The unit tried to repeat the success of its Mohawk human intelligence program in Iraq, but quickly discovered that Afghanistan was not nearly as conducive an environment in which to establish a spy network. "It doesn't work in Afghanistan," said a task force officer. "They tried it. The Mohawk program works because you can get a local Iraqi to go into any [city like] Mosul, Baghdad, and he'll fit in. But if I took my recruited Afghan source and sent him into Sangin [in Helmand], they would know in a fucking heartbeat that this guy didn't belong, and then he would die."

※

In June 2009, Stan McChrystal received his fourth star and took charge of the International Security Assistance Force. He had been in the job a year when a *Rolling Stone* magazine article that quoted his staff speaking in disparaging terms about officials in the administration of President Barack Obama forced his resignation. (Obama, a Democrat, succeeded George W. Bush as president in January 2009, but the change in administration did little to change the White House's reliance on JSOC.) McChrystal was replaced by David Petraeus, whose command lasted until July 2011. During the tenures of each general in Kabul, the twin issues of JSOC's night raids and civilian casualties gained a prominence that they hadn't before. "In '01, '02, '03, the occasional night raid might generate some local [protest] but in those days, the American presence was generally considered to be a good thing [by the Afghans]," said an Army civilian who made numerous visits to Afghanistan in the years after the September 11 attacks. However, with the passage of time, "you had less tolerance among the Afghans for any of that," as the population tired of the corruption in the Karzai government, which Afghans associated with the United States.

In rural Afghan society, even more so than in many other cultures, having foreign, non-Muslim troops force their way into homes was seen as a grave violation of dignity. In particular, it was an offense against the concept of purdah, in which women are kept segregated from men who are not family members. In the later years of the war, JSOC forces were virtually the only Coalition military units conducting night raids, in part because they operated under rules of engagement for Operation Enduring Freedom, the United States' post–September 11 war against Al Qaeda. The conventional U.S. military operated under ISAF rules of engagement, which were much more limiting, requiring an extensive approval process for any night raid. "Our rules were totally different," said a Ranger officer. "That's key. And that's [why] Task Force was able to do this at such a higher level, because we didn't have the bureaucracy or the approval authority [issue]. We could get a target that morning and execute it that night."

As ISAF commanders, McChrystal and Petraeus each adhered to counterinsurgency doctrine that held that victory required separating insurgents from the civilian population so that civilians could be protected and insurgents targeted. This was devilishly difficult in Afghanistan's Pashtun tribal belt, where the insurgents sprang from the local population. It also placed the senior military leaders on the horns of a dilemma. They knew that more than any other Coalition force, it was JSOC that was taking the fight to the Taliban. (The ISAF press office regularly issued press releases about Coalition operations, without detailing the units involved. The vast majority of those that involved offensive action against the Taliban were JSOC operations.)[14] But McChrystal and Petraeus also knew that night raids had become a political sore spot for Karzai and were hugely unpopular with the population, particularly when JSOC made mistakes and killed civilians, threatening the Coalition's ability to remain in Afghanistan.

A series of high-profile episodes in 2010 and 2011 brought this issue to the fore. In the most notorious and controversial incident, on February 12, 2010, Rangers conducted a night raid on a compound in Gardez, the capital of Paktia province in eastern Afghanistan. The raid was based on mistaken intelligence that insurgents in the compound were preparing for a suicide bomb operation. But rather than insurgents, the compound belonged to a local police detective, Mohammed Daoud Sharabuddin, who was hosting a party to celebrate the naming of his newborn son. Daoud had been through numerous U.S. training programs and was, essentially, an American ally. He wasn't even Pashtun, the ethnicity from which the Taliban is drawn almost exclusively. But when Daoud and his fifteen-year-old son went outside to see who was in their yard at 3:30 A.M., they were shot. In a chaotic scene, the shooting continued, and within moments seven Afghans lay dead or dying, including two pregnant women.

The surviving family members later accused the JSOC troops of trying to hide evidence of what had happened by digging bullets from the women's bodies with knives. ISAF headquarters put out a series of erroneous reports that said that the men killed had been insurgents and that the women were victims of "honor killings" by the "insurgents." The ISAF reports also sought to damage the reputation of Jerome Starkey, a Kabul reporter for *The Times* of London, who had started to uncover the deception. The affair came to a bizarre conclusion when, in an extraordinary scene, McRaven himself, accompanied by a large retinue of U.S. and Afghan troops, showed up at the family's home in Gardez with a sheep he was ready to sacrifice in a ritualistic apology. The family invited Starkey and photographer, Jeremy Kelly, to witness the event. Their reporting documented JSOC's involvement.

Several years later, exactly why the JSOC forces raided the compound remained unclear, as the commands involved had failed to release any records of the event.[15] But the incident and others in which civilians were killed by air strikes called in by forces on the ground, resulted in a number of changes. Among these was that JSOC forces were required to do a "call-out" before assaulting a target at night, meaning that they had to surround a compound and then give anyone inside an opportunity to surrender. This was tremendously unpopular with the strike forces,[16] who felt it gave insurgents a chance to destroy phones and other material that could help the task force map the Taliban network and lead to other targets. "You're really ceding the upper hand to the enemy," said a senior Team 6 operator, who added that Team 6 strike forces sometimes ignored the call-out requirement. "If we were sure the bad guy was in there, we weren't going to do a call-out," he said. "We weren't giving him an opportunity to destroy evidence or anything else. We were doing an assault."

Another requirement, which predated the Gardez massacre, was that JSOC would work with Afghan special operations forces on every mission. The Afghan force, recruited from the Afghan Commando units trained by U.S. Special Forces, was called simply the Afghan Partner Unit, or APU. In 2009, the Bagram headquarters insisted that every mission include at least five APU soldiers. By late 2010, that number had increased to seven. Views of the APUs' usefulness varied among strike forces. A Ranger officer who served in Iraq and Afghanistan commented that APU troops were "very tough, much tougher than the Iraqi military." But JSOC was too focused on training the APU troops to clear buildings, he said. If the United States wanted to leave behind a special operations force capable of hunting down Taliban after an American withdrawal from Afghanistan, it should have concentrated instead on training the APU on human intelligence skills, as the U.S. military's departure would deprive the APU of the signals and imagery intelligence assets that drove so many JSOC raids. "We should be focusing them on developing a source network, because that's going to be their only lifeline," he said.

Another Ranger said his strike force only brought along APU soldiers "for show" so that the task force and, ultimately, ISAF press releases, could boast that each raid had been "Afghan-led." The strike force would place a Ranger in charge of the Afghan troops on each mission. The Afghans rarely took part in the fighting. "They would just sit in a corner or hide in a room," the Ranger said. However, he said, that was not the message transmitted up the chain of command: "Was it reported like that on the radio? No, but the higher-ups, as long as I reported it right, they were cool with that. . . . I would always say, 'APU conducting call-out.' They would radio back, 'Okay, good.' Were the APU conducting the call-out? No. 'APU entering the compound.' Were the APU entering the compound? No."

The Ranger acknowledged that other Ranger platoons and Delta troops made more of an effort to get their assigned Afghans involved, but he said Rangers in general were resistant to training and mentoring Afghan forces, which he viewed as a job for Special Forces. "They were a means to an end," he said of the APU. "They helped us get out the door."

The view from the top of the chain of command looked very different. In a March 7, 2012, appearance before the House Armed Services Committee, McRaven, who by then had received his fourth star and been made head of U.S. Special Operations Command, defended night raids as "an essential tool for our special operations forces." But, since the previous summer, "we have really Afghanized our night raid approach," he added. "The Afghans are in the lead on all our night raids," McRaven continued. "They are the ones that do the call-outs, asking people to come out of the compounds, they are the first ones through the door, they are the ones that do all of the sensitive site exploitation."

The civilian casualty, or "civcas," episodes put Petraeus in a difficult position. He was a strong advocate for JSOC, having seen and benefited from the command's effectiveness as the Coalition commander in Iraq. But he also knew Hamid Karzai's patience was wearing thin. "He would just take ass-whipping after ass-whipping when he'd go to talk to Karzai about the civcas stuff," said a senior member of Petraeus's staff. "It was stuff that didn't seem like it needed to happen, if you will. They didn't have to whack these guys." A senior JSOC officer would brief Petraeus every week on the command's activities, and the command's liaisons, who sat a thirty-second walk from his office, spoke with him every day—a validation of McChrystal's insistence on placing talented liaisons in every headquarters that mattered to JSOC. "He spoke their language," said the senior member of Petraeus's staff. "He was very comfortable around those guys. . . . He was a big supporter of what they did, but . . . he was just as hard on them too. When they fucked something up he made them atone for their sins."

The task force committed one of its more egregious "sins" on October 8, 2010, when it tried to rescue British aid worker Linda Norgrove, who had been abducted on September 26. Intelligence traced her location to a compound about 7,000 feet up a mountainside in the Korengal Valley in eastern Afghanistan's Kunar province. Two years previously, the task force had conducted a successful hostage rescue of an American engineer kidnapped in central Afghanistan. In that episode, dubbed Operation Prometheus, Team 6 operators had landed about three miles from the kidnappers' hideout and patrolled through heavy snow to sneak up on and shoot both guards and rescue the engineer.[17]

The Norgrove mission fell to a troop from Team 6's Silver Squadron, the unit's newest assault squadron. As part of the significant expansion of JSOC, Delta and Team 6 were each directed to create a fourth line squadron, notwithstanding the fact that they found it hard to fill their three existing squadrons. Over the course of a couple of years, Team 6 built Silver Squadron by running an additional assessment and selection course, then adding a fourth team to each of the three existing assault squadrons, slowly filling the fourth troop with operators and then moving the three additional troops into the new squadron.[18] The troop that conducted the mission was, with one or two exceptions, filled with seasoned operators and commanded by "a very experienced guy," according to a senior Team 6 operator.

Unlike the operation to rescue the engineer, the geography of the area did not allow for the rescue force to land at an offset location and move on foot to the objective. Instead, it would have to fly straight to the target. The 160th's 4th Battalion flew the mission with Chinooks. There was nowhere to land, so the operators fast-roped down to the ground.[19]

A manned ISR aircraft overhead gave the SEALs second-by-second updates of what it saw. The aircraft reported a figure moving in the bushes. But what the observers in the plane had missed was that the man they'd spotted was dragging Norgrove behind him. On the ground, two SEALs reacted to the new information in different ways. Neither realized that the hostage was in the bushes. The aircraft's last report was that she was in the building. "It all comes down to decision making in that moment," said a senior Team 6 operator. A team leader who had climbed onto the roof saw the kidnapper and fired. At the same moment, another SEAL threw a grenade at the movement in the bushes. The team leader's shot almost certainly killed the kidnapper, but the grenade killed Norgrove. At the time, however, almost nobody on the objective or watching in the operations centers realized that a grenade had caused the explosion.

It took a few seconds for the awful news to reach Bagram. At first the SEALs reported "Jackpot," meaning they'd found Norgrove. "You hear 'Jackpot!' Everybody's like, 'Yes!' in the whole room," said a source who was in the operations center. The next words cut the celebrations cruelly short: ". . . administering CPR at this time." The atmosphere in the operations center deflated. "You just knew something went wrong," said the source.

At first nobody fully understood the truth about what killed Norgrove. Because the operators had been briefed that the kidnappers might be wearing suicide vests, the team leader who fired at the man dragging Norgrove thought that his bullet must have detonated such a vest on the kidnapper, causing the explosion. Even the operator who threw the grenade and his shooting buddy on the team, who was the only other person who knew about the grenade, didn't realize that the grenade had killed Norgrove, in large part because the team leader was so convinced that the kidnapper he'd shot had somehow blown up and that Norgrove had died in that explosion. When the troop returned from the objective to Jalalabad, the grenade thrower and his shooting buddy kept their mouths shut during the mission debrief. This meant that the story told to the British government, Norgrove's parents, and the news media was that a suicide vest explosion killed Norgrove. Shortly after the JSOC task force had put out this official version of events, the operator who threw the grenade finally informed his team leader that he had thrown a fragmentation grenade. "That's when it hit the team leader that, 'Okay, I didn't just shoot a dude that had a vest on, my own teammate threw a grenade,'" said a Team 6 source. The team leader was "horrified," according to a senior Team 6 operator, but rather than report what he knew immediately, he retreated to his living quarters for about another forty hours. "He didn't [report it] because he doesn't want to damage the reputation of the command," said the senior operator. "And throughout the whole next day he's chewing on it."

Meanwhile, Kurilla, JSOC's Afghanistan task force commander, had been poring over the video of the mission and realized that someone had thrown a grenade. "Once you see the video, it's unmistakable," said a Team 6 source. He called the squadron commander and command master chief up to Bagram and showed them the video. They returned to Jalalabad and called in the team leader. He had already decided to tell what he knew, but it was too late. The wheels of investigation had begun to turn.

Norgrove's death in a U.S. mission was already front page news in the United Kingdom and the United States, and a major embarrassment for Petraeus, who was about to travel to the U.K. for a visit planned in advance of the rescue effort. The general called Norgrove's parents and British prime minister David Cameron in the wake of the failure. Kurilla and others from JSOC had briefed Petraeus in the immediate aftermath of the mission. "That day there was just a steady stream of those guys coming in and out," said the senior Petraeus staffer. The revelation that it was a Team 6 operator that had inadvertently killed Norgrove only exacerbated the awkwardness and the anger. "There was some tension in there," said the senior staffer. "They had a great chance to save this lady and we ended up whacking her. . . . People were a little pissed . . . that the story didn't come out right the first time" with regard to how Norgrove was killed, the staffer said. "When it turned out that it was one of our guys, it was just 'Holy shit.' That was definitely a low time for JSOC because they'd built up some equity pulling off missions and then this was a low point for them."

The failure of the Norgrove operation was enormously painful and frustrating for the task force, the members of which knew that they had been one unnecessary mistake away from one of the most difficult, daring hostage rescues in U.S. history. It was "a very gutsy operation," said a Team 6 operator. "There's not another force that could have done it." But it also prompted some introspection in Team 6.

The operator who had thrown the grenade was on his first Team 6 deployment, and had previously been warned about throwing grenades on missions, said a senior Team 6 operator. "They counseled him but didn't do anything," he said. "They probably should have moved him on." But there were other factors behind the mission failure. Silver Squadron did no hostage rescue training during its pre-deployment workup, the senior Team 6 operator said. Instead, the team focused on "combat clearance" techniques. "[In] hostage rescue clearance, there is no scenario—no scenario—where you grab a grenade," the operator said. The same was not true for combat clearance. "So you've got a brand-new guy that made it through selection, gets to the squadron, and doesn't do any hostage rescue training beforehand. So he goes on deployment and he performs as trained." The senior Team 6 operator called into question the decision to use Silver Squadron for the mission: "If you haven't trained to it in six months, you don't do it."

Those who suffered most from the events on the objective were Norgrove herself, of course, and her loved ones. But there were costs on the military side as well. The operator who threw the grenade, his shooting buddy, and the team leader who covered it up were moved out of the unit.

For the latter two, this expulsion was temporary. Each returned to Team 6. For the operator who threw the grenade, the exclusion was permanent. "To this day, the guy that threw the grenade, he's a wreck," said a senior Team 6 operator several years later. Team 6's reputation had also suffered. "This is a big failure for the command," said the senior operator. Within seven months, however, the unit would have a chance to redeem itself.[20]

26

Hit and Miss in Pakistan

The helicopter carrying the Team 6 operators was gaining on the small convoy heading toward the Pakistan border. It was early March 2002, a few days after the bitter, bloody mountaintop battle of Takur Ghar during Operation Anaconda, and some of the same operators who'd fought in that snowy hell and lost their friends there were now being offered what seemed to be a chance at ultimate retribution. Overhead imagery had captured what appeared to be a tall man in a white robe and turban surrounded by other men getting into the vehicles, at least one of which was a late model sport-utility vehicle, at a compound that U.S. intelligence associated with Al Qaeda.

Now, a Predator was following the vehicles as they sped east. In the crowded operations center at the main U.S. military headquarters in Bagram, Major General Franklin "Buster" Hagenbeck, the senior U.S. commander in Afghanistan, was getting impatient as he watched the Predator feed on a flat screen. "Where's the dad-gum air? Push the air!" he shouted. "Sir, we've got two F-16s and a B-1B [bomber] on station and we are getting them in," his deputy chief of operations replied.

The vehicles pulled over and the passengers got out. Hagenbeck announced to the operations center that "all restrictions have been lifted." They were free to hit the vehicles with an air strike. In the helicopter, the Team 6 operators pleaded with Bagram not to bomb the vehicles, but rather to let the SEALs land and get eyes on the targets first. But Hagenbeck and his staff were determined not to miss what might be a fleeting opportunity to kill the man they were fervently hoping was Osama bin Laden. (As a conventional Army general, Hagenbeck would not usually be in a position to order JSOC forces around on the battlefield, but after Takur Ghar, he had asked for and received that authority from General Tommy Franks, the head of Central Command, for the remainder of Operation Anaconda, which was still under way.) "Bombs away!" shouted someone in the operations center. "Go get 'em!" yelled Hagenbeck.

The first F-16 missed the target. Its 500-pound bomb exploded harmlessly near the vehicle. The second F-16 made no mistake. Then, the larger B-1B dropped a dozen 2,000-pound bombs to make sure nobody got away. The operators' mission then changed from a possible ambush to sensitive site exploitation—finding the body of the tall man in white robes and collecting DNA to see if it was bin Laden. The Air Force had used cluster munitions—small bomblets that the SEALs believed had a 50 percent dud rate—against the convoy, heightening the danger to the operators. "We were pissed," said a SEAL.

The operators knew that they would be landing beside a scene of carnage, given the ordnance the Air Force had just dropped. But they were not prepared for what they encountered. Instead of more than a dozen hardened Al Qaeda fighters lying dead by the side of the road, "it was a family," said the SEAL. "It was just, 'Oh my God!'"

The height disparity between the man in white and the others had not been because the white-robed figure was very tall, it had been "because he's an adult and they're kids," the SEAL said. "ISR is a very dangerous thing sometimes," said another operator. "It really allows you to confirm your biases. I think it was seventeen women and children were killed on that target." The SEALs did their best to bury the victims in accordance with Islamic law. "One kid survived," said the first SEAL. "We patched him up and put him on a plane."[1]

JSOC's post–Tora Bora hunt for bin Laden was off to what could charitably be called a bad start.

⁂

A few weeks later Pete Blaber, on orders from Tommy Franks, and Spider from the CIA's Ground Branch, flew into Pakistan's capital city of Islamabad and met with Robert Grenier, the CIA's station chief. "There's no Al Qaeda here," Grenier told them. Amused by Grenier's refusal to acknowledge what was obvious, the pair later met with Pakistan's senior military leaders, who "literally belly-laughed" at their contention that Al Qaeda was regrouping in the tribal areas, according to a source familiar with the conversation. "The trail of tears goes right back into Pakistan," Blaber told the Pakistani flag officers. "We followed it. That's where they are."

With Pakistan's permission, Blaber and Spider stayed. Together with a few U.S. communications and intelligence personnel, they established two advance force operations cells: one in Miram Shah, the all-but-lawless capital of the North Waziristan tribal agency a few miles from the Afghan border; and the other in Wana, about fifty-five miles to the southwest, in South Waziristan. JSOC chose the locations for a reason. The command thought that bin Laden might be hiding out in Waziristan.

By mid-2003, the AFO team in the tribal areas had grown to two Delta operators, a 24th Special Tactics Squadron combat controller, a Team 6 officer, two Orange operatives (one of whom was an Urdu-speaking signals intelligence guy), plus Spider. The intent was to work closely with Pakistan's most elite special operations unit, the Special Services Group, hunting Al Qaeda's leadership throughout the tribal areas.

The Pakistani unit appeared supportive of at least some of the Americans' efforts, according to one AFO operator. Typical missions would begin with JSOC elements in Afghanistan generating intelligence on targets in the tribal areas, which they would transmit via secure satellite communications to the AFO team. The team members and their Pakistani counterparts would jump in their trucks, the Americans would use Global Positioning System devices to locate the targets, and then point and tell the Pakistani troops to search a particular compound. The team operated in Razmak, Miram Shah, Wana, and Parachinar—all towns in the tribal areas—and visited every border crossing. The AFO operators were always in Pakistani uniforms—sometimes dressed as members of the Special Services Group, at other times as border guards.

But the Pakistanis imposed such tight constraints on the team that it was sometimes like being "in jail," the AFO operator acknowledged. The Pakistanis never let the operators go anywhere without their Special Services Group and Inter-Services Intelligence minders. The AFO personnel referred to their Miram Shah outpost as "Miram Shawshank," in reference to the movie *The Shawshank Redemption*, which is set in a state prison. If an American tried to leave the base alone, a Pakistani guard would stop him at gunpoint. The U.S. operators thus became little more than "hostages," said a retired special operations officer, who blamed the Pakistanis. "They talked a good story, but they never would allow us to do anything," he said. "But that was an investment in the future. We knew if we left, we'd never get back in." The arrangement lasted at least several years.

Like others in the U.S. government, JSOC had entertained high hopes of routing Al Qaeda from the tribal areas with the help of their Pakistani "allies." Eventually, however, reality sank in. "It became very apparent that the Pakistanis weren't going to do anything," the retired officer said. But it wasn't just the Pakistani security services blocking JSOC's hunt for bin Laden and other Al Qaeda leaders in the tribal areas. The command also faced opposition from the CIA. "Pakistan was completely an Agency area, and they weren't going to let anybody [from JSOC] come in and do anything," the retired officer said. "It was the Agency's turf. . . . The Agency hired a whole bunch of former [special operations] and Marine guys to go out and do humint collection for them."[2]

Meanwhile, having become the lead special mission unit in Afghanistan almost by default, given Delta's commitment to Iraq, Team 6 set about preparing for any cross-border mission that the National Command Authority might order it to conduct. The first thing the SEALs had to figure out was what mode of transport they might use to cross the border, beyond the obvious helicopter solution. One option was to ride in undercover on specially outfitted "jingle trucks," the ubiquitous brightly painted vehicles that ply the roads of South and Central Asia, so-called because of the little chains that jangle as they move. To a casual observer, the SEALs' trucks looked full of lumber. But each had a hidden passenger compartment that could hold "a couple of assault teams"—between eight and ten operators—according to a special operations source familiar with the vehicle. "This was a Trojan horse kind of deal," he said. In early 2004, Team 6's Afghan agents drove the trucks across the border successfully, but without any operators in the back. "If you're going to blow somebody's cover, you don't want it to be yours," he said.

But the cross-border infiltration method to which Team 6 devoted the most time and money was the use of high-altitude, high-opening (HAHO) freefall parachute techniques. The unit considered HAHO parachuting its forte, so much so that it trained extensively to use the method to get the biggest prize of all: Osama bin Laden. Each Team 6 squadron that deployed to Afghanistan assigned one of its two assault troops the mission to be ready on short notice to conduct a HAHO jump into Pakistan to kill the Al Qaeda leader, if the United States got actionable intelligence on his location. The basic idea would be to load the troop (about fifteen to twenty operators) onto a Combat Talon at Bagram, where the operators would put on oxygen masks at least two hours before jumping, to clear all the carbon dioxide from their systems; fly along—but not over—the Pakistan border, have the SEALs jump at high altitude (probably about 25,000 feet), open their specialized chutes quickly, and then steer themselves on the wind into Pakistan, using handheld Global Positioning System devices. An operator from the squadron's 3 Troop, which at the time was the reconnaissance troop, would usually be the lead jumper, guiding the rest in and then getting them to the target. When done perfectly, a HAHO jump resulted in twenty operators landing close to each other, ready to fight, up to thirty miles from where they'd jumped, with the enemy being none the wiser. But such perfection was difficult to attain. It required hundreds of practice jumps and the use of unreliable computer programs to help a unit determine its "release point"—the exact right time and place at which to jump. While all freefall missions were challenging and dangerous, the operators considered HAHO a much tougher skill to master than HALO. "It's just a difficult process," said a Team 6 SEAL. "There's so many little things that can just go wrong with it."

Training for the HAHO mission consumed three to four weeks of the pre-deployment workup for the troop that had the mission. Much of this training was done in Arizona, home of U.S. Special Operations Command's Parachute Testing and Training Facility at Pinal Airpark northwest of Tucson, but at least one Gold Squadron troop spent part of winter 2003–2004 in Colorado, training for HAHO jumps in the mountains. Upon arriving at Bagram at the start of a rotation, the designated HAHO troop would immediately link up with the Combat Talon crews also on alert for the bin Laden mission and go over what was expected if they got the call. The troop would conduct "fly-away" rehearsals, in which the operators would load onto the plane and fly off, but in order to preserve the secrecy surrounding the HAHO capability, they never jumped.[3] "We did not want to really tip our hand," said a Team 6 source.

In early 2004, intelligence suggested that the SEALs might have an opportunity to put the training to use. A JSOC spy had reported a possibility that bin Laden was in a compound in Miram Shah. "There's a house where we thought bin Laden was at," said a special operations source. "We had a spy that was going in there and saying [it]." The evidence was mostly circumstantial—"movement patterns and vehicles," the source said. There was a tall man living in the compound who always traveled in convoys of multiple vehicles surrounded by numerous people who seemed to act deferentially toward him. "That's what we were looking at: somebody important is in this compound and it appeared to be bin Laden—tall fellow, and it looked like he had four or five security guys with him. That's what this Mohawk was telling us, and so we had planned on this target, got a little overhead stuff, and it was around a thirty-kilometer infiltration, so we were putting together the intel to be able to hit this target, but we were never able to confirm that it was him."

Nonetheless, the Joint Interagency Task Force at Bagram, part of whose mission it was to track Al Qaeda's network in Pakistan, briefed McChrystal on the possibility that bin Laden had been found. McChrystal asked the briefer to put a percentage on the likelihood that it was bin Laden. "I don't know," the briefer replied. "He's either there or he's not." "No, I need at least an 80 percent surety that he's there," the general said. The briefer told him that he couldn't give McChrystal 80 percent surety. "Well then, I'm not going to ask the SecDef for approval to hit this target," McChrystal said. "The threshold for being able to get execution to launch an operation [across the border] was kind of high," said a special operations source familiar with the episode.

A year later, a similar sequence of events took place when a Pakistani source for the CIA reported that Al Qaeda's second- and third-ranking leaders, Ayman al-Zawahiri and Abu Faraj al-Libi, were due to attend a meeting of Al Qaeda's senior leaders in the Bajaur tribal agency. JSOC hastily put together a plan for a Team 6 parachute assault onto the meeting, where they were to capture as many people as possible and take them to a pickup zone from which helicopters would take them back to Afghanistan. McChrystal and CIA director Porter Goss (who had succeeded George Tenet in 2004) were in favor of the plan, but Rumsfeld and his undersecretary of defense for intelligence, Stephen Cambone, thought it too risky. Rumsfeld ordered that more Rangers be added to the plan. The CIA's Islamabad station chief also opposed the plan. The Team 6 operators sat on a Combat Talon for hours before Rumsfeld canceled the mission.[4] "In the end we still believe that who we thought was in that target was there," said a senior Team 6 officer.

But Team 6 kept up its HAHO training, ready for a similar mission, especially if bin Laden—or UBL, as JSOC personnel often referred to him—was spotted in the tribal areas. "We were always training for it," said a senior Team 6 source. "We had a package always on alert to go get UBL with a jump option. If we found him, guys would parachute in—launch in a Talon from Bagram, get their gear on, HAHO, go to altitude, fly across border, twenty-five or thirty kilometers in, land and do the strike, and the rest of the squadron would come in via [helicopters] after it was over. Lots of planning for those."

The troop designated for the HAHO mission was kept on a very short string at Bagram during the first few years. "Then we, the operators, realized, 'Hey, this is futile—why don't we go out and do some other stuff?'" recalled a Team 6 SEAL. So the string gradually loosened to allow the troop to conduct other missions, so long as it could be back at Bagram ready to go within twenty-four hours. No matter where the troop was in Afghanistan when bin Laden was spotted, the mission would launch from Bagram, because that was where the troop kept its freefall gear.

To hide the fact that the unit had this capability available, Team 6 continued to avoid conducting freefall missions in Afghanistan whenever possible. There were some notable exceptions, however. In 2005 the task force got solid intelligence on the location of what a senior Team 6 source described as several "mid- to-upper-level" Al Qaeda figures in eastern Afghanistan. The mission fell to Red Squadron's designated HAHO troop, led by Lieutenant Commander Francis "Frank" Franky. The troop opted to jump in. "It was a big deal for us to use that package because that package was supposed be only for UBL," said another Team 6 operator. The mission was a big success. The troop jumped in and conducted "an extremely arduous long patrol" before catching the Al Qaeda personnel asleep, said the senior Team 6 source. "They nailed it," he said. "That was a big AQ windfall for us. We found all kinds of intel and we captured about seven dudes."

Another HAHO mission later that year did not turn out as well. On August 31 the Taliban abducted David Addison, a former British soldier working as a security adviser for a road-building project in western Afghanistan. JSOC soon had located Addison and his captors in a cave in Farah province, but time appeared to be running out. "We had some sort of report that they were going to kill him," said the senior Team 6 source. The task force quickly put together a rescue plan dubbed Operation Big Ben. The plan, which required a night jump into very rugged mountainous terrain, did not meet with universal acclaim, even from Commander Mike Goshgarian, the Blue Squadron commander, whose operators would be jumping. "Gosh was really against it," said a Team 6 officer. But Bill McRaven, JSOC's deputy commander for operations and the senior JSOC official in Afghanistan, was "really jazzed on it," so the mission was a go, he said.

While ISR aircraft kept the cave under observation, the HAHO troop flew on a Combat Talon from Bagram on September 3 and jumped into the night. Another troop's worth of special operators flew to a military airfield in Herat, from where the plan would have them fly to the objective on Chinooks, arriving almost simultaneously with the HAHO troop.

When the operators landed, "it was like the dark side of the moon," the officer said. "Boulders everywhere, big boulders, and they came down between the boulders." No jumper was seriously hurt—"We were very, very, lucky," he said—but when the operators reached the objective, all they found was Addison's body in the cave with his throat slit. The failure was a reminder that even as JSOC's ability to conduct other types of direct action raids and to hunt high-value targets was steadily improving, hostage rescue—the command's original raison d'être—remained a desperately difficult, unforgiving mission profile.

Team 6 continued to hone its freefall expertise. Its operators considered themselves the best exponents of HALO and HAHO missions in the U.S. military. But the capability did not come without a cost. On February 13, 2008, Senior Chief Petty Officer Tom Valentine, the troop chief for Blue Squadron's 1 Troop, died in a HAHO training accident in Arizona during the troop's workup prior to deploying to Afghanistan as the bin Laden "package."[5] An investigation determined that Valentine's parachute lines became so entangled he was unable to cut away his main chute and deploy the reserve. Three weeks later, Chief Petty Officer Lance Vaccaro, a SEAL going through Team 6's selection and training course, also died during freefall training in Arizona when his main chute failed to open and he did not deploy his backup chute in time.[6]

But for all the resources expended on training for such high-risk missions, during the first few years after the fall of the Taliban, JSOC's cross-border operations existed only in the operators' minds. The only people JSOC was sending into Pakistan were sources recruited from Afghanistan and Pakistan's border regions, said a source who served in the Bagram operations center. "We weren't really sending any of our guys over the border," he added.

That isn't to say that no JSOC personnel were in Pakistan after the AFO missions in the tribal areas finally ended. There were, but they were based in the Islamabad embassy. The command installed a team of about half a dozen personnel at the embassy working for a senior Orange officer, who reported directly to McChrystal. "He was working with our intel agencies and [the Pakistani military] trying to figure out where high-level Al Qaeda guys were in the Northwest Frontier Province," said a source familiar with the mission. While some JSOC personnel in Islamabad functioned mostly as liaisons, Orange also had multiple signals intelligence teams working out of Islamabad with the Pakistani military. "Orange definitely flew [their planes] in Pakistan and they had certain collection capabilities," said a senior Team 6 source. In addition to the collection packages on the aircraft, Orange also used "a handheld collection capability . . . to help the Paks," he said. However, Pakistan continued to keep a tight rein on JSOC's operations, so none of this activity was "unilateral"—i.e., done without Pakistan's consent. "There was nothing that Orange could do without the Pak permission," the Team 6 source said. "It was always with the Paks."

"You can't do anything unilateral in that country," said another special mission unit member. However, the same source declined to say whether Orange had ever placed personnel in Pakistan under nonofficial cover.

In late spring of 2004, there was an embarrassing incident involving a Delta sergeant major who was working as the JSOC team leader's senior enlisted adviser in Pakistan. Security guards at the Islamabad Sheraton Hotel where the sergeant major was staying searched his car and found hand grenades. "He had just come from the Northwest Frontier Province and I think he'd been driving around, so instead of dropping this stuff off at the embassy [as] he should have done, he drove straight to the hotel," said a source familiar with the episode. The team leader fired the sergeant major.

To get around Pakistan's constraints, as the decade wore on, Orange also flew Beechcraft civilian-style propeller planes based in Afghanistan along, but not over, the Pakistan border. The planes contained a "Typhoon Box" into which dozens of phone numbers of interest to JSOC had been entered. The box would register whenever one of them was in use, and then locate the phone.[7]

⁂

In the fall of 2005 Team 6 finally got the chance to cross the border, albeit on foot rather than via parachute. A Gold Squadron troop walked about ten kilometers across the border toward a compound they had named Objective Cottonmouth near the village of Dandi Sedgai in North Waziristan. The targets were Al Qaeda facilitators that intelligence suggested would be meeting at the compound.

The raid turned into a significant firefight. The SEALs killed "about six or eight" militants, said a senior Team 6 officer. One operator was shot in the calf. The wound forced him to medically retire. Another operator was shot in the head. His helmet deflected the round, but the force of impact flipped him over, injuring his ankle. "Cottonmouth was a good shootout," said a senior Team 6 operator. The SEALs captured four men and loaded them onto the Task Force Brown Chinooks that landed to take the operators back to Afghanistan. At first the SEALs didn't think their captives were valuable. "We used to call them dirt farmers," said the senior Team 6 officer. "We thought they were useless. The longer we held them, the more we got on AQ."

Within a few weeks, the "dirt farmers" had given up intelligence that allowed the United States to target Al Qaeda's third in command (which was fast becoming the most dangerous job in the organization), Abu Hamza Rabia. On December 1, 2005, a CIA drone killed Rabia and at least one other militant in the village of Asoray, near Miram Shah.

In a curious attempt to conceal the true nature of the attack, the United States gave the Pakistani military advance notice of the operation so that the Pakistanis could hit the same target with Cobra attack helicopters immediately following the drone strike.[8] Bizarrely, the Pakistani military then concocted a second cover story blaming the deaths on the premature detonation of a bomb it said the militants were building. The deception worked briefly. National Public Radio carried an interview with BBC correspondent Zaffar Abbas in which Abbas reported:

"The Pakistani authorities say there was an explosion inside a house which later on they said was a hideout of al-Qaeda operators in the region. And the suggestion has been that probably they were making some kind of a bomb or explosive device over there which went off. But the local tribesmen over there say that it was part of the Pakistani military's operation in which a number of helicopter gunships were used and rockets were fired at this place. And five people died, two of them believe[d] to be foreign militants, and one of them was Hamza Rabia."[9]

But within a couple of days news organizations had figured out the truth.[10]

Six weeks later, JSOC was involved in another strike in the tribal areas, this time a rare foray over the border by U.S. Air Force F-15E Strike Eagle attack jets. The target was a dinner that intelligence suggested would be attended by Zawahiri and other senior Al Qaeda leaders. "We thought it was [Al Qaeda's] two through five," said a JSOC source. The F-15Es were controlled by JSOC, but as they crossed the border they were placed under Title 50 of the U.S. Code, which governs covert operations, so technically they were flying for the CIA.

The pilots' aim was perfect. The intelligence said the dinner was going to occur in a corner room of the compound. "I watched that corner room disappear and nothing else in that building was impacted," said the JSOC source. "It was brilliant precision targeting." There was only one problem. The dinner had already ended and the guests had departed. "They'd all left just before that," the source said. Reputable news organizations such as *The Washington Post* reported that the strike "killed more than a dozen people," none of them members of Al Qaeda. (However, those same news organizations also described the incident as a drone strike.)[11] The JSOC source was skeptical of such accounts. "Some of those killed were complicit as hell," he said.

In the summer of 2007, U.S. intelligence had what it considered its best lead on bin Laden since the Al Qaeda leader's escape in 2001. The intelligence suggested that bin Laden would be attending a meeting in Tora Bora. JSOC put together Operation Valiant Pursuit. The 160th increased the number of helicopters in Afghanistan from five to eleven. The rest of the plan dwarfed that contingent. Five B-2 Spirit stealth bombers carrying eighty bombs apiece were to pummel Tora Bora. The Team 6 operators who had trained to capture or kill bin Laden were relegated to bit part players in what one senior military officer derided as a "carpet bombing" operation. In the end the expected mass gathering of Al Qaeda leaders never occurred and the mission did not launch. But for years afterward there was grumbling in some quarters that the time it took to gather such a large force together had let an opportunity slip.[12]

✳

After taking command of JSOC in June 2008, Bill McRaven wanted to reenergize the hunt for senior Al Qaeda targets thought to be in Pakistan's tribal areas. The intelligence that supported the search had gone stagnant and the JSOC commander wanted to "shake it up" by taking actions that resulted in phone chatter or other actions on the part of Al Qaeda personnel that would give the United States more targets. "We determined we needed to do a campaign plan," with the goal of launching a series of raids into the tribal areas, said a JSOC source. In effect, JSOC was trying to re-create the success of its man-hunting campaign in Iraq, which was predicated on the idea that when intelligence was in short supply, it was better to raid possible targets in an effort to "pressure the network" than it was to sit back and wait for perfect intelligence to appear. The task force came up with about eight locations that represented JSOC's best guess as to the whereabouts of Al Qaeda "associates" in Pakistan, the JSOC source said. A debate ensued over whether it would be better to hit the least important target first, or to start at the top of the chain and work down. Team 6 leaders argued for hitting the highest-ranking target first, on the grounds that the political reaction in Pakistan to news of U.S. ground forces conducting a combat operation on Pakistani soil might mean that one mission was all the task force would be allowed. McRaven disagreed. He wanted to hit the lowest priority target first, to desensitize the Pakistanis to the strikes and demonstrate how well JSOC could execute them. McRaven was the boss, so his view prevailed.

At the same time, Bush administration officials were debating the potential value of a JSOC raiding campaign. Prompted by a "mountain of [intelligence] reporting" that tied the highest levels of the Pakistani government to the support Inter-Services Intelligence was continuing to provide the Taliban, the administration was more willing to risk a Pakistani reaction in order to hit the terrorists that had found a haven in its tribal areas. "The White House let it be known that nobody wanted to be blamed for the next 9/11," said a Bush administration national security official. Nonetheless, getting the president to sign off on just one raid was a significant achievement for those advocating such a policy shift. "It was a big deal," said the official. "There were a number of meetings getting the president to approve it." The first strike would be McRaven's preferred option: the lowest-ranking target JSOC had, a minor Al Qaeda facilitator. "It was basically for a nobody," a Team 6 operator said.

Blue Squadron's 1 Troop—about two dozen operators—conducted the mission on September 3, flying as close as possible to the Pakistan border and then walking over the border at last light. A quick reaction force on Chinooks was also on standby. The target, named Objective Ax, was in the village of Angoor Adda near Wana in South Waziristan. Although it was a troop-level mission, the political sensitivity meant the Blue Squadron commander came along. Someone high up the chain of command had stipulated "that that level of rank was going to control it on the ground," the operator said. The SEALs arrived at the objective unseen, having walked virtually under the noses of a Pakistani military checkpoint. Operators scaled the compound walls, dropping down into the courtyard and opening the gate for the rest of the troop to enter. Then a door opened. A resident fired a shotgun blast at the SEALs. The next couple of minutes were chaos. "There were women on the target who started tackling our guys, and there were guys having to disarm these women, including throwing them on the floor," said a senior Team 6 source. "Nobody shot any women. They shot a few guys. But all these women started coming at them. . . . Guys were getting away, guys were fleeing." In the midst of the confusion, an aircraft nearby reported that Pakistani forces were moving toward the SEALs. That was all the squadron commander needed to hear. He called in the Task Force Brown helicopters—two MH-60 Black Hawks—and the troop departed at about 3 or 4 A.M., taking a few detainees with them and having suffered one minor wound from a shotgun pellet.

As the Team 6 leaders had predicted, Pakistan's government reacted strongly to the raid. Officials there claimed twenty locals had died. Foreign Ministry spokesman Mohammad Sadiq called it "a grave provocation." U.S. ambassador to Pakistan Anne Patterson was also angry with JSOC, telling task force leaders that they had put her in a very awkward position with the Pakistanis. "There was a lot of damage control and really it got pretty ugly," said a JSOC source. In light of the Pakistani reaction, President Bush forbade further raids. "The value gained from that op," said a senior Team 6 officer, "was zippo."[13]

27

A Reckoning in Abbottabad

In late January 2011, Bill McRaven was in Afghanistan when he received a call from Mike Vickers, the acting undersecretary of defense for intelligence. Vickers had some important news. The CIA thought it had a lead on bin Laden. Soon McRaven was on a plane back to the States, where he visited the Agency's Langley headquarters for a briefing from Michael Morell, the head of Special Activities Division. Morell told McRaven about the intelligence that led the Agency to believe there was a good chance that bin Laden was living in a walled compound in the town of Abbottabad, about fifty miles north of Islamabad.

McRaven said he thought a special operations raid on the compound would be "relatively straightforward," at the tactical level. The challenges would be getting to Abbottabad, which was about 120 miles from the Afghan border. McRaven also said he had two individuals in mind for key roles: a Team 6 squadron commander he liked, who he thought could handle something going wrong on the objective, and a SEAL captain who had long experience in Team 6, whom he soon assigned to work with a planning team at the Agency.[1] (For the captain, there was a certain symmetry about being placed in such a key role: he had been one of the first JSOC officers into the tribal areas on the AFO teams after Anaconda. His career had since taken him to Afghanistan, Iraq, and the Horn of Africa, as he rose to become Team 6's deputy commander.)

There was much speculation later about why Team 6, rather than Delta, was handed the bin Laden mission. Some suggested that it was because the JSOC commander, the head of U.S. Special Operations Command, and the chairman of the Joint Chiefs of Staff were all Navy admirals. The real reason is much simpler: if bin Laden was found in Afghanistan or Pakistan, it was always going to be Team 6's mission. The so-called Af-Pak region was Team 6's theater of operations. The unit had planned and trained for a bin Laden mission for years, and had already conducted multiple cross-border missions into Pakistan.[2]

But beyond deciding that if President Barack Obama ordered him to mount a raid, Team 6 would be the unit for the mission, McRaven did not follow convention. Instead of tapping the Team 6 commander, Captain Pete Van Hooser, or "PVH," as he was known, and letting him decide how to run the mission and whom to send, the JSOC commander declined to inform Van Hooser about the mission immediately. Instead, he went around Van Hooser, reached into Team 6, and selected a particular squadron—Red—and squadron commander for the operation. McRaven also waited several days after informing the Red Squadron leadership about the mission before telling the Team 6 commander, all of which made Van Hooser, the oldest SEAL in the Navy, "just livid," said a Team 6 source. The silver-haired Van Hooser, who had lost a leg in a parachuting accident, had been brought back onto active duty from retirement to run Team 6.[3]

McRaven's selection of Red Squadron, which was not Team 6's Trident, or alert, force at the time, also perplexed some Red Squadron operators, and led to a certain degree of cynicism. "Everyone knew the squadron that was already deployed could have pulled it off just as well as we could," said Matt Bissonnette, a Red Squadron SEAL chosen for the mission. "The only reason we were tasked with this mission was because we were available to conduct the needed rehearsals to sell the option to the decision makers at the White House."[4]

Some in Team 6 viewed the friction between McRaven, fifty-five, and Van Hooser, who at sixty-two was only on active duty by virtue of an age waiver, through the prism of McRaven's personal history with Team 6. As a young lieutenant, McRaven had served in Team 6 during the unit's early years under Richard Marcinko. But after only three months on the job Marcinko had fired him. The setback had no long-term impact on McRaven's career, and in retrospect, getting fired by Marcinko, who served time in jail, did not look so bad on his résumé. But McRaven never served in Team 6 again. Some operators thought he continued to hold a grudge against the unit because of his experience more than a quarter century previously.[5] "He [McRaven] holds his bad time at Dev-Group against everybody," said a Team 6 source, using a common abbreviation for Team 6's cover name. McRaven denied this, making the point to the author in 2014 that if he had held any grudges against Team

6, "it would not have been involved in all the operations it has been involved in over the last five years."[6]

The tension between McRaven and Van Hooser reached a breaking point during an early planning meeting at the CIA attended by a handful of people, including JSOC's deputy commander, Brigadier General Tony Thomas, and Command Sergeant Major Chris Faris, McRaven's senior enlisted adviser. The JSOC commander told Van Hooser that his responsibility for the mission would be limited to overseeing the training in the United States. When the force deployed to Afghanistan, it would be commanded by the Ranger Regiment commander, Erik Kurilla, who was running JSOC's Afghanistan task force at the time. Incensed, Van Hooser tried to resign on the spot, turning as if to leave the room. McRaven called him back, and everyone else left the room while the two SEAL officers hashed out their differences. By the end of the conversation, McRaven told Van Hooser that he could run the operation.[7]

꙼

Shortly thereafter, about thirty Red Squadron operators gathered for a meeting in a secure conference room at Dam Neck. They were told they'd be doing some training down in North Carolina for a joint readiness exercise, but they all understood something else was going on. It was clear from who was and was not in the room that the squadron's commander and command master chief had handpicked the most experienced operators from across the squadron to form a large troop of all-stars, rather than use an existing troop whose operators were used to working with each other in a team. Almost all the operators present "had double digit deployments" to Afghanistan, according to Bissonnette,[8] so the end result was a highly experienced set of individuals. But the decision not to just go with one of the squadron's organic assault troops rankled many operators and left lasting bitterness. "They cherry-picked all the guys that they wanted, who were their friends, and made the 'Super Troop,'" said an operator. "It totally destroyed unit connectivity. . . . A lot of people just up and left after that."

Red Squadron's leadership picked twenty-three operators for the mission, plus a couple of alternates in case someone got hurt during training. The plan was to fly twelve men on each of the two helicopters earmarked for the mission, in addition to the aircrews. The ground force's twenty-fourth man was a CIA interpreter who took part in the training from the beginning. A military working dog—a Belgian Malinois named

Cairo—would complete the ground force, which had about six weeks to prepare.[9]

Team 6 had been training for almost a decade to conduct a freefall parachute assault on bin Laden's location. Even though he had been found deep inside Pakistan, rather than in the tribal areas abutting Afghanistan, some experienced operators saw no reason to abandon that option, even though it would have required a Combat Talon to carry the assault force deep into Pakistani airspace. "The preferred course of action would have been the airdrop one," said a Team 6 source. "The guys would get in virtually undetected. . . . We trained for years for that."

But decisions made far above the operator level had determined that the assault force would infiltrate on helicopters, that it would fly to the X (i.e., fly straight to the objective, rather than landing at an offset location and creeping up to the objective), and that the helicopters carrying the operators on the most important mission of their lives would be like none they had ever seen before.

✳

The 160th Special Operations Aviation Regiment and the combat development organizations that support it had been experimenting with stealth technologies for many years, beginning with a program to create a stealthy Little Bird. The program progressed to include the Black Hawk, the 160th's principal assault aircraft. The work had two overall aims: to reduce a helicopter's radar signature by giving it a different shape and coating it in special materials, and making the aircraft quieter, which usually involved development of a Fenestron, or shrouded tail rotor. (Much of a helicopter's noise signature comes from its tail rotor.) The 160th took the issue of reducing aircraft noise very seriously. In training exercises the unit would time how far from the target—in time of flight—the rotor sounds could be heard. As a rule, the larger the airframe, the farther out the target could hear the helicopter. The 160th wanted to reduce the time between an enemy hearing a helicopter approaching and it arriving overhead by as much as possible. "Even [cutting] fifteen seconds is huge," said a 160th veteran. "And thirty seconds is amazing, because then you can be on top of the target and fast-roping people down."

The stealth Black Hawk gained almost mythical status, like a unicorn. "I remember first hearing about it . . . in 2000 to 2001," said a Delta source. The program quickly gained traction. "I remember in 2004 hearing that it was a line item in the budget," he said. Knowledge of the special access program was on a strictly need-to-know basis, and hardly anyone needed to know. Shortly thereafter the 160th regimental leadership came looking to 1st Battalion—the core unit of Task Force Brown—for two crews to go down to Nellis Air Force Base, Nevada, and start training on the new helicopters. In the end one crew went after a couple of pilots volunteered. "I never saw them again," said a 160th source. "They'd be permanently assigned out there." The program became more formalized. The aircraft were based at Nellis, but 160th crews trained on them at some of the military's other vast landholdings in the Southwest: Area 51; China Lake Naval Air Weapons Station in California; and Yuma Proving Ground, Arizona. U.S. Special Operations Command planned to create a fleet of four and make them the centerpiece of a new covered aviation unit in Nevada. By 2011 Special Operations Command had canceled that plan, but the first two stealth helicopters still existed, and certain 1st Battalion crews would rotate down to Nellis to train on them.

The additional material that made the helicopters invisible to radar also added weight and made them difficult to fly.[10] This gave Team 6's most experienced men pause. Rehearsals had revealed that the "helicopter was very unstable when they tried to hover," said a Team 6 operator. "Those things had been mothballed. The [pilots] hadn't flown them in a while, but they got back out there." However, he added, "rehearsing it in the United States is not like flying the thing in actual combat conditions. Combat is not the first time to try something, and an operation like that—a mission like that—is certainly not." But when David Cooper, Team 6's command master chief, put this view to McRaven early in the planning process and suggested the task force at least plan an alternative infiltration method, the JSOC commander gave the idea short shrift. (In fact, McRaven found Cooper's argument disrespectful and pressured Van Hooser to fire his command master chief, which the Team 6 commander refused to do.)[11]

Training for the operation was divided between Nevada and North Carolina. In North Carolina, the task force rehearsed the assault at a CIA training facility in Harvey Point, where the Agency had built an almost perfect replica of the bin Laden compound. In Nevada the task force flew both the stealth Black Hawks and the Chinooks against Groom Lake's approximation of the Pakistani radars they would be flying against on the mission. What they found, according to a Team 6 source, is that by terrain masking—using the terrain to hide from the radar—the Chinooks "could get in without being spotted by the radar." But JSOC and the CIA nonetheless insisted that the task force use the two-of-a-kind stealth Black Hawks.[12]

"The helicopters were really forced on us," a Team 6 source said. "These newfangled helicopters that had never been used before." During initial planning meetings McRaven had told Red Squadron to "look at all options" as they considered how to conduct the mission. But early on, the JSOC commander told them to forget about jumping in. "McRaven said there were too many wires," said the Team 6 source, who strongly disagreed with the admiral. "Every one of those operators, except maybe [the squadron commander], could have landed inside of that compound under parachute."

In Team 6, there were different opinions about whom to blame for the insistence on using the helicopters. Some operators thought the CIA was driving the decision. Others attributed it to McRaven. "He wanted to use these newfangled helicopters," said an operator. "He sold it to the president that way: These things are invisible to radar, they'll get in, the [Pakistanis] will never know we were there." When the helicopters proved unstable during training, the JSOC commander refused to revisit the decision, the operator said.

As they prepared for the mission, the operators' primary training challenge was to "break the habits from Afghanistan," where the vast majority of their missions had been based on the same template. "There were so many unknowns in Pakistan," said a Team 6 source. "What was the [Pakistani military] going to do? And . . . the civilians—in what was essentially a retired military town, a retired ISI town—what were they going to do?" The Team 6 and Red Squadron leaders put the operators through a variety of contingencies to prepare them mentally for dealing with eventualities that they weren't used to facing in Afghanistan. "There was no clear-cut answer to any of these scenarios," the Team 6 source said. The operators had to figure it out on their own. Their reaction to the initial scenarios was not auspicious. "They started off abysmally, with a sense of, 'kill everybody, even in the surrounding area' kind of thing," the source said. "But as they kept going on and the problems got more and more complex, you could see them self-organize, which is what SEALs do very well, working it out on the ground."

One contingency that those running the training made sure that the operators were as ready as they could be for was a helicopter crash. "We did so many downed helo drills that [the operators] were just sick of it," the Team 6 source said. "But they figured out the answers to these downed helo scenarios themselves. Nothing was ever pushed on them."

Other variations to the plan were considered and discarded. "The initial plan had Agency Ground Branch guys going in on the ground to cut off some of the intersections, but that was ruled out by the Agency as too risky," a Team 6 source said. While CIA operatives had established a safe house[13] and reconnoitered the area previously, by the time of the raid there were no U.S. personnel waiting or watching in the neighborhood, he said. The operators were not particularly intimidated by the tactical challenges or potential threats they might face on the objective. "This target wasn't any more complicated than hundreds of others we'd assaulted over the years," said Bissonnette. For any other target, the amount of rehearsals would have seemed like overkill. "We had never trained this much for a particular objective before in our lives," said Bissonnette. However, he added, "the extra preparation helped us mesh, since we'd been drawn from different teams."[14]

A big question was how the force on the ground should respond if the Pakistani military showed up and surrounded the compound. According to several published accounts,[15] McRaven advised the White House to seek a negotiated solution in that case while the troops strongpointed the compound. But to some operators, it seemed that McRaven told Red Squadron to surrender if they were surrounded. "Then he briefed that to the president," said a Team 6 source. "Thankfully, the president said, 'No, they're not going to surrender, they'll fight their way out and we'll go in and get them if we have to.' The guys were thankful for that. They would not have surrendered anyway. They might have nodded to McRaven, but they would not have surrendered."

The issue of what to do with bin Laden was simpler. "Bin Laden was the first time [we were told], 'This is a kill mission, not a capture mission, unless he was naked with his hands up,'" said the Team 6 source. (In this respect, U.S. policy had not changed since Tora Bora almost a decade previously, when, according to Delta officer Tom Greer, "it was made crystal clear to us that capturing the terrorist was not the preferred outcome.") In planning meetings with the CIA, Team 6 officials had argued that their normal rules of engagement were sufficient. "But they [the CIA] were adamant: kill him," the source said. "That message came from [CIA director Leon] Panetta." One thing the task force didn't have to worry about, a CIA analyst assured them, was Pakistani jets chasing the helicopters. "[He's] telling us that there's no way in hell the Pakistanis can scramble their jets, not at night, not going to happen," the Team 6 source said.

About a week before the end of April, the operators departed Dam Neck to stage at the task force's Jalalabad base. The president had still not approved the mission. Around the time that the bin Laden mission force arrived in Afghanistan, Kurilla and others in the Afghanistan task force were briefed on the operation. They provided the quick reaction force as well as combat jets flying along the border, ready to race to Abbottabad and provide close air support if the assault force needed it.[16]

On April 29, the president told his national security team he had decided to authorize the mission, but left the final call on timing to McRaven, who was in Afghanistan. D-day was set for May 1. But later that night McRaven pushed the mission a day to the right, as the forecast said there would be excessive cloud cover over Abbottabad on April 30.[17] By now the operation had a name: Neptune's Spear.

In one of the final staff meetings with McRaven at Jalalabad, two days before the mission, Colonel John Thompson, the 160th commander, made a final effort to dispense with the stealthy Black Hawks, according to a source in the room. "Sir, I really think we need to use the 47s for this and not these 60s," he told McRaven, noting the success the Chinooks had enjoyed against the Pakistani radar array in Nevada. The admiral was not amused at this late attempt to change the plan, the source said. "McRaven went off on him," he said. "Embarrassed him, belittled him . . . I felt bad for the guy." McRaven disputed this version of events, saying nobody advised him "against any facet of the UBL raid" and that he did not "chew anyone out publicly."[18]

✳

At 11 P.M. on May 1 the stealth Black Hawks took off from Jalalabad, along with three Chinooks carrying a quick reaction force and the gear and personnel for a forward arming and refueling point. The Chinooks were going to set down north of Abbottabad, ready to go to the assistance of the assault force if need be. The plan was for the Black Hawks to refuel there on the way back into Afghanistan. The flight passed uneventfully, the operators dozing in the helicopters until the first shout to alert them that they were nearing the objective: "Ten minutes!"

The operators shook themselves alert and rechecked their gear for the last time. The helicopters had wheeled around to approach Abbottabad from the south. In what was either a fortuitous coincidence or a piece of the operation never publicly acknowledged, the neighborhood in which the compound sat was swathed in darkness from what appeared to be one of the rolling blackouts that regularly afflict Pakistani towns.

With the helicopters a minute or two out, a curious thing happened: someone tried to call a phone associated with one of the two brothers who lived with bin Laden as his aides and couriers. This was unusual because it was the middle of the night and they didn't normally take phone calls there at any time. The call wasn't answered.[19]

Then, with the helicopters hovering over the compound, the operation suddenly teetered on the edge of disaster. As the SEALs got ready to fast-rope out of one of the Black Hawks, it suddenly pitched and seemed to slide toward the ground. The pilot wrestled with the controls, as operators scrambled to get clear of the door so that their legs didn't get crushed when the helicopter hit the earth. Unable to keep the aircraft aloft, the pilot nonetheless managed to slow its descent to such an extent that Bissonnette, who was in the stricken helicopter, said he didn't even notice the impact. "If not for his skill as a pilot it could have been a lot worse," a Team 6 source said.

The cause of the crash was a phenomenon called vortex ring state, or settling with power, which occurs when a helicopter's rotors cannot get the lift required from the turbulent air of their own downwash. It is rare for Black Hawks to settle with power, but these were no ordinary Black Hawks. The problem resulted in part from an oversight in the construction of the mock-up compound at Harvey Point: whereas the Abbottabad compound was surrounded by a brick wall, the Harvey Point replica made do with a chain-link fence. "That air bled out through that chain-link fence" in North Carolina, said the Team 6 source. "But in reality the compound had those solid walls and that bad air just came right back up into the rotor blades and that thing just lost power."

As soon as they touched dirt the operators streamed off the helicopter. Although the crash landing had upset their plans, they were now on familiar ground, in the sense that they were taking down a compound just as they did almost every night in Afghanistan. And unlike some Afghan compounds, this one was not particularly well defended, or at least, not by armed men. But the operators still ran into repeated problems trying to clear the compound. Even with a sledgehammer, Bissonnette and a colleague couldn't bust in the solid metal door to the gatehouse in which they believed bin Laden's courier lived with his family. In a furious exchange of fire the SEALs killed the courier while they were still outside the gatehouse. Operators sighted the other brother and killed him and, accidentally, his wife as she threw herself in front of him.

Climbing the outside staircase to the compound's second story, a SEAL saw a clean-shaven young man put his head briefly round the corner. The operator recognized him as bin Laden's son, Khalid. They called to him. "Khalid!" The youth stuck his head around the corner again and the SEAL shot him dead. "We had planned for more of a fight," Bissonnette said. As Bissonnette and two other SEALs moved past Khalid's corpse to ascend to the third tier, they knew they had killed three of the four men they expected to find on the compound. They had now been on the ground about fifteen minutes, plenty of time for bin Laden to prepare a defense. The point man got to the top of the stairs and saw a head poking out of the bedroom. He fired two rounds and the person disappeared back into the room. The point man moved slowly, keeping his rifle trained on the open door of the room. As he came around the door he saw two women screaming over the body of a man who had taken a bullet through his left eye. The round had continued on, taking a chunk off the top of his head. He was still twitching in his death throes. Bissonnette and a third SEAL, Robert O'Neill, fired several rounds into his chest. Three children sat bunched together in the corner.

Osama bin Laden was dead.[20]

The SEALs turned their attention to dealing with the women and children, collecting as much material of intelligence value as possible—after all, this was the Al Qaeda leader's home and office—and figuring out what to do with the crashed helicopter.

Under pressure to depart before Pakistani security forces realized what was up, the operators were forced to leave a large amount of potentially valuable material on the objective. Bin Laden, it turned out, was something of a pack rat. "There were things piled up along the walls," said a Team 6 source. "You basically walked in paths to get through the house. So who knows what was in all those boxes." The operators grabbed as much as they could of the potentially priceless intelligence material, stuffing computers and other digital devices into the trash bags each had brought for that purpose, "but they simply couldn't carry it all," he said.

"We left drawers unopened," Bissonnette said. "The hallway on the second deck had stacks of boxes untouched. We usually did a better job, but we just ran out of time. We were perfectionists, and while the rest of the operation went smoothly after the crash, the SSE [sensitive site exploitation] wasn't up to standards."[21] The contents of the material left on the objective would remain one of the mission's enduring mysteries.

As their colleagues filled trash bags with Al Qaeda's secrets, other operators set charges to destroy the helicopter that had crashed. The pilots weren't sure such drastic measures were required. They thought they could fly the aircraft out of the compound empty. "But it had already been rigged to blow and [the squadron commander] said, 'No, blow it in place,'" a Team 6 source said.

The operators whose job it was to fix the charges intended to erase all evidence of the helicopter's experimental nature couldn't reach the tail boom, which "was hanging over the wall," the Team 6 source said. But they had put so much explosive on the rest of the helicopter they didn't imagine they'd need to cover the tail as well. "They thought it would explode anyway, but it didn't," he said. "It sheared off. But no one got in trouble for it." The next day that sci-fi-looking tail rotor was the star attraction for the media and onlookers who descended on the compound. It was JSOC's own inadvertent calling card.

Thirty-eight minutes after they had landed, the SEALs were in the air again. Those who had flown in the Black Hawk that had crashed were riding out on a Chinook. But they weren't out of danger just yet. "Shortly after that is when the Pakistanis were able to figure out what happened," the Team 6 source said. "[They] spun up and scrambled their F-16s to hunt down those helicopters," which must have come as something of a surprise to the CIA analyst who had guaranteed it wouldn't happen. It should have been a race to the border, with the helicopters having a head start and the jets a significantly faster speed. But the jets flew off in the wrong direction. After the mission, someone in Task Force Brown sat down and did the math. Even had the F-16s flown straight after the helicopters, "it would've been close but they couldn't have got them" before they crossed the border, the source said.

✳

A day or two later, a C-17 touched down near Virginia Beach and the operators dismounted as if returning from just another mission. There was no fanfare, no ticker tape parade.

A little more than thirty-one years previously, a similar group of operators had quietly returned home from a vital mission overseas, also hidden from the public eye. They too were smart, patriotic, and highly motivated. But that is where the similarities end. Their mission—which had failed—had also involved helicopter flights deep into denied territory. Just to put the task force together had been a monumental effort on the part of the nation's military. In contrast, JSOC had run a dozen other missions on the night that Team 6 killed bin Laden.[22] The extraordinary had become routine.

28

Successes, and a Failure

Spring 2009 found Team 6 newly in charge of JSOC's operations in the Horn of Africa and Yemen. Events off the Somali coast soon gave the unit an opportunity to prove its worth to a new president in a high-profile mission with no margin for error.

On April 8, 2009, four teenage Somali pirates boarded and seized the *Maersk Alabama*, a 155-meter container ship that was traversing the Indian Ocean a little more than 300 miles from Somalia. The twenty-man crew was well trained in how to respond to pirate attacks and most hid from the pirates, even managing to temporarily capture the ring-leader, Abduwali Muse. But the pirates reneged on a deal to trade Muse for the ship's American captain, Richard Phillips, and instead all four pirates took Phillips hostage and sailed off in the *Maersk Alabama*'s large, covered orange lifeboat.[1]

Piracy had been on the rise in the waters off Somalia since the turn of the century, a result of the anarchy plaguing that country and the demise of its fishing business. In 2008 Somali pirates attacked 111 ships, seizing forty-two.[2]

JSOC had not been oblivious to the issue. Around late 2004 McChrystal had asked TF Brown to examine whether it would be feasible to use Little Birds to attack Somali pirates. From late 2004 to late 2005 TF Brown planned against that mission, coming up with a concept that would have had Little Birds operating off a cargo ship. "You could put Little Birds on any cargo ship . . . and no one would have known at night," said a TF Brown source. "Had we done that at night under [night vision] goggles over the water, they would not have known what hit them." The pilots were keen on the concept, so long as it didn't involve "getting stuck on a ship for six months or a year, sitting there waiting to just go shoot boats," he said. But nothing came of the plans, in the face of stiff resistance from Colonels Andy Milani and Kevin Mangum, who commanded the 160th from 2003 to 2005 and 2005 to 2008 respectively.[3]

It might have stayed that way, had the pirates chosen another ship to attack on the morning of April 8, 2009. But their capture—albeit brief—of the *Maersk Alabama* marked the first successful pirate attack on a U.S.-flagged ship since the early nineteenth century. Once they took an American hostage on the open water, the next stage in the drama was almost inevitable. JSOC got the call, and, since it was a maritime scenario, that meant a mission for Team 6.

Plans were soon afoot to deploy Team 6's Red Squadron, which had the Trident alert mission, to a ship off the Somali coast.[4] In the meantime, early on April 9, the *Bainbridge*, a U.S. Navy guided missile destroyer, arrived on the scene and began shadowing the lifeboat containing Phillips and his four captors. It was soon joined by the *Halyburton*, a U.S. Navy frigate. In a desire to get operators into position as soon as possible, while waiting for the White House to decide whether to order the alert package to deploy, JSOC ordered a handful of Team 6 operators from Team Nairobi to fly to Djibouti, pick up some parachutes, and then jump in to the Indian Ocean beside the *Bainbridge*.[5] They arrived on the night of April 8.[6] A little more than twenty-four hours later, in the early hours of April 10, Phillips attempted to escape by jumping into the water, only for the pirates in the lifeboat to catch up with him.[7]

Meanwhile, in and around Dam Neck, Virginia, beepers started going off April 10. Team 6 had been in existence for almost three decades, but the alert standard was still the same. Each operator who got the word had to be ready to launch in four hours. Most of Red Squadron descended on Oceana Naval Air Station, where two J-alert birds, which were now C-17s, not the C-141s of the 1980s and 1990s, were waiting. The SEALs loaded two high-speed assault craft on each plane, and took off for the Indian Ocean. The operation to rescue Phillips now had a name: Lightning Dawn.[8]

After an almost twenty-hour flight, with two aerial refuelings, the planes' back ramps opened, the sunlight streamed in, and the four assault craft flew out, followed by about fifty Team 6 personnel. Those fifty jumping into the Indian Ocean included most of Red Squadron, a few intelligence and communications guys, plus the assault craft boat drivers. (The high-speed boats and crewmen were primarily there in case the pirates managed to get Phillips to land, forcing the SEALs to go ashore to rescue him.) The need to bring the intelligence and communications personnel, for whom military freefall jumping was not usually a job requirement, meant three operators had to tandem jump with them, meaning the inexperienced personnel were strapped to the SEALs under one parachute. For at least one communications tech, this meant his first parachute jump of any kind was a freefall jump into the Indian Ocean on a combat mission. Captain Scott Moore, Team 6's commander, also jumped in to handle the interactions with Rear Admiral (lower half) Michelle Howard, who was commanding Combined Task Force 151, a multinational force assembled to combat piracy in the Indian Ocean. Howard's flagship was the *Boxer*, an amphibious assault flattop sitting over the horizon from the *Bainbridge* and the pirates. It was into the patch of sea beside the *Boxer* that the Team 6 contingent jumped. Moore and the Red Squadron commander stayed on the *Boxer*, while the squadron's executive officer, a lieutenant commander named Walt, took an assault team and some snipers to the *Bainbridge*.[9]

Once on the destroyer, the operators considered the challenge before them. They had, of course, trained for hostage rescue missions at sea, but usually with the idea that the hostages would be on a cruise ship taken over by terrorists, requiring Team 6 to use its trademark "underway" techniques to board the moving ship. "This was a much different problem," said a Team 6 source. "It was a single floating room. . . . It would have been easier for us to clear the *Maersk Alabama* than the *Maersk Alabama* lifeboat, because there's so many ways that you can board the *Maersk Alabama* with the element of surprise and never be seen, and there's so many ways that you can move on that ship without them ever seeing you, and then you can be on them in the bridge in a second." The lifeboat's enclosed design meant it lacked gunwales for boarders to grab on to. "It was like a space capsule," the source said. Moore asked a couple of Red Squadron's senior master chiefs for their thoughts on how to tackle it. "No one had any answers," the source said. "Okay," Moore told them. "We just need to let the situation develop safely." As long as the pirates weren't threatening to kill Phillips immediately, there was time to figure something out, the SEALs thought.

One option that the operators considered and rejected as too risky was swimming up to the lifeboat in the dark and killing the pirates. However, the SEALs did disguise themselves as regular sailors taking food to the lifeboat in order to get a closer look at the pirates and the layout of the small craft. Whether or not the pirates noticed the SEALs' full beards—which had become a tradition for operators headed to Afghanistan, where Red Squadron was due to deploy in a couple of weeks—is a matter of conjecture.

By now the pirates were getting very jumpy. They had run out of khat, the mild narcotic plant to which many Somali men are addicted and which helps prevent seasickness. And the U.S. Navy had surrounded them, preventing their efforts to reach Somalia, even though they were drifting in that direction.[10]

On the morning of April 12 the SEALs persuaded Muse, the pirates' leader, to come aboard the *Bainbridge*, ostensibly to help with negotiations and to get medical treatment for a cut on his hand he had suffered in a fight with a crewman during the initial hijacking. But in Phillips's opinion, Muse had decided to abandon his colleagues. "I think the Leader got off that boat because he saw bad shit coming down the pike," he later wrote in an account of his ordeal.[11]

Meanwhile, the lifeboat was floating toward the twelve-nautical-mile line marking Somalia's territorial waters. No one on the *Boxer* could tell Moore what the legal ramifications would be if the lifeboat crossed that invisible line. So in order to prevent that eventuality, the SEALs persuaded the pirates to allow the *Bainbridge* to attach a line to the lifeboat and tow the small craft, under the rationale that it would ensure a smoother ride for the three pirates (plus Phillips) left on the lifeboat. What it also allowed the *Bainbridge* to do was surreptitiously pull the lifeboat ever closer.

But McRaven, the JSOC commander, had his own ideas about how to solve the problem. From Afghanistan, he had told the White House his men were going to ram the lifeboat, according to Team 6 sources. "Our high-speed assault craft are still on the *Boxer*," recalled a SEAL. "We're using the ship's RHIB [rigid hull inflatable boat] from the *Bainbridge*. He's telling them he's going to launch it to ram the boat."

The operators viewed McRaven's actions as micromanagement. In their view, ramming the boat was "an Israeli tactic" that would have the disadvantage of knocking the SEALs off balance. Moore's goal was to get the pirates to give up peacefully. But figuring out what was going on in their heads was no easy task, once they exhausted their supply of khat. At that point, "they're getting really weird," recalled a Team 6 source.

McRaven wanted the *Bainbridge* to stop towing the lifeboat, but gave

Moore "emergency assault authority," meaning that if there appeared to be an immediate threat to Phillips's life, the Team 6 commander had the authority to act. But while Moore and McRaven were discussing what steps to take next, Walt had taken the initiative and positioned snipers on the destroyer's fantail, ready to take out all three pirates on the lifeboat should the opportunity present itself. That chance came soon. The tension, lack of khat, and sleep deprivation were affecting the three remaining pirates. Phillips was acting belligerently with them. A pirate fired an AK round off the front of the lifeboat. But as the pirates argued with each other and Phillips that night, they finally exposed themselves simultaneously to the snipers on the *Bainbridge*. Walt called Moore. "They're losing it," he said. "We got the third shot." "Cleared hot," Moore replied. "But don't fuck it up."[12]

Half a dozen shots rang out in the space of a couple of seconds and all three pirates dropped dead or dying to the floor. One squeezed off a single harmless AK round as his last act alive. Huddled on the lifeboat floor, Phillips was safe, a fact confirmed by two operators who slid down the rope to get onto the lifeboat as quickly as possible.[13] The snipers had performed perfectly, even though killing the pirates was not the SEALs' most desired outcome. "Our team tried everything in our power to get those fuckers to give up," said a Team 6 source. "We weren't looking to fucking plug 'em."

Walt waited to get Phillips onto the *Bainbridge* before passing the good news to the *Boxer*. In the meantime McRaven called again to order the SEALs to stop towing the lifeboat. Instead, Moore was able to tell him that the pirates were dead and Phillips was on the *Bainbridge*. It was a remarkable success. But it took a while before either JSOC or the Obama administration decided to shower the SEALs with plaudits.[14] "We were not instantly heroes," said a Team 6 source. "It took about twelve hours for . . . JSOC and the administration to realize that the Americans that know about this are like, 'Wow, these are the greatest guys ever!'"

The rescue of Phillips was at the time the most high-profile mission Team 6 had ever undertaken. It was also the first occasion on which the United States' new president, Barack Obama, had had to rely on JSOC. When word of the success reached the White House, Obama called McRaven in Afghanistan. "Great job," he told the admiral.[15] It would not be the last time the president had cause to congratulate him.

Five months later Team 6 was back on a destroyer sailing off the Somali coast. This time their target was Saleh Ali Saleh Nabhan, the senior East African Al Qaeda leader JSOC had been hunting for years and had missed with a cruise missile strike in March 2008.

For several months a combination of human and signals intelligence had allowed JSOC to track Nabhan around the clock. The Al Qaeda figure had become lazy with his security arrangements. "There was a sense that he had gotten very loose and arrogant, using his phone as often as he could," said a military intelligence official. "[He] set a lot of patterns—always traveled certain roads." The analysts had refined Nabhan's pattern of life to the point that they could forecast where and when he would be traveling through Somalia, along what roads, and in what vehicle. With Nabhan's movements so predictable, JSOC began to work on plans to kill or capture him, while at the same time engaging in an arduous process to get White House approval for the mission, just as it had for the previous year's failed strike. The prospect of U.S. special operators fighting it out with Al Qaeda militants on the ground in Somalia made policymakers even more risk averse than usual. Several Obama administration national security officials had been in government at the time of the October 1993 Mogadishu battle in which eighteen U.S. soldiers died, almost all from JSOC's task force. "Any time you say 'Somalia [and] task force,' instantly 1993 gets thrown up in [your] face," said an officer who helped plan the Nabhan mission. But JSOC had assembled its arguments well. Its analysts expected Nabhan to drive along southern Somalia's coast road soon, and they divided the route they expected him to take into red, yellow, and green sections, depending on the risk to civilians of any strike in those areas. They determined that there was an excellent opportunity to strike Nabhan as he drove through an isolated area.[16]

In the second week of September, Chairman of the Joint Chiefs of Staff Admiral Mike Mullen chaired an early evening secure videoteleconference of about forty officials in which McRaven gave a highly classified PowerPoint briefing that detailed three different options for getting Nabhan. The first was a missile strike, delivered either from an aircraft or a Navy ship. This option carried the least risk, but also the least potential reward, as there would be no way to exploit the site for intelligence afterward, and Nabhan would be dead, and therefore unavailable for interrogation. The second option was also a lethal strike, but carried out by two Task Force Brown AH-6 Little Bird attack helicopters, with a small force of less than a dozen Team 6 operators following up on a pair of MH-6 Little Bird lift helicopters to exploit the site and collect Nabhan's body, or at least some DNA extracted from it, to confirm his identity. The third option was a helicopter vehicle interdiction, like the second, but with the aim of capturing Nabhan rather than killing him. This was the highest-risk option. All the forces required for each option were already in position. The SEALs and the Little Birds and crews had flown out to the region almost four weeks previously and were on two destroyers, one of which was the *Bainbridge,* sitting off the coast of Somalia just out of sight of land.

Despite the group's initial reluctance to countenance a mission in which there was any possibility of putting U.S. boots on the ground—"Somalia, helicopters, capture. I just don't like the sound of this," said Daniel Benjamin, the State Department's counterterrorism coordinator during the meeting—the upshot of the meeting was that the president was presented with a kill option and a capture option. However, the officials did not really see the capture option as viable, because the Obama administration had yet to figure out a policy for dealing with terrorists captured by U.S. forces outside Afghanistan and Iraq. If the United States wanted to remove Nabhan from the battlefield, it would have to kill him. JSOC had done its preparatory work well. At the cabinet level, the reaction of the Obama administration's senior national security leaders was, "This is clean," according to a source privy to the discussions. Obama signed off on the lethal strike that night.[17]

The next day, September 14, Nabhan set out with three colleagues to make the 300-mile trip from Merka to Kismayo in southern Somalia, just as JSOC's analysts had predicted. JSOC's plan had evolved since McRaven's PowerPoint briefing. It now involved Task Force Silver, the covered Air Force unit, flying a civilian-style propeller aircraft made by the Spanish firm CASA along Nabhan's route and firing a Griffin missile at his car. Designed to minimize the risk of collateral damage while neutralizing the intended target, the Griffin could be used as a rocket-powered missile or a guided bomb and had only been in production since 2008. But at the last moment, with the plane in the air, clouds rolled in and foiled the plan. "They could not see the car and therefore could not use the Griffin," said a Team 6 source. The backup plan of using Little

Birds and SEALs from Team 6's Gold Squadron was now the last, best option, much to the operators' delight. "They were praying for clouds," the Team 6 source said. The helicopters launched from the destroyer, which was just over the horizon, and flew fast and low in the broad daylight toward the Somali shore. They aimed to intercept Nabhan's vehicle outside the town of Baraawe, about fifteen miles inland.

The AH-6s took the lead, with the MH-6s following about a mile behind, so as to give the gunships time to shoot, turn around, and either shoot again or confirm the vehicle had been stopped. As staff in multiple operations centers around the world followed Nabhan's vehicle on video feeds from a Predator drone and a U-28A manned ISR aircraft, the AH-6 flight lead, Chief Warrant Officer 4 Jay Rathbun, finally got the vehicle in view as it motored along the road through the Somali brush. The four men it held, including Nabhan in the backseat, would have had little if any warning of the danger as the Little Birds closed on them. "It's tough to see them," said a Task Force Brown source. "They're like little gnats, and then you've only got a matter of seconds."

On his first pass, Rathbun had trouble lining up a good shot, but declined to say "alibi," the code word that would pass the target to his Dash-2. "As the flight lead, you're in a once-in-a-lifetime mission, the chances of you saying 'alibi' are just about zero," said a Little Bird pilot familiar with the mission. "So the guy lived probably another fifteen seconds, because that's how long it took to get that aircraft round and take a shot." Rathbun brought his helicopter around to face Nabhan's vehicle before diving in and firing minigun rounds that stopped the vehicle and killed those inside, blowing some of them apart.

Rathbun chose to fire the 7.62mm minigun, rather than the 30mm chain gun or rockets, in order to preserve the bodies as much as possible and to minimize damage to any materials of intelligence value in the car. "If you hit it with rockets or 30[mm] then you're going to destroy it," the Little Bird pilot said. "It's going to be hard to piece together, frankly, who's who. And if you catch the car on fire, that's the worst case, because then it's real hard to get the DNA."

After the car had been stopped, the MH-6s arrived carrying between six and eight Team 6 operators on their pods. At least one SEAL shot at the car, firing a burst from his M240 machine gun while seated on an MH-6 pod, but there was nobody left to kill. JSOC's number one enemy in the Horn of Africa was dead. It had been well worth the wait for the men on the helicopters. However, the Team 6 source said, much of the credit belonged to the analysts who were able to predict Nabhan's route with such accuracy: "Those intel folks really won the day."

The analysts got their reward. After making sure all four vehicle occupants were dead, which didn't take long—"They were picking [body] parts out of the trees," the Team 6 source said—the operators turned to their next tasks: collecting DNA from the corpses and scooping up anything of intelligence value. This was a major advantage of Rathbun firing the minigun instead of rockets. "Had a rocket gone into that thing, everything would have been damaged," said a Team 6 source. Instead, although the minigun rounds had done brutal work to the car and the people inside, a camera was the only sensitive item in the vehicle not to survive the attack unscathed. The SEALs retrieved a trove of valuable information, according to a military intelligence source: "Two laptops, a multitude of disks and then . . . I want to say three phones, but each one had multiple SIM cards," in addition to two "push-to-talk communications devices . . . like walkie-talkies." The SEALs took all four bodies, or what remained of them, out of the car, put them on the aircraft, and flew them back to the ship, where, after Nabhan's corpse had been positively identified, they were buried at sea.[18]

Other than the intelligence value the United States derived from the mission, and the death of Nabhan, the significance of the mission was that it demonstrated to officials both inside and outside JSOC that the command retained the ability to conduct lethal clandestine operations with a small U.S. footprint. This was a relief to some in JSOC, who were growing concerned that so many years spent operating out of large, well-equipped bases in Iraq and Afghanistan had blunted the command's ability to conduct missions in more austere environments. The Nabhan strike allowed JSOC "to get back to the roots of the organization," said an officer who helped plan it.

But the strike had little long-term effect on the war against Al Qaeda and al-Shabaab, said an intelligence officer. "It really had no impact on al-Shabaab's operations, other than they knew that we would be willing to do it," he said.

※

Operation Lightning Dawn, the rescue of Richard Phillips from the clutches of Somali pirates, would spawn a hit movie starring Tom Hanks. But nobody wanted to make a movie about Team 6's next major hostage rescue mission at sea, even though, according to multiple sources in the unit, what transpired was a direct result of the Phillips mission.

The incident began on February 18, 2011, when nineteen pirates, all but one of whom were Somalis, captured the SY *Quest*, a yacht that four middle-aged Americans—two men and two women—were sailing around the world. As the pirates sailed the yacht toward northern Somalia, the U.S. Navy sent four ships to intercept it: the aircraft carrier *Enterprise*, the guided missile cruiser *Leyte Gulf*, and the guided missile destroyers *Sterett* and *Bulkeley*. The ships caught up with the yacht February 19.[19]

Meanwhile, JSOC had dispatched a Gold Squadron contingent under Commander John Rudella to handle the crisis. The operation was called Manor Press. Although the ratio of pirates to hostages was far from ideal, the SEALs realized that only five or six pirates—the ringleaders—had guns. The operators were confident they could handle them. "The boys had a plan to take out the top guys ready to go," said a SEAL officer.

Rudella asked for "emergency assault authority," which McRaven had given Moore during Lightning Dawn. But this time the JSOC commander, who was at Fort Bragg, wanted to keep a tighter rein on the SEALs than he had managed during the earlier crisis, and declined Rudella's request, according to Team 6 sources. In particular, he refused to let them try the sort of tricks that Red Squadron had used on the pirates who took Phillips hostage, they said. "He had felt that [Team 6] had manipulated him during the Captain Phillips rescue," said a senior Team 6 source. "From the time that the guys got on station, McRaven said, 'Hey, you manipulated me during Lightning Dawn, it's not going to happen again,'" said another Team 6 source. "And he made every call, every single call, during [Manor Press]." McRaven told Rudella that if fired upon, his SEALs were not to fire back.

Nonetheless, the Team 6 snipers set themselves up on one of the ships following the sailboat, much as the Red Squadron snipers had done during Lightning Dawn.[20] "They have already figured out who the real bad guys are, who's there really to kill somebody and who's along because they've got to get some money and they have khat and whatever," said the senior Team 6 source. The pirates were all within view of the snipers. "They weren't down belowdecks," the source said. "They were sitting there in the back of the sailboat, underneath the awning." However, the orders prevented the snipers from taking action. "Under no circumstances were they allowed to fire," he said.

The Navy brought two pirates on board the *Sterett* for negotiations. But when one of the ships approached the yacht it unnerved the pirates. On the morning of February 22, a pirate fired a rocket-propelled grenade at the *Sterett*. It missed the ship, which was about 600 meters away, but it was a sign that the pirates' mood had turned ugly. Shortly thereafter, some of the pirates shot the four hostages to death, thinking that the Navy would leave them alone if they killed the Americans.

"They gunned them down as the snipers are watching through their scopes," a Team 6 operator said. The Team 6 force immediately launched a boarding party. The SEALs dove off their high-speed assault craft onto the yacht and rolled into a standing position ready to shoot. But for the hostages, it was too late. All four Americans were dead or mortally wounded. So were two pirates, having died at the hands of their comrades. A third pirate was "playing possum" in the tangle of bodies, then jumped up and attacked one of the SEALs, who wrestled with him briefly before killing him with a combat knife. After another pirate in the cabin was shot by an operator, the remaining pirates surrendered.

The failure left a bitter taste for some of the SEALs. "They weren't allowed to do anything," the operator said. "They had plans that they could have done, things that they could have tried to stop that boat. . . . The snipers . . . were crushed. They knew who the bad guys were. They should have taken the shots, but they obeyed orders. They were crushed."

Some Team 6 operators blamed McRaven for the failure. "He micromanaged it," said one, accusing McRaven of disregarding one of the special mission units' key strengths: "Delta and SEAL Team 6 solve tactical problems." But a retired officer who worked for McRaven for several years said micromanagement wasn't the admiral's style. "One man's micromanagement is another man's attention to detail," he added.

✳

Less than two months later, Team 6 scored a major success in the same waters without having to fire a shot.

U.S. intelligence had been closely tracking Ahmed Abdulkadir Warsame, a Somali in his mid-twenties who was the senior liaison between al-Shabaab and Al Qaeda in the Arabian Peninsula (AQAP), which was Al Qaeda's Yemen offshoot. The February 2006 prison breakout of some of its most ardent and experienced members had rejuvenated AQAP. It had become the most active Al Qaeda branch, demonstrating an ambition to strike U.S. targets—particularly commercial airliners—far from Yemen. As a result, JSOC had increased its presence in Yemen and the U.S. government was keen to get its hands on Warsame. JSOC's planners knew either they or the CIA could kill Warsame in Yemen with a drone strike (each organization had its own drones flying over Yemen—the CIA's from southern Saudi Arabia, JSOC's from Djibouti). The JSOC staff also considered capturing or killing him in Somalia. (Yemeni president Ali Abdullah Saleh had made it clear putting U.S. boots on the ground in Yemen for a capture operation was out of the question.) But Warsame was a potentially invaluable source of intelligence and JSOC wanted to grab him alive. In mid-April 2011 Warsame unwittingly presented JSOC with an opportunity to do just that, when he made arrangements to travel on a small boat from Yemen to Puntland, the semi-autonomous region of northeastern Somalia. Not only was the United States listening to Warsame's cell phone, however. According to author Daniel Klaidman, "Using local spies, JSOC had been able to penetrate his network and manipulate the timing and logistics of his movements," meaning that somehow JSOC had arranged for Warsame to be traveling with just one associate and no guards.

On the evening of April 19, 2011, a troop of around twenty-five operators and support personnel from Team 6's Silver Squadron, dressed as regular Navy sailors rather than special mission unit operators, climbed into their rigid hull inflatable boats. Using a traditional wooden ship common to the region to screen themselves until the last possible moment, they boarded the fishing skiff on which Warsame was traveling through the Gulf of Aden. Taken by surprise, Warsame and his companion surrendered with minimal fuss. The mission marked the United States' "first at-sea counterterrorism mission," according to a senior Team 6 source.

The military held Warsame on the *Boxer* and interrogated him for more than two months before the Obama administration opted to try him in civilian court in New York. As with the Nabhan strike, the mission yielded an intelligence bounty: a laptop, two USB thumb drives, a hard drive, and a memory card. Things got even better for the CIA and JSOC analysts once Warsame began cooperating with his interrogators.[21] "That was a huge one because he was carrying back all kinds of material to take to al-Shabaab from AQAP—huge, huge takeaway," said a senior SEAL officer.

Playing a possible role in the operation was JSOC's own spy-ship-cum-staging-base that the command had operated off Somalia from the winter of 2010–2011. Commanded by a regular Navy officer and known as an afloat forward staging base (the same phrase used for the much larger flattops from which JSOC task forces sometimes operated), the ship fell under Task Force 484, JSOC's task force in the Horn of Africa and Yemen. The ship was leased from the Edison Chouest Offshore firm, and looked like a commercial or scientific craft, but could accommodate operators, SEAL boats, and at least one helicopter. The ship focused mostly on collecting signals intelligence.[22] "We would rely on submarines mostly to pop up there and do sigint collection for us, but we needed a full-time platform," said a Team 6 source. "We couldn't get a Navy ship so we rented and repurposed a civilian ship. . . . It was loaded in terms of all the latest up-to-date sigint equipment." The signals intelligence gear was largely manned by experts from Team 6's White Squadron, which provided signals intelligence support personnel—cryptologists ("crippies") and technical surveillance (TS) troops. (Although it had a squadron designation, White Squadron was commanded by a lieutenant commander, an officer a rank below the commanders who led the other squadrons.)

The ship also came in handy whenever Team 6 needed to conduct an OTB ("over-the-beach") mission in Yemen or Somalia. "What we keep on that thing [are] our boats, our mechanics, a lot of our support dudes, and then the force will jump in," said another Team 6 source. "Sometimes they'll jump boats in . . . but usually it's out there so all you have to do is jump in the force."

By the time Team 6 captured Warsame, Yemen had become a major focus of U.S. counterterrorism efforts. With JSOC's operations in the country—code-named Copper Dune—now under Team 6's command, the task force there enjoyed some success responding to the threat of suicide bombers in Sana'a by using Marine AV-8B Harriers to strike the suicide bombers' safe house north of the capital, and a combination of Harriers and submarine-launched cruise missiles to target AQAP camps in fall 2009. However, Yemeni president Saleh's calculus that his people could tolerate air strikes but not American boots on the ground meant that JSOC's presence in Yemen remained modest. JSOC's numbers rose slowly before being capped at about fifty personnel by Ambassador

Gerald Feierstein, who ran the Sana'a embassy from 2010 to 2013. Known collectively as Team Sana'a, the JSOC element had nonetheless grown too large to remain in the embassy proper and moved into new quarters close by. The team was commanded by a Team 6 troop commander, an officer holding the rank of lieutenant commander. His military chain of command ran through Task Force 484, which from 2009 was the name for the Team 6–led task force in the Horn and Yemen, but he also answered to the CIA chief of station in Sana'a, who, in the 2009–2010 timeframe, was JSOC's old friend Spider.

Team 6's Black Squadron, its advance force operations unit, provided most of the JSOC personnel, with some support from regular assault teams. Delta's Echo Squadron also had a contingent there with four Mi-17 helicopters painted in Yemeni military colors. They were there to fly Yemeni forces on counterterrorism missions, but when Saleh permitted them to fly, which wasn't often, it was mostly for training, not combat operations. In an effort to persuade Saleh that JSOC could conduct effective, stealthy missions in Yemen itself, Team 6 ran a demonstration in which operators flew in from Djibouti and conducted a high-altitude, low-opening parachute jump into the desert. The exercise went smoothly, but Saleh remained unmoved.

The task force also had a few personnel undercover performing advance force operations. These included "a couple of . . . Delta shooters that became Arabic speakers, and they were sensational," said a JSOC source. They and the occasional Team 6 AFO operator worked with female operators from Delta's G Squadron performing low-visibility urban reconnaissance in Sana'a and Aden, much of it focused on collecting signals intelligence from cell-phone networks and Internet cafés.[23]

Into this intelligence stream flowed the information gained from JSOC's April 2011 capture of Warsame. From the U.S. perspective, a benefit of getting Warsame was the detailed intelligence on the movements, security measures, and pattern of life of Anwar al-Awlaki, a U.S. citizen and Islamic cleric who had become a major player in Al Qaeda in the Arabian Peninsula and thus a high-priority target for the United States. Awlaki's citizenship resulted in much debate in the Obama administration and the wider foreign policy community about the appropriateness and legality of targeting him, but Obama had few qualms. Indeed, the president was particularly focused on Awlaki, pressuring his national security team to find and fix the charismatic terrorist.[24]

JSOC had a golden opportunity to kill Awlaki on May 5, 2011, just three days after the Abbottabad raid. Awlaki and at least one companion were driving through a rural part of Shabwah, southeast of Sana'a. Unbeknownst to them, JSOC was tracking them and had lined up three different types of aircraft ready to take a shot. First up was an MC-130W Dragon Spear, a special operations refueling version of the C-130 Hercules retrofitted with a weapons package. The Dragon Spear fired a Griffin missile at Awlaki's truck, but missed due to a problem with its targeting pod. It was out of the fight. As the vehicle raced to evade the barrage, a Marine Corps Harrier jet took its turn, but just nicked the vehicle's rear fender. Those monitoring the Predator feed in Sana'a, Fort Bragg, and the Pentagon watched in amazement as the truck emerged from the fireball and continued across the desert. Short on fuel, the Harrier had to depart. JSOC still had a Predator in the sky. Such drones had eviscerated Al Qaeda's midlevel leadership in Pakistan's tribal areas. But Awlaki was not so easily killed. He had called for help and two brothers who were colleagues in AQAP sped to rendezvous with Awlaki under some trees in a small valley. There, unseen by the JSOC staff watching the video feed, they switched vehicles with Awlaki and his driver, then the two vehicles departed in different directions. The drone followed Awlaki's original vehicle, now with the brothers inside, and destroyed it, killing them. Awlaki escaped.[25]

By the time the next chance to target Awlaki—Objective Troy—arrived at the end of September, the CIA had taken charge of the drone program in Yemen. The opportunity came about when Awlaki made the mistake of remaining in one place for two weeks, far longer than normal. Combined with human intelligence from at least one Yemeni source and the usual array of signals intelligence assets, this allowed the combined CIA-JSOC team to find and fix the cleric in Al Jawf province, northeast of Sana'a.[26] This time the United States was determined not to let Awlaki slip through their fingers. The Agency flew several Reaper drones from a base in Saudi Arabia. (The MQ-9 Reaper was a larger and more heavily armed version of the Predator.) Circling above the compound to which Awlaki had been tracked, they provided a comforting level of redundancy for the CIA planners.

The plan was for the drones to strike Awlaki while he was driving far from any noncombatants. A force comprised of operators from Team 6's Red Squadron; one Delta operator; CIA Ground Branch operatives; and

Yemeni counterterrorism personnel was to land in an Echo Squadron Mi-17 to exploit the site as soon as the drones struck. On September 30, as Awlaki and his colleagues finished breakfast in a small mud house and walked outside to climb into their vehicles and drive away, the CIA was sure it finally had its man. Its confidence stemmed from an extraordinary combination of human and technical intelligence: the Agency had gained access to Awlaki's vehicle and equipped it with a hidden video camera that was transmitting live, so the CIA's watchers actually saw Awlaki getting in the backseat. While this sort of work can be done by having U.S. or local operatives sneaking up to the car and installing the gear when nobody's watching, that wasn't how the CIA accomplished their feat in the case of Awlaki. "The easiest way . . . is to have a source who brings you the car, which is what the Agency would prefer . . . and they did have a source very close to Awlaki," said a JSOC source. "You can do the install inside your comfortable garage and then give the car back to the source and he's gone."

With 100 percent confidence that they had their target in their sights, the Agency's decision makers got impatient and gave the order to strike before the vehicles had gone very far. The drones fired a dozen Hellfire missiles at Awlaki, destroying his vehicle and killing him and several colleagues, including another American, Samir Khan, the editor of AQAP's online magazine, *Inspire*. But the CIA had "fired about forty-five minutes early," meaning the exploitation team had no chance to land to gain intelligence from the site before locals overran it, said a JSOC source. The helicopter carrying the JSOC and Agency personnel turned around in midflight.[27]

29

Extortion 17

The moon had set and the sky was black as the insurgents on a corner turret of a compound 200 meters south of the Logar River scanned the darkness for targets. Looking north, they could see the gray outlines of the mud-brick villages dotting the strip of vegetation that in daylight ran like a green ribbon through the center of the valley, but now was just another shade of black. For years the valley had been inhospitable to invaders. U.S. soldiers built a combat outpost there in spring 2009, but never succeeded in controlling more than a thousand meters around the tiny base, which they abandoned two years later. Now the Americans were back. For hours their airplanes had been circling above the valley, clearly audible in the still of the night. There were also two types of helicopter in the air: the large, twin-rotor ones, a pair of which had landed to the northeast four and a half hours previously, depositing dozens of soldiers who were now scouring a village compound; and the smaller attack helicopters, which the men on the tower had heard firing at their colleagues north of the river.

The helicopters were prize targets for the insurgents, but shooting down a blacked-out helicopter on a dark night using the rudimentary sights on a heavy machine gun or a rocket-propelled grenade launcher was not easy. The Taliban in the valley were getting closer, however. Two months previously they had volley-fired more than a dozen rocket-propelled grenades at one of the twin-rotor helicopters, forcing it to abort its mission and leave the valley.

It was about 2:39 A.M. when the men heard the distinctive sound of another twin-rotor helicopter. Searching the night sky for its black silhouette, they shouldered their rocket-propelled grenade launchers in order to be ready should it appear. The aircraft was coming from the northwest, but approaching quickly.[1]

*

It was the middle of the night of August 5, 2011, a little more than three months since the bin Laden raid. The Ranger strike force that landed at 11:01 P.M. in the Tangi Valley of eastern Wardak province, about thirty-five miles south-southwest of Kabul, was hunting Qari Tahir, who had been the valley's senior Taliban commander since June 6, when the task force had killed his predecessor, Din Mohammad. Signals intelligence had located Qari Tahir (also known as Objective Lefty Grove[2]) in a compound on the river's north side at 6:55 that evening. The strike force quickly put a plan together and, after getting it cleared through the JSOC chain of command in Afghanistan, launched from Forward Operating Base Shank in neighboring Logar province at 10:37 P.M. on two Chinooks. The forty-seven-person force[3] landed unopposed about 2,000 meters to the east of the target compound, and proceeded to walk toward it, a patrol that took place at an altitude of between 6,500 and 7,000 feet.

The Rangers had a lot of friends in the sky: an air weapons team of two AH-64 Apache attack helicopters; an MQ-1 Predator drone; an AC-130 gunship; an MC-12 Liberty surveillance plane; and a PC-12 surveillance plane. The patrol took almost an hour to reach the target compound. Half an hour into that movement, the Apaches watched four individuals leave the compound and join four others. Armed with assault rifles and rocket-propelled grenade launchers, the eight men moved off in a northwesterly direction. The Apache pilots decided the men were displaying hostile intent based on the weapons they carried. After discussing the situation with the ground force, the Apaches attacked at 11:40 P.M., firing sixty rounds of 30mm chain gun ammunition and killing five of the small group. Of the three survivors, one stayed put. The Apaches killed him a few minutes later with another sixty rounds of "thirty mike-mike." The two who were left moved off northwest. Others joined them as they walked parallel to the river.

At 11:54 P.M. the assault force paused about 100 meters east of the compound to prepare for its actions on the objective, before moving forward and, at twenty minutes past midnight, using the seven Afghan Partner Unit soldiers on the mission, beginning the call-out. The assault force then cleared the buildings, finishing just after 2 A.M. The Ranger platoon leader also sent a small element forward to check out the site where the Apaches had killed six men.

Meanwhile, the AC-130 continued to track the two escapees from that attack. Their group had grown until it numbered thirteen men, of whom eight were seen entering a compound about two or three kilometers northwest of the Rangers' original objective at about 1:30 A.M. The usual course of action in the case of "squirters" fleeing the objective or "movers" departing from near it was for some of the assault force already on the ground to interdict them. On other missions, the assault force kept an element aloft in helicopters that could land and intercept suspected insurgents trying to escape. In those cases, the force in the helicopters was called the airborne reaction force or immediate reaction force. But neither option was available that night. The assault force did not have time to clear the objective, sort through their detainees and the corpses of the people the Apaches had killed, and then move northwest and deal with the small but growing group of squirters and movers before daybreak. The Task Force East commander, who was also Team 6's Gold Squadron commander, decided to use an immediate reaction force at Forward Operating Base Shank to fly in to the valley and interdict the group that had escaped the original assault force. Using an immediate reaction force this way—especially when the original assault force was not under attack—was rare. But after checking with the Ranger colonel in charge of the Afghanistan task force, at 2 A.M. the Task Force East commander ordered Gold Squadron's 2 Troop to interdict the suspected insurgents that had gathered northwest of the objective.[4]

With no Task Force Brown MH-47s available, two conventional Army CH-47D Chinooks flew the mission. To minimize the risk to the aircraft, however, the immediate reaction force crowded onto just one helicopter. The other flew empty and broke off a few minutes before the Chinook with the SEALs on board made its final approach. The helicopter carrying the Gold Squadron troop was flown by a mixed five-man Army Reserve and National Guard crew. Its call sign was Extortion 17. It was headed to a landing zone about a kilometer northwest of the compound in which the eight individuals had taken refuge. On the helicopter were fifteen Gold Squadron operators (including the troop's commander, Lieutenant Commander Jonas Kelsall), five Gold Squadron support personnel, two SEALs from a West Coast team, an interpreter, and seven Afghan Partner Unit soldiers, plus a military working dog.[5] The immediate reaction force was wheels up from FOB Shank at 2:24 A.M.

Extortion 17 was flying into a high-threat environment. On June 6, insurgents in the valley had shot fourteen or fifteen rocket-propelled grenades at another Chinook, forcing it to abort its mission to infiltrate U.S. troops. To mitigate the threat to Extortion 17, the AC-130 gunship (7,000 feet above ground level) and both Apaches were supposed to be covering its approach, scanning the ground for insurgents. At 2:38 A.M., flying in a southeasterly direction, the pilots announced they were a minute out from the landing zone. Twenty-three seconds later the Apaches announced that the landing zone was "ice," meaning no Taliban were visible. But as Extortion 17 slowed to about 50 knots on its final approach, insurgents on a turret 220 meters to the south shouldered rocket-propelled grenade launchers and, unnoticed, took aim at the helicopter, which was now no more than 150 feet off the ground and flying across their forward field of view. Their first round missed. But the second was a better—or luckier—shot. The Apache crew members saw a red flash as the round launched, followed by another as the rocket—probably an OG-7V 40mm antipersonnel round—hit an aft rotor blade and exploded on impact, severing about ten feet of the blade. Less than two seconds later the resulting imbalance twisted the aft rotor pylon off the helicopter. The helicopter went into a violent clockwise spin, ripping off the forward pylon. Within five seconds of being hit, the Chinook fuselage fell out of the sky, crashing into the bank of the Logar River in a fiery impact that killed all aboard.

On the AC-130, they'd heard the reports of an RPG and swept the area with their sensors looking for the Chinook. They saw the fireball but initially couldn't believe that was the helicopter. But after several long seconds of searching for Extortion 17 they realized the awful truth. At 2:40 A.M. and ten seconds, one of the Apache pilots reported: "Extortion is down."

As is the norm in all but the largest or most vital operations, the shootdown changed the mission focus, in this case from a raid to personnel recovery. The Ranger assault force released its detainees and moved 3,900 meters on foot to secure the crash site, arriving at 4:45 A.M., just before the arrival of a quick reaction force from the conventional Army.

Later that day JSOC's signals intelligence assets picked up a midlevel Taliban leader saying that his fighter had shot down the helicopter, and that he was moving him to Pakistan for his own protection. The task force followed the phone on which the leader was speaking, tracking it—as well as the guerrilla leader and his RPG gunner—deeper into Wardak province. Lieutenant General Joe Votel, who had assumed command of JSOC from McRaven on June 10, ordered the task force to kill the two insurgents at the first opportunity. Task force aircraft followed the pair's vehicle, waiting for a chance to strike without harming civilians. That came on August 8 when they stopped at a compound and wandered into some nearby trees.[6] With an F-16 waiting to deliver the blow, the task force seized its chance at vengeance. Several 500-pound bombs and Apache gun runs later, both men lay dead. But their demise was little compensation for JSOC's loss.

The downing of Extortion 17 marked the greatest number of casualties ever suffered by U.S. Special Operations Command, as well as the single biggest loss of American lives in the Afghan war. The Naval Special Warfare community reeled in shock.[7] For Team 6, still basking in the glow of the bin Laden operation, the loss was almost immeasurable.

An investigation led by Brigadier General Jeffrey Colt, an experienced special operations aviator, soon determined the facts behind the shootdown of Extortion 17. But in the wake of the tragedy, some saw an opportunity to make political hay. Freedom Watch, a conservative political advocacy group, held a news conference in May 2013 at Washington, D.C.'s, National Press Club with a few of the bereaved families. It was followed by a congressional hearing in February 2014. At these events critics suggested that the Obama administration had "put a target" on the backs of the Team 6 operators by identifying the unit as the one that killed bin Laden. But none of the critics produced evidence that the insurgents who downed the helicopter knew who was on board, nor did they provide proof of any conspiracy or egregious failure beyond what the investigation had revealed.[8]

❋

At the time of the Extortion 17 disaster, JSOC's Afghanistan task force had 3,816 personnel, about 2.4 percent of the Coalition's 155,000 personnel. The command's cutting edge was its nineteen strike forces, divided up between the subordinate Task Forces South, Central, East, and North. The task force's main effort was aimed at enhancing security in Kandahar and Helmand provinces, a task that fell to the Ranger-led Task Force South. Supporting efforts included: expanding what JSOC called Kabul's "security bubble," which was the shared responsibility of the Ranger-led Task Force Central and the Team 6–led Task Force East; "degrading" the Haqqani Network in Paktia, Paktika, and Khost provinces, which fell in TF Central's area of operations; "degrading" Taliban and Islamic Movement of Uzbekistan operations in Kunduz and Baghlan provinces, which was the job of the Delta-led Task Force North; and denying Al Qaeda sanctuary in the eastern provinces of Kunar and Nuristan.

In the year preceding the Extortion 17 shoot-down, JSOC forces in Afghanistan conducted 2,824 missions, of which 2,608 were night raids—an average of more than seven raids a night. Only 301 missions involved shots fired, the vast majority of which occurred during daytime missions (one reason why JSOC was so determined to retain the right to conduct night raids). The "jackpot" rate—the rate at which the assault forces captured or killed the man they were seeking—was 1,381, or about 49 percent.[9] But these numbers hid a growing disillusionment among the operators with the way the war was going. In particular, it was hard for the veterans of JSOC's killing machine in Iraq to muster the same enthusiasm for the command's efforts in Afghanistan.

There were signs by 2012 that JSOC personnel had given up hope of victory in Afghanistan, where, unlike Iraq, it was hard to see tangible benefits from the nightly missions in the form of a declining rate in violence. "In Afghanistan at the strike force level, at the troop level, they knew that this war is not going to end, [that] we're not going to win," said a Ranger officer. "In Iraq I think they knew they could win." This view was not confined to the Rangers. "I don't want to say Green's morale was low, but Green was fucking bitter," the Ranger officer said of his Delta brethren. The attitude of the Green operators in Sharana was "Fuck this, this doesn't make a difference; these raids don't matter." The same was true of the Rangers. In 2011, "I have to convince NCOs to go out," the Ranger officer said. "I have to yell at them to go on a mission. They're like, 'Sir, fuck this. It doesn't matter. I don't want to do this. This raid, for this low-level IED guy is not going to change anything.' Morale changes. They're fucking run ragged . . . They don't want to do this."

30

Old Enemies, New Challenges

In the very early hours of January 25, 2012, the back ramp of an MC-130 Combat Talon opened about 20,000 feet above Somalia. The Blue Squadron operators shuffled forward, rigged for a HAHO jump, and dove out into the moonless night sky. "High altitude, pitch black, out into nothing," a Team 6 source said. They were on a mission that would not garner as many headlines as the bin Laden raid, but which was arguably more tactically challenging. It would showcase the advances Team 6 had made over the previous decade.

The SEALs were on a rescue mission. Three months earlier to the day, Somali pirates had kidnapped American aid worker Jessica Buchanan, thirty-two, and her sixty-year-old Danish colleague, Poul Hagen Thisted, after they had given a workshop on land mines in Galkayo, a city about 350 miles northeast of Mogadishu. (Despite the maritime connotations of the word "pirate," Somali pirates were just as happy to kidnap their victims on land as at sea.) The pirates took the pair to their camp in Hiimo Gaabo, south of Galkayo. Meanwhile, JSOC developed options to free them. Because Somalia fell under Team 6's purview, the Navy unit got the mission, which fell to Blue Squadron, which had the Trident at the time.

JSOC soon figured out where the pirates were holding Buchanan and Thisted and positioned drones overhead, so they were able to track the hostages' movements and daily routines. As negotiations with the kidnappers dragged on—the pirates rejected a $1.5 million ransom offer—U.S. officials became concerned that a urinary tract infection was putting Buchanan's life at risk. President Obama, who had been keeping a close eye on the crisis, authorized JSOC to attempt a rescue mission.

The operators who exited the back of the Combat Talon realized in midair that they couldn't make it to their primary drop zone. "There was so much fog they had to go to an alternate drop zone," said a Team 6 source. For the experienced freefall jumpers this was no great obstacle. Using microphones and earpieces fitted to their helmets, they were able to discuss the change in plans while in midair, and still managed to land far enough away from the camp that the pirates never heard or saw them. The SEALs then moved on foot to the camp so stealthily that the nine kidnappers guarding the hostages had no idea they were under attack until it was far too late. A couple of pirates managed to get some harmless shots off before the SEALs were on top of them, killing all nine with ruthless efficiency as two operators sprinted through the gunfight to cover the hostages with their bodies. Grabbing the hostages, they moved on foot for several minutes to a pickup zone. There Task Force Brown helicopters landed in swirling dust and flew them to Galkayo's airport, where a Combat Talon waited to fly them to Djibouti.[1]

The rescue of Buchanan and Thisted exemplified some of the capabilities and skills JSOC and Team 6 had been perfecting since—and in some cases before—September 11. The positioning of drones over the camp was a testament to the belief of Stan McChrystal and Mike Flynn in the power of the "Unblinking Eye." That President Obama felt comfortable enough to give the go-ahead for the mission was a function of the confidence he had in JSOC, a confidence that was the product of hard work successive JSOC commanders had done building relationships with the White House over two administrations. The perfectly executed freefall jump was a direct result of the time and energy Team 6 had invested in preparing for such missions. "That [mission] would not have been as successful as it was had we not done that profile hundreds and hundreds of times already," said a Team 6 source. The decision to land at an offset location (the "Y"), as opposed to jumping directly onto the objective (the "X"), was based on hard lessons learned from a decade of trial and error in combat. The operators' ability to creep up undetected to the camp—also highlighted during Team 6's October 2010 rescue of the kidnapped American engineer in Afghanistan—was also a skill honed over countless previous missions. The appearance of the Task Force Brown helicopters many hundreds of miles from a friendly air base was a testament to the 160th's vaunted ability to fly its helicopters to wherever the mission demanded "plus or minus thirty seconds" anywhere on the globe. According to one special operations source, the operation to retrieve Buchanan and Thisted became "the gold standard" of hostage rescues within JSOC.

✳

As the twenty-first century stretched toward the middle of its second decade, JSOC had firmly established itself at the top of not only the U.S. military food chain, but also, arguably, the interagency hierarchy inside the Washington Beltway.

To achieve that, successive JSOC commanders had leveraged an organization that McChrystal originally established in 2004 with a more limited mandate. That organization began life as the Joint Reconnaissance and Targeting Force, or JRTF, and was the brainchild of then Colonel Mike Nagata, according to a veteran of the organization. (Other sources credit a slightly wider array of individuals.) The purpose was to achieve a level of synergy among the burgeoning reconnaissance elements of the different JSOC units. At the time, Delta, Team 6, and the Rangers each had units dedicated to deep reconnaissance and advance force operations, and each was growing in size: Delta was expanding Operational Support Troop into what became G Squadron; Team 6 was nurturing Black Squadron from humble beginnings into what would become the unit's largest formation; and the Ranger Reconnaissance Detachment was taking on a broader range of missions and growing into a company designed along the same lines as a Delta reconnaissance troop. All of these reconnaissance units had missions that overlapped with each other and with those of Orange, which saw itself as the premier outfit when it came to clandestine intelligence gathering operations.

Concerned that the units were starting to replicate each other's capabilities, McChrystal originally wanted to pool the reconnaissance assets so they would support all his units. However, relieving the special mission unit and Ranger commanders of their own reconnaissance elements would have been a tough sell, so instead McChrystal and the unit commanders agreed to establish a small task force—the JRTF—whose function would be to plan and, perhaps, command and control, reconnaissance operations that supported JSOC missions. JRTF was "supposed to be the [organization] that tied together [and] synchronized reconnaissance efforts worldwide outside of Iraq and Afghanistan," said a special operations source familiar with its birth. The task force's staff was to be drawn from each of JSOC's major ground units, with the idea that when a potential reconnaissance challenge presented itself, each unit would have a representative in the JRTF who could explain what unique capabilities his or her unit could bring to solving the problem. The task force started small, with barely a dozen members. The JRTF was based at Fort Belvoir, collocated with Orange, because McChrystal thought it needed to be close to one of the special mission units, and Colonel Konrad Trautman, Orange's commander at the time, argued that his unit was the most logical choice. When JRTF officially stood up in the late spring of 2004, Trautman became dual-hatted as commander of both JRTF and Orange. The organization took the place of the advance force operations cell in JSOC headquarters. However, friction soon developed between the JRTF staff and Orange, whose personnel derided their new neighbor as "Junior Task Force."

By the end of 2008, JRTF had outgrown its Fort Belvoir quarters and had moved into an office building in Arlington, Virginia. In keeping with McChrystal's vision of a networked force, JRTF had also begun to exchange liaisons with the major government agencies whose work might have a bearing on JSOC's missions. It had taken on the roles of JSOC's original JIATF's East and West, at Bagram and Balad respectively, which each closed down. "The premise was [that before JRTF] there was no organization holistically looking at the GWOT [global war on terror] as a whole, as it were, the targets outside the major combat zones of Iraq and Afghanistan," a JRTF source said. "What does the rest of the structure, of the enemy order of battle, look like?" JRTF did not have an action arm, but its growing staff would travel abroad, meet with representatives of other U.S. government agencies, as well as foreign governments, "and facilitate operations outside Iraq and Afghanistan," the source said. As the organization increasingly focused on this work with other government departments, it acquired a bulky new name: the Joint Interagency Task Force-National Capital Region, or JIATF-NCR.

The JIATF-NCR commander was a colonel or Navy captain who reported to the JSOC commander. He did not have the authority to task operational units in the field. Instead, if he wanted surveillance of a certain target, for instance, he made a recommendation to that effect to the JSOC commander. The organization, whose staff had grown exponentially, also took up data mining. "You've got an entire floor of the building which is nothing but computers," said a U.S. Special Operations Command staff officer who visited the organization. The staff officer described a demonstration the JIATF-NCR staff gave visitors: "Moham-med So-and-So gets on a plane . . . and you get all his travel documents immediately, up there on the screen . . . now they give you the manifest of every flight he took . . . over the last six months . . . you get the com-plete manifest of all five flights, and you find out five other guys were all on the same five flights . . . and then you cross-reference them . . . and somehow you find out that three of the five are from the same village in Yemen, two or more were in prison together. . . . It's multiple agencies feeding [it] and I was fascinated that we [Special Operations Command and JSOC] were in the lead, because 80 percent of what they were put-ting up there was domestic stuff." (A JSOC staffer credited a program called TRADEWIND with giving JIATF-NCR the ability to call up somebody's travel records immediately.)

A veteran of the organization said it had achieved some major tar-geting successes, starting with some of the Predator strikes in Yemen. However, the Special Operations Command staff officer said, the orga-nization did not exist just to give JSOC targeting data. "If the FBI can pick up a guy landing at Dulles Airport, they do that as well," the officer said. Indeed, by late 2014 JIATF-NCR's mission had evolved away from targeting, and it existed largely to gain concurrence among other govern-ment agencies for specific missions.[2]

JSOC had overhauled its headquarters' intelligence infrastructure to address the weaknesses that hobbled it in the aftermath of September 11. In late 2008 McRaven had established the JSOC Intelligence Brigade (JIB), a 600-person unit based at Fort Bragg and commanded by a col-onel or a Navy captain. Originally conceived by McChrystal to allow the JSOC intelligence director to focus "up and out," while the JIB com-mander focused "down and in," in the words of a JSOC staff officer, the JIB included a full complement of collection, analysis, and dissemina-tion capabilities, including airborne and ground collection platforms, as well as analysts, interrogators, and other specialists in signals, imagery, and human intelligence and counterintelligence. The JSOC director of intelligence remained the command's senior intelligence officer, but his job was to advise the JSOC commander on intelligence missions that the JIB commander executed with his panoply of intelligence capabilities.[3] "You need a commander to be responsible for training, maintaining, commanding and controlling those kinds of assets," said a former senior JSOC officer. "Staff guys can't do that."

"The JIB formalized a lot of talent," said a Team 6 officer. "It enabled [them] to get a lot more bodies and to do a lot more formal training in a more consistent manner."

Meanwhile, in the wake of the U.S. military's departure from Iraq, JSOC and its component units embraced a role that would increasingly see them working closely with the CIA and other intelligence agencies in countries in which the United States was not officially at war. As a result, JSOC continued to expand its espionage capabilities, which were already threatening the CIA's traditional turf. (By 2008, the military had surpassed the Agency's ability to place case officers under nonofficial cover abroad, according to Ishmael Jones, the pen name of a retired CIA nonofficial cover case officer.) For example, in 2014 Orange was largely focused on a global mission to counter what JSOC called the Iranian Threat Network, which included the Quds Force as well as organizations that often acted as Iranian surrogates, such as Hezbollah. And although thousands of JSOC personnel remained busy in Afghanistan, by 2014 Team 6 and Delta had only one troop each in the country. Operations elsewhere indicated the way ahead. In particular, the two missions that occurred two hours and 3,000 miles apart on October 5, 2013: Delta's dawn seizure of Nazih Abdul-Hamed al-Ruqai, also known by his nom de guerre, Abu Anas al-Libi, from outside his home in Tripoli, and a failed attempt by Team 6 in Baraawe, Somalia, to capture Abdikadir Mohamed Abdikadir, otherwise known as Ikrimah, a senior al-Shabaab figure believed to be behind the September 21 attack on Nairobi's Westgate Mall that killed at least sixty-seven people.

The Delta mission, in the capital of a country—Libya—with a weak central government, was smooth, professional, and bloodless. After entering Libya over the beach with Team 6's help, the operators snatched Libi—wanted for his suspected role in Al Qaeda's 1998 embassy bombings, and because intelligence indicated that he was setting up a new Al Qaeda cell in Tripoli—by using two vans to block his car as he returned home from dawn prayers. The operators yanked Libi from his vehicle and sped off with him within sixty seconds. The use of vans with darkened windows suggested that Delta had advance force operations personnel in-country preparing for the mission before the rest of the operators arrived, while the timing of the snatch indicated extensive surveillance of the target to establish his pattern of life.

Team 6 operators almost pulled off an equally impressive tactical feat that morning in Somalia, when they came ashore before dawn and crept toward Ikrimah's house. They had nearly succeeded in entering the building unnoticed when a guard emerged to smoke a cigarette, wandered back inside, and then returned with an assault rifle and began firing. There were enough SEALs to storm the house, but, after the squadron commander on the scene told the task force headquarters in Djibouti that doing so would likely result in the deaths of women and children, the SEALs decided to abort the mission. They withdrew to their boats on the beach and left.[4]

Delta's low-visibility campaign in Libya continued, and on June 15, 2014, the unit again hit the headlines when it seized Islamist militia leader Ahmed Abu Khattala, a ringleader of the September 11, 2012, attack on Benghazi's U.S. consulate. The raid had been a long time in the planning.

JSOC had had a presence in Libya—called Team Libya—since the Arab Spring uprising against Muammar Gaddafi in 2011. Team Libya was part of Task Force 27, which was led by Delta and operated in the Middle East and North and West Africa.[5] When Islamist militiamen overran the Benghazi consulate and attacked a nearby CIA outpost, killing Ambassador J. Christopher Stevens and three other Americans, two Delta operators—one of whom was a Marine—were part of a seven-person team sent from Tripoli that night to mount a rescue mission for the State Department and CIA personnel who had taken refuge in the CIA facility about a mile from the burning consulate. Both operators received high awards for their role in getting the Americans to safety: the Distinguished Service Cross for the Army operator, Master Sergeant David R. Halbruner; and its Navy equivalent, the Navy Cross, for his Marine colleague (whose name was not publicized). "Throughout the operation, Master Sergeant Halbruner continually exposed himself to fire as he shepherded unarmed civilians to safety and treated the critically wounded," reads the citation for Halbruner's award. "His calm demeanor, professionalism and courage [were] an inspiration to all and contributed directly to the success of the mission."[6]

Within hours of the attack, JSOC had determined the identities of the leaders, who were linked to the Ansar al-Sharia militia group. Delta dispatched a team to Libya to hunt them, and by Friday, September 14, three days after the attack, JSOC was briefing U.S. Special Operations Command that it was tracking the militia leaders responsible for the attack, had photographs of them (which were included in the briefing), and information that they had been calling an Islamist figure in jail in Iraq. "They knew who was in command and control of it, they knew it all," said a SOCOM staffer. "I remember them specifically saying the guys on the ground were talking to a guy in prison in Iraq."

From then on, JSOC kept a fix on the militia leaders, information that the command included as one of its handful of top priorities in its weekly Friday briefings to SOCOM. "They were giving the Friday update: 'Hey, we've got a positive ID on X, we know his location is Y, last seen at so-and-so,'" the staffer said. But as to why JSOC didn't launch a mission against Abu Khattala or his associates earlier, the staffer said: "I don't think they ever got permission to."[7] That account was borne out by an October 29, 2013, CNN report that "U.S. special operations forces" were ready to grab Abu Khattala within a day or two of seizing Libi, but the White House never gave the okay, in part due to worries that another raid so soon after the Libi mission might destabilize Libya, leading to the downfall of the weak government in Tripoli, and in part to a desire to gather enough evidence to prosecute Abu Khattala in criminal court.

But the delays gave Delta the time to build a mock-up of Abu Khatta-la's compound at Fort Bragg, allowing them to rehearse the snatch repeatedly. Meanwhile, JSOC kept Abu Khattala under close watch, establishing his daily routine. When the two dozen Delta operators—supported by a couple of FBI agents—struck, they did so with guile, tricking their way into Abu Khattala's compound and seizing him without firing a shot. Delta quickly took him to the *New York*, a Navy ship waiting offshore, where he was interrogated before being brought to the United States to face trial.[8]

※

These sorts of missions placed a premium on exactly the capabilities that McChrystal initially sought to harness with the Joint Reconnaissance and Targeting Force: advance force operations, low-visibility urban re-connaissance, and undercover espionage missions. By 2014 JSOC had replaced the term "advance force operations" with "clandestine," as the former implied the possibility of a follow-on force, which was not always politically acceptable. But the concept remained very much in vogue, so much so that the AFO-type squadrons in the special mission units (Black Squadron in Team 6, G Squadron in Delta) were now regarded as the most prestigious squadrons to command. No wonder that in 2014, there was talk of doing away with Team 6's newest assault squadron, Silver, which had been established at the height of the wars in Iraq and Afghanistan, but no rumors of anything but more growth for Black Squadron. Indeed, the story of Team 6's advanced reconnaissance organization exemplifies the trend toward ever more low-visibility and covert capabilities in JSOC. The squadron didn't even exist until the turn of the century, but by 2014 had become Team 6's largest squadron, with between 150 and 200 personnel. "It was a baby team but now it's a monster," said a Team 6 officer. (During the same period Team 6 had grown from no more than 500 personnel to more than 1,500, of whom only about 300 were SEALs, with the rest consisting of roughly 800 other uniformed Navy personnel and about 400 civilians who together provided administration, intelligence, logistics, communications, and other support.)

As was the case for the assault squadrons, Black's commanding officer was a SEAL commander (the equivalent Navy rank to a lieutenant colonel in the other services), and the squadron had a SEAL operator command master chief. But in 2014 the commander's deputy was a retired Army Special Forces colonel with a great deal of experience in reconnaissance and advance force operations. The vast majority of the squadron's personnel were not SEALs, but other Navy personnel and civilians, including experts in merchant shipping. While the squadron did not have its own fleet, it was capable of using civilian ships to mount operations, and could take advantage of what a JSOC staffer described as Team 6's "natural connection" with the Maritime Branch of the CIA's Special Activities Division. A small number of Black Squadron operators lived abroad under long-term cover.[9] "Their skill sets have exploded over time," said the JSOC staffer, who said the increasingly significant role Black Squadron had assumed as a clandestine organization "absolutely" represented a threat to Orange. Delta's efforts to develop a signals intelligence capability compounded that threat, the staffer added. "If they're developing that capability, what's left for [Orange] to do?" he said. "You can't say." Both Black Squadron and its Delta equivalent, G Squadron, began doing substantial covered work around 2009.[10] But Team 6's maritime bent gave the unit certain advantages, argued a Team 6 source. "What maritime low-level or AFO capability gives you is dwell time," he said. "You have a reason to go in there [to a target location] and stay there for days, weeks, or months. So if you have a maritime company, it comes in from the sea, then it offloads something that goes overland for miles and miles and you can turn a maritime shipping company into a logistics company that goes everywhere."

"If you can conceive of doing it, we're likely doing it," said a Team 6 operator. "It's the things you can't conceive of that we're also likely doing."

＊

The challenge of conducting low-visibility operations in countries in which the United States was not at war was on Joe Votel's mind May 21, 2014, when the JSOC commander made a rare public appearance—and even rarer public remarks—at a special operations conference in Tampa. JSOC developed the "find, fix, finish, exploit, analyze" process in Iraq and Afghanistan, war zones in which the command enjoyed access to "large bases" and "solid infrastructure," he noted. The organization's challenge, he said, is "how do we take that great methodology we refined over the last twelve or thirteen years and apply it to areas outside of declared theaters of armed conflict" in which operators must minimize their "footprint."

When it came to the "find" and "fix" parts of the equation, "a key piece for us" would be figuring out how to maintain the same "level of situational awareness" in austere, remote locations that JSOC enjoyed in mature, built-up combat theaters, Votel said. In Iraq and Afghanistan, JSOC relied heavily on ISR aircraft to build a detailed picture of enemy activity. But that advantage may not be available in other theaters, and JSOC would need technological workarounds, he said. "In some cases we will not be able to operate aerial platforms because the host nation will not allow us to do that," he said. "So we've got to continue to look at long-range, high-fidelity tactical sensors that allow us to see and understand what is happening."

Minimizing civilian casualties when it was time to strike was particularly important in countries that were not declared combat zones, according to Votel. "We have to continue to improve our 'finish' capability—whether it's a lethal finish, or whether it's a nonlethal finish, or whether it's enabling someone else—to be as precise as we possibly can," he said.

Votel also highlighted the continuing priority JSOC placed on counter-proliferation, particularly on preventing "the nightmare scenario" of Islamist terrorists getting their hands on weapons of mass destruction. "We do see violent extremist organizations and others continue to exert a desire to acquire these types of weapons," he said. "So our ability to detect and neutralize them effectively will be a key piece for our country," he told the audience of defense contractors and special operations personnel. "We will only have very limited opportunities to get that right, when the situation is presented to us," he said.

One country Votel highlighted as a place the United States had to be "very, very concerned" about weapons of mass destruction falling into the wrong hands was Syria, where what began as a peaceful uprising against Bashar Assad as part of the Arab Spring movement in 2011 had evolved by 2014 into a multiparty civil war that pitted Assad's military, reinforced by Quds Force and Hezbollah, against rebel forces that were divided between two Sunni Islamist factions and a more moderate group supported by the West. The JSOC commander went on to express his worry that terrorists could use Syria and other unstable countries as safe havens in which to train, but in the case of Syria he wanted to "avoid specific operational details."[11] While his reluctance to open up on the topic was to be expected, Votel had a particular reason to be circumspect: his force was at that moment rehearsing a life-or-death mission deep into rebel-held Syria.

✳

In the early hours of July 3, 2014, two Black Hawks full of Delta operators crossed the border from Jordan into Syria, flying fast across the desert. Their destination was a compound outside the town of Raqqa, on the north bank of the Euphrates in north-central Syria. It was there, U.S. intelligence analysts believed, that a group calling itself the Islamic State—one of the two Islamist factions waging war in Syria—was holding several Western hostages, including at least two Americans: journalists James Foley and Steven Sotloff. The intelligence came from several sources: FBI interviews with two European men that the Islamic State had held as hostages before releasing them, probably as a result of ransoms paid; satellite imagery of a building near Raqqa that matched the descriptions given by the Europeans; and information supplied by Israel.

This was not JSOC's first raid into Syria. But unlike the October 2008 mission to kill Abu Ghadiya, which involved a few minutes' flight across the Iraqi border, this operation involved penetrating 200 miles into Syrian airspace. For that reason, JSOC had chosen to use the latest version of the stealth Black Hawks that flew the bin Laden raid. That mission famously left one of the two such aircraft then in existence burned to a crisp in bin Laden's backyard. But since May 2011 more of the airframes had been constructed, and the program had expanded so that the 160th now kept a unit of about forty personnel under a lieutenant colonel at Nellis Air Force Base in Nevada, where the stealth helicopters were housed.

As the use of the specialized airframes suggested, JSOC had spared little expense to prepare for the operation. The task force had been training for weeks on a replica of the compound they were going to assault. There had been "eyes on the target" for at least a week prior to D-day, reporting what they saw in short, encrypted messages. When the helicopters neared the compound, they were filmed by at least one armed drone overhead.

The Black Hawks touched down and the operators swarmed off, as they had so many times over the previous thirteen years. Moving with their trademark efficiency they swept through the compound, killing about as many as a dozen militants in a firefight that ignited a blaze that would eventually consume the facility. (A helicopter pilot shot in the leg was the mission's only U.S. casualty.) There was little doubt that they were at the location where the Europeans had been held—the internal layout matched the former hostages' descriptions. But to the operators' dismay, they found no sign of the hostages. The militants had moved them to a new location. After spending thirty to forty minutes on the ground, the operators reboarded the helicopters and flew away empty-handed. They were back in Jordan by dawn.[12]

✳

The full cost of the failure to free the hostages in Raqqa would be revealed in horrific fashion in August and early September, when the Islamic State released videos two weeks apart depicting an English-accented militant beheading Foley and Sotloff. The media storm that erupted alerted much of the American public to a menace that had been building for several months, as the Islamic State metastasized from a force focused mostly on fighting the Syrian regime to one that overran much of Sunni Iraq in the first half of 2014. By August, the Islamic State controlled a swath of territory that encompassed eastern Syria and huge chunks of western and northern Iraq. The group, which changed names several times, was the organizational descendant of Al Qaeda in Iraq, but its growth can be traced back to Abu Bakr al-Baghdadi ascending to the leadership of the group in May 2010, and the withdrawal of U.S. forces—including JSOC—from Iraq by the end of the following year. Baghdadi proved himself a charismatic and effective leader who revitalized the organization and expanded its ambitions. In 2012 and 2013 the group emerged as the dominant resistance outfit in Syria, in the process breaking with Al Qaeda leader Ayman al-Zawahiri because of the latter's support for the al-Nusra Front over the Islamic State.

Then, in 2014, having established a secure rear area in eastern Syria, Baghdadi's forces stormed back into Iraq, stunning many Western observers as they swept across the country, whose armed forces put up little effective resistance. On June 29, Baghdadi declared himself head of an Islamic caliphate, a clear challenge to Zawahiri for leadership of the global Islamist movement. For JSOC, it was a bitter experience. The list of Iraqi cities the Islamic State had taken by the end of the summer was a roll call of places where the JSOC task force had engaged in hard, vicious fights to dislodge Saddam Hussein's forces and then to eviscerate Al Qaeda in Iraq: Haditha, where the Rangers withstood a fearsome artillery barrage to take a vital dam during the 2003 invasion; Tikrit, where Task Force Wolverine and Team Tank fought it out with the Fedayeen; Fallujah, where Don Hollenbaugh had earned his Distinguished Service Cross by holding off an insurgent assault single-handedly in April 2004; Rawa, where Doug Taylor's Delta troop had impersonated farmhands to snare Ghassan Amin in April 2005; Al Qaim, where Delta operators Steven Langmack, Bob Horrigan, and Michael McNulty had died in the bloody spring of 2005; and Mosul, where the Rangers killed Abu Khalaf in a perfectly executed assault in 2008.

In response to the Islamic State's expansion, which soon threatened Iraqi Kurdistan, the United States deployed a Delta-led task force to the region. Split between Irbil, where it was headquartered, and a town in southeastern Turkey, its missions included working with the Peshmerga and manning a targeting center that identified and tracked Islamic State fighters for JSOC's fleet of Predator and Reaper drones to kill. On September 10, 2014, President Obama spoke to the nation about his administration's plans to counter the Islamic State. He was at pains to emphasize that his strategy did not "involve American combat troops fighting on foreign soil," but he also compared the approach he intended to take to the campaigns waged in Yemen and Somalia, in which case there appeared to be plenty of work ahead for JSOC. (Much of this work would likely fall under authorities granted by Section 1208 of the defense budget, which provided money for U.S. special operations forces to support regular and irregular local forces that were facilitating U.S.

counterterrorism missions. What that meant in practice was that by Obama's second term, JSOC forces, including the premier direct action operators of Delta and Team 6, were increasingly likely to be found training and directing foreign forces, rather than conducting the direct action missions themselves. In addition to Delta's work with the Peshmerga, other examples included Team 6's work with indigenous security forces in Somalia's breakaway Puntland region, African Union troops in Somalia proper, and Yemen's counterterrorism force.)[13]

But the rise of the Islamic State also held lessons about the limits of JSOC's utility. Through the efforts of countless operators and analysts, and the force of personality of leaders like McChrystal, Flynn, and McRaven, among others, in the years since September 11 JSOC had made itself the go-to force for the National Command Authority for a range of missions far broader than was ever envisioned when the command was established in 1980. But no matter how brilliant the plan, or how accurate the shooters, an elite raiding and intelligence force like JSOC can conduct tactical missions that achieve strategic effects, but it cannot hold ground. It will always rely on the combination of speed, surprise, and violence of action that was the original Delta mantra. In many ways McChrystal, Flynn, McRaven, and their subordinates had designed and built the perfect hammer for the National Command Authority. The risk was that as a result, successive administrations would continue to view too many national security problems as nails.

✳

On July 29, 2014, JSOC underwent its fourth change of command since September 11, 2001, when Lieutenant General Tony Thomas succeeded Joe Votel, who in turn received his fourth star and replaced McRaven as head of U.S. Special Operations Command.[14] (Votel's new position continued the stranglehold that JSOC alumni had on the top position in U.S. special operations. No career Special Forces officer had ever held the job, despite the fact that there were more Special Forces soldiers than any other type of special operations personnel in the military, a fact that spoke volumes about how the Pentagon weighted the perceived, tangible benefits of direct action against the more patient approach of indirect action that Special Forces embodied.) Thomas's thirty-three-year career appeared to have prepared him perfectly for command of JSOC: he had spent more than two thirds of it in the Rangers, Delta, or on the JSOC staff.[15] (His five years at Delta meant Thomas was the first JSOC commander in eighteen years to have spent any portion of his career as an operator in the unit.)

A little over four weeks after Thomas took command, JSOC-controlled manned and unmanned aircraft took to the skies just south of Mogadishu. (The drones might have been Reapers flying from Arba Minch in southern Ethiopia, which JSOC began using in 2011.) Intelligence indicated that a truck in a three-vehicle convoy headed to a facility just south of Mogadishu on September 1 was carrying Ahmed Abdi Godane, the overall leader of al-Shabaab. It had been Godane who formally allied al-Shabaab with Al Qaeda and who had authorized the attack on the Westgate Mall. The aircraft fired a series of Hellfire missiles and other precision-guided munitions, destroying two of the vehicles, but it took several days to confirm the identities of those killed. Meanwhile, Somali and Western experts predicted the group would have difficulties replacing Godane, as he had ruthlessly eliminated any obvious successors and done away with the council that had appointed him. On September 5, the Pentagon announced that Godane had died in the attack.[16]

The hammer had hit the nail. Tony Thomas was off to a good start.

NOTES

Prologue

[1] **As Marwan . . . New Jersey.** http://www.ntsb.gov/doclib/foia/9_11/Flight_Path _Study_UA175.pdf. That Shehhi was piloting UA 175, see *The 9/11 Commission Report* (New York: W. W. Norton, 2004), p. 238.

[2] **. . . a visit to the U.S. embassy . . . Hall.**

[3] **. . . Jackal Cave . . .** *Defusing Armageddon: Inside NEST, America's Secret Nuclear Bomb Squad*, by Jeffrey T. Richelson (New York: W. W. Norton, 2008), p. 178.

[4] **Jackal Cave . . . European Command. Hall.**

[5] **. . . damp, overcast afternoon . . .** E-mail from Eva Mandl, Hungarian Meteorological Service.

[6] **The notional enemy . . . "loose nukes."** A retired special operations officer; a Delta source; a 160th SOAR source. The terrorists in the scenario were not Islamist.

[7] **. . . Taszár . . .** A JSOC staff officer.

[8] **. . . Tuzla, Bosnia . . .** Speech by retired Army Lieutenant General Frank Kearney at the DSI Special Operations Forces symposium, Alexandria, Virginia, November 27, 2012. (Kearney was JSOC's director of operations and was in Tuzla on September 11, 2001.)

[9] **Bolstering . . . in the Balkans.** A Delta source; a retired Special Forces colonel.

[10] **One exercise . . . JSOC headquarters.** Two JSOC staff sources; a Delta source.

[11] **AFO's origins . . . Delta Force . . .** A Delta staff officer; another Delta source.

[12] **Another . . . on a boat.** A JSOC staff officer.

[13] **The AFO cell . . . under JSOC.** *Not a Good Day to Die: The Untold Story of Operation Anaconda*, by Sean Naylor (New York: Berkley, 2005), p. 34.

[14] **In Jackal Cave . . . or kill them.** A Delta source.

[15] **That assault element . . . "jock."** Two Delta sources; a JSOC staff officer.

[16] **(JSOC's . . . Bragg.)** Although JSOC's HQ was technically on the grounds of Pope AFB, in conversation almost everyone in the special operations community referred to Bragg as the command's home.

[17] **Other exercise . . . of its missions.** Two Delta sources.

[18] **By the afternoon . . . the Mediterranean.** A 160th SOAR source.

[19] **. . . end of a taxiway . . . large tents . . .** *Kill bin Laden: A Delta Force Commander's Account of the Hunt for the World's Most Wanted Man*, by Dalton Fury (New

York: St. Martin's Press, 2008), p. 57 (Dalton Fury is the pen name of Delta officer Tom Greer); a Delta source.

[20] **. . . the headquarters . . . the corridor.** A 160th SOAR source.

[21] **Some OST . . . Budapest.** *The Mission, the Men, and Me: Lessons from a Former Delta Force Commander,* by Pete Blaber (New York: Berkley, 2008), p. 144; a Delta source.

[22] **Using small . . . each case.** *Kill Bin Laden,* p. 56.

[23] **Operatives . . . tradecraft.** A Delta source.

[24] **The briefing over . . . the general.** Hall; a JSOC staff officer.

[25] **Alert . . . way you can," he said.** A JSOC staff officer.

Chapter 1: A Phoenix Rises

[1] **It was a late . . . new organization.** Nightingale.

[2] **On April 24 . . . humiliated.** *Guests of the Ayatollah,* by Mark Bowden (New York: Atlantic Monthly Press, 2006), pp. 447–69.

[3] **But the men . . . to Washington.** *Delta Force,* by Col. Charlie Beckwith (Ret.) (New York: Avon, 2000), pp. 326, 330–31; Wayne Long; Nightingale; a JSOC staff officer; a senior JSOC official; a Delta officer; *Crippled Eagle: A Historical Perspective on U.S. Special Operations, 1976–1996,* by Rod Lenahan (Charleston, S.C.: Narwhal, 1998), p. 158. **. . . code-named Snowbird . . .** The project to mount a second attempt to rescue the hostages is often referred to as Honey Badger, but Honey Badger was actually a subcomponent of Snowbird having mostly to do with the program to create a special operations helicopter force.

[4] **A more formal . . . "assigned forces."** The unclassified version of the "Holloway Commission" report, p. 61, accessed at: http://www2.gwu.edu/~nsarchiv/NSAEBB /NSAEBB63/doc8.pdf.

[5] **The military brass . . . beginning.** Nightingale.

[6] **Early one September . . . was concerned.** A senior JSOC official.

[7] **The new . . . or JSOC.** Fitch; a senior JSOC staff member; *FM 100-5— Operations,* published 1976 by the Department of the Army, Appendix B, pp. 2–3, accessed at: http://www.survivalebooks.com/free%20manuals/1976%20US%20 Army%20Vietnam%20War%20OPERATIONS%20201p.pdf.

[8] **At the core . . . "the Unit."** *Delta Force,* pp. 11–40, 132–38; *Inside Delta Force,* by Eric L. Haney (New York: Dell, 2003), pp. 17–103; *Never Surrender,* by LTG (Ret.) William G. Boykin with Lynn Vincent (New York: FaithWords, 2008), pp. 68–83; a Delta officer. **. . . West Virginia . . .** The "Long Walk" was initially held in North Carolina's Uwharrie National Forest, but it had moved to West Virginia by the time JSOC stood up.

[9] **The battalions . . . light infantry.** *The Impact of Leaders on Organizational Culture: A 75th Ranger Regiment Case Study,* by Lieutenant Colonel Francis H. Kearney III, a strategy research project for the U.S. Army War College, Carlisle Barracks, 1997.

[10] **Beckwith envisioned . . . donut's ring.** A Ranger officer. The Ranger battalions were not formally assigned to JSOC, but Scholtes exercised operational control over them.

[11] **Almost simultaneous . . . for Team 6.** *Rogue Warrior*, by Richard Marcinko with John Weisman (New York: Pocket Books, 1992), pp. 192–205, 212–20; *Brave Men, Dark Waters: The Untold Story of the Navy SEALs*, by Orr Kelly (New York: Pocket Books, 1993), pp. 213–18.

[12] **Until . . . Operations Staff.** *No Room for Error: The Covert Operations of America's Special Tactics Units from Iran to Afghanistan*, by Colonel John T. Carney Jr. and Benjamin F. Schemmer (New York: Ballantine, 2002), p. 102; Carney interview.

[13] **Such was . . . full time to JSOC.** A senior JSOC official; Carney.

[14] **A new organization . . . the AH-6.** *The Night Stalkers*, by Michael J. Durant and Steven Hartov (New York: G. P. Putnam's Sons, 2006), pp. 46–56. **But Vaught, who remained . . .** A JSOC staff officer.

[15] **In July . . . agents.** *Secret Warriors: Inside the Covert Military Operations of the Reagan Era*, by Steven Emerson (New York: G. P. Putnam's Sons, 1988), pp. 21–22; *Killer Elite: The Inside Story of America's Most Secret Special Operations Team*, by Michael Smith (London: Weidenfeld & Nicholson, 2006), p. 23.

[16] **Halloween . . . in office.** A senior JSOC official; Nightingale; *The Night Stalkers*, p. 57.

[17] **Although Scholtes . . . December 15.** *Secret Warriors*, p. 26.

[18] **The Pentagon canceled . . . its paces.** A JSOC staff officer.

Chapter 2: JSOC Gets Its Feet Wet

[1] **A February . . . capabilities.** *Secret Warriors*, p. 38.

[2] **At the direction . . . intelligence.** *Killer Elite*, p. 29.

[3] **A day . . . to JSOC.** *Secret Warriors*, pp. 39, 45–47; a senior JSOC official; a JSOC staff officer. **Seaspray** and **Task Force 160** were established with the help of another new organization, the Special Operations Division of the Army's Operations Directorate. The Army created the division in February 1981 to coordinate all Army counterterrorist, special operations, and other covert units and programs.

[4] **Meyer, the Army . . . Team 6 counterpart.** A senior JSOC official; a JSOC staff officer; a Delta officer.

[5] **Marcinko had built . . . beyond.** *Rogue Warrior*, pp. 212–46. . . . **175-man . . .** *Secret Warriors*, p. 26.

[6] **Events came . . . into the future.** A senior JSOC official.

[7] **By early . . . no windows.** A senior JSOC official; a JSOC staff officer. . . . **adjacent to Bragg . . .** Although JSOC's headquarters was technically on the grounds of Pope AFB, in conversation almost everyone in the special operations community referred to Bragg as the command's home.

[8] **Within six . . . such missions.** A senior JSOC official; a JSOC staff officer; two Delta sources.

[9] **For all . . . in combat.** *Rogue Warrior*, p. 245.

[10] **An opportunity . . . overhead reconnaissance.** *Secret Warriors*, p. 78; "The Americans Left Behind," by Doug Waller, *Time*, June 24, 2001; a JSOC staff officer.

[11] **Nonetheless . . . their reporting.** A senior JSOC official; a JSOC staff officer; *Secret Warriors*, pp. 78–79.

[12] **JSOC rehearsed . . . the helicopters.** A senior JSOC official; a JSOC staff officer.

[13] **The Little Birds' role . . . his amazement.** A JSOC staff officer.

[14] **The discovery . . . bitterness.** *Inside Delta Force*, pp. 314–21; *Secret Warriors*, pp. 79–80; a JSOC staff officer; a Delta officer.

[15] **. . . but also . . . he added.** A senior JSOC official.

[16] **As preparations . . . itself.** A Delta officer; *Secret Armies: The Full Story of S.A.S., Delta Force and Spetsnaz*, by James Adams (London: Hutchinson, 1988), pp. 172–77.

[17] **The Italian Red . . . accommodate them.** *Secret Warriors*, pp. 58–70. . . . **Defense Secretary Weinberger . . .** A senior JSOC official.

[18] **Scholtes fought . . . of the 1980s.** A senior JSOC official; a JSOC staff officer; a Pentagon special operations official; three Delta operators. . . . **after the CIA . . . that year . . .** *Veil: The Secret Wars of the CIA, 1981–1987*, by Bob Woodward (New York: Simon & Schuster, 1987), pp. 240–41.

[19] **The initial . . . terrorist incident.** A senior JSOC official; *No Room for Error*, p. 116; a JSOC staffer.

[20] **On Friday . . . friendly fire.** A senior JSOC official; *No Room for Error*, pp. 107–63. . . . **the JSOC task force . . .** The task force was called TF 123 (*Operation Urgent Fury*, by Ronald H. Cole [Washington, D.C.: Joint History Office, 1997], p. 30). . . . **four Team 6 operators who drowned . . .** The four Team 6 operators failed to "neutralize their gear," meaning they did not pack it with buoyancy material like Styrofoam, according to a senior Team 6 officer, who added that "with neutralized gear they could have been floating out there for hours instead of drowning." . . . **three Rangers killed . . .** *Operation Urgent Fury*, U.S. Army Center for Military History monograph, p. 26; a senior JSOC official.

[21] **JSOC was also . . . October 1980.** A senior JSOC official; "Newspaper Reports Special Anti-Terrorism Command," Associated Press, October 8, 1980.

[22] **Scholtes remained . . . his plan.** A senior JSOC official.

[23] **Nor was he . . . the operation.** *No Room for Error*, p. 154. Carney came out of retirement less than two years later.

Chapter 3: Frustration in the Middle East

[1] **In 1981 . . . killed them all.** *Inside Delta Force*, pp. 264–95; a Delta operator.

[2] **Gilden . . . in action.** *Secret Warriors*, p. 184.

[3] **When yet . . . safety.** Two Delta operators.

[4] **(The action . . . an enemy.)** A Delta operator; "Our Hero in Combat," by Wayne Herada, HonoluluAdvertiser.com, January 16, 2002, accessed at: http://the .honoluluadvertiser.com/article/2002/Jan/16/il/il04a.html.

[5] **But according . . . several Marines.** *Inside Delta Force*, pp. 304–14.

[6] **In his autobiography . . . to death.** *Rogue Warrior*, pp. 257–71.

[7] **Intelligence officials . . . next thirty years.** *The Twilight War: The Secret History of America's Thirty-Year Conflict with Iran*, by David Crist (New York: Penguin, 2012), pp. 131–38, 141, 154–55; *The Secret War with Iran*, by Ronen Bergman (New York: Free Press, 2008), pp. 70–72.

[8] **The initial . . . of kidnapping.** A senior JSOC official; a Delta officer.

[9] **The satellite . . . in Curaçao.** A Delta officer; a senior JSOC official; a JSOC staff officer; *Never Surrender*, pp. 143–54; *Killer Elite*, pp. 88–92; *Best Laid Plans: The Inside Story of America's War Against Terror*, by David C. Martin and John Walcott (New York: Touchstone, 1988), pp. 174–75.

[10] **. . . Major General.** Although still a brigadier general at the time, Stiner was "frocked" as a major general, meaning he was allowed to wear two stars before his official promotion date; he was officially promoted to major general July 1, 1985.

[11] **. . . about 120 people . . .** A senior JSOC official.

[12] **Although Scholtes . . . at Langley.** A senior JSOC official.

[13] **Stiner took command . . . J-alert birds.** *Shadow Warriors: Inside the Special Forces*, by Tom Clancy with General Carl Stiner (Ret.) and Tony Koltz (New York: G. P. Putnam's Sons, 2002), pp. 14–27; *Secret Warriors*, pp. 200–211; *Best Laid Plans*, pp. 175–88; *Killer Elite*, p. 135; a JSOC staff officer; a Delta officer. . . . **Laurinburg-Maxton Airport . . .** A Delta operator. **Robert Stethem**'s younger brother, Kenneth, was a SEAL who later joined Team 6.

[14] **In September . . . sidelines.** *Shadow Warriors*, pp. 261–62; a JSOC staff officer; a Delta operator; a Delta officer; a Pentagon special operations official; *Killer Elite*, pp. 125–51. **Nellis Air Force Range** was renamed Nevada Test and Training Range in 2001.

[15] **Four months . . . against risk.** *Shadow Warriors*, pp. 1–2, 27–28; *Best Laid Plans*, pp. 235–39; *Secret Warriors*, pp. 211–12; a JSOC staff officer. . . . **Det 4 NAFCOS . . .** *No Room for Error*, p. 169. . . . **a squadron's worth . . .** Retired Lieutenant Colonel L. H. "Bucky" Burruss.

[16] **Already . . . command down.** *Best Laid Plans*, pp. 237–38.

[17] **Part of . . . that happen.** *Shadow Warriors*, p. 27.

[18] **It took about . . . to plan.** *Shadow Warriors*, pp. 28–32, 265–67; *Best Laid Plans*, p. 238.

[19] **In the best case . . . on the liner.** *Shadow Warriors*, pp. 265–66; *Secret Warriors*, pp. 212–13; *Rogue Warrior*, p. 229; *Best Laid Plans*, p. 243; a senior JSOC official; a senior Team 6 officer. . . . **fast-roped . . .** Fast-roping is a way of putting troops on the ground quickly by having them slide down ropes hanging from a helicopter.

[20] **But circumstances . . . leave Italy.** *Shadow Warriors*, pp. 268–96; *Best Laid Plans*, pp. 238–57; *Secret Warriors*, pp. 213–15.

[21] **The following year . . . matters.** *Special Operations and Low-Intensity Conflict Legislation: Why Was It Passed and Have the Voids Been Filled?*, by Colonel William G.

Boykin, a study project for the Army War College, Carlisle Barracks, 1991, pp. 27–33; a senior JSOC official.

[22] **These steps . . . its campaigns.** A senior Pentagon official.

Chapter 4: Payoff in Panama

[1] **The TWA . . . following Grenada.** *No Room for Error*, p. 167.

[2] **The plan . . . Dutch role.** "Reconstructie: Hoe Nederland een aanval op Suriname overwoog," by Frank van Kolfschooten, *Volkskrant*, 20 November, 2010, accessed at: http://www.volkskrant.nl/vk/nl/2844/Archief/archief/article/detail /1060293/2010/11/20/Reconstructie-Hoe-Nederland-een-aanval-op-Suriname -overwoog.dhtml; "The Netherlands-Planned U.S.-Supported Invasion of Suriname in 1986," BNO News, accessed at: http://wireupdate.com/wires/12538/the -netherlands-planned-u-s-supported-invasion-of-suriname-in-1986/; "Netherlands Was on Verge of Invading Suriname in 1986," DutchNews, November 8, 2011, accessed at: http://www.dutchnews.nl/news/archives/2011/11/netherlands_was _on_verge_of_in.php; a Ranger officer; a Delta operator.

[3] **. . . no special operations assignments . . .** Gary Luck's official Army résumé, provided by Army Public Affairs.

[4] **Delta added . . . 1987.** A Delta officer; *The Commandos: The Inside Story of America's Secret Soldiers*, by Douglas C. Waller (New York: Simon & Schuster, 1994), p. 202.

[5] **The unit . . . support personnel . . .** *Never Surrender*, p. 193. The operators often used "Range 19" to refer to Delta's home.

[6] **In 1989 . . . unit.** A senior JSOC official; special operations sources. . . . **1989 . . .** *The Commandos*, p. 215.

[7] **But Delta's . . . the CIA.** Delta sources; a 160th SOAR source; a retired special operations officer.

[8] **SEAL Team 6 . . . obscurity.** A senior Team 6 officer.

[9] **While Delta . . . on hand.** *No Room for Error*, pp. 173, 297; Carney.

[10] **Also known as . . . own service.** A retired special operations officer. . . . **covered air . . .** A special mission unit commander.

[11] **The Army . . . the battalions.** *To Fight with Intrepidity: The Complete History of the U.S. Army Rangers, 1622 to Present*, by JD Lock (Tucson: Fenestra, 2001), p. 411; Nightingale.

[12] **Once Delta . . . relationship.** A Ranger officer.

[13] **(Team 6 . . . later.)** A senior Team 6 officer.

[14] **In one . . . four helicopters.** *A History of the 160th Special Operations Aviation Regiment (Airborne)*, a report prepared by the Library of Congress Federal Research Division, October 2001, p. 6.

[15] **But the . . . JSOC commander.** 160th SOAR sources.

[16] **In August . . . June 1988.** *A History of the 160th Special Operations Aviation Regiment (Airborne)*, pp. 14–22; *The Night Stalkers*, pp. 77–93; *Shadow Warriors*, pp. 398–405.

[17] **That same . . . years later.** *A History of the 160th Special Operations Aviation Regiment (Airborne)*, pp. 22–24; *The Night Stalkers*, pp. 245–46.

[18] **Tensions . . . the planning.** *Shadow Warriors*, pp. 300–330.

[19] **Army Major General . . . task force . . .** *Shadow Warriors*, pp. 331–32.

[20] **These forces . . . Delta's operators.** *Never Surrender*, pp. 193, 197.

[21] **At 12.45 A.M. . . . ground force.** *Never Surrender*, pp. 198–209; *The Night Stalkers*, pp. 128–32, 148–54; *Shadow Warriors*, pp. 341–43. . . . **CIA operative . . .** *Shadow Warriors*, p. 314; *No Room for Error*, p. 212; a Delta officer. The four officers in the Delta rescue force chain of command—troop commander Major Gary Harrell, squadron commander Lieutenant Colonel Eldon Bargewell, deputy Delta commander Lieutenant Colonel Jerry Boykin, who had been badly wounded in Grenada, and unit commander Colonel Pete Schoomaker—all went on to wear multiple stars on their epaulettes.

[22] **The rest of . . . in action.** *Shadow Warriors*, pp. 355–56, 358–60; *No Room for Error*, pp. 203, 207–9, 214; http://www.suasponte.com/m_fallen.html.

[23] **A third . . . eight wounded.** *At the Hurricane's Eye: U.S. Special Operations Forces from Vietnam to Desert Storm*, by Greg Walker (New York: Ivy, 1994), pp. 144–64; *Brave Men, Dark Waters*, pp. 1–4, 251–71; *No Room for Error*, pp. 220–21.

[24] **For JSOC, the key . . . and the Vatican . . .** *Never Surrender*, pp. 211–12; *Shadow Warriors*, pp. 369–79; a senior Team 6 officer; a Delta officer.

[25] **. . . on January 3 . . . at Bragg.** *Shadow Warriors*, pp. 382–83; *Never Surrender*, pp. 218–20.

[26] **For instance . . . many times.** *Never Surrender*, p. 191.

[27] **In addition . . . the operation.** *Never Surrender*, pp. 210–11.

[28] **Thus Delta . . . "Red."** *Operation Just Cause: The Storming of Panama*, by Thomas Donnelly, Margaret Roth, and Caleb Baker (New York: Lexington, 1991), pp. 81–82; *Shadow Warriors*, pp. 322, 369; a retired special operations officer.

Chapter 5: Manhunts, Motorboats, and Mogadishu

[1] **U.S. Central . . . out of the war."** *The Commandos*, pp. 228–29, 244–51, 335–51; *No Room for Error*, pp. 226–30; *Shadow Warriors*, pp. 397, 405–12, 433–41; *At the Hurricane's Eye*, pp. 197–200; a Delta source; a senior JSOC staff officer; a senior Team 6 officer; a Pentagon special operations source; a former Pentagon special operations official.

[2] **On a warm . . . "dissolved."** Three Team 6 officers; a senior JSOC officer; an Army of Northern Virginia source; *One Perfect Op: An Insider's Account of the Navy SEAL Special Warfare Teams*, by Command Master Chief Dennis Chalker, USN (Ret.) with Kevin Dockery (New York: HarperCollins, 2002), pp. 1–11, 303–15; *The Real Team*, by Richard Marcinko (New York: Pocket Books, 1999), p. 113; a special mission unit source. Chalker's accounts, which appear in his own book and *The Real Team*, differ substantially from the accounts of others involved with the mission. I have relied on the description in *One Perfect Op* for some of what occurred once the Zodiacs left the cruiser, but on other, more senior sources, for the rest of my

account. . . . **Major General Bill Garrison** . . . Garrison was frocked to two-star when he took command of JSOC. . . . **suspected SEALs of telling the press** . . . It was a January 28, 1991, story by Bill Gertz in *The Washington Times* that had infuriated Powell, according to a Pentagon special operations source. The story said Schwarzkopf rejected a SEAL plan to attack the Sea Island oil complex to prevent Iraqi forces from spilling its oil into the Persian Gulf. Iraqi forces did indeed blow up the facility and pump oil into the Gulf to create a massive oil slick.

[3] **Nine months . . . different names.** *Never Surrender*, pp. 223–40; *Killing Pablo: The Hunt for the World's Greatest Outlaw*, by Mark Bowden (New York: Penguin, 2001), passim. . . . **Operation Heavy Shadow** . . . A Delta staff officer. . . . **Eagle Claw veteran** . . . *Crippled Eagle*, p. 255.

[4] **First on the scene . . . cell phone calls.** Special operations sources; *Killer Elite*, pp. 146, 158; Garrison's official Army résumé, provided by Army Public Affairs; *Killing Pablo*, pp. 73–78.

[5] **For more . . . that day.** *Killing Pablo*, pp. 217, 236–61; *Never Surrender*, pp. 232, 240.

[6] **The roughly . . . outside the JOC.** *Black Hawk Down: A Story of Modern War*, by Mark Bowden (New York: Atlantic Monthly Press, 1999), passim; *Never Surrender*, pp. 1–19, 251–90; a Delta officer; a Pentagon special operations official. . . . **a four-man . . . undervalued them.** A Team 6 officer. . . . **J-alert birds taking the task force** . . . The 160th contingent left from Fort Campbell on C-5s.

[7] **. . . disproportionately rose to positions of authority** . . . Boykin would become a lieutenant general. Harrell became Delta commander before going on to head Army Special Forces Command. Captain Scott Miller, who led the Delta assault force, would eventually command Delta during the fiercest period of combat in the unit's history, before becoming a general and commanding all special operations forces in Afghanistan. Lieutenant Tom DiTomasso, a Ranger platoon leader, was selected into Delta and became a squadron commander; Major Craig Nixon, 3rd Ranger Battalion's executive officer, would rise to command the regiment. Navy Captain Eric Olson, a SEAL on the task force staff who received a Silver Star for his actions in the battle, would soon command Team 6 and ultimately U.S. Special Operations Command. Marine officer Gordon Nash, the Task Force Ranger director of operations, rose to become a two-star general, while Army Captain Mike Nagata, an Army of Northern Virginia officer seconded to the CIA chief of station in Mogadishu, went on to command that unit and become a general officer. On the enlisted side, Delta Sergeant First Class Chris Faris would become the command sergeant major of, first Delta, then Army Special Operations Command, before being assigned as the senior enlisted adviser at U.S. Special Operations Command, the top enlisted special operator in the U.S. military.

[8] **There were also . . . 3rd Battalion.** Delta sources; *Black Hawk Down*, p. 334.

[9] **"the Americans ran away".** From Peter Arnett's 1997 interview with bin Laden, a transcript of which I found here: http://www.informationclearinghouse.info/article7204.html.

Chapter 6: Forging Bonds in the Balkans

[1] **Together . . . "force."** A 160th SOAR source.

[2] **A JSOC task force . . . their missions.** Two Delta sources; a Team 6 officer; a 160th SOAR source.

[3] **Although Team 6 . . . and retiring.** Two senior Team 6 officers; a Team 6 operator.

[4] **. . . two very different missions . . .** Speech by retired Army Lieutenant General Frank Kearney at the DSI Special Operations Forces symposium, Alexandria, Virginia, November 27, 2012. (Kearney was JSOC's director of operations in September 2001.) Kearney's exact quote: "The two core tasks of JSOC eleven years ago were hunting PIFWCs and countering WMD."

[5] **The December . . . up seven.** *Clinton's Secret Wars: The Evolution of a Commander in Chief*, by Richard Sale (New York: St. Martin's Press, 2009), pp. 332–43; *Never Surrender*, pp. 297–98, 302–6; a Team 6 source; a senior task force officer; *Code Names: Deciphering U.S. Military Plans, Programs, and Operations in the 9/11 World*, by William M. Arkin (Hanover, N.H.: Steerforth, 2005), p. 255. **. . . reportedly resisted arrest . . .** The following Serbian website presents a detailed argument in English that task force operators deliberately killed Drljaca without provocation: http://www.srpska-mreza.com/guest/LPC/Simo_Drljaca.html. **. . . Red Cross . . .** Junior operators made the decision to impersonate Red Cross personnel. After the mission, the task force decided to never do it again.

[6] **The task force . . . at Srebrenica.** A Delta source; a Team 6 source; a senior task force officer.

[7] **Many operations . . . grab-ass.** A JSOC staff officer; a Team 6 source.

[8] **Amber Star was . . . Security Agency.** Crumpton; a retired special operations officer; a senior special mission unit officer; a Delta source; a senior special operations officer.

[9] **. . . the Counterrorist Center . . .** The center's name changed to the Counterterrorism Center in 2005. *The Way of the Knife: The CIA, a Secret Army, and a War at the Ends of the Earth*, by Mark Mazzetti (New York: Penguin, 2013), p. ix.

[10] **. . . U.S. news media barely registered . . .** An honorable exception is Richard J. Newman's lavishly detailed article in *U.S. News & World Report*, July 6, 1998, titled "Hunting War Criminals—The First Account of Secret U.S. Missions in Bosnia," accessed at: http://www.usnews.com/usnews/news/articles/980706/archive_004280.html.

[11] **The president . . . its success.** "U.S. Troops Arrest Serb War Suspect," by Jeffrey Fleishman, *Philadelphia Inquirer*, January 23, 1998, accessed at: http://articles.philly.com/1998-01-23/news/25748765_1_goran-jelisic-nato-forces-serb-adolf.

[12] **Delta's Operational . . . targets.** Delta sources.

[13] **The women occupied . . . male operators.** A senior special mission unit officer; *The Commandos*, p. 216; Delta sources. One experienced Delta operator interviewed for this book referred to his female colleagues as "props." **. . . almost unique . . .** By the end of the 1980s the Army of Northern Virginia had at least two

female operatives, including an officer who participated in several operations during the early 1990s, according to a senior member of the unit. The assimilation of female operatives was not smooth. "It was very embryonic," the source said. "We were uncomfortable with it."

[14] **Delta's Echo . . . in the Balkans.** Five Delta sources; two 160th SOAR sources; a senior special mission unit officer; a special operations officer; a retired special operations officer.

[15] **Most JSOC operations . . . been considered.** A 160th SOAR source; a senior Team 6 source; two Delta sources; a retired special operations officer; a JSOC staff officer; a Team 6 operator; *Clinton's Secret Wars*, p. 400; USS *Saipan* (LHA-2) Command History—Calendar Year 2000, accessed at: http://www.history.navy.mil /shiphist/s/lha-2/2000.pdf.

[16] **There was . . . years ahead.** Two senior Team 6 sources.

Chapter 7: Loose Nukes and Missed Opportunities

[1] **While JSOC honed . . . closing in.** A retired special operations officer; two Delta operators; a Delta staff officer; three 160th SOAR sources; a senior JSOC officer; a senior special mission unit officer; a Ranger; a senior JSOC staffer; "Deep Underground Tunnels," by Glenn Goodman, *Armed Forces Journal International*, June 1997; "Report to Congress on the Defeat of Hard and Deeply Buried Targets," submitted by the Secretary of Defense in conjunction with the Secretary of Energy, July 2001. . . . **Lincoln Gold** . . . Within the Department of Energy the National Labs team was known as the Lincoln Gold Augmentation Team.

[2] **Delta had a secret . . . similar ones.** A Delta staff officer; a senior JSOC officer; a Delta operator; *Clinton's Secret Wars*, p. 250.

[3] **. . . primary target . . .** A Delta staff officer; a Delta operator; a 160th SOAR source; a retired special operations officer. . . . **John Deutch** . . . "Tarhuna CW Facility" by Jeffrey Lewis, on the Arms Control Wonk blog, March 25, 2007.

[4] **(A decade . . . plant.)** "Tarhuna CW Facility."

[5] **As the new . . . wishful thinking.** A retired special operations officer; a Delta operator.

[6] **While Delta's . . . across the country.** A Team 6 officer; a retired special operations officer; a Delta operator; a Delta staff officer; a JSOC staff officer.

[7] **By the mid-1990s . . . and Jordan.** Two Delta operators; a Delta staff officer; a Team 6 officer; two 160th SOAR sources.

[8] **Among . . . meters long.** Two Delta operators; a Delta staff officer; a retired special operations officer; "Deep Underground Tunnels."

[9] **These exercises . . . operations squadron.** See, for instance, "Memorial to Hail 12 Victims of '92 Copter Crash," *Deseret News*, August 12, 1994, accessed at: http:// www.deseretnews.com/article/369440/MEMORIAL-TO-HAIL-12-VICTIMS -OF-92-COPTER-CRASH.html.

[10] **The command . . . neighborhoods.** A Delta operator.

[11] **Some operators . . . "risk aversion."** "Showstoppers," by Richard H. Shultz Jr.,

Weekly Standard, January 26, 2004; accessed at: http://www.weeklystandard.com /Content/Public/Articles/000/000/003/613twavk.asp.

¹² **In 1998 . . . and Khowst.** *The Mission, the Men, and Me*, pp. 63–85.

¹³ **If the task . . . scratched.** A Team 6 source.

¹⁴ **The Clinton . . . bin Laden.** *The Mission, the Men, and Me*, pp. 63–85; *Ghost Wars*, by Steve Coll (New York: Penguin, 2004), p. 396; *The 9/11 Commission Report*.

¹⁵ **. . . declared war . . .** "Bin Laden's Fatwa," text translated by *PBS NewsHour*, accessed at: http://www.pbs.org/newshour/updates/military/july-dec96/fatwa_1996 .html.

¹⁶ **In 1999 . . . in Hungary.** Two Delta sources; a 160th SOAR source.

Chapter 8: "Fairly Ponderous and Enormously Heavy"

¹ **As if . . . attacks, he said.** A 160th SOAR source.

² **. . . on the tarmac at Dulles airport . . .** Two Delta sources; a senior JSOC staffer.

³ **Hijackings . . . apply.** A Delta source.

⁴ **But with Delta . . . the idea.** A Delta source.

⁵ **Responsibility . . . those targets.** A planning cell source.

⁶ **. . . a September 20 address . . .** http://georgewbush-whitehouse.archives.gov /infocus/bushrecord/documents/Selected_Speeches_George_W_Bush.pdf.

⁷ **At the Pentagon . . . presenting him.** *Known and Unknown*, by Donald Rumsfeld (New York: Sentinel, 2011), pp. 358–59, 392. See also Rumsfeld's October 10, 2001, memo to General Dick Myers and General Peter Pace, "What Will Be the Military Role in the War on Terrorism?" accessed at: www.papers.rumsfeld.com.

⁸ **The warrants and senior . . . could strike.** Hall.

⁹ **The limited . . . darkness."** A planning cell source; a retired special operations officer.

¹⁰ **But Pakistan . . . potential targets.** A planning cell source; Hall.

¹¹ **All but one . . . the Uzbek border.** A planning cell source. The other proposed targets included: a petroleum plant and petroleum storage tanks (considered two different targets) in Jeyretan, directly across from Termez on the south bank of the Amu Darya River, which forms much of Afghanistan's northern border; a petroleum storage facility in Keleft, also on the Amu Darya's south bank, but further west, across from Turkmenistan; an airfield at Sheberghan, about forty-five miles south of the Turkmenistan border; and an airfield at Mazar-i-Sharif.

¹² **It was . . . focus.** A planning cell source; a Delta source; a retired special operations officer.

¹³ **While his planners . . . September 17.** A senior JSOC staff member; *Bush at War*, by Bob Woodward (New York: Simon & Schuster, 2002), pp. 99–100.

¹⁴ **The White House . . . or alive."** http://archives.cnn.com/2001/US/09/17/bush .powell.terrorism/.

¹⁵ **Rumsfeld's office . . . "Poisoning Food Supply."** *Bush at War*, pp. 99–100;

Frank Miller. . . . **faxed** . . . The fax was necessary because the NSC didn't gain access to SIPRNet, the military's classified Internet, until 2002.

[16] **The focus on . . . enough for Dailey.** A planning cell source; a Delta source; a senior JSOC staffer; a retired special operations officer.

[17] **"Tommy . . . persuaded."** *American Soldier,* by General Tommy Franks with Malcolm McConnell (New York: ReganBooks, 2004), p. 280. "Persistent intelligence reports showed al Qaeda members traveling to and from the plant," Franks wrote. "If the terrorists were working on chemical or biological weapons, that was a logical site."

[18] **Several senior . . . radar.** A Delta source; a retired special operations officer. . . . **coherent change detection** . . . A good layman's explanation of coherent change detection can be found here: http://www.sandia.gov/radar/sarapps.html.

[19] . . . **Dailey . . . approach** . . . A former special operations aviation officer who served with Dailey.

[20] . . . **Blaber . . . waste of time** . . . *The Mission, the Men, and Me,* pp. 79–80, 240–41.

[21] **It was late . . . to be avoided.** A planning cell source. . . . **had led a Ranger platoon** . . . *Black Hawk Down,* passim.

[22] **On September 19 . . . September 26.** A planning cell source; a senior JSOC staff member.

[23] **The strike against . . . persisted.** *War and Decision,* by Douglas J. Feith (New York: HarperCollins, 2008), pp. 63–65.

[24] **The two . . . next day.** *Known and Unknown,* p. 370.

[25] **Deeply dissatisfied . . . "prime target."** *War and Decision,* pp. 63–65.

[26] **Early the next . . . and Al Qaeda.** *In My Time,* by Dick Cheney (New York: Threshold, 2011), pp. 336–37; *Known and Unknown,* pp. 370–71; *American Soldier,* pp. 278–82; *Without Hesitation: The Odyssey of an American Warrior,* by General (ret.) Hugh Shelton with Ronald Levinson and Malcolm McConnell (New York: St. Martin's Press, 2010), pp. 447–48.

[27] **Lieutenant Colonel Steve . . . deserts and mountains.** A planning cell source.

[28] **Dailey's perceived . . . rabble.** A Delta source; a planning cell source.

[29] **But the fourth . . . or IO.** A retired special operations officer.

[30] **Planning continued . . . twenty-four aircraft.** A planning cell source. . . . **Dailey attended . . .** A senior JSOC staff member. . . . **160 ground troops and twenty-four aircraft** . . . The "tactical minimum force" (i.e., the force that would assault the objective) included two assault troops (roughly forty operators) from Delta or Team 6 and four Ranger platoons (about 120 paratroops) supported by an AC-130 gunship, two DAPs, two AH-6 Little Birds, four assault Black Hawks, five Chinooks, and a command and control aircraft. The "operational minimum force" (i.e., the total force involved, including supporting elements) included another AC-130, three MC-130H Combat Talon II transport aircraft, two MC-130P Combat Shadow refuelers, two KC-135 Stratotanker refuelers, and another Chinook.

[31] **But the clock . . . not the north.** A planning cell source. . . . **three of the others** . . . The three southern targets were: the "Habash House" (an Al Qaeda guest-

house in Kandahar); the residence of Mullah Mohammed Omar, the Taliban leader; and the Kajaki Dam in Helmand province. The fifth target was the location of two American citizens being held prisoner by the Taliban in Kabul.

³² **With the United States . . . soon."** *American Soldier*, p. 265.

³³ **The solution . . . Navy officer.** *American Soldier*, p. 266.

³⁴ **On September 27 . . . Arabian Sea.** The official Navy history of the *Kitty Hawk*, accessed at: http://www.history.navy.mil/danfs/k4/kitty_hawk-ii.html.

³⁵ **Positioning . . . necessitated.** A retired special operations officer.

³⁶ **Operating from . . . staging base.** A TF Brown source; a Delta source.

³⁷ **Following . . . in Afghanistan.** A retired special operations officer.

³⁸ **By September 20 . . . gunships.** *American Soldier*, pp. 273, 279.

³⁹ **Word that . . . Central Asia.** A planning cell source.

⁴⁰ **It was during . . . didn't pan out.** A Delta source. This appears to be the episode Greer discusses on p. 65 of *Kill bin Laden* in which he says Delta spent several days planning a mission against a target he is not allowed to name in a location he is not allowed to identify.

⁴¹ **A couple . . . at the CIA.** A Langley source.

⁴² **Reese was . . . self-confidence.** Two Delta sources.

⁴³ **Reese flew . . . Agency was doing.** A Langley source.

⁴⁴ **The defense secretary . . . according to Feith.** *War and Decision*, p. 104.

⁴⁵ **In his autobiography . . . were good.** *Known and Unknown*, pp. 375–76.

⁴⁶ **It irked . . . enter Afghanistan.** *War and Decision*, p. 104.

⁴⁷ **As late as . . . no avail.** *First In: An Insider's Account of How the CIA Spearheaded the War on Terror in Afghanistan*, by Gary C. Schroen (New York: Presidio, 2005), p. 148.

⁴⁸ **JSOC's operators . . . "Count us in."** A Delta source.

⁴⁹ **In 1998 . . . capture mission.)** *The Mission, the Men, and Me*, pp. 63–85.

⁵⁰ **Some in Delta . . . "enemy lines."** *First In*, p. 147; a Delta source.

⁵¹ **One of the strongest . . . calling card.** A source familiar with the discussions.

Chapter 9: Risky Missions and Empty Targets

¹ **The vastness . . . the lead.** *Weapon of Choice: ARSOF in Afghanistan*, by Charles H. Briscoe, Richard L. Kiper, James A. Schroder, and Kalev I. Sepp (Fort Leavenworth, Kans.: Combat Studies Institute Press, 2004), pp. 109–14; *American Soldier*, p. 302; a Delta operator. Franks's book lists the time as "1429 hours in Tampa, almost 0100 on October 20 in Afghanistan," but this cannot be true. The time difference between the East Coast of the United States and Afghanistan on that date was eight and a half hours, and multiple sources place H-hour for the missions at 1845 Zulu, or 11:15 p.m. local (Afghan) time. . . . **without the essential context . . .** See, for instance CJCS General Richard Myers's comments in the October 20, 2001, press briefing at the Pentagon: http://www.defense.gov/transcripts/transcript.aspx ?transcriptid=2145. . . . **JSOC was taking the lead.** Several hundred miles to the northeast, pilots from the 160th's 2nd Battalion were pushing their MH-47E

Chinooks "to the limits of design performance" traversing "mountain ranges higher than any the Night Stalkers had ever flown" as they ferried the first two 5th Special Forces Group A-teams into Afghanistan from Kharsi-Khanabad, according to *Weapon of Choice*, p. 96. This reference says the first Special Forces A-team into Afghanistan, ODA 595, landed at 2 A.M. local time, or two hours and forty-five minutes after the JSOC elements at Gecko and Rhino.

[2] **At MacDill . . . said calmly.** *American Soldier*, pp. 302, 304.

[3] **A Predator . . . the target.** A source monitoring the mission from the *Kitty Hawk*.

[4] **Global Positioning . . . Afghan war.** *Weapon of Choice*, pp. 109, 111. (This author was unable to find any other source to confirm this level of Taliban casualties.) **. . . gunships . . .** *Weapon of Choice* says there were multiple AC-130s over Rhino, Franks in *American Soldier* speaks of only one. **. . . 105mm cannon . . .** *American Soldier*, p. 304.

[5] **They were just . . . "the way!"** Rakow; *Weapon of Choice*, pp. 109, 113.

[6] **Now the Talons . . . the jump.** *Weapon of Choice*, pp. 109, 111.

[7] **Outside . . . on the objective.** *Weapon of Choice*, pp. 111, 114.

[8] **For this . . . the night.** Rakow.

[9] **The Masirah . . . began to rise.** *The Mission, the Men, and Me*, pp. 148–49.

[10] **The JSOC advance . . . October 10.** A senior member of the JSOC staff; a 160th SOAR source; Rakow.

[11] **Within a few . . . "UBL."** *The Mission, the Men, and Me*, pp. 149–50. Like many in the U.S. military, Blaber used the alternative spelling—Usama—of bin Laden's first name when referring to the Al Qaeda leader by his initials.

[12] **Despite the size . . . its head.** Senior 160th SOAR source; retired special operations officer; 160th SOAR pilots; Delta sources; a Team 6 source.

[13] **. . . after steaming . . . JSOC personnel.** *American Soldier*, pp. 266, 284–85; http://www.history.navy.mil/danfs/k4/kitty_hawk-ii.html.

[14] **These included . . . aircraft.** Two Delta operators; a JSOC staff officer; Rakow; a senior 160th SOAR source; a TF Brown source; a retired special operations officer; http://www.history.navy.mil/danfs/k4/kitty_hawk-ii.html.

[15] **By October 15 . . . carrier.** http://www.history.navy.mil/danfs/k4/kitty_hawk-ii.html; *American Soldier*, p. 285.

[16] **Task Force Sword's . . . "lot of work."** A 160th SOAR source; http://www.history.navy.mil/danfs/k4/kitty_hawk-ii.html. **. . . only 15 . . .** Eight F/A-18C Hornets, three S-3B Vikings, two C-2A Greyhounds, and two SH-60Bs Seahawks.

[17] **On September 20 . . . "in success."** http://georgewbush-whitehouse.archives.gov/infocus/bushrecord/documents/Selected_Speeches_George_W_Bush.pdf.

[18] **. . . Central Command proposed . . .** A retired special operations officer, who said the decision to make them JSOC's first targets was made between Franks, Dailey, and Franks's director of operations, Air Force Major General Gene Renuart.

[19] **One came . . . southern Afghanistan.** *American Soldier*, p. 303. **. . . 100 miles southwest of Kandahar . . . 6,400-foot paved runway . . .** *From the Sea: U.S. Ma-*

rines in Afghanistan, 2001–2002, by Colonel Nathan S. Lowrey (Washington, D.C.: U.S. Marine Corps History Division, 2011), p. 98.

[20] **The airstrip . . . point there.** A retired special operations officer.

[21] **The Rangers . . . September 11 . . . Rakow.**

[22] **. . . when there were . . . heliborne) missions.** A planning cell source.

[23] **The Gecko . . . Black Hawks.** A planning cell source; a senior 160th SOAR source.

[24] **The Rhino . . . air assault.** A planning cell source.

[25] **Indeed . . . back to the carrier.** A senior 160th SOAR source; a planning cell source.

[26] **Franks himself . . . "territory."** *American Soldier*, p. 303.

[27] **"When an" . . . Blaber wrote.** *The Mission, the Men, and Me*, p. 151.

[28] **In his autobiography . . . American friends.** *American Soldier*, pp. 303–4. . . . **a wealth of exploitable intelligence** . . . Franks said he hoped to find "tactical maps, radio frequencies, satellite telephone numbers, lists of overseas agents, perhaps even the locations of secret refuges in Afghanistan where Taliban or al Qaeda leaders might be hiding."

[29] **"He believed" . . . Blaber wrote.** *The Mission, the Men, and Me*, p. 152.

[30] **Several . . . raids.** A retired special operations officer; a Delta source; Hall.

[31] **JSOC also . . . Kabul itself.** A source on the *Kitty Hawk*.

[32] **Another . . . October 14.** Hall.

[33] **The operation . . . refuelings.** Two 160th SOAR sources.

[34] **A couple of days . . . on the targets.** A TF Sword source.

[35] **Having initially . . . "antiaircraft guns."** A planning cell source; *The Mission, the Men, and Me*, p. 151.

[36] **The mission . . . objectives.** Little Bird pilots; a source on the *Kitty Hawk*.

[37] **In preparation . . . refuel there.** A TF Brown source.

[38] **Unlike the . . . the flight.** Rakow.

[39] **The regimental . . . psychological operations team** . . . *Weapon of Choice*, pp. 113–14.

[40] **The Combat Talons . . . compound itself.** Official Defense Department film of the assault, viewed here: http://www.youtube.com/watch?v=tFk6BmHEROE. . . . **trail formation** . . . *American Soldier*, p. 302.

[41] **After landing . . . surrender.** *Weapon of Choice*, pp. 109, 111.

[42] **. . . quintessential Ranger mission** . . . Once on the ground, securing the airstrip was just one element of Task Force 3/75's mission. The others were: to destroy any Taliban forces there; to gather intelligence materials; to establish a helicopter FARP; to establish a casualty transload site; and "to assess the capabilities of the airfield for future operations." *Weapon of Choice*, p. 109.

[43] **But the presence . . . at Masirah.** *Weapon of Choice*, p. 116.

[44] **The Rangers . . . night air.** *Weapon of Choice*, p. 112.

[45] **As the Rangers . . . "on the run."** *American Soldier*, pp. 304–5.

[46] **But the infiltration . . . pre-assigned targets.** 160th SOAR sources. . . . **flight lead** . . . The flight lead is the pilot—almost always a warrant officer—responsible for

planning, executing, coordinating, and leading the mission. It should be noted that aviation units differentiate between leading and commanding. The air mission commander is almost always a commissioned officer.

[47] **. . . one of four DAPs . . .** A TF Brown source.

[48] **. . . clipped a wall . . .** In *American Soldier* on p. 305 Franks says this accident happened on exfil. Every other source I have says it happened on infil.

[49] **The MH-47 . . . in Panama.** Two Delta sources.

[50] **The accident . . . circumstances.** A TF Brown source.

[51] **Central Command . . . hoped to find.** *American Soldier*, p. 303.

[52] **"The Taliban . . . enemy killed."** *American Soldier*, p. 305.

[53] "Escape and Evasion," by Seymour M. Hersh, *The New Yorker*, November 12, 2001.

[54] **"None of our" . . . wrote Blaber.** *The Mission, the Men, and Me*, p. 172.

[55] **Even Franks . . . book.** "Ground Force Boosted," by Kenneth R. Bazinet, New York *Daily News*, November 5, 2001: http://www.nydailynews.com/archives/news /ground-force-boosted-u-s-sends-troops-set-long-fight-article-1.920839. It is possible Franks knew some operators were wounded by their own grenade and was being disingenuous when he used the phrase "wounded by enemy fire."

[56] **. . . "frags instead of bangers" . . .** A "frag" is a fragmentation grenade, designed to wound and kill; a "banger" is a flash-bang grenade designed to temporarily stun and disorient.

[57] **. . . "ate their own frags" . . .** Two other Delta sources confirmed this account.

[58] **. . . as many as eight . . . earlier that day . . .** A source monitoring the mission on the *Kitty Hawk*.

[59] **At 11:55 P.M. . . . later.** A TF Brown source.

[60] **The Gecko . . . sunrise.** A TF Brown source.

[61] **Once the helicopters . . . on the ground.** *Weapon of Choice*, p. 113; *American Soldier*, p. 305.

[62] **Back in Tampa . . . bad news.** *American Soldier*, p. 305.

[63] **Task Force Sword's . . . were killed.** *Weapon of Choice*, p. 113; a TF Brown source.

[64] **. . . others instantly flashed back to . . .** *From the Sea*, p. 61.

[65] **As the Rangers . . . around the world.** *Weapon of Choice*, pp. 115–17. **. . . who had not watched . . . over the phone . . .** A source in the Office of the Secretary of Defense.

[66] **The Joint Chiefs' . . . to conduct."** The official transcript of Myers's press conference, accessed at: http://www.defense.gov/transcripts/transcript.aspx?transcriptid=2145.

[67] **The task force . . . October 23.** A source on Masirah.

Chapter 10: "Carte Blanche"

[1] **At 10:30 P.M. . . . of the war . . .** *Weapon of Choice*, pp. 140–42. **. . . 24th STS . . .** 160th SOAR sources.

[2] **The first . . . on Kandahar.** A TF Sword planner.

[3] **Operators and planners . . . according to Blaber.** *The Mission, the Men, and Me*, pp. 83, 141, 174–78.

[4] **For once . . . and Herat.** A retired special operations officer; a TF Sword planner; a Delta source.

[5] **Although the . . . Blaber wrote.** *The Mission, the Men, and Me*, pp. 177–78.

[6] **When a reinforced . . . "the bundle" . . .** Three Delta sources; a JSOC staffer; *Kill bin Laden*, p. 73.

[7] **. . . meaning that . . . jumpers.** A special operations source experienced in HALO jumps.

[8] **. . . badly injuring his knee . . .** Two Team 6 sources.

[9] **These rugged . . . upgrade them.** *Special Operations Patrol Vehicles: Afghanistan and Iraq*, by Leigh Neville (Oxford: Osprey, 2011), p. 29; a JSOC staff officer.

[10] **For one TF Sword . . . to prove it.** Little Bird pilots. . . . **Dailey had cut . . .** a TF Sword source.

[11] **As the first . . . cold, dry silence.** Little Bird pilots; *Weapon of Choice*, pp. 140–43; **. . . insisted the Little Bird missions . . .** a TF Sword source.

[12] **Less than three . . . machine gun.** *Weapon of Choice*, p. 143; Little Bird pilots. The **Desert Mobility Vehicle** is also known as the Ground Mobility Vehicle.

[13] **Another two . . . flight to Masirah.** Little Bird pilots.

[14] **While the AH-6s . . . 2:51 A.M.** *Weapon of Choice*, pp. 143–44; Little Bird pilots.

[15] **Not to be . . . pilot said.** JSOC staff officer; Little Bird pilots; Delta operator.

[16] **Those mid-November . . . Afghan desert.** Little Bird pilots.

Chapter 11: Precious Cargo

[1] **That was the situation . . . the meeting.** A TF Sword source who attended the meeting.

[2] **In early November . . . "order out," he said.** A Langley source.

[3] **When Reese . . . director beamed.** A Langley source.

[4] **. . . November 3 . . .** *The Only Thing Worth Dying For*, by Eric Blehm (New York: Harper, 2011), pp. 4, 69. In his autobiography, *At the Center of the Storm: My Years at the CIA* (New York: HarperCollins, 2007), George Tenet, the CIA director at the time, said Karzai made his satellite call to "Greg V." on November 3, but the helicopter mission to pull him out occurred the night of November 4–5. I have gone with the date in *The Only Thing Worth Dying For* because author Eric Blehm appears to have interviewed several individuals—including Hamid Karzai—in detail about the events of those few days.

[5] **. . . two Black Hawks . . .** A TF Brown source. The helicopters were MH-60K models.

[6] **. . . Team 6 SEALs and a bearded case officer . . .** *The Only Thing Worth Dying For*, pp. 4, 62, 69.

[7] **. . . nicknamed . . . Division . . .** *Not a Good Day to Die*, p. 73.

[8] . . . **central province . . . dangerous mission.** *The Only Thing Worth Dying For*, pp. 4, 44–45. . . . **October 8** . . . Tenet gives the date as October 9.

[9] **The Taliban . . . same thing.** *The Afghan Solution: The Inside Story of Abdul Haq, the CIA and How Western Hubris Lost Afghanistan*, by Lucy Morgan Edwards (London: Bactria, 2011), passim.

[10] **In fact . . . mountains of Oruzgan.** *The Only Thing Worth Dying For*, p. 4. . . . **sack of cash** . . . Crumpton.

[11] **Overwatched . . . climbed aboard.** 160th SOAR sources.

[12] . . . **landed at Jacobabad . . . U.S. forces.** *The Only Thing Worth Dying For*, p. 67.

[13] **But Karzai . . . city of Peshawar.** The author met Karzai on several occasions in Peshawar in 1987.

[14] **On November 14 . . . into Afghanistan.** *The Only Thing Worth Dying For*, pp. 12–16; a TF Brown source.

[15] **In his mid-forties . . . and the Balkans.** *Not a Good Day to Die*, p. 73. . . . **a former Marine officer** . . . *Jawbreaker*, by Gary Berntsen and Ralph Pezzullo (New York: Crown, 2005), p. 80. (In *Jawbreaker* Spider is referred to as "Craig.") . . . **Fu Manchu mustache . . . skinny** . . . Two Delta sources.

[16] . . . **less than six months** . . . Crumpton.

[17] **It was Spider . . . uprising."** *At the Center of the Storm*, p. 219.

[18] **Also on . . . darkness.** *The Only Thing Worth Dying For*, pp. 9–12, 90; a Special Forces source who was present. *Weapon of Choice* (p. 156) says there were only four MH-60Ks.

[19] **On August 3 . . . mounted.** *Prisoners of Hope: The Story of Our Captivity and Freedom in Afghanistan*, by Dayna Curry and Heather Mercer with Stacy Mattingly (New York: Doubleday, 2002), passim; *First In*, p. 149.

[20] **The first CIA . . . realistic.** *First In*, pp. 149–50, 156, 190–91, 231, 258, 262–63.

[21] **Just after . . . together.** *First In*, pp. 263–64; a Delta source.

[22] . . . **underwhelmed** . . . *First In*, p. 299.

[23] **(Schroen's assessment . . . Support Troop.)** A JSOC staff officer; . . . **1984** . . . Pardal's LinkedIn page: http://www.linkedin.com/pub/manny-pardal /8/468/829. Referring to Pardal by his first name, Greer describes his initial role in Afghanistan in *Kill bin Laden*, pp. 97–98. (Dalton Fury is the pen name of Tom Greer.)

[24] **After being . . . to safety.** *First In*, pp. 299–300.

[25] **As the three . . . "confrontation."** *Kill bin Laden*, pp. 65–66; a Delta source.

[26] **Schroen's CIA . . . layouts.** *First In*, pp. 177–78.

[27] **Armed with . . . of success.** *Kill bin Laden*, p. 66; a Delta source.

[28] **But Schroen was distinctly . . . "rescue plans."** *First In*, p. 300; a Delta source.

[29] **Nonetheless . . . moot.** *First In*, p. 319; *Jawbreaker*, pp. 159, 167, 180; Crumpton; a TF Sword source.

[30] **That evening . . . the capital.** *Prisoners of Hope*, pp. 254–70.

[31] . . . **using a mobile phone** . . . Crumpton; a TF Sword source.

[32] . . . **November 13 . . . embassy in Islamabad** . . . *Prisoners of Hope*, pp. 271–72, 286.

[33] **The intelligence . . . in twenty minutes.** A TF Sword source.

[34] **But this gave . . . (PZ).** *Prisoners of Hope*, pp. 288–94.

[35] **A Predator was . . . impossible task.** A TF Sword source. . . . **Mitch Bradley . . .** A Team 6 source.

[36] **The hostages . . . away again.** *Prisoners of Hope*, pp. 294–97.

[37] **As Brown . . . figures.** A TF Sword source.

[38] **Twenty agonizing . . . "we say!"** *Prisoners of Hope*, p. 297.

[39] **The aircrew . . . medical care.** A TF Sword source.

[40] **For the Shelter Now personnel . . . Bush.** *Prisoners of Hope*, pp. 300–301.

[41] **"Congrats to the Blue shooters" . . .** A Delta operator.

[42] **The arrival . . . "battlefield."** *From the Sea*, p. 99. TF Sword's desire for what the official history termed an "opportunity to refit and reorganize" is attributed to an interview with Mattis.

[43] **Barely forty-eight . . . small capital.** *The Only Thing Worth Dying For*, pp. 111–137; *Weapon of Choice*, pp. 155–57.

[44] **(Having . . . one account.)** *The Only Thing Worth Dying For*, pp. 113, 117; a Special Forces source who was present.

[45] **From there . . . either direction.** *The Only Thing Worth Dying For*, passim; *Weapon of Choice*, pp. 175–78.

[46] **To the surprise . . . and mobility.** A Special Forces source who was present; *The Only Thing Worth Dying For*, p. 264; a Delta source.

[47] **Later that day . . . in triumph.** *The Only Thing Worth Dying For*, passim.

[48] **. . . December 14 . . .** *From the Sea*, p. 385.

[49] **After the successful . . . "to follow."** *Jawbreaker*, p. 233.

[50] **. . . Erwin . . . Support Troop.** Two Delta sources.

[51] **Erwin had . . . infantry officer . . .** Details on Erwin's soccer career and commissioning are from Wake Forest's website, accessed at: http://www.wakeforestsports .com/trads/hof-2008.html and here: http://www.wakeforestsports.com/genrel /011108aaa.html.

[52] **That job . . . "as nails."** *Jawbreaker*, p. 233. In their books both Berntsen and Greer give Erwin the pseudonym "Lieutenant Colonel Mark Sutter." . . . **November 20 . . .** "Franks: Much Work Ahead," by Liam Pleven, *Newsday*, November 22, 2001. (The *Newsday* article and other news stories say Franks visited Bagram November 20, 2001. However, while not precisely dating the visit, Berntsen in *Jawbreaker* puts it a few days later.) . . . **October 21.** Not a Good Day to Die, p. 29. . . . **rusted hulks . . .** The author has traveled this route on multiple occasions.

[53] **Erwin and Berntsen . . . in country.** *Jawbreaker*, p. 234.

[54] **Dailey thought . . . to Afghanistan.** Tom Greer memo widely circulated in the special operations community and obtained by the author; *Kill bin Laden*, pp. 72–73; *Not a Good Day to Die*, p. 30; a TF Brown source; a Delta source.

[55] **After flying . . . to Japan.** http://www.history.navy.mil/danfs/k4/kitty_hawk-ii .html.

[56] **The move . . . "strength."** *Kill bin Laden*, p. 72; Greer memo; a TF Sword source; a Delta source.

Chapter 12: Rumsfeld Falls for JSOC

[1] **Less than . . . "going to be."** Andrews. . . . **preferred to work through . . .** A JSOC staff officer.

[2] **In his September . . . defeated.** http://georgewbush-whitehouse.archives.gov /infocus/bushrecord/documents/Selected_Speeches_George_W_Bush.pdf.

[3] **The day after . . . "eight years."** A VTC participant.

[4] **Rumsfeld wanted . . . defense for policy.** *War and Decision*, p. 112.

[5] **. . . more than 5,000 flight hours . . . more than 100 combat missions . . .** Holland's official Air Force résumé, accessed at: http://www.af.mil/information/bios /bio.asp?bioID=5834.

[6] **But those who worked . . . very uncomfortable.** A senior member of the Joint Staff; Andrews; another OSD source; a Joint Staff officer; a special operations officer who attended Pentagon meetings with Holland during the post-9/11 period; a retired special operations officer.

[7] **Dailey soon . . . the Pentagon.** An OSD source.

[8] **. . . *JSOC XXI* . . .** A senior JSOC officer.

[9] **On a warm . . . "'effort.'"** Andrews; another OSD source; Hall; a Delta source; *Kill bin Laden*, pp. 66–69.

[10] **But despite . . . militias.** Andrews; another OSD source; a Joint Staff officer; a JSOC staff officer; *Known and Unknown*, p. 654.

[11] **In the late . . . exited.** A source in the briefing. . . . **most senior military and civilian officials . . .** Among those present were Rumsfeld, Wolfowitz, Myers, Marine General Pete Pace, who was the new vice chairman of the Joint Chiefs, Army Lieutenant General John Abizaid, who was the director of the Joint Staff, and Marine Lieutenant General Greg Newbold, the Joint Staff's director of operations.

[12] **Rumsfeld had gotten . . . "times over."** Unless otherwise attributed in the text, this material comes from a Joint Staff officer; Andrews; two JSOC staff officers. . . . **led by Special Forces Colonel David Schroer . . .** Colonel Ron Russell was the first CTCSG commander for a very brief period before he left to command Delta. After retirement David Schroer became Diane Schroer.

[13] **An episode . . . mass destruction.** A senior Joint Staff officer; *Between Threats and War: U.S. Discrete Military Operations in the Post–Cold War World*, by Micah Zenko (Stanford: Stanford University Press, 2010), pp. 91–100.

[14] **For reasons that . . . "six C-17s?"** A special operations officer; *Between Threats and War*, p. 100. (Zenko suggests that Bush vetoed an attack on the camp in summer 2002 because it might have threatened the planned invasion of Iraq.)

[15] **While any . . . JSOC operators.** *Between Threats and War*, p. 94; a senior Joint Staff officer.

[16] **Dailey's . . . closer.** A field grade JSOC staff officer; a Joint Staff officer; a retired special operations officer; Scales.

[17] **Indeed . . . mass destruction.** A Joint Staff officer.

[18] **On August 15 . . . ordered.** A source in the briefing. . . . **code name for JSOC's domestic mission . . .** "Commandos Get Duty on U.S. Soil," by Eric

Schmitt, *The New York Times*, January 23, 2005, accessed at: http://www.nytimes.com/2005/01/23/national/nationalspecial3/23code.html; a JSOC staff officer. There was "a nuclear component" to Power Geyser, the JSOC staff officer said.

[19] **Team 6 was . . . "next week."** An officer in the room.

[20] **The secret unit had . . . commanders-in-chief.** Andrews; a Joint Staff officer; two JSOC staff officers; a retired special operations officer.

[21] **A debate . . . fourth option.** A senior JSOC officer; Andrews; a Joint Staff officer; a retired special operations officer.

[22] **However . . . shift.** A special mission unit officer.

[23] **It was mid-January . . . didn't know it.** Two sources in the briefing.

Chapter 13: Bin Laden Slips Away

[1] **Not long . . . *pakool* caps.** *Kill bin Laden*, p. 153.

[2] **They had been . . . from a Combat Talon.** A Delta operator.

[3] **As for . . . called Tora Bora.** *Kill bin Laden*, pp. 150–53, 167; a Delta operator.

[4] **As it turned . . . in Nangarhar.** *Manhunt: The Ten-Year Search for bin Laden from 9/11 to Abbottabad*, by Peter L. Bergen (New York: Crown, 2012), p. 42; *Jawbreaker*, pp. 239–40, 254.

[5] **In the first . . . stand in Afghanistan.** *The Longest War*, by Peter L. Bergen (New York: Free Press, 2011), pp. 68–69; *Manhunt*, pp. 40–42; *Growing Up bin Laden: Osama's Wife and Son Take Us Inside Their Secret World*, by Najwa bin Laden, Omar bin Laden, and Jean Sasson (New York: St. Martin's Press, 2009), p. 173. . . . **Spin Ghar Mountains** . . . Spin Ghar means "White Mountain" in Pashto; the range is also known as the Safed Koh ("White Mountains") in Urdu.

[6] **As November . . . support operations.** *Kill bin Laden*, pp. 72–74, 80–82. The description of Bagram draws on the author's time there from February to May 2002.

[7] **A lead . . . before them.** *Jawbreaker*, pp. 213–14; *Kill bin Laden*, pp. 69–71, 88.

[8] **. . . 1,500 to 3,000 . . .** *Kill bin Laden*, p. 84.

[9] **(Indeed . . . the capital.)** *Not a Good Day to Die*, p. 11.

[10] **But the Northern . . . in the process.** *Kill bin Laden*, p. 114; *The Longest War*, p. 74.

[11] **Berntsen was about . . . to Jalalabad.** *Jawbreaker*, pp. 213–15.

[12] **After linking . . . hours straight.** *Jawbreaker*, pp. 225, 239–40, 249, 253–54, 265–74; *Kill bin Laden*, pp. 99–100. . . . **December 4 . . .** The date is drawn from *Kill bin Laden*. *Jawbreaker* puts the date about a week earlier. I have chosen to use Greer's date because his operators said his book relied on thorough notes he made throughout the operation.

[13] **Once . . . remained in Bagram.** Two Delta operators; *Kill bin Laden*, pp. 100, 138.

[14] **From the outset . . . to Washington.** *The Art of Intelligence: Lessons from a Life in the CIA's Clandestine Service*, by Henry A. Crumpton (New York: Penguin, 2012), pp. 258–59.

[15] As a result . . . "Definitely not." *The One Percent Doctrine: Deep Inside America's Pursuit of Its Enemies Since 9/11,* by Ron Suskind (New York: Simon & Schuster, 2006), pp. 58–59.

[16] On December 3 . . . at Langley. *Jawbreaker,* p. 277.

[17] Another team . . . infantry force. *The Art of Intelligence,* pp. 258–59.

[18] . . . had told him a month previously . . . *American Soldier,* p. 309.

[19] Franks was . . . later wrote. *American Soldier,* pp. 323–24.

[20] For his part . . . autobiography. *Known and Unknown,* p. 403.

[21] The attitudes . . . disagreed. *Kill bin Laden,* pp. 75–78, 142–43, 293; a Delta operator.

[22] Mulholland's orders . . . in front of them. *Kill bin Laden,* p. 100; *USSOCOM 20th Anniversary History* (an official publication of USSOCOM, 2007), p. 94.

[23] Dailey was . . . "dream." *Kill bin Laden,* pp. 79, 81.

[24] . . . "the most formidable terrain . . ." *Not a Good Day to Die,* p. 19.

[25] Left to . . . the day. *Kill bin Laden,* pp. 238–39.

[26] It didn't . . . overnight. *Kill bin Laden,* pp. 119–20.

[27] "It was" . . . he wrote. *Kill bin Laden,* p. 209.

[28] Greer had received none. *Kill bin Laden,* p. 123.

[29] No Delta . . . the battle. *Kill bin Laden,* p. 292.

[30] Having had . . . armor force. *Kill bin Laden,* pp. 133, 140.

[31] But Greer's . . . radio calls. *Kill bin Laden,* pp. 138, 187, 195.

[32] In the unlikely . . . Greer wrote. *Kill bin Laden,* p. 81.

[33] Meanwhile . . . away!!" *Jawbreaker,* p. 290.

[34] On December . . . their fast. *Kill bin Laden,* pp. 173–75, 180.

[35] At the same . . . "Warpath." *Kill bin Laden,* pp. 166–78. . . . three-man JSOC team . . . One of the three was a Pashto- and Dari-speaking intelligence operative on loan to the CIA from another U.S. government agency, according to both Greer and Berntsen.

[36] With night . . . was gone. *Kill bin Laden,* pp. 185–89.

[37] To the Americans' . . . resumed. *Kill bin Laden,* pp. 212–13.

[38] By December . . . hours. *Kill bin Laden,* p. 246.

[39] Berntsen made . . . "a box!" *Jawbreaker,* p. 307.

[40] With bad . . . the bargain.) *Kill bin Laden,* pp. 243–47.

[41] Sporadic . . . gotten away. *Kill bin Laden,* pp. 277, 289–91.

[42] The U.S. military . . . not American. A Delta operator; *Kill bin Laden,* pp. 272–73.

[43] When A . . . of victory." A Delta operator; *Kill bin Laden,* pp. 270, 291.

Chapter 14: "Patton's Three Principles of War"

[1] After Tora . . . Omar. A Delta operator.

[2] But in January . . . Dailey and Trebon. *Not a Good Day to Die,* passim; two Team 6 sources. . . . "Chewbacca" . . . A TF Sword source.

Chapter 15: Invasion

[1] **On an April night . . . going to lead it.** A Delta source. . . . **Panther . . .** *The Mission, the Men, and Me*, p. 1.

[2] **The JSOC staff . . . previously.** A retired special operations officer; a Delta source.

[3] **December . . . invasion.** A retired special operations officer.

[4] **Not only . . . Task Force 20.** *All Roads Lead to Baghdad: Army Special Operations Forces in Iraq*, by Charles H. Briscoe, Kenneth Finlayson, Robert W. Jones Jr., Cherilyn A. Walley, A. Dwayne Aaron, Michael R. Mullins, and James A. Schroder (Fort Bragg: U.S. Army Special Operations Command History Office, 2006), p. 77.

[5] **Delta was . . . late 2002.** A JSOC staff officer.

[6] **The unit's . . . also there.** A senior special mission unit officer; a Delta source; a Team 6 source.

[7] **If Delta . . . "swarm," Blaber said.** Two Delta sources; *Cobra II: The Inside Story of the Invasion and Occupation of Iraq*, by Michael R. Gordon and General Bernard E. Trainor (New York: Pantheon, 2006), pp. 328–30.

[8] **On the moonless . . . ineffective.** *All Roads Lead to Baghdad*, pp. 169–74; Little Bird pilots.

[9] **As the DAPs . . . in the fight.** *Cobra II*, p. 331; a Delta source.

[10] **The flights . . . airstrike, he said.** A senior JSOC staff officer; three Delta operators; a Delta staff officer; a special mission unit member; a senior special mission unit officer; a former Pentagon special operations official; a special operations source; an intelligence officer; a senior Pentagon official.

[11] **As per Dailey's . . . around Baghdad.** A Delta source; *Cobra II*, pp. 329–30.

[12] **For several . . . suspicious.** *Cobra II*, p. 331.

[13] **In the meantime . . . to Task Force Green.** A Delta source. . . . **March 23 . . .** "A Heart Laid Bare," by Clay Latimer, *Rocky Mountain News*, April 3, 2004.

[14] **The Rangers . . . assault.** *All Roads Lead to Baghdad*, p. 225; "The Haditha Dam Seizure—Part 1," by John D. Gresham, Defense Media Network, May 1, 2010, accessed at: http://www.defensemedianetwork.com/stories/hold-until-relieved-the -haditha-dam-seizure/.

[15] **The Rangers secured . . . ground forces.** TF Brown sources.

[16] **Task Force Green conducted . . . via Coyote.** *All Roads Lead to Baghdad*, pp. 219–25; a JSOC staff officer.

[17] **Task Force Brown . . . refuel at Roadrunner.** *All Roads Lead to Baghdad*, pp. 211–19

[18] **The next night . . . rocky ground.** *All Roads Lead to Baghdad*, pp. 225–28.

[19] **The acting . . . Kearney agreed.** A Delta source; *Cobra II*, p. 331.

[20] **But before . . . "for them."** *All Roads Lead to Baghdad*, pp. 313–19; a TF 20 planner; a Team 6 source; a retired special operations officer; *No Easy Day: The Autobiography of a Navy SEAL*, by Mark Owen with Kevin Maurer (New York: Dutton, 2012), p. 18.

[21] **The tactical . . . two operators.** *Cobra II*, p. 332.

[22] **Defending . . . twenty miles away.** "The Haditha Dam Seizure—Part 1."

²³ **But the assault . . . as well.** *Cobra II*, p. 332; a Delta source.

²⁴ **The request was . . . armored forces.** *All Roads Lead to Baghdad*, pp. 323–24.

²⁵ **Kearney . . . assembling.** Two Delta sources; *All Roads Lead to Baghdad*, pp. 324–26; *Cobra II*, p. 332.

²⁶ **As Celeen . . . to function.** *All Roads Lead to Baghdad*, pp. 292–308; "The Haditha Dam Seizure—Part 1," "The Haditha Dam Seizure—Part 2," and "The Haditha Dam Seizure—Part 3," accessed at: http://www.defensemedianetwork.com /stories/hold-until-relieved-the-haditha-dam-seizure/; a Ranger source. . . . **more than 350 heavy artillery rounds** . . . Gresham gives the incoming artillery caliber as 155mm, while *All Roads Lead to Baghdad* says it was 152mm. . . . **140-man** . . . is as per *All Roads Lead to Baghdad*; Gresham gives the size of the Ranger force at Haditha as 154 personnel.

²⁷ **No Rangers . . . of the Iraq War.** "A Heart Laid Bare"; http://www .leadthewayfund.org/2010/08/captain-russell-brian-rippetoe/; http://www.lead thewayfund.org/2010/08/staff-sergeant-nino-d-livaudais/; http://www.leadthe wayfund.org/2010/08/specialist-ryan-p-long/.

²⁸ **Meanwhile . . . never used.** A Delta source; *Cobra II*, pp. 442–43; *All Roads Lead to Baghdad*, pp. 319–23.

²⁹ **A collection . . . Task Force Wolverine.** A Delta source; *The Mission, the Men, and Me*, p. 5.

³⁰ **During the assault . . . die in the Iraq War.** A Delta source; *Cobra II*, p. 445; "Scott Sather—Strived for Excellence, Influenced Many," by Lieutenant Colonel Darrell Judy, accessed at: http://www.aetc.af.mil/news/story.asp?id=123205410. The military never publicly acknowledged that Sather died in a friendly fire incident. Judy, writing more than seven years later, said he was "killed by enemy fire in southwestern Iraq." . . . **the night of April 8/9** . . . *All Roads Lead to Baghdad* gives the date of the rollover as April 9, while the Defense Department's official announcement of Sather's death listed the date as April 8. A Delta source said both events happened on the same night. I was unable to reconcile these conflicting accounts.

³¹ **Shortly . . . total loss.** *All Roads Lead to Baghdad*, pp. 326–28; *Cobra II*, p. 443; a Delta source.

³² **A week of . . . no casualties.** *The Mission, the Men, and Me*, pp. 1–12; *Cobra II*, pp. 443–44; Delta sources.

³³ **The Wolverines spent . . . from the west.** *Cobra II*, p. 444; a Delta source.

³⁴ **Dailey's preoccupation . . . "came from."** A Delta source.

Chapter 16: The Deck of Cards

¹ **It was . . . the border.** A senior special mission unit officer; a TF Brown pilot; two Delta sources.

² **With U.S. forces . . . had its man.** *All Roads Lead to Baghdad*, pp. 396–401; a Team 6 source. Abu Abbas, whose real name was Mohammed Zaidan, died in March 2004, reportedly of natural causes, while still in U.S. military custody in Iraq.

[3] **As Iraq teetered . . . Hussein himself.** Two Delta sources; two TF Brown pilots; a Ranger officer; *All Roads Lead to Baghdad*, p. 426.

[4] **Task Force 20 . . . was born.** A field grade JSOC staffer. Despite rumors to the contrary, the camp was not named after any service member killed in action named Nama, nor did the acronym stand for "not another motherfucking airfield," however appropriate that might have been.

[5] **The deck of . . . from Nama.** *All Roads Lead to Baghdad*, p. 426; a senior special mission unit officer; a Delta operator.

[6] **But A Squadron . . . villa next door.** A Delta operator; three TF Brown sources; *No Easy Day*, pp. 53–56; *Task Force Black: The Explosive True Story of the SAS and the Secret War in Iraq*, by Mark Urban (London: Little, Brown, 2010), p. 53.

[7] **On June 11 . . . routinely.** *All Roads Lead to Baghdad*, pp. 426–35; Little Bird pilots.

[8] **A week . . . "nonevent."** A senior special mission unit officer; Andrade; two Delta sources; "After the War: Fighting; Syrians Wounded in Attack by U.S. on Convoy in Iraq," by Douglas Jehl, *The New York Times*, June 24, 2003, accessed at: http://www.nytimes.com/2003/06/24/world/after-the-war-fighting-syrians -wounded-in-attack-by-us-on-convoy-in-iraq.html; "U.S. Syria Raid Killed 80," by Richard Sale, UPI, July 16, 2003, accessed at: http://www.upi.com/Business _News/Security-Industry/2003/07/16/US-Syria-raid-killed-80/UPI -78851058396985/.

[9] **Delta's A . . . deck of cards.** Three Delta sources; "The Day My Team and Delta Force Killed Saddam Husseins [*sic*] Two Sons," an account by a 101st infantryman participant in the action, accessed at: http://www.experienceproject.com/stories /Have-Been-To-Iraq-And-Have-A-Story/1543477; a TF Brown source. . . . **$30 million reward . . .** The Rewards for Justice program website's "Frequently Asked Questions" page, accessed at: http://www.rewardsforjustice.net/index.cfm?page =faq&language=english#q14.

[10] **Less than . . . man in Iraq.** A Delta source. . . . **August 17 . . .** "'Chemical Ali' Captured in Iraq," FoxNews.com, accessed at: http://www.foxnews.com/story /2003/08/21/chemical-ali-captured-in-iraq/.

[11] **On October 6 . . . to lead JSOC.** *My Share of the Task: A Memoir*, by General Stanley McChrystal, U.S. Army, retired (New York: Portfolio/Penguin, 2013), pp. 93–94; a Delta source. . . . **Major General . . .** Although the Senate had confirmed McChrystal as a major general in October 2002, the Army did not appoint him to that rank officially until May 2004. In the meantime, the service "frocked" him as a major general, meaning he was entitled to be treated as a major general and wear the insignia that came with the rank, but not to receive a two-star's pay.

[12] **But as McChrystal . . . as a help.** *My Share of the Task*, pp. 93–94, 96; a Delta source.

[13] **A few days . . . Al Qaeda leaders.** *My Share of the Task*, pp. 94–95.

[14] **Within . . . and Afghanistan.** *My Share of the Task*, pp. 99–100.

[15] **When Zarqawi's . . . terrorists in Iraq.** A Delta source.

[16] . . . **the ongoing . . . manpower needs.** A retired special operations officer; a Joint Staff officer.

[17] **Stunned by . . . survived.** *My Share of the Task*, pp. 100–7. . . . **250-person task force** . . . *Top Secret America: The Rise of the New American Security State*, by Dana Priest and William M. Arkin (New York: Little, Brown, 2011), p. 238.

[18] **During . . . ops aviator.** A Delta source; a senior special mission unit source; two special operations aviation sources.

[19] **In November . . . to victory.** *Operation Dark Heart: Spycraft and Special Ops on the Frontlines of Afghanistan—and the Path to Victory*, by Lt. Col. Anthony Shaffer (New York: St. Martin's Press, 2010), pp. 190–98. (The U.S. government destroyed almost all original copies of this book and forced the author to publish a censored version instead. However, I obtained a copy of the uncensored edition. All references to *Operation Dark Heart* are to this version.); *My Share of the Task*, p. 108; a JSOC staff officer; a Ranger officer.

[20] **Then, with . . . compound in Tikrit.** *We Got Him! A Memoir of the Hunt and Capture of Saddam Hussein*, by Lt. Col. Steve Russell, U.S. Army, retired (New York: Threshold, 2011), pp. 307–24; *My Share of the Task*, pp. 110–11; *The Endgame: The Inside Story of the Struggle for Iraq, from George W. Bush to Barack Obama*, by Michael R. Gordon and General Bernard E. Trainor (New York: Pantheon, 2012), p. 38. . . . **nine days after . . .** A Delta operator.

[21] **For the Delta . . . capture.** Two Delta sources.

[22] **As early . . . tenacious insurgency.** *My Share of the Task*, p. 123.

[23] **It was also . . . this influx.** A task force official.

[24] **By fall . . . enemy figure.** A senior JSOC officer.

[25] **Before the year . . . in the country.** *My Share of the Task*, pp. 112–13.

[26] **McChrystal brought . . . Tenet.** A senior JSOC officer.

Chapter 17: Building a Network

[1] **It was still . . . "Grenade!"** Hollenbaugh; "Fort Bragg Soldier Recalls Battle That Won Him Higher Honor," by Kevin Maurer, *The Fayetteville Observer*, syndicated by the Associated Press, June 23, 2005, and accessed at: http://www.freerepublic.com/focus/f-news/1429115/posts; "Battle for Fallujah Forged Many Heroes," by Oren Dorell and Gregg Zoroya, *USA Today*, November 9, 2006, accessed at: http://usatoday30.usatoday.com/news/nation/2006-11-09-medals-fallujah_x.htm; "Heroism Earns Soldier High Award," by Carrie Chicken, *The Walla-Walla Union-Bulletin*, June 14, 2005, accessed at: http://www.professionalsoldiers.com/forums/showthread.php?t=7150; *No True Glory: A Frontline Account of the Battle for Fallujah*, by Bing West (New York: Bantam, 2005), pp. 194–207; *My Share of the Task*, p. 136; a Delta source.

[2] **With Saddam . . . Alexander.** *My Share of the Task*, pp. 116–18; a special operations source familiar with JIATF-East; a senior JSOC officer.

[3] **The JIATF's . . . the tape.** Three sources familiar with JIATF-East.

[4] **As JIATF-East . . . said an officer.** A senior JSOC officer; a Team 6 officer; a special operations source familiar with the mission. . . . **Aristide told CNN . . .**

"Aristide Says U.S. Deposed Him in 'Coup d'Etat,'" CNN, March 2, 2004, accessed at: http://edition.cnn.com/2004/WORLD/americas/03/01/aristide.claim/.

[5] **(Two years . . . news outlets.)** A SEAL Team 6 officer.

[6] **In January . . . U.S. forces.** *My Share of the Task*, pp. 120, 126, 128.

[7] **Residents threw . . . the pilots.** Little Bird pilots.

[8] **The task force . . . gained traction.** *My Share of the Task*, pp. 89–92.

[9] **As it was . . . withdraw.** *The Endgame*, p. 59; *My Share of the Task*, p. 129. McChrystal was largely correct in his assumption that accompanying his troops on missions would bolster their confidence in him. "One of the reasons why I speak with such endearment of General McChrystal is it would not be uncommon for me to hear, 'You have to keep two seats open on vehicle three,' and that would be the extent of what I would be told, and then I would see him and his RTO [radio-telephone operator] come in in kit and go on the op with us," said a junior Ranger officer from that period.

[10] **The episode's . . . of insurgents.** *My Share of the Task*, pp. 122–26.

[11] **(Major General . . . to attack.)** *The Endgame*, pp. 59–60; *My Share of the Task*, p. 130.

[12] **At the urging . . . "the war."** *My Share of the Task*, p. 130; *No True Glory*, p. 155.

[13] **Four Marine . . . April 9.** *The Endgame*, pp. 61–62.

[14] **Surprised by . . . mantra.** *My Share of the Task*, p. 131; a JSOC staff officer; "It Takes a Network—The New Front Line of Modern Warfare," by Stanley A. McChrystal, in ForeignPolicy.com, accessed at: http://www.foreignpolicy.com/articles/2011/02/22it_takes_a_network; *Top Secret America*, p. 242.

[15] **It was on . . . the Silver Star.** Hollenbaugh; "Fort Bragg Soldier Recalls Battle That Won Him Higher Honor"; "Battle for Fallujah Forged Many Heroes"; "Heroism Earns Soldier High Award"; *My Share of the Task*, p. 136; a Delta source. Major Doug **Zembiec** was killed in Baghdad in May 2007. **Boivin** was killed November 15, 2012, when a train crashed into a veterans' float he was on during a parade in Midland, Texas.

[16] **The Marines' . . . the "Unblinking Eye."** *My Share of the Task*, pp. 136–39; a Delta operator. . . . **Mark Erwin's A Squadron** . . . McChrystal gives Erwin the pseudonym "Lieutenant Colonel Steve." . . . **team leaders** . . . A Delta operator who was there gave the team leaders credit for this innovation, whereas McChrystal credited Erwin and Wayne Barefoot, the task force's acting intelligence chief, with the idea.

[17] **The new technique . . . interrogated them.** A Delta operator; *My Share of the Task*, p. 139.

[18] **The boy . . . operators where.** A Delta operator.

[19] **Meanwhile . . . among them.** *My Share of the Task*, pp. 139–43; a Delta operator.

[20] **Another upshot . . . with a Taser.** *My Share of the Task*, pp. 202–3; a Delta operator. **Taser** is the brand name of a handheld nonlethal weapon widely used by police that delivers electric shocks.

[21] **The task force . . . as of 2013.** A Delta operator.

[22] **In his . . . those who did.** *My Share of the Task*, p. 201.

[23] **. . . the operators punished were "scapegoats."** Two Delta sources.

[24] **A March 2006 . . . from Nama.** "In Secret Unit's 'Black Room,' a Grim Portrait of U.S. Abuse," by Eric Schmitt and Carolyn Marshall, *The New York Times*, March 19, 2006, accessed at: http://www.nytimes.com/2006/03/19/international /middleeast/19abuse.html?pagewanted=all.

[25] **In December . . . "about it."** "U.S. Generals in Iraq Were Told of Abuse Early, Inquiry Finds," by Josh White, *The Washington Post*, December 1, 2004, accessed at: http://www.washingtonpost.com/wp-dyn/articles/A23372-2004Nov30.html. . . . **Task Force 121 . . .** TF 121 was so named because 121 is 11 squared, a Delta source said.

[26] **Part of . . . from them.** A congressional staffer familiar with the issue.

[27] **This was . . . in Arabic.** *My Share of the Task*, p. 199.

[28] **JSOC used . . . facilities.** "In Secret Unit's 'Black Room,' a Grim Portrait of U.S. Abuse"; a Delta operator.

[29] **But at McChrystal's . . . at the time.** *Deep State: Inside the Government Secrecy Industry*, by Marc Ambinder and D. B. Grady (Hoboken, N.J.: John Wiley & Sons, 2013), p. 76; a JSOC staff officer.

[30] **Fernandez functioned . . . one bedroom.** A Delta operator.

[31] **But documents . . . occupation of Iraq.** In addition to the articles and books cited above, see "No Blood, No Foul: Soldiers' Accounts of Detainee Abuse in Iraq," by Human Rights Watch, accessed at: http://www.hrw.org/reports/2006/us0706/2.htm; "Camp Nama: British Personnel Reveal Horrors of Secret US Base in Baghdad," by Ian Cobain, *The Guardian*, April 1, 2013, accessed at: http://www.theguardian.com/world /2013/apr/01/camp-nama-iraq-human-rights-abuses; "Former Interrogator Presses for McChrystal's Stance on Abuse," by Spencer Ackerman, *The Washington Independent*, June 1, 2009; "Special Ops Task Force Threatened Government Agents Who Saw Detainee Abuse in Iraq, Documents Obtained by ACLU Reveal," accessed at: https:// www.aclu.org/national-security/special-ops-task-force-threatened-government-agents -who-saw-detainee-abuse-iraq-do; The Report of the Constitution Project's Task Force on Detainee Treatment, pp. 118–21, accessed at: http://detaineetaskforce.org/read/files /assets/basic-html/page118.html; *Task Force Black*, pp. 54–55.

[32] **In midsummer . . . allied representatives.** *My Share of the Task*, pp. 201–2; a Delta source.

[33] **Whether it . . . moved north.** A Delta source.

[34] **There were . . . into reality.** *My Share of the Task*, p. 150.

Chapter 18: "JSOC on Steroids"

[1] **With the move . . . "on terror."** A source familiar with the commanders' conference.

[2] **The JOC . . . on the other.** *My Share of the Task*, pp. 149–51; an officer familiar with the JOC; a field grade JSOC staff officer; *Task Force Black*, p. 82.

[3] **John Abizaid . . . organizations.** *My Share of the Task*, pp. 149–50.

[4] . . . **from fall 2003 . . . and the Rangers.** *My Share of the Task*, p. 158.

[5] **The British SAS's . . . on Zarqawi.** *Task Force Black*, pp. 53–54, 62.

[6] **The size . . . situation morphed.** A Ranger officer.

[7] . . . **as JSOC's intelligence . . . assignment.** Flynn's official Army biography, provided by Army Public Affairs.

[8] **McChrystal understood . . . intelligence chief.** *My Share of the Task*, p. 156.

[9] **Delta had advantages . . . over Iraq.** Two Delta sources.

[10] **By early . . . military bases.** *No True Glory*, p. 48.

[11] . . . **McChrystal made Flynn . . . Baghdad station** . . . *Top Secret America*, pp. 241–42.

[12] . . . **largest in the world** . . . "2 C.I.A. Reports Offer Warnings on Iraq's Path," by Douglas Jehl, *The New York Times*, December 7, 2004, accessed at: http://www.nytimes.com/2004/12/07/international/middleeast/07intell.html.

[13] **The unit recruited . . . with the task force.** An intelligence source; two Delta sources; a special operations source familiar with the Mohawk program; two task force officers.

[14] **The Mohawks also . . . Iraqi sources.** A special operations source familiar with CNOS and the Interagency Support Activity; three Delta sources; three JSOC staff officers; a special mission unit officer; a military intelligence officer. . . . **the Activity** . . . The Interagency Support Activity should not be confused with TF Orange, which early in its existence was renamed the Intelligence Support Activity and which is on occasion also referred to as "the Activity."

[15] . . . **forty aircraft of fifteen different types** . . . A JSOC staff officer; *Top Secret America*, p. 243.

[16] **The aircraft . . . "Northern Virginia."** A TF Brown source.

[17] **By 2004 . . . "[with them]."** A field grade officer familiar with Orange's operations.

[18] **Orange bought . . . intelligence gear.** *My Share of the Task*, p. 157; a TF Brown source.

[19] **The unit experimented . . . miles away.** A field grade officer familiar with Orange's operations.

[20] **Before the . . . Hussein.** *My Share of the Task*, p. 157.

[21] **By May . . . to grow.** *Task Force Black*, pp. 78–79.

[22] **The Confederate . . . device.** A Delta operator; *Top Secret America*, p. 244.

[23] **The divining rod . . . its owner's contacts.** A Delta operator.

[24] **Operators invented . . . phone traffic.** *Task Force Black*, p. 79; *My Share of the Task*, p. 157.

[25] **The NSA placed . . . to the intelligence.** *Top Secret America*, p. 243.

[26] **By late 2003 . . . command center.** A JSOC staffer; *Task Force Black*, pp. 82–83, 127.

[27] **As the task force . . . first place.** A field grade officer familiar with task force missions in Iraq.

[28] **"Strike" . . . catchphrase.** A task force intelligence officer.

[29] **"Our fight" . . . wrote.** *My Share of the Task*, p. 156.

Chapter 19: Snake Eyes

[1] **The Euphrates lapped . . . "that hard."** A senior special mission unit officer; two Delta sources; "Key Zarqawi Aide Captured," a Multi-National Force-Iraq press release number 05-05-09, dated May 7, 2005, accessed at: http://www.freerepublic.com/focus/f-news/1383919/posts?q=1&;page=1901 (the original centcom.mil link is dead); a TF Brown source. . . . **Ghassan Amin . . .** His full name was Ghassan Muhammad Husayn Amin al-Rawi.

[2] **As the Ghassan . . . and Baghdad.** *My Share of the Task*, pp. 167–68, 171–72, 179.

[3] **Realizing . . . DiTomasso's leadership.** *My Share of the Task*, pp. 167–69; Defense Department press release 1317-04, "DoD Identifies Army Casualties," December 24, 2004, accessed at: http://www.defense.gov/Releases/Release.aspx?ReleaseID=8084; a special mission unit officer.

[4] **While JIATF-East . . . unilaterally.** A source familiar with the JIATFs; a military intelligence source; *My Share of the Task*, p. 169. . . . **staffs of fifteen to twenty-five . . .** McChrystal puts the staff size slightly higher, at twenty-five to thirty-five, in *My Share of the Task*, p. 119.

[5] **But as JIATF-West . . . Multi-National Force-Iraq.** *My Share of the Task*, pp. 175–79; *Task Force Black*, pp. 78–79.

[6] **A rapprochement . . . Syrian border.** *My Share of the Task*, p. 179; *Task Force Black*, pp. 80–81; a TF Brown source.

[7] **By fall . . . to Iraq.** *My Share of the Task*, pp. 161–62, 180, 219; a senior Team 6 source; *No Easy Day*, p. 46; two Delta sources.

[8] **McChrystal's announcement . . . refitting, and training.** *My Share of the Task*, pp. 96–99, 180–81; a TF Brown source; two Delta sources.

[9] **The surge west . . . elements.** A TF Brown source.

[10] **Of the three . . . Delta teams.** Three Delta sources; a Ranger source.

[11] **But McChrystal . . . surge work.** *My Share of the Task*, p. 181; a TF Brown source.

[12] **The stakes . . . Snake Eyes.** *My Share of the Task*, pp. 180–82; *The Endgame*, p. 170; *Task Force Black*, pp. 80–81.

[13] **Delta began . . . been done.** A Delta source; *The Endgame*, p. 170; *My Share of the Task*, p. 182; *Task Force Black*, p. 86; http://americanfallensoldiers.com/army-master-sgt-michael-mcnulty/; "The Unknown Soldiers: To Family, Friends, Mike McNulty Will Always Be There," by Tom Sileo, Creators Syndicate, published March 14, 2014, in the Columbus, Georgia, *Ledger-Enquirer*, accessed at: http://www.ledger-enquirer.com/2014/03/15/3002857/the-unknown-soldiers-to-family.html; http://arlingtoncemetery.net/mlmcnulty.htm. McNulty survived long enough to make it to a field hospital, where surgeons were unable to save him. The Army promoted him to master sergeant posthumously. In an odd coincidence, both McNulty and Horrigan had twin brothers who served in the Army.

[14] **The June 17 . . . Austin, Texas.** *My Share of the Task*, p. 182; *Not a Good Day to Die*, pp. 97–98; *Task Force Black*, p. 86; Delta operators.

[15] **. . . and an increasing . . . that risk.** A TF Brown source.

[16] **As Task Force Brown . . . but survived.** *My Share of the Task*, pp. 184–85; Defense Department Press Release 887-05, "DoD Identifies Army Casualties," August 27, 2005, accessed at: http://www.defense.gov/Releases/Release.aspx? ReleaseID=8829; Defense Department Press Release 890-05, "DoD Identifies Army Casualty," August 30, 2005, accessed at: http://www.defense.gov/Releases /Release.aspx?ReleaseID=8831; a task force operator.

[17] **The general . . .** *"It's the fight."* *My Share of the Task*, p. 187.

[18] **Under Mike Flynn's . . . actionable intelligence.** *Top Secret America*, pp. 244–45, 248; *My Share of the Task*, p. 155.

[19] **Meanwhile . . . detainee abuse.** *Deep State*, p. 133.

[20] **At the height . . . in Balad.** *Top Secret America*, p. 251. . . . **"Fox Bravos"** . . . A Ranger officer.

[21] **"No raid force . . . death squads."** *My Share of the Task*, p. 191.

[22] **As the year . . . Snake Eyes.** *My Share of the Task*, p. 186.

Chapter 20: Killing Zarqawi

[1] **In late June . . . "in my mind."** *My Share of the Task*, pp. 188–90.

[2] **To a degree . . . collapse the insurgency.** *Task Force Black*, p. 80.

[3] **On February 20 . . . had vanished.** "Closing in on Zarqawi," by Sean D. Naylor, *Army Times*, May 8, 2006. . . . **between Ramadi and Rawa . . .** *My Share of the Task*, p. 226; *The Endgame*, p. 206; *Task Force Black*, p. 70.

[4] **. . . semi-autonomous . . .** *Top Secret America*, p. 250.

[5] **Zarqawi and McChrystal . . . compelling target.** *Task Force Black*, pp. 84, 133.

[6] **In early January . . . were available.** *My Share of the Task*, pp. 194–95, 198, 203–4.

[7] **. . . February 16 . . .** McChrystal's official Army biography, provided by Army Public Affairs.

[8] **By spring . . . "bigger threat."** "Closing in on Zarqawi."

[9] **On March 18 . . . "here in Iraq."** A task force officer.

[10] **As insurgents figured . . . "awesome."** TF Brown and TF Green sources. A Little Bird–only AVI mission can be seen here: http://www.youtube.com/watch?v =H2tL-T-5IgI.

[11] **. . . "Mossad" . . .** *The Endgame*, p. 233. . . . **"Killer Bees" and "The Little Black Ones."** Little Bird pilots.

[12] **That spring . . . early 2006.** *The Endgame*, p. 205; *My Share of the Task*, p. 204.

[13] **Smack in the heart . . . Site Fernandez.** *My Share of the Task*, p. 206; a TF Brown source.

[14] **In the early . . . in the raid.** *Task Force Black*, pp. 133, 137–45; "Closing in on Zarqawi"; *The Endgame*, p. 206. . . . **elements of B Squadron of the SAS . . .** Technically this was B Squadron of 22 SAS Regiment, the SAS's regular army unit. The Territorial Army—the British Army's rough equivalent of the U.S. Army's National Guard—includes two SAS regiments: 21 SAS and 23 SAS. . . . **Objective**

Larchwood IV . . . *Task Force Black* refers to Larchwood IV as the name of the operation; *The Endgame* says it was the name of the objective.

[15] **Among the . . . getting closer.** "Closing in on Zarqawi"; *Task Force Black*, pp. 146–48, 150–51; *My Share of the Task*, pp. 213–14; *The Endgame*, p. 206.

[16] **Indeed . . . thousand meters away.** "Closing in on Zarqawi"; *Task Force Black*, p. 145.

[17] **The task force continued . . . opening exchanges.** "Closing in on Zarqawi"; an AH-6 pilot; Defense Department press release 366-06, "DoD Identifies Army Casualty," April 27, 2006, accessed at: http://www.defense.gov/Releases/Release.aspx?ReleaseID=9493. . . . **Sergeant First Class Richard J. Herrema . . .** The Army promoted Herrema to sergeant first class posthumously.

[18] **"This has been . . . that objective."** "Closing in on Zarqawi." **. . . about five . . .** *My Share of the Task*, p. 213.

[19] **On May 11 . . . "the cause."** A task force source.

[20] **Life got even . . . early in the fight.** TF Brown sources; a special mission unit officer; *Task Force Black*, pp. 153–56. . . . **Coale was relieved . . .** A Delta source. In his memoir McChrystal refers to Coale only by his first name, and on p. 221 mentions that "Tom D." arrived in Baghdad June 1 to replace "Joe," who was less than two months into a standard 90-100-day deployment.

[21] **Another factor . . . releasing them.** A task force source.

[22] **But McChrystal . . . in front of them.** *My Share of the Task*, pp. 208–12, 214–31; *Task Force Black*, pp. 159–61; *The Endgame*, pp. 206–7. . . . **cheer erupted . . .** A senior JSOC staffer. . . . **died in front of them.** In his memoir on p. 231 McChrystal describes a Delta medic working on Zarqawi. Two task force sources—neither of whom was on site—told me the Delta personnel made no effort to render medical aid.

[23] **The next several . . . in one night.** A JSOC staff officer; *My Share of the Task*, p. 232.

[24] **The task force also . . . as a refuge.** *The Endgame*, p. 208.

[25] **President . . . congratulate him.** *The Endgame*, p. 208; *Task Force Black*, p. 161.

[26] **. . . monthly civilian death tolls . . .** See, for instance, https://www.iraqbodycount.org/database/.

[27] **McChrystal's . . . "too late."** *My Share of the Task*, p. 236.

[28] **At Flynn's . . . start point.** *Task Force Black*, pp. 84–85.

[29] **In August 2004 . . . than 300.** *My Share of the Task*, p. 213; *The Endgame*, p. 205.

[30] **The task force was . . . the fall.** "Closing in on Zarqawi"; a former Delta operator; a senior Special Forces officer; *The Endgame*, p. 234. . . . **Task Force Falcon . . .** In a February 7 speech in Washington, D.C., Lieutenant General John Mulholland, who was deputy commander of JSOC from 2006 to 2007, said TF Falcon was created to get high-value individuals to move so that they could be targeted.

[31] **But one of . . . killing its pilot.** " 'Neither of Us Expected to Get Out . . . Alive,' " by Sean D. Naylor, *Army Times*, July 20, 2008, accessed at: http://www

.armytimes.com/article/20080720/NEWS/807200334/-8216-Neither-us
-expected-get-out-alive-; *The Endgame*, pp. 235–36.

[32] **Other raids . . . from AQI.** *My Share of the Task*, p. 247.

Chapter 21: A New Campaign Against an Old Enemy

[1] **It was July . . . in the shadows.** A source familiar with the conference; a Team
6 source.

[2] **This became clear . . . potential gains.** A Joint Staff officer; *Counterstrike: The
Untold Story of America's Secret Campaign Against Al Qaeda*, by Eric Schmitt and Thom
Shanker (New York: Times Books, 2011), pp. 31–32.

[3] **In 2003 . . . duly impressed.** A source familiar with the mission into Iran; a special mission unit officer; two JSOC staff officers.

[4] **Striding out . . . "protected."** A TF 17 officer; a JSOC staff officer.

[5] **The Quds Force was divided . . . only Coalition forces.** A TF 17 officer. . . .
rather than the foreign ministry . . . "The Shadow Commander," by Dexter Filkins,
The New Yorker, September 24, 2013, accessed at: http://www.newyorker.com
/reporting/2013/09/30/130930fa_fact_filkins?currentPage=all; *The Endgame*, p. 313.

[6] **In early 2005 . . . through December.** "How Iran Used Explosively Formed
Projectiles to Influence Events in Iraq," in Musings on Iraq blog, July 11, 2011, accessed at: http://musingsoniraq.blogspot.com/2011/07/how-iran-used-explosively
-formed.html.

[7] **By early . . . in Iraq.** *Task Force Black*, pp. 206–7.

[8] **. . . in denial . . .** *The Twilight War*, pp. 522–25.

[9] **In summer . . . death squads.** *Known and Unknown*, p. 697.

[10] **George Casey . . . by Iran.** *My Share of the Task*, p. 252.

[11] **JSOC began . . . October 2006.** *My Share of the Task*, p. 252.

[12] **The new missions . . . such missions.** A TF 17 officer.

[13] **In the first . . . days later.** *The Twilight War*, p. 527; *Task Force Black*, pp. 207,
209; *The Endgame*, pp. 322–24; **. . . Objective Clarke . . .** A TF 17 officer.

[14] **In the second . . . "Irbil five."** *My Share of the Task*, p. 253; *Task Force Black*,
pp. 205–6, 208; *The Endgame*, pp. 313, 325.

[15] **The Quds Force struck . . . their escape.** *My Share of the Task*, p. 253; *The Endgame*, p. 312.

[16] **But McChrystal . . . those militias.** A senior special mission unit officer; a TF
17 officer; *My Share of the Task*, pp. 252–53. **. . . about 2,000 . . .** *Task Force
Black*, p. 243.

[17] **Those "assets" . . . on the JSOC staff.** A senior Special Forces officer; a retired
Special Forces officer; a retired special operations officer; a TF 17 officer; *My Share
of the Task*, p. 256.

[18] **The new . . . Operation Canine.** A TF 17 officer.

[19] **In addition to . . . of the Righteous.** *Task Force Black*, pp. 222–26; *My Share of
the Task*, pp. 256–57; *The Endgame*, pp. 351–53; a TF 17 officer.

[20] **Daqduq's role . . . to train others.** A TF 17 officer.

[21] **The task force followed . . . for a period.** A TF 17 officer; *Intelligence Wars: Lessons from Baghdad*, by Steven K. O'Hern (Amherst, N.Y.: Prometheus, 2008), p. 104; *The Twilight War*, p. 521; "Captured Iranian Qods Force Officer a Regional Commander in Iraq," by Bill Roggio, *The Long War Journal*, October 3, 2007, accessed at: http://www.longwarjournal.org/archives/2007/10/captured _iranian_qod.php; "US Released Senior Iranian Qods Force Commander," by Bill Roggio, *The Long War Journal*, July 27, 2009, accessed at: http://www.longwarjournal .org/archives/2009/07/us_released_senior_iranian_qods_force_commander.php; *The Endgame*, p. 439.

[22] **The captures . . . number of assault forces.** A TF 17 officer.

[23] **Almost immediately . . . before striking.** A TF 17 officer; *My Share of the Task*, pp. 267–69; *The Endgame*, pp. 440–43.

[24] **But despite . . . to Petraeus.** A TF 17 officer; a senior Special Forces officer; *My Share of the Task*, p. 269.

[25] **. . . "in competition over the same resources" . . .** *My Share of the Task*, p. 253.

[26] **By 2008 . . . was brief.** A TF 17 officer. **. . . each flight from Tehran . . .** Of course, Quds Force operatives weren't restricted to direct commercial flights from Iran to Iraq. They could also fly to a third location like Jordan or Qatar and then travel to Iraq from there on false passports. "The Quds Force is damn good at putting in people with Jordanian passports or Emirati passports," said a Washington source familiar with special operations in Iraq.

[27] **As JSOC sought . . . fingers of one hand.** A senior special mission unit officer.

[28] **There was a certain . . . treasury.** "U.S. Frees Suspect in Killing of 5 G.I.'s," by Allisa J. Rubin and Michael R. Gordon, *The New York Times*, June 8, 2009, accessed at: http://www.nytimes.com/2009/06/09/world/middleeast/09release.html; *Hezbollah: The Global Footprint of Lebanon's Party of God*, by Matthew Levitt (Washington, D.C.: Georgetown University Press, 2013), p. 306; *Task Force Black*, p. 275.

[29] **. . . Iraqi government released the Hezbollah operative . . .** "Against U.S. Wishes, Iraq Releases Man Accused of Killing American Soldiers," by Michael R. Gordon, *The New York Times*, November 16, 2012, accessed at: http://www.nytimes .com/2012/11/17/world/middleeast/iraq-said-to-release-hezbollah-operative.html.

[30] **(Confusingly . . . G Squadron.)** Delta sources.

[31] **. . . A year later . . .** McChrystal's change of command ceremony was on June 13, 2008.

[32] **(In 2002 . . . about 2,300.)** A field grade JSOC staff officer.

[33] **. . . to declare to author Bob Woodward . . .** *The War Within*, by Bob Woodward (New York: Simon & Schuster, 2008), p. 380.

Chapter 22: Close Target Reconnaissance in Syria

[1] Unless otherwise specified in the text or below, this chapter is based on interviews with the following: four special mission unit veterans; two special operations

sources familiar with operations in Syria; a field grade officer familiar with TF Orange operations; a senior JSOC officer; three TF Brown sources; a CENTCOM source; a Joint Staff officer; a JSOC staffer; a Team 6 source; a Special Forces officer; and a JSOC staffer.

[2] . . . **nom de guerre** . . . "CIA Led Mystery Syria Raid That Killed Terrorist Leader," by Jonathan S. Landay and Nancy A. Youssef, McClatchy Newspapers, October 27, 2008, accessed at: http://www.mcclatchydc.com/2008/10/27/54828/cia-led-mystery-syria-raid-that.html.

[3] . . . **120 to 150 foreign fighters** . . . The CIA's estimates were slightly lower.

[4] . . . **under CIA command.** *The Endgame*, p. 553.

[5] . . . **sometimes wearing Israeli uniforms** . . . When Jerry Boykin included a photograph of himself and Pete Schoomaker wearing Israeli uniforms in his memoir, *Never Surrender*, then JSOC commander Vice Admiral Bill McRaven declared him "persona non grata," essentially directing all JSOC personnel to shun him. See "Blacklisted—Former Delta Force Chief Shunned for Relating Experiences in Book," by Sean D. Naylor, *Army Times*, October 20, 2008.

[6] **But an Army** . . . **"October 2002."** A September 5, 2014, email to the author from Ray Gall, Army Human Resources Command Public Affairs Office. While the operative's name is known to the author, I have chosen not to use it.

[7] **The citation** . . . **classified.** Email to the author from Army Human Resources Command public affairs office, September 2, 2004.

[8] . . . **Cardinal device** . . . The Cardinal device was also used along the Afghanistan-Pakistan border.

[9] . . . **small unit that became Computer Network Operations Squadron** . . . That name dates to about 2005.

[10] . . . **home in Zabadani** . . . "CIA Led Mystery Syria Raid That Killed Terrorist Leader."

[11] . . . **between six and twelve militants** . . . A task force source familiar with the raid estimated that a dozen militants were killed. The McClatchy story referenced above said the Syrian government accused the U.S. forces of killing eight civilians. A photograph accompanying a *New York Times* story showed six coffins for those killed in the raid—"Officials Say U.S. Killed an Iraqi in Raid in Syria," by Eric Schmitt and Thom Shanker, *The New York Times*, October 27, 2008, accessed at: http://www.nytimes.com/2008/10/28/world/middleeast/28syria.html?pagewanted=1&_r=0&hp.

[12] . . . **loading Abu Ghadiya's body aboard a helicopter** . . . "CIA Led Mystery Syria Raid That Killed Terrorist Leader."

Chapter 23: Back to Mogadishu

[1] **It was January** . . . **Yemen and Somalia.** "The Secret War: How U.S. Hunted AQ in Africa," by Sean D. Naylor, armytimes.com, October 30, 2011, accessed at: http://www.armytimes.com/article/20111030/NEWS/110300316/The-Secret-War-How-U-S-hunted-AQ-in-Africa. (This is the first of a six-part series by the

author on the war in the Horn of Africa published in *Army Times*. The sections of this book that deal with JSOC's campaign in the Horn rely heavily upon this series.)

[2] **Sure enough . . . the CIA and JSOC.** "Lack of Human Intel Hampered AQ Hunt in Africa," by Sean D. Naylor, armytimes.com, November 8, 2011, accessed at: http://www.armytimes.com/article/20111108/NEWS/111080316/Lack-of-human -intel-hampered-AQ-hunt-in-Africa (Part Two of the "Secret War" series).

[3] **For the first . . . in Qatar.** "Clandestine Somalia Missions Yield AQ Targets," by Sean D. Naylor, armytimes.com, November 14, 2011, accessed at: http://www .armytimes.com/article/20111114/NEWS/111140317/Clandestine-Somalia -missions-yield-AQ-targets (Part Three of the "Secret War" series); a JSOC staffer; two Team 6 sources; a field grade officer familiar with Orange's operations in the Horn. . . . **Nairobi's Wilson Airport . . .** "Correspondence/Touring Somalia; When All Else Fails (Like the State), Take the Drug Flight into Town," by Donald G. McNeil Jr., *The New York Times*, February 3, 2002, accessed at: http://www .nytimes.com/2002/02/03/weekinreview/correspondence-touring-somalia-when -all-else-fails-like-state-take-drug-flight.html. . . . **crash into each other . . .** "Accident description," accessed at: http://aviation-safety.net/database/record.php ?id=20040523-0.

[4] **After Bennett . . . emplace it.** A Team 6 source.

[5] **While the CIA . . . intelligence official said.** "Years of Detective Work Led to Al Qaeda Target," by Sean D. Naylor, armytimes.com, November 21, 2011, accessed at: http://www.armytimes.com/article/20111121/NEWS/111210315/Years -of-detective-work-led-to-Al Qaeda-target (Part Four of the "Secret War" series); a Team 6 source; a field grade officer familiar with Orange's missions in the Horn.

[6] **The CIA had also . . . went away.** "The Secret War: Tense Ties Plagued Africa Ops," by Sean D. Naylor, armytimes.com, November 28, 2011, accessed at: http:// www.armytimes.com/article/20111128/NEWS/111280320/The-Secret-War -Tense-ties-plagued-Africa-ops (Part Five of the "Secret War" series).

[7] **But the U.S. military . . . to hide.** "Lack of Human Intel Hampered AQ Hunt in Africa"; "Years of Detective Work Led to Al Qaeda Target."

[8] **In late summer . . . about the weapons.** A Team 6 source.

[9] **By late 2005 . . . crime of opportunity.** A Team 6 source; a special mission unit member; a field grade officer familiar with Orange's operations in the Horn.

[10] **In summer . . . affecting it.** A special operations source.

[11] **Two Army of . . . chain of command.** A military source with Yemen experience; a JSOC staffer; *High-Value Target: Countering Al Qaeda in Yemen*, by Amb. Edmund J. Hull, retired (Dulles, Va.: Potomac, 2011), pp. 38–40, 54, 79–80. (Hull refers to "special forces," but from the context it appears he is making the common mistake of not distinguishing between Special Forces and special operations forces.)

[12] **. . . and a national . . . National Security Agency.** "He's in the Backseat!," by James Bamford, *The Atlantic*, April 2006, accessed at: http://www.theatlantic.com /magazine/archive/2006/04/-hes-in-the-backseat/304712/.

[13] . . . **Qaed Salim Sinan al-Harethi** . . . He was also known as Abu Ali al-Harethi.

[14] **Meanwhile . . . "key targets."** "Clandestine Somalia Missions Yield AQ Targets."

[15] **Despite the . . . prison in Afghanistan.** "The Secret War: Africa Ops May Be Just Starting," by Sean D. Naylor, armytimes.com, December 5, 2011, accessed at: http://www.armytimes.com/article/20111205/NEWS/112050312/The-Secret -War-Africa-ops-may-be-just-starting (Part Six of the "Secret War" series).

[16] **While Orange's . . . out of town.** "Somali Islamists Declare Victory; Warlords on Run," by Marc Lacy, *The New York Times*, June 6, 2006, accessed at: http://select .nytimes.com/gst/abstract.html?res=FB0811FB3F550C758CDDAF0894DE404 482.

[17] **The warlords' defeat . . . in Somalia.** A special mission unit member.

[18] **Now, three years . . . assets to the Horn.** "Lack of Human Intel Hampered AQ Hunt in Africa."

[19] **In late 2006 . . . into Somalia.** A Team 6 source.

[20] **The Team 6 operators . . . last resort.** A Team 6 source; "The Secret War: Tense Ties Plagued Africa Ops"; "'Foreign Fighters' Die in Somalia," BBC News, June 3, 2007, accessed at: http://news.bbc.co.uk/2/hi/africa/6716725.stm.

[21] **The operations that led . . . "more aggressive."** "The Secret War: Tense Ties Plagued Africa Ops"; a Team 6 source. . . . **small force at Dire Dawe** . . . *The Way of the Knife*, pp. 149–50.

[22] **The command also . . . shortly thereafter.** "The Secret War: Tense Ties Plagued Africa Ops"; *Dirty Wars: The World Is a Battlefield*, by Jeremy Scahill (New York: Nation Books, 2013), pp. 220–22; *The Way of the Knife*, p. 150. . . . **The Washington Post reported** . . . "U.S. Stages 2nd Airstrike in Somalia; Ethiopians Leaving Capital," by Karen DeYoung and Stephanie McCrummen, *The Washington Post*, January 24, 2007. . . . **a little more than two weeks later** . . . The date of the attack has been variously reported as January 22 (by *The Washington Post*) and January 24 (by Scahill).

[23] **Planned as a . . . and get away.** A Team 6 source; "The Secret War: Tense Ties Plagued Africa Ops"; "U.S. Destroyer Shells Somali Militants," by Jeff Schogol, *Stars and Stripes*, June 5, 2007, accessed at: http://www.stripes.com/news/u-s-destroyer -shells-somali-militants-1.65000; a military intelligence source.

[24] **JSOC's missions . . . intelligence official.** A Team 6 source; "The Secret War: Tense Ties Plagued Africa Ops."

[25] **U.S. intelligence concluded . . . summer 2007.** *Deep State*, p. 157.

[26] **JSOC believed . . . Ras Kamboni.** "Clandestine Somalia Missions Yield AQ Targets."

[27] **Operators also . . . their country.** "The Secret War: Tense Ties Plagued Africa Ops."

[28] **Although the decision . . . official added.** "The Secret War: How U.S. Hunted AQ in Africa."

[29] **With the AC-130s . . . reckoning with Nabhan.** "The Secret War: Tense Ties Plagued Africa Ops"; *My Share of the Task*, pp. 270–71; "U.S. Airstrike Kills Top Qaeda Agent in Somalia," by Jeffrey Gettleman and Eric Schmitt, *The New York Times*, May 1, 2008, accessed at: http://www.nytimes.com/2008/05/01/world/africa /01iht-02somalia.12481389.html.

Chapter 24: Victory in Mosul?

[1] Except where otherwise specified, the account of the assault on Objective Crescent Lake is drawn from an interview with a Task Force North source.

[2] **. . . somehow escaped the Rangers' cordon . . .** JSOC called insurgents who tried to flee "squirters."

[3] **. . . a major . . .** Because command of Ranger platoons, companies, and battalions is limited to officers who have already commanded at that level in a conventional infantry unit, Ranger commanders often hold a higher rank than would be the norm for officers holding the same job in a conventional outfit.

[4] **"I'm tired . . . doing this."** A briefing shown to the author.

[5] **The result . . . twenty-seven to eleven.** A briefing shown to the author.

[6] **Numbers . . . declare victory.** "Winning Isn't News," *Investor's Business Daily,* July 7, 2008; "Al Qaeda Is Driven from Mosul Bastion After Bloody Last Stand," by Marie Colvin, *The Sunday Times* (London), July 6, 2008.

[7] **McRaven was . . . levels of government.** McRaven's official Navy biography, accessed at: http://www.navy.mil/navydata/bios/navybio.asp?bioID=401; *Spec Ops: Case Studies in Special Operations Warfare: Theory and Practice*, by William H. McRaven (New York: Ballantine, 1996), p. 2.

[8] **. . . drove his subordinates slightly harder . . .** A TF Brown source.

[9] **. . . flatten and broaden . . .** Admiral Bill McRaven speech, National Defense Industrial Association Special Operations and Low-Intensity Conflict symposium, January 29, 2013, in Washington, D.C., attended by the author.

[10] **But JSOC's . . . to Afghanistan.** A retired Special Forces officer.

[11] **The task force was now . . . foreign leader.** *The Endgame*, p. 519; "In Maliki's Hometown, Grief and Questions After Deadly U.S. Raid," by Qassim Zein and Hannah Allam, McClatchy Newspapers, June 29, 2008, accessed at: http://www .mcclatchydc.com/2008/06/29/42641/in-malikis-hometown-grief-and.html.

[12] **. . . status of forces agreement . . .** The agreement's full name was "The Agreement Between the United States of America and the Republic of Iraq on the Withdrawal of United States Forces from Iraq and the Organization of Their Activities During Their Temporary Presence in Iraq."

[13] **The agreement's requirement . . . provided one.** "Spec Ops Catches, Iraq Releases," by Sean D. Naylor, *Army Times*, April 19, 2010.

[14] **By early 2010 . . . Salahuddin provinces.** *The Endgame*, p. 623.

[15] **By the first . . . control of Fallujah.** "Al-Qaeda-Linked Force Captures Fallujah Amid Rise in Violence in Iraq," by Liz Sly, *The Washington Post*, January 3, 2014, accessed at: http://www.washingtonpost.com/world/al-qaeda-force-captures-fallujah

-amid-rise-in-violence-in-iraq/2014/01/03/8abaeb2a-74aa-11e3-8def-a33011492df2
_story.html.

Chapter 25: Rangers Step Up in Afghanistan

[1] **After Operation . . . new president.** A senior JSOC officer; a senior Team 6 officer.

[2] **. . . Corporal Pat Tillman . . .** The Army promoted Tillman from specialist to corporal posthumously.

[3] **. . . knew immediately . . .** *Where Men Win Glory: The Odyssey of Pat Tillman*, by Jon Krakauer (New York: Doubleday, 2009), p. 277.

[4] **Around 2005 . . . military skills.** Two senior Team 6 sources; a special operations source familiar with the Counterterrorism Pursuit Teams; *No Easy Day*, p. 67.

[5] **During the decade's . . . chain of command.** Several task force sources. . . . **Niland II . . .** Niland, California, is home to a SEAL training facility.

[6] **Even with . . . aircraft.** Two senior Team 6 sources; a military intelligence source.

[7] **In 2008 . . . 1,000 people.** *Top Secret America*, p. 251.

[8] **". . . our actions were . . ."** *Top Secret America*, p. 229.

[9] **Despite the vastly . . . platoon to Afghanistan.** A Team 6 source.

[10] **Team 6 . . . whenever possible.** *No Easy Day*, pp. 137, 168; Team 6 sources.

[11] **No JSOC . . . "grooming standards."** Ranger sources.

[12] **Several factors . . . and Yemen.** A senior Team 6 source.

[13] **By mid-2009 . . . "least important."** Ranger sources. . . . **shut down their entire networks . . .** "Taliban Cut Cellphone Service in Helmand," by Ray Rivera and Sangar Rahimi, from *The New York Times*'s "At War" blog, March 24, 2011, accessed at: http://atwar.blogs.nytimes.com/2011/03/24/taliban-cuts-cellphone -service-in-helmand/. . . . **on his twelfth combat deployment . . .** "Frederick Army Ranger Killed in Afghanistan," by Megan Eckstein, *The Frederick News-Post* (Maryland), October 5, 2010, accessed at: http://www.fredericknewspost.com/archive/article _fdf2922a-9548-52a0-85e5-de940165f1cc.html?mode=jqm.

[14] **(The ISAF . . . JSOC operations.)** A military public affairs officer.

[15] **In the most notorious . . . of the event.** *Dirty Wars*, pp. 334–47. . . . **Rangers . . .** A JSOC source.

[16] **. . . tremendously unpopular . . .** A senior Team 6 source; *No Easy Day*, p. 141.

[17] **Two years . . . the engineer.** "Exclusive: Inside a U.S. Hostage Rescue Mission," by Sean D. Naylor, *Navy Times*, November 7, 2008, accessed at: http://www.navy times.com/article/20081107/NEWS/811070315/Exclusive-Inside-U-S-hostage -rescue-mission; a senior Team 6 source.

[18] **The Norgrove mission fell . . . into the new squadron.** A senior Team 6 source.

[19] **Unlike . . . to the ground.** A 160th SOAR source; a Team 6 source.

[20] **A manned ISR . . . redeem itself.** Team 6 sources; official investigation into the Norgrove mission, available in redacted form on the Central Command website at: http://www2.centcom.mil/sites/foia/rr/default.aspx.

Chapter 26: Hit and Miss in Pakistan

[1] **The helicopter . . . "on a plane."** Two Team 6 sources; "Inside Command Post in Hunt for bin Laden," by David Wood, Newhouse News Service, March 8, 2002, accessed at: http://community.seattletimes.nwsource.com/archive/?date=20020308 &slug=hunt08. Wood's story, which was written while he was embedded in the Task Force Mountain headquarters at Bagram, and which had material deleted by military censors, makes no mention of the family being victims. However, interviews with SEALs on the mission and a comparison of dates and other details make it clear the mission described in the Wood story and the mission described by the SEALs are one and the same.

[2] **A few weeks . . . "for them."** Three JSOC sources; a Delta operator; a retired special operations officer.

[3] **But the cross-border . . . never jumped.** Three Team 6 sources.

[4] **A year later . . . canceled the mission.** *The Way of the Knife*, pp. 115–16. A senior Team 6 source.

[5] **But Team 6 kept . . . "package."** Team 6 sources. . . . **August 31 . . .** "British Hostage Found Dead in Afghanistan," by Colin Freeman and Tom Coghlan, *The Telegraph*, September 4, 2005, accessed at: http://www.telegraph.co.uk/news/world news/asia/afghanistan/1497611/British-hostage-found-dead-in-Afghanistan.html.

[6] **An investigation . . . chute in time.** "Navy: SEALs' Own Errors Led to Chute Deaths," by Carol Ann Alaimo, *Arizona Daily Star*, February 7, 2009, accessed at: http://tucson.com/news/local/govt-and-politics/navy-seals-own-errors-led-to -chute-deaths/article_e019c515-955f-5d18-9d3d-6ad2116693a9.html.

[7] **To get around . . . locate the phone.** *The Way of the Knife*, p. 134.

[8] **In the fall . . . drone strike.** Two senior Team 6 sources.

[9] **The deception . . . "Hamza Rabia."** "Key Al Qaeda Figure Reported Killed in Blast," National Public Radio, December 3, 2005, accessed at: http://www.npr.org /templates/story/story.php?storyId=5037605.

[10] **But within . . . the truth.** "Shrapnel Points to Drone in Pakistan Attack," Fox News, December 5, 2005, accessed at: http://www.foxnews.com/story/2005/12/05 /shrapnel-points-to-drone-in-pakistan-attack/.

[11] **Reputable news . . . drone strike.** "The New Al-Qaeda Central," by Craig Whitlock, *The Washington Post*, September 9, 2007, accessed at: http://www .washingtonpost.com/wp-dyn/content/article/2007/09/08/AR2007090801845_pf .html.

[12] **In the summer . . . opportunity slip.** *Counterstrike*, pp. 115–18; a 160th SOAR source; *No Easy Day*, pp. 150–52.

[13] **After taking . . . "zippo."** Three Team 6 sources; a 160th SOAR source. **Officials there . . . "provocation."** "U.S. Troops Crossed Border, Pakistan Says," by Candace Rondeaux and Karen DeYoung, *The Washington Post*, September 4, 2008, accessed at: http://www.washingtonpost.com/wp-dyn/content/article/2008/09/03 /AR2008090300523.html?hpid=moreheadlines.

Chapter 27: A Reckoning in Abbottabad

[1] **In late January . . . at the Agency.** *Manhunt*, pp. 165–67.

[2] **There was much . . . missions into Pakistan.** "A Triumph for JSOC," by Sean D. Naylor, *Defense News*, May 9, 2011, accessed at: http://www.defensenews.com/print /article/20110509/DEFFEAT06/105090325/A-Triumph-JSOC.

[3] **Instead of tapping . . . to run Team 6.** Team 6 sources. . . . **Pete Van Hooser . . .** For open sources that Van Hooser was the commander of Team 6, aka Naval Special Warfare Development Group, see his bio on the Academi web page, accessed at: http://academi.com/pages/about-us/management/pete-van-hooser-vp; and the mention of him as a "Leader in Residence" on the Virginia Military Institute's website, accessed at: http://www.vmi.edu/Leadership_and_Ethics/Cadet _Experience/Leader_in_Residence/. **The silver-haired . . . parachuting accident . . .** *No Easy Day*, p. 195.

[4] **McRaven's selection . . . "White House."** *No Easy Day*, p. 187.

[5] **Some in Team 6 . . . previously.** Team 6 sources; "William McRaven: The Admiral," by Barton Gellman, *Time*, December 14, 2011, accessed at: http://content .time.com/time/specials/packages/article/0,28804,2101745_2102133_2102330 -1,00.html; *Brave Men, Dark Waters*, p. 234.

[6] **But McRaven . . . "five years."** Email from Ken McGraw, U.S. Special Operations Command public affairs officer, May 5, 2014, with responses from Admiral McRaven to questions posed earlier by the author to Ken McGraw.

[7] **The tension . . . run the operation.** A source familiar with the episode.

[8] **Shortly thereafter . . . according to Bissonnette . . .** *No Easy Day*, pp. 158, 185–86; a Team 6 source.

[9] **Red Squadron's . . . to prepare.** A Team 6 source.

[10] **The 160th . . . to fly.** "Mission Helo Was Secret Stealth Black Hawk," by Sean D. Naylor, *Army Times*, May 4, 2011, accessed at: http://www.armytimes.com /article/20110504/NEWS/105040314/Mission-helo-secret-stealth-Black-Hawk; two 160th SOAR veterans.

[11] **But when David . . . refused to do.** A Team 6 source; "Shadow Games," by Paul D. Shinkman, *U.S. News & World Report*, November 13, 2013, accessed at: http://www.usnews.com/news/articles/2013/11/14/seal-team-6-chief-demystifies -somalia-capt-phillips-bin-laden-missions.

[12] **Training for . . . stealth Black Hawks.** A Team 6 source.

[13] **. . . established a safe house . . .** *Manhunt*, p. 131.

[14] **The operators were . . . "different teams."** *No Easy Day*, pp. 174–75.

[15] **. . . several published accounts . . .** *Manhunt*, pp. 180–81; *The Finish: The Killing of Osama bin Laden*, by Mark Bowden (New York: Atlantic Monthly Press, 2012), pp. 170–72.

[16] **About a week . . . needed it.** A Team 6 source.

[17] **On April 29 . . . April 30.** *Manhunt*, pp. 205–8.

[18] **McRaven disputed . . . "publicly."** McGraw email, May 5, 2014.

[19] **With the helicopters . . . wasn't answered.** A Team 6 source.

[20] **Then with . . . was dead.** *No Easy Day*, pp. 209–37. O'Neill has disputed the account in *No Easy Day*, and has claimed that he fired the two shots that killed bin Laden. See: "Another Ex-Command Says He Shot Bin Laden," by Nicholas Kulish, Christopher Drew, and Sean D. Naylor, *The New York Times*, November 6, 2014, accessed at: http://www.nytimes.com/2014/11/07/world/asia/another-ex-commando-says-he-shot-bin-laden.html?_r=0, and "Ex-SEAL Robert O'Neill Reveals Himself As Shooter Who Killed Osama Bin Laden," by Joby Warrick, *The Washington Post*, November 6, 2014, accessed at: http://www.washingtonpost.com/world/national-security/ex-seal-robert-oneill-reveals-himself-as-shooter-who-killed-osama-bin-laden/2014/11/06/2bf46f3e-65dc-11e4-836c-83bc4f26eb67_story.html. . . . **settling with power** . . . "Mission Helo Was Secret Stealth Black Hawk."

[21] **. . . stacks of boxes untouched** . . . *No Easy Day*, p. 261.

[22] **. . . a dozen other missions** . . . "Getting bin Laden," by Nicholas Schmidle, *The New Yorker*, August 8, 2011.

Chapter 28: Successes, and a Failure

[1] **On April 8 . . . orange lifeboat.** *A Captain's Duty*, by Richard Phillips with Stephen Talty (New York: Hyperion, 2010), pp. 106–76. . . . **four teenage Somali pirates** . . . "Somalian Pirate Suspect Arrives in New York to Be Tried in U.S. Court," by the Associated Press, April 20, 2009, accessed at: http://www.cbc.ca/news/world/somalian-pirate-suspect-arrives-in-new-york-to-be-tried-in-u-s-court-1.777441.

[2] **In 2008 . . . seizing forty-two.** "Pirates Hijack Two Tankers Within 24 Hours Off Somali Shore," Associated Press, March 26, 2009, accessed on FoxNews.com at: http://www.foxnews.com/story/2009/03/26/pirates-hijack-two-tankers-within-24-hours-off-somali-shore/.

[3] **Around late 2004 . . . respectively.** A TF Brown source.

[4] **Plans were soon . . . off the Somali coast.** Team 6 sources.

[5] **In a desire . . . beside the *Bainbridge*.** Team 6 sources. One of the SEALs was Lieutenant Commander Jonas Kelsall, who died on Extortion 17.

[6] **. . . night of April 8 . . .** *No Easy Day*, p. 89.

[7] **A little more . . . catch up with him.** *A Captain's Duty*, pp. 200–205.

[8] **Meanwhile, in . . . Lightning Dawn.** Team 6 sources.

[9] **After an almost twenty-hour . . . to the *Bainbridge*.** Team 6 sources; *No Easy Day*, pp. 89–94.

[10] **Once on the destroyer . . . in that direction.** Team 6 sources.

[11] **On the morning . . . of his ordeal.** *A Captain's Duty*, p. 255.

[12] **Meanwhile, the lifeboat . . . "don't fuck it up."** Team 6 sources.

[13] **Half a dozen . . . as possible.** *A Captain's Duty*, pp. 261–63; *No Easy Day*, pp. 96–97.

[14] **The snipers had . . . with plaudits.** Team 6 sources.

[15] **It was also . . . told the admiral.** *Manhunt*, p. 148.

[16] **For several months . . . isolated area.** Team 6 sources; military intelligence source.

[17] **In the second week . . . strike that night.** *Kill or Capture: The War on Terror and the Soul of the Obama Presidency*, by Daniel Klaidman (New York: Houghton Mifflin Harcourt, 2012), pp. 122–26; *The Way of the Knife*, pp. 246–47; a White House source; a Team 6 source; two Task Force Brown sources.

[18] **The next day . . . buried at sea.** A Team 6 source; two Task Force Brown sources; a White House source. Other JSOC sources said that there were two destroyers involved, and that the AH-6s also fired into the vehicle, disabling it. . . . **Baraawe . . .** "U.S. Kills Top Qaeda Militant in Southern Somalia," by Jeffrey Gettleman and Eric Schmitt, *The New York Times*, September 14, 2009, accessed at: http://www.nytimes .com/2009/09/15/world/africa/15raid.html?hp. . . . **U-28A . . .** The U-28A is the Air Force Special Operations variant of the Pilatus PC-12.

[19] **The incident . . . February 19.** "Pirates Brutally End Yachting Dream," by Adam Nagourney and Jeffrey Gettleman, *The New York Times*, February 22, 2011, accessed at: http://www.nytimes.com/2011/02/23/world/africa/23pirates.html ?pagewanted=all; "Four American Hostages Killed by Somali Pirates," nbcnews .com, accessed at: http://www.nbcnews.com/id/41715530/ns/world_news-africa/t /four-american-hostages-killed-somali-pirates/#.U3VX6HYglwI.

[20] **Meanwhile JSOC . . . Lightning Dawn.** Team 6 sources.

[21] **U.S. intelligence had . . . with his interrogators.** *Kill or Capture*, pp. 237–39, 251, 262; a Team 6 source; a SEAL officer.

[22] **Playing a role . . . signals intelligence.** Two Team 6 sources.

[23] **With JSOC's operations . . . and Internet cafés.** Two JSOC sources.

[24] **Into this . . . charismatic terrorist.** *Kill or Capture*, pp. 261–63.

[25] **JSOC had a golden . . . Awlaki escaped.** *Dirty Wars*, pp. 454–56; "U.S. Missiles Missed Awlaki by Inches in Yemen," by Martha Raddatz, ABC News, July 19, 2011, accessed at: http://abcnews.go.com/Blotter/us-missed-awlaki-inches-yemen /story?id=14108686.

[26] **By the time . . . northeast of Sana'a.** *Kill or Capture*, p. 263; *Dirty Wars*, pp. 498–500. . . . **Objective Troy . . .** "Al-Awlaki Strike Plan Included Jets, Special Ops," by David Martin, cbsnews.com, September 30, 2011, accessed at: http://www.cbsnews .com/news/al-awlaki-strike-plan-included-jets-special-ops/.

[27] **This time the United States . . . in midflight.** JSOC sources.

Chapter 29: Extortion 17

[1] **The moon . . . approaching quickly.** Except where otherwise indicated, all information on the downing of Extortion 17 is drawn from the official investigation interviews and briefings, redacted copies of which were accessed on the U.S. Central Command website at: https://www2.centcom.mil/sites/foia/rr/centcom%20regulation %20ccr%2025210/forms/allitems.aspx?RootFolder=%2Fsites%2Ffoia%2Frr %2FCENTCOM%20Regulation%20CCR%2025210%2FWardak%20CH-47%20

Investigation&FolderCTID=0x012000BDB53322B36BD84DA24AF0C8F8BC
D011&View={7AED4B57-43F2-4B7D-A38E-4BDDC5BB9BD6}.

[2] . . . **Lefty Grove** . . . Robert "Lefty" Grove was a pitcher for the Philadelphia Athletics and Boston Red Sox from 1925 to 1941.

[3] . . . **forty-seven-person force** . . . The assault force included thirty-five Rangers, seven APU personnel, a U.S. military female cultural support team member, two interpreters, an explosive ordnance detachment member, and a liaison from the "battlespace owner"—the nearest conventional Army unit.

[4] . . . **the Task Force East commander** . . . **Gold Squadron's 2 Troop** . . . A Team 6 source.

[5] . . . **fifteen Gold Squadron operators** . . . "DOD Identifies Service Members Killed in CH-47 Crash," Defense Department Press Release No. 705-11, August 11, 2011, accessed at: http://www.defense.gov/Releases/Release.aspx?ReleaseID=14728; "Tragedy Devastates Special Warfare Community," by Sean D. Naylor, *USA Today*, August 7, 2011, accessed at: http://usatoday30.usatoday.com/news/military/2011-08-07-naval-special-warfare-reaction-afghanistan_n.htm.

[6] . . . **August 8** . . . "Military Killed Taliban Who Downed US Helicopter," by Lolita C. Baldor and Pauline Jelinek, Associated Press, August 10, 2011, accessed at: http://news.yahoo.com/military-killed-taliban-downed-us-helicopter-132740655.html.

[7] **The Naval Special Warfare community reeled in shock.** "Tragedy Devastates Special Warfare Community."

[8] **In the wake . . . revealed.** The author attended the National Press Club event. "Obama 'Put a Target on Their Backs,' SEAL Team 6 Family Members Say," by Paul D. Shinkman, *U.S. News & World Report*, May 9, 2013, accessed at: http://www.usnews.com/news/articles/2013/05/09/obama-put-a-target-on-their-backs-seal-team-6-family-members-say; "Lawmakers Hold Hearing on Deadly 'Extortion 17' Helicopter Crash in Afghanistan," by Jon Harper, *Stars and Stripes*, February 27, 2014, accessed at: http://www.stripes.com/news/lawmakers-hold-hearing-on-deadly-extortion-17-helicopter-crash-in-afghanistan-1.270274.

[9] **At the time . . . 49 percent.** This information is all contained in the in-brief for the Extortion 17 investigation team, included on the Central Command website's collection of documents from that investigation.

Chapter 30: Old Enemies, New Challenges

[1] **In the very early . . . fly them to Djibouti.** A Team 6 source; "U.S. Swoops In to Free 2 from Pirates in Somalia Raid," by Jeffrey Gettleman, Eric Schmitt, and Thom Shanker, *The New York Times*, January 25, 2012, accessed at: http://www.nytimes.com/2012/01/26/world/africa/us-raid-frees-2-hostages-from-somali-pirates.html?pagewanted=1&_r=0; *Impossible Odds: The Kidnapping of Jessica Buchanan and Her Dramatic Rescue by SEAL Team Six*, by Jessica Buchanan and Erik Landemalm with Anthony Flacco (New York: Atria, 2013), pp. 231–68.

[2] **To achieve that . . . specific missions.** A SOCOM staff officer; a special mission unit officer; a retired Special Forces colonel; a military intelligence source; a Delta operator; a special operations source familiar with the JRTF; a JRTF source; a Ranger officer; a U.S. special operations source; a JSOC staffer.

[3] **In late 2008 . . . intelligence capabilities.** *The Command*, an e-book by Marc Ambinder and D. B. Grady (Hoboken, N.J.: John Wiley & Sons, 2012); a former senior JSOC officer; a Team 6 officer; a JSOC staff officer.

[4] **Meanwhile, in the wake . . . and left.** A U.S. special operations source; Team 6 sources; "U.S. Raids in Libya and Somalia Strike Terror Targets," by David D. Kirkpatrick, Nicholas Kulish, and Eric Schmitt, *The New York Times*, October 5, 2013, accessed at: http://www.nytimes.com/2013/10/06/world/africa/Al-Qaeda -Suspect-Wanted-in-US-Said-to-Be-Taken-in-Libya.html?_r=0&hp=&adxnnl=1 &adxnnlx=1400609295-883WHxhUdMWvSh5QaKFkpg; "Inside America's Shadow War on Terror—And Why It Will Never End," by James Kitfield, *Defense One*, May 18, 2014, accessed at: http://www.defenseone.com/threats/2014/05/inside -americas-shadow-war-terrorand-why-it-will-never-end/84685/print/. . . . **military had surpassed the Agency's ability** . . . *The Human Factor*, by Ishmael Jones (New York: Encounter, 2008), p. 357. . . . **at least sixty-seven people** . . . "Terror in Westgate Mall: The Full Story of the Attacks That Devastated Kenya," by Daniel Howden, *The Guardian*, October 4, 2013, accessed at: http://www.theguardian.com/world /interactive/2013/oct/04/westgate-mall-attacks-kenya-terror. . . . **a new Al Qaeda cell** . . . "US Flying Blind to Looming Terror Plots," by James Kitfield, breakingdefense.com, July 17, 2014, accessed at: http://breakingdefense.com/2014/07/us -flying-blind-to-looming-terror-plots/.

[5] **JSOC had had . . . West Africa.** A Ranger source; a Special Forces officer.

[6] **When Islamist . . . success of the mission."** "Two U.S. Commandos Fought in Benghazi Rescue, Privately Honored for Valor," by Rowan Scarborough, *The Washington Times*, October 30, 2013, accessed at: http://www.washingtontimes.com /news/2013/oct/30/us-military-commandos-made-it-to-benghazi/?page=all; "Delta Force Marine Awarded Navy Cross for Fight at CIA Annex in Benghazi," by Rowan Scarborough, *The Washington Times*, November 16, 2013, accessed at: http://www .washingtontimes.com/news/2013/nov/16/delta-force-marine-awarded-navy-cross -fight-cia-an/?page=all; "Delta Force Commando Who Saved 'Numerous Lives' in Benghazi Seige [*sic*] Honored," by Rowan Scarborough, *The Washington Times*, January 25, 2014, accessed at: http://www.washingtontimes.com/news/2014/jan/25 /delta-force-commando-awarded-second-highest-milita/; a SOCOM staffer.

[7] **Within hours . . . permission to."** A SOCOM staffer.

[8] **That account . . . to face trial.** "First on CNN: US Commandos Were Poised for Raid to Capture Benghazi Suspect," by Barbara Starr, CNN, accessed at: http:// security.blogs.cnn.com/2013/10/29/first-on-cnn-us-commandos-were-poised-for -raid-to-capture-benghazi-suspect/; "Why Delta Force Waited So Long to Grab a Benghazi Ringleader," by Eli Lake and Kimberly Dozier, *The Daily Beast*, June 17, 2014, accessed at: http://www.thedailybeast.com/articles/2014/06/17/why-delta

-force-waited-so-long-to-grab-a-benghazi-ringleader.html; "U.S. Captures Benghazi Suspect in Secret Raid," by Karen DeYoung, Adam Goldman, and Julie Tate, *The Washington Post*, June 17, 2014, accessed at: http://www.washingtonpost.com/world /national-security/us-captured-benghazi-suspect-in-secret-raid/2014/06/17 /7ef8746e-f5cf-11e3-a3a5-42be35962a52_story.html.

[9] **These sorts . . . long-term cover.** Three Team 6 sources; a U.S. special operations source; a JSOC staffer.

[10] **Both Black . . . around 2009.** A Team 6 source.

[11] **The challenge of . . . operational details.** "WMDs and Terrorists Among Top Concerns for New Special Ops Pick," by Alex Quade, *The Washington Times*, July 1, 2014, accessed at: http://www.washingtontimes.com/news/2014/jul/1/keeping -wmds-from-terrorists-is-top-priority-for-v/?page=all; "JSOC Commander Speaks, Buckhorn 'Captured' During Exercise," by Howard Altman, *The Tampa Tribune*, May 21, 2014, accessed at: http://tbo.com/list/military-news/jsoc-commander-looks -to-industry-for-new-technologies-20140521/.

[12] **In the early . . . by dawn.** A special operations source familiar with the mission; a former 160th SOAR aviator; "Inside the Failed Raid to Save Foley and Sotloff," by Nicholas Schmidle, *The New Yorker*, September 5, 2014, accessed at: http://www.newyorker.com/news/news-desk/inside-failed-raid-free-foley -sotloff.

[13] **In response . . . counterterrorism forces.)** A U.S. special operations source; "Statement by the President on ISIL," accessed at: http://www.whitehouse.gov/the -press-office/2014/09/10/statement-president-isil-1.

[14] **On July 29 . . . Operations Command.** "New Commander Takes Over Joint Special Operations Command at Fort Bragg," by Drew Brooks, *The Fayetteville Observer*, July 29, 2014, accessed at: http://www.fayobserver.com/military/new -commander-takes-over-joint-special-operations-command-at-fort/article _9382286c-3b36-5cfa-8e50-a983182a770d.html.

[15] **Thomas's career . . . on the JSOC staff.** Thomas's official Army résumé.

[16] **A little over . . . died in the attack.** "US Strike Against al-Shabab Leader Reflects Obama's Counterterrorism Strategy," by Stephanie Gaskell, *Defense One*, September 2, 2014, accessed at: http://www.defenseone.com/threats/2014/09/us -strike-against-al-shabab-leader-reflects-obamas-counterterrorism-strategy/92966 /; "Al-Shabaab Confirms Airstrike Hit Leader," by Abdalle Ahmed Mumim, *The Wall Street Journal*, September 4, 2014; "Attack on Somali Islamist Leader Seen Triggering Power Struggle," by Edmund Blair and Drazen Jorgic, Reuters, September 4, 2014; "U.S. Drone Base in Ethiopia Is Operational," by Craig Whitlock, *The Washington Post*, October 27, 2011, accessed at: http://www.washingtonpost.com/world /national-security/us-drone-base-in-ethiopia-is-operational/2011/10/27/gIQ AznKwMM_story.html; "U.S. Drone Strike in Somalia Targets al-Shabaab Leader," by Craig Whitlock, *The Washington Post*, September 2, 2014, accessed at: http://www .washingtonpost.com/world/national-security/us-drone-strike-in-somalia-targets -al-shabab-leader/2014/09/02/2c833104-32a3-11e4-9e92-0899b306bbea_story

.html; "Statement by the Press Secretary on the Death of Ahmed Godane," a press release from the Office of the Press Secretary, The White House, accessed at: http://www.whitehouse.gov/the-press-office/2014/09/05/statement-press-secretary-death-ahmed-godane.

GLOSSARY

AFO – Advance force operations, the name given to low-visibility missions conducted by **JSOC** operators to prepare for possible future combat operations. The concept was pioneered by Delta's Operational Support Troop, before becoming the name of a cell on the **JSOC** staff. AFO missions are sometimes described as "operational preparation of the battlefield" or "operational preparation of the environment."

AH-6 – The attack, or gunship, version of the two-pilot **Little Bird** helicopter used exclusively by 1st Battalion of the 160th Special Operations Aviation Regiment.

Air assault – A combat mission in which infantry or special operations forces are delivered to the target by helicopter.

Airborne – In the military, this word is normally used to describe parachute troops and missions.

Air strike – An attack that involves munitions—bombs or missiles—delivered from an aerial platform (a plane or helicopter).

Al-Shabaab – A militant group whose name means "the youth," al-Shabaab was part of the Islamic Courts Union, but split off and became the dominant Islamist group in the Horn of Africa after Ethiopia's **JSOC**-assisted 2006 invasion of Somalia. In 2012 al-Shabaab formally allied itself with Al Qaeda.

AQAP – Al Qaeda in the Arabian Peninsula, the name of the Al Qaeda franchise in Yemen, which by the end of the first decade of the twenty-first century U.S. officials had come to view as the terrorist organization that posed the greatest threat to the U.S. homeland.

AQI – Al Qaeda in Iraq, also known as Al Qaeda in Mesopotamia and Al Qaeda in the Land of the Two Rivers. Led at its height by Abu Musab al-Zarqawi, AQI was **JSOC**'s primary enemy during the Iraq War.

The Army of Northern Virginia – One of many nicknames for the Army intelligence unit that began its life in 1980 as the Field Operations Group, and was known for much of the 1980s as the Intelligence Support Activity. Other cover names and nicknames down through the years have included the Tactical Coordination Detachment, the U.S. Army Office of Military Support, Torn Victor, Centra Spike, **Gray Fox**, and **Task Force Orange**.

Asayish – The Kurdish intelligence organization with which **JSOC** worked closely.

Aztec squadron – The Delta Force squadron on call for no-notice deployments. Responsibility to be the Aztec squadron rotated between Delta's assault squadrons.

Black Hawk – The Army's name for its UH-60 utility helicopter (also called an assault or lift helicopter). The MH-60 was the special operations version used exclusively by the 160th Special Operations Aviation Regiment.

Black SOF – The phrase "black **SOF** [special operations forces]" is military shorthand for **JSOC** forces in general, and special mission units in particular. (See also **White SOF**.)

Black Squadron – A SEAL Team 6 unit tasked with advance force operations and other undercover missions.

Brown Cell – A SEAL Team 6 advance force operations unit that grew out of "the Brown Boys," a small group of operators that did undercover work in advance of the 1989 Panama invasion. SEAL Team 6 shut Brown Cell down after a few years.

Bullet Package – The helicopters and personnel kept on alert by the 160th Special Operations Aviation Regiment. The composition of the Bullet Package evolved slightly over the years, but was always based around the regiment's 1st Battalion, plus a couple of 2nd Battalion's Chinooks. Also known as the **Silver Bullet**.

CCO – Commercial cover operative: an intelligence officer operating under commercial cover—i.e., pretending to be a businessman or woman, rather than a U.S. government employee.

CENTCOM – U.S. Central Command, the four-star geographic combatant command responsible for U.S. military operations in the Middle East, southwest Asia, and Central Asia. Headquartered, like U.S. Special Operations Command, at MacDill Air Force Base, Tampa, Florida.

Chinook – The Army's name for its CH-47 twin-rotor cargo helicopter. The MH-47 was the special operations version used exclusively by the 160th Special Operations Aviation Regiment.

CIF – Combatant commander's in-extremis force, a company in each active-duty **Special Forces** group whose mission was to respond quickly to emergencies when **JSOC** forces were not immediately available. (The Army's five active-duty **Special Forces** groups were oriented on geographic regions that roughly aligned with the combatant commanders' geographic areas of responsibility.) Previously called the **CinC**'s in-extremis force before 2002, when then Defense Secretary Donald Rumsfeld banned the use of the phrase "commander-in-chief" to refer to the military's four-star combatant commanders. The CIFs trained closely with Delta and other **JSOC** forces, and sometimes augmented **JSOC** task forces on operations.

CinC – Commander-in-chief, a phrase used to denote the four-star head of one of the military's combatant commands, before Rumsfeld banned its use in 2002.

CNOS – Computer Network Operations Squadron, a Delta offshoot that focused on cyber warfare.

Covered air – A covered air unit is one whose personnel and aircraft operate undercover.

CT – Counterterrorism.

CTCSG – The Counterterrorism Campaign Support Group, a short-lived organization Chairman of the Joint Chiefs General Richard Myers established in October 2001 to support **JSOC**.

DAP – Direct Action Penetrator, a version of the MH-60 **Black Hawk** equipped with weapons mounted on stubby wings, allowing the aircraft to function as an attack helicopter. (In an apparent fit of political correctness, the Army renamed the DAP the Defensive Armed Penetrator, but few in the 160th community refer to it as such.)

Dash-2 – The trail aircraft or "wingman" in any two-aircraft formation.

DevGroup, DevGru – Abbreviations of Naval Special Warfare Development Group, the cover name for SEAL Team 6 since 1989.

DoD – A common abbreviation for the Department of Defense. Pronounced "D-oh-D."

Echo Squadron – Delta's aviation squadron. Headquartered at Fort Eustis, Virginia. For many years its cover name was Flight Concepts Division.

EFP – Explosively formed projectile: a sort of roadside bomb that produced a jet of molten copper that sliced through armored vehicles. EFPs were used in Iraq primarily by Iranian surrogates, who received them from Iran's **Quds Force**.

EOD – Explosive ordnance disposal.

Exfil – Abbreviation of "exfiltrate," the word used in **JSOC** to refer to the act of pulling out of a situation.

The Farm – The CIA's espionage tradecraft training facility at Camp Peary, Virginia.

Fort Bragg – The large Army post in Fayetteville, North Carolina. Home to Delta Force since 1977 and, since 2011, when Bragg absorbed the adjacent **Pope Air Force Base**, to **JSOC** as well.

GAF – Ground assault force, a **JSOC** term that refers to an assault force that uses ground vehicles (as opposed to helicopters) to approach a target. (See also **HAF.**)

GMV – Ground mobility vehicle, a special operations version of the Humvee.

GPS – Global Positioning System, a navigation system that relies on satellites to provide accurate location and time data.

Gray Fox – The name during the immediate post–September 11 period for the special access program for information related to the Army intelligence unit later known as **Task Force Orange**.

GWOT – The Global War on Terror, the collective name the George W. Bush administration gave to the counterterrorism campaigns it launched in the wake of the September 11 attacks.

HAF – Helicopter assault force, a **JSOC** term that refers to an assault force that uses helicopters to approach a target. As with the companion term **GAF**, it became a verb: units either HAF'd (pronounced "haffed") or GAF'd to a target.

HAHO – High-altitude, high-opening: a military freefall parachuting technique that involves jumpers leaping from a plane at altitudes of up to 34,900 feet, opening their parachutes quickly, and then floating on the wind for up to twenty miles before landing.

HALO – High-altitude, low-opening: a military freefall parachuting technique in which jumpers leap from a plane at high altitude, then freefall for many thousands of feet before opening their parachutes as low as 2,500 feet above the ground.

Humint – Human intelligence: i.e., intelligence derived from classic espionage, as well as from interrogations and other nontechnical means.

Imagery – Photographs taken for intelligence purposes by aircraft and satellites.

Infil – Abbreviation of "infiltrate," the word used in **JSOC** to describe the process of moving personnel—often clandestinely—into an area of operations. Sometimes used as an abbreviation of the noun "infiltration" as well.

ISAF – The International Security Assistance Force: the overall military Coalition headquarters in Afghanistan.

ISI – Inter-Services Intelligence: Pakistan's most influential intelligence agency.

ISR – Intelligence, surveillance, and reconnaissance.

Jackpot – The **JSOC** word for a successful direct action mission, i.e., one in which the target of the mission is captured or killed, or, if a hostage rescue mission, one in which the **precious cargo** is rescued.

J-alert birds – The Air Force planes kept on alert to transport a **JSOC** task force from the United States on four hours' notice.

JIATF – Joint interagency task force.

JIB – The **JSOC** Intelligence Brigade: a roughly 600-person unit established in 2008.

JOC – Joint operations center: a field headquarters from which most **JSOC** operations are run.

JSOC – Joint Special Operations Command.

Legend – An undercover intelligence operative's false biography, which provides the basis for a cover story to explain his or her presence in a location from which to conduct espionage.

Little Bird – A small, two-pilot helicopter used exclusively by the 1st Battalion of the 160th Special Operations Aviation Regiment. There are two versions: the **AH-6** gunship and the **MH-6** lift helicopter.

Low-vis – Low-visibility: a term usually used in **JSOC** to refer to operators moving through a town or city in clothes and (sometimes) vehicles that do not draw attention.

LZ – Landing zone: the place where a helicopter lands, as used by the aviators.

MacDill Air Force Base – The installation in Tampa, Florida, that is home to both U.S. Special Operations Command and U.S. Central Command.

MH-6 – The lift variant of the 160th Special Operations Aviation Regiment's **Little Bird** helicopter.

MH-47 – The special operations variant of the CH-47 **Chinook** twin-rotor cargo helicopter. At the time of writing it was flown exclusively by the 160th Special Operations Aviation Regiment.

MH-60 – The special operations variant of the UH-60 **Black Hawk** lift helicopter. At the time of writing it was flown exclusively by the 160th Special Operations Aviation Regiment.

Mission set – The collective term for the range of missions a unit is expected to be able to accomplish.

Mogadishu Mile – The movement made on foot by some Rangers and Delta operators to a rally point toward the end of the October 1993 battle of Mogadishu.

Mohawks – The name given to the Iraqis that Delta recruited and trained in espionage tradecraft.

National Command Authority – The collective term for the president and the defense secretary.

National mission force – a phrase sometimes used in the government to refer to **JSOC** without naming the command.

Night Stalkers – The nickname for the 160th Special Operations Aviation Regiment.

NOC – A nonofficial cover operative, i.e., an intelligence operative whose cover identity is that of someone other than a U.S. government employee. Pronounced "knock."

OCF-I – Other Coalition Forces-Iraq: a phrase used by officials to refer to **JSOC**'s presence in Iraq without naming the command.

Omega teams – The combined CIA-**JSOC** teams that trained and commanded the Agency's Counterterrorism Pursuit Teams, which were Afghan units that reported to the CIA, not to the Afghan government.

Optempo – Operational tempo (also operations tempo, operating tempo): the rate at which a unit conducts operations.

Orange – The one word many **JSOC** personnel use to refer to **Task Force Orange,** the color code name for an intelligence unit known in the 1980s as the Intelligence Support Activity and by a variety of other cover names since then.

OSD – The Office of the Secretary of Defense: the main staff element that supports not just the secretary of defense, him- or herself, but also the deputy defense secretary, the undersecretaries and assistant secretaries of defense, as well as a number of other staff offices.

OST – Operational Support Troop: the Delta unit that specialized in undercover and other **low-vis** work, and pioneered the advance force operations concept. In 2005 OST expanded into D Squadron, which was later renamed G Squadron.

Pandur – A six-wheel-drive armored vehicle used by Delta and SEAL Team 6.

Pathway defeat – A **JSOC** strategy to counter the proliferation of weapons of mass destruction by intercepting components of such weapons before they reached their intended destination.

Peshmerga – Kurdish armed forces. The word means "those who confront death."

Pinzgauer – Rugged six-wheel-drive combat vehicles used by Delta.

Pope Air Force Base – The North Carolina installation that was home to the **JSOC** headquarters since 1981. Adjacent to **Fort Bragg**, the Air Force base was taken over by the much larger Army post in 2011, and was renamed Pope Field.

Precious cargo – The name for the individuals to be safeguarded and rescued in any **JSOC** rescue mission.

PZ – Pickup zone: an alternative name for a helicopter landing zone when the helicopters are landing to pick up troops. Typically used by those on the ground.

Quds Force – Iran's powerful covert operations organization. Officially part of the Islamic Revolutionary Guard Corps, the Quds Force combined the mission sets that in the United States were the provinces of the CIA's Directorate of Operations (later renamed the National Clandestine Service) and U.S. Special Operations Command.

Range 19 – The part of **Fort Bragg** where Delta's new headquarters was built in 1987. The phrase often used by Delta operators to refer to their home base.

RHIB – Rigid hull inflatable boat, a type of boat used by SEALs. Pronounced "rib."

RPG – Rocket-propelled grenade: an antitank weapon ubiquitous among the forces that **JSOC** has often found itself fighting. The RPG can also be used as an anti-helicopter weapon.

Sabre squadron – The generic name both Delta and the British **SAS** gave to their assault squadrons.

SAS – Special Air Service: the British special operations unit on which Charlie Beckwith modeled Delta. (Australia and New Zealand also have special operations units called the SAS.)

Sigint – Signals intelligence: any intelligence derived from intercepting radio, telephone, or other communications.

Silver Bullet – See **Bullet Package**.

SMU – Special mission unit: a specially designated unit in the U.S. military. Special mission units in **JSOC** include Delta, SEAL Team 6, the 24th Special Tactics Squadron, and **Task Force Orange**. Pronounced "smoo."

SOCOM – An abbreviation of U.S. Special Operations Command.

SOF – Special operations forces. Pronounced "soff."

Special Forces – In the U.S. military, the phrase "Special Forces" refers specifically to the five active-duty and two reserve Special Forces groups under U.S. Army Special Forces Command. Often referred to by others as "Green Berets," on account of the color of their headgear, Special Forces soldiers specialize in working "by, with, and through" local forces to either foment rebellion against an enemy of the United States, or to put down an insurgency against an American ally. In other English-speaking countries, the phrase "special forces" is used as a generic term, similar to the use in the United States of the phrase "special operations forces."

SSE – Sensitive site exploitation: the process of collecting all the material of intelligence value from a location (often, but not always, where a direct action mission has taken place).

Stryker – A wheeled armored vehicle used by the Rangers and by conventional Army units.

Task Force – A phrase often used as a generic pseudonym for **JSOC**, as in "those were Task Force aircraft," or "it was a Task Force operation."

Task Force 11 – The name **JSOC** gave its Afghanistan task force from the end of 2001.

Task Force 16 – The name for **JSOC**'s task force in Iraq that focused on fighting Al Qaeda in Iraq.

Task Force 17 – The name **JSOC** gave its task force that focused on countering Iran's **Quds Force** and the Shi'ite militant groups that functioned as its proxies in Iraq.

Task Force Blue – The color code name for SEAL Team 6.

Task Force Gold – The color code name for the Joint Communications Unit.

Task Force Gray – The color code name for 1st Special Operations Wing.

Task Force Green – The color code name for Delta.

Task Force Orange – The color code name for **the Army of Northern Virginia**.

Task Force Purple – The color code name for **JSOC** headquarters.

Task Force Red – The color code name for the Rangers.

Task Force Silver – The color code name for the Air Force **covered air unit.**

Task Force Sword – The name for **JSOC**'s Afghanistan task force, headquartered on Masirah Island, Oman, from September 2001 until the end of that year, when it became **Task Force 11.**

Task Force White – The color code name for the 24th Special Tactics Squadron.

TF – Task Force.

Theater special operations forces – A phrase used by U.S. Special Operations Command and others to refer to U.S. special operations forces that were not part of and had no habitual relationship with **JSOC.** Also known as "**white SOF.**"

Trident – The Trident was the SEAL Team 6 equivalent of Delta's **Aztec squadron**. It was so named because of the Naval Special Warfare insignia of an eagle clutching a trident.

UBL – Usama bin Laden. Although the vast majority of English language sources spelled the Al Qaeda leader's first name Osama, within the U.S. counterterrorism community he was often referred to as "UBL."

Unconventional warfare – The use of proxy forces to foment rebellion against an enemy state. In the U.S. military, this is a primary mission of **Special Forces.**

Wescam ball – A gyro-stabilized camera in a spherical mounting fixed to the underside of an aircraft, the Wescam ball tracked targets and sent live video back to the **JOC.** Used primarily by Delta's **Echo Squadron.**

White SOF – See **Theater special operations forces.**

Winchester – The phrase aviators use when they have run out of ammunition.

WMD – Weapons of mass destruction: nuclear, biological, or chemical weapons.

Workup – The phrase SEALs use for a training cycle, especially one that precedes a deployment.

BIBLIOGRAPHY

Books

The 9/11 Commission Report (New York: W. W. Norton, 2004).

The Afghan Solution: The Inside Story of Abdul Haq, the CIA and How Western Hubris Lost Afghanistan, by Lucy Morgan Edwards (London: Bactria, 2011).

American Soldier, by General Tommy Franks with Malcolm McConnell (New York: ReganBooks, 2004).

The Art of Intelligence: Lessons from a Life in the CIA's Clandestine Service, by Henry A. Crumpton (New York: Penguin, 2012).

At the Center of the Storm: My Years at the CIA, by George Tenet (New York: HarperCollins, 2007).

At the Hurricane's Eye: U.S. Special Operations Forces from Vietnam to Desert Storm, by Greg Walker (New York: Ivy, 1994).

Best Laid Plans: The Inside Story of America's War Against Terror, by David C. Martin and John Walcott (New York: Touchstone, 1988).

Between Threats and War: U.S. Discrete Military Operations in the Post–Cold War World, by Micah Zenko (Stanford: Stanford University Press, 2010).

Black Hawk Down: A Story of Modern War, by Mark Bowden (New York: Atlantic Monthly Press, 1999).

Blank Check: The Pentagon's Black Budget, by Tim Weiner (New York: Warner, 1990).

Blind Spot: The Secret History of American Counterterrorism (New York: Basic Books, 2005).

Brave Men, Dark Waters: The Untold Story of the Navy SEALs, by Orr Kelly (New York: Pocket Books, 1993).

Bush at War, by Bob Woodward (New York: Simon & Schuster, 2002).

A Captain's Duty, by Richard Phillips with Stephen Talty (New York: Hyperion, 2010).

Clinton's Secret Wars: The Evolution of a Commander in Chief, by Richard Sale (New York: St. Martin's Press, 2009).

Cobra II: The Inside Story of the Invasion and Occupation of Iraq, by Michael R. Gordon and General Bernard E. Trainor (New York: Pantheon, 2006).

Code Names: Deciphering U.S. Military Plans, Programs, and Operations in the 9/11 World, by William M. Arkin (Hanover, N.H.: Steerforth, 2005).

Combat Swimmer: Memoirs of a Navy SEAL, by Captain Robert A. Gormly, USN (Ret.) (New York: Dutton, 1998).

The Command, an e-book by Marc Ambinder and D. B. Grady (Hoboken, N.J.: John Wiley & Sons, 2012).

The Commandos: The Inside Story of America's Secret Soldiers, by Douglas C. Waller (New York: Simon & Schuster, 1994).

Counterstrike: The Untold Story of America's Secret Campaign Against Al Qaeda, by Eric Schmitt and Thom Shanker (New York: Times Books, 2011).

Crippled Eagle: A Historical Perspective on U.S. Special Operations, 1976–1996, by Rod Lenahan (Charleston, S.C.: Narwhal, 1998).

The Dark Side: The Inside Story of How the War on Terror Turned into a War on American Ideals, by Jane Mayer (New York: Doubleday, 2008).

Deep State: Inside the Government Secrecy Industry, by Marc Ambinder and D. B. Grady (Hoboken, N.J.: John Wiley & Sons, 2013).

Defusing Armageddon: Inside NEST, America's Secret Nuclear Bomb Squad, by Jeffrey T. Richelson (New York: W. W. Norton, 2008).

Delta Force, by Col. Charlie Beckwith (Ret.) (New York: Avon, 2000).

Dirty Wars: The World Is a Battlefield, by Jeremy Scahill (New York: Nation Books, 2013).

The Endgame: The Inside Story of the Struggle for Iraq, from George W. Bush to Barack Obama, by Michael R. Gordon and General Bernard E. Trainor (New York: Pantheon, 2012).

Fiasco: The American Military Adventure in Iraq, by Thomas E. Ricks (New York: Penguin, 2006).

The Finish: The Killing of Osama bin Laden, by Mark Bowden (New York: Atlantic Monthly Press, 2012).

First In: An Insider's Account of How the CIA Spearheaded the War on Terror in Afghanistan, by Gary C. Schroen (New York: Presidio, 2005).

Ghost Wars, by Steve Coll (New York: Penguin, 2004).

Growing Up bin Laden: Osama's Wife and Son Take Us Inside Their Secret World, by Najwa bin Laden, Omar bin Laden, and Jean Sasson (New York: St. Martin's Press, 2009).

Guests of the Ayatollah, by Mark Bowden (New York: Atlantic Monthly Press, 2006).

Hezbollah: The Global Footprint of Lebanon's Party of God, by Matthew Levitt (Washington, D.C.: Georgetown University Press, 2013).

High-Value Target: Countering Al Qaeda in Yemen, by Amb. Edmund J. Hull (Ret.) (Dulles, Va.: Potomac, 2011).

The Human Factor, by Ishmael Jones (New York: Encounter, 2008).

Impossible Odds: The Kidnapping of Jessica Buchanan and Her Dramatic Rescue by SEAL Team Six, by Jessica Buchanan and Erik Landemalm with Anthony Flacco (New York: Atria, 2013).

In My Time, by Dick Cheney (New York: Threshold, 2011).

Inside Delta Force, by Eric L. Haney (New York: Dell, 2003).

Intelligence Wars: Lessons from Baghdad, by Steven K. O'Hern (Amherst, N.Y.: Prometheus, 2008).

Jawbreaker, by Gary Berntsen and Ralph Pezzullo (New York: Crown, 2005).

Kill bin Laden: A Delta Force Commander's Account of the Hunt for the World's Most Wanted Man, by Dalton Fury (New York: St. Martin's Press, 2008).

Killer Elite: The Inside Story of America's Most Secret Special Operations Team, by Michael Smith (London: Weidenfeld & Nicholson, 2006).

Killing Pablo: The Hunt for the World's Greatest Outlaw, by Mark Bowden (New York: Penguin, 2001).

Kill or Capture: The War on Terror and the Soul of the Obama Presidency, by Daniel Klaidman (New York: Houghton Mifflin Harcourt, 2012).

Known and Unknown, by Donald Rumsfeld (New York: Sentinel, 2011).

The Longest War, by Peter L. Bergen (New York: Free Press, 2011).

Manhunt: The Ten-Year Search for bin Laden from 9/11 to Abbottabad, by Peter L. Bergen (New York: Crown, 2012).

The Mission, the Men, and Me: Lessons from a Former Delta Force Commander, by Pete Blaber (New York: Berkley, 2008).

My Share of the Task: A Memoir, by General Stanley McChrystal, U.S. Army (Ret.) (New York: Portfolio/Penguin, 2013).

Never Surrender, by LTG (Ret.) William G. Boykin with Lynn Vincent (New York: FaithWords, 2008).

The Night Stalkers, by Michael J. Durant and Steven Hartov (New York: G. P. Putnam's Sons, 2006).

No Easy Day: The Autobiography of a Navy SEAL, by Mark Owen with Kevin Maurer (New York: Dutton, 2012).

No Room for Error: The Covert Operations of America's Special Tactics Units from Iran to Afghanistan, by Colonel John T. Carney Jr. and Benjamin F. Schemmer (New York: Ballantine, 2002).

No True Glory: A Frontline Account of the Battle for Fallujah, by Bing West (New York: Bantam, 2005).

Not a Good Day to Die: The Untold Story of Operation Anaconda, by Sean Naylor (New York: Berkley, 2005).

Obama's Wars, by Bob Woodward (New York: Simon & Schuster, 2010).

The One Percent Doctrine: Deep Inside America's Pursuit of Its Enemies Since 9/11, by Ron Suskind (New York: Simon & Schuster, 2006).

One Perfect Op: An Insider's Account of the Navy SEAL Special Warfare Teams, by Command Master Chief Dennis Chalker, USN (Ret.) with Kevin Dockery (New York: HarperCollins, 2002).

The Only Thing Worth Dying For, by Eric Blehm (New York: Harper, 2011).

Operation Dark Heart: Spycraft and Special Ops on the Frontlines of Afghanistan—And the Path to Victory (uncensored version), by Lt. Col. Anthony Shaffer (New York: St. Martin's Press, 2010).

Operation Just Cause: The Storming of Panama, by Thomas Donnelly, Margaret Roth, and Caleb Baker (New York: Lexington, 1991).

Plan of Attack, by Bob Woodward (New York: Simon & Schuster, 2004).

Prisoners of Hope: The Story of Our Captivity and Freedom in Afghanistan, by Dayna Curry and Heather Mercer with Stacy Mattingly (New York: Doubleday, 2002).

The Real Team, by Richard Marcinko (New York: Pocket Books, 1999).

Rogue Warrior, by Richard Marcinko with John Weisman (New York: Pocket Books, 1992).

Rumsfeld's War: The Untold Story of America's Anti-Terrorist Commander, by Rowan Scarborough (Washington, D.C.: Regnery, 2004).

Secret Armies: The Full Story of S.A.S., Delta Force and Spetsnaz, by James Adams (London: Hutchinson, 1988).

Secret Warriors: Inside the Covert Military Operations of the Reagan Era, by Steven Emerson (New York: G. P. Putnam's Sons, 1988).

The Secret War with Iran, by Ronen Bergman (New York: Free Press, 2008).

Shadow Warriors: Inside the Special Forces, by Tom Clancy with General Carl Stiner (Ret.) and Tony Koltz (New York: G. P. Putnam's Sons, 2002).

Spec Ops: Case Studies in Special Operations Warfare: Theory and Practice, by William H. McRaven (New York: Ballantine, 1996).

Special Operations Forces in Afghanistan, by Leigh Neville (New York: Osprey, 2008).

Special Operations Forces in Iraq, by Leigh Neville (New York: Osprey, 2008).

Special Operations Patrol Vehicles: Afghanistan and Iraq, by Leigh Neville (New York: Osprey, 2011).

State of Denial, by Bob Woodward (New York: Simon & Schuster, 2006).

Task Force Black: The Explosive True Story of the SAS and the Secret War in Iraq, by Mark Urban (London: Little, Brown, 2010).

The Threat Matrix: The FBI at War in the Age of Global Terror, by Garrett M. Graff (New York: Little, Brown, 2011).

To Fight with Intrepidity: The Complete History of the U.S. Army Rangers, 1622 to Present, by JD Lock (Tucson: Fenestra, 2001).

Top Secret America: The Rise of the New American Security State, by Dana Priest and William M. Arkin (New York: Little, Brown, 2011).

The Twilight War: The Secret History of America's Thirty-Year Conflict with Iran, by David Crist (New York: Penguin, 2012).

Veil: The Secret Wars of the CIA, 1981–1987, by Bob Woodward (New York: Simon & Schuster, 1987).

War and Decision, by Douglas J. Feith (New York: HarperCollins, 2008).

The War Within, by Bob Woodward (New York: Simon & Schuster, 2008).

The Way of the Knife: The CIA, a Secret Army, and a War at the Ends of the Earth, by Mark Mazzetti (New York: Penguin, 2013).

We Got Him! A Memoir of the Hunt and Capture of Saddam Hussein, by Lt. Col. Steve Russell, U.S. Army, (Ret.) (New York: Threshold, 2011).

Where Men Win Glory: The Odyssey of Pat Tillman, by Jon Krakauer (New York: Doubleday, 2009).

Without Hesitation: The Odyssey of an American Warrior, by General (Ret.) Hugh Shelton with Ronald Levinson and Malcolm McConnell (New York: St. Martin's Press, 2010).

Articles and Reports

"2 C.I.A. Reports Offer Warnings on Iraq's Path," by Douglas Jehl, *The New York Times*, December 7, 2004, accessed at: http://www.nytimes.com/2004/12/07 /international/middleeast/07intell.html.

"After the War: Fighting; Syrians Wounded in Attack by U.S. on Convoy in Iraq," by Douglas Jehl, *The New York Times*, June 24, 2003, accessed at: http://www .nytimes.com/2003/06/24/world/after-the-war-fighting-syrians-wounded-in -attack-by-us-on-convoy-in-iraq.html.

"Against U.S. Wishes, Iraq Releases Man Accused of Killing American Soldiers," by Michael R. Gordon, *The New York Times*, November 16, 2012, accessed at: http://www.nytimes.com/2012/11/17/world/middleeast/iraq-said-to-release -hezbollah-operative.html.

"Al-Awlaki Strike Plan Included Jets, Special Ops," by David Martin, cbsnews.com, September 30, 2011, accessed at: http://www.cbsnews.com/news/al-awlaki-strike -plan-included-jets-special-ops/.

"Al Qaeda Is Driven from Mosul Bastion After Bloody Last Stand," by Marie Colvin, *The Sunday Times* (London), July 6, 2008.

"Al-Qaeda-Linked Force Captures Fallujah Amid Rise in Violence in Iraq," by Liz Sly, *The Washington Post*, January 3, 2014, accessed at: http://www.washingtonpost .com/world/al-qaeda-force-captures-fallujah-amid-rise-in-violence-in-iraq/2014 /01/03/8abaeb2a-74aa-11e3-8def-a33011492df2_story.html.

"Al-Shabaab Confirms Airstrike Hit Leader," by Abdalle Ahmed Mumim, *The Wall Street Journal*, September 4, 2014.

"The Americans Left Behind," by Doug Waller, *Time*, June 24, 2001.

"Aristide Says U.S. Deposed Him in 'Coup d'Etat,'" CNN, March 2, 2004, accessed at: http://edition.cnn.com/2004/WORLD/americas/03/01/aristide.claim/.

"Attack on Somali Islamist Leader Seen Triggering Power Struggle," by Edmund Blair and Drazen Jorgic, Reuters, September 4, 2014.

"Battle for Fallujah Forged Many Heroes," by Oren Dorell and Gregg Zoroya, *USA Today*, November 9, 2006, accessed at: http://usatoday30.usatoday.com/news /nation/2006-11-09-medals-fallujah_x.htm.

"Bin Laden's Fatwa," text translated by PBS Newshour, accessed at: http://www.pbs .org/newshour/updates/military/july-dec96/fatwa_1996.html.

"Blacklisted—Former Delta Force Chief Shunned for Relating Experiences in Book," by Sean D. Naylor, *Army Times*, October 20, 2008.

"British Hostage Found Dead in Afghanistan," by Colin Freeman and Tom Coghlan, *The Telegraph*, September 4, 2005, accessed at: http://www.telegraph.co.uk /news/worldnews/asia/afghanistan/1497611/British-hostage-found-dead-in -Afghanistan.html.

"Camp Nama: British Personnel Reveal Horrors of Secret US Base in Baghdad," by

Ian Cobain, *The Guardian*, April 1, 2013, accessed at: http://www.theguardian
.com/world/2013/apr/01/camp-nama-iraq-human-rights-abuses.

"Captured Iranian Qods Force Officer a Regional Commander in Iraq," by Bill Roggio,
The Long War Journal, October 3, 2007, accessed at: http://www.longwarjournal
.org/archives/2007/10/captured_iranian_qod.php.

"'Chemical Ali' Captured in Iraq," FoxNews.com, accessed at: http://www.foxnews
.com/story/2003/08/21/chemical-ali-captured-in-iraq/.

"CIA Led Mystery Syria Raid That Killed Terrorist Leader," by Jonathan S. Landay
and Nancy A. Youssef, McClatchy Newspapers, October 27, 2008, accessed at:
http://www.mcclatchydc.com/2008/10/27/54828/cia-led-mystery-syria-raid
-that.html.

"Closing in on Zarqawi," by Sean D. Naylor, *Army Times*, May 8, 2006.

"Commandos Get Duty on U.S. Soil," by Eric Schmitt, *The New York Times*, January 23, 2005, accessed at: http://www.nytimes.com/2005/01/23/national
/nationalspecial3/23code.html.

"Correspondence/Touring Somalia; When All Else Fails (Like the State), Take the
Drug Flight into Town," by Donald G. McNeil Jr., *The New York Times*, February
3, 2002, accessed at: http://www.nytimes.com/2002/02/03/weekinreview/cor
respondence-touring-somalia-when-all-else-fails-like-state-take-drug-flight
.html.

"The Day My Team and Delta Force Killed Saddam Husseins [*sic*] Two Sons,"
accessed at: http://www.experienceproject.com/stories/Have-Been-To-Iraq-And
-Have-A-Story/1543477.

"Deep Underground Tunnels," by Glenn Goodman, *Armed Forces Journal International*, June 1997.

"Delta Force Commando Who Saved 'Numerous Lives' in Benghazi Seige [*sic*]
Honored," by Rowan Scarborough, *The Washington Times*, January 25, 2014,
accessed at: http://www.washingtontimes.com/news/2014/jan/25/delta-force
-commando-awarded-second-highest-milita/.

"Delta Force Marine Awarded Navy Cross for Fight at CIA Annex in Benghazi,"
by Rowan Scarborough, *The Washington Times*, November 16, 2013, accessed at:
http://www.washingtontimes.com/news/2013/nov/16/delta-force-marine
-awarded-navy-cross-fight-cia-an/?page=all.

"Escape and Evasion," by Seymour M. Hersh, *The New Yorker*, November 12, 2001.

"Exclusive: Inside a U.S. Hostage Rescue Mission," by Sean D. Naylor, *Navy Times*,
November 7, 2008, accessed at: http://www.navytimes.com/article/20081107
/NEWS/811070315/Exclusive-Inside-U-S-hostage-rescue-mission.

"First on CNN: US Commandos Were Poised for Raid to Capture Benghazi Suspect,"
by Barbara Starr, CNN, accessed at: http://security.blogs.cnn.com/2013/10/29/first
-on-cnn-us-commandos-were-poised-for-raid-to-capture-benghazi-suspect/.

"'Foreign Fighters' Die in Somalia," BBC News, June 3, 2007, accessed at: http://
news.bbc.co.uk/2/hi/africa/6716725.stm.

"Former Interrogator Presses for McChrystal's Stance on Abuse," by Spencer Ackerman, *The Washington Independent*, June 1, 2009.

"Fort Bragg Soldier Recalls Battle That Won Him Higher Honor," by Kevin Maurer, *The Fayetteville Observer*, syndicated by the Associated Press, June 23, 2005, and accessed at: http://www.freerepublic.com/focus/f-news/1429115/posts.

"Four American Hostages Killed by Somali Pirates," nbcnews.com, accessed at: http://www.nbcnews.com/id/41715530/ns/world_news-africa/t/four-american -hostages-killed-somali-pirates/#.U3VX6HYglwI.

"Franks: Much Work Ahead," by Liam Pleven, *Newsday*, November 22, 2001.

"Frederick Army Ranger Killed in Afghanistan," by Megan Eckstein, *The Frederick News-Post* (Maryland), October 5, 2010, accessed at: http://www.frederick newspost.com/archive/article_fdf2922a-9548-52a0-85e5-de940165f1cc.html ?mode=jqm.

"Getting bin Laden," by Nicholas Schmidle, *The New Yorker*, August 8, 2011.

"Ground Force Boosted," by Kenneth R. Bazinet, New York *Daily News* November 5, 2001, accessed at: http://www.nydailynews.com/archives/news/ground-force -boosted-u-s-sends-troops-set-long-fight-article-1.920839.

"The Haditha Dam Seizure—Parts 1, 2, and 3," by John D. Gresham, Defense Media Network, May 1, 2010, accessed at: http://www.defensemedianetwork.com /stories/hold-until-relieved-the-haditha-dam-seizure/.

"A Heart Laid Bare," by Clay Latimer, *Rocky Mountain News*, April 3, 2004.

"Heroism Earns Soldier High Award," by Carrie Chicken, *The Walla-Walla Union-Bulletin*, June 14, 2005, accessed at: http://www.professionalsoldiers.com/forums /showthread.php?t=7150.

"He's in the Backseat!," by James Bamford, *The Atlantic*, April 2006, accessed at: http://www.theatlantic.com/magazine/archive/2006/04/-hes-in-the-backseat /304712/.

"How Iran Used Explosively Formed Projectiles to Influence Events in Iraq," in Musings on Iraq blog, July 11, 2011, accessed at: http://musingsoniraq.blogspot.com /2011/07/how-iran-used-explosively-formed.html.

"Hunting War Criminals—The First Account of Secret U.S. Missions in Bosnia," by Richard J. Newman, *U.S. News & World Report*, July 6, 1998, accessed at: http:// www.usnews.com/usnews/news/articles/980706/archive_004280.htm.

"In Maliki's Hometown, Grief and Questions After Deadly U.S. Raid," by Qassim Zein and Hannah Allam, McClatchy Newspapers, June 29, 2008, accessed at: http://www.mcclatchydc.com/2008/06/29/42641/in-malikis-hometown-grief -and.html.

"In Secret Unit's 'Black Room,' a Grim Portrait of U.S. Abuse," by Eric Schmitt and Carolyn Marshall, *The New York Times*, March 19, 2006, accessed at: http:// www.nytimes.com/2006/03/19/international/middleeast/19abuse.html?page wanted=all.

"Inside America's Shadow War on Terror—And Why It Will Never End," by James Kitfield, *Defense One*, May 18, 2014, accessed at: http://www.defenseone.com /threats/2014/05/inside-americas-shadow-war-terrorand-why-it-will-never-end /84685/print/.

"Inside Command Post in Hunt for bin Laden," by David Wood, Newhouse News

Service, March 8, 2002, accessed at: http://community.seattletimes.nwsource.com /archive/?date=20020308&slug=hunt08.

"Inside the Failed Raid to Save Foley and Sotloff," by Nicholas Schmidle, *The New Yorker*, September 5, 2014, accessed at: http://www.newyorker.com/news/news -desk/inside-failed-raid-free-foley-sotloff.

"It Takes a Network—The New Front Line of Modern Warfare," by Stanley A. McChrystal, in ForeignPolicy.com, accessed at: http://www.foreignpolicy.com /articles/2011/02/22it_takes_a_network.

"JSOC Commander Speaks, Buckhorn 'Captured' During Exercise," by Howard Altman, *The Tampa Tribune*, May 21, 2014, accessed at: http://tbo.com/list/military -news/jsoc-commander-looks-to-industry-for-new-technologies-20140521/.

"Key Al Qaeda Figure Reported Killed in Blast," National Public Radio, December 3, 2005, accessed at: http://www.npr.org/templates/story/story.php?storyId=5037605.

"Lawmakers Hold Hearing on Deadly 'Extortion 17' Helicopter Crash in Afghanistan," by Jon Harper, *Stars and Stripes*, February 27, 2014, accessed at: http://www .stripes.com/news/lawmakers-hold-hearing-on-deadly-extortion-17-helicopter -crash-in-afghanistan-1.270274.

"Memorial to Hail 12 Victims of '92 Copter Crash," *Deseret News*, August 12, 1994, accessed at: http://www.deseretnews.com/article/369440/MEMORIAL-TO -HAIL-12-VICTIMS-OF-92-COPTER-CRASH.html.

"Military Killed Taliban Who Downed US Helicopter," by Lolita C. Baldor and Pauline Jelinek, Associated Press, August 10, 2011, accessed at: http://news.yahoo .com/military-killed-taliban-downed-us-helicopter-132740655.html.

"Mission Helo Was Secret Stealth Black Hawk," by Sean D. Naylor, *Army Times*, May 4, 2011, accessed at: http://www.armytimes.com/article/20110504/NEWS /105040314/Mission-helo-secret-stealth-Black-Hawk.

"The Murder of Simo Drljaca," LPC, accessed at: http://www.srpska-mreza.com /guest/LPC/Simo_Drljaca.html.

"Navy: SEALs' Own Errors Led to Chute Deaths," by Carol Ann Alaimo, *Arizona Daily Star*, February 7, 2009, accessed at: http://tucson.com/news/local/govt-and -politics/navy-seals-own-errors-led-to-chute-deaths/article_e019c515-955f -5d18-9d3d-6ad2116693a9.html.

"'Neither of Us Expected to Get Out . . . Alive,'" by Sean D. Naylor, *Army Times*, July 20, 2008, accessed at: http://www.armytimes.com/article/20080720/NEWS /807200334/-8216-Neither-us-expected-get-out-alive-.

"The Netherlands Planned U.S.-Supported Invasion of Suriname in 1986," BNO News, accessed at: http://wireupdate.com/wires/12538/the-netherlands-planned -u-s-supported-invasion-of-suriname-in-1986/.

"Netherlands Was on Verge of Invading Suriname in 1986," DutchNews, November 8, 2011, accessed at: http://www.dutchnews.nl/news/archives/2011/11/nether lands_was_on_verge_of_in.php.

"The New Al-Qaeda Central," by Craig Whitlock, *The Washington Post*, September 9, 2007, accessed at: http://www.washingtonpost.com/wp-dyn/content/article /2007/09/08/AR2007090801845_pf.html.

"New Commander Takes Over Joint Special Operations Command at Fort Bragg," by Drew Brooks, *The Fayetteville Observer*, July 29, 2014, accessed at: http://www .fayobserver.com/military/new-commander-takes-over-joint-special-operations -command-at-fort/article_9382286c-3b36-5cfa-8e50-a983182a770d.html.

"Newspaper Reports Special Anti-Terrorism Command," Associated Press, October 8, 1980.

"No Blood, No Foul: Soldiers' Accounts of Detainee Abuse in Iraq," by Human Rights Watch, accessed at: http://www.hrw.org/reports/2006/us0706/2.htm.

"Obama 'Put a Target on Their Backs,' SEAL Team 6 Family Members Say," by Paul D. Shinkman, *U.S. News & World Report*, May 9, 2013, accessed at: http:// www.usnews.com/news/articles/2013/05/09/obama-put-a-target-on-their-backs -seal-team-6-family-members-say.

"Officials Say U.S. Killed an Iraqi in Raid in Syria," by Eric Schmitt and Thom Shanker, *The New York Times*, October 27, 2008, accessed at: http://www.nytimes .com/2008/10/28/world/middleeast/28syria.html?pagewanted=1&_r=0&hp.

"Our Hero in Combat," by Wayne Herada, HonoluluAdvertiser.com, January 16, 2002, accessed at: http://the.honoluluadvertiser.com/article/2002/Jan/16/il/il04a .html.

"Pirates Brutally End Yachting Dream," by Adam Nagourney and Jeffrey Gettleman, *The New York Times*, February 22, 2011, accessed at: http://www.nytimes .com/2011/02/23/world/africa/23pirates.html?pagewanted=all.

"Pirates Hijack Two Tankers Within 24 Hours Off Somali Shore," by the Associated Press, March 26, 2009, accessed on FoxNews.com at: http://www.foxnews .com/story/2009/03/26/pirates-hijack-two-tankers-within-24-hours-off-somali -shore/.

"Reconstructie: Hoe Nederland een aanval op Suriname overwoog," by Frank van Kolfschooten, *Volkskrant* November 20, 2010, accessed at: http://www.volkskrant .nl/vk/nl/2844/Archief/archief/article/detail/1060293/2010/11/20/Reconstructie -Hoe-Nederland-een-aanval-op-Suriname-overwoog.dhtml.

The Report of the Constitution Project's Task Force on Detainee Treatment, pp. 118–21, accessed at: http://detaineetaskforce.org/read/files/assets/basic-html/page118 .html.

"The Secret War," Parts 1 through 6, by Sean D. Naylor, October 30 through December 5, 2011, *Army Times*, accessed at: http://projects.militarytimes.com/navy -seals-horn-of-africa/.

"The Shadow Commander," by Dexter Filkins, *The New Yorker*, September 24, 2013, accessed at: http://www.newyorker.com/reporting/2013/09/30/130930fa_fact _filkins?currentPage=all.

"Shadow Games," by Paul D. Shinkman, *U.S. News & World Report*, November 13, 2013, accessed at: http://www.usnews.com/news/articles/2013/11/14/seal-team-6 -chief-demystifies-somalia-capt-phillips-bin-laden-missions.

"Showstoppers," by Richard H. Shultz Jr., *Weekly Standard*, January 26, 2004; accessed at: http://www.weeklystandard.com/Content/Public/Articles/000/000/003 /613twavk.asp.

"Shrapnel Points to Drone in Pakistan Attack," Fox News, December 5, 2005, accessed at: http://www.foxnews.com/story/2005/12/05/shrapnel-points-to-drone-in-pakistan-attack/.

"Somalian Pirate Suspect Arrives in New York to Be Tried in U.S. Court," Associated Press, April 20, 2009, accessed at: http://www.cbc.ca/news/world/somalian-pirate-suspect-arrives-in-new-york-to-be-tried-in-u-s-court-1.777441.

"Somali Islamists Declare Victory; Warlords on Run," by Marc Lacy, *The New York Times*, June 6, 2006, accessed at: http://select.nytimes.com/gst/abstract.html?res=FB0811FB3F550C758CDDAF0894DE404482.

"Special Ops Task Force Threatened Government Agents Who Saw Detainee Abuse in Iraq, Documents Obtained by ACLU Reveal," accessed at: https://www.aclu.org/national-security/special-ops-task-force-threatened-government-agents-who-saw-detainee-abuse-iraq-do.

"Spec Ops Catches, Iraq Releases," by Sean D. Naylor, *Army Times*, April 19, 2010.

"Taliban Cut Cellphone Service in Helmand," by Ray Rivera and Sangar Rahimi, from *The New York Times*'s "At War" blog, March 24, 2011, accessed at: http://atwar.blogs.nytimes.com/2011/03/24/taliban-cuts-cellphone-service-in-helmand/.

"Tarhuna CW Facility," by Jeffrey Lewis, on the "Arms Control Wonk" blog, March 25, 2007.

"Terror in Westgate Mall: The Full Story of the Attacks That Devastated Kenya," by Daniel Howden, *The Guardian*, October 4, 2013, accessed at: http://www.theguardian.com/world/interactive/2013/oct/04/westgate-mall-attacks-kenya-terror.

"Tragedy Devastates Special Warfare Community," by Sean D. Naylor, *USA Today*, August 7, 2011, accessed at: http://usatoday30.usatoday.com/news/military/2011-08-07-naval-special-warfare-reaction-afghanistan_n.htm.

"Transcript of Osama Bin Laden Interview by Peter Arnett," Information Clearing House, accessed at: http://www.informationclearinghouse.info/article7204.htm.

"A Triumph for JSOC," by Sean D. Naylor, *Defense News*, May 9, 2011, accessed at: http://www.defensenews.com/print/article/20110509/DEFFEAT06/105090325/A-Triumph-JSOC.

"Two U.S. Commandos Fought in Benghazi Rescue, Privately Honored for Valor," by Rowan Scarborough, *The Washington Times*, October 30, 2013, accessed at: http://www.washingtontimes.com/news/2013/oct/30/us-military-commandos-made-it-to-benghazi/?page=all.

"The Unknown Soldiers: To Family, Friends, Mike McNulty Will Always Be There," by Tom Sileo, Creators Syndicate, published March 14, 2014, in the Columbus, Ga. *Ledger-Enquirer*, accessed at: http://www.ledger-enquirer.com/2014/03/15/3002857/the-unknown-soldiers-to-family.html.

"U.S. Airstrike Kills Top Qaeda Agent in Somalia," by Jeffrey Gettleman and Eric Schmitt, *The New York Times*, May 1, 2008, accessed at: http://www.nytimes.com/2008/05/01/world/africa/01iht-02somalia.12481389.html.

"U.S. Bombs Pipeline to Stem Oil Flow; Preventive Strike Was Ruled Out," by Bill Gertz, *The Washington Times*, January 28, 1991.

"U.S. Captures Benghazi Suspect in Secret Raid," by Karen DeYoung, Adam Goldman, and Julie Tate, *The Washington Post*, June 17, 2014, accessed at: http://www .washingtonpost.com/world/national-security/us-captured-benghazi-suspect-in -secret-raid/2014/06/17/7ef8746e-f5cf-11e3-a3a5-42be35962a52_story.html.

"U.S. Destroyer Shells Somali Militants," by Jeff Schogol, *Stars and Stripes*, June 5, 2007, accessed at: http://www.stripes.com/news/u-s-destroyer-shells-somali -militants-1.65000.

"U.S. Drone Base in Ethiopia Is Operational," by Craig Whitlock, *The Washington Post*, October 27, 2011, accessed at: http://www.washingtonpost.com/world /national-security/us-drone-base-in-ethiopia-is-operational/2011/10/27 /gIQAznKwMM_story.html.

"U.S. Drone Strike in Somalia Targets al-Shabaab Leader," by Craig Whitlock, *The Washington Post*, September 2, 2014, accessed at: http://www.washingtonpost.com /world/national-security/us-drone-strike-in-somalia-targets-al-shabab-leader /2014/09/02/2c833104-32a3-11e4-9e92-0899b306bbea_story.html.

"US Flying Blind to Looming Terror Plots," by James Kitfield, breakingdefense.com, July 17, 2014, accessed at: http://breakingdefense.com/2014/07/us-flying-blind-to -looming-terror-plots/.

"U.S. Frees Suspect in Killing of 5 G.I.'s," by Allisa J. Rubin and Michael R. Gordon, *The New York Times*, June 8, 2009, accessed at: http://www.nytimes.com/2009 /06/09/world/middleeast/09release.html.

"U.S. Generals in Iraq Were Told of Abuse Early, Inquiry Finds," by Josh White, *The Washington Post*, December 1, 2004, accessed at: http://www.washingtonpost .com/wp-dyn/articles/A23372-2004Nov30.html.

"U.S. Kills Top Qaeda Militant in Southern Somalia," by Jeffrey Gettleman and Eric Schmitt, *The New York Times*, September 14, 2009, accessed at: http://www .nytimes.com/2009/09/15/world/africa/15raid.html?hp.

"U.S. Missiles Missed Awlaki by Inches in Yemen," by Martha Raddatz, ABC News, July 19, 2011, accessed at: http://abcnews.go.com/Blotter/us-missed-awlaki-inches -yemen/story?id=14108686.

"U.S. Raids in Libya and Somalia Strike Terror Targets," by David D. Kirkpatrick, Nicholas Kulish, and Eric Schmitt, *The New York Times*, October 5, 2013, accessed at: http://www.nytimes.com/2013/10/06/world/africa/Al-Qaeda-Suspect-Wanted -in-US-Said-to-Be-Taken-in-Libya.html?_r=0&hp=&adxnnl=1&adxnnlx =1400609295-883WHxhUdMWvSh5QaKFkpg.

"US Released Senior Iranian Qods Force Commander," by Bill Roggio, *The Long War Journal*, July 27, 2009, accessed at: http://www.longwarjournal.org/archives /2009/07/us_released_senior_iranian_qods_force_commander.php.

"U.S. Stages 2nd Airstrike in Somalia; Ethiopians Leaving Capital," by Karen DeYoung and Stephanie McCrummen, *The Washington Post*, January 24, 2007.

"US Strike Against Al-Shabab [*sic*] Leader Reflects Obama's Counterterrorism Strategy," by Stephanie Gaskell, *Defense One*, September 2, 2014, accessed at: http://www .defenseone.com/threats/2014/09/us-strike-against-al-shabab-leader-reflects -obamas-counterterrorism-strategy/92966/.

"U.S. Swoops In to Free 2 from Pirates in Somalia Raid," by Jeffrey Gettleman, Eric Schmitt, and Thom Shanker, *The New York Times*, January 25, 2012, accessed at: http://www.nytimes.com/2012/01/26/world/africa/us-raid-frees-2-hostages -from-somali-pirates.html?pagewanted=1&_r=0.

"U.S. Syria Raid Killed 80," by Richard Sale, UPI, July 16, 2003, accessed at: http:// www.upi.com/Business_News/Security-Industry/2003/07/16/US-Syria-raid -killed-80/UPI-78851058396985/.

"U.S. Troops Arrest Serb War Suspect," by Jeffrey Fleishman, *Philadelphia Inquirer*, January 23, 1998, accessed at: http://articles.philly.com/1998-01-23/news/25748765 _1_goran-jelisic-nato-forces-serb-adolf.

"U.S. Troops Crossed Border, Pakistan Says," by Candace Rondeaux and Karen DeYoung, *The Washington Post*, September 4, 2008, accessed at: http://www.washing tonpost.com/wp-dyn/content/article/2008/09/03/AR2008090300523.html ?hpid=moreheadlines.

"Why Delta Force Waited So Long to Grab a Benghazi Ringleader," by Eli Lake and Kimberly Dozier, *The Daily Beast*, June 17, 2014, accessed at: http://www .thedailybeast.com/articles/2014/06/17/why-delta-force-waited-so-long-to-grab -a-benghazi-ringleader.html.

"William McRaven: The Admiral," by Barton Gellman, *Time*, December 14, 2011, accessed at: http://content.time.com/time/specials/packages/article/0,28804, 2101745_2102133_2102330-1,00.html.

"Winning Isn't News," *Investor's Business Daily*, July 7, 2008.

"WMDs and Terrorists Among Top Concerns for New Special Ops Pick," by Alex Quade, *The Washington Times*, July 1, 2014, accessed at: http://www.washington times.com/news/2014/jul/1/keeping-wmds-from-terrorists-is-top-priority-for-v /?page=all.

Government Publications

20th Anniversary History (an official publication of USSOCOM, 2007). *All Roads Lead to Baghdad: Army Special Operations Forces in Iraq*, by Charles H. Briscoe, Kenneth Finlayson, Robert W. Jones Jr., Cherilyn A. Walley, A. Dwayne Aaron, Michael R. Mullins, and James A. Schroder (Fort Bragg: U.S. Army Special Operations Command History Office, 2006).

"Change Detection," accessed at: http://www.sandia.gov/radar/areas_of_expertise /missions.html.

Flight Path Study—United Airlines Flight 175, a February 19, 2002, briefing by National Transportation Safety Board's Office of Research and Engineering. Accessed at: http://www.ntsb.gov/doclib/foia/9_11/Flight_Path_Study_UA175.pdf.

FM 100-5—Operations, published 1976 by the Department of the Army, Appendix B, pp. 2–3, accessed at: http://www.survivalebooks.com/free%20manuals/1976 %20US%20Army%20Vietnam%20War%20OPERATIONS%20201p.pdf.

From the Sea: U.S. Marines in Afghanistan, 2001–2002, by Colonel Nathan S. Low-rey (Washington, D.C.: U.S. Marine Corps History Division, 2011).

A History of the 160th Special Operations Aviation Regiment (Airborne), a report prepared by the Library of Congress Federal Research Division, October 2001.

The Holloway Commission Report (unclassified version), accessed at: http://www2 .gwu.edu/~nsarchiv/NSAEBB/NSAEBB63/doc8.pdf.

The Impact of Leaders on Organizational Culture: A 75th Ranger Regiment Case Study, by Lieutenant Colonel Francis H. Kearney III, a strategy research project for the U.S. Army War College, Carlisle Barracks, 1997.

"Key Zarqawi Aide Captured," a Multi-National Force-Iraq press release number 05-05-09, dated May 7, 2005, accessed at: http://www.freerepublic.com/focus/f -news/1383919/posts?q=1&;page=1901 (the original centcom.mil link is dead).

Operation Urgent Fury, by Ronald H. Cole (Washington, D.C.: Joint History Office, 1997).

Operation Urgent Fury, U.S. Army Center for Military History monograph.

"Report to Congress on the Defeat of Hard and Deeply Buried Targets," submitted by the Secretary of Defense in conjunction with the Secretary of Energy, July 2001.

"Scott Sather—Strived for Excellence, Influenced Many," by Lieutenant Colonel Darrell Judy, accessed at: http://www.aetc.af.mil/news/story.asp?id=123205410.

"Selected Speeches of President George W. Bush, 2001–2008," accessed at: http:// georgewbush-whitehouse.archives.gov/infocus/bushrecord/documents/Selected _Speeches_George_W_Bush.pdf.

Special Operations and Low-Intensity Conflict Legislation: Why Was It Passed and Have the Voids Been Filled? by Colonel William G. Boykin, a study project for the Army War College, Carlisle Barracks, 1991.

"USS *Kitty Hawk* (CV(A)63)," accessed at: http://www.history.navy.mil/danfs/k4 /kitty_hawk-ii.html.

USS *Saipan* (LHA-2) Command History—Calendar Year 2000, accessed at: http:// www.history.navy.mil/shiphist/s/lha-2/2000.pdf.

Weapon of Choice: ARSOF in Afghanistan, by Charles H. Briscoe, Richard L. Kiper, James A. Schroder, and Kalev I. Sepp (Fort Leavenworth, Kans.: Combat Studies Institute Press, 2004).

"What Will Be the Military Role in the War on Terrorism?," an October 10, 2001, memo from Donald Rumsfeld to Generals Dick Myers and Peter Pace, accessed at: www.papers.rumsfeld.com.

ACKNOWLEDGMENTS

I could not have written this book without the love and support of many people.

My parents, Dave and Verney Naylor, never stopped believing in me, for which I will always be grateful. My brother Mark was a constant source of encouragement, while Hannah and Duncan, my niece and nephew, reminded me that there is more to life than book writing. My sister-in-law Laura and her parents, Peter and Joanne Roth, made me feel welcome as always on my all-too-infrequent visits to New England.

Christine McCann not only showed more patience and love and sacrificed more of herself than I had a right to expect as deadlines came and went. She also copyedited the manuscript, helped organize my time, provided an extraordinarily comfortable desk chair, and was a tireless advocate for the Oxford comma. Henry McCann, meanwhile, graciously allowed me to pet him and feed him "flying" treats, and was a source of enormous joy during the project's darkest days.

I began full-time work on this book at the end of 2011, when my editors at Gannett Government Media Corporation (the company that publishes *Army Times*) allowed me to disappear on unpaid book leave for an indefinite period. I eventually parted ways with *Army Times,* my professional home for more than twenty-three years, but I remain grateful to Tobias Naegele, Alex Neill, and Richard Sandza for supporting my work while I was at the paper, and to the entire newsroom staff for making *Army Times* such a great place to work for so long.

The vast majority of the sources for this book consented to be interviewed on the condition that I not identify them. But I owe all my sources—named and unnamed—a debt of enormous gratitude for having the courage to talk with me. This book would not have been possible without their participation.

While the cloak of secrecy that the Defense Department insists on draping over Joint Special Operations Command meant that no military public affairs officers were empowered to arrange interviews to help in my reporting, Army Colonel Tim Nye, the U.S. Special Operations Command spokesman during the first phase of the research, not only supported my project but went above and beyond the call of duty in trying to persuade his bosses to cooperate with me. His deputy and successor, retired Army Lieutenant Colonel Ken McGraw, was always professional in his dealings with me, answering my questions when he could. Tatjana Christian in the Department of the Army's media relations office in the Pentagon was a model of efficiency in responding to my numerous requests for the official résumés of active duty and retired general officers. Jeanne Bankard, deputy chief of the Army's General Officer Management Office, was very helpful in explaining the "frocking" process as it applied to JSOC commanders. Federal Aviation Authority historian Terry Kraus patiently hunted down post-9/11 hijacking rumors for me, while Donna Tabor, Terry's counterpart at Fort Bragg, provided useful information on the scenes at Bragg in September and October 2001. Retired Army Colonel Rick Kiernan also gave of his time generously.

Several colleagues from the media world were particularly helpful: Rob Curtis placed his knowledge of special operations people and gear at my disposal; Chris Cavas explained how best to track the past movements of Navy ships; David Wood cast his mind back to Bagram in March 2002 on my behalf; and Melinda Day used her deep understanding of the Naval Special Warfare community to put me in touch with good people.

Scott Miller, my long-suffering agent at Trident Media Group, was a source of support and encouragement throughout the process of writing *Relentless Strike*, while Marc Resnick at St. Martin's was as patient and understanding an editor as an author could wish for, and one whose suggestions never failed to improve the manuscript. Responsibility for any flaws that remain is mine alone.

INDEX